W9-DIB-182

THE
JAMES BOND
MOVIE
ENCYCLOPEDIA

Date: 3/17/21

791.43651 RUB
Rubin, Steven Jay,
The James Bond movie
encyclopedia /

STEVEN JAY RUBIN

**CHICAGO
REVIEW
PRESS**

PALM BEACH COUNTY
LIBRARY SYSTEM
3650 Summit Boulevard
West Palm Beach, FL 33406-4198

Pierce Brosnan as James Bond, 007. *Courtesy of the Nicolás Suszczyk Collection*

James Bond's creator, author Ian Fleming, journeys to Istanbul during location shooting for *From Russia with Love* (1963). *Courtesy of the Michael VanBlaricum Collection*

Copyright © 2021 by Steven Jay Rubin
All rights reserved
Published by Chicago Review Press Incorporated
814 North Franklin Street
Chicago, IL 60610
ISBN 978-1-64160-082-8

Library of Congress Control Number: 2020944474

Cover design: Preston Pisellini
Cover photos: Photofest
Print book interior design: Jonathan Hahn

Printed in the United States of America
5 4 3 2 1

INTRODUCTION

Welcome to *The James Bond Movie Encyclopedia*. You're reading this book because you love James Bond movies, and so do I. We're part of an enormous, multigenerational group of worldwide fans who are fascinated by the long history of this storied film franchise. We watch the movies, debate their quality, and share our fondness for the world's most enduring secret agent, James Bond, 007.

This encyclopedia is not just a reference guide, it's a celebration of Bond. Open it to any page and you'll be reminded of some specific details about the world of Bond that you enjoy: a sparkling line of dialogue, a photo of one of the stunning Bond girls, a cool gadget, an exotic location, a thrilling action sequence, the bio of a supporting player, or a behind-the-scenes tidbit. There will be things you know by heart, and some information that may surprise you. For instance, did you know that the first five James Bond mov-ies were released in alphabetical order? *Dr. No*, *From Russia with Love*, *Goldfinger*, *Thunderball*, and *You Only Live Twice*. I didn't even notice that until recently.

The last edition of this book was published in 2003, and I wanted to give this new version as much of a makeover as possible. So 90 percent of the photographs are new to the encyclopedia, thanks to some wonderful ladies and gentlemen all over the world who supplied me with a kaleidoscope of images (please see the acknowledgments). Unlike my recent book *The Twilight Zone Encyclopedia*, which covers the complete span of Rod Serling's original black-and-white series, *The James Bond Movie Encyclopedia* is an ongoing enterprise. You have to keep adding in new details from the newest films to keep the book fresh. Fortunately, there's no reason to think 007's superspy adventures will end anytime soon. *James Bond will return!*

Daniel Craig, the reigning James Bond. *Courtesy of the Anders Frejdh Collection*

Roger Moore received mixed reviews as 007, but he revived the fortunes of the Bond franchise with increasingly spectacular action films in the 1970s and 1980s, which brought in family audiences in unprecedented numbers all over the planet. *Courtesy of the Anders Frejdh Collection*

ACKNOWLEDGMENTS

A James Bond film encyclopedia without photos is going to gather a lot of dust on a bookstore shelf. And a fourth edition that just reprints the same pictures from the first three is also a non-starter. I thus had a huge challenge: to almost completely reillustrate the book. I accomplished it by contacting the world's leading collectors, who offered magnificent cooperation. I owe them all my thanks.

I would like to start with Michael VanBlaricum and the Ian Fleming Foundation in Santa Barbara, California, which is devoted to the major task of preserving the legacy of Bond creator Ian Fleming, his many works, and the films based on them. This organization has also gone to enormous lengths to preserve many of the classic cars and gadgets that have appeared in James Bond's world. In addition, I owe an enormous debt to David Reinhardt, who has meticulously collected thousands of images covering every book edition and film. Based in Canada, David went out of his way to get me the highest-resolution images possible—no small task.

Traveling to Europe in the spring of 2019, I first stopped in London, where I spent some delightful time with special effects tech Brian Smithies, who was part of Derek Meddings's effects team, and who provided me with rare behind-the-scenes shots of the Meddings team's yeoman work on the Bond series. I then flew to Sweden and met with one of Europe's most enthusiastic Bond fans, Anders Frejdh, who has an amazing collection of Bond-related material. Thank you, Anders, for being the perfect host and providing me with some outstanding images. Your enthusiasm for 007 is off the charts. From Sweden, I flew to Paris and met with another enormously enthusiastic Bond fan, Luc Leclech,

who also brought amazing photographic materials to the table, as well as supplying me with some special shots from his friend Joel Villy.

For additional photographs, I would also like to thank David J. Barron, Joyce Bartle, Jon Burlingame (the esteemed author of *The Music of James Bond*), the Film Music Society, Robby Fraser and Kidder Erdman at Endeavor, Las Vegas News Bureau, Paul Maibaum, Malcolm McNeil and his magnificently well-stocked James Bond collection, the National Archives, Lee Pfeiffer and *Cinema Retro* magazine, Steve Oxenrider, Matt Rector at Fort Knox, Charles Sherman, Nicolás Suszczyk, United Artists Releasing, Kenneth Willardt and Ulrich Møller-Jørgensen, and David Williams.

For the first time, I'm featuring some extraordinary original art work supplied by Jeff Marshall of New York. When I first saw some of Jeff's work on one of the 007 pages on Facebook, I was blown away. I immediately contacted him and we, excuse the pun, bonded. Thank you, Jeff, for adding a wonderful new dimension to this tome. The same goes for another terrific artist, Paul Mann, who did the cool *From Russia with Love* and *On Her Majesty's Secret Service* artwork. I am truly blessed by the contribution of these extraordinary men.

Additional kudos to the folks at Chicago Review Press, in particular my editor Devon Freeny, for his long hours at the desk. Devon, you deserve a decoration from the queen.

I would also like to tip my hat to William Koenig at the *Spy Command* blog, and my friend Jeff Hershow and his video archives in Los Angeles. And to my wife, Elisa, and my children, Jaymie and Darren, I dedicate this effort to you. Your love makes it all possible.

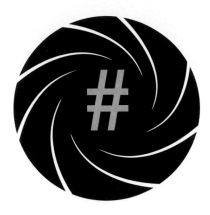

00-: Code prefix granted to select agents of the British Secret Service such as James Bond, 007, which refers to their "license to kill."

003: British Secret Service agent found dead by James Bond (Roger Moore) in the snows of Siberia in *A View to a Kill*. Inside a heart-shaped pendant around the dead agent's neck, 007 finds a microchip that 003 stole from the Russians. According to Q (Desmond Llewelyn) this chip is part of a new line, developed by Zorin Industries, that is totally impervious to damage from electromagnetic pulses.

004: Double-0 agent portrayed by Frederick Warder in *The Living Daylights*, who is assassinated on Gibraltar during Ministry of Defence war games. The killer, working for arms dealer Brad Whitaker (Joe Don Baker) and renegade Russian general Georgi Koskov (Jeroen Krabbé), leaves a tag on 004's body; it reads, Smiert Spionam, Russian for "Death to Spies."

006: British Secret Service code name for Alec Trevelyan (Sean Bean) in *GoldenEye*. Though he was executed by Colonel Ourumov (Gottfried John) during an assault on the Arkangel Chemical Weapons Facility, it's discovered nine years later that he isn't dead at all. He's now Janus, head of a Russian crime syndicate.

007: James Bond's famous code designation. It is also, appropriately, the number that freezes on the countdown panel when a scientist deactivates the A-bomb in *Goldfinger*.

007 Stage: Enormous soundstage constructed on the Pinewood Studios lot outside London in

1976 and first utilized for production designer Ken Adam's gargantuan "Jonah Set" in *The Spy Who Loved Me*. The stage was officially christened "No. 007" on December 5, 1976, in a ceremony attended by Britain's prime minister, Harold Wilson. In 1984, during the filming of Ridley Scott's *Legend*, the soundstage was partially destroyed in a fire, but it was rebuilt the same year for *A View to a Kill*, at which point it was renamed the "Albert R. Broccoli 007 Stage." Two decades later, just a week after filming was completed on *Casino Royale*, the stage burned down again, and was again rebuilt.

The 007 Stage is engulfed in flames during the making of the Tom Cruise fantasy film *Legend* in 1984. *Steve Rubin Collection*

009: British Secret Service agent, portrayed by stuntman Andy Bradford in *Octopussy*, who attempts to steal a counterfeit Fabergé egg from an East Berlin circus run by Octopussy (Maud Adams). Disguised as a clown and chased into the woods near the circus by twin killers Mischka and Grischka (David and Tony Meyer), 009 is climbing a bridge to freedom when a knife finds its mark in his back. He then falls into a flood control basin. Later, at a well-attended party at the residence of the British ambassador to East Berlin, 009 staggers onto the grounds with the knife still embedded in his back, smashes through a window into the ambassador's office, falls to the floor, and dies—the captured egg rolling across the floor.

Another agent with the same numerical designation is assigned to kill kidnapper Victor "Renard" Zokas (Robert Carlyle) in *The World Is*

Stuntman Andy Bradford dons the clown outfit to portray doomed 009 in the *Octopussy* pre-credits teaser. *Steve Rubin Collection*

Not Enough. He does shoot Renard in the head, but the bullet lodges in his medulla oblongata, killing him slowly and leaving him plenty of time to plot his revenge.

Abkarian, Simon (March 5, 1962–   ): French actor who portrayed Alex Dimitrios, a terrorist arms dealer who loses his Aston Martin DB5 to James Bond (Daniel Craig) in a Bahamas poker game in *Casino Royale*. Born into a French Armenian family in Paris, Abkarian made his motion picture debut in director Cédric Klapisch's comedy *Riens du tout* (1992). A decade later, he gave his first performance in an English-speaking film as Lieutenant Dessalines in director Jonathan Demme's *The Truth About Charlie* (2002), a remake of *Charade* (1963).

ACADEMY AWARDS

The Bond series has rarely scored in the annual awards derby of the Academy of Motion Picture Arts and Sciences. In the entire series through 2020, Bond films have earned sixteen Oscar nominations and only five wins:

© Siraanamwong / Dreamstime.com

Wins

1964   *Goldfinger*, Best Sound Effects—Norman Wanstall
1965   *Thunderball*, Best Visual Effects—John Stears
2012   *Skyfall*, Best Song—"Skyfall" by Adele and Paul Epworth
2012   *Skyfall*, Best Sound Editing—Per Hallberg and Karen Baker Landers (tied with Paul N. J. Ottosson for *Zero Dark Thirty*)
2015   *Spectre*, Best Song—"Writing's on the Wall" by Sam Smith and James Napier

Nominations Only

1967   *Casino Royale*, Best Song—"The Look of Love" by Burt Bacharach and Hal David (lost to "Talk to the Animals" from *Doctor Dolittle*)
1971   *Diamonds Are Forever*, Best Sound—Gordon McCallum, John Mitchell, and Alfred E. Overton (lost to *Fiddler on the Roof*)
1973   *Live and Let Die*, Best Song—"Live and Let Die" by Paul and Linda McCartney (lost to the title song from *The Way We Were*)
1977   *The Spy Who Loved Me*, Best Art Direction—art direction by Ken Adam and Peter Lamont, set decoration by Hugh Scaife (lost to *Star Wars*)
1977   *The Spy Who Loved Me*, Best Original Score—Marvin Hamlisch (lost to *Star Wars*)
1977   *The Spy Who Loved Me*, Best Song—"Nobody Does It Better" by Marvin Hamlisch and Carole Bayer Sager (lost to the title song from *You Light Up My Life*)
1979   *Moonraker*, Best Visual Effects—Derek Meddings, Paul Wilson, and John Evans (lost to *Alien*)
1981   *For Your Eyes Only*, Best Song—"For Your Eyes Only" by Bill Conti and Mick Leeson (lost to "Arthur's Theme (Best That You Can Do)" from *Arthur*)
2012   *Skyfall*, Best Cinematography—Roger Deakins (lost to *Life of Pi*)
2012   *Skyfall*, Best Original Score—Thomas Newman (lost to *Life of Pi*)
2012   *Skyfall*, Best Sound Mixing—Scott Millan, Greg P. Russell, and Stuart Wilson (lost to *Les Misérables*)

Acrostar mini jet (a.k.a. Bede jet): Miniature jet aircraft flown by James Bond (Roger Moore) in the *Octopussy* pre-credits teaser. After his plan to destroy a top-secret South American radar system goes awry, Bond escapes in his plane, hotly pursued by a heat-seeking antiaircraft missile. Diving into the radar system's hangar, he's able to maneuver his acrobatic plane through to the other side just as enemy soldiers are closing the hangar doors. As the doors close, the missile enters the hanger and explodes against them—obliterating the hanger, the radar system, and everything else.

Roger Moore and James Bond's Acrostar mini jet,
quite the star in the action-packed *Octopussy* teaser.
Courtesy of the David Reinhardt Collection

The Acrostar jet, designed by Jim Bede and built, modified, and flown by veteran stunt pilot Corkey Fornof, is slightly more than three meters in length and boasts a top speed of 310 mph. It's powered by a Microturbo TRS-18 engine. The jet was initially scheduled to make its Bond debut in *Moonraker*. In that film's original script, 007 and CIA agent Holly Goodhead (Lois Chiles) arrive in Brazil and discover that a fleet of cargo planes owned by Hugo Drax (Michael Lonsdale) are disappearing into the hinterlands. Determined to find them, Bond and Holly climb into their own mini jets and take off for a run across the jungle surrounding Angel Falls in neighboring Venezuela. During one planned action sequence, the two friendly agents engage in a bit of acrobatics that takes them through tight crevices and, at one point, behind Angel Falls itself. Then, just as they're about to find Drax's hidden base, they're jumped by a flight of black twin-boom Vampire jets that try to shoot them down. However, the viability of the sequence depended on the water level in and around Angel Falls. Unfortunately, when it came time to shoot the scene, the riverbed was completely dry. So the Acrostar jet sequence was eliminated from the script, only to be resurrected for the *Octopussy* teaser, where only one jet was used.

Adam, Ken (February 5, 1921–March 10, 2016; birth name: Klaus Adam): Colorful, innovative British production designer who, starting with *Dr. No* in 1962, gave the interior sequences he designed a vibrant, exciting style that would

become the hallmark of the James Bond series for nearly three decades. Adam, a native of Berlin who arrived in England when he was thirteen, came to the 007 series on the recommendation of producer Albert "Cubby" Broccoli, who had worked with him on *The Trials of Oscar Wilde* (1960). Broccoli knew that Adam was innovative and could work within the minuscule production design budget available on *Dr. No*. Given that budget, Adam's design output was nothing short of extraordinary. Dr. No's marvelous reactor room, his eerie Crab Key interrogation chamber, and the underground observation living room were unforgettable. His more realistic settings—M's office, the MI6 communications center, Bond's London apartment, the casino, and Miss Taro's cottage—also belied their actual cost. Adam's designs, along with Terence Young's understated direction, Peter Hunt's slam-bang editing, and the Monty Norman / John Barry music, contributed heavily to the success of *Dr. No* and the emergence of the James Bond films as a pop cultural touchstone of the 1960s.

Adam's location art director on *Dr. No*, Syd Cain, took over production design chores on the next Bond film, *From Russia with Love*, while Adam toiled for director Stanley Kubrick on *Dr. Strangelove*. Adam returned to the Bond fold on *Goldfinger*, once again stretching the limits of contemporary production design with his Fort Knox sets—not just the glittering interior but also the enormous exterior built on the Pinewood Studios lot—and the sprawling Auric Stud ranch, with its intricate and electronically enhanced planning room interior (known as the Auric Stud rumpus room).

Working with special effects supervisor John Stears, Adam also contributed heavily to the design of Bond's customized Aston Martin sports car. Weapon and gadget design, always a vital part of the Bond movie experience, was another of Adam's responsibilities, especially on the next film, *Thunderball*, which featured huge working elements such as the *Disco Volante* hydrofoil and a number of underwater devices employed by villain Emilio Largo (Adolfo Celi). Adam's SPECTRE briefing room, with its modern stainless-steel look, was another design triumph of the period, as was his immense MI6 conference room, complete with animated wall charts and a drawing-room feel.

Production designer Ken Adam's extraordinary interior for Fort Knox, which becomes a glittering battleground for James Bond (Sean Connery) and Oddjob (Harold Sakata) in *Goldfinger*. *Courtesy of the Anders Frejdh Collection*

The international box office success of the early Bond movies meant that the films' budgets began to increase dramatically. With extra money in the bank, Adam began to take on tasks that only the ancient pharaohs would have contemplated. On *You Only Live Twice*, he created the famous volcano set, an enormous and elaborate SPECTRE rocket base supposedly hidden inside an extinct Japanese volcano but actually built full size on the Pinewood Studios lot in 1966. On *Diamonds Are Forever*, Adam designed the garish Las Vegas penthouse of Ernst Stavro Blofeld (Charles Gray), the interior of the moon buggy testing facility, and the oil-rig advance base in Baja California, Mexico, which was actually a portable rig placed off the Southern California coast near Oceanside.

With Syd Cain handling production design chores on *Live and Let Die* and Peter Murton (another former associate of Adam) taking on *The Man with the Golden Gun*, Adam took a five-year 007 hiatus, returning on the mammoth production of *The Spy Who Loved Me* in 1976. This time, working with a design concept built around the circular and ellipse patterns he discovered on a location trip to the Costa Smeralda resort in Sardinia, Italy, Adam created the marvel-ous marine laboratory sets inside the amphibious Atlantis complex of villain Karl Stromberg (Curt Jurgens). But his blockbuster achievement on *Spy* was the "Jonah Set": the incredible interior of the *Liparus* supertanker, which was built inside its own specially constructed soundstage—the 007 Stage—which became the largest soundstage and studio water tank in the world. The glimmering, shimmering interior, with five-eighths-scale nuclear attack submarines, an armored control room, catwalks, a monorail, and assembly and weapons rooms, became one of the most celebrated motion picture interiors of all time.

Following *The Spy Who Loved Me*, Adam came aboard for one more 007 adventure—*Moonraker*. This time, his designs were strongly influenced by three elements: the triangular architecture of the ancient Mayan civilization; the unusual look of the Cathedral of Brasília,

Production designer extraordinaire Ken Adam. *Courtesy of the Charles Sherman Collection*

designed by Oscar Niemeyer, which Adam discovered during a location "recce" to Brazil in 1978; and the work of the painter Mondrian. All of these elements would come together inside the fascinating rocket base of Hugo Drax (Michael Lonsdale), which included "the Great Chamber," an enormous jungle atrium constructed under a Mayan pyramid; the triangular control room with its Perspex floor and colorful viewing panels; and the boxlike space shuttle launching pad. Adam also designed the tubular structure of Drax's radar-proof space station, a multilevel maze of engineering and scientific bric-a-brac that becomes a battleground in the film's closing moments.

Adams, Maud (February 12, 1945–   ; birth name: Maud Wikström): Swedish model turned actress who is the only woman in the Bond series to play two different leading characters—Andrea Anders in *The Man with the Golden Gun* and the title character in *Octopussy*. Adams is also seen briefly in the background of *A View to a Kill*'s Fisherman's Wharf sequence in San Francisco. In *Octopussy*, she was originally summoned to do a screen test with actor James Brolin, who was being considered for the role of Bond. In August 1982, prior to the start of principal photography, she told *Los Angeles Times* columnist Roderick Mann, "The test went well but I was confused—I knew it was policy never to use an actress twice and I'd already been in *The Man with the Golden Gun*. So what was I doing there? Then they called me in for a makeup test and darkened my hair and eyebrows. That was when I realized they had me in mind for *Octopussy*, the villainess of the picture. She's half Indian. I was very excited. After all, a woman has never before played the title role in a Bond film, or been in two films. I came home and waited, and then I got the telephone call saying I had the part. And it's a marvelous one. Everyone

Maud Adams returned to the 007 series as the title character in *Octopussy*. *Steve Rubin Collection*

says it's the best role ever written for a woman in a Bond film. Remember, when I did *The Man with the Golden Gun* all those years ago, I had no acting experience at all. I've done a lot since then so I feel I'm ready to tackle a much more challenging role."[*] A native of Luleå, Sweden, Adams made her film debut as an uncredited photo model in director William Friedkin's 1970 film *The Boys in the Band*. The following year, she made her television debut as Melba Wilde in the *Love, American Style* episode "Love and the Monsters." She was later a regular on the series *Chicago Story* (13 episodes as Dr. Judith Bergstrom, 1982) and *Emerald Point N.A.S.* (22 episodes as Maggie Farrell, 1983–1984).

Adele (May 5, 1988–   ; birth name: Adele Laurie Blue Adkins): British singer-songwriter who won an Academy Award for her title tune to *Skyfall*, which she cowrote with Paul Epworth. The song also won a Golden Globe, a Grammy Award, and the Brit Award for British Single of the Year. A native of Tottenham, London, Adele made her motion picture performing debut in director Nick Moore's romantic comedy *Wild Child* (2008), in which she performed "Chasing Pavements."

The recording artists of a-ha, who warbled the title song to *The Living Daylights*. *Steve Rubin Collection*

a-ha: Norwegian rock 'n' roll trio who performed the title tune to *The Living*

Maud Adams, a stunning Swedish beauty, portrayed Andrea Anders, the title character's girlfriend in *The Man with the Golden Gun*. *Courtesy of the David Reinhardt Collection*

---

[*] Roderick Mann, "Actresses Unruffled in the Battle of the Bonds," *Los Angeles Times*, August 31, 1982.

Daylights (1987). The trio previously scored with the international number-one smash "Take on Me," which featured a most extraordinary music video that combined live action with animation. The group consists of three natives of Oslo, Norway: Pål (pronounced "Paul") Waaktaar-Savoy, Morten Harket, and Magne "Mags" Furuholmen.

Alba, Rose (February 5, 1918–December 2004): Egyptian-born British actress who portrayed the shapely Madame Bouvar, who is seen entering a Lincoln Continental limousine in the *Thunderball* pre-credits teaser. It's all a sham. In actuality, she's SPECTRE agent Jacques Bouvar, who is masquerading as his own widow to escape British intelligence. (Stuntman Bob Simmons portrayed the unmasked Bouvar.) Alba made her feature debut in Italian director Carlo Ludovico Bragaglia's 1955 adventure film *The Golden Falcon*. The following year, she made her first small-screen appearance in the made-for-TV movie *Home Is the Sailor*, which was directed by prolific British television movie producer Michael Barry.

Aldershot, England: Known as the "home of the British Army," it's the town where *Die Another Day*'s hovercraft-chase pre-credits teaser was shot in early 2002. In order to create the sequence, which simulates the demilitarized zone between North and South Korea, the production company rented a Ministry of Defence training center for high-speed driving, located in the middle of dense woodlands.

"Alimentary, Dr. Leiter": The comical medical response given by Bond (Sean Connery) in *Diamonds Are Forever* when Felix Leiter (Norman Burton) asks him where the diamonds are hidden on the body of the late Peter Franks (Joe Robinson). According to screenwriter Tom Mankiewicz, when producer Cubby Broccoli first read the script, he felt that no one would get the line (which refers to Bond shoving the diamonds up Franks's alimentary canal). However, on opening night when Bond said the line, a man in the fourth row of the theater laughed out loud. According to Mankiewicz, Broccoli turned to him and whispered, "It's probably a doctor."*

---

* Tom Mankiewicz, interview by the author, Los Angeles, November 7, 1977.

Alpert, Herb (March 31, 1935–   ): Famous trumpeter, composer, songwriter, and bandleader who played the trumpet during Burt Bacharach's score for the 1967 spoof version of *Casino Royale* and who produced the title song for *Never Say Never Again* (performed by his wife, Lani Hall), for which he also performed another patented trumpet solo.

Ama Island: Secluded Japanese island that is home to a community of fishermen and beautiful pearl divers known as *ama* girls in *You Only Live Twice*. Disguised as a Japanese fisherman, and determined to find a secret SPECTRE rocket base, Bond (Sean Connery) travels to the island, where he "marries" Kissy (Mie Hama), a stunningly beautiful *ama* diver who is actually a top agent of Japanese Secret Service chief Tiger Tanaka (Tetsuro Tamba). Undercover as fisherman and pearl diver, Bond and Kissy eventually find their way through the Rosaki Cave and onto the extinct volcano that Blofeld (Donald Pleasence) uses to disguise his hidden rocket installation.

James Bond (Sean Connery) may be disguised as a docile fisherman, but he's also very handy with a staff in *You Only Live Twice*. *Courtesy of the David Reinhardt Collection*

Amalric, Mathieu (October 25, 1965–   ): Acclaimed French actor, writer, and director who portrayed shady environmentalist Dominic Greene in *Quantum of Solace*. A native of Neuilly-sur-Seine, Hauts-de-Seine, France, Amalric made his motion picture debut as Julien in director Otar Iosseliani's crime drama, *Favourites of the Moon* (1984). He is best known for the roles of Louis in *Munich* (2005), with

Frenchman Mathieu Amalric brought a strictly business aura to the role of key villain Dominic Greene in *Quantum of Solace*. *Courtesy of the Anders Frejdh Collection*

Daniel Craig; Jean-Do in *The Diving Bell and the Butterfly* (2007), which also featured Bond players Max von Sydow (*Never Say Never Again*) and Isaach De Bankolé (*Casino Royale*); and *The Grand Budapest Hotel* (2104), as Serge X. alongside Bond players Ralph Fiennes and Léa Seydoux (*Spectre*, *No Time to Die*).

Amasova, Major Anya: Beautiful but deadly Russian KGB agent portrayed by Barbara Bach in *The Spy Who Loved Me*. Code-named Triple X, she's partnered with James Bond (Roger Moore) on a hunt for freelance madman Karl Stromberg (Curt Jurgens), whose supertanker, the *Liparus*, has been swallowing British and Russian nuclear submarines. Both agents are also looking for a British submarine tracking system that has been developed by Stromberg. Major Amasova is, in effect, the first liberated woman in the James Bond series, reflecting well the mid-1970s movement toward more believable and realistic female characters in film. Having been introduced in the 1960s, when 007's chauvinism was given a free rein, the James Bond films entered their second decade with a considerably more enlightened outlook. Although there would continue to be playmates for Bond in every film, the main female characters began to be drawn with elements of intelligence, independence, and strength. Major Amasova pioneered this trend, as demonstrated in the ruined-temple sequence in which Bond and Anya are trailing Jaws (Richard Kiel). Moving stealthfully among the pillars, Anya (accompanied by Marvin Hamlisch's moody score) shows off a few extremely impressive martial arts stances while dressed in a clingy evening gown. This is no breathless female waiting to be rescued. Later, aboard a train, she's no match for Jaws, but she still fights back. In one of the film's most dramatic moments—an unusual one for a Roger Moore–era Bond film—she even threatens to kill Bond as repayment for the death of her Soviet agent/lover (Michael Billington). The strength and determination in her threat was unprecedented in the series. Bond women were beginning to hold their own at 007's side, and Amasova was the first. Recalled the film's late director, Lewis Gilbert, "Anya is a very independent woman; she's a major in the KGB and Russia's top agent. She's capable of scoring off Bond, and she does. In *The Spy Who Loved Me*, 007 doesn't always win. Sometimes she's smarter than he. This type of interplay makes Bond more human, more like one of us. Being vulnerable with the girl allows Bond's other accomplishments in the film to appear that much more impressive."*

AMC Hornet: American car that Bond (Roger Moore) steals from a Bangkok car showroom in *The Man with the Golden Gun*. Chasing Scaramanga (Christopher Lee) with Sheriff J. W. Pepper (Clifton James) riding shotgun, 007 races through town with half the Bangkok police on his tail. Outdistancing the local authorities, Bond finds himself on one side of a Thai river while Scaramanga and henchman Nick Nack (Hervé Villechaize) are inexplicably on the other. Spying a ruined bridge, Bond does the unthinkable, using the bridge's twisted remains to make a 360-degree spiral jump across the river, landing perfectly on all four tires and continuing the chase. Unfortunately, this incredible stunt, performed by British stunt driver Bumps Willard, was ruined when in postproduction a slide whistle sound effect was added over the jump. It served to cheapen what was actually one of the most incredible stunts ever performed on any film. SEE ALSO "Spiral Jump, the."

Amritraj, Vijay (December 14, 1953–   ): World-famous professional tennis player, commentator, entrepreneur, and sometime actor who made his big-screen debut as Vijay, enthusiastic British Secret Service associate of James Bond (Roger Moore) during scenes shot in India for *Octopussy*. A native of Madras, India, and the brother of producer Ashok Amritraj (*Machete*), he also portrayed a starship captain in *Star Trek IV: The Voyage Home* (1986).

Amsterdam, Netherlands: In *Goldfinger*, one of four cities (along with Zurich, Caracas, and Hong Kong) in which Auric Goldfinger (Gert Fröbe) has stashed the 20 million in pounds sterling worth of gold he has been smuggling out of Great Britain, according to Colonel Smithers (Richard Vernon) of the Bank of England. Amsterdam is also where James Bond (Sean Connery) visits the apartment of diamond smuggler Tiffany Case (Jill St. John), masquerading as

---

* Lewis Gilbert, interview by the author, London, June 15, 1977.

her fellow courier Peter Franks (Joe Robinson), in *Diamonds Are Forever*.

Andalusia, Spain: Region in southern Spain where, near the city of Cádiz, filmmakers shot the scene of lovely Jinx (Halle Berry) coming out of the surf in a stunning orange bikini and meeting James Bond (Pierce Brosnan) in *Die Another Day*. The scene, actually set in Cuba, was written by Robert Wade and Neal Purvis as a nod to the famous introduction of Ursula Andress in *Dr. No*. However, weather problems nearly destroyed the moment. For a few days, the temperature in normally sunny Spain was reduced to fifty degrees, with a forty-mile-per hour wind velocity—not the most ideal circumstances for a frolic in the surf. Fortunately for the production, the sun came out and 007 and Jinx had their day in the sun.

Andermatt, Switzerland: A small village, about fifty miles due south of Zurich, that served as a key exterior location in *Goldfinger*. In the shelter of the Lepontine Alps and not far from the Simplon Tunnel, Bond (Sean Connery) tails the Rolls-Royce of Goldfinger (Gert Fröbe) and later encounters the Mustang convertible of fast-driving Tilly Masterson (Tania Mallet). The warmly romantic strains of John Barry's score in this sequence are a definite highlight.

On the outskirts of Andermatt, Switzerland, director Guy Hamilton's crew prepares to film Tilly Masterson (Tania Mallet) as she attempts to assassinate Auric Goldfinger. *Courtesy of the Anders Frejdh Collection*

Anders, Andrea: Girlfriend of international assassin Francisco Scaramanga (Christopher Lee) in 1974's *The Man with the Golden Gun*. She's portrayed by Maud Adams, who would

go on to play the title character in *Octopussy* in 1983. Theirs is a loveless relationship: Anders sleeps with Scaramanga prior to every kill—a ritual that is also popular among bullfighters. It's supposed to improve their eye. A virtual slave to Scaramanga's will, Anders's only hope is to find the one man—James Bond (Roger Moore)—capable of beating Scaramanga at his own game. So Anders sends one of the assassin's golden bullets to the British Secret Service. In return, she also receives a golden bullet, but at a much higher velocity.

Andress, Ursula (March 19, 1936–   ): Swiss actress who portrayed Honey Ryder in *Dr. No*. A stunning presence in the first Bond film and a fantasy figure for many young men of the 1960s, her entrance on the Crab Key beach—coming out of the water in a white bikini that Andress designed herself—is ranked among the great screen introductions. Unfortunately, thanks to the screen standards of the period, the producers could not recreate the scene as Ian Fleming wrote it. In the book, Honey wears only a belt around her waist, where she carries her knife. When she's spotted by 007 for the first time, she covers her crotch and her broken nose, allowing her magnificent breasts to jut out at Bond. Fleming describes her as the incarnation of Botticelli's Venus—quite a tall order for the film's casting director! A photograph of Andress in a wet T-shirt eventually won her an audition, although her then husband, actor John Derek, had to persuade her to take the part.

Remembered Andress, "We were a small production, and it was like a family that got together to do a movie. We were every day together. We had lunch together, dinner together, and the next morning worked together. It was fabulous. . . . I was supposed to be very tanned, because Honey Ryder was living in Jamaica, a diver looking for shells, but I was snow white, so I had to get makeup from head to the toe. John

Sean Connery and Ursula Andress made a perfect pair in the first James Bond movie, *Dr. No. Courtesy of the David Reinhardt Collection*

Statuesque Ursula Andress made quite an impression in *Dr. No*. Her introduction coming out of the surf is considered one of the the most memorable debuts of an actress in screen history. *Courtesy of the David Reinhardt Collection*

O'Gorman was the makeup man, a lovely man, so he said, 'Okay, take your clothes off.' So I had to stand there all naked in the room, and he began with this pancake, going from top to bottom, covering me in this dark makeup. Then every other second, somebody was knocking on the door. And John would go, 'Come in.' And here I am all nude. They came with the breakfast tray. Finally, when they were finished, I think we had 20 trays of breakfast, because everybody wanted to come in to watch me naked. Sean would come into makeup and there was no room from the door to his makeup chair, because it was full of trays. He'd say, 'Well, we've had a few visitors today.'"

As for the role itself, Andress found it "easy, because I used to do competitive swimming, so the sea was no problem. Running around up and down the hills, through the mud, through this marsh was very easy for me. The difficulty was when I had to speak. I used to be so scared, but Sean helped me a lot and was adorable to me."* Ultimately, Andress was entirely revoiced in post-

* Paul Duncan, "The Gold Standard," *Taschen*, Winter 2012.

production by actress Nikki Van der Zyl, who did all the other female voices in the film other than Miss Moneypenny, Miss Taro and Sylvia Trench.

Andress returned to the Bond world, albeit in spoofy mode, playing seductress and double agent Vesper Lynd in the comedic 1967 adaptation of *Casino Royale*. A native of Ostermundigen, Bern, Switzerland, Andress made her uncredited feature film debut in the Italian comedy *An American in Rome* (1954). Her role in *Dr. No* netted her a Golden Globe for Most Promising Newcomer—Female, an honor she shared that year with Tippi Hedren (*The Birds*) and Elke Sommer (*The Prize*).

Apted, Michael (February 10, 1941–　　): Eclectic British filmmaker who took on the job of directing *The World Is Not Enough* in 1998 and delivered a strong character piece that never allows the slam-bang action to overshadow the story. Easily the best of Pierce Brosnan's forays as 007, *The World Is Not Enough* is filled with little character moments and realistic action that adds dimension to Bond's adventure. Apted wasn't afraid to show 007 beaten up and near death at times—something seldom seen in any of the Roger Moore films.

A native of Aylesbury, Buckinghamshire, England, Apted made his motion picture directorial debut on the war drama *The Triple Echo* (1972). His other film credits include *Coal Miner's Daughter* (1980), *Gorky Park* (1983), *Gorillas in the Mist* (1988), and *Enigma* (2001). He's also the documentarian behind the acclaimed *Up* series, which began with *Seven Up!* in 1964 and has checked in on a group of British-born subjects every seven years from childhood to retirement age.

Director Michael Apted (left), special effects maestro John Richardson (center) and stunt coordinator Vic Armstrong (right) on *The World Is Not Enough*. *Courtesy of the Luc Leclech Collection*

AR-7 folding sniper rifle: A rifle that James Bond (Sean Connery) carries in a trick briefcase in *From Russia with Love*. Though in real life the AR-7 is .22 caliber, Bond's is .25, and Q Branch has equipped it with an infrared telescopic sight. With this rifle, Turkish spymaster Ali Kerim Bey (Pedro Armendariz) kills Krilencu (Fred Haggerty), the Bulgarian agent who was attempting to escape from his apartment's emergency exit in Istanbul—an exit located over the giant mouth of actress Anita Ekberg in a billboard promoting *Call Me Bwana*, an Albert R. Broccoli / Harry Saltzman comedy starring Bob Hope. Bond also makes use of the gun when he wounds a grenade-wielding, helicopter-borne SPECTRE assassin, causing him to drop the grenade and obliterate the chopper.

Ark Royal: SEE "HMS *Ark Royal*."

Arkangel Chemical Weapons Facility: Constructed atop a towering rock precipice in northern Russia and bordered on one side by a huge hydroelectric dam, this secret Soviet storage depot is infiltrated and targeted for destruction by 007 (Pierce Brosnan) and 006 (Sean Bean) during a flashback to the Cold War era in *GoldenEye*. It's commanded by sinister Colonel Ourumov (Gottfried John), who captures 006 and apparently executes him (we find out only later that it was all a setup for 006's defection). Bond engineers his own escape by stealing a motorcycle and effecting an amazing rendezvous with a crashing private plane (reminiscent of stuntman Rick Sylvester's jump off Canada's Asgard Peak in *The Spy Who Loved Me*). Meanwhile, the depot is obliterated by demolition charges set by Bond and 006.

Armendariz, Pedro (May 9, 1912–June 18, 1963): Mexican leading man who, despite a terminal illness, portrayed the exuberant Turkish spymaster Ali Kerim Bey in *From Russia with Love*. Armendariz was perfectly cast as the charming bigger-than-life operative, delivering lines as crisply as a sword point while giving the film an exotic flavor in the manner of classic character actors like Peter Lorre, Sydney Greenstreet, and Basil Rathbone. Armendariz had just finished playing the evil caliph in the King Brothers' 1963 production *Captain Sinbad* (coincidentally, that character was named El Kerim) when director Terence Young signed him to play Kerim Bey.

Because he wanted to improve his family's financial situation, Armendariz told no one that he had cancer of the lymph glands when he came aboard the Bond film. During the final weeks of location shooting in Istanbul, however, Armendariz began to develop a bad limp, and Young finally discovered the truth. His imminent incapacity forced the producers to make some hasty decisions. Could they finish the film with Armendariz, or would they have to find a new actor and reshoot the role?

Young visited Armendariz at his London hotel and asked him about his own plans. The stricken actor mentioned his wife and her need for financial security. "Help me," he asked. "I think I can give you two more weeks. Can you finish with me in that time? I would like to get the money and finish the picture."*

Young, who felt he couldn't do the film without Armendariz, convinced the producers that he could shoot all the remaining Pinewood Studio sequences with Armendariz in the time the dying actor could give them. A meeting was called, and art director Syd Cain and his assistant Michael White were told to begin construction immediately on everything that would require Armendariz, including the sprawling gypsy camp.

Young and cinematographer Ted Moore planned to film all of Armendariz's close-ups by shooting onto the actor over a stand-in's shoulder. Weeks later, Sean Connery would finish his scenes with Terence Young playing Ali Kerim Bey. The atmosphere was heavy at Pinewood Studios during those last weeks of May 1963. For everyone involved in the production, it was as if *From Russia with Love* had taken on a new seriousness.

On Sunday June 9, 1963, Terence Young held a going-away party for Armendariz at his London townhouse. Most of the production cast and crew was there, and Ian Fleming, himself dying of heart disease, arrived in the late afternoon. The two stricken men had met for the first time in Istanbul and had taken a considerable liking to one another. They spent much of the afternoon on a couch in Young's living room, discussing Armendariz's good friend the late Ernest Hemingway. Armendariz mentioned that he had gone to Cuba to visit Hemingway in 1961 before coming to

---

* Terence Young, interview by the author, London, June 25, 1977.

Europe for a part in *Francis of Assisi* for director Michael Curtiz. He remembered that final meeting well, telling Fleming, "On the morning that my boat left for Europe, Ernest came down to my little launch to see me off. We embraced and said farewell. It was sad, because I knew he was dying. As the boat started off, Ernest ran back, jumped into the boat, almost fell in the sea, and put his arms around me, yelling, 'Don't leave! Don't leave me!' He told me that he wouldn't suffer through a long illness. He didn't want to be a vegetable for the rest of his life. He could hardly control himself. But, eventually, with a number of people trying to help him, Ernest left the boat and returned to shore. That was the last time I saw him. Two weeks later, he went to Idaho and shot himself."*

Actor Pedro Armendariz made a strong impression as Turkish spymaster Ali Kerim Bey in *From Russia with Love*. Here he takes aim at Bulgarian assassins sent to kill him at the gypsy camp. *Courtesy of the David Reinhardt Collection*

* Ibid.

After Armendariz had finished his story, Fleming, who was terribly impressed, turned to him and said, "You know [Hemingway's] right; you can never be a vegetable in this life. You've got to go at the right moment." Armendariz nodded, tapped an ash from his long cigar, and said, "You're right, Ian."

On June 18, 1963, nine days later, Pedro Armendariz, lying deathly ill in a hospital bed at UCLA Medical Center in Los Angeles, sent his wife out to have lunch, took a .357 Colt Magnum that he had smuggled in his luggage, and shot himself through the heart with an armor-piercing bullet. Ian Fleming would not last much longer either, dying in August 1964.

Pedro Armendariz was born in Mexico City, raised in the suburb of Churubusco (which was later incorporated into the city itself and became famous for its Churubusco film studio). He eventually moved to Laredo, Texas. After studying at California Polytechnic State University in San Luis Obispo, he returned to Mexico City. Armendariz was discovered by director Miguel Zacarías, who cast him in the drama *Rosario* (1935). After making a number of important, career-building films in Mexico, Armendariz made his US film debut as a police lieutenant in director John Ford's *The Fugitive* (1947). Ford loved his work and continued to cast him in such classic westerns as *Fort Apache* (1948), as former Confederate cavalryman Sergeant Beaufort, and *3 Godfathers* (1948), both opposite John Wayne. It is believed that Armendariz was one of ninety-one people, along with fellow actors John Wayne, Susan Hayward, and Agnes Moorehead, who contracted cancer as a result of exposure to radioactivity from atomic bomb testing while working on the film *The Conqueror* (1956).

armored train: Headquarters of the Janus crime syndicate in *GoldenEye*. A former missile transporter, this railroad juggernaut is home to Alec Trevelyan (Sean Bean), Bond's former close friend and fellow double-0 agent, who is revealed as the head of Janus. When Bond is captured, along with systems programmer Natalya Simonova (Izabella Scorupco), he's brought to the train. Fortunately, he escapes, killing renegade General Ourumov in the process. When Bond targets the train for demolition, Trevelyan and his ace killer, Xenia Onatopp (Famke Janssen), escape in a handy helicopter stored onboard.

James Bond (Pierce Brosnan) and Natalya Simonova (Izabella Scorupco) escape from the disintegrating Janus organization armored train in *GoldenEye*. *Courtesy of the Luc Leclech Collection*

Armstrong, Louis (August 4, 1901–July 6, 1971): Legendary trumpet player and New Orleans native who sang "We Have All the Time in the World" in *On Her Majesty's Secret Service*. In 1969, Armstrong had been in a New York hospital for nearly a year when composer John Barry and lyricist Hal David decided that he was the best person to sing the main song in the film. They needed a man in the autumn of his years who could, with true emotion, sing the line "We've got all the time in the world," which was taken from the last scene in Ian Fleming's original novel.

"Louis Armstrong was the sweetest man alive," recalled John Barry solemnly, "but having been laid up for over a year, he had no energy left. He couldn't even play his trumpet. And still he summoned the energy to do our song. At the end of the recording session in New York City, he came up to me and said, 'Thank you for this job.' He was such a marvelous man. He died soon after that.

"The song didn't do a thing when the film came out. It was a very heavy song, so we couldn't use it as the title track. It was buried inside the film and that probably hurt its chances for success. Interestingly, two years later, it suddenly became number one in Italy."*

Arnold, David (January 23, 1962–   ): Top British film composer who composed the scores for *Tomorrow Never Dies*, *The World Is Not Enough*, *Die Another Day*, *Casino Royale*, and *Quantum of Solace*. A native of Luton, England, Arnold composed his first feature motion picture score for the crime drama *The Young Americans* (1993). His inspired work on the movie *Stargate* (1994), as well as on *Independence Day* (1996), increased his profile considerably and brought him to the attention of the Bond producers.

Arterton, Gemma (February 2, 1986–   ): British actress who portrayed MI6 field agent Strawberry Fields in *Quantum of Solace*. A native of Gravesend, Kent, England, Arterton made her motion picture debut as Kelly in the family comedy *St. Trinian's* (2007), which also featured

---

* John Barry, interview by the author, Los Angeles, December 12, 1977.

Actress Gemma Arterton portrayed MI6 agent Strawberry Fields in *Quantum of Solace. Courtesy of the Anders Frejdh Collection*

Bond player Caterina Murino (*Casino Royale*). After her Bond appearance, she returned as Kelly in *St Trinian's 2: The Legend of Fritton's Gold* (2009), then segued to *Clash of the Titans* (2010), portraying Io.

Asgard Jump, the: Celebrated July 1976 ski/parachute jump off Canada's Asgard Peak by ace ski-jumper Rick Sylvester for *The Spy Who Loved Me*. The idea for this stunt, the most daring of the James Bond series, came to producer Albert R. "Cubby" Broccoli via a Canadian Club whisky advertisement in which Sylvester was pictured flying off the Asgard. Sylvester later admitted that the Asgard jump for Canadian Club had been faked, and that he had really jumped off El Capitan in Yosemite National Park.

For *The Spy Who Loved Me*, Sylvester accepted a $30,000 fee to jump the Asgard for real. He would be doubling Bond (Roger Moore). While on a mission in fictional Berngarten, Austria, Bond is attacked on the ski slopes by four Russian agents carrying machine guns. After killing their leader (Michael Billington) and performing some amazing stunt maneuvers, Bond reaches the edge of an enormous cliff—which he jumps without hesitation, eventually losing his poles and skis.

Will he plunge to his death? Of course not. At the perfect moment, a parachute billows forth, adorned with his country's Union Jack. It is one of the most spectacular moments in the entire Bond series.

Rick Sylvester explained why Asgard Peak was chosen in the first place. "The first requirement is a vertical cliff. Not vertical in the layman's sense, but

in the climber's denotative, meaning a true ninety degrees. Overhanging would be even nicer. Once I sail over the edge with the skis and a closed parachute, I achieve very little horizontal distance.

"Second, there has to be skiable terrain—snow—leading to the edge.

"Third, the cliff should be high, the higher the better. In fact, the higher, the more spectacular—but actually safer too. More vertical means more time to get rid of the skis and deploy the chute, not to mention more time to react if something goes wrong, like bindings not releasing, chute malfunctioning—the usual unthinkables.

"Fourth, I need a suitable landing area, and fifth, suitable wind conditions."*

For Sylvester, the Asgard proved ideal. It was a three-thousand-foot narrow-ledged peak in the Auyuittuq National Park, an arctic wonderland on Canada's Baffin Island, fifteen hundred miles north of Montreal in Inuit country. The Asgard's summit was a football field's length, covered with a carpet of snow and accessible only by helicopter.

While the world prepared for the 1976 Summer Olympics in Montreal to the south, second unit director John Glen assembled his crew of fourteen. In addition to Sylvester, the group included his friend Bob Richardson, an expert climber who would handle safety on the Asgard, working with the camera rigs and keeping a watchful eye on those less experienced in mountain work; Jim Buckley, a parachute expert, who would be in charge of repacking Sylvester's chute, if need be, and keeping track of wind conditions; Monsieur Claude, the proprietor of a Montreal film production company, who would serve as local liaison; a doctor; René Dupont, the film's production coordinator in Canada; Alan Hume, the principal cameraman; two other cameramen and one assistant cameraman; two helicopter pilots; one helicopter mechanic; and director Glen.

John Glen's crew was airlifted out of Montreal in early July 1976, and headed north to Frobisher Bay (now Iqaluit), Baffin Island's largest settlement. From Frobisher Bay, they boarded a DC-3 for a two-hour ride over Cumberland Sound to the little village of Pangnirtung, which in the local vernacular means "place where the bull caribou meet." Here in Pang, ensconced in a comfort-

---

* Rick Sylvester, interview by the author, Los Angeles, January 15, 1978.

Stuntman Rick Sylvester, who jumped Canada's Asgard Peak in *The Spy Who Loved Me* pre-credits teaser. *Steve Rubin Collection*

able hunting lodge, the advance guard of *The Spy Who Loved Me* waited for the appropriate weather conditions.

The Asgard was fifty miles away, a quick hop in the unit's $400-a-day rent-a-copter. For ten days, they waited for the perfect conditions that would allow Sylvester to make his stunt magic. During the interim, Glen shot some test footage, as well as the approach shot showing Sylvester skiing to the takeoff point.

Long hours were spent determining responsibilities and camera positions. Glen had to make sure the stunt was captured properly on film. After ten days of waiting, the calls began to come in from London: "Has he done it yet?"* Back came the negative replies and the grumbling. But there was no other choice. Sylvester wasn't going to risk his life unless the conditions were perfect, and Glen wasn't going to be able to shoot the stunt unless the clouds cleared away from their perch above the Asgard.

The crew remained in Pang, playing cards, watching the Olympics with a decidedly Cana-

dian slant on the cable television, exercising, and making the twice-daily reconnaissance trips to the Asgard. Sylvester had to continually refurbish the prepared run with ice rakes to assure a smooth takeoff.

On a crisp Monday morning, after a night of late television and beer, a tired, grumpy Sylvester took the morning patrol up to the Asgard. After 5:00 AM, the helicopter entered the valley. But the clouds were still there, and a heavy rain had set in. Sylvester yawned, Glen frowned, and the crew returned to base. Sylvester went back to sleep.

Six hours later, the noon reconnaissance returned to the peak and found the Asgard spotlighted in sunshine and the clouds backing off. Glen radioed the base camp and ordered the crew to scramble. It was time. "What?" mumbled Sylvester into the shortwave. "It's okay," replied Glen. "The wind's died down and the clouds are staying away."

The wind was Sylvester's biggest fear. A harsh breeze could push him against the cliff face, making his parachute useless. He recalled those moments in preparation: "The operation suddenly geared up. I was on the first shuttle. We flew in and found the Asgard surrounded by clouds but standing out. And somehow hardly any wind stirred. We had to hurry, though—the clouds looked like they were regrouping for another move."*

At midafternoon, the cameramen were in position. The Jet Ranger helicopter hovered nearby, out of range of the cliff face so that the propeller draft wouldn't interfere with Sylvester's parachute. Alan Hume manned the helicopter camera, which was to take the master shot of the sequence. The other two cameras, positioned on the edge of the cliff itself, were of secondary importance.

Exactly three minutes before a huge cloud blotted out the sun and enshrouded the Asgard in shade, Sylvester received his confirmation from Glen, drew in a sharp breath, dropped down into the egg position, and started his ski run. He bumped across a miniature ice bulge, remained steady, and then shot over the cliff, virtually inches above the head of one of the cliff-positioned cameramen.

Down, drop poles, his mind cried mechanically, and the ski poles went shooting off into space.

---

* Ibid.

* Ibid.

The Canadian Club whisky ad that prompted producer Cubby Broccoli to contact stuntman Rick Sylvester. *Steve Rubin Collection*

Pull off the skis, and his skis fell.

Pop open the chute, and it opened.

"I see the skis rush by. Hmmm, seemed to take a long time for them to catch up with me. How am I doing? Not bad. Heading out from the wall beautifully, toward the broad silky glacier below.

"I see one ski hit at the wall's base, roll down, then get stuck somewhere on a series of ledges.

"The other one swooshes down the steep snow slope leading from the base of the wall. A strange spectacle. Now gently gliding to a stop. And down I come, under the nylon. Lower, lower, lower, touchdown! Up to my knees in snow. It's over. Again?"*

On top of Asgard Peak, Glen was too busy cueing his cameramen to actually see Sylvester's stunt. He was already learning that despite the tests and the painstaking precautions, Hume, in the helicopter, had lost Sylvester soon after he

---

* Ibid.

dropped over the cliff wall. It was up to the ledge cameramen to save the day.

After the doctor confirmed that Sylvester was okay, the film was rushed by helicopter to Pang, where René Dupont personally transported it to Montreal and to a Canadian processing facility. All hands waited for the news. Sylvester anxiously wondered whether the stunt would have to be performed again.

In a very emotional moment, the telephone rang in the crew's converted hunting lodge, and everyone crowded around Glen. "Really?" Glen smiled as Dupont described the film as adequate. The helicopter had indeed lost Sylvester, but one of the ledge cameramen had found him and had caught the entire stunt intact. The parachute had opened, if not perfectly, to reveal the Union Jack—and it looked beautiful.

Glen hung up and smiled at everyone. A cheer went up and Sylvester bought a round of drinks. It was time to pack up and go home.

Aston Martin DB5 with modifications: James Bond's fabulous sports car, featured in *Goldfinger, Thunderball, GoldenEye, Tomorrow Never Dies, Skyfall, Spectre,* and *No Time to Die.* Billed as "the most famous car in the world," it replaced Bond's Bentley, which is seen briefly in *From Russia with Love.*

An Aston Martin was originally introduced in Ian Fleming's 1960 *Goldfinger* novel, but it was a low-tech DB3 with just a few secret compartments and a homing device. But when it came time for 007 producers Albert R. Broccoli and Harry Saltzman to adapt the novel, fresh from their success with the rigged briefcase in *From*

James Bond (Daniel Craig) and his Aston Martin DB10 in action in Rome in *Spectre. Courtesy of the Anders Frejdh Collection*

Russia with Love, they were ready to introduce the ultimate gadget: a car with much more elaborate upgrades.

Buying three silver cars from the Aston Martin plant in England, production designer Ken Adam and special effects supervisor John Stears went to work, taking the cue from the checklist of modifications presented in the screenplay by Q (Desmond Llewelyn): 1) revolving license plates, valid in all countries; 2) bulletproof front, side, and rear windows; 3) audiovisual reception on the dashboard, tied to a magnetic homing device—with a range of 150 miles—placed in the car 007 is tailing (a device that predated modern car GPS capability by nearly forty years); 4) defense mechanism controls built into the car's armrest, including left and right front-wing machine guns, smoke screen and oil slick ejectors, and a switch to raise the rear bulletproof screen; 5) electrically operated and retractable tire shredders, built into the wheel hubs; and 6) a passenger ejector seat activated by a red button hidden atop the gearshift.

The special effects department gave these modifications an assist. The machine guns were actually thin metal tubes activated by an electric motor connected to the car's distributor. Acetylene gas (the kind used in a blowtorch) was discharged into the tubing to give the impression of the guns firing. Insert shots of actual machine guns were also used.

The tire shredder, or "chariot scythe" (named for the same device on Messala's chariot in *Ben Hur*) was really an enormous screw knife welded to a spare knock-on wheel nut. The car had to be stopped to exchange the nut, but thanks to cinematographer Ted Moore's photography and Peter Hunt's editing, the finished film shows it emerging automatically from the hub center.

Bond's 1960s-era GPS, which allows him to track Goldfinger (Gert Fröbe), was another nonworking feature that appears in the film via an insert shot, showing the lighted map, its dialing feature, and the moving blip that indicates the position of Goldfinger's Rolls. The same device is deployed in Kentucky by CIA agent Felix Leiter (Cec Linder).

The ejector seat worked, but it was more a prop than part of the real Aston Martin. The actual seat came from a fighter plane. It was spacious and could be mounted only immediately before the actual shot, in which one of Gold-

Although it appears in a number of Bond films, the Aston Martin DB5 with modifications was introduced to James Bond (Sean Connery) in *Goldfinger. Courtesy of the David Reinhardt Collection*

finger's Chinese guards is thrown through the car's roof. As in a plane, the seat was triggered by compressed air cylinders. For close-ups of the car's interior, the air-powered device was replaced by a non-ejecting passenger seat.

Working features included the electrically operated rotating license plates, which gave Bond three alternative numbers for his car (hardly the "valid all countries" boast that Q makes during his briefing). Bond's smoke screen also worked and was operated by army-type smoke canisters that were discharged into the car's tailpipe. The bulletproof screen, which wasn't really bulletproof, was built into the car's trunk and could be raised or lowered electrically.

The special effects department attached electronic squibs to the car's metal surfaces to simulate ricocheting bullet hits. Into the car's rear light cluster, Stears built two chambers that could be opened to reveal an oil slick sprayer that contained fifteen gallons of colored water, and a supply of caltrops that could be blown out onto the highway by compressed air. The car was completed on schedule in the spring of 1964.

According to Aston Martin, the caltrop ejector was never used in the film because it might have inspired children to spike the tires of vehicles in their neighborhood. Only one car contained all of the special effects modifications, and it was sold to Broccoli and Saltzman's Eon Productions rather than given away free as was originally believed. However, all the subsequent interest in the car, once *Goldfinger* was released, forced the automaker to build two more replicas. These were sent to carnivals, festivals, and other events (including the 1964 New York World's Fair) until the early 1970s, when they were sold to collectors. The replicas' interiors include features that weren't showcased in the film, including a telephone built right into the driver's door, a five-speed manual transmission, a reserve gas tank, a speedometer toplined at 150 mph, a handcrafted body, and very luxurious antelope-hide seat upholstery.

In *Goldfinger*, after planting the homing device in his adversary's Rolls-Royce, Bond (Sean Connery) has the Aston Martin transported to the European mainland via British United Air Ferries. He then follows Goldfinger's Rolls-Royce Phantom III to Switzerland, where he meets and shreds the tires of the very attractive Tilly Masterson (Tania Mallet), the revenge-seeking, poor-shooting sister of the late Jill Masterson (Shirley Eaton). Having accidentally heard Goldfinger utter the words "Operation Grand Slam" to Mr. Ling (Burt Kwouk) the Red Chinese agent, Bond (with Tilly in tow) hops in his DB5 and attempts to escape Goldfinger's factory complex with three Mercedes-Benzes filled with Chinese guards on his tail.

The DB5's defense mechanism controls are immediately put to work. The smoke screen eliminates one Mercedes, which smashes blindly into a tree; a second Mercedes runs into Bond's manufactured oil slick, skids off the road, and explodes into the side of Goldfinger's factory; but the third enemy car corners Bond at a dead end.

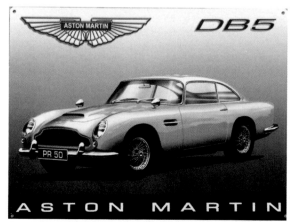

A catalog shot of the world's most famous car.
Courtesy of the David Reinhardt Collection

After Tilly is killed by Oddjob (Harold Sakata), Bond surrenders to his Chinese and Korean pursuers. In one of the great blunders, they allow him to drive his own car back to the factory, guarded by one gun-toting guard in the passenger seat. Make that one *former* gun-toting guard, since Bond immediately triggers the ejector seat.

Back in business, he nonetheless is stymied by a machine gun–wielding gatekeeper (Varley Thomas) and forced back into the factory complex, where he leads two enemy Mercedes sedans on a high-speed chase, which was effectively punched up in editing by Peter Hunt.

Finally, blinded by what he thinks are automobile headlights headed straight for him, 007 crashes his Aston Martin into a brick wall. It turned out that Oddjob rigged a mirror that reflects Bond's own headlights back at him; 007 is captured again.

The Aston Martin DB5 is also featured briefly in the *Thunderball* pre-credits teaser outside Paris, when 007 (Sean Connery once again) activates his rear bulletproof screen and then unleashes a powerful jet of water at SPECTRE guards. As the torrent of water washes over them, the screen dissolves into the arresting nude bathers featured in Maurice Binder's evocative title sequence.

That same trusty Aston Martin DB5 makes a cameo return thirty years later in *GoldenEye* (1995), when Bond (Pierce Brosnan) races it against a Ferrari. It cameos again in *Tomorrow Never Dies* (1997), taking Brosnan's 007 to the Ministry of Defence. Then, fifteen years after that, "the most famous car in the world" makes a more dramatic entrance in *Skyfall* (2012). Unable to secure official transportation from MI6, Bond (Daniel Craig) retrieves his DB5 from a London garage and heads out to Skyfall, his family's country estate in the highlands of Scotland. In one of its saddest moments on screen, the car is raked from end to end by enemy machine gun fire. But just as 007 always manages to regain his footing, this wonderful vehicle is returned to the Q workshops in *Spectre* (2015), where it is completely rebuilt so that Bond (Daniel Craig) can drive it away at the film's conclusion.

Newer-edition Aston Martins are further sprinkled throughout the series. A 1968 Aston Martin makes a splash in the pre-credits teaser of *On Her Majesty's Secret Service*, when Bond (George Lazenby) rescues Tracy (Diana Rigg) from some

A modified 1986 Aston Martin V8 Vantage Volante, equipped with skis for *The Living Daylights*. *Courtesy of the David Reinhardt Collection*

Prince Charles visits 007 (Daniel Craig) and his signature cars on the set of *No Time to Die*. *Courtesy of the Anders Frejdh Collection*

of her father's own hoodlums. At the end of the film, the Aston Martin becomes the honeymoon car for newlyweds Bond and Tracy. Because friends have attached a conspicuous JUST MARRIED sign to the car's rear, Bond stops on the highway to remove it. At that very moment, Blofeld (Telly Savalas) and Irma Bunt (Ilse Steppat) race by, spraying the car with machine gun fire.

In *The Living Daylights*, the new James Bond (Timothy Dalton) is assigned a brand-new 1986 Aston Martin V8 Vantage Volante, which is equipped with its own parcel of customized defense mechanisms designed for snow warfare, including retractable skis that can maneuver the vehicle on ice. A laser mounted in the wheel hubs performs practically the same function, albeit more cleanly, as the spinning chariot-scythe knives in *Goldfinger*; a rocket launcher has a visible target display in the windshield; and a rocket-boosted engine allows the car to virtually fly over a towering roadblock. This Aston Martin is also equipped with a self-destruct mechanism so that it doesn't fall into the wrong hands. Although I wouldn't want to be the one to tell Q that his pride and joy is a bunch of twisted metal.

Pierce Brosnan's 007 definitely gets an upgrade in *Die Another Day*, when he's assigned a gadget-rigged 2002 Aston Martin V12 Vanquish, but many fans thought the writers had jumped the shark when they gave the vehicle "adaptive camouflage"—a device that makes the car invisible. Though a common trope in science fiction films, this modification was altogether wrong for a James Bond adventure. Not to mention, Bond deploys this feature only once, to

roll across the snow to the Ice Palace of Gustav Graves (Toby Stephens).

When Daniel Craig takes over the role in 2006's *Casino Royale*, he's supplied with an Aston Martin DBS V12. About the only thing interesting about this car is that it's supplied with an emergency medical link to MI6 headquarters in London and, thankfully, a defibrillator, which saves Bond's life when he's poisoned by Le Chiffre's girlfriend Valenka (Ivana Milicevic). However, it wasn't the gadgets that distinguished this DBS, it was the extraordinary stunt in which Bond nearly runs over Vesper Lynd (Eva Green) and rolls the car. That stunt broke the international record for most barrel rolls assisted by a special effects cannon. A special air-powered cannon was deployed that allowed the car to complete seven full rolls. Three DBSs, valued at $300,000 each, were destroyed in the stunt.

Basically the same car returns in *Quantum of Solace*, as Bond uses it to chase down his prey in Siena, Italy. In *Spectre*, Bond swipes an Aston Martin DB10 that was earmarked for 009 and gets involved in a huge chase across Rome, during which he deploys a rear-facing double barreled gun, a rear-facing flamethrower, and an ejection seat with parachute. Unfortunately, this beautiful piece of automobile engineering winds up sinking in the dark waters of the Tiber River.

Atkinson, Rowan (January 6, 1955–): British actor, comedian, and television personality who portrayed bumbling foreign service officer Nigel Small-Fawcett in *Never Say Never Again*, his feature film debut. Constantly a royal pain to

007 (Sean Connery), Small-Fawcett yells James Bond's name across a crowded harbor—effectively blowing his cover—and at the end of the movie he disturbs a hot-tub tryst between Bond and Domino Petachi (Kim Basinger).

A native of Consett, County Durham, England, Atkinson first came to the public's attention with his various roles on the award-winning British sketch show *Not the Nine O'Clock News* (1979–1982). His comedy skills were further showcased in the series *The Black Adder* (1982–1983), which was followed by the sequels *Black Adder II* (1986), *Black Adder the Third* (1987), and *Blackadder Goes Forth* (1989). After making a number of video shorts and a television series that introduced his comical Mr. Bean character, he brought him to the big screen in *Bean* (1997). In all these projects, he collaborated with writer/director Richard Curtis, who also cast Atkinson in memorable roles in two of his best-known films: the novice priest in the seminal comedy *Four Weddings and a Funeral* (1994), and Rufus the impossibly precise jewelry salesman in the classic Christmas film *Love Actually* (2003). Atkinson also portrayed the title character in the hilarious spy spoof *Johnny English* (2003) and its two sequels, *Johnny English Reborn* (2011) and *Johnny English Strikes Again* (2018).

Atlantic Iron & Metal Company: Auto-wrecking yard featured in *Goldfinger*. The firm's crane and electromagnet lift the body of the Lincoln Continental belonging to Oddjob (Harold Sakata) and place it into the metal compactor, crushing it into a small metal lump that fits nicely into the bed of Oddjob's Ford Ranchero. As the Lincoln is being lifted, you can see that this car has no engine; only a body shell was crushed. In real life this facility was in Miami, though in the film it's located in a town in Kentucky.

Atlantis (a.k.a. Stromberg Marine Research Laboratory): Huge spider-like amphibious structure located off the coast of Sardinia in *The Spy Who Loved Me*. It's the centerpiece of the undersea city of the future conceived by billionaire shipping magnate Karl Stromberg (Curt Jurgens). Explained production designer Ken Adam, "The idea for Atlantis was not in the original script for *The Spy Who Loved Me*. Cubby [Broccoli], [director] Lewis Gilbert, and I went out to Okinawa, because we had heard about

Bond (Roger Moore) and Anya (Barbara Bach) attempt to escape from a flooding Atlantis in *The Spy Who Loved Me*. *Courtesy of the David Reinhardt Collection*

a Japanese structure that could rise out of the water.

"When we got there, it turned out to be a white elephant. It was something the Japanese government had spent $77 million on for Expo '75, a huge floating exhibition hall called the Aquapolis. It looked like a big floating oil platform, and since it looked so much like an oil rig, I didn't like it.

"It was gigantic, though, and at first I tried to make it work for us." Adam brainstormed ways to augment the real location through the use of models and matte paintings. "But I never could get anywhere on that. It had an immense heliport on the top of the structure, which wasn't necessary. You didn't need a heliport that big.

"Since the Aquapolis was a big disappointment, I decided to design something entirely new. And for the interiors, I wanted to get away from my old straight-line concepts. This time I was going to use circles and ellipses, a concept partly influenced by our location scouting in Sardinia, where much of the architecture along the Costa Smeralda utilizes that style."*

---

* Ken Adam, interview by the author, London, June 17, 1977.

Adam found it interesting that his concepts ended up echoing the cutting-edge real-world design trends of the late 1970s. "As it turned out, this concept was in line with the future of design, in which we see a lot of plastic furniture and prefabricated housing in those shapes. All of the fish tanks in Atlantis were elliptical, the escape corridors featured elliptical exit ways, and Stromberg's big shark pond was circular in shape."

Auger, Claudine (April 26, 1941–December 18, 2019): Stunningly beautiful French actress and Miss France 1958 who perfectly portrayed Dominique "Domino" Derval in *Thunderball*. Her last name is pronounced "aw-JHAY." A native of Paris, Auger made her uncredited film debut in writer/director Pierre Gaspard-Huit's period romantic drama *Christine* (1958). She followed her yeoman outing in *Thunderball* with roles in many international films, including *Triple Cross* (1966), directed by Terence Young and costarring Bond veterans Gert Fröbe and Francis De Wolff); *The Bastard* (1968); *The Bermuda Triangle* (1978); *Fantastica* (1980); *Black Jack* (1981); and many more. Like Ursula Andress in *Dr. No*, her *Thunderball* role was revoiced by actress Nikki Van der Zyl.

Auric Stud: Kentucky estate, built full scale in England at the Pinewood Studios backlot paddock, where Auric Goldfinger (Gert Fröbe) breeds racehorses and plans Operation Grand Slam. Goldfinger's huge ranch house is equipped with a rumpus room where a "hoods convention" assembles to hear the plan. Designed by Ken

The wardrobe requirements for Domino (Claudine Auger) in *Thunderball* were quite abbreviated. *Steve Rubin Collection*

Adam, the room is rigged with a number of electronic controls that can transform it into a high-tech war room, replete with huge maps and photographs and a model of Fort Knox that rises majestically from the floor.

Actress Claudine Auger portrayed Domino in *Thunderball*. *Steve Rubin Collection*

Director Guy Hamilton lines up an establishing shot at Auric Stud, Goldfinger's Kentucky horse-breeding ranch and American base of operations in *Goldfinger*. *Courtesy of the Anders Frejdh Collection*

B-1 bomber: Supersonic US Air Force plane that carries the cruise missiles hijacked by SPECTRE in *Never Say Never Again*. In actuality, the B-1 seen in the film was a three-foot model designed and animated by effects supervisor David Dryer and the effects team from Apogee. A larger, six-foot model, incorporating the plane's bomb bay, was used for the sequence in which the missiles are launched.

B-17 Flying Fortress: Heavy bomber developed for the US Army Air Corps in the 1930s, a converted version of which helps rescue 007 (Sean Connery) and Domino (Claudine Auger) in *Thunderball*. Having obliterated the *Disco Volante* yacht on the nearby reef, 007 and Domino climb from the water into a life raft dropped by the B-17, inflate its signal balloon, and then strap themselves to a harness connected to the balloon's cable. The B-17—equipped with a V-shaped metal catcher on its nose—then snags the balloon, which lifts Bond and Domino skyward and into the rescue plane.

It's not the most dignified form of rescue, but it nonetheless provides a rousing conclusion to what is by some measures still the most popular James Bond film of all time.

baccarat: Blackjack-like card game, popular internationally, that is the focus of both the 1954 CBS TV movie version of *Casino Royale* and the 1967 *Casino Royale* spoof. In the TV movie, Soviet master spy Le Chiffre (Peter Lorre) has been losing heavily at the game. Unless he comes up with the 80 million francs he's illegally borrowed from Soviet coffers, the KGB will target him for assassination. With 26 million francs left, Le Chiffre plans to win back his fortune at the tables. James Bond (Barry Nelson) is assigned the task of playing against him and bankrupting him.

As in blackjack, the object of baccarat is to accumulate a card total closest to a specific number—in this case, the number 9, as compared with blackjack's 21. Players are dealt two cards and choose whether to draw one more. Picture cards are worth nothing. If a player draws only picture cards, he has zero, which is called "baccarat." If a player draws a third card and acquires a total higher than nine, he is busted, which is also called "baccarat."

Traditional baccarat, a.k.a. chemin de fer, differs from blackjack in that it has no house dealer. One of the players serves as the "bank," dealing the cards and putting up a specific amount of his or her own money for other players to wager against. That player remains the bank until he or she can no longer put up a stake or decides

BACCARAT HANDS IN CASINO ROYALE (1954)			
Le Chiffre	Bond	Stake	Le Chiffre's Winnings
baccarat	9	4 million francs	25 million francs
7	5	2 million francs	27 million francs
9	7	4 million francs	31 million francs
6	3	8 million francs	39 million francs
9	7	16 million francs	55 million francs
At this point, Bond is broke, but he suddenly receives a mysterious envelope filled with 35 million francs that replenishes his own coffers.			
3	4	32 million francs	23 million francs
baccarat	9	23 million francs	busted

James Bond (George Lazenby) plays baccarat in *On Her Majesty's Secret Service. Courtesy of the David Reinhardt Collection*

to quit. The other players may risk up to the full amount of the bank's current stake. If they win, they take a corresponding share of the bank's money; if they lose, their wager is added to the bank. A player who wishes to wager the full amount of the stake declares "*banco*," meaning he or she challenges the bank to a one-on-one game.

In the TV film *Casino Royale*, Le Chiffre is the bank, and Bond goes *banco* against him. (No chintzing on Bond's part— he's playing for keeps.) The table on the previ-

After defeating Emilio Largo at the tables in Nassau in *Thunderball*, James Bond (Sean Connery) now moves on to another conquest: Domino (Claudine Auger). *Steve Rubin Collection*

ous page shows the full results of their face-off, including all of Bond's and Le Chiffre's hands, the stake of each game, and the rise and fall of Le Chiffre's total winnings. Having won two preliminary hands against another opponent, Le Chiffre's winnings are up to 29 million francs when Bond enters the game.

In Eon Productions' first 007 film, James Bond (Sean Connery) is introduced playing baccarat at London's Les Ambassadeurs club. But when Eon got around around to remaking *Casino Royale* decades later, in 2006, baccarat was replaced by a high-stakes, no-limit Texas hold'em poker tournament.

Bach, Barbara (August 27, 1947–   ; birth name: Barbara Ann Goldbach): American actress and the wife of former Beatle Ringo Starr who portrayed resourceful KGB agent Major Anya Amasova in *The Spy Who Loved Me*.

Recalled the late director Lewis Gilbert, "Barbara was a very serene kind of girl, very quiet, and thus very effective as the Russian agent. We didn't want anyone flashy or loud. And we couldn't have someone too young either—a girl in her early twenties—because she wouldn't match up with Roger [Moore]. She had to be a mature woman, especially since she was playing a top KGB assassin."[*] Beginning with Major Amasova in *The Spy Who Loved Me*, the Bond filmmakers began to replace the breathless, bosomy Bond girls of the 1960s with more believable female protagonists who could defend themselves and show 007 a thing or two. Bach's Major Amasova demonstrates these qualities throughout the film.

A New York City native, Bach married Italian citizen Augusto Gregorini in 1968 and moved to Italy. She made her feature debut in director Antonio Racioppi's 1971 comedy *Mio padre Monsignore*. That same year she was featured opposite Bond veteran Claudine Auger in two films: Paolo Cavara's horror thriller *The Black Belly of the Tarantula* and Jacques Deray's *A Few Hours of Sunlight*. Bach's additional feature credits include *Stateline Motel* (1973), opposite fellow Bond actress Ursula Andress; *Force 10 from Navarone* (1978), opposite Bond veterans Robert Shaw, Edward Fox, and Richard Kiel and directed by 007 vet Guy Hamilton; *The Humanoid* (1979), once again teaming with Richard Kiel and joined

---

* Lewis Gilbert, interview by the author, London, June 15, 1977.

Newcomer to American film and future wife of Ringo Starr, Barbara Bach shines as Major Anya Amasova in *The Spy Who Loved Me. Courtesy of the David Reinhardt Collection*

NASA engineer in *You Only Live Twice*, and he later returned to the Bond fold as Royal Navy captain Benson in *The Spy Who Loved Me*. According to *Dr. No* director Terence Young, Baker was one of the actors considered for the part of 007.

Born in Varna, Bulgaria, where his father was a British consul, Baker made his feature debut in the war drama *The Intruder* (1953), working for future Bond director Guy Hamilton. His feature credits include *The Dam Busters* (1955); *The Moonraker* (1958), a period adventure that takes place in England in the time of Oliver Cromwell (sorry, no space shuttles); *Sword of Lancelot* (1963), alongside fellow Bond vet Walter Gotell; *The Executioner* (1970), alongside Bond vet Charles Gray; and *ffolkes* (1980), reteaming with Roger Moore,

Actor George Baker was Sir Hilary Bray in *On Her Majesty's Secret Service*. *Steve Rubin Collection*

alongside actor David Hedison and stuntmen George Leech and Richard Graydon.

by another Bond vet, Corinne Cléry; *Jaguar Lives!* (1979), surrounded by another bevy of Bond vets, including Christopher Lee, Donald Pleasence, and Joseph Wiseman; and *Give My Regards to Broad Street* (1984).

Baja California, Mexico: Site of the offshore oil-rig headquarters of Ernst Stavro Blofeld (Charles Gray) in *Diamonds Are Forever*. Bond (Sean Connery) and billionaire Willard Whyte (Jimmy Dean) discover the base when they notice that Blofeld has augmented Whyte's Las Vegas penthouse floor map of his holdings with an oil well in Baja. "Baja!" cries Whyte. "I haven't got anything in Baja!"

Baker, George (April 1, 1931–October 7, 2011): British stage, screen, and television actor who portrayed heraldry expert Sir Hilary Bray in *On Her Majesty's Secret Service*. Baker also dubbed George Lazenby's voice for the sequences in which Bond impersonates Bray at Piz Gloria, the mountain hideaway of Blofeld (Telly Savalas). Baker previously appeared uncredited as a

Baker, Joe Don (February 12, 1936–   ): American tough-guy actor who portrayed shady arms dealer and military memorabilia connoisseur Brad Whitaker in *The Living Daylights*. Baker returned to the Bond fold as CIA agent Jack Wade in *GoldenEye* and *Tomorrow Never Dies*. A native of tiny Groesbeck, Texas, Baker made his film debut as a fixer in *Cool Hand Luke* (1967). He later played Steve McQueen's younger brother in Sam Peckinpah's seminal rodeo drama *Junior Bonner* (1972), but it was his appearance the following year as Sheriff Buford Pusser in Phil Karlson's slam-bang action drama *Walking Tall* that gave his career a major boost—further cementing his reputation as a tough action player.

Going for a more lighthearted approach to the CIA, the producers brought back Joe Don Baker to play Wade in *GoldenEye. Courtesy of the Nicolás Suszczyk Collection*

Bambi: One of the acrobatic ladies whom

Actress Lola Larson (right) portrayed Bambi in *Diamonds Are Forever*, here opposite her partner, Thumper (Trina Parks). *Courtesy of the David Reinhardt Collection*

Blofeld (Charles Gray) assigns the task of guarding Willard Whyte (Jimmy Dean) in *Diamonds Are Forever*. Portrayed by Lola Larson, Bambi and her partner Thumper (Trina Parks) take on James Bond (Sean Connery) when he arrives to rescue Whyte. Agent 007 finally gets the better of them in the swimming pool.

Bardem, Javier (March 1, 1969–   ): Marvelous Academy Award–winning Spanish actor who portrayed Raoul Silva, cyberterrorist and SPECTRE operative, in *Skyfall*. A native of Las Palmas de Gran Canaria, Canary Islands, Spain, Bardem made his credited motion picture debut as Jimmy in director Bigas Luna's *The Ages of Lulu* (1990). A decade later, he made his English language debut as Reinaldo Arenas in director Julian Schnabel's biographical drama *Before Night Falls* (2000), a role for which he received his first Academy Award nomination for Best Actor in a Leading Role (he lost to Russell Crowe in *Gladiator*). He was the first Spanish actor

Traitorous Silva (Javier Bardem) has a charged encounter with James Bond (Daniel Craig) on an abandoned island off the coast of China in *Skyfall*. *Steve Rubin Collection*

to receive an Oscar nomination, and in 2007 he was the first Spanish actor to win an Oscar, scoring his Best Supporting Actor trophy for his role as crazed killer Anton Chigurh in the Coen brothers' crime drama *No Country for Old Men*, which also won Best Picture. He was also nominated for an Academy Award for Best Actor in a Leading Role for *Biutiful* (2010), losing to Colin Firth in *The King's Speech*.

Bardot, Brigitte (September 28, 1934–   ): Iconic French sexpot actress who was director Peter Hunt's first choice for the part of Contessa Tracy di Vicenzo in *On Her Majesty's Secret Service*. Said Hunt, "She would have looked a lot like the Tracy in the book. So Harry Saltzman and I went down to the south of France to see her. We had dinner, twice actually, and she was delightful. But on the second night she informed us that she had just signed a deal to do *Shalako* with Sean Connery."* Diana Rigg was eventually signed to play the woman who marries James Bond at the film's conclusion.

Barnes, Priscilla (December 7, 1954–   ): American actress and comedienne who portrayed Della Churchill, doomed bride of CIA agent Felix Leiter (David Hedison), in *Licence to Kill*. She's murdered by the henchmen of drug lord Franz Sanchez (Robert Davi); the same hoodlums leave Leiter for dead. Born in Fort Dix, New Jersey, Barnes is best known for replacing Suzanne Somers on the sitcom *Three's Company* (70 episodes as nurse Terri Alden, 1981–1984). She made her uncredited feature debut as a bar girl in *Tintorera: Killer Shark* (1977). The following year she played Weena opposite John Beck's Neil Perry in the television adaptation of H. G. Wells's *The Time Machine*. Director Steven Spielberg originally wanted her to play the Willie Scott character in *Indiana Jones and the Temple of Doom*, but Barnes was under contract to *Three's Company* and had to turn down the role, which eventually went to Kate Capshaw, Spielberg's future wife. More recently, she played the recurring role of Magda on *Jane the Virgin* (41 episodes, 2014–2019).

Barrelhead Bar: Seedy watering hole on the Bahamian island of Bimini where Bond (Timothy

---

* Peter Hunt, interview by the author, London, June 21, 1977.

Dalton) meets undercover CIA operative Pam Bouvier (Carey Lowell) in *Licence to Kill*. Equipped with a formidable Mossberg "Rogue" shotgun, Pam is observing the activities of some drug runners employed by Franz Sanchez (Robert Davi) when she's joined by Bond. After Sanchez's henchman Dario (Benicio Del Toro) joins the party, a brawl breaks out, with Bouvier and Bond putting on a good show until Pam blasts a hole in the barroom wall so they can escape. Dario shoots Pam in the back as they flee, but she survives, thanks to some body armor. The Barrelhead Bar was actually an interior designed by Peter Lamont and filmed at Churubusco Studios in Mexico City. The exterior where Bond's motorboat arrives at the dock was filmed at the Harbor Lights Bar in Key West, Florida.

Barry, John (November 3, 1933–January 30, 2011; birth name: John Barry Prendergast): Five-time Oscar-winning British film composer best known for his work on the James Bond films. Barry's contribution to the series was enormous, especially in the early days, when the tenor of the films was deadly serious.

Iconic Bond composer John Barry. *Courtesy of the Film Music Society*

Barry's Bond theme, officially credited to Monty Norman, is arguably the most famous signature theme in film history and a trademark of the Bond movies produced by Eon Productions. When the Jack Schwartzman–produced *Never Say Never Again* opened in 1983 without the signature theme, one of the common complaints was the lack of "real James Bond music."

Barry's show business roots date back to his maternal grandfather, a sea captain who used his pension to purchase a repertory theater in Lancaster, England, which he owned and operated until his death. Barry's mother was an accomplished piano player, and his father, John Xavier Prendergast, took over his father-in-law's theatrical operation, later expanding it into a chain of theaters and cinemas.

Young Barry attended convent school until the age of nine, when he left for a public school education in London. He followed his mother's example at first and practiced piano, but by the time he was sixteen he had taken a liking to the trumpet. He was also studying harmony and orchestration with Dr. Francis Jackson, the master of music at York Minster cathedral, while also playing trumpet in a local dance band. In 1952, Barry was drafted and spent three years in the Green Howards Regiment, which was sent to Egypt and Cyprus. Draftees were required to spend only two years in the service, but Barry wanted to continue to study music in the regimental band, so he agreed to sign on for the extra year.

On Cyprus, he started a practical correspondence course with Bill Russo, jazz bandleader Stan Kenton's orchestra arranger in the United States. Barry began to arrange the music for his regiment, and when he left the army in 1955, he was practically guaranteed a good orchestral job in London.

It was at this point that Bill Haley and Elvis Presley appeared on the music scene, affecting the futures of all young musicians everywhere. Barry was no exception; he spent every spare moment listening to the new sound and preparing his own first rock and jazz rendition.

In 1956, Barry formed the John Barry Seven in London with three army buddies and their friends. He was the first bandleader in England to employ an electric bass guitar player. Barry and his band dived headfirst into the rock 'n' roll revolution, and within two years they were the leading jazz-oriented group in England.

Their success led directly to offers to score feature films, the first of which was a little movie entitled *Beat Girl*, which was released by Renown Pictures in 1960. Between 1960 and 1962, Barry

Composer John Barry and the Norwegian pop group a-ha. *Courtesy of the Film Music Society*

Trumpeter John Barry (front left) and his signature 1960s pop group the John Barry Seven. *Courtesy of the Film Music Society*

and his group toured England and worked on the scores of three more films: *Never Let Go* (1960), *The Amorous Mr. Prawn* (1962), and *The L-Shaped Room* (1962).

Barry's involvement with the Bond movies began in late 1962, when he received a call from Noel Rogers of United Artists Records. Barry had recorded two hit records for United Artists. One called "Hit and Miss" was a signature tune for a BBC program called *Juke Box Jury*, and the other was an English version of the American hit "Walk Don't Run." With two important instrumentals on the charts, UA was interested in Barry for the first Bond film, *Dr. No*. Barry learned from Rogers that 007 producers Broccoli and Saltzman were disenchanted with a Bond theme created by composer Monty Norman and that *Dr. No* needed a vibrant theme as soon as possible.

Considering the impact his theme would have on the future of the series, it is ironic that Barry completed his job without ever having seen *Dr. No*. He was simply handed a timing sheet and told to come up with a two-and-a-half-minute theme that could fit conveniently into the film's title track. Although he composed the piece from scratch, it was not entirely original. He borrowed from his own instrumental compositions, especially a little tune titled "Bee's Knees," which featured that same distinctly plucked guitar.

Little did Broccoli and Saltzman know when they first heard the Bond theme how popular it would become. Barry's fee for the James Bond theme was 200 pounds, less than $1,000. Because of the producers' contract with Monty

Norman, Barry would never receive credit for creating the most famous theme in movie history. In fact, it is Norman's name—not Barry's—that always appears in a film's credits if the Bond theme is used.

Still, the success of the first film encouraged the creative relationship between Barry and the producers, which extended to *From Russia with Love*, *Goldfinger*, *Thunderball*, *You Only Live Twice*, *On Her Majesty's Secret Service*, *Diamonds Are Forever*, *The Man with the Golden Gun*, *Moonraker*, *Octopussy*, *A View to a Kill*, and *The Living Daylights*. Although his Bond work never netted him Academy Award consideration, Barry won five other Oscars, for *Born Free* (song and score, 1966), *The Lion in Winter* (score, 1968), *Out of Africa* (score, 1985), and *Dances With Wolves* (score, 1990).

Bartle, Joyce: Top Wilhelmina model , a native of Astoria, Queens, whose famous legs were featured in the sexy poster art advertising *For Your Eyes Only*. An experienced dancer, she

Lingerie model Joyce Bartle's legs in the poster for *For Your Eyes Only*. To accentuate the look, the bathing suit is backward. *Courtesy of the David Reinhardt Collection*

Stunning Joyce Bartle shows off some of the form that won her the leg assignment on the *For Your Eyes Only* poster. *Courtesy of the Joyce Bartle Collection*

made the jump to modeling, and her early career involved a great deal of lingerie and panty hose work, which brought her to the attention of the Bond advertising team. Bartle later became a conflict manager and mediator, while doing considerable philanthropic work and personal style consultation.

Bartlett, Ruby: A British patient at the Bleuchamp Institute for Allergy Research, portrayed by actress Angela Scoular in *On Her Majesty's Secret Service*. Ruby's from Morecambe Bay, Lancashire, and she's terribly allergic to chicken. She also develops a passionate interest in James Bond (George Lazenby), who has infiltrated the institute as heraldry expert Sir Hilary Bray, Baronet. She astutely recognizes his title as designating "a kind of inferior sort of baron," but "Hilary" doesn't take it as an insult. Patients are not allowed to give their room numbers to strangers, so Ruby writes hers in lipstick on 007's inner thigh (it's helpful that he's wearing a kilt). Later, Bond manages to sneak into her room. They're about to make love when Blofeld (Telly Savalas) begins Ruby's nightly brainwashing regimen—revealing the institute's true purpose.

Basinger, Kim (December 8, 1953–   ; birth name: Kimila Ann Basinger): Gorgeous American actress and former model who portrayed Domino Petachi, mistress to SPECTRE master spy Maximilian Largo (Klaus Maria Brandauer), in *Never Say Never Again*. The spectacularly proportioned Basinger was the perfect love interest

for Sean Connery, returning as 007 outside Eon Productions' main Bond series. Unlike Eon's Bond at the time, Roger Moore, who spent a limited amount of time making love to his leading ladies, Connery in *Never Say Never Again* is very much attached to Domino in the film's second half. The steamy highlights include their massage rendezvous in the south of France, their shower in the American nuclear sub, and their hot-tub scene at the film's conclusion.

Basinger, a native of Athens, Georgia, began her career in television (she scored the Donna Reed role in the 1979 television remake of *From Here to Eternity*), and made her feature film debut opposite Jan-Michael Vincent and Michael Parks in *Hard Country* (1981). After her Bond appearance, her career blossomed, with major roles in such high-profile films as *The Natural* (1984); *9½ Weeks* (1986); *Batman* (1989), as photojournalist Vicki Vale; Robert Altman's *Ready to Wear* (1994); *8 Mile* (2002), as Eminem's mother; *The Door in the Floor* (2004); and *The Nice Guys* (2016). In 1997, she won the Oscar for Best Supporting Actress for her role in *L.A. Confidential*.

Bass, Alfie (April 8, 1916–July 15, 1987): British character comedian, best remembered as Shorty in *The Lavender Hill Mob* (1951), who went on to do three Bond cameos. As the astonished drunk with wine bottle in hand, he does classic double takes at Bond's miraculous feats: in *The Spy Who Loved Me*, as 007's Lotus Esprit submarine car emerges onto the Sardinian beach; in St. Mark's Square in *Moonraker*, as his gondola hovercraft passes by; and at a Cortina ski resort in *For Your Eyes Only*, as Bond is pursued by enemy skiers. Bass is credited only for *Moonraker*, as the "Consumptive Italian." Bass made his feature film debut in director Charles Frend's romantic comedy *Johnny Frenchman* (1945).

Bassey, Shirley (January 8, 1937–   ): International recording artist and diva of rhythm and blues who recorded the title songs for three James Bond films: *Goldfinger* (her film debut), *Diamonds Are Forever*, and *Moonraker*. Born in Tiger Bay, Cardiff, Wales, Bassey was discovered in 1955 at the Astor Club by music impresario Jack Hylton, who signed her to appear in *Such Is Life*, a show built around comedian Al Read. Bassey was making records by 1956, and had a run of respectable hits by the time she was

Taking over a crane, James Bond prepares to deliver Blofeld's bathosub to oblivion during oil-platform action in *Diamonds Are Forever*. *Courtesy of the Anders Frejdh Collection*

twenty-three. Her music has also appeared in such films as *The Liquidator* (1965), *Murphy's Law* (2001), *The Life and Death of Peter Sellers* (2004), *Cats & Dogs: The Revenge of Kitty Galore* (2010), and *Nocturama* (2016). In 2000, for her services to entertainment, Bassey was awarded Dame Commander of the Order of the British Empire.

bathosub: One-man submarine utilized by Ernst Stavro Blofeld (Charles Gray) in *Diamonds Are Forever*. Realizing his situation aboard his Baja California oil rig base is hopeless, Blofeld enters the sub and orders his crane driver to lower him into the ocean. Bond (Sean Connery), however, knocks out the driver and gains control of the crane and the sub. Literally in the driver's seat, he begins to play with his longtime nemesis, eventually smashing the sub into the wall of a building, where it explodes.

"Originally," recalled screenwriter Tom Mankiewicz, "in my first version of the ending, Blofeld was escaping underwater in his bathosub when Bond sees the submarine idling in twelve feet of water. Bond dives off the oil rig, holding the long string of a huge weather balloon, which he ties to the sub's conning tower . . . And they were going to wind up in a giant salt mine. But this was all very long and involved. . . .

"First of all, Blofeld was going to die in the salt mine. . . . At that particular point, nobody knew what was going to happen in the next film. . . . Blofeld might have been in the next film, especially if somebody had a good idea."[*]

But, he added, "the picture was quite long at the time and . . . something had to go. So we said, 'Let's deal with Blofeld on the rig.' Because, as

---

[*] Tom Mankiewicz, interview by the author, Los Angeles, November 7, 1977.

you remember, we still had to get to our tag with Mr. Wint and Mr. Kidd on the ocean liner."

Bautista, Dave (January 18, 1969–   ): Champion wrestler turned actor who portrayed the formidable Mr. Hinx, an assassin, in *Spectre*. Best known for his role as Drax the Destroyer in the *Guardians of the Galaxy* film series, Bautista, a native of Washington, DC, made his motion picture debut as Ray in director Brian A. Miller's crime drama *House of the Rising Sun* (2011). The following year he played Brass Body in the action drama *The Man with the Iron Fists*, directed by RZA of the Wu-Tang Clan and also featuring Bond player Rick Yune (*Die Another Day*).

Dave Bautista, as Hinx the assassin in *Spectre*, joins a long line of physically imposing killers who fall short against James Bond. *Courtesy of the Anders Frejdh Collection*

bauxite mine: The perfect cover for the operations of Dr. No (Joseph Wiseman) on Crab Key in *Dr. No*. The mine scenes were filmed at an actual bauxite facility on the Jamaican coast near Ocho Rios. In Fleming's original novel, the operations were disguised within a guano, or bird dung, processing facility.

Bean, Sean (April 17, 1959–   ): Popular English character actor who played Alec Trevelyan, a.k.a. 006, a.k.a. Janus, an ex-double-0 agent turned traitor, in *GoldenEye*. Bean first received international attention when he portrayed Sean Miller, an Irish terrorist who confronts Harrison Ford in *Patriot Games* (1992). He later played Boromir, the doomed prince of Gondor, in *The Lord of the Rings: The Fellowship of the Ring* (2001), and ten years later he starred as Eddard

"Ned" Stark, the charismatic patriarch of the Stark family, in the HBO series *Game of Thrones*. A native of Sheffield, South Yorkshire, Bean made his feature film debut in director Roy Battersby's romantic drama *Winter Flight* (1984).

Bedfont Lakes, Middlesex, England: Location where the filmmakers shot the cocktail party thrown by Elliot Carver (Jonathan Pryce) for the launch of his cable news network in *Tomorrow Never Dies*. The offices of IBM were used as the network's new studio, which in the film was located in Hamburg.

Bedi, Kabir (January 16, 1946–   ): Tall, deep-voiced veteran Indian actor who portrayed Gobinda, bodyguard and chief henchman of Kamal Khan (Louis Jourdan) in *Octopussy*. A native of Lahore, Punjab, Bedi made his film debut in director Surendra Mohan's *Seema* (1971). He made his English language debut opposite Bond players Britt Ekland and Lana Wood in James Polakof's *Satan's Mistress* (1982), followed by the warmly received war drama *Forty Days of Musa Dagh* (1982), in which Bedi starred as Armenian resistance leader Gabriel Bagradian. Since *Octopussy*, Bedi has worked

Indian actor Kabir Bedi portrayed Gobinda, formidable majordomo of Kamal Khan (Louis Jourdan) in *Octopussy*. *Courtesy of the David Reinhardt Collection*

constantly in Bollywood films, as well as such international titles as *The Beast of War* (1988, released in the US as *The Beast*), *Beyond Justice* (1991), and *The Broken Key* (2017).

Bell Rocket Belt: A one-man, jet-propelled flying apparatus worn by James Bond (Sean Connery) during his escape from the French chateau of Jacques Bouvar (Bob Simmons) in the pre-credits teaser of *Thunderball*. As 007 remarks to his French contact Mademoiselle LaPorte (Mitsouko), "No well-dressed man should be without one." The suit was real and actually flew, though it was piloted by a US Army jet-pack specialist assigned to the film crew. The stunt was performed outside France's Château d'Anet on the afternoon of February 19, 1965. Bond's escapades with the jet pack became a prominent element of the film's poster and trailer campaign, alongside his underwater antics.

"No well-dressed man should be without one." James Bond (Sean Connery) escapes from enemy gunmen using a Bell Rocket Belt. *Courtesy of the Michael VanBlaricum Collection*

Bellucci, Monica (September 30, 1964–   ): Italian beauty who portrayed Lucia Sciarra, widow of an enemy operative in *Spectre*. Born in Città di Castello, Umbria, Bellucci made her feature film debut as Francesca, the lead in director Francesco Laudadio's drama *La riffa* (1991). However, it was her charismatic performance as the title character Malèna Scordia in Giuseppe Tornatore's *Malèna* (2000) that brought her to the attention of international audiences. She

Director Sam Mendes (right) with actress Monica Bellucci while shooting the funeral of her character's husband in *Spectre*. *Courtesy of the Anders Frejdh Collection*

later played Persephone in *The Matrix Reloaded* and *The Matrix Revolutions* (both 2003).

belly dancers: Given its exotic locations and beautiful women, the James Bond series features an unsurprising number of belly dancers. With their jingling costumes, voluptuous figures, and alluring artistry, they titillate audiences while keeping the sexual content within the PG-13 range.

Belly dancers figure prominently in *From Russia with Love*. Not only does a dancer credited as Leila perform for Bond (Sean Connery) at the gypsy camp, but she is featured prominently in the title credits designed by Robert Brownjohn and Trevor Bond. According to the late cinematographer Frank Tidy (*Dracula* starring Frank Langella; *Spacehunter: Adventures in the Forbidden Zone*), who broke into the film business as an assistant to Brownjohn and Bond, the idea for the *From Russia with Love* titles came when Brownjohn's wife walked in front of a slide show he was projecting. From that idea came the concept of projecting the titles on the undulating form of a belly dancer. Among cinematographers, it was an in-joke that cinematographer Ted Moore's credit was projected on Leila's posterior.

In *The Man with the Golden Gun*, on the trail of Francisco Scaramanga (Christopher Lee), Bond (Roger Moore) ends up in Beirut tracking down the bullet that killed British agent Bill Fairbanks. A golden "dumdum bullet" that flattens on impact for maximum wounding effect, it's the lucky charm of belly dancer Saida (Carmen Sautoy), and she will not dance without it. Bond swallows the bullet during a fight with enemy agents.

Belly dancers also appear as ornaments in the tent of Sheik Hosein (Edward de Souza), Bond's contact in Egypt in *The Spy Who Loved Me*.

beluga caviar: Exotic appetizer ordered by Bond (Sean Connery) but never served during a romantic evening encounter with Domino (Claudine Auger) in *Thunderball*. It's also a prominent item in the suitcase of gourmet provisions 007 smuggles into the Shrublands health clinic in *Never Say Never Again*. Rather than commit himself to the clinic's healthy dietary regimen, Bond packs "emergency" rations including the beluga, quail's eggs, foie gras from Strasbourg, and vodka. It's also what black-marketeer Valentin Zukovsky (Robbie Coltrane) manufactures at his plant on the Caspian Sea in *The World Is Not Enough*. When the plant is obliterated by buzz-saw-wielding helicopters deployed by Renard (Robert Carlyle), Zukovsky ends up in a vat of caviar that nearly drowns him, until

he supplies useful information to Bond (Pierce Brosnan).

Bennett, Charles (August 2, 1899–June 15, 1995): British screenwriter and playwright who cowrote CBS's 1954 live-TV adaptation of *Casino Royale* with Antony Ellis. Bennett was born in Shoreham-by-Sea, West Sussex, England, earned his first on-screen writing credit as the original playwright on director Alfred Hitchcock's *Blackmail* (1929), and later reteamed with Hitchcock as a screenwriter on such classics as *The Man Who Knew Too Much* (1934), *The 39 Steps* (1935), and *Foreign Correspondent* (1940), the last of which earned him an Oscar nomination for for Best Original Screenplay, which he shared with cowriter Joan Harrison. Bennett also wrote director Jacques Tourneur's atmospheric supernatural thriller *Curse of the Demon* (1957), as well as Irwin Allen's colorful dinosaur film *The Lost World* (1960), which costarred future Bond players Jill St. John and David Hedison.

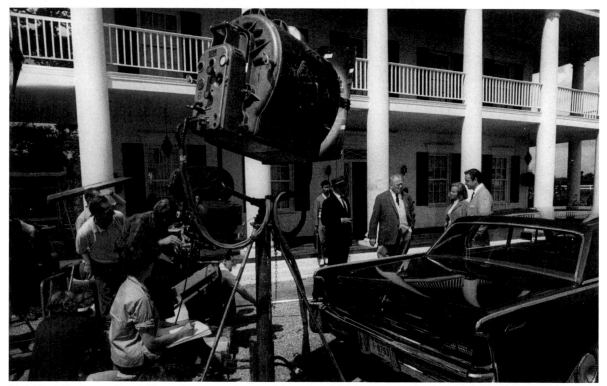

Right to left: James Bond (Sean Connery), Pussy Galore (Honor Blackman), and Goldfinger (Gert Fröbe) say good-bye to Mr. Solo (Martin Benson), the one hood who won't go along with Operation Grand Slam in *Goldfinger*. *Courtesy of the Anders Frejdh Collection*

Benson, Martin (August 10, 1918–February 28, 2010): Sinister-looking British character actor who portrayed doomed mob kingpin Mr. Solo, who has a "pressing engagement" in *Goldfinger*. A native of London, Benson garnered the first film credit of his lengthy career as Count Stephan Mikla in director Harold French's drama *The Blind Goddess* (1948). Benson's other feature appearances include *The King and I* (1956), as Kralahome; *The 3 Worlds of Gulliver* (1960), as villainous Flimnap; *Exodus* (1960); *Gorgo* (1961); *Cleopatra* (1963); *A Shot in the Dark* (1964); and *The Omen* (1976), as doomed Father Spiletto.

Benz, Commissar: Mustachioed Russian agent based in Istanbul, portrayed by actor Peter Bayliss in *From Russia with Love*. As the agent in charge of surveillance at the local railroad station, it is Benz who spots Bond (Sean Connery) and Tatiana Romanova (Daniela Bianchi) as they board the Orient Express with Ali Kerim Bey (Pedro Armendariz).

To ensure a safe journey for his friends, Kerim Bey later tricks Benz into opening his door for the ticket agent, only to brandish a loaded pistol in the Russian's face. Trussed up like a turkey, Benz is left alone with Kerim Bey, who will keep the Russian company until Bond escapes across the Turkish/Bulgarian border. Meanwhile, Benz gets to hear Kerim Bey's life story.

Unfortunately, these events are observed by SPECTRE assassin Donald Grant (Robert Shaw) who eventually murders both Kerim Bey and Benz, making it appear as if they killed each other.

Beretta 418: Italian-made .25 caliber semiautomatic pistol that is 007's weapon of choice prior to the start of *Dr. No*. According to Bond (Sean Connery), he's used it for ten years, since 1952, and he's never missed with it. However, Major Boothroyd the armorer (Peter Burton) believes the Beretta is too light a weapon for a double-0 agent, with no stopping power, deeming it more appropriate for "a lady's handbag." Consequently, since it jammed on 007 on his last mission, sending him to the hospital for six months, M (Bernard Lee) orders Boothroyd to show Bond the finer points of the Walther PPK.

Beretta 950 Jetfire: Model of .25 caliber semiautomatic pistol used by CIA undercover operative Pam Bouvier (Carey Lowell) in *Licence to Kill*. Bouvier carries hers in a special lace-garter leg holster designed by Jodie Tillen.

Berkoff, Steven (August 3, 1937–   ): Acclaimed British actor, director, and playwright who portrayed fanatical Soviet general Orlov in *Octopussy*. In a film brimming with interesting characters and mysterious events, it's a bravura performance, enhanced by Berkoff's unusual look and his wild mannerisms and gestures. Even his dialogue, delivered in a measured tone from an obnoxious, strutting carriage, lands with additional impact, especially during his lecture to the Soviet leadership on the possibility of a military breakthrough in the West. Berkoff's skill at portraying a textured villain has elevated other films and television programs as well, including the miniseries *War and Remembrance* (1988–1989), in which he portrayed Hitler. A London native, Berkoff received his dramatic training in England and France and formed the London Theatre Group in 1968. He made his uncredited feature debut as a teenager in *The Sheriff of Fractured Jaw* (1958) and later appeared in *Nicholas and Alexandra* (1971); *A Clockwork Orange* (1971); *Barry Lyndon* (1975); *Outland* (1981), opposite Sean Connery; *Beverly Hills Cop* (1984), as

General Orlov (Steven Berkoff) attempts to escape across the border between East and West Germany in *Octopussy*. *Steve Rubin Collection*

businessman Victor Maitland; *Rambo: First Blood Part II* (1985); *The Krays* (1990); and *The Girl with the Dragon Tattoo* (2011).

Berry, Halle (August 14, 1966–   ): Academy Award–winning actress and former teen beauty queen who portrays Jinx, a sultry American NSA operative in *Die Another Day*. Her intro-duction—emerging from the surf in a striking orange bikini—was the writers' homage to Ursula Andress's debut in *Dr. No*. Her torture scene in the ice-structure lab of Gustav Graves (Toby Stephens) is also an homage, to Bond's laser beam near-castration in *Goldfinger*. During shooting in Cádiz, Spain, Berry suffered a minor scare when a fragment from a smoke grenade got lodged in her left eye. At a nearby hospital, Berry underwent a thirty-minute procedure to remove the fragment, which fell on her in a

Halle Berry cuts an impressive figure as NSA agent Giacinta "Jinx" Johnson in *Die Another Day*. *Courtesy of the David Reinhardt Collection*

sequence where Bond (Pierce Brosnan) shoots down an enemy helicopter.

As to following her Oscar-winning perfor-mance in *Monster's Ball* (2001) with a part in a James Bond movie, Berry told the television program *Entertainment Tonight*, "People love James Bond. Being in a Bond movie right after winning an Oscar is the best thing I can do. It's a big movie around the world, it's splashy, it's exciting, it's sexy, it's provocative, it's fun, and it will keep me still out there after winning an Oscar. I can assure myself I'm not going to fall into obscurity after that grounding achieve-ment."* A native of Cleveland, Ohio, Berry made her motion picture debut in Spike Lee's romantic drama *Jungle Fever* (1991). Her additional feature film credits include *The Last Boy Scout* (1991); *The Flintstones* (1994); *The Rich Man's Wife* (1996); *Bulworth* (1998); *X Men* (2000), as the mutant Storm; *Swordfish* (2001); *X-Men 2* (2003); *Gothika* (2003); *Catwoman* (2004); *X-Men: The Last Stand* (2006); *New Year's Eve* (2011); *Cloud Atlas* (2012); *X-Men: Days of Future Past* (2014); and *Kingsman: The Golden Circle* (2017).

Beswick, Martine (September 26, 1941–   ): Jamaican-born British actress who scored roles in two separate Bond films directed by Terence Young. In *From Russia with Love*, her film debut, she's statuesque Zora, the gypsy girl who battles fellow gypsy Vida (Aliza Gur) in a memorable girl fight. A favorite of Young's, Beswick returned in *Thunderball*, portraying Paula Caplan, assistant to James Bond (Sean Connery) in Nassau. Beswick also appeared as the barmaid in *Saturday Night Out* (1964), a musical comedy that costarred fellow Bond vet-erans Bernard Lee and Margaret Nolan. She also starred opposite Raquel Welch in *One Million Years B.C.* (1966), where she met her then hus-band John Richardson. In 1980, she starred as celebrated real-life madam Xaviera Hollander in *The Happy Hooker Goes to Hollywood*. NOTE: In the *From Russia with Love* opening credits, her name is misspelled as "Martin Beswick." Geez!

bezants: Ornamental gold balls featured on various medieval coats of arms, including that of the Bond family. The Bonds have three bezants on theirs, according to the research done by Sir

---

* Halle Berry, interview, *Entertainment Tonight*, Paramount Domestic Television, November 18, 2002.

Hilary Bray (George Baker) in *On Her Majesty's Secret Service*. During his conversation with Ruby Bartlett (Angela Scoular) at Piz Gloria, 007 (George Lazenby) incorrectly tells her that his coat of arms has four bezants instead of three. It's not clear whether this was an unintentional blooper or Bond is simply inflating his ball count. NOTE: The Bond coat of arms seen in the film was created by production designer Syd Cain.

Bianchi, Daniela (January 31, 1942–   ): Voluptuous Italian leading lady and Miss Rome 1960, who won the part of reportedly defecting Russian cipher clerk Tatiana "Tanya" Romanova in *From Russia with Love*—a character described in Ian Fleming's original novel as looking like a "young Greta Garbo." A truly stunning beauty and a highlight of the series, Bianchi worked well with Sean Connery, and their scenes together have a polish and a realism that is uncommon in the series, probably because this is the best Bond script. Her seduction scene in the bridal suite of an Istanbul hotel was pretty steamy for 1963, especially with SPECTRE movie cameras recording it from inside the *cabinet de voyeur*.

Between takes on the Orient Express with Sean Connery and Daniela Bianchi in *From Russia with Love*. When the cameras roll again, Daniela's character, Tanya, is going to get slipped a mickey. *Courtesy of the David Reinhardt Collection*

Italian beauty Daniela Bianchi made a memorable impression as seductive Russian cipher clerk Tatiana Romanova in *From Russia with Love*. *Courtesy of the David Reinhardt Collection*

In postproduction another actress, Barbara Jefford, entirely revoiced the part, which was Bianchi's English-language debut.

Daniela Bianchi made her European motion picture debut uncredited in the French film *Love Is My Profession* (1958). Four years later came her first two credited appearances: in another French film, *Demons at Midnight*, and in Italian director Giulio Petroni's *Always on Sunday*. In 1967, Bianchi teamed with fellow Bond veterans Adolfo Celi, Bernard Lee, Anthony Dawson, and Lois Maxwell, as well as Sean Connery's brother Neil, in the spy thriller/spoof *Operation Kid Brother*. In 1970, she married Italian cargo shipping company president Alberto Cameli and retired from show business. They have a son, Filippo.

Actress Daniela Bianchi behind the scenes on *From Russia with Love*. *Courtesy of the David Reinhardt Collection*

Big, Mr.: Tough Harlem drug kingpin portrayed by Yaphet Kotto in *Live and Let Die*. Mr. Big is actually the sinister Dr. Kananga, a diplomat and drug smuggler from the mythical Caribbean island of San Monique. The Mr. Big disguise allows Kananga to maintain a disciplined crime syndicate in the States while performing the sensitive duties of a UN diplomat in New York City. Moving between the two identities can be difficult, so Kananga employs a number of hide-outs, secret passageways, and electronic ruses that confuse CIA surveillance teams.

Harlem crime lord Mr. Big (Yaphet Kotto, center) is really sinister Caribbean diplomat Kananga in disguise in *Live and Let Die*. *Courtesy of the Anders Frejdh Collection*

Binder, Maurice (August 25, 1925–April 9, 1991): Renowned American artist, title designer, trailer maker, marketing specialist, and longtime resident of England whose stylishly photographed nude models and world-famous title sequences were a mainstay of Eon Productions' Bond series for decades.

The pattern was established practically from the beginning. Composer John Barry's staccato 007 theme rings out as Binder's twin white dots roll across the screen, gradually turning into a through-the-gun-barrel portrait of James Bond. Agent 007 walks across the screen, turns, and fires his pistol. The gun view wavers and a red shroud washes across it. Is there a more recognizable title graphic in the world? An incredible pre-title teaser sequence usually follows, setting the audience on the edge of their seats. Then, as they recover, Binder's titles and requisite nudes strike, perfectly matched to the opening-titles song by a popular recording artist of the period.

Like a circus ringmaster's oratory, Binder's titles prepare the audience for the adventures to come.

They've become as integral a part of the series as the phrase "Bond, James Bond." And subsequent title designers have continued the tradition.

What would the films be like without them? Just look at the opening sequence of *Never Say Never Again*, the non-Eon Bond film from 1983. Producer Jack Schwartzman told me that by the time they got to postproduction, there wasn't much money left in the bank to cover either evocative titles or a pre-credits sequence, the latter of which was planned but never shot.* So all the film can offer is Lani Hall's title song, which is catchy—but it plays over a bland helicopter shot of the Bahamas that's totally underwhelming.

Maurice Binder was the son of a New York City manufacturer who grew up studying ship and architectural design. Attending Stuyvesant High School, his ambition was to become a naval architect. He was a precocious, energetic kid, and his mother shipped him off to the Art Students League and sketching classes to quiet him down.

In 1939, at the age of fourteen, Binder began to edit a company newspaper produced by the advertising department of Macy's department store. He also produced a radio program on WOR in Newark called the *Macy-Bamberger Boys' Club*. As a teenager working on the show, Binder received an education in radio production, sound effects, and special effects. After graduating from high school at fifteen, Binder attended City College of New York and night school at St. John's University. At seventeen, he became the assistant art director at Macy's, in charge of catalog and mail order.

"In those days," he remembered, "we had dozens of publications. There were piles of advertising layouts to do, and it took someone who could work quickly."[†]

His burgeoning art career, however, was put on hold as World War II heated up in Europe. In 1941, as a civilian administrative assistant attached to the War Department on a diplomatic passport, he embarked on a two-and-a-half-year building program throughout the Middle East and North Africa. Binder helped build airports, hospitals, roads, and military bases in Aden, Oman, Masirah Island, Syria, Lebanon, Palestine, Cairo, and Dakar. From the Allied air bases he helped

---

* Jack Schwartzman, interview by the author, Los Angeles, November 2, 1984.
† Maurice Binder, interview by the author, London, June 16, 1977.

construct, military aircraft were shuttled into the China-Burma-India theater.

In 1943, as German forces under Rommel were being forced out of North Africa, Binder returned to the United States and enrolled in sea navigation school. When the war in Europe ended in May 1945, Binder was a lieutenant (j.g.) on the LT-60, a salvage tug. He served until the end of the war in the Pacific, then navigated, he recalled, "the Panama Canal to Universal Pictures' backlot."*

Still in the navy, Binder began to do freelance advertising work for Mischa Kallis at Universal, the only studio that created its own advertising on the West Coast (the other studios did their advertising work in New York City). Kallis was dubious about Binder's qualifications, but he gave him a test on a cheap little western entitled *The Daltons Ride Again* (1945). Binder returned to his ship with pad and pencils and generated thirty-five designs in one night.

He remembered, "My job at Macy's had primed me for pressure. We were doing thirty-five pages of advertising a day at one time, so Kallis's assignment wasn't extreme." Binder was given $125 for his sketches and another assignment on an Yvonne De Carlo western, *Frontier Gal* (1945).

After being discharged from the navy, Binder worked for Arthur A. Schmidt, who was assistant to Harry Cohn at Columbia Pictures. Schmidt needed a sketch artist to help him visualize ad campaigns. Binder posed the stars for photo layouts and sketched ads. His first full campaign was for the classic *Gilda* (1946). He eventually became West Coast art director for Columbia, working on campaigns for movies such as *The Jolson Story* (1946), *Down to Earth* (1947), *Dead Reckoning* (1947), and *The Lady from Shanghai* (1948). Binder also freelanced for other production companies.

Although Binder had been introduced to Albert R. "Cubby" Broccoli when the latter was an agent with Charles K. Feldman, their creative relationship didn't begin until 1961, when Broccoli and his producing partner, Harry Saltzman, attended the premiere of *The Grass Is Greener*, a Stanley Donen film. Binder had designed the title sequence, which featured a group of infants. It so charmed the audience that Broccoli and Saltzman immediately thought of him for their new James Bond series.

Binder's storyboard for the James Bond logo—designed in ten minutes—consisted of a series of white sticky-backed price tabs placed to simulate the bullet holes of gunshots going off across the screen. One of the bullet holes would appear as if you were looking through a gun—the barrel, not the gun sight. At a miniatures studio, Binder filmed his through-the-gun-barrel spiral logo shot.

The shot of 007 walking and firing was a separate piece of film shot later. For that sequence, stuntman Bob Simmons doubled Sean Connery. The footage of Simmons was used in the first three films—*Dr. No, From Russia with Love* and *Goldfinger*, which were shot at an aspect ratio of 1.85:1 (known as "flat" ratio). When *Thunderball* was lensed in 2.35:1 widescreen (known as "scope," after Cinemascope), Binder was forced to reshoot the logo. This time, he used Sean Connery. In the walk-and-fire footage of both Bob Simmons and Sean Connery, and later of George Lazenby, Bond always wore a fedora. When Roger Moore entered the series in 1973, the hat was discarded.

Though Binder's logo kicked off each movie, he did not design the opening credits for the second and third films in the series, *From Russia with Love* and *Goldfinger*. He came back in *Thunderball* with an idea he had seen in the Raymond Revuebar in Soho: a woman swimming in a tank above the bar. From that springboard, Binder designed his first live-action title sequence, using carefully photographed nudes. Binder's use of slow motion, colorful lighting, rippling bubbles, and the silhouettes of shapely female torsos—a pattern that continued in subsequent Bond titles—were all elements that worked in perfect synch with Tom Jones's rousing title song.

One of the more comical stories associated with Binder's title sequence shoots occurred at Pinewood Studios on *The Man with the Golden Gun*. Binder was shooting a nude woman's silhouette. Conscious of rating codes and censors, he noted that from a certain angle the woman's pubic hair was a little too noticeable on camera. When the model refused to shave, Binder realized that the only way to make the shot work was to brush her hair into place and use Vaseline to hold it there. "You do it," she said, and Binder dutifully got down on his knees and put things right. At that exact moment—so the story goes—Roger Moore and Cubby Broccoli walked onto the stage.

* Ibid.

Roger turned to Cubby and said, "I thought you were the producer on this picture." And Cubby replied, "It doesn't seem right, does it?"*

Binder's creativity was tested over the years as he searched for ways to keep his title sequences from becoming repetitive. For the Roger Moore films, he enlisted the cooperation of the lead actor, and Moore became a prime character in the sequences. In *For Your Eyes Only*, he was impressed with the beauty of title-song singer Sheena Easton and decided to feature her on screen.

Binder coordinated with composer Bill Conti to ensure that the title song meshed with the titles. "I've always wanted the song synchronized so that when I show the title of the film, the singer sings it," Binder explained. "Unfortunately, on *For Your Eyes Only*, the song title came in

Title specialist Maurice Binder, whose use of back-lit nudes was a highlight of many James Bond title sequences. *Courtesy of the Michael VanBlaricum Collection*

* Ibid.

ninety seconds after the song began. I asked Bill Conti to help, and we rewrote the song in two days."

In addition to title sequences, Binder was also heavily involved in designing the trailers for most of the early Bond films. He was the one who created the sequence in which the Doberman guard dogs track down and kill Corinne Dufour (Corinne Cléry) for the *Moonraker* teaser trailer, which was partially narrated by actress Lise Hilboldt.

In addition to the Bond films, Binder worked on the titles for movies including *The Long Ships* (1964); *Battle of Britain* (1969), for producer Harry Saltzman; *The Private Life of Sherlock Holmes* (1970); *The Wild Geese* (1978); *The Last Emperor* (1987); and Mel Gibson's *Hamlet* (1990), his last film.

Bird 1: See "*Intruder.*"

Birds of the West Indies: A book that became one of author Ian Fleming's primary reference guides during his vacations in Jamaica. In 1952, searching for a name with which to christen the hero of his new novel, Fleming noticed the simple name of the book's author, ornithologist James Bond. The name struck a chord, and the world's greatest secret agent was born.

Bishop, Ed (June 11, 1932–June 8, 2005; birth name: George Victor Bishop): American actor who appeared first as the space tracking technician based in Hawaii in *You Only Live Twice* and later returned in *Diamonds Are Forever* as radiation shield inspector Klaus Hergersheimer, who's impersonated by James Bond (Sean Connery). A native of Brooklyn, Bishop received a scholarship to study drama at the London Academy of Music and Dramatic Art in 1960—and England soon became his permanent base. He made his credited feature debut as Vogt, a US Army Air Forces officer in the Steve McQueen–Robert Wagner World War II film *The War Lover* (1962). Three years later, he was Lieutenant Hacker, a communications officer aboard the American destroyer commanded by Captain Finlander (Richard Widmark) in director James B. Harris's gripping Cold War thriller *The Bedford Incident*. Bishop is also known for his role as Commander Ed Straker on the British sci-fi series *UFO* (1970–1971), and many other important film and television roles.

Black Park: An area of rural England, not far from Pinewood Studios, where part of the *Goldfinger* Aston Martin car chase was filmed. The factory element of that chase was filmed on the Pinewood studio grounds.

Blackman, Honor (August 22, 1925–April 5, 2020): Sultry British actress who starred in *Goldfinger* as Pussy Galore, the title character's resourceful pilot and confederate in Operation Grand Slam. Blackman won the part after impressing producers Albert R. Broccoli and Harry Saltzman with her continuing role as the leather-clad, judo-proficient Cathy Gale in the second and third seasons of the British spy duo series *The Avengers* (1962–1964). Leaving the series, she was replaced by Diana Rigg, who would later star in *On Her Majesty's Secret Service* (1969). The male half of *The Avengers*—Patrick Macnee—would join the 007 series in *A View to a Kill* (1985).

Said Blackman, "The fighting in *Goldfinger* was really quite easy as compared to *The Avengers*. . . . Sean is a lovely gent, and who doesn't want to fight in the hay or do anything with Sean? Secondly, they provide you with hay, the soft stuff. In the television studio, you're bouncing around on the cement all over the place. You don't have to wait until you get to the fighting sequences when you're with Sean, he just says, 'Uh, just a minute,' and he gets hold of you, and you've gone through to the bone because he is so tough. There is one scene where he just has to yank me back and [my] arm was just in a disgusting condition for about a week because of the brute force of the fist, you know.

"Before Bond, I was sweet, innocent, peaches and cream and golden hair. I really couldn't help it, I took an awful long time to grow up, I think. When you get past twenty-five, you want to start growing out of that. I was always looked upon as terribly kind and understanding and I never got any lovely bitch parts. And I was never really intelligent—I was usually the one who says, "Darling, I'll make the cocoa. You just go to bed and don't worry about it."*

Born in Plaistow in London's East End and a dispatch rider during World War II, Blackman made her uncredited feature film debut in the drama *Fame Is the Spur* (1947), and her credited debut the following year in the horror drama *Daughter of Darkness*. Just prior to *Goldfinger*, Blackman made a strong impression as a very fetching Hera, Queen of Gods in *Jason and the Argonauts* (1963), working with future Bond players Laurence Naismith (*Diamonds Are Forever*) and Douglas Wilmer (*Octopussy*). Later appearances included a starring role in the British sitcom *The Upper Hand* (95 episodes, 1990–1996) and a memorable cameo in *Bridget Jones's Diary* (2001).

Blades health club: London private club, featured prominently in the Ian Fleming's original Bond novels, that has morphed into a fencing club in the film *Die Another Day*. In that stuffy arena, Bond (Pierce Brosnan) and Gustav Graves (Toby Stephens) engage in what could arguably be the best action sequence in the Brosnan-era Bonds: a fencing duel that goes from spirited to no-holds-barred deadly.

Bleuchamp Institute for Allergy Research: Cover organization run by SPECTRE chief Ernst Stavro Blofeld (Telly Savalas) in *On Her Majesty's Secret Service*. Located at Piz Gloria, an Alpine peak accessible only by funicular, the institute treats allergy patients—a group of beautiful women. As part of Blofeld's scheme to blackmail the free world, the girls are systematically brainwashed so they will distribute a terrifying toxin that can completely destroy the agricultural and livestock capabilities of the targeted nations. The institute is named after "Count Balthazar de Bleuchamp," the royal moniker Blofeld is

Actress Honor Blackman achieved 007 legend status with her perfect portrait of Pussy in *Goldfinger*. Courtesy of the David Reinhardt Collection

---

* Special features, Goldfinger, James Bond Ultimate Edition (1964; MGM, 2006), DVD.

attempting to claim as his own. His aristocratic aspirations give James Bond (George Lazenby) an opening to infiltrate the institute, posing as London College of Arms heraldry expert Sir Hilary Bray. The structure is eventually obliterated in a dawn helicopter assault, led by Bond and Marc-Ange Draco (Gabriele Ferzetti), by gunmen from the Union Corse crime syndicate.

Bliss, Caroline (July 12, 1961–   ; birth name: Carol Gatehouse): Statuesque blonde British actress, the granddaughter of composer Sir Arthur Bliss (*Things to Come*), who made her debut as the new Miss Moneypenny—M's proud but love-starved secretary—in Timothy Dalton's first 007 film, *The Living Daylights*. Bliss reprised the role in *Licence to Kill* (1989). A native of Hammersmith, London, Bliss made a high-profile debut as Lady Diana Spencer in the TV movie *Charles & Diana: A Royal Love Story* (1982), working with fellow Bond players Christopher Lee and Charles Gray.

Blofeld, Ernst Stavro: Bond's longtime nemesis and the head of SPECTRE, the enormous international crime syndicate introduced in Ian Fleming's novel *Thunderball*. The novel was actually based on a film treatment by Fleming, screenwriter Jack Whittingham, and producer Kevin McClory, an early attempt to get a James Bond film adaptation off the ground. SPECTRE and Blofeld are also featured in the novels *On Her Majesty's Secret Service* and *You Only Live Twice*.

In the movies, Blofeld is first featured with his back to camera in *From Russia with Love* (portrayed, uncredited, by *Dr. No* veteran Anthony Dawson). Eric Pohlmann portrayed Blofeld's voice in both *From Russia with Love* and *Thunderball* (once again, you never see his face). He makes his

British character actor Donald Pleasence takes on the role of Ernst Stavro Blofeld, here complete with his number-one companion, the iconic white cat, in *You Only Live Twice. Courtesy of the David Reinhardt Collection*

on-camera debut in *You Only Live Twice*, with Donald Pleasence in the role, complete with an incredible scar supplied by the makeup department; according to film critic Alexander Walker, the character looked like "an egg that had cracked on the boil."*

Telly Savalas takes on the role of Ernst Stavro Blofeld in *On Her Majesty's Secret Service. Courtesy of the David Reinhardt Collection*

In *You Only Live Twice*, Blofeld hatches a scheme to start World War III on behalf of the Red Chinese, building a secret rocket base inside an extinct Japanese volcano. From this enormous cavern, he launches his *Intruder* rocket—a spaceship that opens its jaws and captures Soviet and American capsules. When Bond (Sean Connery) invades the base with the help of an army of ninja warriors, Blofeld escapes to return in the next film, *On Her Majesty's Secret Service*, in the guise of Telly Savalas.

This time, Blofeld is sequestered in the Swiss Alps, posing as a world-famous allergist. In reality, he is developing a terrifying form of germ warfare that will destroy the agricultural and livestock production of the world's leading nations. His agents are unsuspecting young, female allergy patients who have been brainwashed to distribute the toxin. Once again, Bond (George Lazenby) comes in to mess up the works. During a climactic chase on a bobsled run, Blofeld appears to have been killed when his skull is cracked by an overhanging branch—but he returns in the climax with Frau Irma Bunt (Ilse Steppat) to murder Bond's bride, Tracy (Diana Rigg).

In the next film, *Diamonds Are Forever*, Charles Gray portrays a very sophisticated Blofeld, with smart tailored suits, a cigarette holder, and erudite quotations. Gray's Blofeld is also the most fantastical version; his plot is nothing less than nuclear blackmail from outer space, thanks to his diamond-powered satellite and its laser cannon. Eventually, Blofeld gets trapped in his own bathosub, with Bond (Sean Connery) controlling the crane that lowers it into the water. The sub later explodes, but Blofeld's body is never found.

---

* John Brosnan, *James Bond in the Cinema*, 2nd ed. (San Diego: A. S. Barnes, 1981), 144.

Blofeld was supposed to return as the key villain in *The Spy Who Loved Me*, but the appearance was scuttled because of threats from Ian Fleming's *Thunderball* collaborator Kevin McClory, who had won all rights to SPECTRE and Blofeld after

Charles Gray portrays a particularly annoyed Ernst Stavro Blofeld in *Diamonds Are Forever*. *Courtesy of the David Reinhardt Collection*

a legal battle with Fleming back in 1961. McClory had teamed up with Eon Productions to produce the movie version of *Thunderball*, but by the mid-1970s he was attempting to mount his own James Bond film series, beginning with a project called *James Bond of the Secret Service*. Eon's Cubby Broccoli had screenwriter Richard Maibaum change the *Spy Who Loved Me* antagonist from SPECTRE's Blofeld to a purely independent villain, Karl Stromberg (Curt Jurgens).

Eon did get away with featuring a Blofeld lookalike—never identified by name in the credits—in the pre-titles teaser of *For Your Eyes Only*. The bald-headed, wheelchair-bound, beige-suited figure, with his trademark white cat, is snared by the skid of the helicopter Bond (Roger Moore) is piloting and deposited in the nearest industrial smokestack—which would appear to be his final demise.

It would take a non-Eon Bond production to resurrect the SPECTRE chieftain, after Kevin McClory licensed the *Thunderball* rights to producer Jack Schwartzman and he produced a new

Christoph Waltz portrays Blofeld in *Spectre*; a captured Dr. Madeleine Swann (Léa Seydoux) doesn't appear too happy about it. *Courtesy of the Anders Frejdh Collection*

adaptation of Fleming's original novel as *Never Say Never Again*. Played by actor Max von Sydow, this film's Blofeld resembles the never-fully-seen versions in the early 007 films: he simply announces the latest extortion plan and leaves most of the details to his field commander, Maximilian Largo (Klaus Maria Brandauer).

Today, all rights to SPECTRE and Blofeld are controlled by Eon Productions. Hence, producers Barbara Broccoli and Michael G. Wilson brought them both back for *Spectre* and *No Time to Die*. This time, however, the writers added a huge twist to the story. In this adjusted 007 universe, Bond (Daniel Craig) and Blofeld (Christoph Waltz) are revealed to be foster brothers. However, it's hardly a friendly family relationship—Blofeld is still an international criminal, and he doesn't hesitate to capture, torture, and attempt to kill Bond.

Blue Grass Field, Kentucky: In *Goldfinger*, the final destination of the title character's private Lockheed JetStar, which carries the recently captured and tranquilized 007 (Sean Connery). On arrival, Bond is driven to Auric Stud, the Kentucky home of Goldfinger (Gert Fröbe). In the real world, the airfield, located in Lexington, is now known as Blue Grass Airport.

Blush, Fatima (a.k.a. Number 12): Truly wicked SPECTRE executioner portrayed by Barbara Carrera in *Never Say Never Again*. Fatima is introduced as a private-duty nurse assigned to Captain Jack Petachi (Gavan O'Herlihy), a US Air Force communications officer who has been turned by SPECTRE. Bribed, seduced, drugged, and beaten into submission by Fatima, Petachi has received a corneal implant so that he now possesses the same eye print as the president of the United States. With that startling enhancement, he can bypass a top-level security check and arm two cruise missiles equipped with nuclear warheads. Petachi succeeds in his mission—and is promptly eliminated by Fatima, who tosses a snake into his car, distracting him into a head-on collision with a stone wall.

Turning her attentions to James Bond (Sean Connery), Fatima meets him at a "wet" bar in Nassau, Bahamas, and takes him for a diving excursion off Bluebeard Reef. After they make torrid love, she attaches a homing device to Bond's diving gear that summons a group of

Sexy Barbara Carrera stole the show as wicked SPECTRE assassin Fatima Blush in *Never Say Never Again. Courtesy of the Michael VanBlaricum Collection*

The 750iL wasn't 007's first BMW; here Q (Desmond Llewelyn) supplies Bond (Pierce Brosnan) with a sparkling BMW Z3 in *GoldenEye. Courtesy of the Luc Leclech Collection*

radio-controlled sharks ready for the kill. Bond eludes them, hooks up with a sexy deep-sea diver (Valerie Leon), and evades another attempt on his life when Fatima detonates a bomb in his hotel suite.

In Nice, France, she leads a motorcycle-riding 007 on a merry chase that winds up in a tunnel, where Bond is surrounded by her henchmen. Employing the rocket-motor capabilities of his bike, Bond escapes from the nest of enemies, only to be cornered by Fatima in a warehouse. Forced to his knees, Bond is about to have his genitals blown off when Blush orders him to confess in writing that their sex was the best he ever had.

Bond stalls for time, then deploys and fires his rocket-loaded fountain pen, plunging an explosive dart into Fatima's chest. For an agonizing moment, nothing happens, but then she's blown to kingdom come. Like a latter-day wicked witch, only her high heels remain.

BMW 750iL: Q Branch marvel supplied to Bond in *Tomorrow Never Dies*. A new variation on the trick Aston Martin introduced in *Goldfinger*, this "bimmer" has what Q (Desmond Llewelyn) refers to as the "usual refinements," including rockets, bulletproof (although not rocket-proof) windows, a GPS tracking system, and the most extraordinary remote-control capability, operated via special cell phone. Using a mouse-like control pad with a closed-circuit video screen that shows him where he's headed, Bond (Pierce Brosnan) can literally sit in the back of the car and drive without using a steering wheel or gas pedal. This device comes in handy when Elliot Carver (Jonathan Pryce) sends the bad guys after him; their pursuit is easily the best scene in the film. Unfortunately, the wear and tear on Q Branch toys like this is just too much. As a colossal distraction to ease his getaway, Bond drives the trick BMW off the top story of the parking structure of Hamburg's Hotel Atlantic and into a local Avis Rent-a-Car agency. Fifteen BMWs were destroyed in the making of the film.

Boa, Bruce (July 10, 1930–April 17, 2004; birth name: Andrew Bruce Boa): Canadian character actor, mostly in Britain from 1958, who portrayed the US Air Force commander of Feldstadt Air Base in *Octopussy*. Born in Calgary, Boa made his feature film debut in director Basil Dearden's romantic space comedy *Man in the Moon* (1960), working alongside future Bond players Charles Gray and Nikki Van der Zyl (who redubbed many of the female characters in the early Bond films). In addition to his yeoman work in the Bond picture, Boa is known for playing General Rieekan, the Rebel base commander on Hoth in *The Empire Strikes Back* (1980), as well as for many television appearances in Great Britain and the United States.

Bogner, Willy, Jr. (January 23, 1942–): Accomplished German cameraman, director, writer, and former Olympic skier whose uncanny ability to capture the movement of skiers has provided the James Bond series with some of its most breathtaking action sequences. A native of Munich, Bogner gained prominence with *On Her Majesty's Secret Service*, most of which takes place in the snows of Switzerland.

Bond producer Albert R. Broccoli had seen some of Bogner's early films, including *Skifascination* (1966), a forty-seven-minute 35mm documentary that won first prize at sports festivals in Cortina D'Ampezzo and Grenoble. He enlisted the filmmaker to shoot the ski sequences for *OHMSS*. Equipped with a modified Arriflex camera and an adapted Hasselblad viewfinder, Bogner held his camera while skiing backward to catch the swiftly moving Olympic-level skiers as they flew down the slopes above the Swiss village of Mürren. Sometimes he shot backward looking through his legs. His skis were modified with curved tips at both ends to allow him the proper mobility.

OHMSS director Peter Hunt remembered, "I've never seen anyone manipulate skis and a camera like Willy. Of course, in the rushes, we got lumps of sky, bits of his bottom, and somebody's shoe—things like that—but when you took all of the best pieces, you had some exciting material."* After the success of his work on *On Her Majesty's Secret Service*, Bogner was hired to handle the acrobatic ski sequences on *The Spy Who Loved Me*, once again photographing his stunt performers while skiing himself.

For the close-ups of Bond (George Lazenby or Roger Moore), Bogner placed his actors on a sled that was pulled forward at 40 to 50 mph while the cameras rolled. Bogner returned to handle ski stunts on *For Your Eyes Only* in 1981. Four years later, he journeyed to Iceland to shoot the teaser sequence for *A View to a Kill*, which involved not only ski scenes but also "snow surfing" to the Beach Boys tune "California Girls."

bombe surprise (pronounced "BOM-buh sir-PREEZ"): The dessert delivered to James Bond (Sean Connery) and Tiffany Case (Jill St. John) by phony ocean liner waiters Mr. Wint (Bruce Glover) and Mr. Kidd (Putter Smith) in *Diamonds Are Forever*. It disguises a time bomb. During a fight with the two unorthodox SPECTRE assassins, Bond attaches the bomb to Wint and kicks him overboard, where he is blown to bits.

Bond, James (January 4, 1900–February 14, 1989): American ornithologist and author of the famous book *Birds of the West Indies*. Because that book occupied a prominent place on author Ian Fleming's coffee table in his vacation home in Jamaica, it inspired him, in 1952, to choose

"James Bond" as the name of his British Secret Service agent.

Fleming later signed a copy of *You Only Live Twice* for the ornithologist, writing, "To the real James Bond from the thief of his identity. Ian Fleming February 5, 1964 (A great day!)"*

James Bond, the ornithologist, a native of Philadelphia and a graduate of Cambridge University, was a former curator of ornithology at the Academy of Natural Sciences in his hometown. He was the leading authority on birds of the West Indies for more than half a century, and he is best known among scientists for proving that birds of the Caribbean originated in North America, not South America.

Bond, Mrs. James: Short-lived identity of the Contessa Teresa "Tracy" di Vicenzo (Diana Rigg) in *On Her Majesty's Secret Service*. Only a few minutes after her wedding to Bond (George Lazenby), she's machine-gunned by Irma Bunt (Ilse Steppat) from a car driven by Ernst Stavro Blofeld (Telly Savalas). "Mrs. Bond" is also the cover identity of CIA agent Rosie Carver (Gloria Hendry) in *Live and Let Die*. When James Bond (Roger Moore) arrives at his hotel on the island of San Monique, he finds she's used that name to check into his room ahead of him.

Bond, Samantha (November 27, 1961–   ): Shakespearean stage actress who won the coveted part of Miss Moneypenny in *GoldenEye*. She continued in the role of as trusted secretary to M (Dame Judi Dench) in *Tomorrow Never Dies*, *The World Is Not Enough*, and *Die Another Day*. She's not the first real-life Bond to be involved in the series—Trevor Bond handled pre-title-sequence work on *From Russia with Love* and *Goldfinger*.

Samantha Bond brought new dimensions to the role of Miss Moneypenny in *The World Is Not Enough*. *Courtesy of the Joel Villy Collection*

Bond girls: S<small>EE</small> "Women of the James Bond films."

Bond's Office: Featured only once—in the sixth James Bond film, *On Her Majesty's Secret Service*. Resigning from the British Secret Service when M (Bernard Lee) fails to permit him to continue his search for the missing Blofeld (Telly Savalas), Bond (George Lazenby) retreats to his own office to clean out his desk.

In the film, screenwriter Richard Maibaum's homage to the series' rich history, 007 pulls out three souvenirs from previous adventures: the belt and knife worn by Honey (Ursula Andress) in *Dr. No*, the strangler's watch used by Grant (Robert Shaw) in *From Russia with Love*, and the miniature rebreather from *Thunderball*. He then takes out a flask and toasts a portrait of the queen.

When Moneypenny (Lois Maxwell) summons him back to M's office, Bond learns that his resignation has turned into a much-needed vacation. What would we do without you, indeed, Miss Moneypenny?

Bonita: Fiery South American flamenco dancer portrayed by actress Nadja Regin in the *Goldfinger* pre-credits teaser. Definitely working for the drug cartel that has been using heroin-laced bananas to finance a revolution, she lures

Lovely Nadja Regin, who had previously appeared as Kerim Bey's girlfriend in *From Russia with Love*, returned in the *Goldfinger* pre-credits teaser as Bond's South American conquest Bonita, a ravishing dame with very reflective pupils. *Courtesy of the David Reinhardt Collection*

Bond (Sean Connery) to her dressing room after he blows up Mr. Ramirez's drug operation. There he picks her up out of the bathtub, kisses her—and then sees an assassin (Alf Joint), a.k.a. the *capungo*, reflected in her pupils. Whirling around, Bond shoves Bonita in front of the *capungo*'s billy club, and she gets a good thwacking.

Boothroyd, Major: The no-nonsense armoror, played by Peter Burton, who supplies James Bond (Sean Connery) with his new Walther PPK pistol in the first Bond film, *Dr. No*. When Burton was unable to return in the second film, *From Russia with Love*, he was replaced by tall, aristocratic Desmond Llewelyn, who would go on to portray 007's long-suffering quartermaster in seventeen James Bond films. Though Llewelyn's character is also credited as "Boothroyd" in his first appearance, and KGB agent Anya Amasova (Barbara Bach) addresses him by that name in his eighth film, *The Spy Who Loved Me*, he's generally referred to only by his British Secret Service code, Q.

Boren, Lamar (May 3, 1917–January 15, 1986): Veteran cinematographer and underwater specialist who was responsible for the large-scale battle sequences in *Thunderball*, the opening underwater sequences in Victoria Harbour, Hong Kong, in *You Only Live Twice*, and the adventures of the Lotus submarine car in *The Spy Who Loved Me*. He also filmed James Bond's duel with a giant water snake in *Moonraker*.

Unlike dozens of "diving for sunken treasure" or "monsters from the deep" exploitation films, *Thunderball* was conceived of as an ambitious, widescreen underwater epic. United Artists, perched on a tidal wave of 007 interest in early 1965, was ready to pour nearly $6 million into the next Bond adventure. It was going to be the biggest Bond film yet, with underwater battles with dozens of spear-gun-carrying frogmen, a trip to an underwater garage where stolen atomic bombs were hidden, a romantic swim with Bond (Sean Connery) and Domino (Claudine Auger), and a tense encounter between Bond and an underwater sentry guarding the *Disco Volante* hydrofoil. The task of photographing these landmark underwater sequences fell to Lamar Boren.

Boren, who claimed to have taken part in his first dive at eleven years old, had been shooting underwater films since the late 1940s. He knew about *Thunderball*, because producer Albert R. "Cubby" Broccoli had first contacted him in the summer of 1961, when it was slated to be the first Bond film. But *Thunderball* had been shelved due to a copyright dispute between Ian Fleming and one of his collaborators on the original story, producer Kevin McClory. Boren returned to the Bahamas to wind up his fourth season on the popular *Sea Hunt* television series. As the Bond films grew in size and importance, he remained in the Caribbean working for Ivan Tors Studios, a Miami-based production company that specialized in underwater adventure shows and films, including *Sea Hunt* and *Flipper*.

Underwater photography had come a long way since 1914, when a photographer named Ernie Williamson hand-cranked the original version of Jules Verne's *20,000 Leagues Under the Sea* off Nassau in the Bahamas. In those days, Williamson worked on a specially built catamaran on which a photosphere was balanced between two pontoons. The photosphere—a glass canopy in which Williamson placed himself and his camera—was then lowered into the water to photograph the various divers and props that had been assembled for the film. Boren knew Williamson and admired his techniques, but his own dream was to physically follow the underwater action with an airtight camera that could operate under its own power.

In his early days at RKO, around 1950, Boren designed an airtight stainless steel camera case for an old Eyemo camera, and he was followed around the studio tank by a stagehand carting a car battery for the power supply. This worked well enough for the studio tank, but when Boren began filming *Sea Hunt* in the Caribbean, an independent power source was needed. He didn't want generator cords or battery cables to inhibit his progress underwater.

The solution came in 1957 when he acquired some miniature silver cells from a friend. The tiny batteries were part of the guidance system of an air-to-air missile, and they were being manufactured in limited quantities by the Yardney company of New York. Boren incorporated this portable power source into his Eyemo, creating one of the first independent underwater cameras. He was now free to explore the full breadth of the ocean. The quality of his work and the variety of his subject matter improved considerably, and

it was not long before a number of production companies were hiring him to do underwater work.

By the early 1960s, he had replaced his Eyemo with Panavision cameras, two of which would film all the underwater action in *Thunderball*. Boren recalled, "*Thunderball* was the most ambitious underwater film in history. Cubby [Broccoli] and Harry [Saltzman] were so pleased with our footage that they kept increasing its importance in the film. One thing that made the whole project even more interesting was the creation of so many functional underwater props and gadgets."[*]

Boren worked closely on the film with a unit from Ivan Tors that would eventually number more than sixty professional divers and employ $85,000 worth of Voit diving equipment. Production designer Ken Adam and art director Peter Lamont also designed several futuristic underwater vehicles, including several one-man, electric-powered, spear-gun-equipped scooters and the two-man sled designed to carry the hijacked A-bombs. The vehicles were built by Miami underwater engineer and cameraman Jordan Klein.

Boren also put to good use the filming techniques he had perfected earlier on *Sea Hunt*. To adjust the level of his camera, he used his lungs like an elevator. To rise up, he took a deep breath of oxygen. And to drop down, he exhaled. By controlling his breathing in such a fashion, he was able to keep himself perfectly balanced—which contributed to the steadiness of his camera and the crystal clarity of his underwater shots.

Thanks to Boren, the ocean itself became a character in *Thunderball*. Married to composer John Barry's beautifully mellow musical score, the underwater sequences lent the film a unique atmosphere of enchantment, just as exotic Jamaica had enlivened *Dr. No*.

The freshness and otherworldliness is evident from the start, in the early sequence in which James Bond (Sean Connery) meets Domino (Claudine Auger) in the sea off Nassau. Agent 007 sees her swimming underwater among the exotic tropical fish that inhabit the Caribbean coral. As she glides through the underwater scenery, Bond is entranced by her wonderful form.

---

[*] Lamar Boren, interview by the author, La Jolla, CA, August 17, 1976.

And when her foot gets caught in an outcropping of coral, Bond comes to her rescue. He helps her to the surface, where he introduces himself. It's a short sequence, but it perfectly captures the magic of the tropics and the romance that is such an integral part of the film. NOTE: Claudine Auger's stunt double during these sequences was Lamar Boren's wife, Evelyne.

Bouquet, Carole (August 18, 1957–   ): Hauntingly beautiful French actress who portrayed the vengeful Melina Havelock in *For Your Eyes Only*. Bouquet was a casting coup for the Bond producers—perfectly suited to playing a half-Greek, half-British archaeologist's daughter whose parents are brutally murdered early in the film. When Havelock's beautiful eyes are featured in close-up after her parents' deaths, they perfectly convey her seething desire to avenge her family. Armed with a crossbow, she's an impressive sight skulking through the woods of Spain in pursuit of Cuban hit man Hector Gonzales (Stefan Kalipha).

A native of Neuilly-sur-Seine (now Hauts-de-Seine), Bouquet made her film debut in director Luis Buñuel's *That Obscure Object of Desire* (1977), which was nominated for the Best Foreign Film Oscar. She later won the César for Best Actress for playing Gérard Depardieu's wife in Bertrand Blier's *Trop belle pour toi* ("Too Beautiful for You," 1989).

French actress Carole Bouquet brought a simmering sexuality to the role of revenge-minded Melina Havelock in *For Your Eyes Only*. *Courtesy of the David Reinhardt Collection*

Bourton-on-the-Water: Village in England's Cotswolds that doubled as the surface of an Icelandic glacier in *Die Another Day*. To supplement action previously filmed on the Vatnajökull ice cap in Iceland, the producers took over a Bourton parking lot and dressed it as a slippery ice cap, across which Bond (Pierce Brosnan) drives his Aston Martin V12 Vanquish as he's chased by a machine gun–equipped Jaguar XKR driven by Zao (Rick Yune).

Bouvar, Colonel Jacques (a.k.a. Number 6): SPECTRE agent portrayed by stuntman Bob Simmons and assassinated by James Bond (Sean Connery) in the *Thunderball* pre-credits teaser. Attending the colonel's supposed funeral at a cathedral outside Paris, Bond and his French contact Mademoiselle LaPorte (Mitsouko) notice that upon leaving, Bouvar's widow (Rose Alba) suspiciously opens a car door by herself—something French widows are obviously not supposed to do. Bond follows her back to a French chateau and promptly offers his personal condolences in the form of a solid punch to the face—revealing that the widow is none other than Colonel Bouvar in drag.

A particularly vicious fight ensues, especially for Bond, who knows that Bouvar has already murdered two double-0 agents. Whacked by a fireplace poker, Bond finally gets the best of Bouvar and breaks the enemy agent's neck. Stopping to toss flowers on the corpse, he then escapes from the chateau in a Bell jet pack.

NOTE: Although Richard Maibaum's script gives the colonel's name as "Boitier," it's pronounced "Bouvar" in the finished film.

Bouvier, Pam: Undercover CIA operative and former US Army pilot portrayed fabulously by Carey Lowell in *Licence to Kill*. In the Michael G. Wilson–Richard Maibaum screenplay, Bouvier is an ode to the woman of the 1980s: a tough, no-nonsense player who doesn't like warming her behind on the sidelines. Glimpsed briefly in the Key West office of Felix Leiter (David Hedison), she gets her true introduction at the seedy Barrelhead Bar in Bimini, Bahamas—and quite an introduction it is.

Tipped off by Leiter's computer that Bouvier is shadowing operatives of drug lord Franz Sanchez (Robert Davi) in Bimini, Bond (Timothy Dalton) joins her at the Barrelhead. Pam is seated at

Newcomer Carey Lowell took on the role of resourceful CIA pilot Pam Bouvier in *Licence to Kill*.
Courtesy of the David Reinhardt Collection

a table surrounded by the slime of the Caribbean and wielding a hidden shotgun. She's very unimpressed with Bond's own firepower—his trusty Walther. But there's no time to wait for reinforcements, as the two are quickly joined by Sanchez's henchman Dario (Benicio Del Toro), who is very suspicious of Pam and her English friend.

After Pam shoves her shotgun up against Dario's crotch, a brawl breaks out. Outnumbered and outgunned, 007 holds back the tide until Pam creates her own escape route by blasting a hole in the barroom wall. They escape in Bond's motorboat. Pam is shot by Dario, but fortunately she's wearing body armor. After a rather abrupt moonlight tryst in the boat, Pam agrees to fly 007 into the lion's den—Isthmus City, where Sanchez has his stronghold.

Posing as 007's secretary, with a new hairdo and wardrobe to match, Pam becomes a passive observer as Bond skillfully infiltrates the drug empire. However, her skills come in handy when she impersonates the Isthmus harbor pilot and rams the *Wavekrest* research vessel of Sanchez ally Milton Krest (Anthony Zerbe) into the dock—a diversion that helps Bond plant drug loot in the decompression chamber.

Pam is also very handy at the Olimpatec Meditation Institute, run by hapless televangelist and Sanchez henchman Joe Butcher (Wayne Newton). She seduces Butcher, locks him in his bedroom, and goes off to help Bond escape from the on-site laboratory where Sanchez's cocaine is dissolved in gasoline so it can be transported undetected.

Later, while piloting a crop-dusting plane, Pam drops 007 on top of one of the tanker trucks carrying this liquid cocaine. As Bond systematically obliterates Sanchez's drug convoy, Pam keeps watch from above—a sort of friendly guardian angel version of villainous pilot Naomi (Caroline Munro) in *The Spy Who Loved Me*. With Sanchez dead and his empire ruined, there's a major celebration at the drug lord's home, where Pam sees Bond kissing Lupe Lamora (Talisa Soto).

Unaware it's a good-bye kiss—Lupe is now a fixture on the arm of President Lopez (Pedro Armendariz Jr.)—a teary-eyed Pam runs off. Bond sees her and jumps into Sanchez's pool, where they enjoy a passionate embrace in the water, where most Bond movies seem to end.

Brandauer, Klaus Maria (June 22, 1943–   ): Marvelous Austrian character actor of stage and screen who made his English-speaking screen debut as Maximilian Largo in *Never Say Never Again*. The previous year, Brandauer had attracted worldwide attention with his starring role in István Szabó's *Mephisto*, which won the 1982 Academy Award for Best Foreign Film, and the notice of producer Jack Schwartzman. He cast Brandauer as Largo, resulting in the most interesting 007 villain since Auric Goldfinger. Youthful, handsome, and urbane, Brandauer also gave Largo a fascinating touch of the psychotic, particularly in his moments with Domino Petachi (Kim Basinger).

A native of Bad Aussee, Styria, Brandauer made his feature acting debut in the Cold War thriller *The Salzburg Connection* (1972). He was later nominated for an Oscar and won a Golden Globe for Best Supporting Actor for playing Meryl Streep's husband Baron Bror von Blixen in *Out of Africa* (1985). He later joined Sean Connery again in director Fred Schepisi's romantic thriller *The Russia House* (1990).

Brandt, Helga (a.k.a. Number 11): Female nemesis of James Bond (Sean Connery) in *You Only Live Twice*, portrayed by German beauty Karin Dor. Posing as the confidential secretary of Mr. Osato (Teru Shimada), the spectacularly built Brandt is in reality a SPECTRE agent.

SPECTRE agent Helga Brandt (Karin Dor) has James Bond (Sean Connery) just where she wants him in *You Only Live Twice. Courtesy of the David Reinhardt Collection*

Schooled in the Fiona Volpe style of assassination, she unsuccessfully tries to kill Bond by leaving him trapped in a disabled private plane. Her failure spells her own doom when a dissatisfied Ernst Stavro Blofeld (Donald Pleasence) opens a mechanical footbridge, causing her to fall into his private piranha pool. When it comes to his agents' failed assassination attempts against 007, Blofeld never has a reassuring word or a forgiving heart.

Brausch: The (fictional) brand of silencer attached to the Walther PPK provided to Bond (Sean Connery) in *Dr. No*. According to the armoror, Major Boothroyd (Peter Burton), it offers very little reduction in muzzle velocity.

Bray, Sir Hilary: British heraldry expert at the London College of Arms, portrayed by George Baker in *On Her Majesty's Secret Service*. Bray is busy determining whether fugitive SPECTRE chief Ernst Stavro Blofeld (Telly Savalas) has a claim to the royal bloodline of the de Bleuchamp family.

Sensing an opportunity to apprehend Blofeld, Bond learns all he can from Bray about heraldry, then takes on Bray's identity for a trip to Blofeld's Swiss hideaway of Piz Gloria. His mission: to convince Blofeld to visit the de Bleuchamp ancestral home in Augsburg for research purposes. There the British Secret Service can arrest him. Unfortunately, Bond's cover is blown during his stay in the Alps after he begins bed-hopping among the luscious allergy patients that Blofeld is brainwashing.

Brayham, Peter (July 12, 1936–December 7, 2006): British stuntman/actor who portrayed Rhoda, the SPECTRE agent driving the Chevrolet stake truck in *From Russia with Love*. He stalls the truck on the railroad tracks to stop the Orient Express and provide an escape option for Grant (Robert Shaw). Having killed Grant in a vicious fight on the train, Bond (Sean Connery) surprises Rhoda, knocks him out, ties him up, and captures the truck.

Later, after he's destroyed a SPECTRE helicopter, Bond arrives at the dock where Rhoda has tethered a motorboat. When Bond and Tanya (Daniela Bianchi) head for Venice, Rhoda is untied and tossed into the water off Istria, where he cusses unintelligibly. It just wasn't his day.

Born in England, Brayham made his acting debut as Rhoda, but he was known more for his forty-plus years as a stunt performer and coordinator, which began with *The Guns of Navarone* (1961) and included work on *Goldfinger*, *You Only Live Twice*, and *Live and Let Die*. He was also the stunt arranger on *Time Bandits* (1981), in which he once again teamed with Sean Connery. His final credits were as a stunt coordinator for the BBC's time-hopping police drama *Life on Mars* (2006–2007).

Bree, James (July 20, 1923–December 1, 2008): British actor, mostly in television, who portrayed Swiss lawyer Gebrüder Gumbold in *On Her Majesty's Secret Service*. Gumbold is working for Blofeld (Telly Savalas) to establish the SPECTRE chief's blood connection to the royal line of the de Bleuchamps—prompting Bond (George Lazenby) to pay a little visit to his office in Bern. A native of East Coker, Somerset, England, Bree made his uncredited feature debut in director John Paddy Carstairs's comedy *Just My Luck* (1957), which also featured Michael Brennan (*Thunderball*). Three years later, he appeared in John Guillermin's crime drama *Never Let Go* alongside future Bond player Cyril Shaps (*The

Spy Who Loved Me). Later, he portrayed three characters—the Security Chief, Nefred, and the Keeper of the Matrix—on the BBC's *Doctor Who* (1969–1986).

Brennan, Michael (September 25, 1912–June 29, 1982): Tough, beefy British actor who portrayed Janni, a SPECTRE henchman in *Thunderball*. Working for spymaster Emilio Largo (Adolfo Celi), Janni is mostly teamed with Largo's top henchman, Vargas (Philip Locke). A native of London, Brennan made his uncredited feature debut as a camp guard in director Leslie Howard's adventure thriller *Pimpernel Smith* (1941). Nine years later, future James Bond film director Terence Young hired him to play Smoke O'Connor in the World War II drama *They Were Not Divided*, which also featured future Bond players Edward Underdown, Desmond Llewelyn, Anthony Dawson, Christopher Lee, and Peter Burton—all of whom would work in Young's three Bond pictures. Brennan also appeared in two adaptations of Sir Walter Scott's *Ivanhoe*, the 1952 MGM version as Baldwin, a confederate of Prince John's, and the 1970 BBC miniseries as villainous Norman knight Front de Beouf.

Brent Cross Shopping Centre: A shopping center in Hendon, London, where the underground garage chase in *Tomorrow Never Dies* was shot. It's supposed to be Hamburg, Germany.

bridal suite: The accommodations offered to James Bond (Sean Connery) in an Istanbul hotel in *From Russia with Love*, after he discovers that his original room is filled with listening devices. In actuality, the desk clerk who recommends the new room (Arlette Dobson) and the hotel's concierge (Andre Charisse) are working for SPECTRE. The bridal suite has been selected as the site where Tatiana Romanova (Daniela Bianchi) will seduce Bond so that, unbeknownst even to her, the scene can be filmed from a *cabinet de voyeur* behind the bed while SPECTRE agent Rosa Klebb (Lotte Lenya) observes.

briefcase (a.k.a. trick briefcase): A smart piece of luggage supplied to Bond (Sean Connery) by Q Branch in *From Russia with Love*. The briefcase saves his life in the final duel with SPECTRE assassin Donald Grant (Robert Shaw) on the Orient Express. Equipped with a number

of lethal weapons, the briefcase proved such an important element of the story that it influenced many future Bond films. From this point on, nearly every film contained a Q Branch sequence in which Bond is outfitted with various gadgets. Even the Aston Martin car that became a sensation in the next film, *Goldfinger*, was essentially the briefcase's automotive equivalent.

By the early 1960s, Western nations saw science and technology as one of the keys to defeating their Communist adversaries. Not only were they scrambling to land a man on the moon by the end of the decade, but technology was on the march in every facet of human life. So it's not surprising that Bond producers Albert R. Broccoli and Harry Saltzman were always looking for the latest high-tech gadgets to add to the Q Branch's arsenal. Having once scouted for vaudeville acts in New York City in the 1930s, Saltzman was especially adept at seeking out new toys that would work wonders in the latest Bond movie. The briefcase was the first.

In fact, Bond's briefcase figured into the very first day of shooting on *From Russia with Love*—April 1, 1963—during the scene in which Q (Desmond Llewelyn) comes to M's office to explain the case's various features: a special .25 caliber AR-7 folding sniper rifle with an infrared telescopic site; twenty rounds of ammunition hidden in two metal rods; fifty gold sovereigns hidden in the back; a flat-bladed throwing knife hidden in the front; and a metal tin of talcum powder that is actually a tear-gas cartridge, magnetically affixed to an inside wall of the case as a security precaution. As Q explains, when you ordinarily open a briefcase like this one, you move the catches to the side and open. If you do this, the tear-gas cartridge will explode in your face. Bond is then advised to first turn the catches horizontally and then move them to the side. The case can then be opened without triggering the gas.

Whimsical editor Peter Hunt actually played a trick on director Terence Young during one of the screening sessions in which this scene was shown. During the screening, when Bond attempts to properly open the briefcase using Q's instructions, Hunt cut in footage of an explosion that obliterates Bond, M, and Q. According to Hunt, it gave Young quite a start and, of course, kept everyone in stitches for days.*

---

* Peter Hunt, interview by the author, London, June 21, 1977.

In the finished movie, the briefcase is identified as standard field issue. In addition to Bond, it is carried by Captain Nash (production manager Bill Hill), Bond's doomed Yugoslavian contact, who is murdered by SPECTRE agent Grant. The briefcase is then involved in one of the most thrilling fight sequences in the entire series— inside the train compartment on the Orient Express, where 007 is about to be murdered by Grant. On his knees, staring at Grant's silenced automatic, Bond plays his final card. He asks for a cigarette, but Grant refuses. Bond then offers to pay for it. Considering that Grant has already taken Bond's bankroll, the request intrigues him. Grant asks him how he's going to pay for the cigarette, and Bond replies that there are fifty gold sovereigns in his briefcase. Grant then makes his worst mistake by letting Bond retrieve them.

Knowing how the trick case works, Bond opens it correctly (out of Grant's sight) and retrieves the sovereigns, which he throws on the floor. The ever-greedy Grant then asks if there are any more in Nash's case, and Bond adroitly replies in the affirmative, even taking the step of offering to open the other case himself. Grant falls right into the trap, thinking that Bond has a weapon hidden inside and insisting on opening the case himself. Of course, the tear gas cartridge explodes in his face. (Thanks to screenwriter Richard Maibaum, Bond's gambit is a distinct improvement over the corresponding moment in Fleming's original novel, in which 007's cigarette case deflects the assassin's bullet.)

The fight—one so brutal it used to be cut when the film run on network television—then begins. Despite his prowess in fisticuffs, Bond is about to be strangled with the garrote wire hidden in Grant's watch when 007 trips a catch on the briefcase, revealing the hidden knife. Bond stabs a surprised Grant in the arm, then strangles him with his own garrote.

The briefcase is mentioned one other time in the series, on the private jet in *Goldfinger*, when stewardess Mei-Lei (Mai Ling) informs Bond that his briefcase was damaged upon examination. "So sorry," she says. In real life, a plastic version of the briefcase was later sold commercially; not surprisingly, it became a popular toy.

Brigadier: The American commanding officer portrayed by John McLaren in *Goldfinger*. He leads the US infantry assault against Goldfinger (Gert Fröbe) and his forces after they break into Fort Knox. Another brigadier, portrayed by Paul Carpenter, bids farewell to Bond (Sean Connery) at the airport after the battle. NOTE: In the real US military, there is no rank of brigadier, only brigadier general, and an officer of that rank would be addressed as "General." Why these two officers are referred to "Brigadier" is a bit of a mystery—but it sounds very British.

British United Air Ferries: The airline that transports Goldfinger (Gert Fröbe), his henchman Oddjob (Harold Sakata), and his Rolls-Royce Phantom III to Geneva in *Goldfinger*, on flight VF 400. Tracking his adversary's progress thanks to a homing device concealed in the Rolls, Bond (Sean Connery) and his Aston Martin sports car follow them a half hour later on the next Air Ferries flight to Geneva.

Broadchest, Miss Stephanie: The comical cover name that James Bond (Daniel Craig) gives to Vesper Lynd (Eva Green) in *Casino Royale*. Needless to say, she doesn't see the humor.

Broccoli, Albert Romolo "Cubby" (April 5, 1909–June 27, 1996): American film producer who devoted himself almost exclusively to making James Bond films from 1962 until his death in 1996. Originally partnered with Harry Saltzman in the first nine films in the series, Broccoli later shared producing chores with his stepson, Michael G. Wilson. Broccoli's daughter Barbara now shares those duties with Wilson, making the continuing adventures of 007 a true family affair.

Albert Broccoli was the son of Giovanni Broccoli, who, along with his brother, immigrated to New York City from Calabria, Italy around 1900. According to research done in Florence by Broccoli's wife Dana, the brothers are descended from the Broccolis of Carrera, who first crossed two Italian vegetables—cauliflower and rabe—to produce the vegetable that took their name, and eventually supported them in the United States.

Although Giovanni made a comfortable living as a civil engineer, his plan to retire to truck farming in the early 1900s did not prove successful. The Broccoli children were forced to toil in the family garden and sell their vegetables in the Harlem produce market. It was not an easy life. Expenses mounted, and when the market was flooded with too many vegetables, prices plummeted. Many times, Albert and his brother had to dump their vegetables in the sewers rather than truck them back to the family farm in Astoria.

For a time, Albert's father operated a successful citrus farm in Florida, but the venture proved disastrous in the late 1920s when the farm was bombarded by hurricanes. Albert Broccoli soon realized that he could not survive in America by following in the footsteps of his ancestors. He would have to seek another calling.

After his father died, he went to live with his grandmother in downtown Astoria and began working as an assistant pharmacist. After a few months, he quit to work for a cousin named D'Orta who ran a casket company. D'Orta needed an office manager, so eighteen-year-old Broccoli began a successful new career as a casket salesman and accountant.

Although young Broccoli made a great deal of money working for his cousin, he was not happy. In 1934, his wealthy cousin Pat De Cicco invited him out to California. De Cicco, then married to actress Thelma Todd (*Horse Feathers*), introduced Broccoli to the movie industry, and it wasn't long before the casket salesman from Astoria was hobnobbing with such Hollywood notables as Howard Hughes, Howard Hawks, and Joe Schenck.

When his vacation time ended, Broccoli decided to uproot himself from the coffin business and move west. It was not easy to make a living in Hollywood unless you were in the entertainment business. And Broccoli was not in the business. However, he was a very good salesman, and he soon amassed a bankroll selling beauty supplies in the Los Angeles area. His movie contacts paid off when Howard Hawks offered him a "gofer" job on Howard Hughes's new film *The Outlaw*.

As Hawks's able assistant, Broccoli plunged into the film industry, learning the business end of the creative medium, meeting new people, getting married, and continuing to socialize with the upper strata of Hollywood. When Howard Hawks was fired from *The Outlaw* in 1941, Broccoli stayed on the film. He worked closely with Howard Hughes, who took over personal control of the film, which starred his muse, the voluptuous Jane Russell.

On the recommendation of Joe Schenck, Broccoli later transferred over to 20th Century Fox to become director Henry King's production assistant on such classics as *A Yank in the R.A.F.*

Producer Albert R. Broccoli, one of the most successful producers in show business history, focused on the Bond pictures almost exclusively for over thirty years. *Courtesy of the Anders Frejdh Collection*

(1941), *The Black Swan* (1942), and *The Song of Bernadette* (1943). In 1942, Broccoli left Fox to join the US Navy.

After World War II ended in September 1945, Broccoli returned to Hollywood to become a successful talent agent. His boss was Charles K. Feldman, who would later produce the 1967 Bond spoof *Casino Royale*. As a member of Feldman's extremely successful Famous Artists Agency, Broccoli resumed his film education. He learned about casting, bargaining, contract negotiations, and percentages—in short, a lawyer's course in how to make movies and turn a profit.

Broccoli and his wife mingled freely with the Hollywood community, giving sumptuous parties and acquiring an impeccable social standing. Broccoli still couldn't hide a desire to try something else. He wanted to enter the creative side of show business. Feldman had already started to produce on the side as early as 1942, and Broccoli began considering a career as a producer.

Friends encouraged him, but it was challenging to begin a producing career in Hollywood after the war. Money was extremely tight, and the studios were relying on their own proven stable of producers. The time of the independent producer was still a good decade away, so Broccoli bode his time at Famous Artists. In 1951, he resumed a high school friendship with Irving Allen, a Polish-born director who was then between jobs. With slim prospects of landing a film project on their own, the discontented pair decided to pool their talents and resources, form their own company, and move to London.

Their company was called Warwick Film Productions, named after the New York hotel where they made the deal. With the backing of the British government—which had recently begun subsidizing companies that employed British artists—and a hard-won distribution deal with Columbia Pictures, Broccoli and Allen signed Alan Ladd to a three-picture contract.

After establishing himself in a townhouse in London's Portland Place, Broccoli began acquiring British talent so that Warwick could benefit from the government subsidies. Remembered Broccoli, "If you went over to England to make a picture and you hired 80 percent British technicians, you got a slice of what they called Eady money," after the former UK Treasury official, Sir Wilfrid Eady, who gave his name to the subsidy program. "In other words, you got a British subsidy, and it could amount to 2 or 3 million pounds."*

Warwick's first project was a little war drama titled *The Red Beret* (1953). Budgeted at $1.1 million, cowritten by Richard Maibaum, and directed by Terence Young, it told the story of a young paratrooper (Alan Ladd) who fights to escape his reputation for cowardice. Retitled *Paratrooper* for its American debut, this first Warwick entry became an overnight sensation for Columbia Pictures at a time when the studio desperately needed revenue to counter the postwar slump at the box office.

The surprising success of their first film was encouraging to Broccoli and Allen. For their second Alan Ladd feature, they chose another action story, British writer Hammond Innes's novel *The White South*, about a two-fisted sailor who helps a young lady search for her father's killer in Antarctica. Their adaptation, *Hell Below Zero* (1954),

spearheaded by veteran American director Mark Robson, scored again for Warwick. It was the second in a string of successes that would last for seven years, making the transplanted Americans the kings of the independent film business in England.

Their features were all strong on American actors, British supporting players, colorful location backgrounds, and action-packed plots. And during those successful years, Broccoli established lasting relationships with many artists who would later contribute heavily to the success of the Bond pictures. Warwick's personnel included cinematographer Ted Moore, who started as a camera operator on *The Red Beret*; that film's screenwriter Maibaum, who also cowrote the very successful *Cockleshell Heroes* (1955); and art director Ken Adam, who designed the last Warwick feature, *The Trials of Oscar Wilde* (1960).

Two years before future partner Harry Saltzman acquired an option from Ian Fleming for his Bond novels, Broccoli was given the opportunity to start a 007 project. In the summer of 1958, while he was still partnered with Allen, he received a call from Ned McLaine, a wealthy London businessman who was one of Fleming's good friends. Broccoli was in New York taking care of his two children while his first wife fought a losing battle with cancer. It was a trying time for the producer, and had the project been anything else, Broccoli would probably have said no. But Bond was a different story.

Ever since reading *Dr. No*, Broccoli had become fascinated by Fleming's writing and the exciting life of Britain's most famous Secret Service agent. Thus, not surprisingly, the chance of doing an action-packed James Bond film appealed to him. McLaine advised Broccoli to contact his partner, Irving Allen, as soon as possible. Fleming, he was told, was anxious to make a deal.

Two weeks later, a luncheon was arranged at the Les Ambassadeurs club in London (which would later host the pivotal meeting between Saltzman and Fleming). Accompanying Fleming were the McLaine brothers—Ned and Jacque—and Fleming's agent at MCA, Bob Fenn, who prefaced the meeting by discussing the recent deal with CBS for thirty-two half-hour episodes of a Bond TV series (a deal that would promptly collapse), the latest publishing figures on *Dr. No*, and Mr. Fleming's eagerness to make a lucrative film deal.

---

* Albert R. Broccoli, interview by the author, Los Angeles, April 10, 1977.

Producer Albert R. "Cubby" Broccoli (center) with production designer Ken Adam (left) and director Lewis Gilbert (right) on the "Jonah Set" for *The Spy Who Loved Me. Courtesy of the David Reinhardt Collection*

Fifty-three-year-old Irving Allen seemed content to let Broccoli do all of the talking. He listened to Fenn, nodding occasionally to Fleming, who seemed to have a voracious appetite for scrambled eggs; the whole proceeding seemed to bore him. After Fenn declared that the rights to all of the Bond books could be optioned for $50,000, Allen couldn't stand it anymore.

"Come on," he said, "how can you talk figures like that?"

Fenn replied, "Excuse me?"

Allen then declared, "I'm sorry, gentlemen, but these books aren't even television material." Broccoli tried to argue the point, but it was hopeless.*

---

* Ibid.

Having said his piece, Allen grabbed his hat and left the luncheon. Broccoli mumbled an apology and also left. For a few seconds, the remaining gentlemen sat in stunned silence, wondering why they had journeyed to London to hear such claptrap. Even more exasperating to Ned McLaine was the fact that Allen had left him with the luncheon check. Allen's failure to support a project that was deep in Broccoli's heart contributed to the gradual disintegration of their partnership and the final collapse of Warwick Film in 1960.

Now alone, but wealthy and resourceful, Broccoli began to search for a new project. For two years he thought about how the Bonds had slipped through his fingers, his memory rekindled each time Fleming wrote a new novel.

Then, in the summer of 1961, Broccoli was approached by screenwriter Wolf Mankowitz, whose friend producer Harry Saltzman had optioned the film rights to the Bond novels. With only twenty-eight days left until that option expired, Saltzman needed a production deal fast. Extremely dubious about making any deals with Fleming after the fiasco at Les Ambassadeurs, Broccoli reluctantly agreed to meet Saltzman in Audley Square in June 1961. A partnership deal was struck, and Eon Productions was born.

Soon after the Audley Square meeting, Broccoli took the Fleming project to his old cohorts at Columbia Pictures. He left copies of the Bond novels with production chief Mike Frankovich. Frankovich gave the novels to a story editor for an opinion, who quickly advised him that James Bond was a poorly conceived British version of Mickey Spillane's detective Mike Hammer, and that the character would never work in the United States. Frankovich, though, had a great deal of respect for Cubby Broccoli and his track record. He decided to call a board meeting and briefly postpone making a final decision.

Meanwhile, there were rumors going around that the story editor had never even read the Bond books, and even that someone had mistakenly given him copies of Peter Fleming's travel novels instead. Broccoli waited in London for an answer, and when the phone failed to ring, he decided to take the project to his friend Arthur Krim at United Artists

On June 20, 1961, Broccoli and Saltzman, accompanied by their wives, Dana and Jacqueline, and Broccoli's one-year-old daughter, Barbara, flew into New York City for a meeting with Krim. Frankovich had called the previous week, stating that Columbia could not pick up the Bond option, so it was either UA or back to square one. Fortunately for the future of James Bond, United Artists was ready to deal.

Broccoli related the facts of the meeting: "Harry Saltzman and I walked into 729 Seventh Avenue in New York, to United Artists, for a meeting with Arthur. I found ten people at the meeting, including young David Picker, who had just been given the job of head of production. Arthur said, 'Now, Cubby, tell me about James Bond.' And I did. I was the salesman. But Picker said, 'I'm very familiar with James Bond.' He wanted to know how I planned to make the pictures. I had budgeted the first one at $1.1 million. They

agreed to $1 million. In forty-five minutes we put together a deal for six pictures.

"When Arthur and I shook hands, I suddenly remembered that it was my second wedding anniversary. I thought, I'm here in New York with my wife, Dana, and our baby daughter, Barbara—and I've got a deal to make James Bond pictures. I'm flying high."[*]

Since 1975, when Harry Saltzman sold his share of Eon to United Artists, the Broccoli family has been the sole production conduit for James Bond's film adventures—except for the 1983 film *Never Say Never Again*, which was a new adaptation of Fleming's novel *Thunderball* (the rights to which were controlled by producer Kevin McClory at the time). Even when the Fleming titles ran out, Broccoli had permission from Fleming's estate to create new Bond stories. *Licence to Kill*, Broccoli's sixteenth 007 film, released in 1989, was the first non-Fleming title. Additional non-Fleming titles have included *GoldenEye*, *Tomorrow Never Dies*, *The World Is Not Enough*, *Die Another Day*, *Skyfall*, *Spectre*, and *No Time to Die*.

In 1981, the Academy of Motion Picture Arts and Sciences awarded Albert R. Broccoli its prestigious Irving G. Thalberg Award for his illustrious producing career. Broccoli also received the Order of the British Empire from the Queen of England, as well as the French Commandeur des Arts et des Lettres.

Since 1962, the Bond movie franchise Albert Broccoli initiated has grossed over $7 billion dollars in revenue. And there appears to be no end in sight. The catchphrase that first appeared after Broccoli's second film, *From Russia with Love*, still rings true: "James Bond Will Return."

Broccoli, Barbara (June 18, 1960–): American film producer and daughter of legendary Bond producer Albert R. Broccoli, who made her producing debut on *GoldenEye* and has continued in that capacity on every Bond film since. Having gained experience on previous Bond films in virtually every department—including production, casting, and music supervision—Broccoli received credit as an executive assistant on *Octopussy*, graduating to assistant director on *A View to a Kill*. She received associate producer credit on both of Timothy Dalton's Bond entries, *The Living Daylights* and *Licence to Kill*. Now,

---

[*] Ibid.

Producer Barbara Broccoli, along with her half brother Michael Wilson, has carried the heavy weight of the James Bond series on her shoulders for over thirty years. *The Ander Frejdh Collection*

along with half brother Michael G. Wilson, she guides the future of the James Bond films.

Brosnan, Pierce (May 16, 1952–   ): Handsome Irish actor who, in *GoldenEye*, became the fifth man to portray James Bond in the United Artists series of 007 adventures. Brosnan was originally signed to play Bond in *The Living Daylights*, but in a much-publicized decision, NBC executives refused to let the actor out of his contract for the series *Remington Steele*, and Timothy Dalton was his last-minute replacement. In addition to *GoldenEye*, Brosnan portrayed James Bond in *Tomorrow Never Dies*, *The World Is Not Enough*, and *Die Another Day*. He was also married to the late Cassandra Harris, who appeared in *For Your Eyes Only*.

Back in June 1994, at a press conference announcing his casting in *GoldenEye*, Brosnan promised "a Bond for the '90s." Asked how he would play Bond, he said, "He has to go back to being a more flinty character. But we are now in 1994. I think that has to be addressed." The new

Pierce Brosnan as James Bond, Secret Agent 007. *Courtesy of the Luc Leclech Collection*

Bond would be no "new man," however. "In a piece like this, which is fantasy," he continued, "I think the political correctness has to be eased up a little." Brosnan also revealed that the earliest film he could remember seeing as a boy was *Goldfinger*. "I remember sitting in that cinema on a Saturday afternoon with my parents, seeing this magnificent thing unfold before me, and I remember Sean!"* Brosnan lived up to the Bond legacy, propelling *GoldenEye* to the biggest box office haul in 007 history to that point.

At a press conference in Hong Kong for *The World Is Not Enough*, however, Brosnan was somewhat critical of his own initial turn as 007. "In *GoldenEye*, I was cautious; this was my first time and I didn't want to blow it. So when you're cautious, you're not as free with your performance

---

* Special features, GoldenEye, James Bond Ultimate Edition (1995; MGM, 2006), DVD.

and your knowledge of the character because you censor yourself, but I got away with it." His ambition going forward was to stretch the character beyond the familiar tropes. "The essence of James Bond is cruelty, vodka martinis, sex, his weapon—because the man deals with killing. He has this license to kill. There is a dark side to him. . . . And then you have all the wit and the charm and the throwaway one-liners. It is formulaic, which is its strong point. But I also think that's a weakness. I'd like to see one where they take the formula away—to give the illusion of it at the beginning, but then to surprise, because if you can surprise and have growth, then you have interest. But I do know we can push it further. This man is fallible. He has feelings and doubts. And there's moral ambiguity there. And I think when you go into the gray area of any character, that's when you get interesting drama—it's in the books. Fleming does make this character fractured."*

But for all the talk of Bond's fractured fallibility, Brosnan recognized that the movies needed to retain a sense of playful romance. "The women in Bond movies have got to be sexy, they have to be beautiful, they have to have a sense of who they are. And when you get the really good ones, they're played by actresses who are right on the money with their own sensuality and sexuality and they play it to the hilt. And they play it with a wiggle. So they're not going to go away, otherwise we wouldn't have a Bond movie. That would be very sad. Bond without babes?"

A native of Drogheda in County Louth, Brosnan made his feature debut in director John Mackenzie's crime drama *The Long Good Friday* (1980). However, it was his starring role as roguish frontman to the private investigator played by Stephanie Zimbalist in NBC's *Remington Steele* that won him international stardom and a prominent career as a leading man in features.

Brosnan's first post–*Remington Steele* feature, *The Fourth Protocol* (1987), reteamed him with director John Mackenzie in a film that also featured Bond player Julian Glover. His numerous feature credits include *Dante's Peak* (1997); the remake of *The Thomas Crown Affair* (1999); *The Matador* (2005), spoofing his Bond persona; *Mamma Mia!* (2008); *Percy Jackson & the Olympians: The Lightning Thief* (2010); and *No Escape* (2015).

---

* Special features, *The World Is Not Enough*, James Bond
  Ultimate Edition (1999; MGM, 2006), DVD.

Brown, Earl Jolly (October 18, 1939–August 24, 2006): Portly American actor, briefly in film and television, who portrayed the extremely soft-spoken henchman Whisper in *Live and Let Die*, his film debut. The following year, he portrayed Jelly in director Robert Clouse's action comedy *Black Belt Jones* (1974), which costarred his *Live and Let Die* castmate Gloria Hendry.

Rotund Earl Jolly Brown portrayed soft-spoken Whisper, a confederate of Kananga's in *Live and Let Die*. *Courtesy of the Anders Frejdh Collection*

Brown, Robert (July 23, 1921–November 11, 2003): Authoritative British character actor who became the second person to portray British Secret Service chief M in the James Bond series. Brown was actually introduced as Admiral Hargreaves, Flag Officer, Submarines, in *The Spy Who Loved Me*. When Bernard Lee, the first M, died prior to the making of *For Your Eyes Only*, his role was temporarily assumed by Chief of Staff Tanner (James Villiers). Brown became M in *Octopussy*, and played that part in every Bond until he was replaced by Dame Judi Dench in *GoldenEye*. A native of Swanage, Dorset, England, Brown made his feature film debut as a British military policemen in director

British character actor Robert Brown took over the role of M, James Bond's boss, in *Octopussy*. *Steve Rubin Collection*

Carol Reed's classic mystery thriller *The Third Man* (1949), which featured Bernard Lee. After a number of minor parts, Brown's career began to pick up in the late 1950s and early 1960s. The roles were still small—but the movies were more important, including *Ben Hur* (1959), as the chief of rowers; *Sink the Bismarck!* (1960), as the gunnery officer on the battleship *King George V*, who orders all batteries to fire by yelling "*Shoot!*"; *It Takes a Thief* (1960); *The 300 Spartans* (1962); *Billy Budd* (1962); *Operation Crowbow* (1965); and *One Million Years B.C.* (1966).

Browning, Ricou (November 23, 1930–   ): Underwater director, cameraman, actor, and stuntman who worked on both *Thunderball* and *Never Say Never Again*. Although he achieved international popularity as the gruesome Gill Man in *The Creature from the Black Lagoon* (1954), Browning spent most of his professional life behind the underwater cameras.

While directing the *Thunderball* underwater sequences, Browning began a typical shooting day at 9:00 AM. "We needed sunlight," he recalled. "Then we would rehearse the sequence before we went into the water. Everything on *Thunderball* was orchestrated underwater with hand signals— no radio communicating like we do today. If we had a problem, we would never correct it underwater. We'd surface, discuss it, and go back down to complete the sequence."

Most of the time, the underwater team filmed in shallow water—between fifteen and twenty feet. The deepest they went on *Thunderball* was fifty feet, when they worked around the ditched NATO bomber. The final battle sequence was conducted off Clifton Pier in Nassau, Bahamas, in fifteen to twenty feet of water around an old wrecked US Navy landing craft.

Eighteen years later, Browning began work on *Never Say Never Again*—a shoot that was bedeviled by bad weather. For the sequence in which Bond (Sean Connery) is chased by sensor-equipped sharks, the crew shot around a wrecked fishing boat that was located only two hundred feet from the carcass of the *Thunderball* NATO bomber, only the framework of which remained. The crew also shot in the waters of Silver Springs, Florida, where Jordan Klein had constructed the exterior superstructure of the *Flying Saucer* yacht, through which a new generation of underwater scooters travels.

A native of Fort Pierce, Florida, the multitalented Browning reprised his Gill Man character in two sequels, *Revenge of the Creature* (1955) and *The Creature Walks Among Us* (1956). But it was his introduction to Ivan Tors Studios that led Browning into the production of underwater television shows, including the iconic *Sea Hunt*, *The Aquanauts*, and *Flipper*, the last of which Browning cocreated. He would later become president of Tors's Florida studios.

Brunskill: The servant of Colonel Smithers (Richard Vernon) at the Bank of England dinner attended by Bond (Sean Connery) and M (Bernard Lee) in *Goldfinger*. Portrayed by Denis Cowles, he's the one who served the "rather disappointing brandy."

Brunskill (Denis Cowles), Colonel Smithers's servant, offers James Bond (Sean Connery) a cigar during a strategy session on dealing with big-time gold smuggling in *Goldfinger*. *Courtesy of the Anders Frejdh Collection*

Bunt, Frau Irma: The ruthlessly efficient personal secretary to Ernst Stavro Blofeld (Telly Savalas) in *On Her Majesty's Secret Service*, perfectly portrayed by German actress Ilse Steppat, who, sadly, died soon after the film's release. Showing off some of his knowledge of family names and lineages, Bond (George Lazenby), masquerading as Sir Hilary Bray of the London College of Arms, informs Irma that *bunt* is a nautical term referring to the "baggy or swollen parts of a sail." However, it is Bunt who pierces Bond's cover when she discovers him sneaking into the bedroom of luscious allergy patient Ruby Bartlett (Angela Scoular). Surviving the Union Corse crime syndicate's helicopter assault on Blofeld's Piz Gloria fortress, Bunt is the one who machine-guns Tracy (Diana Rigg) minutes after her wedding to Bond.

Buoy Point, Florida: Fictional location off the coast of Miami of a wrecked ship where SPECTRE intends to place one of the two hijacked A-bombs in *Thunderball*. It is also the site of an underwater battle between Emilio Largo's black-suited frogmen and a platoon of orange-suited US Navy aqua-paras led by James Bond (Sean Connery). Thanks to 007, who performs the same chores he did at the gypsy camp in *From Russia with Love*—in other words, he's everywhere—the Americans win and the bomb is recovered.

Burton, Norman (December 5, 1923–November 29, 2003): American character actor who portrayed CIA operative Felix Leiter in *Diamonds Are Forever*. Burton's Leiter was similar to the version of the character introduced by Cec

Actor Norman Burton (second from right) joins fellow *Diamonds Are Forever* cast members Lana Wood and Bruce Glover (far right) and host/author Steven Jay Rubin at the July 1981 James Bond Weekend, held at the Playboy Club in Century City, Los Angeles. *Steve Rubin Collection*

Linder in *Goldfinger*. In *Diamonds Are Forever*, however, Leiter is a little funnier and a bit more exasperated with his buddy 007 (Sean Connery). The fact that Bond has broken every law in the Las Vegas vehicle code has something to do with Leiter's annoyance. A New York City native, Burton made his feature debut as Thompkins the reporter in director W. Lee Wilder's horror film *Fright* (1956). Moving frequently between increasingly more important film and television assignments (he played an office worker in "Miniature," the Robert Duvall episode of *The Twilight Zone*), Burton put on full ape makeup as the hunt leader in the original *Planet of the Apes* (1968), and later was featured as Will Giddings opposite Paul Newman in *The Towering Inferno* (1974). Sadly, Burton was killed in a car crash on the California/Arizona border while returning to his home in Mexico.

Burton, Peter (April 4, 1921–November 27, 1989): British actor and member of director Terence Young's stock company who portrayed armoror Major Boothroyd in the first James Bond film, *Dr. No*. When Burton proved unavailable, actor Desmond Llewelyn took over the role in *From Russia with Love* but quickly became more commonly known as Q—a role that lasted decades. A native of Bromley, Kent, England, Burton made his feature debut in Young's World War II film *They Were Not Divided* (1950), which also featured future Bond players Edward Underdown (*Thunderball*), Anthony Dawson, Michael Brennan, Christopher Lee, and Desmond Llewelyn. That same year, he was once again featured with Anthony Dawson, this time as Nigel in *The Wooden Horse* (1950), another war picture. Following *Dr. No*, Burton played an Arab sheik in *Lawrence of Arabia* (1962), a minister's aide in *A Clockwork Orange* (1971), and Douglas Ransom in Terence Young's *The Jigsaw Man* (1983), which featured the director's usual stock company of Bond players: Yuri Borienko (*On Her Majesty's Secret Service*), Anthony Dawson, Vladek Sheybal, and Charles Gray.

Butcher, Professor Joe: Soft-spoken international televangelist portrayed by Wayne Newton in *Licence to Kill*. In reality, he's a sleazy, lecherous henchman of South American drug kingpin Franz Sanchez (Robert Davi). Like real-life televangelist and convicted con man Jim Bakker,

Las Vegas singing legend Wayne Newton (pictured here with costar Carey Lowell) took on the role of smarmy televangelist Professor Joe Butcher, who helps a drug lord with his money laundering operation in *Licence to Kill*. *Courtesy of the David Reinhardt Collection*

Butcher is a high-rolling charlatan who lives in a pleasure palace called the Olimpatec Meditation Institute. But his institute actually houses the laboratories that dissolve Sanchez's cocaine in gasoline. And through a code developed by Sanchez's financial expert William Truman-Lodge (Anthony Starke), Butcher's television show actually broadcasts the current price of cocaine to an international clientele. Thus, in addition to receiving donations from devoted viewers, Butcher's telephone operators also take major drug orders. His cushy lifestyle is disrupted when Bond (Timothy Dalton) and Pam Bouvier (Carey Lowell) destroy the institute and its cocaine cargo.

Butler, Dick (May 8, 1936–December 3, 2013; a.k.a. Richard E. Butler): Top American stuntman who doubled Sean Connery in sections of the fight between Bond and Bambi (Lola Larson) and Thumper (Trina Parks) in *Diamonds Are Forever*. In one sequence, Butler is kicked into the metal tubes (actually cardboard) in Willard Whyte's living room, and in another he's thrown into the swimming pool. According to writer/director Robert Short, who in 1971 visited Elrod House in Palm Springs, California, where this sequence was filmed, Sean Connery did most of his own stunts and enjoyed every minute of it.

Byron Lee and the Dragonaires: Jamaican band, discovered by composer Monty Norman, that performed as the house band at the hotel in Jamaica in *Dr. No*. Led by Chinese Jamaican musician Byron Lee, the band also contributed three songs to the film's soundtrack—"Under the Mango Tree," "Jump Up," and the calypso version of "Three Blind Mice"—though the solo guitar work on their songs was provided by Ernest Ranglin. Lee died of cancer at seventy-three on November 4, 2008.

C: Nickname of Max Denbigh (Andrew Scott), the head of Britain's new Joint Intelligence Service, formed by the recent merger of MI5 and MI6 in *Spectre*. A bureaucratic little snot who has moved England's intelligence networks into a high-tech London complex bankrolled by money from the private sector, C is pushing for Britain to join a global surveillance and intelligence initiative dubbed "Nine Eyes," which would combine the intelligence streams of nine countries—and he is determined to close down the double-O field agent program. M (Ralph Fiennes) and Bond (Daniel Craig) loathe this know-it-all, but they're unaware that he has been compromised by Blofeld (Christoph Waltz) and SPECTRE.

Andrew Scott portrayed duplicitous C, a British spymaster who wants to eliminate the double-O section in *Spectre*. *Courtesy of the Anders Frejdh Collection*

cable car: Form of transportation that plays a dramatic role in both *On Her Majesty's Secret Service* and *Moonraker*. In the former film, a cable car connects the tiny Swiss village of Mürren with the mountaintop refuge of Piz Gloria, from which Ernst Stavro Blofeld (Telly Savalas) is plotting his latest scheme to blackmail the free world. James

Bond (George Lazenby) infiltrates Blofeld's headquarters disguised as a British heraldry expert, but when his cover is blown, he's imprisoned by Blofeld in the cable car's wheelhouse—a complicated mass of cables and gears that resembles the mechanism of a watch.

Bond realizes that if he can make it through a window to the outside, he can escape. Tearing out the pockets of his pants to create a pair of makeshift gloves, Bond carefully winds his way through the gear system, catches hold of the departing cable, and is whisked out of the mechanical prison. Once he's in the open air, 007 holds on to the cables and then jumps aboard an arriving cable car that takes him back into the Piz Gloria reception area, where he steals a pair of skis and heads into Mürren.

The interior of the wheelhouse was filmed at Pinewood Studios on a set designed by Syd Cain. Stuntman Chris Webb and Richard "Dicky" Graydon did the dangerous location work in which Bond clings to the icy cables. Remembered stunt arranger George Leech, "I was supposed to be George Lazenby's double in that sequence, but when I started doing the cable climb, I fell off and twisted my arm. It was a dangerous stunt to do in freezing cold weather, ten thousand feet up. We were working on the last station of the Schilthorn cable run. Below was at least a one-hundred-foot drop, and the cables were extremely greasy and caked with ice."*

Since Leech was injured, he employed Chris Webb and Dicky Graydon to double for Lazenby. To protect them, Leech fastened a metallic rigging device inside their sleeves. In case they lost their grip, the metal hook would prevent them from falling. As a second safety precaution, a drop bed was placed below the cable to catch the stuntmen if their primary device failed them. Director Peter Hunt asked Leech if the stunt was possible without the metallic aid, but as the day wore on and it became colder, Leech felt it was impossible to do the stunt without some metallic safeguard.

"It was so cold," said Leech, "that Dicky couldn't get a grip on the moving wire. He began to slide down the mountain on the cable. Luckily, I had stationed somebody at the first piling who stuck his foot out in time and prevented Dicky

---

* George Leech, interview by the author, London, June 23, 1977.

The funicular from Mürren to Piz Gloria, which became an icy escape route for James Bond (George Lazenby) in *On Her Majesty's Secret Service*
Steve Rubin Collection

while Jaws, the controls on his cable car shot, crashes spectacularly into the wheelhouse—later emerging, in typical Jaws fashion, unscathed.

The fight between Bond and Jaws was performed on a stage at Pinewood, with the actors trading blows in front of a blue screen so the Brazilian skyline could later be matted in. Master shots of the stalled cable cars and the wheelhouse were shot on location in Brazil.

Cabot, Bruce (April 20, 1904–May 3, 1972; birth name: Etienne Pelissier Jacques de Bujac): American tough-guy actor who portrayed casino boss Bert Saxby in *Diamonds Are Forever*. Cabot's rugged features were perfectly suited to the film's Las Vegas atmosphere, crowded with underworld diamond smugglers, tough-talking women, and mysterious assassins. A native of Carlsbad, New Mexico, Bruce Cabot made his credited featured debut as Fred Dykes in director J. Walter Ruben's *The Roadhouse Murder* (1932) for RKO Pictures. The following year, he won what was to be his most celebrated role: John Driscoll, the writer who rescues Ann Darrow (Fay Wray) from the eponymous giant ape in *King Kong* (1933). In 1947, he costarred in *Angel and the Badman*, the first of many films he made with his good friend John Wayne.

Café Martinique: Romantic outdoor Nassau, Bahamas, nightclub featured in *Thunderball*, where Bond (Sean Connery) dances with Domino (Claudine Auger) and discovers that she is leaving Nassau in two days' time. The real Café Martinique lies on Paradise Island, a two-mile strip of sand and rock that forms the outer edge of Nassau Harbor. Here, in the mid-1960s, Nassau's elite arrived every evening in their motor launches to eat, drink, and dance to the wonderful melodies of the tropics. In this lush atmosphere, Domino begins to fall in love with Bond.

How do you cast 150 extras to play a group of rich socialites and tourists? If you're Cubby Broccoli and Harry Saltzman, you don't use extras at all. With the help of Patty Turtle of the Nassau Tourist Board and an offer to donate a sum of money to the local Red Cross, the producers convinced a group of Nassau's social elite to portray themselves at two all-night parties, during which director Terence Young shot his key sequences. Eon Productions threw in a bucket of the finest

from sliding any farther. He could have eventually slid all the way to Mürren."*

A much larger cable car is featured in *Moonraker*, during a hair-raising sequence filmed partially on stage and partially in Rio de Janeiro. Bond (Roger Moore) and Holly Goodhead (Lois Chiles) are making their way from Sugarloaf Mountain to the Brazilian mainland when a crony of Jaws (Richard Kiel) halts their cable car midway on its run. Jaws then climbs aboard a second car, which is carefully maneuvered alongside a trapped Bond and Holly.

A fight ensues between 007 and his steel-toothed nemesis, with each jumping in, around, and between the two stalled cars. Eventually 007 grabs hold of one of the cables and, using a chain, slides downhill with Holly in tow. Jaws follows in a cable car controlled by his wheelhouse assistant and nearly runs Bond down. At the last possible moment, Bond and Holly jump to safety,

---

* Ibid.

caviar and several cases of Dom Pérignon champagne. The same group was later hired to attend the special Junkanoo parade, which was organized especially for *Thunderball*.

Note: When *Thunderball* was being produced, the only way to get to Paradise Island was by motor launch. Thanks to a bridge that was constructed in 1967 (and others that followed), motor launches are no longer necessary.

Cain, Syd (April 16, 1918–November 21, 2011): Resourceful British production designer who joined the James Bond series as location art director on *Dr. No*, and later served as art director on *From Russia with Love*, production designer on *On Her Majesty's Secret Service*, and supervising art director on *Live and Let Die*. Born in Grantham, Lincolnshire, England, Cain received his first job as an uncredited draftsman on director Charles Frank's drama *The Inheritance* (1947). Fifteen years later, he jumped to art director on director Norman Panama's Bing Crosby / Bob Hope comedy *The Road to Hong Kong* (1962), which featured a plethora of future Bond veterans, including Peter Madden (*From Russia with Love*), Irvin Allen (*On Her Majesty's Secret Service*), Walter Gotell, Bob Simmons, and the two lady island assistants of *Dr. No*—Michel Mok and Yvonne Shima. Three years later, and once again working with director Terence Young, he received his first credit as production designer on *The Amorous Adventures of Moll Flanders*, which also featured other members of Young's "stock company," including Anthony Dawson, Bernard Lee, and Desmond Llewelyn, and *Thunderball*'s Reginald Beckwith, Leonard Sachs, and Michael Brennan.

Cairo: Egyptian capital featured in *Diamonds Are Forever* and *The Spy Who Loved Me*. In *Diamonds*, the city is the second stop for James Bond (Sean Connery) on his ruthless search for Ernst Stavro Blofeld (Charles Gray), the man behind the murder of Bond's wife in the previous film. Tipped off in Tokyo, Bond goes to a Cairo casino and meets a fez-wearing blackjack player whose card request, "Hit me," is happily obliged—literally—by Bond. To avoid a further beating, he in turn directs Bond to Marie (Denise Perrier), a bikini-clad jet-setter who tells Bond everything when he rips her top off and nearly strangles her with it. The information eventually leads him to the jungles of South America and to Blofeld's cloning experiments.

In *The Spy Who Loved Me*, Cairo becomes the scene of a number of strange encounters between Bond (Roger Moore) and KGB major Anya Amasova (Barbara Bach), who are competing for a nuclear submarine tracking system that is being offered on the open market by anonymous sources. Bond also receives an equipment briefing from Q (Desmond Llewelyn) inside an Egyptian tomb turned headquarters of the British Secret Service in Cairo. All exterior sequences were shot on location in the Egyptian capital, including a visit to a spectacular nightly light show conducted on the Giza Plateau with the pyramids in the background.

"California Girls": Classic Beach Boys tune, covered by Gidea Park in the pre-credits teaser of *A View to a Kill*. It accompanies the sequence in which Bond (Roger Moore) takes the runner from a disabled snowmobile and surfs down a glacier—continuing a trend in the Moore-starring 007 films toward including memorable musical tracks as comic relief.

"California Girls," however, represented a low point in the trend. In the early Bond films, the filmmakers had stretched the bounds of moviemaking to create the ultimate in white-knuckle action sequences. Eventually, they started to toss in a little humor to bring the audience back into their seats. But by the time they were backing a well-directed snow-surfing sequence with a Beach Boys song, this tendency had started to undercut the audience's suspension of disbelief. Fortunately, such touches were abandoned during the Daniel Craig era of super-serious Bond epics.

Call Me Bwana (1963): A Bob Hope / Anita Ekberg jungle comedy produced by Albert R. Broccoli and Harry Saltzman. To publicize their rare producing detour from the Bond series, Broccoli and Saltzman featured the film on the billboard containing the trapdoor to the apartment of Bulgarian agent Krilencu (Fred Haggerty) in *From Russia with Love*. In the film, Krilencu crawls through Anita Ekberg's mouth and is promptly shot by his longtime nemesis Kerim Bey (Pedro Armendariz).

In Ian Fleming's original novel, the billboard was from the 20th Century Fox film *Niagara* (1953), starring Marilyn Monroe, whose mouth served as the trapdoor. Monroe died from an overdose of sleeping pills shortly before *From Russia with Love* went into production. It is doubtful that *Niagara* would have been used anyway, since the billboard sequence provided an excellent promotional opportunity for the producers' own more recent film and their star Anita Ekberg.

Cambridge University: Alma mater of James Bond (Sean Connery), who mentions in *You Only Live Twice* that he "took a first in oriental languages" there. In *The Spy Who Loved Me*, Sheik Hosein (Edward de Souza) also remembers Bond (Roger Moore) from their Cambridge days.

Cameron, Earl (August 8, 1917–July 3, 2020): Bermuda native who portrayed Pinder, an able British Secret Service operative who assists Bond (Sean Connery) in Nassau, Bahamas, in *Thunderball*. Cameron made his feature film debut in director Basil Dearden's *Pool of London* (1951), which also featured future Bond player Laurence Naismith (*Diamonds Are Forever*). His additional feature credits include *Tarzan the Magnificent* (1960); *Guns at Batasi* (1964); *Battle Beneath the Earth* (1967); *Cuba* (1979), reteaming with Sean Connery; *The Queen* (2006); and *Inception* (2010).

Campbell, Martin (October 24, 1943–   ): New Zealand–born film director, adept at slam-bang action, who helmed *GoldenEye*, which introduced Pierce Brosnan as Bond in 1995. He returned to the series a decade later to introduce Daniel Craig in *Casino Royale*, arguably the best Bond picture since *Goldfinger*. A native of Hastings, New Zealand, Campbell made his motion picture directing debut on *The Sex Thief* (1973), then followed that with a number of formative directing assignments on top British television series, particularly *The Professionals* (5 episodes, 1978–1980); *Reilly: Ace of Spies* (6 episodes, 1983); and *Edge of Darkness* (6 episodes 1985), with Bond player Joe Don Baker. Following the international success of *GoldenEye*, he began to get top feature directing assignments that took him all over the world, including *The Mask of Zorro* (1998); *Vertical Limit* (2000); *Beyond Borders* (2003); *The Legend of Zorro* (2005); *Edge of Darkness* (2010); *Green Lantern* (2011); and *The Foreigner* (2017), reteaming with Brosnan.

Director Martin Campbell brought his considerable action film skills to *GoldenEye*. *Courtesy of the David Reinhardt Collection*

Caplan, Paula: Assistant to James Bond (Sean Connery) in Nassau, portrayed by Martine Beswick in *Thunderball*. She is later captured in her hotel room by Fiona Volpe (Luciana Paluzzi) and her SPECTRE thugs, drugged, and brought to the Palmyra estate of Emilio Largo (Adolfo Celi). Tortured by Vargas (Philip Locke), Largo's main henchman, Paula takes a cyanide pill and kills herself to avoid revealing any information.

Capri: A popular tourist island off the coast of Southern Italy that is mentioned by Domino (Claudine Auger) in *Thunderball*. It's where she says she first met Emilio Largo (Adolfo Celi).

capungo: The Latino assassin portrayed by stuntman Alf Joint in the pre-credits teaser of *Goldfinger*. According to Ian Fleming's original novel, it's not a proper name but the Mexican term for a petty bandit. The *capungo* sneaks up behind Bond (Sean Connery) while he is embracing Bonita the flamenco dancer (Nadja Regin), but 007 sees his approach reflected in Bonita's pupils. As they struggle, the *capungo* gets thrown into the bathtub and reaches for

Bond's gun, which is hanging on a peg. Bond then tosses an electric heater into the tub, electrocuting the assassin. Shocking, positively shocking, indeed.

Caracas, Venezuela: In *Goldfinger*, one of four cities (along with Zurich, Amsterdam, and Hong Kong) in which Auric Goldfinger (Gert Fröbe) has stashed the 20 million in pounds sterling worth of gold he has been smuggling out of Great Britain, according to Colonel Smithers (Richard Vernon) of the Bank of England.

"Card Sense Jimmy Bond": The nickname of American agent James Bond (Barry Nelson) in the TV adaptation *Casino Royale* (1954). It's mentioned by British agent Clarence Leiter (Michael Pate), who knows Bond's reputation as an expert baccarat player. Bond's card shark persona is a cover for his espionage work with America's Combined Intelligence Agency.

Carlyle, Robert (April 14, 1961–   ): Scottish character actor who portrayed doomed villain Victor "Renard" Zokas in *The World Is Not Enough*. Carlyle achieved something quite rare in the Bond series—evoking sympathy for the villain. It's not easy to get on with your daily villainy with a bullet lodged in your brain, especially one that is robbing you of your senses. Sure, you're impervious to pain, but it plays hell in the boudoir. A native of Glasgow, Carlyle first came to the attention of American audiences when he portrayed Franco in the tense drama *Trainspotting* (1996). However, it was the hit dramedy *The Full Monty* (1997) that really put him on international radar. More recently, he played John Lennon, uncredited, in Danny Boyle's whimsical *Yesterday* (2019).

Carrera, Barbara (December 31, 1945–   ): Nicaraguan actress and former model who shone as SPECTRE executioner Fatima Blush in *Never Say Never Again*. Carrera took an exuberant approach to the part, and in her delightfully animated hands, Fatima is a colorful psychotic who revels in her killing—a pure comic book villainess. Cackling like a witch, dancing down staircases, and sashaying across hotel lobbies, employing every possible approach to assassinating Bond (all unsuccessful, of course), Carrera is such a lively element in *Never Say Never Again*

that the film's pacing never recovers from her character's death. Deprived of her presence in the film's final third, the movie stumbles along with very little drama. As in *Thunderball*, the movie's remaining villain Maximilian Largo (Klaus Maria Brandauer) does not make a very formidable opponent for Bond—nothing approaching the hysterically fiendish zeal for killing that is the essence of Fatima Blush.

Born in Bluefields, Nicaragua, Carrera moved to New York City when she was sixteen, where she pursued what would become a major career as a fashion model. Her sultry presence would eventually grace over three hundred magazine covers. She made her feature film debut portraying a model in director Jerry Schatzberg's drama *Puzzle of a Downfall Child* (1970). More important roles followed, and her film credits include *The Master Gunfighter* (1975); *The Island of Dr. Moreau* (1977); *I, the Jury* (1982); *Lone Wolf McQuade* (1983); and *Wild Geese II* (1985), with *Never Say Never Again*'s Edward Fox.

Carter, Reggie (1936–September 2, 1995): Jamaican actor who portrayed Mr. Jones, the mysterious chauffeur who poisons himself with cyanide rather than submit to interrogation by 007 (Sean Connery) in *Dr. No*. According to the *Jamaica Gleaner* newspaper, Carter was also a journalist, and in 1959 he was the first on-air announcer for the Jamaican Broadcasting Corporation. He later became a partner in the advertising firm PKC Advertising and a founding director of CGR Communications.* Though a leading man in the Jamaican theater, Carter made only three other on-screen appearances following his debut in *Dr. No*: the miniseries *Return to Treasure Island* (1986) and two features, *The Lunatic* (1991) and *Sankofa* (1993).

Cartlidge, William P. (June 16, 1942–   ): British producer and longtime associate of director Lewis Gilbert, who served as an associate producer on both *The Spy Who Loved Me* and *Moonraker*. Cartlidge began his career as a third assistant director on director Laslo Benedek's *Malaga* (1960), a crime drama that featured among others, *Thunderball*'s Paul Stassino. He was later a first assistant on *Born Free* in 1966,

---

* "Icon: Reggie Carter—the Famous Mr Blackburn," *Jamaica Gleaner*, April 15, 2008, http://old.jamaica-gleaner.com/gleaner/20080415/ent/ent3.html.

the same year he went to work for Gilbert on *Alfie*. Prior to *The Spy Who Loved Me*, Cartlidge served as an assistant director on two other Lewis Gilbert films, *The Adventurers* (1970) and *Friends* (1971), and he was an associate producer on Gilbert's *Paul and Michelle* (1974).

On *The Spy Who Loved Me*, he worked closely with Albert R. Broccoli and Michael Wilson on that film's complicated international shooting schedule. Remembered Cartlidge, "We had found that we couldn't get access to Sardinia until the tourist season ended in September [1976]. And we couldn't shoot in Egypt in the summer because of the incredible heat. So we ended up starting in the studio, on the smaller sets.

"The big 007 Stage was still under construction and wasn't going to be ready until Christmas. What we decided to do was build all the smallish sets, the ones that would require only a day's shooting or less; and when they were finished, we could strike them down and go off to locations. This procedure gave the studio back its valuable space for other productions, and it allowed us to get rid of a lot of actors who were only scheduled for a short period.

"You can't book supporting players for a shot in August and another shot in November. You have to take them when they're available. So we got rid of the little scenes that take place in, say, Gogol's office in Moscow; in the pyramid complex when M (Bernard Lee) and Gogol (Walter Gotell) supervise the search operations; the Q laboratories, and the ski chalet where you first see Bond (Roger Moore). When we came back from Egypt and Sardinia, the only things we had left to do were the Atlantis and supertanker sets, which were just about finished."*

Caruso, Miss: Curvy Italian Secret Service agent, portrayed by Madeline Smith in *Live and Let Die*. She's Roger Moore's first playmate in his series of 007 adventures.

Madeline Smith as Miss Caruso in *Live and Let Die*. *Steve Rubin Collection*

* William P. Cartlidge, interview by the author, London, June 2, 1977.

Carver, Elliot: Billionaire British media mogul portrayed by Jonathan Pryce in *Tomorrow Never Dies*. Combining the entrepreneurial qualities of early Rupert Murdoch and Ted Turner with the terror tactics of your average Nazi megalomaniac, the writers came up with this nefarious character, who probably skipped journalism school and an internship at the *London Times*. Intent on scooping the competition at all costs, Carver has just launched Carver Media Group Network (CMGN), an international cable network that trades on the worst kind of tabloid journalism. Now he plans to initiate World War III, pitting Britain against China, just so he can get the exclusive news footage for his network of television stations, newspapers, and magazines. Fortunately, James Bond (Pierce Brosnan) is around to stop the presses.

Carver, Paris: Sultry wife of billionaire media mogul Elliot Carver, portrayed by Teri Hatcher in *Tomorrow Never Dies*. Unbeknownst to her jealous husband, she's also an ex-flame of James Bond (Pierce Brosnan), a connection that unfortunately spells her doom. When she tries to help Bond thwart her out-of-control husband, she's bumped off by Carver's henchman Dr. Kaufman (Vincent Schiavelli). Paris, like Jill Masterson (Shirley Eaton) in *Goldfinger*, has only a few minutes on screen in the film.

Teri Hatcher portrayed Paris Carver, an ex-flame of James Bond (Pierce Brosnan) who is now married to a megalomaniac media mogul in *Tomorrow Never Dies*. *Courtesy of the David Reinhardt Collection*

Carver, Rosie: Inept CIA liaison to Bond (Roger Moore) in *Live and Let Die*, portrayed by former Playboy bunny Gloria Hendry. In actuality, Carver's CIA cover is a sham; she's really working for Kananga (Yaphet Kotto). Solitaire (Jane Seymour) gives Bond a tarot card clue—the queen of cups in the upside-down position—that Carver is not what she claims. Rosie is eventually killed when she blunders into one of Kananga's jungle booby traps.

Rosie Carver (Gloria Hendry) is exposed as a double agent by James Bond (Roger Moore) in *Live and Let Die. Courtesy of the Anders Frejdh Collection*

Case, Tiffany: Cocky redheaded diamond smuggler portrayed by Jill St. John in *Diamonds Are Forever*. When Bond (Sean Connery) questions the derivation of her name, she explains that she was born on the first floor of Tiffany's in New York while her mother was looking for a wedding ring.

Tiffany Case (a feisty Jill St. John) is about to show a little too much cheek as she attempts to switch programming cassetes aboard Blofeld's oil-platform base in *Diamonds Are Forever. Courtesy of the Anders Frejdh Collection*

Living in a third-floor apartment in Amsterdam, Case is a crafty courier for an international diamond smuggling syndicate that is being decimated by Ernst Stavro Blofeld (Charles Gray). Tiffany's mission is to supervise the smuggling of a huge diamond cache into the United States through Los Angeles. British smuggler Peter Franks (Joe Robinson) will be the courier, but 007 kills Franks and assumes his identity.

When Bond hides the real diamonds and substitutes fake ones, Case joins her smuggling cohorts in Las Vegas to track down the real stuff. Later, she reluctantly joins forces with Bond against Blofeld, who kidnaps her. She winds up on Blofeld's oil rig in Baja California, where Bond and the CIA disrupt SPECTRE's latest caper to blackmail the planet with a laser satellite—powered by diamonds.

Casey, Bernie (June 8, 1939–September 19, 2017): Tough-guy actor and former professional football player who portrayed CIA agent Felix Leiter in *Never Say Never Again*. Casey was the first African American actor to play James Bond's counterpart in the Central Intelligence Agency. His part was small and underwritten.

Joining Bond (Sean Connery) in the south of France, where the *Flying Saucer* yacht belonging to Maximilian Largo (Klaus Maria Brandauer) is under surveillance, Leiter helps Bond escape from local authorities after 007 eliminates Fatima Blush (Barbara Carrera) with his rocket pen. He later joins Bond in the climactic assault on Largo's archaeological dig in the Tears of Allah, where he keeps some SPECTRE operatives pinned down with submachine gun fire. Born in Wyco, West Virginia, Casey played wide receiver for the San Francisco 49ers (1961–1966) and Los Angeles Rams (1967–1968). He made his feature film debut as Cassie in *Guns of the Magnificient Seven* (1969), working with future Bond player Joe Don Baker. Moving between film and television roles, Casey played the main creature in the memorable CBS television film *Gargoyles* (1972). His additional feature film credits include *Boxcar Bertha* (1972), *Cleopatra Jones* (1973), *Cornbread, Earl and Me* (1975), *The Man Who Fell to Earth* (1976), *Sharky's Machine* (1981), *Revenge of the Nerds* (1984), *Spies Like Us* (1985) *Bill & Ted's Excellent Adventure* (1989), *Another 48 Hrs.* (1990), *Under Siege* (1992), and many others.

CASINO ROYALE

(CBS, 1954) ★★: TV adaptation of Ian Fleming's first James Bond novel, which aired at 8:30 PM EST on Thursday, October 21, 1954, as the third live one-hour episode of CBS's Climax Mystery Theater anthology series.

THE SETUP

Technically the first Bond movie, *Casino Royale* is a small-scale, studio-bound thriller that introduces James Bond (Barry Nelson) as an American agent up against a Russian master spy named Le Chiffre (Peter Lorre). The battlefield: a Monte Carlo baccarat table.

BEHIND THE SCENES

CBS purchased the television rights to Fleming's novel for $1,000, and the result was this terribly dated and low-key effort, directed by William H. Brown from a script by Antony Ellis and Charles Bennett. The story nonetheless conveys a sense of Fleming's style and that of the Bond films to come: the high-stakes gambling, the larger-than-life villain, the beautiful woman (Linda Christian as beautiful double agent Valerie Mathis, the film's take on the novel's Deuxième Bureau agent Rene Mathis), and the loyal friend—in this case, Michael Pate as British agent Clarence Leiter, the movie's version of CIA agent Felix Leiter. It's not clear whether it was the decision of screenwriters Ellis and Bennett or that of producer Bretaigne Windust to change the names and backgrounds of the characters for American television, or to give the main character the ridiculous nickname "Card Sense Jimmy Bond." When *Casino Royale* was broadcast live in 1954, the adventures of James Bond were still largely unknown in the United States, so no one paid much attention to the changes in the story. The film is also introduced in an unusual fashion by series host William Lundigan, who brings out a baccarat "shoe" at the beginning of the show and explains its significance to the story.

Lost for nearly thirty years, the TV *Casino Royale*

The US paperback cover of Ian Fleming's *Casino Royale.*

surfaced in 1981 when Jim Shoenberger, a Chicago airline executive and film collector, was rummaging through some old film cannisters that were marked *Casino Royale*. Thinking that the 16mm print was a battered copy of the 1967 *Casino Royale* spoof, he was about to cut up the film for leader when he noticed that it was in black and white. Remembering that the David Niven / Woody Allen spoof was in color, he was curious enough to run the film, and discovered that it was a perfectly preserved kinescope copy of the 1954 Climax Mystery Theater broadcast. The rediscovered film was first shown publicly in July 1981 at the James Bond Weekend in Los Angeles—a 007 luncheon and trivia marathon. Barry Nelson was a featured guest.

THE CAST

James Bond	Barry Nelson
Le Chiffre	Peter Lorre
Valerie Mathis	Linda Christian
Clarence Leiter	Michael Pate
Chef de Parte	Eugene Borden
Croupier	Jean Del Val
Le Chiffre's Henchmen	Gene Roth
	Kurt Katch
Himself–Host	William Lundigan

THE CREW

Director	William H. Brown
Written for television by	Antony Ellis
	Charles Bennett
Based on the novel by	Ian Fleming
Producer	Bretaigne Windust
Associate Producer	Elliott Lewis
Art Directors	Robert Tyler Lee
	James Dowell Vance
Camera Operator	Ben Wolf

 ## CASINO ROYALE

(Columbia Pictures, 1967) ★: James Bond spoof produced by Charles K. Feldman and Jerry Bresler. US release date: April 19, 1967. Budget: $9 million. Worldwide box office gross: $41.7 million (US gross: $22.7 million; international gross: $19.0 million).* Running time: 131 minutes.

---

* "Casino Royale (1967)," The Numbers, accessed April 27, 2020, https://www.the-numbers.com/movie/Casino-Royale.

THE SETUP

In this undisguised parody, which has little to do with any of Ian Fleming's original books, Sir James Bond (David Niven) emerges from retirement to confront twin evils: the nefarious activities of Soviet master spy and super gambler Le Chiffre (Orson Welles) and the more deadly international scheme of Bond's own nephew Jimmy Bond (Woody Allen). His plan: confuse his enemies by giving his name to dozens of other agents, male and female. All roads eventually lead to the baccarat table in Monte Carlo, where agent James Bond / Evelyn Tremble (Peter Sellers) takes on Le Chiffre in a high-stakes card game.

BEHIND THE SCENES

With five directors, eight writers (only three credited), two second unit directors, and plot holes you could drive Aston Martins through, *Casino Royale* is one of the worst film spoofs ever made. Producer Charles Feldman controlled the rights to Ian Fleming's first novel but was unable to make a deal with Albert R. Broccoli and Harry Saltzman to produce a serious James Bond adaptation (Feldman turned down $500,000 for the rights). So he decided to produce a big, lumbering satire on the world of Bond that comes across like a misfired television variety special. However, because he was one of the most successful talent agents of all time and knew virtually everyone on Hollywood's A-list, Feldman was able to assemble an incredible cast. The few high points include the Herb Alpert title track, the Dusty Springfield song "The Look of Love," Barbara Bouchet as Moneypenny's luscious daughter, and the performances by Peter Sellers and Woody Allen. Otherwise, it's just a series of long set pieces that are not in the least bit funny.

THE CAST

Evelyn Tremble / James Bond	Peter Sellers
Vesper Lynd	Ursula Andress
Sir James Bond	David Niven
Le Chiffre	Orson Welles
Mata Bond	Joanna Pettet
The Detainer / Lady James Bond	Daliah Lavi
Jimmy Bond / Dr. Noah	Woody Allen
Agent Mimi / Lady Fiona	Deborah Kerr
Ransome	William Holden
Le Grande	Charles Boyer
McTarry/M	John Huston
Smernov	Kurt Kasznar
Himself	George Raft
French Legionnaire	Jean-Paul Belmondo
Cooper/James Bond	Terence Cooper
Miss Moneypenny	Barbara Bouchet
Agent Buttercup	Angela Scoular
Eliza	Gabriella Licudi
Heather	Tracey Crisp
Peg	Elaine Taylor
Miss Goodthighs	Jacqueline Bisset
Meg	Alexandra Bastedo
Frau Hoffner	Anna Quayle
Hadley	Derek Nimmo
Polo	Ronnie Corbett

THE CREW

Presented by	Charles K. Feldman
Directors	John Huston
	Ken Hughes
	Val Guest
	Robert Parrish
	Joseph McGrath
Screenplay by	Wolf Mankowitz
	John Law
	Michael Sayers
Suggested by the novel *Casino Royale* by	Ian Fleming
Producers	Charles K. Feldman
	Jerry Bresler
Director of Photography	Jack Hildyard
Additional photography	John Wilcox
	Nicolas Roeg
Music composed and conducted by	Burt Bacharach
Title song performed by	Herb Alpert and the Tijuana Brass
"The Look of Love" performed by	Dusty Springfield
Lyrics by	Hal David
Production Designer	Michael Stringer
Costume Designer	Julie Harris

 CASINO ROYALE

(Sony/MGM, 2006) ★★★★: The twenty-first film in the Eon Productions James Bond series. US release date: November 17, 2006. Budget: $150 million. Worldwide box office gross: $594.4 million (US gross: $167.4 million; international gross: $427.1 million).* Running time: 144 minutes.

---

* "Casino Royale (2006)," The Numbers, accessed April 28, 2020, https://www.the-numbers.com /movie/Casino-Royale-(2006).

James Bond (Daniel Craig) confronts a terrorist bomber in the courtyard of a foreign embassy in *Casino Royale*. Remember the days when Roger Moore rarely got his hair mussed as James Bond? This is not that kind of 007. *Courtesy of the Anders Frejdh Collection*

THE SETUP

A mysterious financial expert named Le Chiffre (Mads Mikkelsen) is introduced to an African rebel leader (Isaach De Bankolé) who decides to funnel him a huge trove of cash for investment purposes. Although he informs his new client that there will be no risk, Le Chiffre immediately uses most of the money to short stock in an aeronautics company—knowing that the terrorist organization he belongs to (what we later learn is a reincarnation of SPECTRE) will blow up their touted airliner prototype. When James Bond (Daniel Craig) foils that plot, Le Chiffre is forced to enter a no-limits, winner-take-all poker tournament in Montenegro to win back the money he lost. To prevent this, Bond joins the tournament, using funds supplied by the government and supervised by Vesper Lynd (Eva Green), a woman who initially despises 007's arrogance.

BEHIND THE SCENES

One of the great challenges facing the Bond series as it entered the twenty-first century was competition. As Hollywood studios began focusing on big tentpole franchises, the action genre started to grow crowded. Bond suddenly was competing for box office dollars with the likes of Jason Bourne, the *Mission: Impossible* films, and the *Fast and the Furious* series. This new breed of action film featured a high level of gritty violence and sophisticated action set pieces and stunt work. Although the Pierce Brosnan era had done well financially, producers knew that Bond stories would have to change with the times. That change came with the introduction of a new James Bond: Daniel Craig.

Many Bond fans were not initially thrilled with the casting of Craig. Some even referred to him disparagingly as "that blond Bond." But once *Casino Royale* opened, most critics found their initial skepticism giving way to jaw-dropping awe. The film essentially rebooted the series, remaking Ian Fleming's first James Bond novel and reimagining 007 as a gritty, extremely physical, and vulnerable secret agent. Gone were many staples of the previous films—the comedy one-liners, the bed-hopping, the larger-than-life supervillains—in favor of more grounded plots, mainly terrorism. The new focus played to Craig's strengths. He possesses a thuggish quality—he is no longer the

Casino Royale art by Jeff Marshall.
Courtesy of Jeff Marshall

Daniel Craig makes the cover of *Premiere* magazine prior to the 2006 premiere. *Steve Rubin Collection*

suave, polished agent who knew the right wines—but that thuggishness gives him believability as a twenty-first-century double-0: essentially a hired government killer.

Eva Green and Mads Mikkelsen are also terrific as Vesper Lynd and Le Chiffre. Martin Campbell's direction is truly thrilling—he does action like few other directors—and David Arnold's score is wonderful. The decision to change the penultimate card game from baccarat to no-limit poker was also brilliant. The film garnered the most nominations ever from the British Academy of Film and Television Arts: nine BAFTAs, including Best British Film, Adapted Screenplay, Actor in a Leading Role (Craig, the first Bond to be nominated),

Film Music, Cinematography, Editing, Production Design, Sound, and Special Visual Effects. Its only win: Sound. *Casino Royale* also featured a number of firsts for an Eon Productions Bond film, including: first to have a major black and white sequence; first not to feature Miss Moneypenny; first to place the gun-barrel sequence after the pre-credits teaser, without Bond's signature walk; first to have a blond James Bond; first since *Dr. No* to have an animated opening sequence; and first since *Live and Let Die* not to feature the character of Q.

THE CAST

James Bond	Daniel Craig
Vesper Lynd	Eva Green
Le Chiffre	Mads Mikkelsen
M	Dame Judi Dench
Felix Leiter	Jeffrey Wright
Rene Mathis	Giancarlo Giannini
Solange	Caterina Murino
Alex Dimitrios	Simon Abkarian
Steven Obanno	Isaach De Bankolé
Mr. White	Jesper Christensen

Valenka	Ivana Milicevic
Villiers	Tobias Menzies
Carlos	Claudio Santamaria
Mollaka	Sébastien Foucan
Dryden	Malcolm Sinclair
Mendel	Ludger Pistor

THE CREW

Director	Martin Campbell
Writers	Neal Purvis & Robert Wade
	Paul Haggis
Producers	Barbara Broccoli
	Michael G. Wilson
Director of Photography	Phil Meheux
Music by	David Arnold
Production Designer	Peter Lamont
Costume Designer	Lindy Hemming
Casting by	Debbie McWilliams
Stunt Coordinators	Gary Powell
	Pavel Cajzl
Title Designer	Daniel Kleinman
Editor	Stuart Baird

Celi, Adolfo (July 27, 1922–February 19, 1986): Heavyset Italian character actor (his last name is pronounced CHELL-ee) who played Emilio Largo, the ruthless, one-eyed SPECTRE spymaster in *Thunderball*. Commanding in bearing and mannerisms, Celi was well cast as Largo, a big operator who can easily turn from charmer to killer when SPECTRE business is at stake. His voice, however, was redubbed by London-born actor Robert Rietty.

Fine Italian character actor Adolfo Celi appeared to be having fun with his seething, one-eyed portrayal of SPECTRE chief Emilio Largo in *Thunderball*. *Courtesy of the David Reinhardt Collection*

A native of Messina, Sicily, Celi made his feature film debut in director Luigi Zampa's *Un americano in vacanza* (1946). After many Italian films, Celi was featured in *That Man from Rio* (1964), director Philippe de Broca's terrific spoof of the James Bond movies that starred Jean-Paul Belmondo. The following year, Celi portrayed Battaglia, the corrupt prison camp warden in the Frank Sinatra World War II classic *Von Ryan's Express*, and Cardinal Giovanni de'Medici in *The Agony and the Ecstacy*. In 1967, Celi joined fellow Bond veterans Daniela Bianchi, Bernard Lee, Anthony Dawson, and Lois Maxwell in another 007 spoof, *Operation Kid Brother*, starring Sean Connery's brother Neil.

centrifuge trainer: A simulator of gravitational force found at the industrial space complex run by Hugo Drax (Michael Lonsdale) outside Los Angeles in *Moonraker*. Touring the facilities with Dr. Holly Goodhead (Lois Chiles), Bond (Roger Moore) accepts her offer to test his skills on the simulator. According to Goodhead, the maximum speed of the trainer is 20 Gs, a fatal force, while 3 Gs is equivalent to takeoff pressure and 7 Gs is the point at which most people pass out.

Unbeknownst to Holly, when she's called away from the training area to receive a bogus phone call, Chang (Toshiro Suga) sabotages the trainer, intending to kill Bond with a lethal force. As the trainer builds speed like an amusement park attraction, Bond begins to push a "chicken switch" that is supposed to automatically shut down the system. It doesn't work.

As the force continues to build, rippling the skin on 007's face, Bond tries to use his wrist-activated dart gun. He finally shoots out the controls of the trainer after enduring a force of 13 Gs. A returning Holly rushes to his side, but Bond wants none of her comforting. He staggers away—totally disoriented but alive.

The sequence, which owes a great deal to the motorized traction table incident in *Thunderball*, is one of the few times that the film takes on a chilling realism. (Another is Corinne Dufour's death in the forest.) Otherwise, most of the action sequences in *Moonraker* are either unbelievable (the gondola chase, the space station assault), overstaged (the glass museum fight with Chang), or just plain dull (the motorboat chase in South America).

Ceylan, Hasan (February 24, 1922–December 1980): Beefy Turkish character actor who played the persistent, mustachioed Bulgarian agent with the beret in *From Russia with Love*. Ceylan's character is the one who tails 007 (Sean Connery) from the Istanbul airport to the office of Kerim Bey (Pedro Armendariz). And he then tails defecting Russian cipher clerk Tatiana Romanova (Daniela Bianchi) to the St. Sophia Mosque, where he is struck and killed by Grant (Robert Shaw) before he can intercept the map of the Russian consulate that Tatiana is leaving for Bond. Another sequence, in which Ceylan tails Bond to the Bosphorus ferryboat but gets into an automobile accident planned by Bond and Kerim Bey, was cut from the film when the son of director Terence Young pointed out that Ceylan's character had already been killed in the mosque. The story sounds improbable, but in the heat of postproduction, scenes may be moved around in the edit; it's likely that the ferryboat sequence was originally scripted to precede the Bulgarian agent's death.

A native of Istanbul, the prolific Ceylan made his feature film debut in director Münir Hayri Egeli's historical romance *Sultan Selim and Hasan the Janissary* (1951). He spent his entire career as a major player in the Turkish film industry. *From Russia with Love* was his sole foray into English-language filmmaking.

Chamonix, France: Resort community in southeastern France where the ski sequences were shot in *The World Is Not Enough*. They were doubling Azerbaijan in the former USSR.

Champagne, Barry (June 18, 1952–February 8, 2009): Assistant aerial stunt coordinator and engineer who worked closely with aerial stunt supervisor Corkey Fornof on *Licence to Kill*. One of Champagne's key sequences was the stunt where CIA pilot Pam Bouvier (Carey Lowell) maneuvers her Piper Cub crop-dusting plane so that James Bond (Timothy Dalton) can jump onto a moving tanker-trailer truck.

For that sequence, shot in the mountains outside Mexicali, Mexico (near the border with the US), English stuntman Simon Crane doubled Dalton, and aerial stunt coordinator Fornof flew the Piper. A padded "bed" was placed atop the tanker truck, and Fornof slowed the aircraft down to about 70 mph so that Crane could jump onto the truck.

For the pre-credits teaser sequence in which Bond captures Sanchez's Cessna 172 private plane, Champagne explained that three aircraft were actually used. Fornof flew the in-flight Cessna, a second plane was hung upside down in the Coast Guard helicopter snare, and a third was mounted on the ground rig (where close-ups of Dalton were shot). All three aircraft were purchased from a Florida aircraft junkyard. The plane that the Coast Guard helicopter snares was equipped with an engine built by John Richardson's special effects department. Its tail section was also reinforced to accommodate the helicopter's winch cable.

Champagne Section: Flight ID for the five Piper Cherokee monoplanes that participate in Operation Rockabye Baby in *Goldfinger*. Trained in stunt flying by Pussy Galore (Honor Blackman), the five voluptuous women flyers, dressed in black jumpsuits, are led by the Champagne Leader (Aleta Morrison).

Pussy Galore (Honor Blackman, center/front) and her Flying Circus, designated as Champagne Section in Goldfinger's plot to detonate an atomic device inside Fort Knox in *Goldfinger*. Aleta Morrison (second from right) is the Champagne Leader. *Steve Rubin Collection*

Château d'Anet, France: Glitzy location, the residence of sixteenth-century French noblewoman Diane de Poitiers, that's used in the *Thunderball* pre-credits teaser to portray the estate of SPECTRE agent Jacques Bouvar (Bob Simmons) when he returns home disguised as his own supposed widow. Located near Paris, the elegant surroundings were the jumping-off point for James Bond (Sean Connery) to take flight in the Bell jet pack.

Château de Chantilly, France: Ornate French estate that doubled as the home and stables of Max Zorin (Christopher Walken) in *A View to a Kill*. The buildings were completed in the eighteenth century by an aristocrat who was convinced he would be reincarnated as a horse. Zorin relates that story in the film to Bond (Roger Moore), but he incorrectly dates his home as being from the sixteenth century.

Chiffre, Le: Soviet master spy and obsessed gambler, created by Ian Fleming as the first Bond villain in his novel *Casino Royale*. He's been portrayed in various permutations in three James Bond films. Le Chiffre's name comes from the French word meaning "cipher" or "number." According to Fleming's original novel, British Secret Service records identify Le Chiffre as a displaced concentration camp survivor after World War II who could not remember his name. Since he became a simple number on a list of displaced persons, he took the name Le Chiffre. He eventually becomes a top agent for the Soviet Union, working in the area of southern France and Monte Carlo. His penchant for high-stakes gambling and high-stakes losing (using Soviet funds) comes to the attention of both the Soviets and Western intelligence. The latter enlists James Bond to bankrupt Le Chiffre in one last grand game of chance, believing that this will convince the Soviets to take matters into their own hands and liquidate Le Chiffre before he becomes a source of embarrassment.

In CBS's 1954 live adaptation of the novel, Le Chiffre is portrayed by Peter Lorre. An American agent nicknamed "Card Sense Jimmy Bond" (Barry Nelson) is sent to Monte Carlo to outplay Le Chiffre at baccarat. With the help of the Deuxième Bureau's double agent Valerie Mathis (Linda Christian), he succeeds. However, while searching for Mathis, Bond is captured and tortured by the Russian master spy, who is determined to take back a check worth 87 million francs that Bond won at the tables. While Le Chiffre briefly leaves Bond alone while he goes off to search for the missing check, 007 manages to free himself, and he eventually shoots and kills Le Chiffre and one of his thugs.

The same character, albeit in a comic vein, was portrayed by actor Orson Welles in producer Charles K. Feldman's *Casino Royale* spoof in 1967. In that goofy film, the Soviet master spy still plays

Mads Mikkelsen portrays the mysterious Le Chiffre in *Casino Royale*, a man with a desperate reason to win a huge poker tournament. *Courtesy of the Anders Frejdh Collection*

baccarat in Monte Carlo with stolen Soviet funds, but he's also a magician who practices his tricks right at the table. Le Chiffre is eventually defeated at the baccarat table by Evelyn Tremble / James Bond (Peter Sellers) and later killed by the KGB.

The most realistic portrayal of Le Chiffre was that of distinguished Danish actor Mads Mikkelsen in the 2006 blockbuster reboot of *Casino Royale*, which introduced Daniel Craig as the newest James Bond. Mikkelsen's Le Chiffre is a ruthless sponsor of international terrorism, no longer working for the Soviets but affiliated with an international crime organization that is later revealed to be SPECTRE. The film adds a nice touch to the villain: he weeps blood from one of his eyes, a malady caused by a derangement of one of his tear ducts. He also suffers from asthma and uses an inhaler.

This version of Le Chiffre acts as an international investment strategist, and he has secured funds from Steven Obanno (Isaach De Bankolé), an African rebel leader who has been recommended to Le Chiffre by SPECTRE operative Mr. White (Jesper Christensen). Obanno trusts that Le Chiffre will invest his money wisely, with no risk. No sooner is the money secured than Le Chiffre shorts a million shares of the aeronautics company Skyfleet—betting the company's stock will go down because Le Chiffre's organization plans to blow up their sophisticated airliner prototype. However, when Bond thwarts that sabotage operation, Le Chiffre is forced to use the remaining hunk of Obanno's investment to enter a no-limit, winner-take-all game of Texas hold'em poker. Bond tracks him to Montenegro and enters the marathon game, which Le Chiffre must win at all costs. At one point, Le Chiffre has Bond poisoned—sending 007 into cardiac arrest—but he's saved by Her Majesty's treasury liaison Vesper Lynd (Eva Green), who reattaches the line to the heart defibrillator that jolts Bond back to life.

In a nail-biting gambling confrontation, Bond eventually beats Le Chiffre, leaving him penniless. But the villain captures Bond and submits him to one of the most gruesome torture scenes ever conceived for mainstream PG-13 audiences—one taken directly from Ian Fleming's own description in the book. Bond is stripped and tied to a rattan chair, the seat of which has been removed. Le Chiffre then wields a carpet beater, which he continuously twirls and slams into James Bond's exposed privates. It's one of those scenes that's hard to watch, but Craig is brilliant as he fails to give in to Le Chiffre—even managing to laugh as he's also screaming in pain. Fortunately, Le Chiffre's failure to pay back the funds he acquired from Obanno comes back to bite him: he's assassinated before he can kill Bond.

Chiles, Lois (April 15, 1947–   ): American leading lady and former fashion model who portrayed brainy and slinky CIA agent Holly Goodhead in *Moonraker*. Born in Houston, Chiles made her film debut as the female lead in director Michael Schultz's drama *Together for Days* (1973), which also marked the film debut of actor Samuel L. Jackson. Although that film was not a hit at the box office, her next movie—the Barbra Streisand / Robert Redford starrer *The Way We Were* (1973)—was a smash, with Chiles

Lois Chiles was well-cast as icy astrophysicist Holly Goodhead in *Moonraker. Courtesy of the David Reinhardt Collection*

playing Redford's rich girlfriend Carol Ann. Some of Chiles's other feature film credits include *The Great Gatsby* (1974), reteaming with Robert Redford); *Coma* (1978); *Death on the Nile* (1978); *Sweet Liberty* (1986); *Creepshow 2* (1987); *Broadcast News* (1987); *Twister* (1989); and *Speed 2: Cruise Control* (1997). In 2005, Chiles married New York investor and philanthropist Richard Gilder, and she retired from acting.

Chin, Tsai (November 30, 1933–   ): Chinese actress, director, teacher, and author who portrayed Ling, Hong Kong girlfriend to Bond (Sean Connery) in *You Only Live Twice*. (Ling's signature line: "Darling, I give you very best duck.") She returned to the Bond series in 2006 to cameo as Madame Wu, one of the poker tournament players in *Casino Royale*. Chin told interviewer Mark Cerulli of her original Bond appearance, "[Director] Lewis Gilbert and his wife, Hilda, were good friends of mine . . . It's always lucky to be in a Bond film, so I did it. My costar from [the play] *The World of Suzie Wong*, Gary Raymond, was great friends with Sean, so we all mixed together. Sean wasn't a star then. . . . I think I saved the producers money, because in those days you had to do everything twice—one for the American audience, who were prudish, and once for the continental European audience. So I had 'taped' myself—and I'm very good at it—so you couldn't see anything you shouldn't see so they only had to shoot it once. . . . Sean was always teasing me, saying, 'Oh, I can see you now.'"*

Chin was born in Shanghai, the third daughter of Zhou Xinfang, one of the most celebrated Chinese actors of the twentieth century. Trained at the Royal Academy of Dramatic Art in London, she made her feature film debut in director Michael Anderson's war drama *Battle Hell* (1957). That same year, director David Lean cast her as the voice of Tokyo Rose in *The Bridge on the River Kwai*. Chin's additional feature film credits include *The Inn of the Sixth Happiness* (1958); *The Face of Fu Manchu* (1965), with fellow Bond players Christopher Lee, Karin Dor (*You Only Live Twice*), and George Leech (*Thunderball*); *Blow-Up* (1966); *The Joy Luck Club* (1993); *Memoirs of a Geisha* (2005); and *Now You See Me 2* (2016).

Chinese junk: Ship belonging to Scaramanga (Christopher Lee) in *The Man with the Golden Gun*. It transports him to and from his island home off the coast of mainland China. Bond (Roger Moore) and Mary Goodnight (Britt Ekland) use it to escape from the island when Scaramanga's solar energy station is obliterated. After his attempt to kill Bond is foiled, Nick Nack (Hervé Villechaize) is netted and hoisted into the rigging of the junk for safekeeping.

Chinnor Cement Works: A large, abandoned quarry in Chinnor, England, where the pre-credits hovercraft chase sequence for *Die Another Day* was shot. The quarry, which is located on Station Road next to an old railway line, contains hilly and rough terrain together with large waterways. Location work was begun on April 2, 2002, and filming was completed by June 20. Large, ornate temple gates were constructed next to one of the waterways, giving the location an ambiance befitting the sequence's Korean setting.

Chitwood, Joie (April 14, 1912–January 3, 1988): American stunt daredevil whose Greatest Show on Wheels troupe was featured prominently in

Live and Let Die. Chitwood, among other things, portrayed Charlie, the doomed CIA chauffeur who is killed by Whisper (Earl Jolly Brown) while driving Bond (Roger Moore) in New York City. A native of Denison, Texas, Chitwood made his uncredited feature film debut in the crime drama *Fireball Jungle* (1968). In addition to his work on *Live and Let Die*, Chitwood handled stunt driving work on, among others, *A Small Town in Texas* (1976), *Stunts* (1977), and *Smokey and the Bandit Part 3* (1983).

chloral hydrate: A sleeping powder that Grant (Robert Shaw) slips into the champagne glass of Tatiana Romanova (Daniela Bianchi) on the Orient Express in *From Russia with Love*. According to Grant, posing as British agent Captain Nash, the drug is "quick but mild." As to why he drugged the defecting Russian cipher clerk, Grant explains to Bond (Sean Connery) that his escape route is only for one. This tidy bit of information appears to satisfy Bond, who then lowers his gun—one of 007's biggest mistakes in the series.

Chloral hydrate is also used by Kara Milovy (Maryam d'Abo) to drug James Bond (Timothy Dalton) in *The Living Daylights*. She's been told, mistakenly, by renegade general Georgi Koskov (Jeroen Krabbé), that Bond is a KGB agent.

Christensen, Jesper (May 16, 1948–   ): Danish film, television, and stage actor who portrayed the mysterious Mr. White in *Casino Royale*, *Quantum of Solace*, and *Spectre*. A native of Copenhagen, Christensen made his motion picture debut in director Anders Refn's Danish crime drama *Cop* (1976). Working in primarily Scandinavian films and television shows, Christensen made his English-language debut in Sydney Pollack's *The Interpreter* (2005), a film that also featured Bond players Earl Cameron and Tsai Chin, and that undoubtedly brought him to the attention of the Bond producers.

Christian, Linda (November 13, 1923–July 22, 2011; birth name: Blanca Rosa Welter): Mexican-born leading lady who portrayed Valerie Mathis, a French double agent who became the first Bond girl, opposite Barry Nelson's American 007, in the live television version of *Casino Royale* in 1954. Although she appears to be working for Soviet master spy Le Chiffre (Peter Lorre), Mathis is actually an agent with the French Deuxième Bureau who supplies Bond with 35 million crucial francs during the climactic baccarat game with Le Chiffre. A native of Tampico who traveled around the world with her oil executive father, Christian made her feature film debut—under the name Linda Welter—in *The Rock of Souls* (1943), a Spanish-language romantic drama directed by Miguel Zacarías. After some uncredited performances in American films, she portrayed Hine-Moa in the adventure romance *Green Dolphin Street* (1947). Two years later, she married actor Tyrone Power, a union that produced two children, Taryn and Romina.

Chu Mi: Poolside bathing beauty portrayed by Francoise Therry, who is one of the women in the harem of Hai Fat (Richard Loo) in *The Man with the Golden Gun*. Bond (Roger Moore) meets her when he impersonates Scaramanga to infiltrate the grounds of Hai Fat's estate in Bangkok. NOTE: Some sources spell her name Chew Mee.

Churchill, Della: The doomed bride of longtime 007 friend and compatriot Felix Leiter (David Hedison), portrayed by *Three's Company* veteran Priscilla Barnes in *Licence to Kill*. Married to Leiter in Key West, Florida, Della is later murdered when the henchmen of escaped drug lord Franz Sanchez (Robert Davi) break into her house. Leiter himself is thrown to the sharks in the marine warehouse of Sanchez ally Milton Krest (Anthony Zerbe); he loses his left leg. Della's

The day starts out festive for bride Della Churchill (Priscilla Barnes) and groom Felix Leiter (David Hedison) in *Licence to Kill*. It doesn't end well. *Courtesy of the David Reinhardt Collection*

murder and Felix's mutilation send a revenge-crazed Bond (Timothy Dalton) after Sanchez.

Churubusco Studios: Studio complex in Mexico City that was the base of operations for the filming of *Licence to Kill*. Financial considerations forced Cubby Broccoli's team to investigate alternatives to their usual base, England's Pinewood Studios.

Circus Circus: Colorful, raucous Las Vegas hotel and casino chosen by Bond (Sean Connery) for his rendezvous with Tiffany Case (Jill St. John) in *Diamonds Are Forever*. Tipped off by Bond, Felix Leiter (Norman Burton) fills the place with radio-equipped CIA agents who monitor Tiffany's every move.

Circus Circus is known for it high-wire acts and many carnival games designed for young tourists left to wait while their parents gamble. The film features a virtual guided tour of the casino circa the early 1970s, including stops at the blackjack table, where Tiffany receives a card that reads "Why don't you play the water bal-

The Circus Circus Hotel and Casino in Las Vegas became a critical meeting point for Tiffany Case and James Bond in *Diamonds Are Forever*. *Steve Rubin Collection*

loons?"; the water balloon game, where she wins a stuffed animal filled with diamonds; and the sideshow attraction featuring Zambora, a woman who transforms into a huge rampaging gorilla—after which Tiffany escapes from Bond and his CIA associates.

Citroën 2CV (a.k.a. Deux Cheveaux): Compact getaway car driven by Melina Havelock (Carole Bouquet) in *For Your Eyes Only*. When Bond (Roger Moore) loses his deluxe Lotus Esprit to a self-destruct explosion, he's forced to take the wheel of Melina's vehicle in a wild chase through the backcountry outside Madrid. Pursued by heavily armed agents of hit man Hector Gonzales (Stefan Kalipha), Bond and Melina somehow survive, putting the frail compact through some very unlikely maneuvers, including a calculated roll.

Clavell, Michaela: British actress, the daughter of bestselling author and screenwriter James Clavell, who was introduced as Penelope Smallbone, new assistant to Miss Moneypenny (Lois Maxwell) in *Octopussy*. Initially, it was thought that Clavell would replace Maxwell as M's secretary, but she did not return in *A View to a Kill*. When Timothy Dalton took over the role of Bond in *The Living Daylights*, he was greeted by an entirely new Moneypenny, portrayed by Caroline Bliss. *Octopussy* is Clavell's only feature credit.

Cleese, John (October 27, 1939–): Tall British character actor and former member of the fabled Monty Python comedy troupe who assisted Desmond Llewelyn as "R" in *The World Is Not Enough* and took over for him as as Q in *Die Another Day*. Though Cleese's appearance in *The World Is Not Enough* seemed like an attempt to pass the torch to him from Llewelyn, who died in a car crash just a month after the movie's release, in 2002 Cleese denied that he and his late costar had any such understanding. "He was such fabulous company, that Desmond, and [we] had struck a deal. I was 60 when I started and Desmond was 80. So we agreed to go on together until he was 100, at which point I would have had enough experience to take over."* A native of Weston-Super-Mare,

* William Keck, "John Cleese Steps in as Bond's Beloved Q," *Entertainment Weekly*, June 7, 2002, https://ew.com /article/2002/06/07/john-cleese-steps-bonds-beloved-q/.

Somerset, England, Cleese made his motion picture debut in director Kevin Billington's romantic drama *Interlude* (1968). Having honed his comedy skills on BBC Radio (*I'm Sorry, I'll Read That Again*) and such television programs as *The Frost Report* (1966–1967) and *Marty* (1968–1969), starring Marty Feldman, Cleese cocreated *Monty Python's Flying Circus* (1969–1973), which debuted on British television and led to his involvement in a series of internationally successful Monty Python films, including *Monty Python and the Holy Grail* (1975) and *Life of Brian* (1979). Cleese also performed in such films as *Time Bandits* (1981), with Sean Connery; the comedy classic *A Fish Called Wanda* (1988); *Rat Race* (2001); and the first two *Harry Potter* movies, as Nearly Headless Nick.

Cléry, Corinne (March 23, 1950– ; birth name: Corinne Picolo): Beautiful French actress who portrayed Corinne Dufour, Hugo Drax's doomed helicopter pilot and executive assistant in *Moonraker*. Cléry is actually one of the highlights

Although her role was short lived, French actress Corinne Cléry's portrait of helicopter pilot Corinne Dufour was a highlight of *Moonraker*. *Courtesy of the David Reinhardt Collection*

of the film. Cool and resourceful, she has all the classic attributes of a Bond girl. Unfortunately, she also has an extremely short life span. Her death scene in the forest, where she's attacked and killed by Drax's Dobermans, became the basis for *Moonraker*'s unusual teaser trailer. It's one of the best-directed scenes in the film—and totally out of synch with the movie's tongue-in-cheek approach. Cléry, a Parisian native, made her feature debut in director Joël Le Moigné's drama *Les poneyttes* (1968). The same year she did *Moonraker*, Cléry costarred with fellow Bond players Richard Kiel and Barbara Bach in *The Humanoid* (1979).

Clifton Pier: Harbor installation in Nassau, Bahamas, off which the final underwater battle takes place in *Thunderball*. This sequence, the most ambitious of all the film's underwater sequences, was handled by the full underwater film crew from Ivan Tors Studios—sixty divers strong. It was filmed by Lamar Boren, who single-handedly paddled through the underwater war zone.

cloaking device: The Q Branch gadget supplied to Bond (Pierce Brosnan) with his new Aston Martin V12 Vanquish in *Die Another Day*: "adaptive camouflage" that renders the vehicle invisible. Perhaps Q's archaeological team stumbled upon a downed Klingon Bird of Prey. You never know with these guys.

cobalt and iodine: The special ingredients in the "atomic device" given to Auric Goldfinger (Gert Fröbe) by the Red Chinese government in *Goldfinger*. Activated by Mr. Ling (Burt Kwouk), a specialist in nuclear fission, the bomb is set to detonate inside the American gold repository at Fort Knox, Kentucky. The cobalt and iodine will render the fallout "particularly dirty," with the goal of irradiating America's entire gold supply for fifty-eight years.

cocoon: The stern section of the *Disco Volante* yacht in *Thunderball*, which becomes a heavily-armed decoy when its aft section is transformed into a swift hydrofoil craft. Dead in the water with a US Coast Guard flotilla closing in, the doomed cocoon fights a delaying action, until one well-placed shell from an American warship obliterates the decoy and its crew.

Coffey, Al: World-class springboard diver whose ability is on brief display at the Fontainebleau Hotel pool in *Goldfinger*.

Coltrane, Robbie (March 30, 1950–   ; birth name: Anthony Robert McMillan): Rotund Scottish character actor who portrayed colorful Russian mafioso Valentin Dmitrovich Zukovsky in *GoldenEye* and *The World Is Not Enough*. He's best known today as giant gamekeeper Rubeus Hagrid in eight *Harry Potter* movies. Born in Rutherglen, Scotland, Coltrane made his motion picture debut in director Bertrand Tavernier's science fiction drama *Death Watch* (1980), which also featured Bond player Max von Sydow (*Never Say Never Again*). Coltrane's additional feature credits include *Krull* (1983), as Rhun; *Defense of the Realm* (1985); *Absolute Beginners* (1986); *Henry V* (1989), as Sir John Falstaff; *Van Helsing* (2004); and *Ocean's Twelve* (2004).

Columbo, Milos: Pistachio-chewing Greek smuggler, ex-resistance fighter, and casino owner on Corfu, perfectly portrayed by Israeli actor Topol in *For Your Eyes Only*. The first impression James Bond (Roger Moore) gets of Columbo is based on the lies of Soviet agent Aris Kristatos (Julian Glover), who claims Columbo is a drug smuggler, sex trafficker, and contract murderer. In reality, Columbo is a smuggler known as "the Dove," but his activities are limited to gold, diamonds, cigarettes, and pistachio nuts—not heroin, which is Kristatos's domain. Columbo also runs a fleet of intercoastal freighters in the Aegean Sea.

Israeli actor Topol was well cast as pistachio-chewing smuggler Milos Columbo, a former World War II partisan, in *For Your Eyes Only*. *Courtesy of the David Reinhardt Collection*

There is a blood feud between Columbo and Kristatos, dating back to World War II, when both fought the Nazis as resistance fighters on Crete. Unfortunately, Kristatos was a double agent who betrayed his countrymen to the Germans—an act that Columbo will never forget.

Columbo eventually captures Bond on a beach in Corfu—after Kristatos's henchman Locque (Michael Gothard) runs down Columbo's mistress, Lisl (Cassandra Harris). The smuggler sets the record straight about Kristatos's true identity and joins forces with 007, helping Bond track his foe to the monastery/fortress of St. Cyril's in the Meteora cliffs, where a wounded Columbo finally takes care of Kristatos with a knife.

Combined Intelligence Agency: A fictional CIA-type organization that employs James Bond (Barry Nelson) in the CBS live TV adaptation of *Casino Royale*. Bond's card-playing skills, which have won him the sobriquet "Card Sense Jimmy Bond," are a front for his intelligence activities.

Commander Jamaica: Title proposed by multi-millionaire producer Henry Morgenthau III for a 1956 NBC television series he developed with Ian Fleming. Set aboard a thirty-foot yacht moored at Morgan's Harbour in Jamaica, the story pitted an agent named James Gunn against a gang threatening to deflect the course of American missiles from nearby Cape Canaveral. If the plot sounds familiar, it should. When NBC failed to pick up Morgenthau's proposed series, Fleming took the plot outline back and wrote his sixth James Bond novel, *Dr. No*.

Connery, Sean (August 25, 1930–   ; birth name: Thomas Sean Connery): Legendary Scottish leading man, the first actor to play 007 for the big screen—and, for many, the best of all possible Bonds. Early in his career, he developed a unique screen presence and a dashing romantic manner—à la Cary Grant or Errol Flynn—that became overwhelmingly appealing to both men and women. It was that quality that led to the enormous success of the early James Bond films, both commercially and critically. In many ways, he paved the way for dozens of Commonwealth actors—from Wales, Scotland, Ireland, England, New Zealand, and Australia—who have become top leading men in Hollywood in the intervening decades.

It was serious looks like this that cemented actor Sean Connery's portrait of James Bond—not a guy you want to mess with. *Courtesy of the David Reinhardt Collection*

What Connery brought to the character of Bond was a sexual magnetism that few actors possess, combined with a palpable sense of danger. Screenwriter Tom Mankiewicz once said, "When Connery walks into a bar, you know he could probably kill somebody if he had to. When Roger Moore walked into a bar, you knew he would probably say something glib to get out of the situation."* Both actors were successful 007s, but Connery's was the tougher, more serious-minded secret agent.

Although a London newspaper poll at the turn of the 1960s picked Connery as the perfect actor to play Bond in a feature film, it was his appearance in two earlier movies that brought him to the attention of the producers. Albert R. Broccoli spotted him in the Walt Disney fantasy *Darby O'Gill and the Little People* (1959), while

---

* Tom Mankiewicz, interview by the author, Los Angeles, November 7, 1977.

Harry Saltzman caught him in the British service comedy *On the Fiddle* (1961), playing opposite British comedian Alfie Lynch. Saltzman had screened the latter film upon the suggestion of editor Peter Hunt, who was friendly with *On the Fiddle* producer Benjamin Fisz.

The odds were against Connery, who was referred to at that time by American film executives as "that limey truck driver" (Connery had driven a truck at one time in his native Edinburgh). But Broccoli was especially impressed by Connery's stature and the fact that for a big man, he moved "like a cat." For Broccoli, Bond had to be an Englishman who was good with his fists—a combination he felt he could sell to US film audiences, who were used to the two-fisted handiwork of American detectives like Mike Hammer and Sam Spade.

When Connery was eventually signed to a seven-year contract, he underwent a transformation, courtesy of director Terence Young. Having

grown up in the Fountainbridge slums of Edinburgh, the very rugged and wild Connery was hardly Fleming's dashing upper-class hero. Young brought him to his own tailor and carefully outfitted him for the role of Bond.

Connery may not have been Fleming's prototypical 007, but from the fans' point of view—and there would be millions—he was the best possible choice for the film series. Serious, sexy, deadly, and unbeatable, he was also extremely glib with writer Richard Maibaum's throwaway humor, a factor that contributed to the series' long-standing success (although throwaway humor has almost completely disappeared from the contemporary Bonds).

In an interview with the BBC during his Bond tenure, Sean Connery evaluated the experience. "It's very good entertainment. They obviously like it. And one every year or fourteen months is a healthy issue. I came straight to London because I doubt anyone in Scotland would have employed

Twelve years after he appeared in *Diamonds Are Forever*, Sean Connery returned as James Bond one last time in *Never Say Never Again*—looking better than ever. *Courtesy of the David Reinhardt Collection*

Sporting the kind of physique that won him significant positions in bodybuilding competitions in the UK, Sean Connery catches up on his reading in Jamaica during production on *Dr. No. Courtesy of the David Reinhardt Collection*

me. They employed me for other jobs, but certainly not as an actor."* From 1962 to 1967, Connery appeared in five films in the series: *Dr. No* (1962), *From Russia with Love* (1963), *Goldfinger* (1964), *Thunderball* (1965), and *You Only Live Twice* (1967). Then, tired of the extremely long shooting schedules that prohibited him from doing more than a handful of non-Bond films, plus the grueling pressure of being an international media star, Connery departed the series.

But following George Lazenby's solo performance as 007 in *On Her Majesty's Secret Service* (1969), United Artists lured Connery back to the role. UA exec David Picker offered to back two of Connery's personal film projects, in addition to giving him a salary of $1.4 million plus profits for the next film in the series. Connery was back as Bond for *Diamonds Are Forever* (1971), donating $1 million of his fee to the Scottish International Education Trust, a charity he founded to aid deprived Scottish children. Connery left the series again after *Diamonds Are Forever*, ushering in the Roger Moore era. However, thanks to producer Jack Schwartzman and his breakaway *Never Say Never Again* project, Connery returned to play 007 one more time in 1983.

Connery is the son of Euphemia McBain, a cleaning lady, and Joseph Connery, a factory worker and truck driver. Connery, living in difficult economic times, worked many jobs before entering the acting ranks—including the aforementioned truck driver, milkman, laborer, artist's model, coffin polisher, and bodybuilder. He also briefly served in the Royal Navy, and considered a career in professional soccer.

He made his credited big-screen debut as Spike in director Montgomery Tully's British crime

Sean Connery as James Bond, 007 by Jeff Marshall. *Courtesy of Jeff Marshall*

drama *No Road Back* (1957). In addition to *Darby O'Gill and the Little People* and *On the Fiddle*, Connery played a villainous member of Anthony Quayle's band of murderers in *Tarzan's Greatest Adventure* (1959), director John Guillermin's terrific adventure film, which starred Gordon Scott as the title hero.

In between Bond roles, Connery worked for directors Alfred Hitchock in *Marnie* (1964), Sidney Lumet in *The Hill* (1965) and *The Anderson Tapes*

---

* Special features, *Dr. No*, James Bond Ultimate Edition (1962; MGM, 2006), DVD.

(1971), Irvin Kershner in *A Fine Madness* (1966), and Martin Ritt in *The Molly Maguires* (1970). Post Bond, Connery's roles increased in stature and quality, including *Murder on the Orient Express* (1974), again for Sidney Lumet; *The Wind and the Lion* (1975); *The Man Who Would Be King* (1975); *A Bridge Too Far* (1977); *The Great Train Robbery* (1978); *Time Bandits* (1981); *Highlander* (1986); *Indiana Jones and the Last Crusade* (1989); *The Hunt for Red October* (1990); *The Rock* (1996); and *Finding Forrester* (2000). In 1987, the Academy of Motion Picture Arts and Sciences rewarded him with the Oscar for Best Supporting Actor for director Brian De Palma's *The Untouchables*. Connery's Chicago street cop Jimmy Malone was cut from the same two-fisted, no-nonsense playbook as his James Bond.

Connery vs. Japan: One of the major reasons why actor Sean Connery decided to leave the James Bond series after *You Only Live Twice* was his experience in Japan during that movie's location filming in July and August 1966. For an actor who was rapidly tiring of the James Bond films' long and difficult shooting schedules, the Japanese location was the proverbial last straw.

His frustration began on July 27, 1966, when Connery and his first wife, actress Diane Cilento, arrived in Tokyo and were mobbed by 007 fans. Already hugely popular in Japan, James Bond enthusiasm had increased exponentially when it was announced that the latest film would be shot practically in the Japanese fans' own backyard.

Hundreds of journalists and photographers—virtually anyone who could carry a camera—were sent to record the six-week-long Bond invasion. The torrent of coverage began at 5:00 PM on July 27, at the Tokyo Hilton, where a hasty press conference was arranged to greet the exhausted Connery. Agent 007 appeared rumpled and bleary-eyed, minus his toupee and dressed in baggy knockabout trousers, shower sandals, and a blue shirt open at the neck to reveal his hairy chest. "Is this the way James Bond dressed?" asked one reporter, who had waited in the hotel lobby for six hours. "I'm not James Bond," Connery replied politely. "I'm Sean Connery and I like to dress comfortably, except for formal occasions."*

Sensing that an international incident was brewing unless he appeared more cordial, Con-

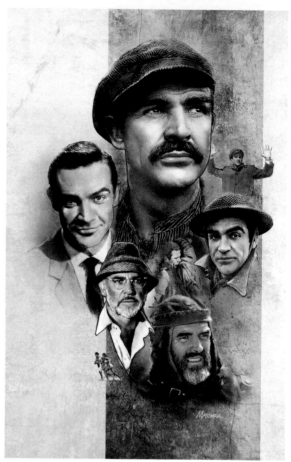

The magnificent career of actor Sean Connery, partially encapsulated by artist Jeff Marshall. *Courtesy of Jeff Marshall*

nery summoned his patented Bond charm and even managed a few weak jokes about his fondness for Scotch cooking and whisky. He let the reporters inspect the tattoos on his arms—one reading Scotland Forever and the other Mother and Father—and offered some words of praise for Japanese cooking. Connery also confessed that he enjoyed the *ofuro*, the Japanese bath. "It's wonderful," he beamed, "all that splashing around after you've washed yourself clean, and then getting back into a deep tub of hot water. The soaking is marvelous."

After about twenty minutes of good-natured discussion, everyone was smiling, even publicist Tom Carlile, who had been nervous about the awesome crowd of camera-clicking reporters. And then the bombshell was dropped.

---

* Andy Adams, "Bond Kicks Up a Furore in Japan," *Asian Adventure*, August 1967.

A reporter asked, "What do you think of Japanese women?" Connery thought for a second, according to a reporter from *Asian Adventure* who attended the press conference, and then smiled, answering the question honestly—if not diplomatically. "Japanese women are just not sexy," he said. "This is even more so when they hide their figures by wearing those roomy kimonos."

After Connery's comment, the *Asian Adventure* reporter related, "There was a rather strained silence in the room. . . . National pride was aroused." To avoid a confrontation, Carlile, the quick-witted PR pro, stepped in, asking the crowd's indulgence so that Connery could get some rest after the long jet flight from London. Connery offered to pose once more for the cameras, then retired to his room.

The press conference was a bad omen, and it only led to more press scrutiny on *You Only Live Twice*. During the six weeks of filming in Japan, reporters were everywhere—hiding behind fences, hanging from trees, lurking in restrooms—all armed with cameras and ready to capture their own private scoop. Such coverage made the film front-page news for weeks, and at times put the Eon Productions crew under a microscope.

When a stuntman mistimed his throw and catapulted a steel dart into the wall of historic Himeji Castle, it seemed that every paper in Japan got wind of it. Official protests were lodged, the Eon crew was banned from the castle grounds—where the ninja training was being shot—and it was only after a judicious amount of apologizing and repeated offers to pay for any damages that the crew was once more permitted inside the grounds of the historic fortress.

Filming on the streets of Tokyo was at times impossible. No sooner would director Lewis Gilbert's hidden camera begin recording Connery's progress than the actor would be mobbed by fans. After location filming was completed in Japan, Connery returned to London to finish the picture. However, the seeds of discontent were already sown. After 1967, producers Albert R. Broccoli and Harry Saltzman would be looking for a new actor to play Bond.

Constantine, Emperor: The fourth-century Byzantine monarch who commissioned an underground reservoir in Istanbul that Kerim Bey (Pedro Armendariz) uses as a clandestine route into the Russian consulate in *From Russia with Love*. Bey makes the journey twice a day, at 11:00 AM and 3:00 PM.

Conti, Bill (April 13, 1942–   ): Academy Award–winning American film composer, well known for his *Rocky* music, who contributed the light-hearted score on *For Your Eyes Only*. He also collaborated with lyricist Mick Leeson to craft the film's title song, for which they received an Oscar nomination for Best Original Song, losing to "Arthur's Theme (Best That You Can Do)" from the Dudley Moore comedy *Arthur*. A native of Providence, Rhode Island, Conti received his Oscar for scoring *The Right Stuff* (1983). Along with lyricists Carol Connors and Ayn Robbins, Conti was also nominated for the song "Gonna Fly Now" from *Rocky* (they lost to the song "Evergreen" from *A Star Is Born*). Conte made his film-composing debut on the Spanish-language feature *A Candidate for a Killing* (1969). In addition to assignments on multiple *Rocky* and *Karate Kid* films, some of his more notable movie scores include *Blume in Love* (1973), *Harry and Tonto* (1974), *Next Stop, Greenwich Village* (1976), *Broadcast News* (1987), and *The Thomas Crown Affair* (1999).

Coolidge, Rita (May 1, 1945–   ): Soulful American pop singer with country music roots who sang "All Time High," the opening-titles song for *Octopussy*. Before embarking on a solo career, Coolidge performed with Delaney & Bonnie and Friends, Joe Cocker, Leon Russell, and Kris Kristofferson. When it was released in 1983, "All Time High" became a Top 10 hit in nine countries.

Rita Coolidge sang "All Time High," the opening-titles tune to *Octopussy*. *Steve Rubin Collection*

Corfu: Greek island in the Ionian Sea that is a principal setting in *For Your Eyes Only*. Corfu's sandy beach proved to be difficult terrain for assassin Emile Locque (Michael Gothard) and his dune buggies, which are supposed to run down and kill Bond (Roger Moore) and his lady friend

Lisl (Cassandra Harris). It was also a particularly difficult filming location for fledgling director John Glen, who quickly fell three days behind schedule. Despite the delay, producer Cubby Broccoli stood by Glen, and somehow the crew managed to unstick themselves and finish the frenetic dune-buggy chase.

corneal implant: Surgical enhancement that gives *Never Say Never Again*'s US Air Force captain Jack Petachi (Gavan O'Herlihy) an exact duplicate of the cornea of the president of United States' right eye. Petachi's new, extremely blue eye allows him to breach a top-level security check and arm two cruise missiles with nuclear warheads.

Corsican brandy: The usual drink of choice of Union Corse kingpin Marc-Ange Draco (Gabriele Ferzetti) in *On Her Majesty's Secret Service*. During his initial meeting with Bond (George Lazenby) at his Draco Construction offices, he forgoes the brandy for a glass of Campari, an Italian aperitif.

Cortina d'Ampezzo: Winter resort city in the Italian Alps that is a key setting in *For Your Eyes Only*. Tipped off by the Italian Secret Service that Emile Locque (Michael Gothard) is in Cortina, Bond (Roger Moore) goes there and meets Aris Kristatos (Julian Glover), who claims to be a former World War II resistance fighter and Anglophile. He's actually a Russian agent preparing to retrieve vital equipment from the sunken hulk of the *St. Georges* surveillance ship.

Kristatos lies and tells Bond that Locque is working for Milos Columbo (Topol), a man he also claims is involved in drug smuggling, sex trafficking, and contract murder. Bond also meets Kristatos's protégée, ice skater Bibi Dahl (Lynn-Holly Johnson), her teacher, Jacoba Brink (Jill Bennett), and another enemy agent, East German biathlon champion Erich Kriegler (John Wyman), who is working for Kristatos.

Bond's local Secret Service contact, Luigi Ferrara (John Moreno), is later murdered by Locque, who leaves Columbo's symbol—the white dove—on the body. Bond, meanwhile, has been chased on skis by Kriegler, assaulted by ski-borne motorcycles, and, later, at a hockey rink, attacked by three hapless hockey players, who end up sprawled in their own net.

Cosio, Joaquín (October 4, 1962–   ): Mexican actor who portrayed renegade Bolivian general Medrano in *Quantum of Solace*. A native of Tepic, Nayarit, Cosio made his motion picture debut in director Walter Doehner's romantic drama *The Blue Room* (2002). The Bond movie was his English-language debut.

Courtleigh Manor Hotel: The base of operations for the crew of *Dr. No* in Kingston, Jamaica, in January 1962.

Coventry Climax: British forklift manufacturer whose name is painted on the side of the Auric Stud forklift that loads gold bars into the Lincoln Continental that will take Mr. Solo (Martin Benson) to the local airport in *Goldfinger*. Although this scene takes place in Kentucky, it was actually shot on the Pinewood Studios backlot outside London—which explains why the scene features British machinery.

Coward, Sir Noël (December 16, 1899–March 26, 1973): British actor/writer/director/composer who was author Ian Fleming's first choice to play the title character in *Dr. No*. However, after receiving Fleming's cable, the actor replied, "Dear Ian. The answer to *Dr. No* is No! No! No! No!"

Crab Key: A fictional island off the coast of Jamaica that was turned into a fortress by SPECTRE operative Dr. No (Joseph Wiseman) in the movie of the same name. Disguised inside a bauxite mine, the facility deploys a nuclear-powered jamming signal that is tampering with the guidance systems on US rockets fired from nearby Cape Canaveral, Florida. Protecting the operation is a diesel-powered amphibious vehicle equipped with a flame-thrower and disguised as a dragon to frighten off the locals, as well as Dr. No's private army, which is equipped with machine guns, guard dogs, and high-powered boats.

Craig, Daniel (March 2, 1968–   ; birth name: Daniel Wroughton Craig): Rugged British actor who made his dynamic debut as James Bond in 2006's *Casino Royale*, and completely transformed the 007 series for a new generation of fans. Craig brought a visceral, feral quality to the part of Bond in his first film and its follow-ups *Quantum of Solace*, *Skyfall*, *Spectre*, and *No Time to Die*.

Relative unknown Daniel Craig achieved international stardom practically overnight when he brought his considerable acting chops to the rebooted role of James Bond in *Casino Royale*. *Courtesy of the Anders Frejdh Collection*

In *Skyfall*, actor Daniel Craig was wearing the Bond character like a perfectly fitted glove. *Courtesy of the Anders Frejdh Collection*

A native of Chester, Cheshire, England (near Liverpool), and well educated in the British theater (Joseph Fiennes and Ewan McGregor were classmates at the Guildhall School of Music & Drama in London), Craig made a modest film debut in 1992 as Sergeant Botha, a pro-apartheid cadet in *The Power of One* (1992). Moving easily between TV and film assignments on both sides of the Atlantic, his profile began to rise when he appeared in such films as *Lara Croft: Tomb Raider* (2001), as Angelina Jolie's boyfriend; Steven Spielberg's *Road to Perdition* (2002), opposite Tom Hanks as Paul Newman's gangster son; *Layer Cake* (2004); *Munich* (2005), once again for Spielberg, portraying a Mossad assassin; and *Infamous* (2006), as one of the *In Cold Blood* killers.

Taking on the iconic role of 007 was not an easy choice for Craig to make. He knew it would change his life, not only as an actor but as a human being. As for every new 007, the stakes were enormous. A success would make him an international superstar; a failure would turn him into a cocktail party joke. He consulted friends, family, business associates. Hampering his decision was the lack of a final script—often a problem on Bond movies. But when producers Barbara Broccoli and Michael G. Wilson finally shared the screenplay with him, he was thrilled. However, he still had the same concern that Sean Connery had half a century earlier: would he be typecast as Bond? Would he be denied an eclectic career on the big screen? Craig told *Esquire* magazine, "I mean, of course, I want to win Oscars. Every actor wants to win Oscars. But then it sunk in: If I don't take something like this

when it comes around and have a go at it, then what? Yeah, there's gonna be negatives, but . . . I figured, Fuck it, it's *Bond*. Enjoy it."[*]

To prepare for *Casino Royale*, Craig read all of Ian Fleming's novels and talked with Mossad and British Secret Service agents who worked on Craig's *Munich* as technical advisers. In the beginning, Bond fans were skeptical; he was hardly the tall, dark, and handsome poster boy previous 007s Roger Moore and Pierce Brosnan had been. He was disparaged as "James Bland" and "that blond Bond." There was even something thuggish about him. But as soon as *Casino Royale* was released, fans abandoned their criticism for elation. Ironically, Craig's less polished and more ruthless air was just what the part now called for.

When asked about these aspects of the new Bond, Craig told *Playboy*, "For [*Casino Royale*], my feeling was he should look like the man who had yet to make his first kill. I wanted to play around with the flaws in his character. . . . In the books, Bond is suave and sophisticated, yes—Sean Connery really nailed it—but there's also a flawed aspect of Bond. In the novels, he is quite a depressive character. When he's not working, he's at his worst."[†] Craig told *Hello!* magazine in London, "The character of Bond is nothing new. In every culture there's a character like this, a lone warrior who goes after the bad guys. But he's a bad man, too, and that, I think, is part of his attraction. He burns brightly, both for men and for women."[‡]

---

[*] David Katz, "Bond Is Dead, Long Live Bond!," *Esquire*, September 2006.
[†] Daniel Craig, interview by David Sheff, *Playboy*, November 2008.
[‡] Daniel Craig, interview by Gabrielle Donnelly, *Hello!*, November 20, 2006.

Even in noirish shadow, Daniel Craig's presence was felt. *Steve Rubin Collection*

Craig's arrival to the series also coincided with a severe reduction in humor, wordplay, and ardent sexism. A vibrant realism took over. Said Craig, "These days I don't think you can make puns as easily. . . . They've been sent up in such a way they almost ring like parody. *Austin Powers* did them in the extreme. So making a Bond movie, you have to keep that in mind. As soon as you go that way, you're making a parody of a parody. It looks like you're doing Mike Myers."[*]

Another factor that separated Craig from some of the other 007 actors was his ability to dive into the action sequences with an exuberant physicality. It used to be somewhat of a joke that Roger Moore could vanquish the bad guys without getting his hair mussed. Timothy Dalton and Pierce Brosnan were polished fighters whom the writing didn't ask much of on an action level. But Craig came to the Bond series when the writers were creating pulse-pounding action sequences that harked back to the early days of Bond, when Sean Connery used his fists to make a point. Said Craig, "I wanted to make my role as physical as possible—if you don't get bruises on a Bond film, you're not doing it properly."[†]

Now seasoned in the role, Daniel Craig brings his world-weary best to *No Time to Die. Courtesy of United Artists Releasing*

---

[*] Craig, interview by Sheff.
[†] Craig, interview by Donnelly.

It wasn't just his physical prowess in action scenes; right out of the gate in *Casino Royale*, Craig worked beautifully with his female costar, actress Eva Green. In doing his research, Craig had developed definite opinions on Bond's relationships with women; as he explained to *Playboy*, "In Fleming, there's misogyny till the end. Rereading the books reminds you of the time they were written. They are sexist and racist. It's time to put all that in its place. One thing that remains from Fleming is that the women always leave Bond—as opposed to his leaving them. It's the opposite of the way we think of him, that he beds a woman and says bye-bye and flies out the window. In the books, he has relationships and occasionally is nearly getting married when she dumps him because he turns moody and dark . . . his true personality comes out, and he's impossible to live with."[*]

Crete: Greek island in the Mediterranean that was a World War II battleground for resistance fighters Milos Columbo (Topol) and Aris Kristatos (Julian Glover), as revealed in *For Your Eyes Only*. Columbo later tells James Bond (Roger Moore) that Kristatos turned traitor, working as a double agent for the Nazis.

Crewdson, Captain John (May 15, 1926–June 26, 1983): Former Royal Air Force officer who flew the helicopter for the scene in which SPECTRE chases Bond (Sean Connery) across the foothills of Yugoslavia in *From Russia with Love*. The sequence was actually filmed near Lochgilphead, Scotland. Crewdson returned to fly Draco's helicopter in *On Her Majesty's Secret Service*, and he was also part of the aerial crew on both *The Spy Who Loved Me* and *For Your Eyes Only*. Crewdson, a native of Horley, Surrey, England, made his motion picture flying debut as a helicopter pilot on director Joseph Sterling's thriller *Operation Conspiracy* (1956), the cast of which included Bill Nagy (Mr. Midnight in *Goldfinger*). He later coordinated all the aerial sequences in *The War Lover* (1962).

Crinan: A coastal town in Scotland where the motorboat chase finale in *From Russia with Love* was filmed. The sequence was originally to be shot in the waters off Pendik, Turkey, but bad

---

[*] Craig, interview by Sheff.

weather, malfunctioning motorboats, and inexperienced support crews shifted it to Scotland.

crocodile farm: A principal setting in *Live and Let Die*, where James Bond (Roger Moore) is left to die by Tee Hee (Julius Harris). Captured in New Orleans, Bond is brought out to the farm, where he is stranded on an island in the middle of a small stream infested with hundreds of crocodiles and alligators. Convinced that his enemy is doomed, Tee Hee chuckles and returns to the drug lab that refines heroin for crime boss Kananga (Yaphet Kotto). As the crocodiles prepare for their human lunch, 007 sees his chance and jumps to safety over their aligned backs.

This sequence was shot at an actual Jamaican crocodile farm owned by a part-Seminole man named Ross Kananga. To determine how Bond could escape from a stream full of crocs, screenwriter Tom Mankiewicz went to the real Kananga and asked him what he would do if he found himself in a similar situation. Kananga told him that he would try to jump over their backs. The actual stunt, however, could be done safely only if the crocodiles were immobilized. The entire pond was cleared of excess crocodiles so that director Guy Hamilton could bring in his small team of filmmakers, including a contingent of London construction workers who fashioned the little retractable bridge that strands Bond on the island.

Kananga tied the feet of half a dozen reptiles to weights on the bottom of the pond so they couldn't move, while their jaws and tails remained free. When the crocodiles were finally tethered in place, creating a reptilian bridge of snapping teeth and swishing tails, Kananga himself prepared to jump their backs—a stunt he had never before attempted. He had to wear a pair of pants and shoes resembling the outfit worn by Moore, who would be watching his own escape from a safe distance.

The first four times Kananga tried the stunt, he slipped and fell into the pond. On the third time, one of the crocs actually nipped at his foot. He soon discovered that the street shoes he was forced to wear were preventing him getting across the strange, slippery surfaces. Even with specially prepare soles, which were designed to give him traction, he continued to slip and land in the water. Each time, he had to return to the wardrobe shack, change into a fresh pair of dry trousers, and row out to the little concrete island.

TRESPASSERS WILL BE EATEN, indeed! James Bond's nemesis in *Live and Let Die*. *Steve Rubin Collection*

Kananga also told Hamilton that each time he failed, it made the stunt more difficult, because the crocodiles knew he was coming. The element of surprise was especially important with those huge jaws only inches away. On the fifth try, Kananga finally managed to keep his footing and raced to the shore across the croc's backs. One small step for Kananga, one huge step forward for *Live and Let Die*.

Crow, Sheryl (February 11, 1962–   ): American singer who performed the soulful title song in *Tomorrow Never Dies*. A native of Kennett, Missouri, Crow was nominated for a Golden Globe for her Bond song, sharing the Best Original Song nomination with Mitchell Froom (they lost to "My Heart Will Go On" from *Titanic*). Her music made its film debut in director Michael Fields's thriller *Bright Angel* (1990), on which she sang "Heal Somebody." She was nominated for a second Golden Globe for Best Original Song for "Try Not to Remember" from *Home of the Brave* (2006). She also sang the title tune "Real Gone" in the Pixar animated feature *Cars* (2006).

Songstress Sheryl Crow warbled the title tune to *Tomorrow Never Dies*. *Courtesy of the Anders Frejdh Collection*

Cucinotta, Maria Grazia (July 27, 1968–): Italian actress who portrayed Julietta the Cigar Girl in *The World Is Not Enough*. Cucinotta first came to the attention of American audiences when she portrayed the fetching love interest of the poor postman in the international hit *Il Postino* (1994). In *The World Is Not Enough*, she's called the Cigar Girl because she offers a cigar to Bond (Pierce Brosnan) in the teaser sequence set in Bilbao, Spain. Later, she leads 007 on an exciting motorboat chase after she blows up a chunk of MI6 headquarters in London. A native of Messina, Sicily, Cucinotta made her motion picture debut as Arabella in director Enrico Oldoini's romantic comedy *Vacanze di Natale '90* (1990), which also featured Bond player Corinne Cléry.

The Cigar Girl (Maria Grazia Cucinotta) leads Bond on a spirited motorboat chase along the Thames in *The World Is Not Enough. Courtesy of David Williams, Bondpix*

Cumming, Alan (January 27, 1965–): Scottish character actor who shone as obnoxious, egotistical computer programmer Boris Grishenko in *GoldenEye*. His exclamation of choice, "I am invincible," was memorable, and so was his character's death as a liquid-oxygen-encased icicle. A native of Aberfeldy, Perthshire, Cumming made his

Alan Cumming as Boris Grishenko in *GoldenEye. Steve Rubin Collection*

motion picture debut as Alexander Novak in director Ian Sellar's drama, *Prague* (1992). His post-Bond film credits include *Eyes Wide Shut* (1999), *The Flintstones in Viva Rock Vegas* (2000), *Spy Kids* (2001), *Nicholas Nickleby* (2002), *X-Men 2* (2003), and *Battle of the Sexes* (2017). American audiences know him as Eli Gold on the TV series *The Good Wife* (119 episodes, 2010–2016).

Cummings, Bill (1928–2002): British stuntman, a veteran of the 007 team, who portrayed Quist, one of Emilio Largo's henchmen in *Thunderball*. It is Quist who attempts to assassinate Bond (Sean Connery) in 007's Nassau hotel room. Bond surprises Quist, disarming him, then sends him back to Largo with the message "The little fish I throw back in the sea." Cummings made his uncredited feature debut as an archer and stunt performer in MGM's *Ivanhoe* (1952), which also featured fellow Bond stuntmen Bob Simmons and George Leech. Cummings performed stunt chores on *Dr. No*, *From Russia with Love*, *Goldfinger*, *You Only Live Twice*, *On Her Majesty's Secret Service*, *Diamonds Are Forever*, *Live and Let Die*, *The Man with the Golden Gun*, *The Spy Who Loved Me*, and *For Your Eyes Only*.

Cuneo, Ernest (May 27, 1905–March 1, 1988): American lawyer, newspaperman, author, and former pro football player, a friend of Ian Fleming and a partner in Ivar Bryce's Xanadu Productions, who contributed early story elements to the late-1950s James Bond film adaptation project that eventually became the novel *Thunderball*. A former legal advisor to Franklin D. Roosevelt, Cuneo wrote a memorandum to Bryce, dated May 28, 1959, that was, in effect, the project's first story outline.

In it, a Russian agent poses as a US Army sergeant working on board a celebrity-filled USO airliner that is constantly flying to top-secret US bases. James Bond discovers that the Russians plan to detonate atomic bombs on those same bases.

When the sergeant transfers to the Caribbean USO, Bond follows, disguised as a British entertainer. In Nassau, he discovers that a mysterious power is commanding a fleet of Bahamian fishing boats, all of which are equipped with watertight underwater hatches just like those used by the Italian navy during World War II. Atomic bombs are to be delivered by Russian submarines to these fishing boats and hoisted through their watertight trapdoors by frogmen.

Cuneo finished the outline by detailing an underwater battle between the enemy frogmen and Bond's unit that takes place during an outdoor USO concert in Nassau. Cuneo centered his outline around the heavy use of both American and British celebrities, an idea given to him by producer Kevin McClory, who had featured a number of celebrity cameos in *Around the World in 80 Days* (1956). Cuneo also felt that the American government would be willing to cooperate by allowing a British camera crew to film at certain US installations, perhaps even aboard their new aircraft carrier the USS *Independence*.

Bryce showed Cuneo's outline to Fleming, who scribbled his own pointed comments. His two biggest criticisms concerned the lack of a Bond heroine, and the use of the Russians as the principal villains.

Following Cuneo's initial outline, Fleming created a film treatment in which the Russians are replaced by the Mafia in the A-bomb conspiracy. The latter is headed by a capo named Cuneo, whose principal lieutenant is a huge bear of a man named Largo. The role of Largo was written for American actor Burl Ives, who had already expressed interest in the project—and had recently won a Best Supporting Actor Oscar for his part in *The Big Country* (1958).

Largo and his handpicked team break into an American atomic base in Britain and steal an A-bomb. They transfer the bomb to a helicopter, which transports it to a tramp steamer anchored in the English Channel. The steamer passes the bomb to a Sunderland flying boat, which then speeds across the Atlantic and deposits its cargo in the water near Largo's huge yacht, the *Virginia*, where a complement of divers transfer it through the yacht's watertight underwater hatch.

Much of the early action in Fleming's treatment takes place at a public house in the British countryside, where Bond tracks Largo and meets a British agent named Domino Smith, who has infiltrated the Mafia gang. Screenwriter Jack Whittingham would later alter many of these story elements, and the Mafia villains would be replaced by Fleming's own SPECTRE organization.

Da Vinho Estate: The location in Zambujal, Portugal, used for the home of Marc-Ange Draco (Gabriele Ferzetti) in *On Her Majesty's Secret Service*. Site of Draco's birthday celebration in the film, the estate sported a private bullring and sumptuous gardens. Said screenwriter Richard Maibaum, who departed somewhat from Fleming's description of the head of the Union Corse crime syndicate, "What I thought we should do to Draco, our sympathetic Mafioso, was to give him some interest in livestock. In this case, we made him a cattleman, someone who raised bulls as a pastime. Such a background gave some weight to Draco's decision at the end of the film to support Bond's attack on Piz Gloria. The birthday sequence was also helped when we discovered the Da Vinho estate in Portugal, which I thought was absolutely right for this man's background."*

d'Abo, Maryam (December 27, 1960–   ): British actress of Dutch and Russian heritage who portrayed Kara Milovy, the Czechoslovakian cellist who falls in love with James Bond (Timothy Dalton) in *The Living Daylights*. She had terrific chemistry with Dalton, who was making his auspicious debut as 007. D'Abo was the perfect mate—an elegant, well-mannered, soulful woman dedicated to her musical craft and dreams of a solo career, who is tossed headlong into the adventure of a lifetime. Their pairing infused the story with a sense of romance that had been missing from many of the Roger Moore 007 movies. Not since *The Spy Who Loved Me* had Bond been given the special time to develop a believable relationship with a woman.

Actress Maryam d'Abo brought Czech cellist Kara Milovy to life in *The Living Daylights*. *Courtesy of the David Reinhardt Collection*

Speaking in Vienna prior to the star of shooting on *The Living Daylights*, d'Abo said, "The first time I heard of James Bond, I must have been eleven or twelve, it was the [Sean Connery films] and I just loved it. The character of James Bond from the Ian Fleming books is a man who lives in a world where every day is unexpected." She added, "I would never want to compare myself to any of the other Bond leading ladies, because every leading lady we've had in the Bond movies have had their own qualities. I'm not playing someone who is sophisticated and so and so, because I wouldn't have been chosen otherwise. I'm a very natural girl. And I have a very genuine character and I think that I have been chosen for that reason."* D'Abo, a native of London, made her feature film debut in the sci-fi horror film *Xtro* (1982).

Dahl, Bibi: Randy Olympic ice-skating hopeful portrayed by blonde Lynn-Holly Johnson in *For Your Eyes Only*. The teenage protégée of sinister

---

* Richard Maibaum, interview by the author, Los Angeles, April 30, 1977.

* Special features, *The Living Daylights*, James Bond Ultimate Edition (1987; MGM, 2006), DVD.

Olympics-bound ice skater Bibi Dahl (Lynn-Holly Johnson) takes a shining to James Bond (Roger Moore) in *For Your Eyes Only*. *Courtesy of the Anders Frejdh Collection*

millionaire Aris Kristatos (Julian Glover), Bibi meets James Bond (Roger Moore) in Cortina d'Ampezzo, where she is training under Jacoba Brink (Jill Bennett). 007 returns to his hotel at one point and finds Bibi waiting invitingly in his bed. Ever the wit, Bond offers her an ice cream cone instead.

Bibi eventually discovers that her patron is a ruthless Soviet agent who virtually imprisons her in his fortress at St. Cyril's in Greece. When Kristatos is killed, Bibi discovers a new and more suitable patron: amiable Milos Columbo (Topol).

Dahl, Roald (September 13, 1916–November 23, 1990): Legendary, whimsical Welsh author and screenwriter who was enlisted to write *You Only Live Twice* in 1966. Recalled Dahl, "I remember the phone ringing and this man saying his name was Broccoli. I thought he was joking. After all, a man with the last name of a vegetable? It was funny. I really hadn't heard of him.

"He told me about the Bond films and about *You Only Live Twice*, the latest in the series. And then he asked me if I would like to write a script.

Now that was an exciting proposition, because I had admired the films. I had seen one or two and I had known Ian Fleming well. My wife [actress Patricia Neal] and I had often stayed at his home in Oracabessa. So I went up to London right away, to Audley Square, where I met Cubby [Broccoli] and Harry Saltzman. And they asked me right off whether I could deliver a first draft in eight weeks, a second in four more, and a complete script in twenty weeks. I said I could, and that was that.

Celebrated author Roald Dahl took a rare screenwriting gig when he was assigned the job of adapting *You Only Live Twice*. *Steve Rubin Collection*

"*You Only Live Twice* was the only Fleming book that had virtually no semblance of a plot that could be made into a movie. The concept of Blofeld patrolling his garden of poison plants in a medieval suit of armor and lopping off the heads of half-blinded Japanese was ridiculous. When I began the script, I could retain only four or five of the original novel's story ideas. Obviously, the movie had to take place in Japan. We kept Blofeld and Tiger Tanaka and Bond's pearl-diving girlfriend, Kissy. And we retained the ninjas— those masters of oriental martial arts who use their talents to raid Blofeld's hideout. But aside from those bits, I had nothing except a wonderful Ian Fleming title."*

A native of Llandaff, Cardiff, who flew Hawker Hurricanes as a fighter pilot with the RAF in World War II, Dahl was the author of many famous children's books, including *Charlie and the Chocolate Factory*, *The Witches*, *Matilda*, *The BFG*, *James and the Giant Peach*, and *Fantastic Mr. Fox*. Cubby Broccoli hired him again the year after *You Only Live Twice* to write *Chitty Chitty Bang Bang* (1968), based on another novel by Ian Fleming.

Daily Gleaner: Actual newspaper in Kingston, Jamaica, that is the supposed employer of the devious photographer Bond calls "Freelance" (Margaret LeWars) in *Dr. No*.

---

* Roald Dahl, interview by the author, London, June 19, 1977.

Dalton, Timothy (March 21, 1946–): Classically trained Welsh actor, known for his costume films and stage work, who became the fourth actor to portray James Bond in the Eon Productions series of 007 films. When he replaced Roger Moore starting with *The Living Daylights* in 1987, the series underwent a major about-face in focus and tone. Moore's comfort with witty lines, light comedic situations, and fantasy plots was replaced by a hard-edged reality and moments of unflinching violence that reflected Dalton's more realistic approach to the character of 007.

Dalton told film journalist Craig Modderno in 1989, "I think Roger was fine as Bond, but the movies had become too much techno-pop and had lost track of their sense of story. I mean, every movie seemed to have a villain who had to rule or destroy the world. If you want to believe in the fantasy on screen, then you have to believe in the characters and use them as a stepping stone to lead you into this fantasy world. That's a demand I made, and Albert Broccoli agreed with me."*

Timothy Dalton had the perfect Bond qualities. He was tall, handsome, athletic, commanding. He was believable as a British secret agent with a license to kill who can bed any lady he wants. Most of all, Dalton was an excellent actor who brought a wealth of experience to the set.

In interview after interview, the new Bond told reporters that he was rereading the Fleming novels, especially his favorite, *Casino Royale*, in order to research his new role. This James Bond was not going to play second fiddle to gadgets and breathless females. In Vienna for the start of filming on *The Living Daylights*, Dalton said, "I intend to approach this project with a sense of responsibility to the work of Ian Fleming and to the project *The Living Daylights* as written by Michael Wilson and Richard Maibaum. I have to make it my own. . . . I think the essential quality of James Bond is that he's a man who lives on the edge. He never knows when at any moment he might be killed, therefore I think some of the qualities we associate with Bond . . . reflect that

Following the light comedic Roger Moore films, Timothy Dalton brought a serious, no-nonsense approach to the character of James Bond. *Courtesy of the David Reinhardt Collection*

sense of danger in his own life. We know that he drinks—lines like 'shaken not stirred' reflect that sense of drinking. We know he smokes and likes to drive fast cars. I think the qualities of the man are really the qualities of a man who's living very much on the edge of his life. He's always liked his women. I suppose he can take them or leave them, or maybe take them and leave them."*

Dalton's debut in *The Living Daylights* was terrific. His first close-up on the Rock of Gibraltar, as he spies the death of a fellow agent, is riveting. His arrival via parachute onto the yacht of a playgirl is equally perfect. There was no hesitation in his performance. His fisticuffs appeared genuine—especially compared to Moore, who had a tendency to use too much kickboxing—and he could underplay situations.

---

* Timothy Dalton, interview by Craig Modderno, Los Angeles, June 30, 1989.

* Special features, *The Living Daylights*, James Bond Ultimate Edition (1987; MGM, 2006), DVD.

He didn't play humor well—but, then, the humor in his films was not written well, especially in the virtually humorless *Licence to Kill*. In *The Living Daylights*, Dalton can be forgiven for not putting across his punning remarks, because they were probably written to be delivered by Pierce Brosnan, the original choice for the next Bond until he was unable to get out of his contract with NBC's *Remington Steele*. In *Licence to Kill*, however, Dalton was saddled with a dead-serious story with very little room for humor, especially from the villains. It was a James Bond circus without the clowns.

Unlike Moore, who always seemed to be in command, Dalton's Bond seems like a candidate for the psychiatrist's couch—a burned-out killer who may have just enough energy left for one final mission. That was Fleming's Bond: a man who drank to diminish the poison in his system, the poison of a violent world with impossible demands. Dalton's was the suffering Bond.

A native of Colwyn Bay, Wales, Dalton made his promising feature debut as Philip II in director Anthony Harvey's sumptuous biographical drama *The Lion in Winter* (1968), which also featured a memorable score from frequent Bond composer John Barry.

Dario: Cold-blooded killer and former Contra rebel portrayed by Benicio Del Toro in *Licence to Kill*. Employed by drug lord Franz Sanchez (Robert Davi), knife-wielding Dario is introduced almost immediately as the man who cuts out the heart of Alvarez (Gerardo Albarrán), the unfortunate lover of Lupe Lamora (Talisa Soto). Dario later confronts Bond (Timothy Dalton) and Pam Bouvier (Carey Lowell) in the Barrelhead Bar, and takes a solid punch from 007.

As Pam escapes to 007's waiting motorboat, Dario shoots her in the back. She survives, thanks to her body armor. During a laboratory demonstration at the Sanchez's Olimpatec Meditation Institute, Dario recognizes Bond, who, up until this point, has been trusted in the drug lord's company. Bond is quickly disarmed and nearly thrown into a cocaine-bundle shredder when Pam arrives to save him. As the laboratory explodes in flames, Bond and Dario engage in a desperate fight above the shredder, which 007 eventually wins—shredding the cowardly killer in the process.

dart-firing wristwatch: A weapon supplied to James Bond (Roger Moore) by Q (Desmond Llewelyn) in *Moonraker*. The watch is equipped with ten darts. Five are blue-tipped and have armor-piercing heads. Five are red-tipped and coated with cyanide, which causes death in thirty seconds. Later, trapped in an out-of-control centrifuge trainer, Bond uses one of the armor-piercing darts to disable the machine.

DATES OF NOTE IN THE JAMES BOND FILMS

- **January 16, 1962**: First day of shooting on the first 007 film, *Dr. No*. The crew went on location at Jamaica's Palisadoes Airport to film Bond (Sean Connery) arriving on the island.
- **April 1, 1963**: First day of shooting on *From Russia with Love*. Director Terence Young shot the scene in M's office in which Q (Desmond Llewelyn) familiarizes Bond (Sean Connery) with the many special features of his field-issue briefcase.
- **March 19, 1964**: Sean Connery's first day of shooting on *Goldfinger*. He reported to Stage D at Pinewood Studios, which was set up as the El Scorpio nightclub in South America.
- **February 16, 1965:** Principal photography on *Thunderball* began at the Château d'Anet in France.
- **July 4, 1966**: The first day of shooting on *You Only Live Twice*. Director Lewis Gilbert filmed the sequence in which Bond (Sean Connery) is apparently murdered in the Hong Kong apartment of Ling (Tsai Chin).
- **October 21, 1968**: The first day of shooting on *On Her Majesty's Secret Service*. The location was the mountaintop Piz Gloria restaurant in Switzerland, where filming began at 7:45 AM with new 007 George Lazenby and ten gorgeous women.
- **November 6, 1973**: The first day of shooting on *The Man with the Golden Gun*. Director Guy Hamilton and a skeleton crew motored out to Victoria Harbour, Hong Kong, to film the wreck of the *Queen Elizabeth I* ocean liner. For this early sequence, actor Mike Lovatt doubled Roger Moore, who wasn't due in Hong Kong until the following April.
- **September 27, 1982**: The first day of shooting on *Never Say Never Again*. The location was Nice, France.

- **August 10, 1982**: The first day of filming on *Octopussy*. The sequence follows James Bond (Roger Moore) as he arrives at Checkpoint Charlie in West Berlin.
- **June 27, 1984**: Date of a disastrous fire that destroyed the 007 Stage at Pinewood Studios and changed the production plans for the fourteenth James Bond film, *A View to a Kill*. Fed by exploding gas cylinders that had been used to fuel some campfires on a large forest set for director Ridley Scott's fantasy film *Legend*, the blaze leveled the structure. Despite costing more than 1 million pounds to rebuild the stage, the disaster added little to the budget for *A View to a Kill*, although it did extend the film's shooting schedule for three weeks. The set for the abandoned Main Strike silver mine was actually constructed simultaneously with the laying of the roof on the newly reconstructed stage.
- **July 18, 1988**: First day of shooting on *Licence to Kill*. Working in Mexico City's Churubusco Studios, director John Glen filmed the interior of the love nest on Cray Key in the Bahamas where Lupe Lamora (Talisa Soto) and her lover (Gerardo Albarrán) are surprised by Sanchez (Robert Davi) and his henchmen. A second location that day was the interior of the bedroom of Felix Leiter (David Hedison) in Key West, where James Bond (Timothy Dalton) finds the body of Leiter's bride, Della Churchill (Priscilla Barnes).
- **January 14, 2002**: First shooting day on *Die Another Day*. The location: the office of Miss Moneypenny (Samantha Bond) on Pinewood Studios' Stage B. Scene 135 begins with MI6 operative Charles Robinson (Colin Salmon) passing through on his way to see M (Dame Judi Dench).
- **July 30, 2006**: Date when the 007 Stage burned down for a second time, only a week after shooting ended on *Casino Royale*. Crews were dismantling a huge replica of Venice featured in the film when the fire broke out.
- **November 15, 2013**: Date of a joint announcement by MGM and the estate of producer Kevin McClory, announcing that the studio had acquired all the rights to the James Bond novel *Thunderball*, previously controlled by McClory, who cowrote the original story treatment with Ian Fleming and screenwriter Jack Whittingham. This agreement officially brought Blofeld and SPECTRE back into the Eon Productions 007 universe.

Davi, Robert (June 26, 1951–   ): Charismatic American character actor who portrayed ruthless South American drug lord Franz Sanchez in *Licence to Kill*. Davi was a breath of fresh air after the comic book Bond villains of the Roger Moore films and the buffoons in *The Living Daylights*.

Actor Robert Davi played suave drug lord Franz Sanchez in *Licence to Kill*. *Steve Rubin Collection*

Like Timothy Dalton's version of Bond, Davi's Sanchez is a darker, more realistic character who is totally immersed in his corrupt world. Such a villain was necessary in order to give Bond's revenge mission credibility—in line with the way Ian Fleming portrayed the relationships between Bond and the villains in his first 007 novel, *Casino Royale*. Remembered Davi, "Timothy and I were fans of the Bond books. We went back to *Casino Royale* because they wanted a grittier Bond. Fleming never thought of Bond as a goody two shoes. I call Timothy Dalton the father of Daniel Craig. . . . Timothy brought that intensity and darkness as an actor."*

Born in Astoria, Queens, Davi made his motion picture debut as Vito Genovese in director Richard C. Sarafian's period crime drama *Gangster Wars* (1981). Two roles in the 1980s raised his profile considerably: opera-singing villain Jake Fratelli in *The Goonies* (1985) and FBI special agent Big Johnson in *Die Hard* (1988). His costar in the latter film, Grand L. Bush, was also cast in *Licence to Kill*, as Hawkins.

Dawson, Anthony (October 18, 1916–January 8, 1992): Lean-faced Scottish character actor who portrayed villainous Professor R. J. Dent in *Dr. No*. He also portrayed Ernst Stavro Blofeld in *From Russia with Love* (though his voice was dubbed by Eric Pohlmann). Prior to his Bond experience, Dawson had the memorable role of Grace Kelly's attempted murderer in director

---

* George Simpson, "James Bond Villain Robert Davi 'Timothy Dalton Is the Father of Daniel Craig's Darker 007,'" *Daily Express*, June 11, 2019.

Alfred Hitchcock's 1954 thriller *Dial M for Murder*. . A native of Edinburgh, Dawson made his credited motion picture debut in director Anthony Asquith's *Johnny in the Clouds* (1945), a.k.a. *The Way to the Stars*. A favorite of director Terence Young, he was cast in Young's World War II drama *They Were Not Divided* (1950), which also featured future Bond players Edward Underdown (*Thunderball*), Michael

British character actor Anthony Dawson portrayed the nefarious Professor Dent, an agent of the title character in *Dr No*. *Courtesy of the David Reinhardt Collection*

Brennan, Desmond Llewelyn, Christopher Lee, and Peter Burton. In 1967, Dawson joined fellow Bond players Daniela Bianchi, Adolfo Celi, Bernard Lee, and Lois Maxwell in the Bond spoof *Operation Kid Brother*, which starred Sean Connery's kid brother, Neil Connery.

Day of the Dead (a.k.a. Dia de los Muertos): Mexican holiday often celebrated with elaborate parades and pageantry, which become the backdrop for the *Spectre* pre-credits teaser set in Mexico City. Working without MI6 authorization, James Bond (Daniel Craig) assassinates terrorist Marco Sciarra (Alessandro Cremona) during a tense mano a mano inside a helicopter that threatens to kill festivalgoers below. Thanks to the modern world's ubiquitous surveillance cameras—not to mention everyone's handy iPhone—it's another example of Bond flouting the "secret" aspect of being a secret agent. Certainly his highest-profile incident since he killed another terrorist inside a foreign embassy compound in *Casino Royale*.

de Armas, Ana (April 30, 1988–   ): Cuban leading lady who portrayed Paloma in *No Time to Die*. A Havana native, she made her motion picture debut as Marie in director Manuel Guitiérrez Aragón's crime drama *Virgin Rose* (2006). Her subsequent feature film credits include *Knock Knock* (2015); *War Dogs* (2016); *Blade*

It's macabre party time in Mexico City during Day of the Dead festivities in the *Spectre* pre-titles teaser. *Courtesy of the Anders Frejdh Collection*

Sultry Ana de Armas. *Steve Rubin Collection*

Isaach De Bankolé portrayed African rebel leader Steven Obanno in *Casino Royale*. *Courtesy of photographer David J. Barron*

Runner 2049 (2017); *Yesterday* (2019), alongside fellow Bond player Robert Carlyle, who portrayed John Lennon uncredited; and Rian Johnson's murder mystery *Knives Out* (2019), in which she played unassuming nurse Marta Cabrera opposite Daniel Craig's southern detective Benoit Blanc.

Cuban actress Ana de Armas as Paloma in *No Time to Die*. *Courtesy of the Anders Frejdh Collection*

De Bankolé, Isaach (August 12, 1957–   ): Ivory Coast native who portrayed African rebel leader Steven Obanno in *Casino Royale*. Born in Abidjan, De Bankolé made his motion picture debut in director Jean-Paul Feuillebois's comedy *Comment draguer tous les mecs*, or "How to Flirt

with All the Guys" (1984). More recently, he portrayed the River Tribe elder with the distinctive lip plate in *Black Panther* (2018).

De Beers: Famous European diamond broker that agrees, should it become necessary, to supply NATO with the $280 million ransom in *Thunderball*.

de Bleuchamp, Count Balthazar: Title to which Ernst Stavro Blofeld (Telly Savalas) aspires in *On Her Majesty's Secret Service*. Masquerading as a world-famous allergist who runs an exclusive clinic high in the Swiss Alps, Blofeld has also been tracing his ancestral line and now wishes to claim the de Bleuchamp title. He hopes that the London College of Arms will validate such a claim—a connection that leads James Bond (George Lazenby) to impersonate the college's Sir Hilary Bray (George Baker) to infiltrate Blofeld's fortress of Piz Gloria. It is 007's

Cinematographer Roger Deakins (second from left) goes over a scene with director Sam Mendes (in white) while Daniel Craig waits patiently during location work off Macao on *Skyfall*. *Steve Rubin Collection*

hope that he can lure Blofeld to Augsburg, the ancestral home of the de Bleuchamps, where he can be arrested by the British Secret Service. Unfortunately, Blofeld is too busy to travel—he's about to unleash a deadly germ strain to threaten the world's livestock and agriculture—and Blofeld orders Bond/Sir Hilary to finish his research within the walls of Piz Gloria.

de Keyser, David (August 22, 1927–   ): British actor who portrayed the unnamed plastic surgeon in charge of creating clones of Blofeld (Charles Gray) in *Diamonds Are Forever*. He also dubbed the voice of Marc-Ange Draco (Gabriele Ferzetti) in *On Her Majesty's Secret Service*. A native of London, De Keyser made his credited motion picture debut in director John Boorman's musical comedy *Having a Wild Weekend* (1965).

De Wolff, Francis (January 7, 1913–April 18, 1984): British character actor who portrayed Vavra the fiery gypsy leader in *From Russia*

with Love. A native of Essex, England, De Wolff made his credited motion picture debut in director Bernard Vorhaus's crime drama *Ten Minute Alibi* (1935). A versatile character actor for decades, De Wolff played swarthy Norman knight Front De Boeuf in *Ivanhoe* (1952), with future Bond stuntmen Bob Simmons and George Leech doing his stunt riding during the jousting matches. He reprised the role of Front De Boeuf in a BBC television miniseries in 1970. De Wolff also played Albert Hardcastle, the corrupt theater owner opposite Bill Travers, Virginia McKenna, Peter Sellers, and Margaret Rutherford in the delightful British comedy *The Smallest Show on Earth* (1957), a.k.a. *Big Time Operators*.

Deakins, Roger (May 24, 1949–   ): Academy Award-winning British cinematographer, frequently associated with the Coen brothers, who shot *Skyfall*, receiving an Oscar nomination for his work on the film. Born in Torquay, Devon, England, Deakins made his feature film debut as a cinematographer on director Chris Boger's period drama *Marquis de Sade's Justine* (1977). His credits include, with his Academy Award nominations noted via boldface: *Mountains of the Moon* (1990); *Barton Fink* (1991); ***The Shawshank Redemption*** (1994); ***Fargo*** (1996); *Courage Under Fire* (1996); ***Kundun*** (1997); *The Big Lebowski* (1998); ***O Brother, Where Art Thou?*** (2000); ***The Man Who Wasn't There*** (2001); *A Beautiful Mind* (2001); ***No Country for Old Men*** (2007); ***The Assassination of Jesse James by the Coward Robert Ford*** (2007); ***The Reader*** (2008), nomination shared with Chris Menges; ***True Grit*** (2010); ***Prisoners*** (2013); ***Unbroken*** (2014); ***Sicario*** (2015), ***Blade Runner 2049*** (2017), and ***1917*** (2019), the last two of which won the Oscar for Best Achievement in Cinematography.

Dean, Jimmy (August 10, 1928–June 13, 2010): American musician, actor, and entrepreneur who portrayed kidnapped billionaire Willard Whyte in *Diamonds Are Forever*. Probably better known for founding the company that created "Jimmy Dean Pure Pork Sausage" than his acting career, Dean nevertheless made his feature film debut in the Bond movie. Dean's number-one hit song "Big Bad John" was adapted into a feature film of the same name in 1990, with Dean playing his only other feature part as Cletus Morgan.

defibrillator: What saves the life of James Bond (Daniel Craig) when his martini is poisoned by Valenka (Ivana Milicevic), girlfriend of master spy Le Chiffre (Mads Mikkelsen) in *Casino Royale*. Built into the glove compartment of Bond's Aston Martin, the defibrillator fails to work and Bond passes out. Fortunately, Vesper (Eva Green) comes to his aid, reattaching a disconnected electrode and hitting the proper button to unleash a powerful charge and bring Bond back to life.

Dehn, Paul (November 5, 1912–September 30, 1976): Academy Award–winning British screenwriter and lyricist who received cowriting credit with Richard Maibaum on *Goldfinger*. When the script won an Edgar Award from the Mystery Writers of America in 1964, the witty Dehn sent a telegram to Rex Stout, president of the Mystery Writers, expressing his thanks but claiming that his contribution was only .007

percent of the finished script. Dehn went on to write four sequels for the *Planet of the Apes* series. A native of Manchester, Dehn made his motion picture debut by contributing the Oscar-winning original story (with James Bernard) for the thriller *Seven Days to Noon* (1950), which also featured future Bond players Geoffrey Keen (Defence Minister Freddie Gray in the Moore and Dalton eras), Willoughby Gray, and Patrick Macnee. He was later nominated for the Oscar for Best Writing, Screenplay Adapted from other Material, for *Murder on the Orient Express* (1974), his final feature credit.

Deighton, Len (February 18, 1929–   ): British thriller author who, according to director Terence Young, wrote the first draft of *From Russia with Love* in 1962 and accompanied Young on the first location trip to Istanbul. Richard Maibaum wrote the final script and received sole screenplay credit. Deighton, born in Marylebone, London, also collaborated with Sean Connery and Kevin McClory on an early draft of *James Bond of the Secret Service* (a.k.a. *Warhead*), the proposed remake of *Thunderball* that was never shot. Deighton is the author of the popular Harry Palmer series of spy novels, three of which were made into films by producer Harry Saltzman: *The Ipcress File*, *Funeral in Berlin*, and *Billion Dollar Brain*.

Del Toro, Benicio (February 19, 1967–   ): Academy Award–winning Puerto Rican character actor who portrayed deadly Dario, one of Franz Sanchez's killers in *Licence to Kill*. Born in San Germán, Puerto Rico, Del Toro won his Oscar for Best Supporting Actor when he played an honest Mexican policeman in director Steven Soderbergh's *Traffic* (2000). He made his feature film acting debut as Duke the Dog-Faced Boy in *Big*

Actor Benicio Del Toro portrayed Sanchez's knife-wielding henchman Dario in *Licence to Kill*. *Steve Rubin Collection*

Top Pee-Wee (1988). Now one of Hollywood's most popular actors, Del Toro's credits include: *The Usual Suspects* (1995), *Sin City* (2005), *The Wolfman* (2010), *Guardians of the Galaxy* (2014), *Sicario* (2015), *Star Wars: The Last Jedi* (2017), *Avengers: Infinity War* (2018), and *Sicario: Day of the Soldado* (2018).

"delicatessen in stainless steel": Wheelchair-bound Ernst Stavro Blofeld's desperate and basically ludicrous bribe to prevent Bond (Roger Moore) from dumping him into an industrial chimney in the *For Your Eyes Only* teaser. It is certainly one of the most ridiculous lines of dialogue ever uttered by a Bond villain. Interestingly, it is a line that screenwriter Richard Maibaum denies ever writing. NOTE: Although he was dressed like Blofeld, the wheelchair-bound villain went unidentified in the film—unsurprising, since producer Kevin McClory owned the film rights to *Thunderball*, the SPECTRE organization, and Blofeld at that time.

Delta-9: A toxic gas that Goldfinger (Gert Fröbe) intends to spray into the atmosphere above Fort Knox, Kentucky, in order to immobilize the garrison of forty-one thousand US soldiers in *Goldfinger*. Although he tells Pussy Galore (Honor Blackman) and his gangster associates that the gas will merely put the soldiers to sleep, in actuality it is a deadly nerve agent. The gas is effectively tested on the "hoods convention" at Goldfinger's Auric Stud ranch. Fortunately, thanks to her interest in James Bond (Sean Connery), Pussy switches out the gas in the canisters at the last minute before they can be deployed against the soldiers.

Dench, Dame Judi (December 9, 1934–   ): Academy Award–winning British actress who won the part of M opposite Pierce Brosnan in *GoldenEye* and continued to play the part into the Daniel Craig era, appearing in *Tomorrow Never Dies*, *The World Is Not Enough*, *Die Another Day*, *Casino Royale*, *Quantum of Solace*, and *Skyfall*. Her style: tough, no-nonsense, ballsy. She seldom cut James Bond a break but respected the hell out of him. Their relationship culminated in *Skyfall*, when she herself became the target of Silva (Javier Bardem), a ruthless former MI6 operative with revenge on his mind. A native of York, North Yorkshire, England,

Dame Judi Dench added a new chapter in James Bond film history when she took on the role of M
Courtesy of the Anders Frejdh Collection

Dench has been nominated seven times for an Academy Award, winning for Best Supporting Actress as a marvelous Queen Elizabeth in *Shakespeare in Love* (1998). She was also nominated for *Mrs. Brown* (1997), Best Actress; *Chocolat* (2000), Best Supporting Actress; *Iris* (2001), Best Actress; *Mrs. Henderson Presents* (2005), Best Actress; *Notes on a Scandal* (2006), Best Actress; and *Philomena* (2013), Best Actress. Dench made her feature debut as Miss Humphries in director Charles Crichton's crime drama *The Third Secret* (1964).

Dent, Professor R. J.: Dr. No's chief operative in Jamaica, portrayed by Anthony Dawson in *Dr. No*. An oily-haired, suspicious-looking local geologist who runs Dent Laboratories in Kingston, Dent leads a team of assassins that kills John Strangways (Tim Moxon) and his new secretary (Dolores Keator) but bungles all attempts to take out Bond (Sean Connery).

After Bond disposes of the famous tarantula in his bed, Dent tries again to kill Bond at Miss Taro's cottage in the Blue Mountains. But 007 is sitting behind Dent in the darkened bedroom as the assassin pumps six shots from his Smith & Wesson automatic into a bundle of sheets and pillows designed to look like Bond and Taro. Ordered to drop his gun, Dent confesses that Strangways was killed and starts to explain other details in the hopes of distracting Bond long enough so that he can retrieve his pistol.

Finally diving for his gun, Dent comes up empty, prompting 007's classic remark: "That's a Smith & Wesson. You've had your six." Dent is then promptly blown away by Bond in a manner that pretty much defines his double-0 prefix—licensed to kill. It would, however, be one of the last times that 007 would shoot down an unarmed assailant. The series would head in a lighter direction—until Daniel Craig assumed the Bond helm in 2006.

Derval, Dominique "Domino": Emilio Largo's French mistress in *Thunderball*, and the sister of murdered NATO aerial observer François Derval (Paul Stassino). Portrayed by actress and former Miss France Claudine Auger, her nickname is "Domino," which appears on her ankle bracelet.

Bond (Sean Connery) first sees Domino's photograph in his official dossier for Operation Thunderball. Their first meeting is quite romantic, occurring underwater in the Caribbean when Bond gallantly removes her trapped foot from the coral. He gradually learns that she's Largo's unhappy mistress, and that she has no idea that he's involved in anything criminal. Later, when Bond tells Domino that Largo had her brother murdered, she becomes vengeful. In the film's dramatic conclusion, she kills Largo with a speargun.

Domino will always be my favorite Bond girl, and I consider her probably the most beautiful woman in the series. She also appears in one of the most romantic films in the series. Her encounters with Bond on Love Beach, in the casino, underwater, and at the Palmyra pool are all wonderful sequences that work particularly well with John Barry's intimate musical score. And she's dressed in a series of breathtaking bikinis and bathing suits selected by wardrobe designer Anthony Mendleson. Claudine Auger fills the role so perfectly, it's no wonder producers Broccoli and Saltzman chose her over consummate English actress Julie Christie, another possibility for the part.

Derval, Major François: A NATO aerial observer, portrayed by actor Paul Stassino, who is murdered by SPECTRE in *Thunderball*. Referred to as "Commandant" despite his rank of major, he's assigned to a nuclear bomber squadron based in rural England. Derval is seduced by SPECTRE assassin Fiona Volpe (Luciana Paluzzi) and murdered by Angelo Palazzi (also Stassino), a mercenary who, thanks to plastic surgery, is now an exact duplicate of Derval.

James Bond (Sean Connery) discovers Derval's body at the Shrublands health clinic. This clue leads him to Nassau in the Bahamas and to Derval's sister, Dominque "Domino" Derval (Claudine Auger), who happens to be the mistress of the mysterious Emilio Largo (Adolfo Celi), a multimillionaire and SPECTRE spymaster.

Swimming to a downed NATO bomber that has been hijacked to the Bahamas by Palazzi, Bond finds the doppelganger's body in the plane's cockpit, where he drowned when Largo cut his air hose. Among his effects, Bond finds Derval's identification disk and watch—clues that finally convince Domino that Largo is her enemy.

Di Portanova, Sandra and Ricky: American owners of the fabulous Acapulco house that became the Isthmus City home of Franz Sanchez (Robert Davi) in *Licence to Kill*. With its Moorish arcades, wide decks, and terraces, the house became the perfect Bond film location.

di Vicenzo, Contessa Teresa "Tracy": SEE "Tracy."

DIAMONDS ARE FOREVER

(United Artists, 1971) ★★★: The seventh James Bond film produced by Albert R. Broccoli and Harry Saltzman. US release date: December 17, 1971. Budget: $7 million. Worldwide box office gross: $116.0 million (US gross: $43.8 million; international gross: $72.2 million).* Running time: 119 minutes.

THE SETUP

Following the murder of his wife Tracy in *On Her Majesty's Secret Service*, James Bond (Sean Connery) is tracking her murderers, focusing on SPECTRE chief Ernst Stavro Blofeld (Charles Gray). What 007 doesn't know is that Blofeld is conducting a cloning experiment to create duplicates of himself, while simultaneously planning another one of his outlandish blackmail capers by sending a powerful laser-equipped satellite into orbit. Bond goes undercover as a diamond

* "Diamonds Are Forever (1971)," The Numbers, accessed May 11, 2020, https://www.the-numbers.com/movie/Diamonds-Are-Forever.

smuggler, a ruse that eventually leads him to Amsterdam and the apartment of sexy diamond courier Tiffany Case (Jill St. John). She leads him to Las Vegas, where Blofeld is posing as mysterious billionaire Willard Whyte.

—— BEHIND THE SCENES ——

Having lost their box office momentum with *On Her Majesty's Secret Service*, starring George Lazenby as Bond, producers Broccoli and Saltzman offered Sean Connery a sizable incentive to return to his signature 007 role. And Connery delivered, producing another epic Bond hit.

Connery was frank about his motivations for returning, and aware that the *OHMSS*'s disappointing $23 million domestic gross had garnered him some leverage. "Coming back to do this one, the wicket was better for me to make the conditions," he told a BBC interviewer in 1971. "Of not being such a pawn in the circumstances. Also to be able to get a two-picture deal as well with United Artist and myself as partners, to produce, act, or whatever." Asked whether his character had changed since *You Only Live Twice*, Connery replied "I suppose I'm a bit slower. Not quite as fit. . . . I have no real dissatisfaction with the character as such. I only read three Bond novels. I read *Thunderball*, because that was the first one we were supposed to do. And I read *Live and Let Die* and *From Russia with Love*."*

In their efforts to recapture the old Bond magic, the producers knew that a return to the seriousness of *From Russia with Love* was not a wise move. They took the *Goldfinger* approach

Stuntwoman Donna Garrett works on a move with stunt arranger Bob Simmons (doubling Sean Connery) while director Guy Hamilton (right) looks on during shooting on *Diamonds Are Forever*. *Courtesy of the Anders Frejdh Collection*

to 007 filmmaking, which meant an outrageous caper, plenty of gorgeous women to dally with Bond, and action sequences that bordered on the unbelievable. *Diamonds Are Forever* has these elements in good quantity. A more mature-looking Sean Connery has liaisons with Tiffany Case (Jill St. John) and Plenty O'Toole (Lana Wood), and battles bodyguards Bambi (Lola Larson) and Thumper (Trina Parks). He performs unbelievable stunts in a stolen moon buggy

---

* Special features, *Diamonds Are Forever*, James Bond Ultimate Edition (1971; MGM, 2006), DVD.

Screenwriter Tom Mankiewicz said that Sean Connery had a pro's grace in his return to 007 duty in *Diamonds Are Forever*. *Courtesy of the David Reinhardt Collection*

and a swift Ford Mustang fastback. And he faces some of his most unusual enemies, including the gay assassins Mr. Wint (Bruce Glover) and Mr. Kidd (Putter Smith); the burly diamond smuggler Peter Franks (Joe Robinson); and, of all things, a foppish Blofeld, played in ham fashion by Charles Gray, who previously played a deadpan Dikko Henderson in *You Only Live Twice*. Producers would continue to follow the *Goldfinger* model for an uninterrupted decade, before returning to a more serious tone in *For Your Eyes Only*.

THE CAST

James Bond	Sean Connery
Tiffany Case	Jill St. John
Ernst Stavro Blofeld	Charles Gray
Plenty O'Toole	Lana Wood
Willard Whyte	Jimmy Dean
Bert Saxby	Bruce Cabot
Mr. Wint	Bruce Glover
Mr. Kidd	Putter Smith
Felix Leiter	Norman Burton
Professor Dr. Metz	Joseph Furst
M	Bernard Lee
Q	Desmond Llewelyn
Sir Donald Munger	Laurence Naismith
Maxwell	Burt Metcalfe
Slumber	David Bauer
Shady Tree	Leonard Barr
Mrs. Whistler	Margaret Lacey
Miss Moneypenny	Lois Maxwell
Peter Franks	Joe Robinson
Bambi	Lola Larson
Thumper	Trina Parks
Klaus Hergersheimer	Ed Bishop
Barker	Larry Blake
Dr. Tynan	Henry Rowland
Plastic Surgeon	David de Keyser
Doorman (Tropicana)	Nicky Blair
Aides to Professor Dr. Metz	Constantin de Goguel
	Janos Kurucz
Tom	Shane Rimmer
Immigration Officer	Clifford Earl
Agent	Karl Held
Airline Representative	John Abineri
Blofeld's Double	Max Latimer

THE CREW

Director	Guy Hamilton
Screenplay by	Richard Maibaum
	Tom Mankiewicz
Producers	Harry Saltzman
	Albert R. Broccoli
Associate Producer	Stanley Sopel
Director of Photography	Ted Moore
Music by	John Barry
Title song performed by	Shirley Bassey
Lyrics by	Don Black
Production Designer	Ken Adam
Art Directors	Jack Maxsted
	Bill Kenney
Set Decorators	Peter Lamont
	John Austin
Production Managers	Claude Hudson
	Milton Feldman
Stunt Arrangers	Bob Simmons
	Paul Baxley
Title Designer	Maurice Binder
Visual Effects	Albert Whitlock
	Wally Veevers
Dubbing Mixer	Gordon McCallum
Sound Recordists	John Mitchell
	Alfred E. Overton
Editors	Bert Bates
	John W. Holmes

DIE ANOTHER DAY

(United Artists, 2002) ★★★: The twentieth James Bond movie produced by Eon
Productions. US release date: November 22,
2002. Budget: $142 million. Worldwide box
office gross: $431.9 million (US domestic gross:
$160.9 million; international gross: $271.0 million).* Running time: 133 minutes.

─────────────── **THE SETUP** ───────────────

After an unsuccessful attempt to thwart an
arms-for-conflict-diamonds deal by North
Korean colonel Tan-Sun Moon (Will Yun Lee),
James Bond (Pierce Brosnan) is captured and
tortured by the colonel's father, General Moon
(Kenneth Tsang). Fourteen months later, Bond
is exchanged for Tan-Sun Moon's assistant
Zao (Rick Yune); however, he is informed by M
(Dame Judi Dench) that his double-0 status is
suspended under suspicion that he leaked information to the North Koreans. Bond later escapes
from MI6 custody and tracks Zao to Cuba, where
he meets NSA agent Giacinta "Jinx" Johnson
(Halle Berry). He follows Jinx to a gene therapy
clinic, where he nearly kills Zao but manages to
retrieve a pendant that leads Bond to a cache
of conflict diamonds—jewels that bear the crest
of British billionaire businessman Gustav Graves
(Toby Stephens).

─────────────── **BEHIND THE SCENES** ───────────────

Perhaps to honor the Bond film franchise's
fortieth anniversary and the upcoming fiftieth
anniversary of the Ian Fleming 007 novels, the
producers went all out. They reached deep
into their pockets to cast a pedigreed leading
lady, bringing no less than the 2001 Academy
Award winner for Best Actress, Halle Berry, into
the Bond fold. Not since actress Diana Rigg
traded in her patented leather catsuit from
The Avengers for marriage vows with Bond in
On Her Majesty's Secret Service had a leading
lady been so heralded. Pop superstar Madonna
was hired to record the title tune and appear
in a cameo role as a fencing instructor. Touché!
And the filmmakers loaded the new film with
what was formerly a taboo practice: references

─────────────────────────
* "Die Another Day (2002)," The Numbers, accessed May 11,
2020, https://www.the-numbers.com/movie/Die-Another-Day.

and homages to the last nineteen James Bond
movies.

    Die Another Day is one of those Bond films
that is hard to pin down. It's entertaining and at
times boldly effective, especially the opening
teaser inside North Korea, Bond's torture scenes
when he's captured by the North Koreans, the
dramatic sword fight in London between Bond
and Graves, and the thrilling ending aboard a
transport plane. At other times, it strays too
far from the Bond formula, particularly when it
introduces an invisible car—which, by the way,
is barely used in the film. A true jump-the-shark
moment. But Brosnan is great, as is the supporting cast—particularly Berry, Toby Stephens, and
Rosamund Pike as Graves's assistant, the icy
Miranda Frost—and the film, though a bit of a
bust for some fans, was a huge box office hit.

─────────────── **THE CAST** ───────────────

James Bond	Pierce Brosnan
Jinx	Halle Berry
Gustav Graves	Toby Stephens
Miranda Frost	Rosamund Pike
Zao	Rick Yune
Colonel Moon	Will Yun Lee
General Moon	Kenneth Tsang
Damian Falco	Michael Madsen
M	Dame Judi Dench
Q	John Cleese
Miss Moneypenny	Samantha Bond
Charles Robinson	Colin Salmon
Raoul	Emilio Echevarría
Verity	Madonna

─────────────── **THE CREW** ───────────────

Director	Lee Tamahori
Screenplay by	Neal Purvis & Robert Wade
Producers	Barbara Broccoli Michael G. Wilson
Director of Photography	David Tattersall
Music by	David Arnold
Title song performed by	Madonna
Production Designer	Peter Lamont
Supervising Art Director	Simon Lamont
Costume Designer	Lindy Hemming
Second Unit Director	Vic Armstrong
Stunt Coordinator	George Aguilar
Surfing Coordinator	Laird Hamilton
Title Designer	Daniel Kleinman
Editors	Andrew MacRitchie Christian Wagner

Dimitrios, Alex: Terrorist arms dealer whom Bond (Daniel Craig) tracks to Paradise Island in the Bahamas in *Casino Royale*. It was Dimitrios who was picked up on the hotel surveillance camera answering the call that bomb maker Mollaka (Sébastien Foucan) made from Madagascar. Bond enters a poker game and wins Dimitrios's Aston Martin DB5 (Bond: three aces, Dimitrios: three kings), then beds his neglected wife, Solange (Caterina Murino), before tailing Dimitrios to Miami.

Dink: Statuesque blonde masseuse portrayed by Margaret Nolan, seen briefly in *Goldfinger* administering to Bond (Sean Connery) at the Fontainebleau Hotel pool in Miami Beach. She's dismissed by Bond when Felix Leiter (Cec Linder) arrives to brief him. Reason he gives: "Man talk."

"I thought I'd find you in good hands": Bond (Sean Connery) and his Miami Beach masseuse Dink (Margaret Nolan) greet Felix Leiter in *Goldfinger*. *Steve Rubin Collection*

disclaimer: Unusual legal language featured at the beginning of *A View to a Kill*. It reads, "Neither the name 'Zorin' nor any other name or character in this film is meant to portray a real company or actual person." The message was included because the name of villain Max Zorin's company, Zorin Industries, was similar to that of a real company, Zoran Ladicorbic Ltd. The real Zoran was a fashion design company, quite different from Max Zorin's microchip manufacturer, but the legal departments at Eon Productions and United Artists thought it prudent to feature the unusual disclaimer. Another disclaimer

concerning the use of the Red Cross insignia was featured at the beginning of *The Living Daylights*.

Disco Volante: Italian name for the fabulous yacht belonging to Emilio Largo (Adolfo Celi) in *Thunderball*. In English, the name translates as "Flying Saucer." Equipped with a false bottom through which SPECTRE frogmen can deposit their hijacked A-bombs, the yacht's normal speed is twenty knots. However, at the drop of a switch, the *Disco Volante* can jettison its rear superstructure—the cocoon—and transform into a swift hydrofoil craft. To fight a delaying action, the cocoon is equipped with machine guns and an artillery piece.

In *Thunderball*, 007 (Sean Connery) discovers the *Disco Volante*'s false bottom and photographs it with an infrared underwater camera supplied by Q (Desmond Llewelyn). The pictures convince him that the yacht could have picked up the stolen A-bombs without generating surface activity. When 007 later disrupts Largo's NATO project, Largo orders the cocoon jettisoned and makes his escape in the hydrofoil, which eventually grounds on a coral reef and disintegrates. The cocoon is obliterated by US Coast Guard warships.

To build the hydrofoil, production designer Ken Adam was sent to Puerto Rico in December 1964 to purchase the *Flying Fish*, an old Rodriguez hydrofoil that had once carried passengers between Venezuela and Mexico. Rodriguez was the manufacturing firm in Messina, Sicily, that had originally built swift hydrofoils for use in the Adriatic Sea.

The rusty craft was driven under its own power to a Miami shipyard for a complete overhaul. Its 1,320 horsepower Mercedes-Benz diesel engine was put into top condition to propel the extra fifty-foot cocoon that Adam was constructing nearby.

"We had two slip bolts holding the cocoon," said Adam, who used a real pleasure yacht as the prototype for his own creation. "Some of our naval experts thought it wouldn't work, but we had less trouble with the *Disco* than with any other gadget.

"The cocoon itself was about fifty feet long. We fitted it out with a yellow smokestack, two lifeboats, and a functional sundeck. Once the hydrofoil drove off, we were able to turn the cocoon into a floating arsenal. I installed the type of armament you would find on a destroyer, including an antiaircraft cannon, heavy machine guns, and armor plating."*

Special effects expert John Stears later constructed a model of both the hydrofoil and the cocoon. Both were blown apart in the water tank at Pinewood Studios.

dislocated collarbone: What Bond (Pierce Brosnan) suffers when he falls from an obliterated hot air balloon in the pre-credits teaser for *The World Is Not Enough*. To avoid sick leave, he uses his legendary sexual charms to convince Secret Service physician Dr. Molly Warmflash (Serena Scott Thomas) to send him back into action. However, the disability hampers his mobility at key times, a bit of intelligence that Elektra King (Sophie Marceau) passes on to her villainous lover Renard (Robert Carlyle).

DNA replacement therapy: Novel medical procedure sought out by sinister North Korean army officers Colonel Moon (Will Yun Lee) and Zao (Rick Yune) in *Die Another Day*. Disfigured by Bond (Pierce Brosnan) in the film's teaser, Moon and Zao attempt to alter their appearance—a procedure that could prove catastrophic for Bond and the world.

Doleman, Guy (November 22, 1923–January 30, 1996): New Zealand–born character actor who portrayed SPECTRE agent Count Lippe in *Thunderball*. After bungling his mission to kill Bond at the Shrublands health clinic, Lippe is, in turn, assassinated on the highway by motorcycle-riding Fiona Volpe (Luciana Paluzzi). A native of Hamilton, New Zealand, Doleman made his motion picture debut in director T. O. McCreadie's war drama *Always Another Dawn* (1948). He later portrayed Lieutenant Commander Farrel, a US nuclear submarine officer working for Commander Dwight Towers (Gregory Peck) in director Stanley Kramer's powerful anti-nuclear-war film *On the Beach* (1959). And he was spy Colonel Ross in the trilogy of thrillers based on Len Deighton's Harry Palmer books: *The Ipcress File* (1965), *Funeral in Berlin* (1966), and *Billion Dollar Brain* (1967).

Dolly: Buxom blonde, portrayed by Blanche Ravalec, who falls in love with Jaws (Richard Kiel) in *Moonraker*. NOTE: She has no dialogue.

---

* Ken Adam, interview by the author, London, June 17, 1977.

America's couple of 1979—Jaws (Richard Kiel) and his girlfriend Dolly (Blanche Ravalec). It takes one helluva woman to settle this man down. *Courtesy of the David Reinhardt Collection*

Domination: A fascinating 3-D video game played by Maximilian Largo (Klaus Maria Brandauer) and James Bond (Sean Connery) in *Never Say Never Again*. A mid-1980s equivalent of the obligatory game of chance between 007 and his nemesis, Domination is a high-tech battle for power as opponents fight for countries chosen at random by the machine.

Seated at opposite ends of a long table, both players face a 3-D map of the world, which then zeroes in on the randomly selected target country. Target areas light up on the country map. Whoever hits them first with the joystick-controlled laser beam scores points. Another way to win is to employ missiles. The left joystick controls two nuclear missiles, and the right one controls a shield to block the missiles. Fail to block the incoming missile and you lose the game. Winning totals are calculated in dollar amounts.

Largo chooses blue, and 007 plays red. When Bond begins the game against Largo, they're fighting for Spain at a value of $9,000, but as he struggles to keep up with his opponent, he's jolted with an electric shock and lets go of the joysticks. Largo apologizes and explains to 007 that, unlike armchair generals who never feel their soldiers' pain, the players must endure electric shocks as they fight for control. If a player lets go of the controllers to escape the shocks, he loses the game.

In the next game, fighting for Japan at a value of $16,000, Bond suffers an even larger electric shock and lets go of the joysticks again. Explaining that as the stakes increase, so does the level of pain, Largo wins again. In the third game, fighting for the United States at a value of $42,000, Bond begins to get used to the apparatus but loses anyway, after getting such a powerful shock that it throws him to the floor.

Getting to his feet, Bond is informed by Largo that he owes $67,000. Bond then says he'll play one more game, fighting for the rest of the world at a value of $325,000. This time Bond masters the machine and beats Largo at his own game, giving his nemesis such a powerful electrical shock that he's forced to forfeit. Bond then tells Largo that he'll forgo his winnings in return for one dance with his mistress Domino Petachi (Kim Basinger).

The live-action element of the Domination game sequence was filmed in a huge French rococo room inside Waddesdon Manor, the home of the Rothschild family in England. David Dryer's effects team then spent months creating the game effects, matting in elaborate laser effects over the live-action photography.

Dominique and the Enchanted Papillon: Cabaret act at the Eiffel Tower Restaurant in *A View to a Kill*. While Bond (Roger Moore) and French detective Achille Aubergine (Jean Rougerie) discuss the possibility that Max Zorin is fixing horse races, Dominique (Dominique Risbourg) performs onstage with dozens of butterflies—some of which are controlled by her dark-suited puppeteers on the balcony. Unbeknownst to Bond and Aubergine, Zorin's murderous bodyguard May Day (Grace Jones) has knocked out one of the puppeteers and assumed her identity. Her butterfly is equipped with a poisonous barb that strikes Aubergine in the face and kills him. Bond chases after May Day, but she escapes by jumping off the Eiffel

Tower and parachuting to safety—an incredible stunt performed by stuntman B. J. Worth.

Domino: The nickname of Dominique Derval (Claudine Auger) in *Thunderball*. The name, given to her by her friends, appears on her ankle bracelet. It's also the name of Maximilian Largo's mistress Domino Petachi, portrayed by Kim Basinger in *Never Say Never Again*.

Actress Claudine Auger was the perfect Domino in Thunderball. The Steve Rubin Collection

Dor, Karin (February 22, 1938–November 6, 2017; birth name: Kätherose Derr): Statuesque German actress who portrayed SPECTRE agent Helga Brandt in *You Only Live Twice*. Masquerading as the confidential secretary of Mr. Osato (Teru Shimada), she fails in her attempt to assassinate Bond and ends up as fish food in Blofeld's private piranha pool. Born in Wiesbaden, Hesse, Dor made her feature film debut in director Franz Antel's comedy *Rosen aus dem Süden* (1954). She made her English-language debut in *The Bellboy and the Playgirls* (1962), a comedy codirected by Francis Ford Coppola. Two years after *You Only Live Twice*, director Alfred Hitchcock cast the redheaded Dor as Cuban resistance leader Juanita de Cordoba in *Topaz* (1969), what she considered a highlight of her career.

double six: A specific dice combination featured in the rigged backgammon game in *Octopussy*. In order to cheat Major Clive (Stuart Saunders) out of 200,000 rupees, Kamal Khan (Louis Jourdan) has been using loaded dice that can produce a double six at will. When challenged on his uncanny ability to throw that number, Kamal shrugs and says, "It's all in the wrist."

When Bond (Roger Moore) takes over the major's game, Kamal throws another double six and 007 loses a quick 100,000 rupees. However, when the bet is doubled, Bond calls "player's privilege" and uses Kamal's loaded dice to score a double six and win the game. Such trickery recalls the golf course shenanigans in *Goldfinger*.

Dove, the: The nickname of charismatic Greek smuggler Milos Columbo (Topol) in *For Your*

Where else would Domino (Claudine Auger) end up but in the arms of 007 (Sean Connery) at the conclusion of *Thunderball? Courtesy of the David Reinhardt Collection*

Eyes Only. The moniker dates back to his days with the resistance during World War II. A white dove symbol adorns the wet suits of his divers.

 ## DR. NO

(United Artists, 1962) ★★★⯪ : The first James Bond movie produced by Albert R. Broccoli and Harry Saltzman. US release date: May 8, 1963. Budget: $1 million. Worldwide box office gross: $59.6 million (US domestic gross: $16.1 million; international gross: $43.5. million).* Running time: 111 minutes.

THE SETUP

British Secret Service operative John Strangways (Tim Moxon) has been murdered in Jamaica, and James Bond (Sean Connery)

* "Dr. No (1963)," The Numbers, accessed May 12, 2020, https://www.the-numbers.com/movie/Dr-No.

is summoned from a posh London private club to receive his briefing from M (Bernard Lee). M informs Bond that Strangways was working with the Americans to track down the source of massive interference that is disrupting their latest rocket program—and there is a possibility that the source of that interference is in the Caribbean. Bond is then sent to Jamaica to investigate—a trail that leads to a mysterious island called Crab Key and the equally mysterious man who runs it: Dr. No.

BEHIND THE SCENES

In the beginning, there was *Dr. No.* Long before the Marvel Cinematic Universe, *The Fast and the Furious, Jason Bourne,* or the *Mission: Impossible* film series, secret agent 007 appeared on the scene and ushered in an ongoing series of high-tech thrillers, loaded with sex and violence. James Bond may not have introduced sex to the cinema—moral codes had begun to relax toward the end of the 1950s, thanks to such pioneers as Elvis Presley, Marilyn Monroe, and Marlon Brando—but no film series presented sex on the big screen quite like the Bond movies. And it started with *Dr. No*.

Sylvia Trench, Miss Taro, Honey Ryder—they were extremely desirable women, filmed in various states of dress and undress, all in big-screen color. The scene on Crab Key in which Ursula Andress emerges from the water in a skimpy bikini is one of the most famous introductions of a new performer in screen history, paralleling Omar Sharif's arrival on a camel in *Lawrence of Arabia* the same year. However, producers Broccoli and Saltzman were shrewd enough to maintain a suggestive rather than an explicit approach to sex, which guaranteed that their film series would be embraced by family audiences. Like P. T. Barnum, the producers were selling the circus to everyone in town.

But it wasn't just the hint of sex that guaranteed the success of the first James Bond movie. *Dr. No* (and *From Russia with Love*, which followed) tells a realistic story—one that begins innocently enough with a bridge game in Jamaica. What remains fascinating about the first 007 adventure is its almost documentary-like approach and, at times, deadly seriousness.

You also see the last trappings of the 1950s reflected in the conservative clothing of the Secret Service communications personnel (sweaters and bow ties), the elegantly dressed women (evening gowns in major motion pictures were on their way out), and the businesslike approach to investigating a crime in the tropics. Helping flesh out the film's world are a group of colorful, extremely interesting background characters: Strangways, Professor Dent, Quarrel, M, Boothroyd, Leiter, even Sylvia Trench.

And Joseph Wiseman brought to life Dr. No— the first megalomaniac supervillain of the atomic age. No's sinister modus operandi reflected the archvillains of the past—Fu Manchu, Professor Moriarty, Ming the Merciless. But his high-tech island fortress, with its ruthlessly efficient garrison, were trappings of the modern world.

Dr. No by Jeff Marshall. *Courtesy of Jeff Marshall*

America had invented the bomb and other super-weapons, and Dr. No was the first in a gallery of supercrooks who were prepared to abuse them.

To defeat this threat required a new kind of hero as well. *Dr. No* introduced international audiences to Sean Connery—the perfect actor to bring Bond to life. He was handsome, enormously charismatic, and when he punched someone, they stayed down. For US audiences, such a two-fisted approach to the character was a key ingredient in the film's success. Producers Broccoli and Saltzman had been pushing all along for a tough main character in the style of hard-boiled American detectives like Mike Hammer or Philip

Marlowe. With Connery in the role, they got it.

Credit Broccoli and Saltzman for also assembling a fine creative team to put the first adventure together. Director Terence Young was mostly a B movie director until the Bond series. With 007, he found a character with whom he had plenty in common. Young himself was a dashing tank commander with the Irish Guards during World War II. A contemporary of Ian Fleming, Young had his own stylish savoir faire that blended perfectly with the author's work. Young was also friendly with American director John Ford, who influenced Young's filmmaking style, particularly when it came to action scenes.

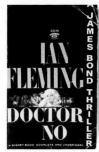

The cover of Signet's American paperback edition of the original *Dr. No* novel. *Steve Rubin Collection*

Working with Young was screenwriter Richard Maibaum, a talented, extremely witty ex-playwright who could perfectly capture the essence of Fleming's character—but with a touch of humor that wasn't present in any of the books. That Maibaum wrote with a light touch guaranteed that the Bond films would never be spoofed into oblivion (the fate of many adventure series).

Also on the Bond team was editor Peter Hunt, whose urge to bring commercial cutting styles to the feature film business would be a tremendous boon to the production. Ted Moore's camera work, Bob Simmons's stunt arranging, John Barry's plucked-guitar opening theme, Monty Norman's Caribbean-flavored score, Maurice Binder's colorful titles, John Stears's special effects— everything added up to a powerful debut.

Still, due to the reluctance of United Artists to give the film a big splash in the United States, the film opened in America with no premiere and little fanfare. If you'd have called a San Fernando Valley theater in Los Angeles in the spring of 1963, you would have been told that the picture was called "Doctor Number" and the star was "Seen Connery."

Despite its halfhearted release, *Dr. No* made a tidy profit and guaranteed the production of a second Bond film, *From Russia with Love*. After the success of *Goldfinger* in 1964–1965, *Dr. No* and *From Russia with Love* were rereleased and became the most successful second-run double feature in film history.

THE CAST

James Bond	Sean Connery
Honey	Ursula Andress
Dr. No	Joseph Wiseman
Felix Leiter	Jack Lord
M	Bernard Lee
Professor Dent	Anthony Dawson
Quarrel	John Kitzmiller
Miss Taro	Zena Marshall
Sylvia Trench	Eunice Gayson
Miss Moneypenny	Lois Maxwell
Puss-Feller	Lester Pendergast
John Strangways	Tim Moxon
Girl Photographer	Margaret LeWars
Mr. Jones	Reggie Carter
Major Boothroyd (Armorer)	Peter Burton
Duff	William Foster-Davis
Playdell-Smith	Louis Blaazer
Sister Rose	Michel Mok
Sister Lily	Yvonne Shima
Mary, Strangways' Secretary	Dolores Keator

THE CREW

Director	Terence Young
Screenplay by	Richard Maibaum
	Johanna Harwood
	Berkely Mather
Based on the novel by	Ian Fleming
Producers	Harry Saltzman
	Albert R. Broccoli
Director of Photography	Ted Moore
Music by	Monty Norman
Orchestrated by	Burt Rhodes
Conducted by	Eric Rodgers
James Bond theme played by	John Barry Orchestra
"Three Blind Mice," "Jump Up,"	
and "Under the Mango Tree"	Byron Lee and the
	Dragonaires
Production Designer	Ken Adam
Art Director	Syd Cain
Makeup	John O'Gorman
Hairstylist	Eileen Warwick
Production Manager	L. C. Rudkin
Assistant Director	Clive Reed
Continuity	Helen Whitson
Camera Operator	John Winbolt
Title Designer	Maurice Binder
Special Effects	Frank George
Animation	Trevor Bond
	Robert Ellis
Editor	Peter Hunt

Sean Connery and his bevy of women in *Dr. No* (left to right: Eunice Gayson, Zena Marshall, and Ursula Andress).
Courtesy of the David Reinhardt Collection

Bond (Sean Connery) and Honey (Ursula Andress) prepare to meet Dr. No. *Courtesy of the David Reinhardt Collection*

Dr. Shatterhand's castle: A feudal stronghold in Kyushu, Japan, introduced by author Ian Fleming in the novel *You Only Live Twice*. Honeycombed with deadly volcanic fumaroles, poisonous plants, and terrifying insects, the castle becomes a magnet for locals eager to commit suicide. Its owner is none other than SPECTRE chieftain Ernst Stavro Blofeld, now retired to private life and masquerading as the very neutral Swiss citizen Dr. Shatterhand. For the movie adaptation, producer Cubby Broccoli tried to replicate this medieval bastion on a location scout to Japan in March 1966. Crisscrossing the island of Kyushu in a French-built Alouette helicopter that spring were Broccoli, director Lewis Gilbert, cinematographer Freddie Young, production designer Ken Adam, and military liaison Charles Russhon. Nowhere could they find a location that matched the description of the castle in Fleming's book.

Remembered Gilbert, "We didn't see one castle on the Japanese coastline, for the very simple reason that the Japanese don't build castles on the coast. Because of the typhoons, it's too dangerous. Any castles were built inland to defend strategic mountain passes and valleys. It was frustrating for us, because we couldn't find the most important setting in Fleming's book. We searched every inch of the Japanese coastlines and drew an entire blank. Not one battlement."*

---

* Lewis Gilbert, interview by the author, London, June 15, 1977.

The trip was not entirely without results. During one of the helicopter scouts, the crew came across a Japanese national park filled with dormant volcanoes, one of which was a crater lake. The scenery inspired Ken Adam to instead build Blofeld's base inside the cone of one of the volcanoes. Its roof would be made out of solid metal, camouflaged to look like the surface of a crater lake.

Draco, Marc-Ange: Head of the notorious Union Corse—one of the biggest crime syndicates in Europe—and the father of Contessa Teresa "Tracy" di Vicenzo (Diana Rigg), portrayed by actor Gabriele Ferzetti and voiced by David de Keyser in *On Her Majesty's Secret Service*. One of the most sympathetic Mafia dons ever to grace the screen, Draco runs several legitimate business fronts, including construction, electronics, and agricultural concerns. Bond (George Lazenby) meets Draco at his offices at Draco Construction in Portugal. A native of Corsica, Draco met Tracy's mother, an English girl, when he was on the run from the authorities. She died when Tracy was twelve.

Draco is determined to help his daughter find the right husband (her first husband killed himself in a Maserati with one of his mistresses), so he likes the fact that Bond is interested in her. He offers 007 a dowry of 1 million pounds sterling. Bond declines the generous offer but does mention an interest in Draco's intelligence sources, particularly in regard to the whereabouts of mysterious SPECTRE chief Ernst Stavro Blofeld (Telly Savalas). Draco will only admit that some of his men have defected to SPECTRE.

However, when Tracy threatens to run away unless he tells Bond what he needs to know, Draco admits that there may be a lead through a lawyer named Gebrüder Gumbold (James Bree), who has offices in Bern, Switzerland. Later, when Tracy is captured by Blofeld, Draco joins Bond in a full-scale assault on their mutual enemy's mountain fortress of Piz Gloria. And, true to his promise, he gives Bond a check for 1 million pounds when 007 weds his daughter at the film's conclusion. Bond, of course, returns the money.

"dragon" tank: Dr. No's diesel-powered anti-personnel ATV on Crab Key in *Dr. No*. Equipped with a flamethrower and armor plate, and painted with dragon markings to frighten superstitious locals, the vehicle doesn't deter Bond and Quarrel, who launch an ill-fated assault on the "monster." The vehicle was based on a swamp vehicle first seen by Ian Fleming on the island of Inagua, Bahamas, in 1956.

Drax, Hugo: Fanatical billionaire industrialist, portrayed by Michael Lonsdale in *Moonraker*, who plans to destroy the human population of Earth with a strain of toxic nerve gas dispersed from outer space. His plan for mass murder completed, Drax will the repopulate the planet with his own master race.

Drax is the head of Drax Industries (a.k.a. Drax Enterprise Corporation), a multinational company that, among other things, manufactures space shuttles—known as Moonrakers—in California with components from countries around the world. His own fleet of Moonraker shuttles, which are based in South America, will transport his master race into space. There they will live on a radar-invisible space station until Earth's depopulation has been completed. When his orbiting

Moonraker's billionaire aerospace entrepreneur Hugo Drax—another megalomaniac in a long line of megalomaniacs in the Bond series. *Courtesy of the Anders Frejdh Collection*

installation is overrun by US astro forces, Drax is cornered by James Bond (Roger Moore) and tossed out of the station's air lock into airless outer space oblivion.

Dryden: Duplicitous British agent portrayed by Malcolm Sinclair in the *Casino Royale* pre-credits teaser. He's assassinated by Bond (Daniel Craig), becoming his second kill and making him eligible for double-0 status.

Dubin, Gary (May 5, 1959–October 8, 2016): Kid actor in *Diamonds Are Forever* who competes against Tiffany Case (Jill St. John) to win a stuffed dog in the water gun concession at the Circus Circus Hotel and Casino in Las Vegas. "I saw the whole thing. The machine's fixed! Who's she? Your mother?!" the boy protests to the barker. Probably best known for playing Danny Bonaduce's friend Punky Lazaar on the TV series *The Partridge Family* (6 episodes, 1971–1974), Dubin went on to play one of the hapless teenagers victimized by Bruce the Shark in *Jaws 2* (1978). A Los Angeles native, Dubin made his uncredited feature film debut in director Delbert Mann's romantic comedy *Fitzwilly* (1967), which also featured an uncredited Laurence Naismith (*Diamonds Are Forever*).

Duck Inn: A seventeenth-century pub near Canterbury, England, that was a favorite watering hole of Bond author Ian Fleming, who lived nearby. It was featured in the book *Moonraker* and inspired Fleming to give James Bond his famous numerical designation. According to an item published in the *London Daily Telegraph* on September 18, 1991, Fleming always took the 007 bus to the pub. Hence Bond became agent 007.

Dufour, Corinne: Hugo Drax's beautiful executive assistant and helicopter pilot, portrayed by Corinne Cléry in *Moonraker*. Based at Drax's enormous French estate, which has been rebuilt brick by brick near Drax's Los Angeles space shuttle manufacturing plant, Dufour becomes an early bedmate for Bond (Roger Moore). Unfortunately, in Drax's eyes her dalliance with Bond also marks her for early termination.

After being unceremoniously dismissed, she is chased through a nearby forest and devoured by Drax's vicious Dobermans. This sequence was featured effectively in the film's unusual teaser trailer campaign, which contrasted the tranquility of a picturesque forest scene with the deadly hounds killing their human prey.

Duggan, Gerry (July 10, 1909–March 27, 1992): Irish character actor who portrayed Bond's affable caddy Hawker in *Goldfinger*. Born in Dublin, Duggan made his motion picture debut in *The Siege of Pinchgut* (1959), a.k.a. *Four Desperate Men*, a crime drama that netted Duggan a British Academy of Film and Television Arts (BAFTA) nomination for most promising newcomer of the year (he lost to Hayley Mills in *Tiger Bay*).

Duke of Wellington portrait: A painting by Goya found in the living room of the underground fortress of Dr. No (Joseph Wiseman) in the film of the same name. The real Duke of Wellington portrait was actually stolen from the National Gallery in London in August 1961, just six months prior to the start of principal photography on *Dr. No*. Hence Bond's double take upon seeing the portrait in Dr. No's lair. The Wellington's appearance was suggested by director Terence Young's script supervisor, Johanna Harwood, who received cocredit on the script with Richard Maibaum and Berkely Mather. Originally, the scene was going to feature a recently heisted Picasso.

Duran Duran: British pop group who recorded the rousing title track for *A View to a Kill*. As of this book's press time, it's the only Bond opening-titles track ever to have reached number 1 on *Billboard's* Hot 100 singles chart. Duran Duran, which at the time of their Bond performance included Simon Le Bon, Nick Rhodes, and John Taylor, adapted their name from that of the wacky character with the "orgasmatron" in the science fiction film *Barbarella* (1968). The band first surfaced in 1978 in a club called Barbarella's.

John Taylor, Nick Rhodes, and Simon Le Bon of Duran Duran *Steve Rubin Collection*

Easton, Sheena (April 27, 1959–   ; birth name: Sheena Shirley Orr): Scottish pop singer who sang the title track to *For Your Eyes Only* (1981). Thanks to opening-titles producer Maurice Binder, Easton is the only musical performer, to date, to sing on camera in the Bond film series.

Eaton, Shirley (January 12, 1937–   ): The famous "golden girl" of *Goldfinger*, Eaton portrayed the villain's girl Friday, Jill Masterson, who dies of skin suffocation when her entire body is painted gold by Oddjob. Who could ever forget Eaton's introduction in the film? She's lying on a chaise lounge on the balcony of Goldfinger's Miami Beach hotel suite, attired in a black bra and panties, while she uses binoculars and a radio transmitter to help her boss cheat at gin. When 007 (Sean Connery) sneaks into the suite and turns off the transmitter, she whirls around, showing plenty of cleavage, and asks, "Who are you?" Bond gives his standard retort, "Bond, James Bond," while, thanks to composer John Barry, moody Bond music rises in the background. Definitely one of the great moments in the series.

A native of Edgware, Middlesex, England, Eaton made her credited motion picture debut as Millicent "Milly" Groaker in director Ralph Thomas's comedy *Doctor in the House* (1954), which also featured future Bond player Geoffrey Keen (Defence Minister Freddie Gray in the Moore and Dalton eras). As a fan of crime novelist Mickey Spillane, producer Albert R. Broccoli no doubt saw Eaton in director Roy Rowland's Spillane adaptation *The Girl Hunters* (1963) before casting her in *Goldfinger*. Post-Bond, Eaton made a memorable impression as Dr. Margaret E. "Maggie" Hanford opposite Lloyd Bridges, Brian Kelly, David McCallum, and Keenan Wynn in the rousing adventure film *Around the World Under the Sea* (1966). Two years later, she costarred opposite future Bond players Christopher Lee and Tsai Chin in *The Blood of Fu Manchu* (1968). She soon retired from acting to raise a family.

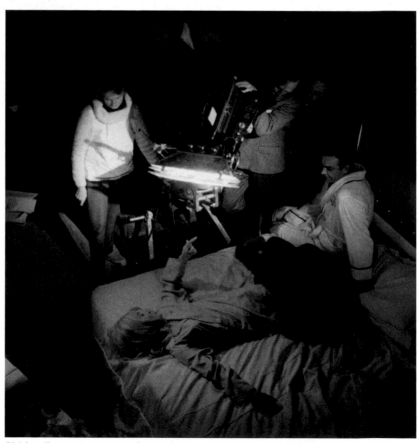

Shirley Eaton gets some last-minute staging instructions during bed-play with Sean Connery in *Goldfinger*. In this shot, you can see how intimate staged love scenes can be. *Courtesy of the Anders Frejdh Collection*

Eden Project, the: A botanist's playground of biodomes filled with one hundred thousand plants from five thousand species, this real-life international destination was a principal location in *Die Another Day*. Located in Cornwall, in remote southwestern England, the Eden Project served as the showroom of environmentalist Gustav Graves (Toby Stephens). Graves is supposed to be keen on transforming barren icebound northlands into gardens, but that public facade is at odds with his real intentions. Due to the delicate nature of the actual facility, the production was given extremely limited access. Additional sequences were shot on a lush Eden Project facsimile built by production designer Peter Lamont on Stage E at Pinewood Studios.

Eilean Donan Castle: Real Scottish castle used as an MI6 field headquarters in *The World Is Not Enough*. It's located near the Isle of Skye in western Scotland. The same castle was used in the 1986 film *Highlander*, which costarred the most famous man of Scotland, Sean Connery.

Eilish, Billie (December 18, 2001   ; birth name: Billie Eilish Pirate Baird O'Connell): Ethereal American singer-songwriter, of Irish and Scottish descent, who warbled the soulful title tune to *No Time to Die*, and cowrote it with her brother, Finneas O'Connell. She is the youngest artist to ever record a James Bond title tune. A native of Los Angeles, and the daughter of voice actor and screenwriter Maggie Baird and construction worker and amateur musician Patrick O'Connell, Eilish began her career performing with Finneas's band, the Slightlys. Her debut single was "Ocean Eyes" (2015), and her first album was *When We All Fall Asleep, Where Do We Go?* (2019), which debuted at number one on the *Billboard* 200, making Eilish the first artist born after the turn of the millennium to have a number-one album in the United States. She made her television performing debut in 2016, when she sang "Six Feet Under" on the television series *Pretty Little Liars*. She made her feature film debut on the romantic drama *Everything, Everything* (2017), on which she sang "Ocean Eyes." Eilish won five Grammy Awards in 2020.

Ekberg, Anita (September 29, 1931–January 11, 2015): Voluptuous Swedish actress whose mouth became a key plot point in *From Russia with Love*. Alerted to an unannounced police search—the cops are actually the sons of sympathetic Turkish agent Kerim Bey (Pedro Armendariz)—Bulgarian assassin Krilencu (Fred Haggerty) attempts to sneak out of his Istanbul apartment by using a trapdoor built inside a billboard featuring an advertisement for the 1963 Albert R. Broccoli / Harry Saltzman production *Call Me Bwana*. Ekberg starred in the film, and she's prominently featured on the billboard; in fact, the door actually opens right into her mouth. Krilencu never makes it to safety, as he's gunned down by Kerim Bey—prompting another one of Richard Maibaum's great lines for Sean Connery: "She should have kept her mouth shut."

Born in Malmö, Ekberg was Miss Sweden 1950 and made her credited feature film debut as Wei Ling opposite John Wayne and Lauren Bacall in *Blood Alley* (1955). However, it was her appearance as the mesmerizing Sylvia in Federico Fellini's *La Dolce Vita* (1960) that rocketed her to stardom. She married *Thunderball*'s Felix Leiter, Rik Van Nutter, in 1963, a union that lasted twelve years before they divorced in 1975.

Ekland, Britt (October 6, 1942–   ; birth name: Britt-Marie Eklund): Swedish actress—ex-wife of comedy legend Peter Sellers, onetime lover of

Gorgeous Britt Ekland won many fans as James Bond's secretary Mary Goodnight in *The Man with the Golden Gun*. *Courtesy of the David Reinhardt Collection*

Director Guy Hamilton checks a camera angle with actress Britt Ekland during the filming of *The Man with the Golden Gun. Courtesy of the Anders Frejdh Collection*

rocker Rod Stewart—who portrayed daffy Mary Goodnight in *The Man with the Golden Gun*. Ekland impressed producers Albert R. Broccoli and Harry Saltzman with her voluptuousness, although the producers were later surprised to discover that she was pregnant at the time.

Indeed, her full, sensuous lips, gorgeous eyes, and enticing accent enhanced a character that in the Bond books had been nothing more than Bond's secretary. But the impact was blunted by the pure silliness of her role. She spends most of the film either locked in the trunk of Scaramanga's flying car or stuck in the closet of 007's hotel room while Bond (Roger Moore) makes love to Andrea (Maud Adams).

A native of Stockholm, Ekland made her credited motion picture debut in director George Marshall's crime comedy *The Happy Thieves* (1961), which also featured future Bond player Joseph Wiseman (*Dr. No*). Specializing in light comedy (hence her comfort in the Mary Goodnight role), Ekland later appeared in *After the Fox* (1966); *The Bobo* (1967), opposite her husband, Peter Sellers; and *The Night They Raided Minsky's* (1968). One of her steamier roles was playing Willow the island barmaid in *The Wicker Man* (1973), which also featured her costar in *The Man with the Golden Gun*, Christopher Lee. Interestingly, Ekland starred in the 1983 crime drama *Doctor Yes: The Hyannis Affair*.

El Scorpio nightclub: The tough South American bar featured in the *Goldfinger* pre-credits teaser, where Bond (Sean Connery) arrives in a spotless white dinner jacket after setting demolition charges that will destroy Mr. Ramirez's illegal drug operation. In that sequence, shot on Pinewood Studios' Stage D, a crowd of thirty-five men and fifteen women, all playing South American locals, crowded onto the stage as choreographer Selina Wylie worked with shapely actress Nadja Regin, who dances for the crowd before she joins Bond in her dressing room. Jack Dawkes, Sid Abrams, and Harry Thorne portrayed a typical flamenco trio on a small stage in the center of the room, though John Barry's flamenco music was piped in electronically.

electromagnetic pulse: Featured in *GoldenEye*, this is a weapon developed by the US and Soviets during the Cold War. Discovered after atomic weapons were first used against Hiroshima and Nagasaki, it can destroy a city's entire electrical grid, which is what renegade British Secret Service agent/traitor Alec Trevelyan (Sean Bean) wants to do to London.

electromagnetic RPM controller: A comical gadget that Q (Desmond Llewelyn) deploys to beat Las Vegas slot machines in *Diamonds Are Forever*. I wonder what the Nevada Gaming Commission thought of this device.

Ellery, Margaret: A pretty British Overseas Airways Corporation stewardess—playing herself on the morning of Tuesday, January 16, 1962—who competes with 007 (Sean Connery) for a taxi at Kingston, Jamaica's Palisadoes Airport. It was the first day of shooting on *Dr. No*.

Ellipsis: Code word in communications between agents of what is later revealed to be the reconstituted SPECTRE organization, as first introduced in *Casino Royale*. When Bond (Daniel Craig) recovers the cell phone belonging to Mollaka (Sébastien Foucan), a mysterious text message containing only this word leads him to Paradise Island in the Bahamas and the next link on the trail of his enemies.

Elrod House: Real name of the futuristic house featured as the desert residence of billionaire Willard Whyte (Jimmy Dean) in *Diamonds Are Forever*. Designed by the late architect John Lautner and valued at nearly $8 million in a 2016 sale, the concrete-and-glass house has nearly eight thousand square feet of space and is situated on about twenty-three acres in Palm Springs, California. Built for interior designer Arthur Elrod in 1968, the house, likened to a spaceship, has a circular living room sixty feet across with skylights radiating from the center like the petals of a desert flower. The home also has an indoor/outdoor pool and a two-bedroom guest house. Lautner, one of the greatest American contemporary architects, was still actively working on projects at the time of his death at age eighty-three, in October 1994.

Eon Productions Ltd.: The production company that has produced the James Bond movies since 1962. It's actually an acronym that stands for "Everything or Nothing." Eon is a subsidiary of Danjaq LLC, a US-based company named after the wives of its founders, producers Albert R. Broccoli and Harry Saltzman—Dana and Jacqueline, respectively. Producer Harry Saltzman sold off his interest in the company in 1975, and it is currently owned by the late Albert Broccoli's daughter, Barbara Broccoli, and his stepson, Michael G. Wilson.

Fabergé eggs: The extremely rare jeweled eggs originally designed by Carl Fabergé as Easter gifts for the Russian royal family. One of the eggs becomes a key plot element in *Octopussy*.

The movie begins when 009 (Andy Bradford) steals a Fabergé egg from the circus in East Berlin run by Octopussy (Maud Adams). Agent 009 dies with a knife in his back, and the jeweled egg falls into the hands of the British ambassador. It is eventually sent to British Secret Service headquarters, where it is revealed as a fake.

The genuine article—the Coronation egg, which contains a tiny model of the Russian imperial coach—is up for auction at Sotheby's. Suspiciously, it is the fourth egg to be auctioned in a single year. The seller is anonymous and has a numbered Swiss bank account.

Meeting with James Bond (Roger Moore), M (Robert Brown) and Defence Minister Freddie Gray (Geoffrey Keen) reason that the egg could

Attending a major London art auction in *Octopussy*, Magda (Kristina Wayborn) and Kamal Khan (Louis Jourdan) wonder who is suddenly bidding for a prized Fabergé egg. *Courtesy of the Anders Frejdh Collection*

be a part of a Soviet plot to raise currency for payoffs or covert operations abroad. What they don't know is that renegade Soviet general Orlov (Steven Berkoff) is stealing a huge cache of Kremlin jewelry to purchase the services of ruthless Kamal Khan (Louis Jourdan), an exiled Afghan prince, his associate Octopussy (Maud Adams), and her circus performers.

A Fabergé egg. *Steve Rubin Collection*

This cover force is going to help engineer Orlov's terrifying plan to detonate a nuclear device on the US Air Force's Feldstadt Air Base in West Germany. The general knows that the Europeans would believe it was an American bomb triggered accidentally and demand that the United States unilaterally disarm. And without the American nuclear deterrent, Orlov can then carry out his plan to invade the West with Soviet forces.

The phony Fabergé egg stolen by 009 is part of a fake trove that Orlov's jewel forgery expert, Lenkin (Peter Porteous), is substituting for the real jewels in the Kremlin Art Repository. But with the intended replacement stolen and the repository conducting a surprise audit of its collection, the conspirators' only option is to buy back the original at any cost.

Meanwhile, M orders Bond to accompany Secret Service art expert Jim Fanning (Douglas Wilmer) to the auction, where the Coronation egg is identified in the program simply as "The Property of a Lady." Their mission's code name: Operation Trove.

At Sotheby's, the auction begins, and Kamal Khan is quickly identified as a principal bidder. Fanning doesn't like what Kamal Khan usually sells at auctions—what he refers to as "marginal quality from dubious sources." But, as a buyer, it looks like Kamal Khan will acquire the egg—that is, until Bond, to Fanning's astonishment, starts to bid against him. At one point, Bond asks the auction assistant if he can see the egg up close. Unbeknownst to anyone in the gallery, 007 then substitutes the phony egg stolen by 009 for the real item.

The bidding continues, reaching an unimaginable figure of 500,000 pounds, until Bond lets Kamal Khan win. Fanning, about to suffer a heart attack, can't believe what he's seen. "He had to buy it," says Bond. Determined to find out why, Bond follows Kamal Khan to Udaipur, India, later using the real Fabergé egg he switched at the gallery as collateral in a high-stakes backgammon game with Kamal Khan, which 007 wins.

Like the golf match in *Goldfinger*, the Sotheby egg auction in *Octopussy* is one of those perfectly dramatized sequences that matches 007 against a villain without the typical gunplay and mayhem associated with secret agent derring-do. Sumptuously re-created by producer Albert R. Broccoli's veteran production designer, Peter Lamont, the auction house sequence stands out in the Bond series as another breath of fresh air.

Fairey Marine: A British boat-building company that supplied the motorboats to the *From Russia with Love* crew in 1963. The boats, which were driven by Bond (Sean Connery) and a group of SPECTRE agents in the film's finale, were loaded onto trucks in Glasgow, Scotland, and taken to the coastal village of Crinan, where they were deposited on an estuary and then motored out into the Atlantic. Fairey Marine's Peter Twiss, a former Royal Air Force pilot who was the first man to fly a jet aircraft faster than 1,000 mph, was in charge of the flotilla.

fake fingerprints: An ingenious invention supplied by Q (Desmond Llewelyn) in *Diamonds Are Forever*. Convinced that a diamond smuggling syndicate has elaborate methods of confirming the identity of its couriers, Q provides James Bond (Sean Connery) with a set of these phony fingerprints, which 007 wears to Amsterdam when he takes on the identity of smuggler Peter Franks (Joe Robinson). Sure enough, when he arrives at the apartment of fellow smuggler Tiffany Case (Jill St. John), she takes his drinking glass, dusts it for fingerprints, and then compares them to those of the real Peter Franks. They match, and Bond's cover is left intact.

fake manta ray: Giant underwater costume worn by James Bond (Timothy Dalton) in *Licence*

to Kill. A throwback to the fake seagull on the diving mask in *Goldfinger*, the manta-ray disguise helps Bond sneak aboard the *Wavekrest* research vessel, where he proceeds to sabotage a major drug deal.

fake rubber seagull: Perched on 007's head, the seagull was camouflage for Bond (Sean Connery) as he swam up to an enemy dock in the *Goldfinger* pre-credits teaser. From this point on, the tone of the Bond series changed.

Up until *Goldfinger*, the James Bond series had walked a careful line, remaining faithful to the straight and serious tone of Ian Fleming's original Bond stories but adding a touch of screenwriter Richard Maibaum's self-mocking humor. Humor was an important element in American suspense films at that time, including most of Alfred Hitchcock's films, especially the very Bond-like *North by Northwest* (1959). Maibaum reasoned correctly that to make American audiences accept the completely preposterous 007 plots, there had to be moments in which the story gave a wink: *We know this is completely ridiculous, but isn't it also extremely fun?* In the early films, Sean Connery mastered the deadpan throwaway delivery that sold Maibaum's humor to the masses.

Unfortunately, with the "fake rubber seagull" gag in *Goldfinger*, the humor started to become less subtle. Putting a rubber bird on 007's head was like a popping a red ball on his nose. In *From Russia with Love*, 007 was a British Secret Service agent. But in *Goldfinger*, he began to take on the trappings of a clown. It was not yet a full-bore transformation; *Goldfinger*, *Thunderball*, and *You Only Live Twice* were still very serious spy adventures. But the table was being set for the comedy Bond of the upcoming Roger Moore era—culminating in 007 literally dressing up in a red nose and white face paint in *Octopussy*. It was an unfortunate shift in the character, which even the technicians on the set during the seagull scene saw coming. There was considerable grumbling when the prop department brought out the phony seagull rig.

Falmouth, Jamaica: Site of a tropical quagmire on Jamaica's north shore—about twenty miles east of Montego Bay—that served as the location for the swamp country in *Dr. No*, where Bond (Sean Connery), Quarrel (John Kitzmiller), and Honey (Ursula Andress) run into the "dragon" tank.

fan-tan parlor sequence: The original pre-credits teaser, written by Richard Maibaum, for *Thunderball*. It takes place in a Hong Kong fan-tan parlor—actually a strip joint—where a beautiful girl dressed from head to toe like a peacock sits in a golden cage above the main room. Bond gives her the eye and later follows her into a dressing room, where he enters into polite conversation and then slugs her in the mouth. Her peacock head comes off, revealing a man—the very enemy agent Bond is searching for. The teaser was abandoned in favor of a similarly themed sequence that takes place at the Château d'Anet in France

Faslane submarine base: An actual British Royal Navy base for Polaris nuclear submarines, located on the Clyde River near Glasgow, on the southwestern coast of Scotland. It served as a background for an exterior sequence in *The Spy Who Loved Me*, in which Bond (Roger Moore) is briefed about a missing nuclear submarine while an actual British nuclear submarine navigates the channel behind him.

Fearing, Patricia: Curvaceous physical therapist portrayed by British actress Molly Peters in *Thunderball*. At the Shrublands health clinic in rural England, Patricia not only helps Bond (Sean Connery) recover from a nasty poker wound inflicted by SPECTRE agent Jacques Bouvar (Bob Simmons) in the teaser but is also involved with SPECTRE agent Count Lippe (Guy Doleman), who's enrolled at the clinic while a plastic-surgery-aided duplicate is substituted for NATO aerial observer François Derval (Paul Stassino).

When Lippe nearly kills Bond by increasing the tension on his motorized traction table, Patricia pleads with 007 not to tell her boss. The price of Bond's silence is a tryst in the steam room and another in Bond's suite, where he works a mink glove over Patricia's nude back.

The Patricia Fearing character resurfaces in *Never Say Never Again*, with actress Prunella Gee in the role. This time, Bond (Sean Connery) seduces her with a suitcase full of gourmet foods, including beluga caviar, quail eggs, foie gras from Strasbourg, and vodka. While sleeping with Patri-

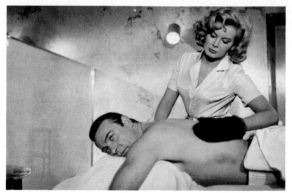

Molly Peters played the comely physical therapist Patricia Fearing in *Thunderball*, here in an image that reverses what actually happens in the finished film, in which Bond (Sean Connery) gives Patricia a mink glove rubdown. *Courtesy of the David Reinhardt Collection*

cia, Bond hears a scuffle in another room, where SPECTRE agent Fatima Blush (Barbara Carrera) is beating up nervous airman turned drug addict and sex slave Jack Petachi (Gavan O'Herlihy).

Feirstein, Bruce (1956–   ): American humorist, columnist, screenwriter, producer, and director who wrote/cowrote *GoldenEye* (his motion picture screenwriting debut), *Tomorrow Never Dies* (sole credit), and *The World Is Not Enough*. Feirstein, who wrote a column for the *New York Observer*, was born in Maplewood, New Jersey, and started his career in advertising, working on the "Ultimate Driving Machine" campaign for BMW. His writing career took off in 1983 when he wrote the worldwide bestseller *Real Men Don't Eat Quiche*.

Feirstein came to the Bond series through his longtime friendship with top Broadway and film producer Fred Zollo, husband to Bond producer Barbara Broccoli. During the long incubation period of *GoldenEye*, Broccoli and Zollo had discussed the possibility of having Feirstein contribute to the script. Though he'd yet to have one of his screenplays produced, they were impressed with his screenwriting talent and saw that he had the sensibility they were looking for.

Feirstein understood the dynamic of Bond to a T. "Barbara Broccoli and I had talked about Bond many times," he remembered. "I once pointed out something to her that I thought was wrong with *Octopussy*. In that film's teaser, you recall, Bond's baby jet is low on fuel, and he ends up taxiing into a rural gas station in Cuba and tells the attendant to fill it up. That wasn't very Bondian. What he should have done was flown the baby jet into the rear of an in-flight C-5 transport plane, where he would be greeted by Miss Moneypenny, who would take him to his briefing with M. That was the way the original movies worked. The humor had to be smart."*

In September 1994, Feirstein received a phone call from Barbara Broccoli informing him that he had a meeting the next day with *GoldenEye* director Martin Campbell. Suddenly, the fate of the *GoldenEye* script was placed in his hands.

Feirstein was canny about his contributions to the screenplay, but he did admit that he came in primarily to work on the characters, including Bond; the third act of the film; and making the humor smarter. "My favorite scenes in the movie are the ones with M and Q," he laughed. "Martin Campbell came up with the idea of making M a woman. My assignment was to see if I could make it work. M is not a Maggie Thatcher. She smokes, drinks; she's tough. She's not politically correct and she's certainly not from the same old boys' club as the previous M."

As for 007 himself, Feirstein had a clear vision of the character for the 1990s and beyond. "In order for you to understand Bond, you have to realize that a lot of him is not on screen. There was a great deal of darkness in the original novels and in the first films. Sean Connery brought that to life. You really believed that this was a guy you'd love to go drinking with up to a point. You knew he was dangerous—he's a man who lives every day of his life as if it were his last."

Feirstein also described a scene between M and Bond in one of the *GoldenEye* drafts in which Bond says, "I've never forgotten that a license to kill is also a certificate to die." Said the writer, "That's the character. He's someone who understands that and lives his life accordingly. During one of the love scenes, I heard someone on the set say, 'This is a guy who isn't sure he's going to live for six months, what does he care about safe sex? His job is death.'"

Fekkesh, Aziz: Egyptian black-market trader, portrayed by Nadim Sawalha in *The Spy Who Loved Me*, who is one of the mysterious characters involved in the peddling of a nuclear

submarine tracking system. James Bond (Roger Moore) learns of Fekkesh's identity from Sheik Hosein (Edward de Souza), a British agent masquerading as a desert chieftain outside Cairo.

Unfortunately, Fekkesh is murdered by Jaws (Richard Kiel) during a huge outdoor show at the pyramids. Inside the dead man's coat, Bond finds a datebook that indicates a meeting with Max Kalba (Vernon Dobtcheff), a Cairo nightclub owner who may or may not have the missing microfilm copy of the tracking system.

In an early draft screenplay of *The Spy Who Loved Me*, Fekkesh was first identified as a curator for the Cairo Museum of Antiquities, and Bond goes to the museum instead of to the pyramids for his first rendezvous. In the museum, he encounters two Russian agents, and a big fight occurs in the mummy room. Glass cases are smashed, mummies disintegrate, and inane one-liners prevail. In one sequence, after one of the Russians hurls a bust of King Tutankhamen at Bond and misses, Bond quips, "Tut Tut." Bond is eventually overpowered by the Russians and knocked out. The idea of fighting in such a delicate environment was later used in *Moonraker*, in which Bond fights Chang (Toshiro Suga) in the Venice Glass Museum.

Feldman, Charles K. (April 26, 1904–May 25, 1968; birth name: Charles Gould): Brilliant American producer and former talent agent who purchased the feature film rights to Ian Fleming's *Casino Royale* from actor/director Gregory Ratoff for $75,000, and brought it to the big screen in 1967 as a $9 million spoof for Columbia Pictures. His coproducer on the project was Jerry Bresler.

A New York City native, Feldman was one of the most successful talent agents of his era. He made his motion picture producing debut on *The Lady Is Willing* (1942), a romantic comedy that starred Marlene Dietrich and Fred MacMurray. Prior to *Casino Royale*, his other feature producing credits included: *Red River* (1948), uncredited; *The Glass Menagerie* (1950); *A Streetcar Named Desire* (1951); *The Seven Year Itch* (1955); *Walk on the Wild Side* (1962); *What's New Pussycat* (1965); and *The Group* (1966), uncredited.

It was not Feldman's initial intention to make a spoof of Bond's world. However, when he failed to make a deal with established 007 producers Albert R. Broccoli and Harry Saltzman

---

* Bruce Feirstein, telephone interview by the author, June 1, 1995.

or to lure Sean Connery away from their stable, he realized that a serious Bond was not in the cards. Given that he knew virtually everyone in Hollywood, he assembled an astonishing number of writers, directors, and stars to create the big, lumbering lummox of a spoof that *Casino Royale* became. An oddity in the 007 canon, it nonetheless featured Peter Sellers, Woody Allen, and Orson Welles in the same film—certainly an accomplishment.

Feldstadt Air Base: Fictional US Air Force base in West Germany that is targeted for nuclear destruction in *Octopussy*. In order to force Western Europe to unilaterally disarm, renegade Russian general Orlov (Steven Berkoff) is determined to detonate an A-bomb at Feldstadt and make it look like the Americans exploded one by mistake. He reasons that the resulting outrage

will force the US to disarm, leaving European borders clear for a massive Soviet invasion.

Unbeknownst to Octopussy (Maud Adams), who thinks she's involved in a typical jewel smuggling operation with her partner, Kamal Khan (Louis Jourdan), her own circus is being used as cover for the bomb, which has been planted in the base of the circus cannon. Despite being thrown off the circus train and left far behind, James Bond (Roger Moore) manages to steal a car and head for Feldstadt to prevent the "accident." Pursued by angry West German police and a platoon of base security troops, 007 disguises himself as a clown and quickly enters the circus tent. There he fights his way to the cannon's base and, with Octopussy's help (she shoots the lock off), deactivates the bomb.

Felton, Norman (April 29, 1913–June 25, 2012) British American television producer who, in New York during the spring of 1962, began a short-lived collaboration with author Ian Fleming on what would eventually become the MGM/NBC television series *The Man from U.N.C.L.E.* The sum of Fleming's involvement in the series consisted of notes written hurriedly to Felton on a pad of blank Western Union telegram forms. Much of it was useless, but Felton did make note of the names Fleming gave to his two principal agents: Napoleon Solo and April Dancer.

Returning to Hollywood and working with writer Sam Rolfe, Felton created a pilot script, titled "Solo," about an international crime-fighting organization named U.N.C.L.E. (United Network Command for Law and Enforcement) and its various operatives, one of which, Napoleon Solo, was a secret agent like James Bond.

One year later, Felton again tried to interest Fleming in the venture, but this time the author was advised to stay away from any television projects that involved secret agents. Already embroiled in a lawsuit over the screen rights to his novel *Thunderball*, Fleming was not about to risk another, especially since Bond producers Albert R. Broccoli and Harry Saltzman were already aware of the Felton series and were dead set against it.

In January 1964, Eon Productions brought a suit against Felton's production company, claiming that by using the title *Solo* for their proposed series, they were in effect stealing an actual character name from *Goldfinger*, then in

Roger Moore dons clown garb as James Bond desperately tries to prevent a nuclear accident on a US Air Force base in *Octopussy*. *Steve Rubin Collection*

production at Pinewood Studios. Felton pointed out that Mr. Solo in *Goldfinger*, a Mafia chieftain, was certainly not the same man as Napoleon Solo in their series. After he brought MGM's best lawyer into the case, Eon Productions backed down, demanding only that Felton change the name of the series. Felton's Arena Productions agreed, and *Solo* was changed to *The Man from U.N.C.L.E.*, which made its debut on American television in the fall of 1964.

A native of London, Felton immigrated to the United States with his family in 1929 and settled in Ohio. His television producing career emerged in full flower when he came aboard the anthology series *Studio One in Hollywood*, where he produced sixteen episodes between 1957 and 1958. While producing *The Man from U.N.C.L.E.*, Felton also produced its spinoff, *The Girl from U.N.C.L.E.*, which starred Stefanie Powers as April Dancer.

Ferzetti, Gabriele (March 17, 1925–December 2, 2015; birth name Pasquale Ferzetti): Suave Italian leading man who portrayed Marc-Ange Draco, the head of the Union Corse crime organization in *On Her Majesty's Secret Service*. He's also the father of Contessa Teresa "Tracy" di Vicenzo (Diana Rigg), wife-to-be of Bond (George Lazenby). Well-groomed and impeccably mannered, Ferzetti's Draco is probably one of the most sympathetic Mafia dons ever presented on screen. NOTE: Ferzetti's voice was redubbed by actor David de Keyser.

A native of Rome, Ferzetti made his feature film debut during World War II, when he was featured in director Luigi Chiarini's romantic drama *Via delle cinque lune* ("Street of the Five Moons,"1942). American audiences first took note of Ferzetti when he starred as Fabius Maximus opposite Victor Mature in *Hannibal* (1959). The year before he did *On Her Majesty's Secret Service*, Ferzetti portrayed Morton the railroad baron in director Sergio Leone's *Once Upon a Time in the West* (1968).

Fields, Strawberry: MI6 operative portrayed by Gemma Arterton in *Quantum of Solace*. Attached to the British consulate in La Paz, Bolivia, Fields is tasked with convincing 007 (Daniel Craig) to return to London. Instead, Fields accompanies him to the ritzy Andean Grand Hotel, succumbs to Bond's charms, goes to bed with him, and is later killed by Quantum

agents (she's left on the bed in Bond's hotel room à la Jill Masterson in *Goldfinger*, her lungs filled with crude oil).

Fiennes, Ralph (December 22, 1962–   ): Two-time Academy Award–nominated British actor—his name is pronounced "Rafe Fines"—who was cast as Gareth Mallory, the new M, in *Skyfall* and has continued in that role ever since. A native of Ipswich, Suffolk, England, Fiennes made his big-screen debut as Heathcliff in director Peter Kosminsky's 1992 adaptation of *Wuthering Heights*. The following year he became internationally known for his role as concentration camp commandant Amon Goeth in director Steven Spielberg's acclaimed World War II drama *Schindler's List* (1993), a role for which he was awarded his first Oscar nomination for Best Supporting Actor (he lost to Tommy Lee Jones in *The Fugitive*). Showing his versatility, Fiennes's next film was director Robert Redford's historical drama *Quiz Show* (1994), in which he portrayed patrician game show contestant Charles Van Doren. In 1996, he was cast as Almásy in Anthony Minghella's epic war drama *The English Patient*, which netted Fiennes his second Oscar nomination, this time for Best Actor (he lost to Geoffrey Rush in *Shine*). He later took on one of his most popular roles, playing the evil Lord Voldemort in *Harry Potter and the Goblet of Fire* (2005) and three subsequent films in the smash-hit series.

Actor Ralph Fiennes jumped from Harry Potter to Bond, portraying MI6 spymaster Gareth Mallory. *Courtesy of the Anders Frejdh Collection*

Fillet of Soul: A fictional chain of US restaurants that are used as distribution points for illegal narcotics in *Live and Let Die*. The Harlem and New Orleans franchises are featured in the film.

Finney, Albert (May 9, 1936– February 7, 2019): Versatile, five-time Academy Award– nominated British actor whose final feature film performance was the role of game warden and caretaker Kincade in *Skyfall*. A native of Salford, Lancashire, England, Finney came to

Actor Albert Finney portrayed shotgun-carrying Bond family game warden Kincade in *Skyfall*. *Steve Rubin Collection*

international prominence in 1963 when he portrayed the rakish title character in director Tony Richardson's bawdy eighteenth-century comedy adventure *Tom Jones*, which went on to win the Best Picture Oscar that year. A decade later, he scored with the celebrated role of detective Hercule Poirot in director Sidney Lumet's crime drama *Murder on the Orient Express* (1974), which also starred Sean Connery and was written by Bond veteran Paul Dehn (*Goldfinger*). Finney received his Academy Award nominations for *Tom Jones* (1963), *Murder on the Orient Express* (1974), *The Dresser* (1983), *Under the Volcano* (1984), and *Erin Brockovich* (2000).

Fleming, Ian Lancaster (May 28, 1908–August 12, 1964): British author, newspaper columnist, and former British naval intelligence officer who invented the character of James Bond, Secret Agent 007. Fleming's novels and short stories were modern fairy tales for adults: fantastic globe-trotting adventure stories about a British Secret Service agent with a license to kill. Loaded with sexual references, sadomasochistic violence, and edge-of-your-seat suspense, they captured the imagination of thrill-seeking readers around the world.

President John F. Kennedy was a big Fleming fan, as was author Raymond Chandler, who encouraged Fleming to continue his writing career even though his first books were not big sellers. Fleming based many of his novels on his experiences as a naval intelligence officer

Author Ian Fleming didn't have to travel very far to have an on-set discussion with Ursula Andress on *Dr. No*. He lived just down the road at his GoldenEye residence. *Courtesy of the David Reinhardt Collection*

during World War II. It wasn't until 1975, though, that Fleming was identified as a close associate of British spymaster Sir William Stephenson, whose Ultra network had broken the German diplomatic code in 1939. Through Ultra, Fleming was involved in some of the greatest espionage capers in military history.

In 1944, during a wartime trip to Jamaica, Fleming decided that he would make the island his postwar retreat. Before returning to London, he asked his good friend American millionaire Ivar Bryce to secure some Jamaican beach property for him. Bryce purchased a beachfront

Ian Fleming chats with Sean Connery during location filming in Turkey on *From Russia with Love*. *Courtesy of the David Reinhardt Collection*

parcel near the deserted donkey track at Oracabessa, a fruit-trading center on Jamaica's beautiful north shore. So was born the Caribbean vacation home Fleming dubbed GoldenEye.

Two years later, Fleming was hired by newspaper magnate Lord Kemsley to manage the foreign news section of a large group of English papers. He took the job on the condition that his contract include a two-month vacation each year. He would spend it at his little beach house in Jamaica—a routine that was to continue for the rest of his life.

For nearly six years, he toyed with the idea of writing during his tropical vacations. He even completed a few local color articles for *Horizon* magazine, but it was not until a few weeks before his 1952 marriage to Lady Anne Rothermere that Ian Fleming decided to write a novel in Jamaica. He took the name of his main character from the author of a book that graced his coffee table there: *Birds of the West Indies* by American ornithologist James Bond. Within six weeks, *Casino Royale* was completed, and Fleming was off to find a suitable publisher.

He approached venerable old Jonathan Cape, who had published several of his brother Peter Fleming's travel books. Cape accepted the manuscript on the recommendation of several people, including Fleming's good friend William Plomer, and scheduled the book for publication in England in the spring of 1953.

Between 1952 and his death in 1964, Fleming wrote twelve James Bond novels and two collections of short stories. In order of their publication dates, they were: *Casino Royale* (1953); *Live and Let Die* (1954); *Moonraker* (1955); *Diamonds Are Forever* (1956); *From Russia with Love* (1957); *Dr. No* (1958); *Goldfinger* (1959); *For Your Eyes Only* (short stories, 1960); *Thunderball* (1961), based on a screen treatment by Fleming, Kevin McClory and Jack Whittingham; *The Spy Who Loved Me* (1962); *On Her Majesty's Secret Service* (1963); *You Only Live Twice* (1964); *The Man with the Golden Gun* (1965); and *Octopussy/The Living Daylights* (short stories, 1966).

In 1961, producers Albert R. Broccoli and Harry Saltzman acquired film rights to all of

Ian Fleming on one of his final visits to a Bond set, visiting Sean Connery and Shirley Eaton during the filming of *Goldfinger*. *Courtesy of the David Reinhardt Collection*

Fleming's novels and short stories except two: *Casino Royale*, which had been previously sold to actor Gregory Ratoff in 1956 (Ratoff later sold the rights to agent turned producer Charles K. Feldman, who adapted it into a 007 spoof in 1967), and *Thunderball*, the rights of which were won by producer Kevin McClory in a copyright infringement suit (McClory joined forces with Broccoli and Saltzman to produce *Thunderball* in 1965). Fleming's James Bond character continued in literature after his death, first in *Colonel Sun* by Kingsley Amis (1968), and then in many subsequent books by authors such as John Gardner and Ray Benson.

Over the years Broccoli and Saltzman and their successors at Eon Productions adapted all available Fleming titles—including *Casino Royale*, having finally obtained the rights in 1999. (In

James Bond (Sean Connery) meets the desirable Jill Masterson (Shirley Eaton) in a Fontainebleau hotel suite in Miami. It soon leads to "the best place in town." *Courtesy of the Anders Frejdh Collection*

2013, Eon secured the rights to *Thunderball* as well.) Subsequently, the producers have chosen, with the permission of the Fleming estate, to invent their own stories rather than dramatize any of the non-Fleming Bond titles. With a bit of luck, we should see James Bond movies into the twenty-third century.

Floating Palace, the: Nickname for the lavish island home of Octopussy (Maud Adams) in India. Surrounded by watery gardens, streams, bathing ponds, and pools, it appears to be floating on the lake. In actuality, the floating palace is an island in the middle of Udaipur's Lake Pichola. Unfortunately, Octopussy's defenses do not include serious walls or barricades. Thus, a group of criminals-for-hire from downtown Udaipur can gain entrance with little trouble. Hired by Kamal Khan (Louis Jourdan), their mission is to kill James Bond.

Flying Saucer: The name of the enormous yacht belonging to Maximilian Largo (Klaus Maria Brandauer) in *Never Say Never Again*. In Italian, "flying saucer" translates to *Disco Volante*—the name Ian Fleming, Kevin McClory, and Jack Whittingham gave to the yacht in the original novel *Thunderball*. For *Never*, producer Jack Schwartzman received permission to film aboard Saudi billionaire Adnan Khashoggi's yacht, the *Nabila*. Nearly three hundred feet long, the *Nabila* had a helicopter pad and eleven guest suites, many of which had gold bathroom fittings.

Fontainebleau: The famous Miami Beach hotel that served as a key location at the beginning of *Goldfinger*. It is first seen from an aerial view as a plane tows a promotional banner proclaiming WELCOME TO MIAMI BEACH.

James Bond (Sean Connery) thinks he's being booked into "the best hotel in Miami Beach" as a holiday gift from M. In actuality, he's been ordered to observe the suspicious activities of one Auric Goldfinger (Gert Fröbe). Bond's orders are delivered via CIA agent Felix Leiter (Cec Linder), who makes his film introduction while walking through the hotel's famous ice rink and pool area. There he finds 007 getting a massage from Dink (Margaret Nolan), a fabulously proportioned blonde.

Leiter briefs Bond on his mission and then points to a spot near the Fontainebleau pool where Goldfinger is cheating a Mr. Simmons (Austin Willis) at gin. Equipped with a radio transmitter disguised as a hearing aid, Goldfinger is being aided by his girl Friday, Jill Masterson (Shirley Eaton), who, while looking out a window of Goldfinger's hotel suite, spies on Simmons's hand with a pair of binoculars. Masterson is discovered by Bond, who orders Goldfinger to start losing or else he'll be turned over to the Miami Beach police. Helpless to defend himself lest he give himself away, Goldfinger nods his head, then proceeds to lose $15,000 to Mr. Simmons.

Cec Linder related a funny story about filming at the Fontainebleau Hotel pool in 1964. Said Linder, "The scene in which Felix Leiter strolls past the pool in search of Bond called for a background of voluptuous bathing beauties in bikinis. However, this is not the usual clientele at the Fontainebleau pool. On an average day, the pool is populated instead by a large group of older, silver-haired ladies and their card-playing husbands. Because of hotel restrictions, the film crew could not prevent the vacationers from relaxing by the pool, so the production company had to do some quick thinking to get their bathing beauties in place. What they decided to do was pure subterfuge.

"At the pool that morning, it was announced that at five o'clock in the afternoon, the crew would be shooting the pool area and that since the vacationers were going to be on camera, it would be a good idea for the women to go out and have their hair done. No sooner did all the older ladies leave the area than the crew brought in their voluptuous extras and shot Linder's walk-by. When the older ladies returned at 4:30 PM, the crew shot the pool a second time—but there wasn't any film in the camera."* M couldn't have planned a more successful caper.

---

* Cec Linder, telephone interview by the author, July 17, 1989.

Fool, the: A tarot card selected by James Bond (Roger Moore) from the deck offered by Solitaire (Jane Seymour) in *Live and Let Die*. After the selection, she replies, "You have found yourself."

FOR YOUR EYES ONLY

(United Artists, 1981) ★★★: The twelfth James Bond film produced by Albert R. Broccoli. US release date: June 26, 1981. Budget: $28 million. Worldwide box office gross: $195.3 million (US domestic gross: $54.8 million; international gross: $140.5 million).[†] Running time: 127 minutes.

--- **THE SETUP** ---

Operating in the Ionian Sea off the coast of Albania, the *St. Georges*, a British surveillance ship disguised as a harmless fishing boat, strikes a World War II–era mine and sinks. On board are sensitive instruments—including ATAC, the Automatic Targeting Attack Communicator, a top-secret device that can launch ballistic missiles. Thus begins a race between the British and the Russians to retrieve ATAC. James Bond (Roger Moore) is sent into action, while Greek marine archaeologist Melina Havelock (Carole Bouquet) is out to avenge her parents, who were brutally machine-gunned on the deck of their research vessel. Complicating their efforts are two former Greek resistance fighters and bitter enemies, Aris Kristatos (Julian Glover) and Milos Columbo (Topol)—one of whom is working for the Russians. To accomplish his mission, Bond eventually teams with Melina, while trying to figure out which resistance fighter is the good guy.

--- **BEHIND THE SCENES** ---

Having followed the *Goldfinger* formula for many years—bigger-than-life villains with outlandish schemes—Cubby Broccoli reeled in the fantasy in his twelfth outing, returning to the serious spying that was the hallmark of *From Russia with Love*. Richard Maibaum returned to write the screenplay, which was inspired by two Fleming short stories, "For Your Eyes Only" and "Risico."

[†] "For Your Eyes Only (1981)," The Numbers, accessed May 18, 2020, https://www.the-numbers.com/movie/For-Your-Eyes-Only.

This time Maibaum shared scripting duties with Broccoli's stepson Michael G. Wilson, and John Glen, an editor and second unit director, was given the directing reins. The result is another high point in the Roger Moore era: a fascinating spy adventure with plenty of mysterious characters, plot twists, romance, and the perfect Bond heroine in Melina Havelock (Carole Bouquet).

There are, indeed, no fantasy elements in *For Your Eyes Only*. Aris Kristatos (Julian Glover) and Milos Columbo (Topol) are flesh-and-blood human beings who have very real reasons for hating one another. Hate and revenge—two very real human emotions—play important parts in the film. Melina is determined to avenge her parents at all costs. She's Greek, and she takes her logic from the legend of Electra, who avenged her loved ones.

High points beside the meaty roles of Havelock, Kristatos, and Columbo include: the Meteora climb; the underwater search for the *St. Georges* surveillance ship; the teaser's solemn beginning, which takes place in the cemetery, where Bond places flowers on his late wife Tracy's grave; and the comic ending of the film, which has Margaret Thatcher (a dead-on Janet Brown) on the phone with Max the parrot.

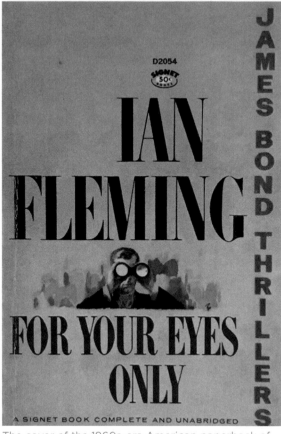

The cover of the 1960s-era American paperback of Ian Fleming's *For Your Eyes Only*

--- **THE CAST** ---

James Bond	Roger Moore
Melina Havelock	Carole Bouquet
Milos Columbo	Topol
Bibi Dahl	Lynn-Holly Johnson
Aris Kristatos	Julian Glover
Countess Lisl	Cassandra Harris
Jacoba Brink	Jill Bennett
Emile Leopold Locque	Michael Gothard
Erich Kriegler	John Wyman
Timothy Havelock	Jack Hedley
Miss Moneypenny	Lois Maxwell
Q	Desmond Llewelyn
Minister of Defence	Geoffrey Keen
General Gogol	Walter Gotell
Tanner	James Villiers
Ferrara	John Moreno
Claus	Charles Dance
Karageorge	Paul Angelis
Iona Havelock	Toby Robins
Apostis	Jack Klaff
Santos	Alkis Kritikos
Nikos	Stag Theodore
Hector Gonzales	Stefan Kalipha
First Sea Lord	Graham Crowden
Vice Admiral	Noel Johnson
McGregor	William Hoyland
Bunky	Paul Brooke
Rublevitch	Eva Rueber-Staier
Vicar	Fred Bryant
Girl in Flower Shop	Robbin Young
Mantis Man	Graham Hawkes
Denis	John Wells
The Prime Minister	Janet Brown

--- **THE CREW** ---

Director	John Glen
Screenplay by	Richard Maibaum
	Michael G. Wilson
Executive Producer	Michael G. Wilson
Producer	Albert R. Broccoli
Associate Producer	Tom Pevsner
Director of Photography	Alan Hume
Music by	Bill Conti

Title song performed by	Sheena Easton
Lyrics by	Mick Leeson
Production Designer	Peter Lamont
Art Director	John Fenner
Set Decorator	Vernon Dixon
Costume Designer	Elizabeth Waller
Production Supervisor	Bob Simmonds
Production Managers	Mara Blasetti
	Philip Kohler
	Aspa Lambrou
Assistant Director	Anthony Waye
Second Unit Direction and Photography	Arthur Wooster
Continuity	Elaine Schreyeck
Camera Operator	Alec Mills
Casting by	Maude Spector
	Debbie McWilliams
Action sequences arranged by	Bob Simmons
Driving stunts arranged by	Remy Julienne
Underwater Photography	Al Giddings
Ski Photography	Willy Bogner Jr.
Aerial Photography	James Devis
Climbing Team	Rick Sylvester
	Herbert Raditschnig
	Chester Brown
	Bill Fox
Title Designer	Maurice Binder
Special Effects Supervisor	Derek Meddings
Visual Effects Photography	Paul Wilson
Sound Mixer	Derek Ball
Editor	John Grover

Ford Mustang: Cream-colored 1964½ sports car with red upholstery belonging to Tilly Masterson (Tania Mallet) in *Goldfinger*. After her failed assassination attempt against Goldfinger (Gert Fröbe) on a Swiss mountain highway, Tilly is chased by 007 (Sean Connery), who shreds her tires with his trick Aston Martin. The Mustang, the first of its model line to be featured in a major motion picture, was also the first of many Ford Motor Company cars to appear in the James Bond series.

SPECTRE assassin Fiona Volpe (Luciana Paluzzi) also drives a Mustang in *Thunderball*. It's a light blue 1965 model with a white top. When 007 (Sean Connery) leaves the water after his underwater escapade underneath the anchored *Disco Volante*, he hitches a ride with Volpe in this car. The same car is parked outside Emilio Largo's Palmyra estate—another clue that Largo and Volpe are in cahoots.

James Bond's Mustang does some fancy manuevering during a wild parking lot chase in Las Vegas in *Diamonds Are Forever*. *Courtesy of the Anders Frejdh Collection*

In *Diamonds Are Forever*, James Bond (Sean Connery) drives a 1971 red hardtop Mustang, with California license plate CA52H6. (Technically speaking, this is a blooper; a Mustang rented in Nevada should have Nevada plates.) The car figures in the hilarious chase down Fremont Street between Bond and the Las Vegas Police Department, ending up in a parking lot behind the Mint Hotel (in reality, the backlot of Universal Pictures). In the final moment, Bond appears to be stopped at a narrow alley, but he manages to prop the car up on two wheels and escape. You'll notice that Bond drives into the alley on his right tires (with the left side of the car up in the air) but exits on his left tires (with the right side of the car up in the air). To cover for the discontinuity, the filmmakers inserted a shot of the car's interior implying that 007 somehow rocked the car from one side to the other in the middle of the narrow alley!

Ford Mustangs figure prominently in the James Bond series. *Steve Rubin Collection*

Ford Ranchero: A light blue 1964 model was driven by Oddjob (Harold Sakata) in *Goldfinger*. In the truck's bed, he transports the remains of a 1964 Lincoln Continental that has been crushed into a neat pile of metal by a compactor in a Kentucky auto wrecking yard (actually shot in Miami Beach).

A 1964 Ford Ranchero— perfect for carrying a crushed Lincoln Continental, gold bullion, and the remains of Mr. Solo in *Goldfinger*. *Steve Rubin Collection*

Fornof, J. W. "Corkey" (December 5, 1945–   ): Aerial stunt coordinator, pilot, engineer, and inventor who flew his Acrostar Bede mini jet in *Octopussy*, and later took over aerial action chores on *Licence to Kill*. On the latter film, Fornof coordinated the sequence in which Bond (Timothy Dalton) captures the getaway plane of Sanchez (Robert Davi), 007's water-skiing stunt behind the seaplane, and the crop-duster hijinks of Pam Bouvier (Carey Lowell). Fornof was originally hired to fly twin mini jets in *Moonraker*, but the stunt sequence was canceled when the riverbed feeding Venezuela's Angel Falls went dry.

Forster, Marc (November 30, 1969–   ): German-born director, writer, and producer who directed *Quantum of Solace*. A native of Illertissen, Bavaria, Forster's breakout feature as a director was the romantic drama *Monster's Ball* (2001), which netted Bond actress Halle Berry (*Die Another Day*) a Best Actress Oscar. His follow-up feature was *Finding Neverland* (2004), about the life of *Peter Pan* creator J. M. Barrie. Forster's additional directorial credits include *The Kite Runner* (2007), *Machine*

Director Marc Forster helmed *Quantum of Solace. Courtesy of the Anders Frejdh Collection*

Gun Preacher (2011), *World War Z* (2013), and *Christopher Robin* (2018). He was the first non-Commonwealth director to helm an Eon Productions Bond film.

Fort Knox, Kentucky: A US Army base protecting the gold depository of the United States, where, in 1964, $15 billion in gold bullion was stored. It is named after General Henry Knox, America's first secretary of war.

In *Goldfinger*, the plan of the title character (Gert Fröbe) is to detonate a small but "particularly dirty" atomic bomb—supplied by the Red Chinese—in the repository, thereby effectively eliminating access to the entire US gold reserve for fifty-eight years. The resulting economic chaos in the West will please the Chinese, and the value of Goldfinger's smuggled gold hoard will increase tenfold.

Although director Guy Hamilton's film crew was allowed to film on the base, where his cameras caught the actions of hundreds of US soldiers as they fall "unconscious," the crew was forbidden to film inside or near the actual gold repository. With the building and its vaults a key setting in the film, production designer Ken Adam was asked to recreate the full-size exterior of the repository on the backlot at England's Pinewood Studios. It was built complete with a huge concrete driveway and iron fencing. Its enormous, multistory interior was constructed inside a soundstage, where Adam stacked gold four stories high.

Explained Adam, "The very nature of a gold repository is very dull. You can't stack gold very high because of weight problems and questions of transportation. The ingots need to be stored in small chambers situated along narrow tunnels. And there's simply no drama in a series of little rooms. In my case, I stacked gold bars forty feet high under a gigantic roof. I had a whole crew of men polishing the metalwork so that it would shine when we turned the lights on. And it was the perfect place to stage the final battle between Bond (Sean Connery) and Oddjob (Harold Sakata). It was like a golden arena, and Bond was able to use gold bars as weapons."*

Film editor Peter Hunt, who marveled at Adam's creations, remembered the day the two of them were told they couldn't visit the interior

---

* Ken Adam, interview by the author, London, June 17, 1977.

His wrist tied to a portable nuclear device that is ticking down, James Bond (Sean Connery) navigates inside Fort Knox in *Goldfinger*. *Courtesy of the Anders Frejdh Collection*

of the real Fort Knox repository. "I told this nice American liaison from the Treasury Department that it was ridiculous not to let us take a look at the vault area," said Hunt. "After all, what were they afraid of, anyway? And he told me, 'Don't you understand? You all think there is a lot of gold in there, but in actuality there is nothing in there at all. We can't let you know that.' Whether he was telling the truth or not, both Ken and I thought that would have been a great ending

The actual Fort Knox depository in Kentucky, which was reproduced on the Pinewood Studios lot by Ken Adam. *Courtesy of the National Archives*

for the film: Goldfinger breaks into the world's largest bank and finds nothing."*

Foucan, Sébastien (May 27, 1974–): Fleet-footed, acrobatic French actor and parkour specialist who portrayed Mollaka, the terrorist bomb maker in *Casino Royale*, his big-screen debut. Born in Paris, Foucan spent three months in the Bahamas on the Bond film. His amazing ability at what he coined "free running" first came to the public's attention in Great Britain after the release of the television documentary film *Jump London* (2003) and its follow-up *Jump Britain* (2005). Foucan's work in *Casino Royale*—leaping from impossible heights and landing unscathed—is truly jaw-dropping. The sequences also served to introduce the raw physicality of the new James Bond, Daniel Craig.

Fox, Edward (April 13, 1937–): Aristocratic British actor who portrayed Bond's superior, M, as a hot-tempered, impatient bureaucrat in *Never Say Never Again*. The performance was a striking contrast to that of the previous actor to play opposite Sean Connery in the role, the fatherly Bernard Lee. But *Never Say Never Again* doesn't hesitate to place the British Secret Service in a more contemporary era of tight operational constraints and squeezed budgets. In the 1980s, in the eyes of the new M and perhaps the government more broadly, the double-0 section has become more of an embarrassment than an asset. Once again, it's up to James Bond to prove them wrong.

Fox, a London native, made his credited

motion picture debut in writer/director Herbert J. Leder's sci-fi horror film *The Frozen Dead* (1966). After years of television work and mostly modest feature roles, Fox's career reached another level when he played the title character in director Fred Zinnemann's *The Day of the Jackal* (1973). His additional feature credits include *A Bridge Too Far* (1977), with fellow Bond player Sean Connery; *Soldier of Orange* (1977), with future Bond player Jeroen Krabbé; *Force 10 from Navarone* (1978), with Bond players Robert Shaw, Richard Kiel, Barbara Bach, and Paul Angelis (*For Your Eyes Only*); *Ghandi* (1982); *The Dresser* (1983); *Robin Hood* (1991); *Nicholas Nickleby* (2004); and the spy spoof *Johnny English Strikes Again* (2018), starring Rowan Atkinson.

France, Michael (January 4, 1962–April 12, 2013): American screenwriter who received story credit on *GoldenEye*. France always wanted to do a Bond movie, but it wasn't until 1991, when he sold his spec script for what would become the Sylvester Stallone hit *Cliffhanger* (1993), his produced screenwriting debut, that he was given the chance. Recalled France, "I learned how to write action movies from watching Bond films. I always wanted to write one, and I had my agent pester Michael Wilson and Barbara Broccoli. Once they got past the legal problems they had faced for a couple of years, I was invited to lunch with Barbara and Michael at an Italian restaurant on Pico Boulevard in West Los Angeles called Osteria Romana Orsini. This was in January 1993. Before the meeting I crammed on everyone's bios, and as soon as I showed up they started quizzing me, basically on what my attitude toward the character was, what I knew about 007, what I could bring to a new film to make it fresh and different from the blizzard of action movies that had come out in recent years. They liked the fact that I knew the movies. Many people didn't know the characters. They were pitching old stories. I decided I wanted to be a writer when I was watching *Goldfinger*. When I was a kid, I wanted to be Richard Maibaum, not Bond."*

France's meeting with the producers lasted over ninety minutes. But for two months, France heard nothing. Finally, in March 1993, they called back, and France was given the opportunity to

---

* Peter Hunt, interview by the author, London, June 21, 1977.

* Michael France, telephone interview by the author, June 15, 1995.

come up with a new story line. He explained, "We were all in agreement that we needed to treat Bond seriously and not to do one of the more comedic, sillier Bonds like *Moonraker*. By the same token, they didn't want to be as serious as *Licence to Kill*. *Goldfinger* was considered the model Bond. They didn't lay down the law—no formulas were mentioned. But it was very collaborative. We had meetings twice a week for several months with Michael, Barbara, Cubby, and Dana [Broccoli, Cubby's wife]—either at Cubby's house in Beverly Hills or at MGM. I also talked to some technical people like stuntman B. J. Worth and aviation coordinator Corkey Fornof.

"The movies that we kept coming back to as inspiration were the earlier Connery Bonds like *From Russia with Love*. That's where we wanted the character and situations to be. We also wanted a villain on the level of *Goldfinger*—with an elaborate, unsinkable plot. At the same time, we also want him to be credible as a threat—that all of the story elements were based in reality, that these things could happen."

France placed much of the story in Russia following the fall of the Soviet Union, with the island location in Cuba saved for the ending. He finished his final draft in February/March 1994, a full year after his first meeting with Wilson and Broccoli. British writer Jeffrey Caine was brought in to write the next draft of the screenplay. And he in turn was followed by Kevin Wade and Bruce Feirstein. Final credits gave Caine and Feirstein the screenplay credit and France the story.

A native of St. Petersburg, Florida, France also cowrote the films *Hulk* (2003), *The Punisher* (2004), and *Fantastic Four* (2005). After battling complications from diabetes, he died in 2013 at age fifty-one.

Francisco the Fearless: Circus daredevil, portrayed by veteran Bond stuntman Richard "Dicky" Graydon, who flies out of a cannon in *Octopussy*. It is within the base of this cannon that General Orlov (Steven Berkoff) and Kamal Khan (Louis Jourdan) have placed an atomic device that

will be exploded on a US Air Force base in West Germany. As the timer of the bomb counts down, Francisco and his cannon are rolled into the circus big top. However, his entrance is upstaged when James Bond (Roger Moore) arrives in a clown's suit. As the crowd watches, Bond disarms the A-bomb, after which Francisco looks out from the cannon's barrel and says, impatiently, "Now?"—one of the film's best laughs.

Franks, Peter: Tough British diamond smuggler portrayed by actor/stuntman Joe Robinson in *Diamonds Are Forever*. Franks is an international courier for a diamond smuggling syndicate that is being decimated by Ernst Stavro Blofeld

James Bond (Sean Connery) battles diamond smuggler Peter Franks (Joe Robinson) in an Amsterdam elevator in *Diamonds Are Forever*. *Courtesy of the Anders Frejdh Collection*

(Charles Gray) and SPECTRE. Captured by the British Secret Service on his way to Amsterdam for a pickup, Franks is replaced in the pipeline by James Bond (Sean Connery), who assumes Franks's identity. He receives his credentials from Miss Moneypenny (Lois Maxwell) at the English Channel crossing.

Bond also benefits from a fantastic invention from Q Branch: phony fingerprints that convince smuggler Tiffany Case (Jill St. John) that he's the genuine Franks. Unfortunately, Franks escapes from the British and arrives at Case's Amsterdam apartment, where he is killed by 007 in a vicious elevator fight. Bond then switches wallets with the dead man and allows Tiffany to discover his identification on the corpse, leading her to declare, "You've just killed James Bond!"

Friendship Airport: Airfield outside Baltimore, now known as BWI Thurgood Marshall Airport, that is the destination of the title character's private jet in *Goldfinger*. The plane leaves Switzerland with a tranquilized James Bond (Sean Connery) on board. Having entered the States, the Lockheed JetStar, piloted by Pussy Galore (Honor Blackman), will then fly to its final destination: Blue Grass Field, Kentucky.

Fröbe, Gert (February 25, 1913–September 4, 1988; birth name: Karl-Gerhart Fröbe): Rotund German character actor who portrayed the iconic title character in *Goldfinger*—perhaps the best of all the Bond villains. Although his voice was later completely redubbed by a British actor, Michael Collins, Fröbe's mannerisms were perfectly suited to the fabulously wealthy megalomaniac who is intent on exploding an atomic device inside Fort Knox, Kentucky—home of America's gold reserves.

Israel banned the release of *Goldfinger* in 1964 when it was discovered that Fröbe had been a member of the Nazi Party during World War II. However, after the ban, a Jewish man named Mario Blumenau came forward and told the world that Fröbe had saved his and his mother's lives by hiding them during the war. The ban was lifted after Fröbe also proved he had not been active in the party.

Born in Oberplanitz (now Zwickau), Saxony, Fröbe made his credited motion picture debut in director R. A. Stemmle's musical comedy *The Berliner* (1948), playing Otto Normalverbraucher.

German actor Gert Fröbe was perfect as the title character in *Goldfinger*. *Courtesy of the David Reinhardt Collection*

American audiences first discovered him as oafish Sergeant Kaffekanne, the mounted German soldier who brings the beach gunners their milk every morning in *The Longest Day* (1962), a film that also featured Sean Connery. Two years after *Goldfinger*, he portrayed Colonel Manfred Von Holstein in Ken Annakin's *Those Magnificent Men in Their Flying Machines or How I Flew from London to Paris in 25 hours 11 minutes* (1965).

FROM RUSSIA WITH LOVE

(United Artists, 1963) ★★★★: The second James Bond film produced by Albert R. Broccoli and Harry Saltzman. US release date: April 8, 1964. Budget: $2.2 million. Worldwide box office gross: $78.9 million (US domestic gross: $24.8 million; international gross: $54.1 million).*
Running time: 118 minutes.

---

* "From Russia with Love (1964)," The Numbers, accessed May 19, 2020, https://www.the-numbers.com/movie/From-Russia-With-Love.

THE SETUP

To exact revenge for the death of their operative Dr. No, SPECTRE chief Ernst Stavro Blofeld assembles a rogues' gallery of villains to blackmail and murder James Bond (Sean Connery). They include planner Kronsteen (Vladek Sheybal), a master chess player; operations chief Rosa Klebb (Lotte Lenya), a former Soviet master spy; and Grant (Robert Shaw), a blond-pated killer. The bait: a Russian Lektor decoding machine to be turned over to 007 in Istanbul by voluptuous Soviet cipher clerk Tatiana Romanova (Daniela Bianchi). Despite the warnings of his friend and local spy chief Kerim Bey (Pedro Armendariz), Bond is snared in the elaborate trap. Only a rigged briefcase stands between 007 and certain death.

The cover of the 1960s-era American paperback edition of Ian Fleming's *From Russia with Love*. *Steve Rubin Collection*

BEHIND THE SCENES

A classic adventure thriller, *From Russia with Love* was the most serious film in the series until the release of *Casino Royale* in 2006. Its tone derives from that of Ian Fleming's original novel, probably his best. With *From Russia with Love*, Fleming attempted to upgrade the character of Bond and create an incredibly intricate blackmail and murder plot, involving the most dastardly group of villains ever assembled. In that novel's concluding scene, when Klebb kicks Bond with one of her poison-tipped shoe spikes, it looks like the end of 007. And it actually was supposed to be. Fleming was upset with the disappointing sales of the Bond books at the time, and his intention was to kill off 007 once and for all. It was only through the intervention of American author Raymond Chandler, who was a big Bond fan, that Fleming was encouraged to revive Bond in his next book. Thus, *From Russia with Love* was grounded in a seriousness that was well preserved in Richard Maibaum's thoughtful adaptation.

Having scored well with location photography on *Dr. No*, the producers wisely decided to shoot much of *From Russia with Love* on location in Istanbul. Casting was particularly effective in this entry. Robert Shaw and Lotte Lenya stole the picture as blond ice-water-in-his-veins assassin Grant and his spymaster Rosa Klebb, respectively. And the charming Pedro Armendariz—in his final film role—brought Kerim Bey to vibrant life.

Like many Alfred Hitchcock classics, which served as inspiration for both Maibaum and director Terence Young, this Bond film has many memorable set pieces, including the gypsy camp where Bond (Sean Connery) witnesses a particularly nasty girl fight and then has to stave off an attack by Bulgarian agents; the assassination of Krilencu (Fred Haggerty), who attempts to exit his apartment through a movie billboard; Tanya (Daniela Bianchi) seducing Bond in his Istanbul hotel suite, filmed by a hidden movie crew; the fight on the train between Grant and Bond, probably the best screen fight ever choreographed; and the famous helicopter and motorboat chase that concludes the film. *From Russia with Love* lacks the humor some fans expect from a Bond film, and the typical 007 gadgets are kept to a minimum. But it's still one of the best adventure films ever made.

THE CAST

James Bond	Sean Connery
Tatiana Romanova	Daniela Bianchi
Kerim Bey	Pedro Armendariz
Rosa Klebb	Lotte Lenya
Grant	Robert Shaw
M	Bernard Lee
Sylvia Trench	Eunice Gayson

Injured Kerim Bey (Pedro Armendariz, left) uses the shoulder of James Bond (Sean Connery) to take out Krilencu the Bulgarian killer in *From Russia with Love*. *Courtesy of the David Reinhardt Collection*

Morzeny	Walter Gotell	Orchestral music composed and conducted by	John Barry
Vavra, the Gypsy Leader	Francis De Wolff	Title song performed by	Matt Monro
Train Conductor	George Pastell	Title song written by	Lionel Bart
Kerim's Girl	Nadja Regin	James Bond theme written by	Monty Norman
Miss Moneypenny	Lois Maxwell	Art Director	Syd Cain
Vida	Aliza Gur	Assistant Art Director	Michael White
Zora	Martine Beswick	Set Dresser	Freda Pearson
Kronsteen	Vladek Sheybal	Costume Designer	Jocelyn Rickards
Belly Dancer	Leila	Wardrobe Mistress	Eileen Sullivan
Bulgar Agent	Hasan Ceylan	Wardrobe Master	Ernie Farrer
Krilencu	Fred Haggerty	Makeup	Basil Newall
Rolls Chauffeur	Neville Jason		Paul Rabiger
Commissar Benz	Peter Bayliss	Hairstylist	Eileen Warwick
Mehmet	Nushet Atear	Production Manager	Bill Hill
Rhoda	Peter Brayham	Assistant Director	David Anderson
Major Boothroyd	Desmond Llewelyn	Continuity	Kay Mander
Grant's Masseuse	Jan Williams	Second Unit Cameraman	Robert Kindred
McAdams	Peter Madden	Camera Operator	John Winbolt
Nash	Bill Hill	Location Manager	Frank Ernst

THE CREW

Director	Terence Young	Istanbul Production Assistant	Ilham Filmer
Screenplay by	Richard Maibaum	Stunt work arranged by	Bob Simmons
Adapted by	Johanna Harwood	Title Designer	Robert Brownjohn
Producers	Albert R. Broccoli	Assistant Title Designer	Trevor Bond
	Harry Saltzman	Special Effects	John Stears
Director of Photography	Ted Moore	Special Effects Assistant	Frank George
		Editor	Peter Hunt

From Russia with Love by Jeff Marshall. *Courtesy of Jeff Marshall*

Frost, Miranda: World champion fencer and undercover MI6 agent portrayed by Rosamund Pike in *Die Another Day*. Bond (Pierce Brosnan) meets the icy Frost (pun intended) at the Blades fencing club, where she's sparring with Gustav Graves (Toby Stephens), her boss. However, we soon learn that Miranda's loyalties are not with the British government, and that she was the one who betrayed Bond in North Korea.

Fukunaga, Cary Joji (July 10, 1977–   ): Stylish American film and television director, writer, and producer who became the first Yank to helm an Eon Productions 007 pic when he came aboard *No Time to Die*. Born in Oakland, California (his father is of Japanese descent, his mother of Swedish ances-

try), Fukunaga made his feature direc-torial debut on the Spanish-language crime drama *Sin Nombre* (2009). However, what put him on Hollywood's radar was his yeoman work directing the first season of the HBO television series *True Detective* (2014), for which he won the Emmy Award for

Cary Fukunaga was the first American to direct an Eon Pro-ductions Bond film, bringing his skills to *No Time to Die. Courtesy of the Anders Frejdh Collection*

Outstanding Directing for a Drama Series. He followed that success with the acclaimed African war drama *Beasts of No Nation* (2015), which he wrote, produced, and directed (and which also featured actor Idris Elba, who has been touted as a future James Bond candidate).

Fullerton, Fiona (October 10, 1956–   ): Nigerian-born British actress who portrayed Soviet KGB agent Pola Ivanova in *A View to a Kill*. Fullerton also portrayed Tatiana Romanova in screen tests with Timothy Dalton prior to his Bond debut in *The Living Daylights*. (They

re-created the scene in *From Russia with Love* in which Bond finds Tanya in his hotel suite bed).

Born in Kaduna, Nigeria, Fullerton made her feature film debut as a teenager in director Richard C. Sarafian's family drama *Run Wild, Run Free* (1969). Three years later, she got her big break playing the title character in William Ster-ling's *Alice's Adventures in Wonderland*. In 1996, Fullerton had a strange encounter at her front door with a supposed fan, who later confessed in a letter from prison that he had come to kill her but decided not to when she answered the door with her infant daughter in her arms. She was so haunted by this revelation, she later said, that that she decided to retire from show business to pursue her interests in writing and real estate while raising her family.*

fun house: Training ground for Francisco Scaramanga (Christopher Lee) in *The Man with the Golden Gun*. This atmospheric location, built inside his fabulous island home, comes com-plete with false doorways and exits, a mirror maze to confuse his opponents, and a shooting gallery in which wooden dummies fire back with live ammunition. To help keep his eyesight and reflexes at their sharpest levels, Scaramanga invites the world's top guns to this maze, where they are at a distinct disadvantage. While Scaramanga stalks his targets, his associate Nick Nack (Hervé Villechaize) controls the audio and visual elements of the fun house, which serve to further startle all visitors. Scaramanga's challenge: to reach his own golden gun before exposing himself to his opponent's firepower.

Rodney (Marc Lawrence), a slick syndicate hit man, is Scaramanga's first victim, and Bond (Roger Moore) is nearly his second. A sign of Scaramanga's respect for 007 is a wooden figure of 007 that stands in the midst of the maze. In the final shoot-out, Bond impersonates that figure and wins a gun duel with his ultimate nemesis.

The fun house set was designed by Peter Mur-ton and built at Pinewood Studios. Setting the moody stage for these indoor gun duels is John Barry's score—a definite plus in the film.

---

* Fiona Fullerton, "The Day a Stalker Came to Kill Me," *Daily Mail*, August 3, 2008, https://www.dailymail.co.uk/femail /article-1041249/The-day-stalker-came-kill-Fiona-Fullerton -reveals-terrifying-ordeal.html.

Galore, Pussy: Auric Goldfinger's personal jet pilot and co-conspirator in Operation Grand Slam, portrayed by athletic British actress Honor Blackman in *Goldfinger*. Pussy is also the leader of a group of acrobatic aerial pilots: Pussy Galore's Flying Circus. The circus, composed of five voluptuous blondes flying Piper Cherokee monoplances, will spray the deadly Delta-9 nerve gas into the atmosphere over Fort Knox, taking out forty-one thousand US Army troops that guard the gold repository.

Honor Blackman brought a fresh sexuality to the ultimate Bond girl: Pussy Galore in *Goldfinger*. *Courtesy of the David Reinhardt Collection*

Honor Blackman burned herself into the memory of Bond fans in 1964 as the ultimate Bond girl, Miss Pussy Galore. *Courtesy of the David Reinhardt Collection*

In Ian Fleming's original novel, Pussy is a lesbian gang leader. That's not the case in the Richard Maibaum / Paul Dehn screenplay, but she is a resourceful woman who prefers the company of her fellow pilot-acrobats. I don't blame her.

Pussy was the first in a long line of James Bond females with blatantly sexual names. Her introduction on Goldfinger's jet does generate one of the biggest and best laughs in the series. Bond: "Who are you?" Pussy: "My name is Pussy Galore." Bond: "I must be dreaming."

The producers of *Goldfinger* were prepared to change her name to Kitty Galore if the censors objected. But Eon Productions' publicity man, Tom Carlile, defused that possibility by granting an exclusive to a London newspaper if their photographer would snap a picture of Honor Blackman and Prince Philip at a charity ball and give it the caption "Pussy and the Prince." When the photo and caption appeared the next day and no one objected, the producers were emboldened to use the name in the final cut of the film.

gamma gas: Poison gas employed by SPECTRE mercenary Angelo Palazzi (Paul Stassino) to murder NATO aerial observer François Derval (Paul Stassino) and the members of his nuclear bomber crew in *Thunderball*.

Garbage: Scottish American alternative pop-rock group, featuring lead singer Shirley Manson, who performed the title song in *The World Is Not Enough*. Its other members include Duke Erikson (guitar, bass, keyboards), Steve Marker (guitars, keyboards), and Butch Vig (drums, percussion). In 1997, they were nominated for a Grammy Award for Best New Artist. They made their motion picture debut performing "#1 Crush" in *Romeo + Juliet* (1996).

Garden of Remembrance: The final resting place in Las Vegas for Peter Franks (Joe Robinson) in *Diamonds Are Forever*. Located at the Slumber Inc. funeral home, the ashes are placed in a niche adorned by "restful chartreuse curtains and angel's breath gold trim."

garlic incident, the: A funny off-screen incident in *On Her Majesty's Secret Service* that involved actors George Lazenby and Diana Rigg. The incident supposedly took place in the Pinewood Studios commissary on a Wednesday afternoon prior to their first love scene. As Lazenby told it, midway through their lunch, Rigg called over to him and jokingly shouted, "Hey George, I'm having garlic with my pâté; I hope you are too." Lazenby smiled and went back to his meal. The headlines the next day read, DIANA RIGG EATS GARLIC BEFORE KISS WITH GEORGE LAZENBY.

"The press kept feeding the fire to keep the story going," said Lazenby. "Contrary to the newspaper accounts, Diana and I didn't hate each other. But Diana did have a big ego—after all, she had been around for a while, and I was just an upstart. I'm sure she didn't like us being treated on the same level. Also, the press was very interested in me because I was new, while they had all done interviews with Diana before. Even Telly Savalas was affected. He kept saying, 'Why am I the best-kept secret on this picture?'"[*]

Gavin, John (April 8, 1931–February 9, 2018; birth name: Juan Vincent Apablasa): Handsome American actor of Mexican, Chilean, and Spanish ancestry who was actually signed to play James Bond in *Diamonds Are Forever* but lost the role to Sean Connery when UA executive David Picker made the veteran 007 one final offer he couldn't refuse.

It's hard to believe that Eon Productions would hire an American to play James Bond. But Gavin isn't the only Yank to be seriously considered for the role. Throughout the years, names like Paul Newman, Steve McQueen, Burt Reynolds, James Brolin, and even Jimmy Stewart were considered. As for Gavin, he went on to become a diplomat; President Ronald Reagan appointed him as the US ambassador to Mexico in May 1981.

Gayson, Eunice (March 17, 1928–June 8, 2018): British actress who portrayed Bond's fetching girlfriend Sylvia Trench in *Dr. No* and *From Russia with Love*. According to Gayson, her role was going to recur throughout the series, but when director Terence Young left the franchise during preproduction on *Goldfinger*, her part was eliminated.[*] It was to Sylvia that Bond (Sean Connery) uttered his first line of dialogue, "I admire your courage, Miss . . . ?"

Actress Eunice Gayson, who portrayed fetching society girl Sylvia Trench in *Dr. No* and *From Russia with Love*. *Courtesy of the David Reinhardt Collection*

A native of Purley, Surrey, England, Gayson made her feature film debut in director Harold French's romantic drama *My Brother Jonathan* (1948). Prior to *Dr. No*, she had costarred in *Zarak* (1956), an adventure film starring Victor Mature that was produced by Albert R. Broccoli, directed by Terence Young, and written by Richard Maibaum—all future Bond filmmakers. Gayson retired from acting after her appearance as Countess Marie in the television series *The Adventurer* (1972), which costarred Bond veteran Catherine Schell (*On Her Majesty's Secret Service*).

---

* George Lazenby, interview by the author, Los Angeles, July 1, 1981.

* Eunice Gayson, interview by the author, London, June 1977.

Gee, Prunella (February 17, 1950–   ): British actress who portrayed Shrublands physical therapist Patricia Fearing in *Never Say Never Again*, a role that was originated by the late Molly Peters in *Thunderball* (1965). A native of London, Gee made her feature film debut as Rina Van Niekirk in director Ralph Nelson's action adventure *The Wilby Conspiracy* (1975). She was later cast as Doreen Heavey in the television series *Coronation Street* (69 episodes, 1999–2004). She retired from acting in 2004.

Giannini, Giancarlo (August 1, 1942–   ): Academy Award–nominated Italian actor who portrayed Rene Mathis, local liaison to James Bond (Daniel Craig) in Montenegro in *Casino Royale*. He returned in *Quantum of Solace*, helping Bond infiltrate the SPECTRE organization. Giannini received his Academy Award nomination for Best Actor in a Leading Role for *Pasqualino Settebellezze* (1975). Born in La Spezia, Liguria, Giannini first appeared on the big screen under the name John Charlie Johns in the crime thriller *Libido* (1965). The following year, he portrayed the title character in an Italian television miniseries production of *David Copperfield*. He made his English-language debut as Saverio in director Mauro Bolognini's comedy *Arabella* (1967).

Actor Giancarlo Giannini portrayed mysterious French agent Rene Mathis in both *Casino Royale* and *Quantum of Solace. Courtesy of the Anders Frejdh Collection*

Gilbert, Lewis (March 6, 1920–February 23, 2018): British director, actor, and documentary filmmaker who helmed *You Only Live Twice*, *The Spy Who Loved Me*, and *Moonraker*. Having originally turned down *You Only Live Twice*, Gilbert was persuaded to accept the assignment when producer Albert R. Broccoli convinced him that a huge audience was waiting to see his work. Said Gilbert, "When you make an ordinary film, you never know what your audience is going to be like. You have no idea. It may be twenty people or twenty million. But when you make a

Bond, you know that whether the film is good or bad, there is going to be a huge audience waiting to see it. To me, that became an important challenge."*

A native of London, Gilbert made his feature directorial debut on the dance drama *The Little Ballerina* (1947), which featured future Bond player Sydney Tafler (the captain of the *Liparus* in *The Spy Who Loved Me*, and Gilbert's brother-in-law). Gilbert later directed *Sink the Bismarck!* (1960), one of the great World War II films, during which he collaborated with future Bond editor Peter Hunt. Prior to *You Only Live Twice*, Gilbert produced and directed *Alfie* (1966), which starred Michael Caine and was nominated for five Oscars, including one for Gilbert for Best Picture. Gilbert's additional feature directing credits include *Damn the Defiant!* (1962), *The 7th Dawn* (1964), *Educating Rita* (1983), and *Shirley Valentine* (1989).

girl fight: The fight to the death in rural Istanbul between two beautiful gypsy girls (Martine Beswick and Aliza Gur) who love the same man, in *From Russia with Love*. One of the James Bond series' best moments takes place in art director Syd Cain's sprawling gypsy camp, which was built in an area of Pinewood Studios called the "Pinewood paddock." Peopled with an assortment of exotic characters, including 007 (Sean Connery), Kerim Bey (Pedro Armendariz), Vavra the gypy leader (Francis De Wolff), and a belly dancer (Leila), this sequence benefits strongly from John Barry's staccato theme music and the raw sexual energy that both girls brought to the battle.

Martine Beswick, who would go on to play 007's assistant Paula Caplan in *Thunderball*, described the action in the girl fight: "We were like two wild cats, crashing about, crying out—all to the tune of Terence Young, who was terribly vocal. He was yelling all the time, saying things like 'Kill her, Martine! Now hit her, get her foot, that's right, now turn over. Go, Aliza! Jump on her.'

"Stuntman Peter Perkins was doing the same thing. Both of them were very involved. And it was wonderful that they did that, because it gave us the impetus to make it real. We needed that impetus, because it was cold out there at night, simply freezing, and all we had to wear were

---

* Lewis Gilbert, interview by the author, London, June 15, 1977.

those torn scarves and rags. It was like running around in our bloomers.

"But we didn't show a thing, and still it turned out to be a terribly erotic sequence. Just the sight of two women fighting like that at close quarters was a big turn-on to everybody on the set, including Sean Connery, who seemed to be having a ball."*

Glen, John (May 15, 1932–): British film director who joined the Bond series as a second unit director and editor on *On Her Majesty's Secret Service*, later directed the famous Asgard Jump on *The Spy Who Loved Me*, then went on to direct five James Bond films—*For Your Eyes Only*, *Octopussy*, *A View to a Kill*, *The Living Daylights*, and *Licence to Kill*—more than any other director.

A native of Sunbury-on-Thames, England, Glen had worked for several years as a supervising editor and a director on various TV series when director Peter Hunt invited him to become the editor and second unit director on *OHMSS*. Having a solid background in action film editing and second unit work, Glen still found it difficult to convince producer Albert R. Broccoli that he should direct *For Your Eyes Only* in 1981. Glen eventually won the assignment and delivered a terrific 007 adventure.

Reflecting on the longevity of the series, he told film journalist Craig Modderno in 1989, "Bond has never been corrupted and has always been a citizen above suspicion doing the right thing. In times of mixed morality and abuse of power by many of the people we admire, it's nice to know James Bond is still around to show what heroes are all about!"†

Glover, Bruce (May 2, 1932–): American character actor who portrayed the gay assassin Mr. Wint in *Diamonds Are Forever*. Partnered with bald-pated Mr. Kidd (Putter Smith), Glover picks up a scorpion and kills Dr. Tynan, the motorcycle-riding diamond smuggler, in an early scene. And in the film's concluding scene, Glover ends up going

over the rail of a luxury liner with a time bomb attached to his privates.

Initially, Glover was told that he was much too "normal" for the part of Mr. Wint. As he explained, the casting director was going for a modern version of a Sydney Greenstreet / Peter Lorre type of relationship. "However," recalled Glover, "when they went for the rather wild look of Putter Smith [as Mr. Kidd], they suddenly decided they had enough of that kind of look and felt I was fine."* Interestingly, up until filming began, Glover still wasn't sure which part he was going to play.

---

* Bruce Glover, interview by the author, Los Angeles, December 1, 1977.

American character actor Bruce Glover brings Mr. Wint to glorious life in *Diamonds Are Forever*, here trying to deliver the coup de grâce to James Bond (Sean Connery) *Courtesy of the Anders Frejdh Collection*

---

* Martine Beswick, interview by the author, Los Angeles, November 12, 1977.
† John Glen, interview by Craig Modderno, Los Angeles, June 30, 1989.

Thus, he decided not to memorize his lines. It wasn't until the stuntman handed him a scorpion in the middle of the Nevada desert on the first day of shooting that he realized he was to play Mr. Wint.

At first, Glover was concerned whether the gay element of Mr. Wint and Mr. Kidd's relationship was believable. "After all," he smiled, "I looked over at Putter's mouth and realized that kissing that was an impossibility. He was so wild looking. Eventually, I simply decided that he was a giant teddy bear—my plaything. There were really no sexual thoughts at all. However, I was very possessive of him. After we shot the hand-holding sequence, I looked over at Putter and saw that he had turned beet red, he was so embarrassed." NOTE: The hand-holding scene was initially cut from network television broadcasts of *Diamonds Are Forever*.

A Chicago native, Glover made his feature film debut as an uncredited stevedore in director Charles Lederer's musical comedy *Never Steal Anything Small* (1959). His additional feature credits include *C.C. & Company* (1970), *Walking Tall* (1973), *Chinatown* (1974), *Hunter's Blood* (1986), *Big Bad Mama II* (1987), *Ghost World* (2001), *Simon Says* (2006), and many others. He's the father of actor Crispin Glover, best known for playing George McFly in *Back to the Future* (1985).

Glover, Julian (March 27, 1935–   ): British character actor who portrayed well-tailored heroin smuggler and Soviet agent Aris Kristatos in *For Your Eyes Only*. A native of London, Glover made his feature film debut in *Tom Jones* (1963), which won the Oscar for Best Picture. Glover is probably best known as duplicitous antiquities dealer Walter Donovan in *Indiana Jones and the Last Crusade* (1989), or as the weaselly Grand Maester Pycelle in HBO's hit series *Game of Thrones* (31 episodes, 2011–2016).

His additional feature film credits include *The Alphabet Murders* (1965); *Five Million Years to Earth* (1967), a.k.a.

Actor Julian Glover portrayed the nefarious Kristatos in *For Your Eyes Only*. *Steve Rubin Collection*

Quatermass and the Pit; *Alfred the Great* (1969); *Wuthering Heights* (1970); *Nicholas and Alexandra* (1971); *Antony and Cleopatra* (1972); *Hitler: The Last Ten Days* (1973); *Star Wars: Episode V—The Empire Strikes Back* (1980), as General Maximillian Veers; *The Fourth Protocol* (1987), with fellow Bond player Pierce Brosnan; *Cry Freedom* (1987); *King Ralph* (1991); *Troy* (2004); and *Alien Uprising* (2012).

Gobinda: Giant bodyguard to Kamal Khan (Louis Jourdan), portrayed by veteran Indian actor Kabir Bedi in *Octopussy*. Unsmiling and unsympathetic, with hands that can crush dice cubes—reminiscent of Oddjob and the Slazenger 1 golf ball in *Goldfinger*. Gobinda also has that semi-Jaws quality of gaining the audience's respect even as he's trying to kill Bond. His attempts on 007 become increasingly difficult. First, there's the wild three-wheeler chase through Udaipur, followed by the raucous tiger hunt through the bush that surrounds the Monsoon Palace, then the train-hopping escapade in West Germany.

Finally, Kamal asks the ever-dutiful Gobinda to climb outside their twin-engined plane and battle Bond in midair. In a classic moment in the series, Gobinda sticks a blade in his mouth,

Actor Kabir Bedi portrayed Gobinda, Kamal Khan's formidable and dutiful right arm, in *Octopussy*. *Steve Rubin Collection*

Roger Moore and Kabir Bedi have a humorous moment during midair action filmed on a blue screen stage for *Octopussy. Steve Rubin Collection*

summons up his resolve, and crawls outside the aircraft for one final confrontation. As they're maneuvering for position on the plane's fuselage, Bond is able to whip the radio antenna into Gobinda's face. Stunned, his burly adversary loses his grip and falls to his death.

Gogol, General Alexis: Senior KGB officer who became a recurring character in the James Bond series. Portrayed by actor Walter Gotell, who first appeared in *From Russia with Love* as SPECTRE field commander Morzeny, General Gogol was introduced as M's opposite number in *The Spy Who Loved Me*. Pitted against freelance madman Karl Stromberg (Curt Jurgens), James Bond (Roger Moore) joins forces with KGB agent Anya Amasova (Barbara Bach). This alliance—a tip of the cap to Cold War détente—includes their respective bosses, M and Gogol, the latter of whom operates offices in the underground chambers of an Egyptian tomb.

Portrayed as a humanistic Soviet military man, Gogol is definitely a new breed of Russian char-

acter in Western cinema. As the series evolved, he became even more sympathetic. After brief appearances in *Moonraker* and *For Your Eyes Only* (in the latter, he arrives by helicopter only to discover that the ATAC computer has been destroyed), Gogol returns in *Octopussy* as the counterpart to fanatical General Orlov (Steven Berkoff), who is ready to create a nuclear "accident" on a US Air Force base in West Germany in order to force unilateral disarmament throughout Western Europe. Determined to avoid confrontation with the West, Gogol stands firmly against Orlov and eventually wins over his Russian superior (Paul Hardwick). When Orlov's smuggling activities are exposed, Gogol launches the investigation to find and arrest the renegade Russian general—which leads to the final confrontation on the train tracks near the West German border, where the fleeing Orlov is machine-gunned by border guards.

Gogol returns in *A View to a Kill* to warn Max Zorin (Christopher Walken) that his murderous activities are not sanctioned by the KGB. When

Bond kills Zorin, Gogol is delighted to award 007 (Roger Moore) the Order of Lenin. In *The Living Daylights*, Gogol made his final appearance in the series, this time as a high-ranking foreign service bureaucrat who allows Kara Milovy (Maryam d'Abo) to perform in Austria.

NOTE: Although the character is credited in his final appearance as "General Anatol Gogol," the only mention of his given name in the films themselves is in *The Spy Who Loved Me*, in which M calls him Alexis and he refers to M by his first name, Miles.

golden bullet: The trademark of assassin Francisco Scaramanga (Christopher Lee) in *The Man with the Golden Gun*. These "dumdum bullets" are designed to flatten upon impact for maximum wounding effect. Scaramanga has them custom manufactured in Macao by Lazar the gunsmith (Marne Maitland), who also designed the fascinating weapon that shoots them.

Because of the types of security checks he often faces, Scaramanga must have a weapon that, when disassembled, doesn't look like a weapon. His golden gun thus converts to a ballpoint pen, a cuff link, a cigarette lighter, and cigarette case—a fact he reveals just prior to the assassination of heavily guarded industrialist Hai Fat (Richard Loo). Scaramanga hides his bullet in his belt buckle.

At the beginning of *The Man with the Golden Gun*, one of the custom gold bullets, with an engraved 007, is sent to the British Secret Service. M (Bernard Lee) points out that in the past an engraved bullet has been used by Scaramanga to terrify his intended victims. Rather than go into hiding, Bond (Roger Moore) takes the fight to the assassin.

Golden Grotto: Fictional area of the Caribbean Sea, not far from Nassau in the Bahamas, that is the habitat for an especially deadly species of shark in *Thunderball*. It's also where Emilio Largo (Adolfo Celi) hides his hijacked British nuclear bomber.

After a prolonged NATO search of the Atlantic fails to find the bomber, Bond (Sean Connery) and Felix Leiter (Rik Van Nutter) are about to end their own search when their helicopter passes over an area that Leiter identifies as the Golden Grotto. Remembering that Largo's sharks are

It is in the Bahamas' fictional Golden Grotto that James Bond and Felix Leiter go hunting for the downed Vulcan bomber in *Thunderball*. *Steve Rubin Collection*

of the Golden Grotto variety, Bond realizes that they've found their prize at last.

For the scene in which Bond is trapped in Largo's pool with his Golden Grotto sharks, Connery really did film underwater alongside the creatures, which were actually tiger sharks. Underwater cinematographer Lamar Boren explained, "Those sharks weren't drugged, nor were their jaws wired. They were the real thing, and Sean was depending on us to keep him out of trouble. But you really don't have to worry about sharks anyway, unless there's blood in the water or a lot of garbage. . . . The sharks were very sluggish. They ended up ignoring Sean and just swimming around."[*]

GoldenEye: The nickname of author Ian Fleming's beachfront vacation home in Jamaica—where, between 1952 and 1964, he wrote his James Bond novels and short stories. Eon Productions' seventeenth Bond film borrowed the term as the code name for a secret, space-based Russian weapons system. This system is taken over by the sinister Janus crime syndicate in *GoldenEye*.

GOLDENEYE

(MGM/United Artists, 1995) ★★★: The seventeenth James Bond movie produced by Eon Productions, it marked the debut of Pierce Brosnan as James Bond. US release

---

[*] Lamar Boren, interview by the author, La Jolla, CA, August 17, 1976.

date: November 17, 1995. Budget: $60 million. Worldwide box office gross: $356.4 million (US domestic gross: $106.4 million; international gross: $250.0 million).* Running time: 130 minutes.

THE SETUP

A throwback to the intrigue-laden Bond films of the '60s, *GoldenEye* pits 007 (Pierce Brosnan) against an old friend and double-0 comrade, Alec Trevelyan (Sean Bean), who is now the head of a fanatical splinter group of the Russian mafia. His plot: revenge against his native England through the destruction of its economic system. His method: unleashing a deadly electromagnetic pulse from a commandeered Russian space satellite code-named GoldenEye—an attack that will disable Britain's entire electrical grid. In a nod to previous female assassins like Fiona Volpe in *Thunderball* and Fatima Blush in *Never Say Never Again*, the writers introduced the amazingly athletic Xenia Onatopp (Famke Janssen), a gorgeous assassin who knocks off her victims with her "killer thighs." Bond is helped along the way by another beauty, computer expert and love interest Natalya Simonova (Izabella Scorupco).

BEHIND THE SCENES

Audiences had been waiting for Pierce Brosnan to assume the James Bond mantle ever since it was announced that he couldn't get out of his *Remington Steele* contract to star in *The Living Daylights*. He was a perfect choice for 007—handsome, cool as a cucumber, good with his fists, comfortable with the opposite sex, and adept at the type of witty throwaway humor that had been missing from the deadly serious Timothy Dalton Bond films. When asked what it meant to play Bond at the opening press conference for the film, Pierce Brosnan responded, "It's pretty emotional in many ways—actually only because it was in my life in '86 and it went out of my life in '86. When something happens in your life, [then] happens for a second time, it carries a certain significance."

Brosnan assured fans that his character was "still a ladies man—he has an eye out for the women. It's a classic Bond; he gets the women. As a boy of eleven years old, Sean was the first

After an unprecedented six-year absence from the big screen, James Bond returned in the personage of Pierce Brosnan in *GoldenEye*. Not surprisingly, Brosnan was a terrific Bond. *Courtesy of the David Reinhardt Collection*

Bond I ever saw." But he wasn't going to lean on nostalgia; he noted that as he waited for the press conference to begin, "I stood there and I could hear the clamor outside of the press, and everything went into slow motion, and then they put the music on, the Bond music, and suddenly I'm doing this—I'm about to stand in front of all these people and announce to the world that I'm going to do this role and also have colossal fun. There's no ghosts here. There's no ghosts of Sean, there's no ghosts of the '60s, there's no ghosts of Roger . . . it's like a fresh, clean slate."*

The early 1990s had been a difficult time for the Bond franchise, stuck in a complicated legal war over Bond distribution rights that stalled the series for six years. However, given all that time, the writers came up with a believable story that

---

* "Goldeneye (1995) ," The Numbers, accessed May 20, 2020, https://www.the-numbers.com/movie/Goldeneye.

* Special features, *GoldenEye*, James Bond Ultimate Edition (1995; MGM, 2006), DVD.

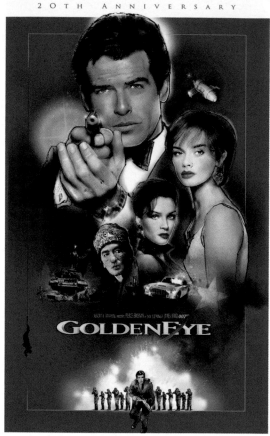

GoldenEye by Jeff Marshall. *Courtesy of Jeff Marshall*

won over international audiences. Highlights: the exciting teaser sequence involving Bond racing over a cliff in a motorcycle and skydiving into a crashing private plane; Famke Janssen chewing the scenery so well as Onatopp; and Dame Judi Dench as a new M with "balls."

THE CAST

James Bond	Pierce Brosnan
Alec Trevelyan	Sean Bean
Natalya Fyodorovna Simonova	Izabella Scorupco
Xenia Zaragevna Onatopp	Famke Janssen
Jack Wade	Joe Don Baker
M	Dame Judi Dench
Valentin Dmitrovich Zukovsky	Robbie Coltrane
Defense Minister Dmitri Mishkin	Tcheky Karyo
General Arkady Grigorovich Ourumov	Gottfried John
Boris Grishenko	Alan Cumming

Q	Desmond Llewelyn
Miss Moneypenny	Samantha Bond
Bill Tanner	Michael Kitchen
Caroline	Serena Gordon
Severnaya Duty Officer	Simon Kunz
French Warship Captain	Pavel Douglas
French Warship Officer	Olivier Lajous
Admiral Chuck Farrell	Billy J. Mitchell
IBM Computer Store Manager	Constantine Gregory
Irina (Zukovsky's Mistress)	Minnie Driver
Anna	Michelle Arthur

THE CREW

Presented by	Albert R. Broccoli
Director	Martin Campbell
Screenplay by	Jeffrey Caine
	Bruce Feirstein
Story by	Michael France
Executive Producer	Tom Pevsner
Producers	Barbara Broccoli
	Michael G. Wilson
Associate Producer	Anthony Waye
Director of Photography	Phil Meheux
Music by	Eric Serra
Title song performed by	Tina Turner
Production Designer	Peter Lamont
Costume Designer	Lindy Hemming
Casting by	Debbie McWilliams
Stunt Coordinator	Simon Crane
Title Designer	Daniel Kleinman
Editor	Terry Rawlings

 ## GOLDFINGER

(United Artists, 1964) ★★★★: The third James Bond film produced by Albert R. Broccoli and Harry Saltzman. US release date: December 25, 1964. Budget: $3.5 million. Worldwide box office gross: $124.9 million (US domestic gross: $51.1 million; international gross: $73.8 million).* Running time: 111 minutes.

THE SETUP

Having devastated a heroin smuggling operation in South America, James Bond (Sean Connery) is sent to Miami's swanky Fontainebleau Hotel to observe one Auric Goldfinger (Gert Fröbe), a suspected gold smuggler. Bond foils Goldfinger's rigged gin game with Mr. Simmons

* "Goldfinger (1964)," The Numbers, accessed May 20, 2020, https://www.the-numbers.com/movie/Goldfinger.

(Austin Willis), beds the suspect's stunning girlfriend, Jill Masterson (Shirley Eaton), gets knocked out by his Korean manservant (Harold Sakata), then witnesses Masterson's unusual death: she's painted from head to toe in gold. Returning to London, Bond is ordered to tail Goldfinger to Austria, where he discovers that not only is his nemesis a gold smuggler, with a pilot named Pussy Galore (Honor Blackman), but he's also planning something much bigger—something called Operation Grand Slam.

BEHIND THE SCENES

Although *From Russia with Love* has a better story, *Goldfinger* is the best film in the James Bond series. It elevated the series to a level of pop entertainment that very few films achieve. Indeed, when *Goldfinger* was released during Christmastime 1964, it became a worldwide phenomenon, with many theaters staying open twenty-four hours a day to accommodate the crowds. It was the first megahit film of the modern era. Past box office winners had established their records over a long period of release time, but *Goldfinger* rewrote the record book from its first day in release. No film had ever made as much money in so little time. Why? *Goldfinger* was a big fantasy story with three elements that have never quite been equaled.

First, it has Goldfinger himself, the best of all possible villains, with the most perfect of all schemes. He's also accompanied by Oddjob, a wicked manservant who talks through a very lethal bowler. Second, the film has the most alluring gallery of women ever seen in the series, and introduces them in outrageous fashion. Third, it has that Aston Martin DB5 with modifications. No film prop or gadget has ever been idolized more than that car. Remember, this was the mid-1960s, the era of the space race between the United States and the Soviet Union, when high technology was all the rage. For months, the Aston Martin was the talk of every school campus in the world.

Pussy (Honor Blackman) tries to pilot the doomed presidential jet, while Bond explains that Goldfinger is playing his golden harp. *Courtesy of the Anders Frejdh Collection*

However, there were some problems along the way. According to editor Peter Hunt, the first assembly of the film was so bad that producers Albert R. Broccoli and Harry Saltzman were actually prepared to shelve the film and release *Thunderball* next.* It's hard to believe considering how amazingly good the finished film was, but apparently the producers were concerned that Bond is a rather inactive hero for a good chunk of the film (from the time he's shot with the tranquilizer dart until he battles Oddjob inside Fort Knox). After the first cut, Hunt said, shots were inserted that improved the way the film played, the shelving idea was abandoned, and *Goldfinger* became a legendary addition to the series. That's thanks in large part to Richard Maibaum's script, which cleverly updated the Ian Fleming novel, Guy Hamilton's slam-bang direction, and John Barry's memorable score.

---

* Peter Hunt, interview by the author, London, June 21, 1977.

THE CAST

James Bond	Sean Connery
Auric Goldfinger	Gert Fröbe
Pussy Galore	Honor Blackman
Jill Masterson	Shirley Eaton
Oddjob	Harold Sakata
M	Bernard Lee
Q	Desmond Llewelyn
Mr. Solo	Martin Benson
Felix Leiter	Cec Linder
Mr. Simmons	Austin Willis
Miss Moneypenny	Lois Maxwell
Midnight	Bill Nagy
Capungo	Alf Joint
Old Lady Gatekeeper	Varley Thomas
Bonita	Nadja Regin
Sierra	Raymond Young
Colonel Smithers	Richard Vernon
Brunskill	Denis Cowles
Kisch	Michael Mellinger
Mr. Ling	Burt Kwouk
Strap	Hal Galili
Henchman	Lenny Rabin
Sydney	Tricia Muller
Dink	Margaret Nolan
Mei-Lei	Mai Ling

THE CREW

Director	Guy Hamilton
Screenplay by	Richard Maibaum
	Paul Dehn
Producers	Harry Saltzman
	Albert R. Broccoli
Director of Photography	Ted Moore
Music composed and conducted by	John Barry
Title song performed by	Shirley Bassey
Title song lyrics by	Leslie Bricusse
	Anthony Newley
Production Designer	Ken Adam
Art Director	Peter Murton
Assistant Art Directors	Michael White
	Maurice Pelling
Set Dresser	Freda Pearson
Wardrobe Supervisor	Elsa Fennell
Wardrobe Mistress	Eileen Sullivan
Wardrobe Master	John Hilling
Makeup	Paul Rabiger
	Basil Newall
Hairstylist	Eileen Warwick
Production Manager	L. C. Rudkin
Assistant Director	Frank Ernst
Continuity	Constance Willis

Camera Operator	John Winbolt
Action sequences by	Bob Simmons
Stuntman	George Leech
Choreographer	Selina Wylie
Title Designer	Robert Brownjohn
Special Effects	John Stears
Special Effects Assistant	Frank George
Sound Recordists	Dudley Messenger
	Gordon McCallum
Editor	Peter Hunt
Assembly Editor	Ben Rayner
Dubbing Editors	Norman Wanstall
	Harry Miller

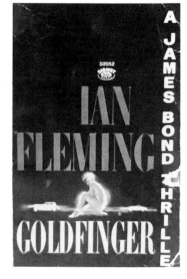

The cover of the 1960s-era paperback edition of Ian Fleming's *Goldfinger*. Steve Rubin Collection

Goldfinger, Auric—The title character in the third James Bond film produced by Albert R. Broccoli and Harry Saltzman, and arguably the best villain in the entire series, portrayed by Geman actor Gert Fröbe, although his voice was entirely redubbed by British actor Michael Collins.

A British citizen, Goldfinger is a fabulously wealthy man with worldwide interests, including a country club and a metallurgical facility in England, a factory in Switzerland, and a stud farm in Kentucky, in addition to a fleet of cars, a private jet, and a private army of Chinese and Korean retainers. As Felix Leiter (Cec Linder) puts it, he's a "big operator."

In the story, the Bank of England suspects that Goldfinger has been smuggling large amounts of gold bullion out of England. It's true, but it barely scratches the surface of his real

Goldfinger (Gert Fröbe) battles James Bond (Sean Connery) aboard his private jet in *Goldfinger*. He's about to learn that it's extremely dangerous to fire guns in planes. *Courtesy of the David Reinhardt Collection*

caper. His plan is to, with the help of the Red Chinese, detonate an atomic bomb inside the gold repository at Fort Knox, Kentucky, where America's entire $15 billion gold reserve is stored. With the US gold radioactive and useless for fifty-eight years, economic chaos in the West will result, pleasing the Chinese and making Goldfinger's own stock of gold increase in value by a factor of ten.

Why is Goldfinger the best villain in the series? Because he is one of the best-drawn characters, combining a realistic greed and obsession for gold with an outsized, almost fantastical personality. Like Dr. No and the villains in *From Russia with Love*, Goldfinger could easily be the perfect cartoon villain, but thanks to Richard Maibaum's marvelous script, he's also totally convincing in the role.

And Gert Fröbe is perfectly cast. He's an overweight man, but he has a certain lightness and grace to him. He's also supremely confidant, self-assured, and resourceful. And even though Bond keeps thwarting him, nothing can shake his will to succeed.

His roly-poly panache doesn't disguise pure ruthlessness and evil, however. Only a twisted, demented megalomaniac would have Oddjob (Harold Sakata) murder Jill Masterson (Shirley Eaton) by covering her body with gold paint or kill Mr. Solo (Martin Benson) by crushing a brand-new Lincoln Continental around him. Worse yet, Goldfinger plans to spray poison gas into the air and kill forty-one thousand American soldiers who guard the Fort Knox installation. This is not

the type of man you want pointing a laser beam at your privates.

***Goldfinger* theme**: It's being whistled by the janitor (Norman McGlen) when Bond (George Lazenby) is brought to the office of Marc-Ange Draco (Gabriele Ferzetti) in *On Her Majesty's Secret Service*—another of screenwriter Richard Maibaum's references to the rich 007 legacy.

Goldfinger's twin brother: The original villain in an early draft of Richard Maibaum's *Diamonds Are Forever* screenplay. Moving away from the serious approach of the previous film, *On Her Majesty's Secret Service*, the draft introduced Goldfinger's brother as a power-mad Swedish shipping magnate who houses a laser cannon in the hull of one of his fleet's supertankers. Plans were even made to have Gert Fröbe play the "twin." This story idea was later abandoned when producer Albert R. Broccoli came up with the idea of Blofeld impersonating a reclusive Howard Hughes–like billionaire. However, aspects of the character resurfaced in the character of Karl Stromberg in *The Spy Who Loved Me*.

golf match: One of the highlights of *Goldfinger*. Ordered to probe the activities of suspected gold smuggler Auric Goldfinger (Gert Fröbe) and supplied with a bar of gold loaned to him by the Bank of England to use as bait, Bond (Sean Connery) tricks Goldfinger into a high-stakes gold challenge match at an English golf club.

For a series in which the action seldom slows down and characters and situations tend to be larger than life, the golf match in *Goldfinger* stands out as a simple but superbly effective battle of wills. Directed at the perfect easygoing pace by Guy Hamilton and tightly written by Richard Maibaum, who abbreviated Ian Fleming's original eighteen-hole match to two holes, it's one of the few times in the franchise when the characters all catch their breath for a moment and forgo the comic book stakes for human-level intensity.

As the competitors navigate the beautifully serene fairways and putting greens of the club, Bond is nattily dressed in a sports shirt, a V-neck sweater, and slacks, while Goldfinger looks amazing in a pair of plus four knickers. Bond's gift for quick thinking—which the series would often lose track of through too much reliance on Q Branch gadgets—is perfectly demonstrated here, when he thwarts a cheating adversary by cheating him one better. The first Daniel Craig 007 film, *Casino Royale*, would explore similar territory, with director Martin Campbell adhering to the same relaxed pacing for the extended Texas hold'em poker match in which Bond takes on another terrific villain, Le Chiffre (Mads Mikkelsen).

Incidentally, it was while taking golf lessons for *Goldfinger* that Sean Connery developed his great passion for the sport.

Goodhead, Dr. Holly: Tall and slinky American astrophysicist and undercover CIA agent portrayed by Lois Chiles in *Moonraker*. On loan to Drax Industries from NASA, Holly isn't too impressed with Bond (Roger Moore) at the start, since it was his government that lost the shuttle in the film's teaser. Gradually, they learn to respect one another, and eventually they link company head Hugo Drax (Michael Lonsdale) to secret operations in Rio de Janeiro and the jungles of Brazil.

Captured by Drax, Holly and Bond are about to be roasted by a shuttle engine when they

Tall, willowy Lois Chiles joined Roger Moore as Holly Goodhead in *Moonraker*. Talk about a character name that wouldn't work today. *Courtesy of the David Reinhardt Collection*

manage to escape through a ventilation shaft. Eventually they steal aboard a shuttle and participate in the final assault on Drax's radar-proof space station. Their shuttle finally destroys the nerve gas pods Drax plans to use to depopulate the Earth.

Holly and Bond are assuming a tender position aboard their returning shuttle when closed-circuit video reveals them to M (Bernard Lee), Q (Desmond Llewelyn), and Defence Minister Freddie Gray (Geoffrey Keen). What is he doing? Q replies, "He's achieving reentry"—a standard Roger Moore–era quip.

Goodnight, Mary: Far Eastern liaison and in-between lover to James Bond (Roger Moore) portrayed by Swedish beauty Britt Ekland in *The Man with the Golden Gun*. Having been assigned to staff intelligence for two years, Mary feels qualified to give Bond an assist on his present assignment. Unfortunately, the lovely British agent spends most of her time sleeping in closets, while Bond makes love to the mysterious Andrea Anders (Maud Adams).

Although quite the bumbler, Goodnight's ability to get herself locked in the trunk of a flying car belonging to Scaramanga (Christopher Lee) actually helps Bond track the dangerous assassin to his private island off the coast of China. There she is completely helpless to prevent the duel of the century—Bond's Walther PPK versus Scaramanga's golden gun.

Britt Ekland portrayed Mary Goodnight, daffy field secretary to James Bond (Roger Moore), in *The Man with the Golden Gun. Courtesy of the David Reinhardt Collection*

Gotell, Walter (March 15, 1924–May 5, 1997): German-born character actor, long in Great Britain, who rose in rank throughout the James Bond series. Born in Bonn, Gotell started out as SPECTRE tactical chief Morzeny in *From Russia with Love*; he was promoted to the role of the KGB's General Gogol in *The Spy Who Loved Me*, *Moonraker*, *For Your Eyes Only*, *Octopussy*, and *A View to a Kill*; and then Gogol rose to a high-ranking position in the Soviet diplomatic corps in *The Living Daylights*.

Specializing in playing German soldiers in Britain during World War II, Gotell made his credited debut in *At Dawn We Die* (1943). Ten years later, he portrayed a German sentry in *Paratrooper*, directed by future 007 helmer Terence Young and produced by Albert R. Broccoli and his partner at that time, Irving Allen.

Gotell's additional feature credits include *Duel in the Jungle* (1954); *Ice Cold in Alex* (1958); *The Bandit of Zhobe* (1959), again for Broccoli and Allen; *Sink the Bismarck!* (1960), for future Bond director Lewis Gilbert; *The Guns of Navarone* (1961); *These Are the Damned* (1962); *55 Days at Peking* (1963), as sympathetic Captain Hoffman of the German legation; *Attack on the Iron Coast* (1968); *Black Sunday* (1977); *The Boys from Brazil* (1978); *Cuba* (1979), joining Sean Connery; and *Prince Valiant* (1997), his final film.

Gothard, Michael (June 24, 1939–December 2, 1992): British actor who portrayed villainous Emile Locque in *For Your Eyes Only*. A native of Hendon, Middlesex, England, Gothard made his feature film debut as Max, the young poet star of director Don Levy's drama *Herostratus* (1967).

Specializing in characters with odd traits and personalities, Gothard also appeared in *Scream and Scream Again* (1970), with Bond player Christopher Lee; *The Last Valley* (1971); *The Devils* (1971); *Whoever Slew Auntie Roo?* (1972); *The Three Musketeers* (1973); *Warlords of the Deep* (1978), with fellow Bond veterans Hal Galili (*Goldfinger*), Shane Rimmer, and Robert Brown;

Michael Gothard of *For Your Eyes Only*.
Steve Rubin Collection

Lifeforce (1985); and *Christopher Columbus: The Discovery* (1992), with fellow Bond vets Robert Davi and Benicio Del Toro, directed by 007 veteran John Glen.

Sadly, while under treatment for depression, Gothard died by suicide in 1992.

GPS: Acronym for Global Positioning System, a worldwide radio navigation system formed from a constellation of twenty-four satellites and their ground stations, allowing the average person on the street to establish his or her exact position on the planet at any moment. Widely available today in everything from smartphones to cars to planes, it was introduced to the world of James Bond in 1997's *Tomorrow Never Dies*, as a plaything of billionaire media mogul Elliot Carver (Jonathan Pryce). It's actually one of Carver's employees, ace computer terrorist Henry Gupta (Ricky Jay), who tampers with a GPS satellite, throwing off a British warship's ability to establish its actual position and allowing its crew to think they're in Chinese territorial waters when they're not.

In addition, although it wasn't identified as such, the tracking device built into the dashboard of James Bond's Aston Martin in *Goldfinger* was an early form of GPS.

Grace, Martin (September 12, 1942–January 27, 2010): Top Irish stunt coordinator who arranged the action sequences on *A View to a Kill* and who had doubled Roger Moore on the previous five James Bond movies, *The Man with the Golden Gun*, *The Spy Who Loved Me*, *Moonraker*, *For Your Eyes Only*, and *Octopussy*.

During the train stunts for *Octopussy*, Grace was involved in an accidental collision that resulted in a broken pelvis and eight months of recuperation. On *A View to a Kill*, Grace supervised more than a hundred British, French, Swiss, and American stuntmen. In the latter film, Grace coordinated the scene in which May Day (Grace Jones) jumps from the Eiffel Tower (accomplished by American stuntman B. J. Worth); the chaotic flooding and dynamiting of the Main Strike Mine, which includes the machine-gunning of its mine workers; and the amazing fight between Bond (Roger Moore) and Max Zorin (Christopher Walken) atop the Golden Gate Bridge, most of which was shot on a duplicated set at Pinewood Studios.

Grace described his first look at the real bridge: "Three people can fit in the elevator going up to the top of the Golden Gate Bridge, and one of them was the elevator operator. So, I went up with Karen [Price], the double for Tanya Roberts. When we arrived at the top—this is about 750 feet from the water—I got out and walked straight on and straight down the cables. I didn't hesitate.

"The cables are surrounded by a great big cylinder, which is about three feet wide. It's circular, which means that you only have about 18 inches at the top that you actually walk on; the rest is curving away from you. But there is a handrail on both sides. If you have people with you, if you give them confidence, you have no problems. If you don't give them confidence, you have problems.

"Roberts's double was actually a high-wire artist in her own right, but she had never been up that high. During a high-wire act, she was probably up about 40 feet. And 700 feet is quite a bit higher, so the first reaction can be a little tricky. For her, the best thing that could happen was that I went up and walked down and pretended I was going to lunch. And then she was okay.

"So we established that, and then we came back to the studio, where we had a duplicate of the bridge's top section, and we actually did the real fight there with Roger, Chris and Tanya. The highest point was about 50 feet from the ground, and we had a duplicate airship swinging from the top."

Grace also carefully coordinated the sequence in which Bond rides the blimp's mooring cable to the bridge. Said Grace, "When Bond's being carried to the bridge, he's wearing a harness. We had a wire running through the rope so that he was harnessed from the waist onto a little loop coming out of the wire; we also had a foot stirrup made for him so he could put his foot in it and rest.

"It almost sounds too easy, but the thing is, hanging from a helicopter for fifteen minutes without those little aids—you couldn't do it. It's impossible to hang that long. There's a limit to how long even the strongest man can hold onto a hanging rope. . . . So, obviously, there must be these safety precautions."

A native of Lisdowney, County Kilkenny, Ireland, Grace made his debut as a utility stuntman on *You Only Live Twice* (1967).

Grand Slam Task Force: The code name given to the convoy of military vehicles that will assault Fort Knox in *Goldfinger*. Smuggled across the Mexican border by underworld confederates of Mr. Strap (Hal Galili), the convoy consists of jeeps, trucks, and an ambulance equipped with Goldfinger's laser. In the jargon of Operation Grand Slam, Goldfinger is the Grand Slam Task Force Leader. NOTE: If you want to see how the convoy transitions from shooting at the real Fort Knox to the Pinewood Studios backlot, just look at the last vehicle in line. In Kentucky, it's a US Army Dodge Weapons Carrier. At Pinewood, it's a standard pickup truck.

Grant, Donald: Agent 007's cool and deadly adversary in *From Russia with Love*, portrayed by Robert Shaw. A convicted murderer, the blond-pated Grant escaped from Dartmoor Prison in England in 1960 and was recruited by SPECTRE in 1962. According to their records, as quoted by Morzeny (Walter Gotell), Grant has been diagnosed as a "homicidal paranoiac," which is considered superb material for their assassination training.

Working under the command of SPECTRE agent number 3 Rosa Klebb (Lotte Lenya) and SPECTRE agent number 5 and head of planning Kronsteen (Vladek Sheybal), Grant's mission is to kill James Bond on the fabled Orient Express and capture the Lektor decoding machine that 007 has stolen from the Russian consulate in Istanbul. He will then return it to the Russians for a huge reward.

Deadly SPECTRE agent Donald Grant (Robert Shaw), posing as British agent Nash, introduces himself to James Bond (Sean Connery) on the Orient Express in *From Russia with Love*. *Courtesy of the David Reinhardt Collection*

Assassin Donald Grant looms out of the background of artist Paul Mann's evocative painting of *From Russia with Love*. *Courtesy of the Paul Mann Collection*

Graves, Gustav: Impossibly rich and extremely smarmy environmental entrepreneur portrayed by Toby Stephens in *Die Another Day*. On the surface, Graves appears determined to turn the world's icy reaches into gardens with a satellite-mounted heat ray, which goes through glaciers like a knife through butter. With such a working device, he manages to impress the scientific community as well as the queen of England, who knights him. But appearances are deceiving. Graves is actually renegade North Korean officer Colonel Moon, who has gone through a radical form of gene replacement therapy that has completely altered his appearance. Graves/Moon's intention is to use the satellite to blow a hole in the demilitarized zone between North and South Korea, paving the way for a full-scale invasion of the south. In addition to operating a dangerous satellite, Graves is also a member of the Blades fencing club in London—where he challenges 007 to a deadly match—the highlight of the film.

Gray, Charles (August 29, 1928–March 7, 2000; birth name: Donald M. Gray): British character actor who portrayed grim-faced Dikko Henderson in *You Only Live Twice* and Ernst Stavro Blofeld in *Diamonds Are Forever*. The latter role was a much bigger one for Gray, who became the third actor to portray Blofeld on screen (following Donald Pleasence and Telly Savalas).

Gray's Blofeld was certainly the most flamboyant of the series, but he's hardly threatening. Spouting philosophical bilge and strutting around

Ernst Stavro Blofeld (Charles Gray) appears to hold all the cards in *Diamonds Are Forever*. Gray's portrait of the SPECTRE chief was much lighter than the others have been. *Courtesy of the David Reinhardt Collection*

in smart tunics, an expensive cigarette holder dangling from his lips, he's more an elegant cad than a true Bond villain. No wonder writers Tom Mankiewicz and Richard Maibaum stuffed him into a bathosub at the end of the film rather than have him face off against the two-fisted 007. Sean Connery versus Charles Gray? No contest.

Commented Mankiewicz, "It was wonderful to write this 'piss elegant' dialogue for Charles. You could give him lines like 'The great powers flexing their military muscles like so many impotent beach boys' because he could say them so well."*

In *You Only Live Twice*, Gray's Dikko Henderson is a pained civil servant who's embraced a Japanese way of life. Moments after greeting Bond, he's stabbed by a henchman of Mr. Osato (Teru Shimada).

A native of Bournemouth, Dorset, England, Gray made his feature film debut as Captain Brossard in actor/director José Ferrer's biographical drama *I Accuse!* (1958), working alongside future Bond players Laurence Naismith (*Diamonds Are Forever*) and Eric Pohlmann. Gray's other feature credits include *The Night of the Generals* (1967), as pompous General von Seidlitz-Gabler; *The Secret War of Harry Frigg* (1968); *The Executioner* (1970); *Cromwell* (1970), as the Earl of Essex; *The Rocky Horror Picture Show* (1975), as the Criminologist; *The Seven-Per-Cent Solution* (1976), as Mycroft Holmes; and *The Jigsaw Man* (1983), with fellow Bond veterans Yuri Borienko (*On Her Majesty's Secret Service*), Anthony Dawson, Peter Burton, and Vladek Sheybal, directed by Bond veteran Terence Young.

Gray, Willoughby (November 5, 1916–February 13, 1993): British character actor who portrayed renegade Nazi scientist Dr. Carl Mortner in *A View to a Kill*. Born in London, Gray made his credited feature film debut in director Roy Kellino's crime drama *Guilt Is My Shadow* (1950), which featured a bit role for Desmond Llewelyn. He later played the elderly king in *The Princess Bride* (1987), before ending his career as Sir John

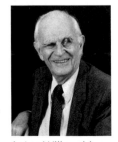

Actor Willoughby Gray was nefarious Dr. Mortner in *A View to a Kill*. *Steve Rubin Collection*

---

* Tom Mankiewicz, interview by the author, Los Angeles, November 7, 1977.

Stevens in the television series *Howards' Way* (40 episodes, 1985–1990).

Green, Eva (July 6, 1980–   ): Charismatic French actress who portrayed Vesper Lynd, a member of Her Majesty's Treasury's Financial Action Task Force in *Casino Royale*. A native of Paris, Green made her motion picture debut in director Bernardo Bertolucci's romantic drama *The Dreamers* (2003). Just prior to *Casino Royale*, she costarred opposite Orlando Bloom and Liam Neeson in Ridley Scott's medieval adventure film *Kingdom of Heaven* (2005). Green's more recent credits include *300: Rise of an Empire* (2014), *Sin City: A Dame to Kill For* (2014), *Miss Peregrine's Home for Peculiar Chlidren* (2016), and *Dumbo* (2019). She also starred in Showtime's Victorian-era horror series *Penny Dreadful* (27 episodes, 2014–2016), alongside former Bond Timothy Dalton.

Eva Green by Jeff Marshall. *Courtesy of Jeff Marshall*

Eva Green brought her considerable charms to the role of Vesper Lynd in *Casino Royale*. Her on-screen chemistry with Daniel Craig was palpable. *Courtesy of the Anders Frejdh Collection*

Greene, Dominic: Sinister SPECTRE operative portrayed by Mathieu Amalric in *Quantum of Solace*. On the surface, he's is a wealthy international environmentalist, but despite the fact that his last name is Greene, in reality he has no intention of saving the planet. Greene is part of an international crime organization known as Quantum—which we learn in *Spectre* is one of the tendrils of a rebooted SPECTRE. His rather low-octane scheme is to corner the freshwater market in Bolivia by making a deal with the renegade General Medrano (Joaquín Cosio), who is trading what he thinks is useless desert for a Quantum-engineered coup that will make him Bolivia's next president. Did you get all that?

Bond (Daniel Craig) first sees Greene in Port-au-Prince, Haiti, where 007 rescues Greene's girlfriend, Camille (Olga Kurylenko), from Medrano. Bond later keeps tabs on Greene's organization during a performance of *Tosca* in Bregenz, Austria, then tracks him back to Bolivia for a final encounter at a desert hotel, where Bond takes out Greene's henchmen and captures Greene—eventually leaving him stranded in the desert with a just a can of engine oil. According to M (Dame

On the surface, Dominic Greene (Mathieu Amalric, right) appears to be an environmentalist. In reality, he is a nefarious operative of SPECTRE. *Courtesy of the Anders Frejdh Collection*

Judi Dench), Greene's body is later found by British intelligence with two bullets in his head and engine oil in his stomach.

grilled sole: The dinner order on the Orient Express for Bond (Sean Connery), Tatiana Romanova (Daniela Bianchi), and Donald Grant (Robert Shaw) in *From Russia with Love*. Bond orders for Tatiana; Grant follows suit.

Grindelwald: Swiss village, located two miles from the village of Mürren and the mountaintop restaurant Piz Gloria, which served as the location for the skating rink sequence in *On Her Majesty's Secret Service*. In that sequence, Bond (George Lazenby) attempts to escape from SPECTRE ski troops and is rescued by Tracy (Diana Rigg), the woman he will marry.

Recalled director Peter Hunt, "The skating rink was melting as we shot on it. Some nights we had to wait and see if the temperature would drop below zero. We would wait until midnight or one o'clock in the morning and then ask, 'Is it freezing yet?' and we would be informed, 'No way.' So, in the end, I just had to mark off certain areas and make sure the skaters didn't wander."[*]

Adding visual interest to the skating sequences were Rudi and Gerda Johner, a skating duo who were given the center spotlight on the festive evening. Since Diana Rigg couldn't skate with any degree of proficiency, the key sequence in the film in which Tracy skates up to the bedraggled Bond was done with Rigg's skating double. Hunt kept his camera focused on the double's legs as she skates up to Bond, and then he cut to Rigg.

Grishenko, Boris: Smarmy, egotistical computer hacker portrayed by Alan Cumming in *GoldenEye*. He works with Natalya Simonova (Izabella Scorupco) and loves tormenting her with his risqué passwords. In a company with policies against sexual harassment, this guy would have been booted to Siberia in twelve seconds. Eventually, he finds a more suitable position working for criminal mastermind Alec Trevelyan (Sean Bean). And he gets his cool comeuppance when Bond unleashes a flood of deadly liquid oxygen into Trevelyan's Cuban control room, turning Grishenko into an ice sculpture.

Guincho Beach: A Portuguese beach where the opening fight sequence between Bond (George Lazenby) and some Union Corse thugs was filmed for *On Her Majesty's Secret Service*. Shot in May 1969, the sequence was prepared carefully by the movie's stunt coordinator, George Leech. Remembered Leech, "It was one of the most enjoyable fights in the film, but it worried me at first. It looked okay in the script, but when we actually got down to that empty beach, we realized there weren't any props of any kind.

"I wondered how we could create a spectacular fight on a plain beach. So I got a few fishing boats lined up near the waterline, and these had some oars and nets lying around—props we could use. We were always looking for something different in the Bond fights, and this time I thought we would take the fight into the water, where just before sundown, it would photograph well.

"So with the water, the boats, the nets, the oars, and a few anchors, we were able to work up a good fight. It wasn't easy. Terry Mountain, Takis Emmanuel, and I sat on that beach for days trying to plan the fight."[*]

Gupta, Henry: American cyberterrorist portrayed by real-life card magician Ricky Jay in *Tomorrow Never Dies*. According to British intelligence, Gupta practically invented techno-terrorism. He started out as a student at Berkeley in the '60s and now sells his expertise for cash. Current employer: billionaire media mogul Elliot Carver (Jonathan Pryce).

Gur, Aliza (April 1, 1944–   ): Israeli-born actress who portrayed Vida, the smaller gypsy who battles Zora (Martine Beswick) in the celebrated girl fight in *From Russia with Love*. It was her credited feature film debut, although she had earlier played an extra in Cecil B. DeMille's *The Ten Commandments* (1956). A native of Ramat Gan, Israel, Gur emigrated to the US in her twenties and began booking film and television assignments. She was also Miss Israel 1960.

---

[*] Peter Hunt, interview by the author, London, June 21, 1977.

[*] George Leech, interview by the author, London, June 23, 1977.

Haggerty, Fred (July 14, 1918–2002): Hungarian-born actor/stuntman who portrayed Krilencu the Bulgarian assassin in *From Russia with Love*. A native of Budapest, Haggerty was a working stuntman and stunt coordinator when he was cast as Krilencu. As an actor, he had previously worked with *Russia* costar Pedro Armendariz in *Captain Sindbad* (1963). Haggerty later returned to stunt work in the Bond series, making uncredited contributions to *The Spy Who Loved Me*, *For Your Eyes Only*, *Octopussy*, and *A View to a Kill*. His last stunt role was on *Who Framed Roger Rabbit* (1988). His final acting credit was as the gatekeeper in director Jonathan Lynn's crime comedy *Nuns on the Run* (1990), which starred Bond veteran Robbie Coltrane.

Haggis, Paul (March 10, 1953–   ): Two-time Academy Award–winning Canadian screenwriter and producer who cowrote *Casino Royale* and *Quantum of Solace* with Neal Purvis and Robert Wade. Born in London, Ontario, Haggis worked in television for many years—creating, among other series, *Walker, Texas Ranger* (195 episodes, 1993–2001)—before making his motion picture writing and directing debut on the musical drama *Red Hot* (1993). His breakout motion picture hit was *Crash* (2005), which won Haggis two Oscars, for Best Picture (shared with producer Cathy Schulman) and Best Original Screenplay (shared with cowriter Bobby Moresco). He also scored a Best Director nomination that year. The previous year, he received an Oscar nomination for Best Adapted Screenplay for that year's Best Picture winner, *Million Dollar Baby*. He was the first screenwriter to write back-to-back Best Picture winners.

Hai Fat: Sinister Bangkok-based industrialist and the head of Hai Fat Enterprises, portrayed by Hawaiian Chinese actor Richard Loo in *The Man with the Golden Gun*. Determined to acquire a monopoly on solar energy, Hai Fat hires Francisco Scaramanga (Christopher Lee) to kill a British solar energy scientist and steal the revolutionary "solex agitator" device.

When Bond (Roger Moore) tries to impersonate Scaramanga, he's captured by Hai Fat's minions and brought to a karate school. Agent 007 holds his own with some formidable kickboxers until he escapes. Meanwhile, Hai Fat is assassinated by Scaramanga, who steals the solex for himself.

Haines, Guy: Special envoy to the prime minister of England, portrayed by Paul Ritter in *Quantum of Solace*. Haines is actually working for Quantum, an international crime syndicate that's later revealed to be a branch of SPECTRE. Bond (Daniel Craig) encounters Haines's bodyguard during a performance of *Tosca* in Bregenz, Austria, and throws him off a roof. Although the guard is obviously an enemy agent, MI6 identifies him as a member of Britain's Special Branch, and subsequently revokes 007's passport and credit cards. NOTE: "Guy Haines" was also the name of the character played by Farley Grainger in Alfred Hitchcock's acclaimed 1951 thriller *Strangers on a Train*.

Hall, Lani (November 1, 1945–   ): Smooth Latin songstress—and wife of music superstar Herb Alpert—whose title song for *Never Say Never Again* was a highlight of the film. It was the feature film debut for this Chicago native.

Songstress Lani Hall warbled the catchy title tune to *Never Say Never Again*. *Steve Rubin Collection*

Hama, Mie (November 20, 1943–   ): Beautiful, charismatic Japanese actress—her name is pronounced: MEE-ay HAH-mah—who portrayed Kissy, the Japanese Secret Service agent who marries Bond (Sean Connery) on Ama Island in

You Only Live Twice. Although the Bond film was her most famous English-language credit, Hama was also featured in *King Kong vs. Godzilla* (1962) and *King Kong Escapes* (1967), as well as over seventy Japanese films.

She became a major media star in her native Japan, hosting talk programs similar to the *Today* show and *Good Morning America*. She shared memories of her Bond experience with *New York Times* writer Martin Fackler. "It was an honor to be a Bond girl, but once was enough," she said. "I didn't want that image to stick with me. I am actually a subdued and steady person, but I felt that somewhere beyond my control, others were creating a character named 'Mie Hama.'"*

Hama believed that Bond director Lewis Gilbert cast her after seeing her in *King Kong vs. Godzilla*. "I had never seen a 007 movie, and had no idea 007 was such a huge international hit." Hama regretted not speaking more with actor Sean Connery, whom she respectfully referred to as "Sean Connery-san." After the film's release, they never met again.

Hamilton, Guy (September 16, 1922–April 20, 2016): British director who helmed *Goldfinger*, *Diamonds Are Forever*, *Live and Let Die* and *The Man with the Golden Gun*. Hamilton deserves much credit for *Goldfinger*'s perfect balance of comic and serious elements; the deadly earnestness of *Dr. No* and *From Russia with Love* was gone, but the broad comedy of the future Bond films was still in check. Hamilton would later direct Sean Connery's return to the role of 007 in 1971's *Diamonds Are Forever*, as well as Roger Moore's debut as Bond in 1973's *Live and Let Die*.

Born in Paris, where his father was a British diplomat, Guy Hamilton made his feature film debut as an uncredited assistant director on director Alberto Cavalcanti's crime drama

* Martin Fackler, "From Bond Girl to 'a Normal Life,'" *New York Times*, March 5, 2017.

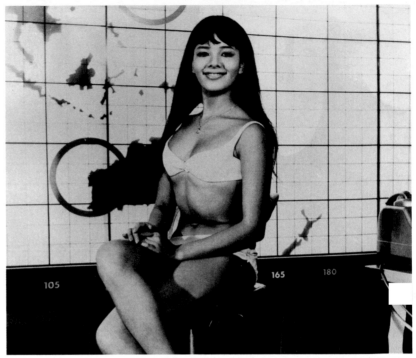

Japanese beauty Mie Hama took on the role of Kissy in *You Only Live Twice*. *Courtesy of the David Reinhardt Collection*

I Became a Criminal (1947), which featured future Bond player Michael Brennan. He then graduated to assistant director assignments on major films such as *The Third Man* (1949) and *The African Queen* (1951). He later made his directing debut on another crime drama, *The Ringer* (1952).

Hamilton's additional feature film directing credits include *The Colditz Story* (1955); *The Devil's Disciple* (1959); *The Best of Enemies* (1961); *Funeral in Berlin* (1966), for Bond producer Harry Saltzman, with Bond veteran Guy Doleman;

Director Guy Hamilton goes over a move with Sean Connery during oil-platform action in *Diamonds Are Forever*. *Courtesy of the Anders Frejdh Collection*

Director Guy Hamilton, on location with Roger Moore in New Orleans on *Live and Let Die*. *Courtesy of the Anders Frejdh Collection*

Battle of Britain (1969), again for producer Harry Saltzman, this time featuring Bond players Robert Shaw, Curt Jurgens, Edward Fox, and Nikki Van der Zyl (who dubbed voices for Saltzman's movie just as she did for many of the early Bond films); and *Force 10 from Navarone* (1978), with Bond players Robert Shaw, Edward Fox, Barbara Bach, and Richard Kiel.

Director Guy Hamilton works with Hervé Villechaize during shooting in Nick Nack's communications lair in *The Man with the Golden Gun*. *Courtesy of the Anders Frejdh Collection*

Hamlisch, Marvin (June 2, 1944–August 6, 2012): Three-time Academy Award–winning American film composer who created the fanciful music of *The Spy Who Loved Me*, for which he received two Academy Award nominations, for Best Song ("Nobody Does It Better," shared with lyricist Carole Bayer Sager) and Best Score.

Hamlisch's music perfectly sets up the incredible pre-credits teaser—the famous Asgard Jump, in which James Bond (Roger Moore) skis off a Swiss mountaintop and parachutes to safety. Hamlisch's music for the chase sequence that featured the Lotus Esprit submarine car was also excellent.

A New York City native who, at seven, became the youngest student ever admitted to the prestigious Juilliard School of Music, Hamlisch received his first composing credit on *The Swimmer* (1968). He earned his three Oscars for the title song (with lyricists Alan and Marilyn Bergman) and score for *The Way We Were* (1973) and his adapted score for *The Sting* (1973). Hamlisch was also nominated for seven other Oscars: *Kotch* (1971), Best Original Song ("Life Is What You Make It," with lyricist Johnny Mercer); *Same Time, Next Year* (1978), Best Original Song ("The Last Time I Felt Like This," with lyricists Alan and Marilyn Bergman); *Ice Castles* (1978), Best Original Song ("Through the Eyes of Love," with lyricist Carole Bayer Sager); *Sophie's Choice* (1982), Best Original Score; *A Chorus Line* (1985), Best Original Song ("Surprise, Surprise," with lyricist Edward Kleban); *Shirley Valentine* (1989), Best Song ("The Girl Who Used to Be Me," with lyricists Alan and Marilyn Bergman); and *The Mirror Has Two Faces* (1996), Best Original Song ("I Finally Found Someone," with Barbra Streisand, Bryan Adams, and Robert "Mutt" Lange).

hang glider: A method of airborne transportation used by James Bond (Roger Moore) in both *Live and Let Die* and *Moonraker*. In actuality,

Behind the scenes as Roger Moore prepares to arrive on San Monique while piloting a hang glider in *Live and Let Die*. *Courtesy of the Anders Frejdh Collection*

the idea originated with *Diamonds Are Forever* screenwriter Richard Maibaum. In one of the early drafts of that film, Bond uses a glider to find Marie, the woman who knows the whereabouts of Ernst Stavro Blofeld (in the film, Bond strangles her with her own bikini top until she gives him the information).

Screenwriter Tom Mankiewicz later used the same sequence in *Live and Let Die* when Bond (Roger Moore) hang-glides his way from the cabin cruiser of Quarrel Jr. (Roy Stewart) to the cliff-top sanctuary of Solitaire (Jane Seymour). In *Moonraker*, Bond is piloting an armored motorboat in South America and is about to go over the falls, but he escapes in another hang glider that lands him gently in the jungle—not far from the secret rocket base of Hugo Drax (Michael Lonsdale).

Harrier jump jet: Celebrated British jet fighter, with the ability to take off vertically, that carries defecting Russian general Georgi Koskov (Jeroen Krabbé) from Austria to England in *The Living Daylights*.

Harris, Cassandra (December 15, 1942–December 28, 1991; birth name: Sandra Colleen Waites): Australian actress and late wife of actor Pierce Brosnan, who portrayed Countess Lisl Von Schlaf, mistress of Milos Colombo (Topol) in *For Your Eyes Only*. Born in Sydney, Harris made her feature film debut in *The Greek Tycoon* (1978), working alongside fellow Bond players Luciana Paluzzi and Roland Culver (*Thunderball*). Harris also appeared in her husband's celebrated television series *Remington Steele* (4 episodes, 1982–1985). It was Harris who introduced Brosnan to producer Albert R. Broccoli during the production of *For Your Eyes Only*. Sadly, after a four-year battle with ovarian cancer, Cassandra Harris died in December 1991, of the same disease that killed her mother and would kill her daughter, Charlotte Brosnan, in 2013 at age forty-one.

Harris, Julius W. (August 17, 1923–October 17, 2004): African American character actor of film and television who portrayed the chuckling Tee Hee, henchman to Mr. Big/Kananga (Yaphet Kotto) in *Live and Let Die*. Born in Philadelphia, Harris made his feature film debut in director Michael Roemer's romantic drama *Nothing but a Man* (1964), joining a cast that included his

future *Live and Let Die* castmate Kotto. Prior to the Bond picture, Harris had been in a number of blaxploitation films of the 1970s, including *Shaft's Big Score!* (1972); *Super Fly* (1972); and *Black Caesar* (1973), with another *Live and Let Die* cast member, Gloria Hendry. One year after *Live and Let Die*, Harris costarred opposite Walter Matthau and Bond veteran Robert Shaw, portraying Inspector Daniels in Joseph Sargent's terrific thriller *The Taking of Pelham One Two Three* (1974). Harris's additional feature film credits include *King Kong* (1976), *Islands in the Stream* (1977), *Looking for Mr. Goodbar* (1977), *Split Decisions* (1988), and *Harley Davidson and the Marlboro Man* (1991).

Julius Harris portrayed Tee Hee, Kananga's prosthetic hook–equipped associate in *Live and Let Die*. *Courtesy of the Anders Frejdh Collection*

Harris, Naomie (September 6, 1976–   ): Accomplished British actress of Jamaican and Trinidadian descent who made her debut as M's aide Eve Moneypenny in *Skyfall* and reprised the role in *Spectre* and *No Time to Die*. Harris was raised by her mother, TV writer Lisselle Kayla (*EastEnders*), and began acting in British television at age eleven. She later attended the Anna Scher Theatre, a prestigious acting school in Islington, before making her feature film debut in director John Miller's comedy *Living in Hope* (2002). However, it was her costarring role as Selena in Danny Boyle's stunning post-apocalyptic thriller *28 Days Later* (2002) that jump-started Harris's feature film career. She also played the scene-stealing witchy woman Tia Dalma in Gore Verbinski's *Pirates of the Caribbean* sequels, and costarred as Winnie Mandela opposite Idris Elba's Nelson Mandela in the biopic *Mandela: Long Walk to Freedom* (2013).

Moneypenny's introduction in *Skyfall* is atypical for a character that had been a part of every Bond movie between 1962 and 2002. After sitting out the first two films of the Daniel Craig era, she returns as a field agent who is forced to take a

Naomie Harris joined the ranks of MI6 as Moneypenny, as always one of Bond's closest allies. *Courtesy of the Anders Frejdh Collection*

desperate shot to stop an enemy agent engaged in a fight with 007. She flirts quite a bit with Bond, but Harris was well aware of the ground rules: "The Bond girl has to die, and Moneypenny can't have sex."* Her field agent experience was short lived. Said Harris, "By the end of *Skyfall* my character realises that she doesn't have the stomach for killing people and being shot at. I imagine her to be someone very academic and thorough, better suited to being behind a desk doing research. She's happier now, she's found her feet and anyway she's not M's secretary; she's more like an advisor."† Amusingly, after spending two months learning the ins and outs of stunt sequences for *Skyfall*, to prepare for her second film in the series she was offered a typing course, though she insisted that "if you see me at a computer screen, it's because I'm accessing top secret files." As for her relationship with Bond, Harris admitted that in *Spectre*, "I see them as

friends. She's the only person Bond can trust. . . . He may have gone rogue. Everyone thinks he has lost his mind because of M dying. Moneypenny is the only one he can confide in about the true nature of his mission."*

For every role she plays, Harris creates a biography; for Moneypenny, she explained, "I imagine she comes from the Home Counties, is very bright, a tomboy and much closer to her father than her mother. He was in the military and she wants to impress him. She was recruited by MI6 at university and the only person who knows what she does is her dad."†

In 2016, Harris was nominated for the Academy Award for Best Supporting Actress for *Moonlight*, that year's unexpected Best Picture winner. The following year, she was awarded the Officer of the Order of the British Empire (OBE) designation by Queen Elizabeth II.

Hartford, Diane (birth name: Diane Brown): British actress who portrayed the partying tourist at the Kiss Kiss Club in Nassau, Bahamas, whom Bond (Sean Connery) grabs for a dance in *Thunderball*. They're rudely interrupted by SPECTRE assassin Fiona Volpe (Luciana Paluzzi). Hartford, the former wife of multimillionaire Huntington Hartford, returned to the Bond series as one of the poker players opposite Daniel Craig in *Casino Royale*.

Harwood, Johanna (1930–   ): Irish screenwriter, playwright, and former script supervisor who worked with Bond director Terence Young and received cowriting credit on *Dr. No* and an adaptation credit on *From Russia with Love*. According to Young, it was Harwood who suggested that they feature the stolen Goya portrait of the Duke of Wellington for use in Dr. No's living room in the first film—a painting that everyone in England at the time would recognize. Harwood began her career as a continuity assistant on *Paratrooper* (1953), a.k.a. *The Red Beret*, one of producer Albert R. Broccoli's early producing credits with partner Irving Allen. She later received a cowriting credit on Broccoli and Saltzman's *Call Me Bwana* (1963), the billboard of which figures into Krilencu's death in *From Russia with Love*. She was married to French

* "Emerging Icon: Naomie Harris," *Elle*, November 2013.
† "Spectre: Naomie Harris on Playing Miss Moneypenny, 'the Only Person Bond Can Trust,'" *Radio Times*, November 8, 2017.

* Ibid.
† Ibid.

director René Clément (*Forbidden Games*) until his death in 1996.

Hatcher, Teri (December 8, 1964–   ): American film and television actress who portrayed Paris Carver, the doomed wife of a megalomaniac media mogul in *Tomorrow Never Dies*. It's also revealed that she's a former lover of James Bond (Pierce Brosnan). The role's practically a cameo for the sultry actress, who is well known for her television series work on *Lois & Clark: The New Adventures of Superman* (87 episodes, 1993–1997) and *Desperate Housewives* (180 episodes, 2004–2012). Born in Palo Alto, California, Hatcher made her motion picture debut as Gretchen in director Christopher Guest's comedy *The Big Picture* (1989), which also featured Bond player John Cleese.

Havelock, Melina: Tall, statuesque, hauntingly beautiful half-Greek woman with a crossbow, portrayed by Carole Bouquet in *For Your Eyes Only*. The daughter of British marine archaeologist Timothy Havelock (Jack Hedley) and native Greek Iona Havelock (Toby Robins), Melina doesn't know that her father is secretly working for the British in an effort to salvage the sunken *St. Georges* surveillance ship.

When the Havelocks are killed by Cuban hit man Hector Gonzales (Stefan Kalipha), Melina vows to avenge their deaths with her crossbow. She kills Gonzales, but, unfortunately, she also stumbles into a much bigger plot, involving 007 (Roger Moore)

Charismatic French actress Carole Bouquet portrayed revenge-crazed Melina Havelock, hunting down the men who murdered her parents in *For Your Eyes Only*. *Courtesy of the David Reinhardt Collection*

James Bond (Pierce Brosnan) and the Carvers (Teri Hatcher, Jonathan Pryce) in *Tomorrow Never Dies*. *Courtesy of the David Reinhardt Collection*

Don't ever mess with a woman armed with a crossbow—unless you want a bolt in your belly from Melina Havelock (Carole Bouquet) in *For Your Eyes Only*. *Courtesy of the David Reinhardt Collection*

and a Soviet-British race to recover the ATAC device that was lost aboard the *St. Georges*.

Involved in the salvage operation—using her father's *Neptune* submarine—Melina and Bond are later captured and nearly flayed on a reef, in a scene right out of the novel *Live and Let Die*. Surviving, she joins 007 on the final mission to St. Cyril's church atop Greece's famous Meteora cliffs.

Hawker: Feisty and all-knowing caddy to Bond (Sean Connery) during the celebrated golf match in *Goldfinger*, portrayed by Gerry Duggan. When Bond and Hawker see that Oddjob has recovered Goldfinger's ball in the rough, Hawker offers the immortal retort "If that's his original ball, I'm Arnold Palmer."

Gerry Duggan portrayed Hawker, capable caddy to James Bond (Sean Connery) in *Goldfinger*. *Courtesy of the Anders Frejdh Collection*

Hayward Fault: Earthquake-sensitive region of Northern California that is key to the plan by Max Zorin (Christopher Walken) to destroy Silicon Valley in *A View to a Kill*.

"He Disagreed With Something That Ate Him": Message on a crumpled piece of paper that is stuffed into the mouth of Felix Leiter (David Hedison) after Bond's CIA friend is thrown to the sharks in *Licence to Kill*. It actually mirrors an incident that occurs in author Ian Fleming's novel *Live and Let Die*. In both cases, Leiter survives but is maimed; in the film he loses his left leg below the knee.

heart-shaped pendant: What James Bond (Roger Moore) recovers from around the neck of a dead agent 003 in *A View to a Kill*. It contains a new-generation microchip that British intelligence has determined is impervious to magnetic pulse damage from a nuclear explosion. Ordinary microchips, on the other hand, could be rendered useless by such a calamity—for instance, shutting down every computer in Britain at a strategic moment.

heat-signature recognition: A sophisticated electronic method of pinpointing the position of a submerged nuclear submarine by tracking its wake, a technique explained by Q (Desmond Llewelyn) after the disappearance of the British nuclear submarine *Ranger* in *The Spy Who Loved Me*. Q compares it to using an infrared satellite to track the tail fire of nuclear missiles. Billionaire shipping magnate Karl Stromberg (Curt Jurgens) has enlisted a scientific duo—Dr. Bechmann (Cyril Shaps) and Professor Markovitz (Milo Sperber)—to develop a heat-signature recognition system that Stromberg uses to find and trap three nuclear submarines. However, Stromberg's system is betrayed by his secretary (Marilyn Galsworthy), who tries to make a fortune by selling the system on the open market. The ploy eventually leads James Bond (Roger Moore) and KGB major Anya Amasova (Barbara Bach) to Stromberg's Atlantis hideaway off the coast of Sardinia.

Hedison, David (May 20, 1927–July 18, 2019; birth name: Albert David Hedison Jr.): Distinctive-voiced American character actor of Armenian descent who was the first person to play CIA agent Felix Leiter twice— in *Live and Let Die* and *Licence to Kill*. In the latter film, Leiter is captured and mutilated by drug lord Franz Sanchez (Robert Davi), who throws him to the sharks.

Actor David Hedison, who portrayed Felix Leiter in *Live and Let Die* and *Licence to Kill*. *Steve Rubin Collection*

The event sends James Bond (Timothy Dalton) on a desperate, unauthorized mission of revenge.

Born in Providence, Rhode Island, Hedison made his big-screen debut, using the name Al Hedison, in director Dick Powell's gritty World War II film *The Enemy Below* (1957), playing young Lieutenant Ware opposite Robert Mitchum. Hedison went on to star in a number of feature films—many of them revered by genre fans—including *The Fly* (1958); *The Lost World* (1960), with future Bond player Jill St. John; *The Greatest Story Ever Told* (1965); and *ffolkes* (1980), reteaming with Roger Moore. Hedison was best known for playing submarine skipper Lee Crane on the Irwin Allen–produced TV series *Voyage to the Bottom of the Sea* (110 episodes, 1964–1968).

Hemingway House: Landmark in Key West, Florida, where M (Robert Brown) confronts revenge-crazed James Bond (Timothy Dalton) in *Licence to Kill*. M's top agent has not reported for his next assignment in Istanbul. Worried that Bond will insist on revenge after drug runners mutilate his CIA chum Felix Leiter (David Hedison) and murder Leiter's bride, Della Churchill (Priscilla Barnes), M realizes that the only way to stop 007 is to revoke his license to kill. That doesn't work either, as Bond defies his superior, fights off a couple of fellow British agents, and disappears.

Located at 907 Whitehead Street in Key West, the Hemingway House is where American author Ernest Hemingway spent the last thirty years of his life, until his death in 1961.

Henderson, Dikko: British Secret Service operative whom Bond (Sean Connery) visits in Tokyo, portrayed by Charles Gray in *You Only Live Twice*. Although British, Henderson has adopted many Japanese customs, including the kimono and an appropriately furnished apartment. Although his part is very brief, Gray captures the spirit of the Dikko Henderson portrayed in the original Fleming novel.

How does Bond check Henderson's identity during their first meeting? He takes Henderson's cane and bashes his right leg, which turns out to be wooden. He lost it in Singapore in 1942. Unfortunately, before we can get to know Henderson, he is knifed by a henchman of Mr. Osato (Teru Shimada).

Hendry, Gloria (March 3, 1949–　　): American actress and former Playboy bunny who portrayed the inept double agent Rosie Carver in *Live and Let Die*. Born in Winter Haven, Florida, Hendry made her feature film debut as a cocktail waitress in director Daniel Mann's *For Love of Ivy* (1968). Her other feature credits include *The Landlord* (1970); *Across 110th Street* (1972); *Black Caesar* (1973), with her *Live and Let Die* costar Julius Harris, for director Larry Cohen; *Slaughter's Big Rip-Off* (1973); *Hell Up in Harlem* (1973); and *Black Belt Jones* (1974).

Gloria Hendry portrayed comical agent Rosie Carver in *Live and Let Die*. *Courtesy of the Anders Frejdh Collection*

Hergersheimer, Klaus: The innocent radiation shield inspector portrayed by Ed Bishop in *Diamonds Are Forever*. He's spent three years in G Section at Tectronics, a top-secret division of Willard Whyte's global conglomerate specializing in satellite research and space

James Bond (Sean Connery) impersonates radiation shield inspector Klaus Hergersheimer in *Diamonds Are Forever*. *Courtesy of the David Reinhardt Collection*

exploration. When Bond (Sean Connery) sneaks into Tectronics, it is Hergersheimer whom he impersonates, gaining entrance to the lab of Professor Dr. Metz (Joseph Furst). When the real Hergersheimer shows up, Metz sounds the alarm.

Hey, Virginia (June 19, 1952–   ): Australian actress who portrayed Rubavitch, girlfriend of Russian general Leonid Pushkin (John Rhys-Davies) in *The Living Daylights*. A native of Coogee, New South Wales, Hey made her feature film debut as the tall, white-suited Warrior Woman in George Miller's epic postapocalyptic action thriller *The Road Warrior* (1981). She's also known for playing blue-skinned alien priestess Zhaan in the television series *Farscape* (50 episodes, 1999–2002).

Hill, Bill (1921–   ; birth name: Edward William Hill): British producer, production manager, and assistant director who served as production manager on *From Russia with Love* and also took a small but critical acting part, portraying Captain Nash, the Yugoslavia-based British Secret Service agent who is murdered by Donald Grant (Robert Shaw) in the Zagreb train station restroom. Hill always joked about his brief nonspeaking part. "If you thought about it, it was totally preposterous," he remembered. "Here I am, arriving in Zagreb station on this terribly important mission to assist a fellow agent, and after we trade the recognition signal, we're on our way to the bathroom. What were we supposed to be saying anyway? 'Let's have a pee and then we'll board a train'?"*

A native of London, Hill made his big-screen debut as an assistant director on director Julian Amyes's war drama *Hell in Korea* (1956). Two years later, he rose to production manager on John Guillermin's biographical feature *I Was Monty's Double*, a.k.a. *Hell, Heaven or Hoboken*, which featured future Bond players Bill Nagy (Mr. Midnight in *Goldfinger*), Walter Gotell, Marne Maitland, and Steven Berkoff. Hill made his producing debut as an associate producer on *The Curse of the Mummy's Tomb* (1964).

Himeji Castle: Historic Japanese feudal castle that was used as the ninja training grounds in

You Only Live Twice. Also known as White Heron Castle, due to its striking white appearance, it is considered Japan's most imposing medieval fortress.

Hinx, Mr.: Formidable SPECTRE assassin portrayed by Dave Bautista in *Spectre*. It is Hinx who engages Bond (Daniel Craig) in a spirited car chase across Rome after 007 infiltrates the SPECTRE meeting at the (fictional) Pallazzo Cardenza. Bond loses his Aston Martin DB10 in the Tiber River, but he manages to escape from the killer—who nonetheless shows up later in Austria, where he kidnaps Dr. Madeleine Swann (Léa Seydoux). Bond rescues her and they head for Tangier, but once again Hinx arrives with murder on his mind. But in a deadly train fight, 007 tosses the assassin off the train.

SPECTRE assassin Hinx (Dave Bautista) attempts to kill Bond on the train in *Spectre*. *Courtesy of the Anders Frejdh Collection*

HMS *Ark Royal*: British aircraft carrier where James Bond (Roger Moore) once saw active service, according to Admiral Hargreaves (Robert Brown), Flag Officer Submarines, in *The Spy Who Loved Me*. It's the first time in the series that mention is made of Bond's previous naval assignment. The real HMS *Ark Royal*—an honored World War II British flattop that participated in the sinking of the German battleship *Bismarck*—was sunk by German U-boat U-81 on November 14, 1941.

HMS *Chester*: Fictional British missile frigate, featured in *Tomorrow Never Dies*, that launches a cruise missile against a terrorist arms bazaar in the pre-credits teaser, unaware that nuclear weapons are present. Fortunately, Bond (Pierce

---

* Bill Hill, interview by the author, London, June 20, 1977.

A miniature Royal Navy warship is prepared for action on *Tomorrow Never Dies*. *Courtesy of the Brian Smithies Archive*

Brosnan) hijacks the nuclear torpedo–equipped Russian fighter before the missile can do its dirty work.

HMS *Devonshire*: British anti-submarine frigate that Elliot Carver (Jonathan Pryce) attacks and sinks with his stealth ship in *Tomorrow Never Dies*. Interior sequences were shot inside the HMS *Dryad* ship simulator at Portsmouth, Hampshire, England.

HMS *Tenby*: Whitby-class anti-submarine frigate of the Royal Navy that, anchored in Gibraltar Harbour in December 1966, served as the location for the military "funeral" of James Bond (Sean Connery) in *You Only Live Twice*. In the film, Gibraltar is playing Victoria Harbour in Hong Kong.

When Bond's "body" is dumped into the harbor, the film, in reality, cuts to the Bahamas, where underwater cinematographer Lamar Boren filmed the body floating to the ocean floor. Two scuba divers then rescue it and bring it to a waiting British submarine. The actual interior of the sub was located in the east tunnel of Pinewood Studios, and was completed in mid-October 1966.

HMS *Tenby* was sold to the Pakistan Navy in 1975 and scrapped in 1977.

Holder, Geoffrey (August 1, 1930–October 5, 2014): Tall (six feet, six inches), imposing actor/dancer/choreographer who portrayed the mystical Baron Samedi in *Live and Let Die*. Better known at the time for his soft drink commercials than his film and television roles, Holder was perfectly cast as the giant henchman of Kananga (Yaphet Kotto) who may or may not be a supernatural being.

A native of Trinidad and Tobago, Holder made his motion picture debut as a voodoo dancer in director Harold Young's *Carib Gold* (1957). His other big-screen credits include *Doctor Dolittle* (1967); *Everything You Always Wanted to Know About Sex* (*But Were Afraid to Ask)* (1972); *Annie* (1982), as Punjab; and *Charlie and the Chocolate Factory* (2005), as the voice of the narrator.

Tall, charismatic Geoffrey Holder scored in *Live and Let Die* as Baron Samedi, a villainous henchman who may also have supernatural powers. *Courtesy of the Anders Frejdh Collection*

Holt, Patrick (January 31, 1912–October 12, 1993; birth name: Patrick G. Parsons): British character actor who portrayed deep-voiced RAF group captain Dawson in *Thunderball*. A native of Cheltenham, Gloucestershire, England, Holt made his credited motion picture debut, using the name Patrick Parsons, in director Brian Desmond Hurst's drama *Hungry Hill* (1947). Five years later, he portrayed the Norman knight Philip DeMalvoisin, who jousts with Robert Taylor's title character in *Ivanhoe* (1952), a film that also featured future Bond stuntmen Bob Simmons and George Leech as jousting knights.

Holywell Bay: Remote location in southwestern England, near Newquay, Cornwall, that was transformed into a Korean beach for the *Die Another Day* pre-credits teaser. For the sequence, the local Holywell surf hut was transformed into a North Korean pillbox, and a small forest of pine trees was planted in the dunes behind to mimic a remote shore.

homer: A small electronic surveillance device designed to track both friendly and enemy agents in *Goldfinger*. In order to follow "the man with the Midas touch" (Gert Fröbe) to his Swiss base, Bond (Sean Connery) plants one of the magnetic homers in Goldfinger's Rolls-Royce. The signal is then received on an audiovisual panel built into the dashboard of 007's Aston Martin DB5. Its range is 150 miles.

A smaller homer is standard field issue and is fitted into the heel of James Bond's shoe. This device allows the CIA to determine that Bond has been captured by Goldfinger and transported to the United States on a private jetliner headed for Friendship Airport outside Baltimore. In order to alert the CIA to Goldfinger's plan to detonate an A-bomb in Fort Knox, Bond removes the homer

James Bond (Sean Connery) attaches a "homer" to Goldfinger's Rolls in *Goldfinger*. The idea of tracking a suspect with a device that feeds an audiovisual display predicted GPS tracking almost fifty years before it became standard issue in civilian cars and cell phones. *Courtesy of the Anders Frejdh Collection*

from his shoe and places it in the suit pocket of mafioso Mr. Solo (Martin Benson), who is supposedly headed to the local airport for a trip to New York. Unfortunately, when Oddjob (Harold Sakata) murders Solo and completely crushes his Continental, the homer is destroyed, and Felix Leiter (Cec Linder) is unable to receive the message.

In *The Man with the Golden Gun*, Bond (Roger Moore) employs a similar audiovisual receiver in the cockpit of his seaplane when he tracks Mary Goodnight (Britt Ekland) to Scaramanga's remote island off the coast of China.

The idea of a homer and its audiovisual tracker in 007's Aston Martin presages the development of GPS—now a staple in all modern automobiles and smartphones.

Hong Kong: Bustling metropolitan area on the South China Sea that figures in several Bond films. In *Goldfinger*, it's one of four cities (along with Zurich, Amsterdam, and Caracas) in which Auric Goldfinger (Gert Fröbe) has stashed the 20 million in pounds sterling worth of gold he has been smuggling out of Great Britain, according to Colonel Smithers (Richard Vernon) of the Bank of England. In *You Only Live Twice*, it's the location where Bond (Sean Connery) has his tryst with Ling (Tsai Chin) and stages his faked assassination. In *Diamonds Are Forever*, it's the destination of Tiffany Case (Jill St. John) once she gets the diamonds from James Bond. In *The Man with the Golden Gun*, British Secret Service headquarters in the Far East is located aboard the twisted wreckage of the *Queen Elizabeth I*, which caught fire and partially sank in Victoria Harbour, Hong Kong, on January 9, 1972. And in *Skyfall*, it's where former MI6 agent Raoul Silva (Javier Bardem) defied M (Dame Judi Dench) and tried to disrupt the region's handover to the Chinese in 1997, forcing M to give him up to Chinese intelligence and prompting Silva to swear revenge against her.

Hong Kong Macau Hydrofoil Co. Ltd.: Company offering a sea link between Hong Kong and Macao that is featured in *The Man with the Golden Gun*. (Note the alternate spelling "Macau.") While aboard one of this firm's hydrofoils, James Bond (Roger Moore) follows Francisco Scaramanga's girlfriend, Andrea Anders (Maud Adams), to Hong Kong.

"hoods convention": The nickname given to the group of international gangsters who arrive at the Auric Stud ranch to collect the $1 million promised to them by the title character in *Goldfinger*. Gathered in the ranch's huge rumpus room, they soon find themselves being lectured on the potential of Operation Grand Slam, the plan Goldfinger (Gert Fröbe) has formulated to rob Fort Knox, Kentucky. Every hood is given a choice: they can leave, if they like, with their $1 million, or they can participate in the robbery and come away with $10 million each. Impressed by their host's plan, every hood agrees, except for Mafia kingpin Mr. Solo (Martin Benson), who wants to leave with his $1 million.

What the hoods don't know is that Goldfinger has no intention of stealing the fort's gold. He's instead going to detonate a small atomic device inside the repository that will make America's gold supply useless for fifty-eight years. They're also doomed men, because no sooner does Goldfinger leave the room to provide Solo with his gold than his assistant Kisch (Michael Mellinger) hermetically seals it off and sprays Delta-9 poison gas inside, killing everyone.

To save on the cost of transporting international actors to the Auric Stud set at Pinewood Studios outside London, the producers cast the hoods with foreign-born performers already living in England, including Hungarian Bill Nagy (Mr. Midnight), New Yorker Hal Galili (Mr. Strap), and Canadian Bill Edwards.

Hotel Cala di Volpe: Real-life hotel on the island of Sardinia that was featured in *The Spy Who Loved Me*. Part of the enormous Costa Smeralda resort financed by Karim al-Husayn Shah, the business magnate and spiritual leader known as the Aga Khan, it hosted James Bond (Roger Moore) and Major Anya Amasova (Barbara Bach) prior to their visit to the Atlantis base of Karl Stromberg (Curt Jurgens).

hovercraft: Large passenger vessel that takes James Bond (Sean Connery) across the English Channel to Holland in *Diamonds Are Forever*, riding above the water on a current of air. In the real world, the last hovercraft to ply the channel was retired from service in October 2000, its end undoubtedly hastened by the completion of the Channel Tunnel in 1994.

Several one-man hovercraft—air-cushion assault vehicles—are featured during a high-speed chase in the pre-credits teaser of *Die Another Day*. These craft are utilized by renegade North Koreans to navigate across the mine-strewn demilitarized zone between the two countries, where they've secreted an arms trove. The chase involves Bond (Pierce Brosnan) and Zao (Rick Yune), who is working with rogue North Korean army colonel Tan-Sun Moon (Will Yun Lee).

Hughes, Howard (December 24, 1905–April 5, 1976): Billionaire business magnate and film mogul who inspired the main plot of *Diamonds Are Forever*. Bond producer Albert R. "Cubby" Broccoli had always maintained a friendship with Hughes, his first boss in the film business, whom he referred to as Sam. While *Diamonds* was in development, Broccoli had a dream in which he visited the aging Hughes at his luxurious suite in Las Vegas. It was midafternoon, and Broccoli found himself peeking through a window in Hughes's suite, where he saw a familiar figure sitting behind a huge oak desk. The man turned around, and Broccoli started. It wasn't Hughes at all, but an imposter.

The producer described the dream and its eerie details at his next script conference with writer Richard Maibaum. Said Broccoli on that day, "What would happen, Dick, if someone kidnapped Howard Hughes and substituted an imposter for him? Since no one has seen the real Howard Hughes for years, no one would even know that he was gone."[*]

Maibaum replied, "Sounds like just the right caper for Blofeld."

Hunt, Peter Roger (March 11, 1925–August 14, 2002): British editor turned film director who cut the first four James Bond films before first assuming the mantle of director for *On Her Majesty's Secret Service*. Hunt contributed greatly to the visual style and pacing of the early Bond films.

Starting with *Dr. No*, Hunt and director Terence Young used a film editing technique comparable to television commercial cutting at the time, which produced a very lean visual style. For instance, if an actor walked out a doorway and headed for his car, Hunt would get him there as quickly as possible—"cutting to the chase," as

---

[*] Albert R. Broccoli, interview by the author, Los Angeles, April 10, 1977.

Diana Rigg and George Lazenby help director Peter Hunt celebrate his forty-third birthday on March 11, 1968, during production on *On Her Majesty's Secret Service. Courtesy of the David Reinhardt Collection*

it were. Said Young, "We used to cut in the middle of pans. There was no dissolving. You went straight into flash cuts. There were a lot of sound cuts and an enormous number of tracks and pans so that one always got the impression that something was moving on screen."*

The idea of keeping *Dr. No* moving at all times was a key to its success. Everyone, including producers Albert R. Broccoli and Harry Saltzman, was concerned that American audiences would not accept a Scottish actor as a leading man and hero. Consequently, much of *Dr. No*'s screen time is devoted to movement, action, and fights, and Sean Connery has a minimum of dialogue in the first film. And, as Young pointed out, the zippy pace helped audiences breeze through any ques-

tionable logic in the story: "It was only on the way home that the husband turned to the wife and said, 'It was rather nonsense, wasn't it!' But people would qualify their criticism with 'Look, you enjoyed it for a couple of hours, what else do you want?'"*

Peter Hunt's pacing, combined with Terence Young's precise direction, Richard Maibaum's script, and John Barry's music, initiated a new style in filmmaking. Hunt's editing technique owes a debt to his early schooling at the London College of Music, where he studied music theory and violin and developed an appreciation for musical timing.

Hunt was also responsible for suggesting Sean Connery as a possible James Bond in 1961. At that time, Hunt was editing the movie *On the*

_____
* Terence Young, interview by the author, London, June 25, 1977.

_____
* Ibid.

Fiddle, a British service comedy in the vein of an Abbott and Costello vehicle, with Alfie Lynch and Connery in the leads. One night, while having dinner at London's Polish Club with the film's producer Benjamin Fisz, Hunt bumped into producer Harry Saltzman, who was then conducting the 007 casting search. Hunt suggested Connery for the part, and Saltzman eventually looked at some footage. He came to the same conclusion that his partner Albert R. Broccoli would have in Los Angeles while screening Walt Disney's *Darby O'Gill and the Little People*—that Sean Connery was their Bond.

By the release of *Thunderball* in 1965, Hunt had begun to tire of the editing chores on the Bond films and was eager to make his directing debut. He agreed to return as editor and second unit director on *You Only Live Twice* only if producers Broccoli and Saltzman would let him direct the next picture in the series. The producers kept their part of the bargain, and Hunt was signed to direct an adaptation of perhaps the best of Ian Fleming's novels, *On Her Majesty's Secret Service*.

Unfortunately, Sean Connery had left the series by then, so Hunt was forced to find his own Bond. Australian model George Lazenby won the role in 1968. Hunt's own editorial style was carried on by new editor John Glen, who also served as the film's second unit director.

Ironically, considering the tight pacing Hunt had brought to the series, his directorial debut was the longest film in the series, at 140 minutes, until it was eclipsed by *Casino Royale*'s 144 minutes in 2006. However, *OHMSS* is also one of the most interesting 007 films to delve into as a fan. Determined to make an impact in his directorial debut, Hunt studied the original novel and worked closely with screenwriter Maibaum to create what is probably, along with *From Russia with Love*, the most faithful dramatization of an Ian Fleming work—down to the naval cannon in the driveway of M's home.

Pay particular attention to the opening teaser sequence, which serves to introduce George Lazenby as Bond. The action sequences are quick and boisterous, particularly a fight in the surf, and a quick battle outside Marc-Ange Draco's office in Portugal.

A London native, Hunt made his motion picture debut as an uncredited associate editor on *The Thief of Bagdad* (1940), working with editor Charles Crichton. He rose to editor himself on director Burt Balaban's science fiction thriller *Stranger from Venus* (1954), a.k.a. *Immediate Disaster* and *The Venusian*, and later worked as future Bond director Lewis Gilbert's editor on *Sink the Bismarck!* (1960). Hunt's directing credits include *Gold* (1974), with Bond veterans Roger Moore, Bernard Horsfall (*On Her Majesty's Secret Service*), and Nadim Sawalha (*The Spy Who Loved Me*, *The Living Daylights*); *Shout at the Devil* (1976), again with Moore and Horsfall; *Death Hunt* (1981); *Wild Geese II* (1985), with Bond players Barbara Carrera and Edward Fox; and *HyperSapien: People from Another Star* (1986).

hydrofoil: What the slow-moving yacht *Disco Volante* converts to in *Thunderball*. Leaving its "cocoon" behind to deal with a flotilla of US Coast Guard warships, Emilio Largo (Adolfo Celi) orders the hydrofoil to head for Miami with an A-bomb on board.

hydrogen cyanide: Poison in a hidden suicide capsule that the MI6 agent later known as Silva (Javier Bardem) ingests after he's turned over to the Chinese in *Skyfall*. The poison doesn't kill him, but it does destroy his mouth. Every day he looks in the mirror, he's probably thinking of new ways to kill the woman who gave him up: M (Dame Judi Dench).

"I admire your courage, Miss . . . ?": The first line of dialogue spoken by James Bond in *Dr. No*—and thus his first line in Eon Productions' 007 series as a whole. It is delivered by Sean Connery at a baccarat table to actress Eunice Gayson, portraying playgirl Sylvia Trench. The location is Les Ambassadeurs, a private club in London. Gayson replies, "Trench, Sylvia Trench. I admire your luck, Mr. . . . ?" to which Connery replies, "Bond, James Bond," as he finishes lighting his cigarette.

When director Terence Young first shot this sequence, Connery timed the flick of his lighter to the beginning of the line, which caused a few chuckles among the crew. Young suggested that Connery open his lighter sooner. Thus, when the scene cut to reveal Bond, he would be pictured in a swirl of cigarette smoke, there would be a beat, then one of the most famous lines of dialogue in screen history would be uttered. The technique obviously worked.

Ian Fleming Foundation (IFF): According to the foundation itself, the IFF is "a public benefit nonprofit US 501(c)3 California corporation formed in July of 1992 . . . dedicated to the study and preservation of the history of Ian Lancaster Fleming, Ian Fleming's literary works, the James Bond phenomenon, and their impact on popular culture. One of the IFF's goals is procuring, restoring, preserving, archiving, and displaying the original works of Ian Fleming and all of the subsequent products of that original body of work. These include the films, as well as the merchandise and memorabilia spawned by the films." Over the past two-plus decades, the IFF has archived, restored, and maintained over thirty-five original film vehicles, including the badly damaged Lotus underwater effects car from *The Spy Who Loved Me* and the Neptune submarine from *For Your Eyes Only*. The foundation published *GoldenEye* magazine and the *Shaken, Not Stirred* newsletter, fan publications that contained current Bond news as well as detailed research articles on James Bond and Ian Fleming's work. Most recently, the IFF has provided fifteen vehicles to the *Bond in Motion* exhibition in the London Film Museum. The current board of directors of the Ian Fleming Foundation consists of Michael VanBlaricum, president; David Reinhardt, secretary and Canadian representative; George Martin, treasurer; Brad Frank and Colin Clark of the US; and Dave Worrall and Matthew Field, UK representatives. The Ian Fleming Foundation can be contacted at PO Box 61908, Santa Barbara, CA, 93160, or via the website www.ianflemingfoundation.org.

ice cubes: Pleasure device deployed by stunningly beautiful but treacherously duplicitous heiress Elektra King (Sophie Marceau) in *The World Is Not Enough*. She uses them on Bond first and then brings them out for her real lover (thanks to Stockholm syndrome), the terrorist Renard (Robert Carlyle). Unfortunately, having gotten a bullet lodged in his brain in an assassination attempt, Renard has no sense of touch and can't feel the cubes. It's a vulnerable moment for the character—who would gain more sympathy from us if he stopped murdering everyone in his path. The cubes, by the way, are the perfect metaphor for Elektra, a true ice princess. Ice cubes were previously used as a torture device by Emilio Largo (Adolfo Celi) on Domino (Claudine Auger) in *Thunderball*.

Ice Palace: Fantastic structure built in Iceland by Gustav Graves (Toby Stephens) to house his visiting guests in *Die Another Day*. Constructed in real life on the cavernous 007 Stage at Pinewood Studios, it's another design triumph from Oscar-winning production designer Peter Lamont, who had to create a structure strong enough to accommodate the amazing car chase that takes place within the walls.

IDA physicist: Official role of nuclear expert Christmas Jones (Denise Richards) in *The World Is Not Enough*. Although it's never explained in dialogue, props used in the film indicate that the acronym stands for International Decommissioning Agency—appropriate for a scientist involved in cleaning up shuttered nuclear test sites.

identigraph: Computerized 3-D visual identification system employed by Q Branch in *For Your Eyes Only*. Once a composite of the suspect is created, the identigraph can tap into the photographic files of the French Sûreté, Interpol, the CIA, Mossad, and the West German police. Bond (Roger Moore) uses the experimental system to identify Emile Leopold Locque (Michael Gothard) as the man who paid off Cuban hit man Hector Gonzales (Stefan Kalipha) for murdering Timothy and Iona Havelock (Jack Hedley and Toby Robins).

iguana: Unusual lizard pet of drug lord Franz Sanchez (Robert Davi) in *Licence to Kill*. It wears an expensive diamond collar that is coveted by Sanchez's girlfriend, Lupe Lamora (Talisa Soto). In the end, thanks to the efforts of James Bond (Timothy Dalton), Lupe wins the sparkler.

Imminent: Code name for a possible American nuclear attack against the Soviet Union in *You Only Live Twice*. Having lost one Jupiter space capsule to what they think is a Soviet plot to control outer space, the US government announces that if anything should happen to their second Jupiter capsule, they will launch an attack. Little do they know that SPECTRE, courtesy of their *Intruder* spaceship, is playing the Americans off against the Russians on behalf of the Red Chinese. Thanks to James Bond (Sean Connery), who gets to the control panel in time and triggers the *Intruder*'s self-destruct mechanism, a nuclear nightmare is averted.

International Brotherhood for the Assistance of Stateless Persons: A philanthropic organization based in Paris that in actuality is a SPECTRE front in *Thunderball*. Beneath its offices is the sleek, modern, stainless steel headquarters of Ernst Stavro Blofeld.

International Hotel: Las Vegas hotel (now the Westgate Las Vegas Resort & Casino) that provides a penthouse suite for billionaire Willard Whyte (Jimmy Dean) in *Diamonds Are Forever*.

Sean Connery is dressed for action while Jill St. John (left) takes a break during Las Vegas location filming on *Diamonds Are Forever*. *Las Vegas News Bureau*

When Whyte is abducted, the penthouse is occupied by Whyte's successor: SPECTRE's Ernst Stavro Blofeld (Charles Gray).

Intruder: The name given to the SPECTRE rocket in the script for *You Only Live Twice*. It is also code-named Bird 1 on its final mission. The instrument by which Ernst Stavro Blofeld (Donald Pleasence) plans to aid the Red Chinese by igniting World War III between the United States and the Soviet Union, the *Intruder* is designed to literally swallow enemy space capsules. Equipped with an electronically operated snout that opens like the mouth of a whale, the *Intruder* performs effectively, capturing one Soviet and one US Jupiter spacecraft. Having snatched the ships from orbit, the *Intruder* then returns to its secret rocket base, hidden inside the cone of an extinct Japanese volcano.

On its third mission to capture a second Jupiter spacecraft, a hostile act that the Americans will be led to believe is precipitated by the Russians (this time, the *Intruder* is emblazoned with the Red star of the Soviet Union to further mislead US authorities), James Bond (Sean Connery) is able to break into Blofeld's rocket base and activate the self-destruct mechanism on the *Intruder* before it accomplishes its mission.

The idea of playing the Russians and Americans off against one another is typical of SPECTRE, which had initiated another such caper in *From Russia with Love*. And when the earlier film's screenwriter, Richard Maibaum, joined forces with *You Only Live Twice* director Lewis Gilbert on *The Spy Who Loved Me*, they went back to the same premise again, only this time billionaire Karl Stromberg (Curt Jurgens) replaced Blofeld as the megalomaniac who's intent on provoking war between Russia and the West for his own selfish gain. The submarine-swallowing supertanker of that film—the *Liparus*—was simply a seaborne version of the *Intruder* rocket.

Sean Connery and Daniela Bianchi take a break from shooting in Istanbul's St. Sophia Mosque in *From Russia with Love*. *Courtesy of the David Reinhardt Collection*

Ionian Sea: Body of water off the coast of Albania where the *St. Georges* surveillance ship is sunk in *For Your Eyes Only*.

Istanbul: Largest city in Turkey and headquarters of the British Secret Service's Station T–Turkey in *From Russia with Love*. It is in this city on the Bosphorus strait that SPECTRE initiates its plan to steal a Russian Lektor decoding machine and humiliate and murder James Bond (Sean Connery). In *The World Is Not Enough* it's also the target of the plot by Renard (Robert Carlyle) and Elektra King (Sophie Marceau) to

detonate a nuclear device aboard a ditched submarine. With Istanbul devastated and the Bosphorus tanker route closed to the sea, Elektra's oil pipeline will triumph over its three Russian competitors. M (Dame Judi Dench), 007 (Pierce Brosnan), and Dr. Christmas Jones (Denise Richards) are all held captive in the middle of the strait, on a tiny island known as the Maiden's Tower.

In *Skyfall*, Bond (Daniel Craig) and Moneypenny (Naomie Harris) are in Istanbul to pursue the mercenary Patrice (Ola Rapace), who has stolen a hard drive containing information on friendly agents all over the world. Their pursuit leads to a desperate fight on the roof of a train, during which Moneypenny accidentally shoots Bond, allowing Patrice to escape. Like Tilly in *Goldfinger*, Moneypenny is a lousy shot.

Isthmus City: Fictional South American coastal city that is actually the cocaine capital of the drug empire run by Franz Sanchez (Robert Davi) in *Licence to Kill*. Ruled by puppet president Hector Lopez (Pedro Armendariz Jr.), the city has been essentially bought by Sanchez, who owns the main hotel and bank.

Many interior and exterior sequences in Isthmus City were actually filmed in Mexico City. The city's Main Post Office became the interior of the Banco de Isthmus, where Sanchez launders all of his drug loot. The hotel where Bond (Timothy Dalton) stays, El Presidente, was filmed inside the Gran Hotel Ciudad de México. Its exterior was shot outside the Biblioteca del Banco de México—the Library of the Bank of Mexico. The exterior shots of Sanchez's office building were filmed outside the famous El Teatro de la Ciudad (Theater of the City). The casino where elegant blackjack dealer Lupe Lamora (Talisa Soto) helps Bond meet Sanchez was filmed inside Mexico City's Casino Español, at the time a private club.

Istria: A peninsula on the Adriatic Sea that circa 1963 was part of the now defunct nation of Yugoslavia. It is the closest point of reference when Bond (Sean Connery) and Tanya (Daniela Bianchi) depart Yugoslavia on their motorboat trip to Venice in *From Russia with Love*.

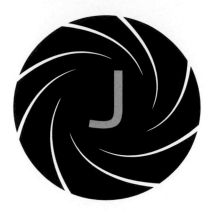

James, Clifton (May 29, 1920–April 15, 2017): Rotund American character actor who portrayed bumbling Louisiana sheriff J. W. Pepper in both *Live and Let Die* and *The Man with the Golden Gun*. Born in Spokane, Washington, James made a career of playing law enforcement officers (serious and comedic) and criminals. His motion picture debut was as Colonel Ramey in director Jack Garfein's film noir drama *The Strange One* (1957). His additional feature credits include *The Last Mile* (1959); *Something Wild* (1961); *Experiment in Terror* (1962); *David and Lisa* (1962); *Invitation to a Gunfighter* (1964); *The Chase* (1966); *Cool Hand Luke* (1967); *Will Penny* (1967); *Tick, Tick, Tick* (1970), as redneck D. J. Rankin; *The New Centurions* (1972); *Silver Streak* (1976), as J. W. Pepper clone Sheriff Chauncey; *Superman II* (1980); and *Eight Men Out* (1988), as baseball commissioner Charles Comiskey.

Comical American character actor Clifton James won many fans as bumbling southern sheriff J. W. Pepper in *Live and Let Die*. *Courtesy of the Anders Frejdh Collection*

James Bond of the Secret Service: Early working title of a script by Kevin McClory, Len Deighton, and Sean Connery that was planned as a remake of *Thunderball* but was never produced. McClory had cowritten the original story for *Thunderball* with Ian Fleming and screenwriter Jack Whittingham as part of an early attempt to adapt Fleming's Bond novels to the screen, and he controlled all rights to that particular Bond adventure. In 1965 he'd partnered with Albert R. Broccoli and Harry Saltzman to produce the original film version, under an agreement that prevented him from producing another adaptation for ten years. Promptly in 1975, McClory announced *James Bond of the Secret Service*—later known as *Warhead*—which would feature the return of Sean Connery as 007.

By this point Broccoli was producing the Bond series alone for United Artists, and he remembered the competition provided by Columbia Pictures' *Casino Royale* spoof in 1967. He was not about to let a rival Bond into the marketplace without a fight. A long legal battle with McClory soon began, and it wasn't until 1982, when producer and top entertainment lawyer Jack Schwartzman entered the fray, that a *Thunderball* remake finally went before the cameras. Based on an entirely different script, it became *Never Say Never Again*.

James Bond theme: Although it is officially credited to *Dr. No* composer Monty Norman, the true creator of arguably the most famous theme in motion picture history was John Barry, who joined the creative team on the first James Bond movie quite late in the game after producers rejected the original theme tune composed by Norman. Writing in his incredibly detailed book *The Music of James Bond*, author and music historian Jon Burlingame explained the theme's musical origins:

> Although Barry cited "Bees Knees," a 1958 John Barry Seven recording that was guitar-driven with a similarly dark tone, it was really his theme for the film *Beat Girl* to which the "James Bond Theme" owes the biggest debt: low, sinister twangy guitar, insistent beat and high, blaring brass—an early and surprising combination of jazz and rock elements for a film about

juvenile delinquents in London. Issued as a soundtrack album in 1960. Barry's catchy, hip *Beat Girl* music became England's first long-playing record devoted to a single movie score.*

The James Bond theme has been recorded over five hundred times and has sold over twenty million records over the years, and was given a special Ivor Novello Award. Of the various orchestrations of the signature 007 theme throughout the years, I have always been partial to the one used in the opening of *From Russia with Love*, which represents John Barry at his most dramatic.

JAMES, LOVE ALWAYS, DELLA & FELIX: Sentiment engraved on the back of the silver cigarette lighter given to James Bond (Timothy Dalton) by Della (Priscilla Barnes) and Felix Leiter (David Hedison) after their wedding in *Licence to Kill*. Later, 007 uses that same lighter to ignite gasoline-drenched Franz Sanchez (Robert Davi), who maimed Felix and murdered his bride.

Famke Janssen as Xenia Onatopp in *GoldenEye*. *Courtesy of the Nicolás Suszczyk Collection*

Janssen, Famke (November 5, 1964–   ): Dutch beauty who portrayed Xenia Zaragevna Onatopp, the larger-than-life psychotic assassin in *GoldenEye*. Costumed by Lindy Hemming, Janssen is stunning as the top killer for crime boss Alec Trevelyan (Sean Bean). Onatopp has a black-widow streak in bed—she crushes her lovers with her "killer thighs." She even draws some blood when she kisses Bond in the steam room. Tall, athletic, and deliciously murderous, she's definitely one of the great Bond villainesses— ranking right up there with Fiona Volpe (Luciana Paluzzi) in *Thunderball* and Fatima Blush (Barbara

Famke Janssen, echoing the unabashed wickedness of Barbara Carrera's Fatima Blush in *Never Say Never Again*, took on the role of Xenia Onatopp in *GoldenEye*. *Courtesy of the David Reinhardt Collection*

Carrera) in *Never Say Never Again*. Born in Amstelveen, Noord-Holland, Janssen made her motion picture debut as Kyle Christian in writer/director Paul Mones's dramatic thriller *Fathers & Sons* (1992). Her post-*GoldenEye* credits include *House on Haunted Hill* (1999) and *Love & Sex* (2000), and she's starred in three *Taken* movies as Liam Neeson's ex-wife, Lenore, and five *X-Men* films as Jean Grey/Phoenix.

Janus: Code name for turncoat British agent Alec Trevelyan (Sean Bean) in *GoldenEye*. It's rumored that Trevelyan/Janus lives on a converted Soviet missile train, but no one has ever seen him. His alias is an appropriate one, since Janus is the name of the Roman god with two faces. It's also the name given to Trevelyan's crime syndicate, which is behind a plot to destroy England's economy by setting off a destructive electromagnetic pulse from a Russian space satellite. Specializing in arms trading, the syndicate was the first outfit to supply the Iraqis during the original Gulf War.

Japan: Setting of the fifth James Bond film, *You Only Live Twice*. It also figures in a

---

* Jon Burlingame, *The Music of James Bond* (Oxford: Oxford University Press, 2012), 15.

curious blooper. In the film, British agent Dikko Henderson (Charles Gray) asks Bond (Sean Connery) if he's ever been to Japan before. He replies, "No, never." However, in *From Russia with Love*, during the comical sequence in which Miss Moneypenny is listening to Bond's Istanbul tape recording of Tatiana Romanova, Bond responds to Tanya's question of "Am I as exciting as all those Western girls?" with "Once when M and I were in Tokyo . . ." So Bond *has* been to Japan before.

Japan is also the second target selected in the Domination video game battle between Maximilian Largo (Klaus Maria Brandauer) and Bond (Sean Connery) in *Never Say Never Again*. It's worth $16,000, and Largo wins.

Jaws: Enormous, apparently invulnerable, steel-toothed assassin portrayed by Richard Kiel in *The Spy Who Loved Me* and *Moonraker*. In *Spy*, Jaws is introduced in the employ of fanatical billionaire shipping magnate Karl Stromberg (Curt Jurgens). His mission is to retrieve a microfilm copy of the nuclear submarine tracking system that Stromberg is using to capture enemy subs. Partnered initially with bald Sandor (Milton Reid, a veteran of *Dr. No*), Jaws continues solo when Sandor is killed by Bond (Roger Moore) in Cairo. Huge but clumsy, Jaws battles Bond, losing each contest, including a fight at an Egyptian tomb, where he's buried under a mountain of rubble; in a train compartment, where his steel teeth are electrocuted and he's tossed through the compartment window; on the Sardinia roadway, where his car goes off a cliff and into the roof of a peasant's house; and in Stromberg's Atlantis lair, where he's fastened to the plate of an electromagnet and thrown into the shark pen.

At first glance, the Jaws character seemed to take the Bond series across the thin line between plausibility and fantasy. Up until *The Spy Who Loved Me*, the films had prided themselves on presenting flesh-and-blood heroes and villains. No matter how wild the story lines became, villains were eventually eliminated for good—except Blofeld, who had a strange habit of reappearing in successive films—and peace was somehow restored to the world. Jaws, on the other hand, was a character right out of the comic books: a killer on the loose who can't be stopped or killed, with a touch of Wile E. Coyote from the Road Runner cartoons.

Yet, in retrospect, Jaws was a very shrewd addition to the series at the time. By the mid-1970s, most of the people who had grown up with Bond were growing out of the core movie audience of twelve- to twenty-four-year-olds. In other words, they were getting too old to be considered guaranteed ticket buyers. Producer Albert R. Broccoli needed to freshen up the series to appeal to the new generation of filmgoers that would soon turn fantasy adventures like *Star Wars* and *E.T.* into megahits. Bigger-than-life characters like Jaws were the answer. His appearance in *The Spy Who Loved Me* certainly helped revive the series' sagging box office numbers.

Eager to capitalize on the character's huge popularity, Broccoli asked screenwriter Christopher Wood to revive Jaws as one of the assassins working for Drax (Michael Lonsdale) in *Moonraker*. In that film, Jaws appears in the amazing pre-credits teaser, in which he throws James Bond (Roger Moore) out of an airplane without a parachute. Unfortunately, his own ripcord malfunctions, and Jaws lands on top of a huge circus tent, which, of course, collapses. Later, he masquerades as a Mardi Gras mummer in Rio, where he's whisked away by revelers before he can deal with Bond. An amazing fight erupts between Bond, CIA agent Holly Goodhead (Lois Chiles), and Jaws atop two cable cars high above the Rio harbor. Once again, Jaws is revealed as huge but clumsy and surrounded by incompetence. As the two secret agents jump to safety, the assassin's cable car loses its braking capability and crashes into the wheelhouse. He survives, of course, dusts

Having steel teeth can come in handy, as Jaws (Richard Kiel) demonstrates on a cable car line in *Moonraker*. *Courtesy of the David Reinhardt Collection*

himself off, and meets his first girlfriend, buxom Dolly (Blanche Ravalec).

Later, all four characters become passengers on one of the space shuttles carrying Drax's master race to his radar-proof space station. But Jaws soon realizes that he and his girlfriend are not to be included in Drax's mad scheme. At the last minute, he joins Bond in the furious assault on the space station. Victorious, Bond and Holly leave Jaws and Dolly to ride home with the US space troopers. Opening a bottle of champagne, Jaws proposes a toast to Dolly, uttering his only dialogue in the series, "Well, here's to us."

Jaws was also the name of the surf break on the north shore of Maui, Hawaii, where filmmakers shot James Bond (Pierce Brosnan) riding a massive wave onto a North Korean military base for the pre-credits teaser of *Die Another Day*. In real life, the wave was ridden by expert surfer/stuntman Laird Hamilton.

Jay, Ricky (June 26, 1946–November 24, 2018; birth name: Richard Jay Potash): Card magician, showman, author, scholar, and actor who portrayed cyberterrorist Henry Gupta, henchman to billionaire media mogul Elliot Carver (Jonathan Pryce) in *Tomorrow Never Dies*. Born in Brooklyn, New York, Jay made his feature motion picture debut as George in the crime thriller *House of Games* (1987), directed by his close friend writer/director David Mamet. He later appeared in six other Mamet films. His additional motion picture credits include *Homicide* (1991); *Boogie Nights* (1997), as cameraman Kurt Longjohn; *Magnolia* (1999); *State and Main* (2000); *Heist* (2001); and *The Prestige* (2006). Jay was a master at sleight of hand, and his stage magic shows, including *Ricky Jay and His 52 Assistants*, were celebrated around the world. His consulting company, Deceptive Practices, devised the wheelchair that let actor Gary Sinise play double amputee Lieutenant Dan in *Forrest Gump* (1994). Jay was listed in the *Guinness Book of World Records* for throwing a playing card 190 feet at ninety miles an hour.

jet boat: Tiny rocket-powered craft commandeered by Bond (Pierce Brosnan) in the pre-credits teaser for *The World Is Not Enough*, to track down and destroy the Cigar Girl (Maria Grazia Cucinotta) after she blows a huge hole in MI6 headquarters on the Thames. Q (Desmond Llewelyn) later claims that it was his own private fishing boat, but we know better. After all, it has the usual Q Branch gizmos beyond the rocket-powered engine: heat-seeking torpedoes, submersible capabilities, and the ability to drive down a city street. The only problem is that it's so tiny that it's hard to maneuver in a high-speed chase with a larger boat, as Bond eventually finds out.

jet pump powerboats: The high-speed motorboats featured in *Live and Let Die* that use jets of water for propulsion. The engines on these unusual boats suck in the water and pump it out in a fast stream that propels the boat forward and provides rudder control. Without the jet stream, the boat cannot change direction—a dangerous fact that actor Roger Moore learned during location shooting in Louisiana. Moore had been practicing some tight turns on a bayou waterway when his motor cut out, leaving him with no steering at 45 mph. Losing control, he smashed into a dock—an unfortunate accident that sent the new James Bond to the local doctor with a jammed leg, a fractured front tooth, and general bruising.

JIM: Specialized deep-sea diving equipment featured in *For Your Eyes Only*. Designed, according to Bond (Roger Moore), "for salvage work at depths of more than three hundred feet," the equipment comes in handy when 007 and Melina (Carole Bouquet) must retrieve the ATAC computer from the wreck of the *St. Georges* surveillance ship. Breathing a mixture of oxygen and helium, they have a total of eight minutes to spend at 584 feet, where the wreck lies.

Jinx (a.k.a. Giacinta Johnson): Resourceful, athletic NSA agent portrayed by Halle Berry in *Die Another Day*. James Bond (Pierce Brosnan) meets her in Cuba when she comes out of the water in an eye-popping orange bikini, an obvious nod to Ursula Andress's entrance in *Dr. No*. After a passionate tryst, 007 follows Jinx to a gene therapy clinic, where he discovers and tries to kill his North Korean nemesis Zao (Rick Yune), who is undergoing facial restructuring. On the trail of suspicious billionaire Gustav Graves (Toby Stephens), Bond reunites with Jinx in Iceland, where Graves is demonstrating his Icarus orbital mirror satellite laser. When Jinx is captured and nearly tortured to death with mobile lasers, 007 rescues her, then leads Zao on a wild chase across an icy escarpment to rescue her a second time when she's trapped in Graves's disintegrating Ice Palace. They both later stow away on Graves's cargo plane headed for Korea, where Jinx eventually does battle with Graves's duplicitous associate Miranda Frost (Rosamund Pike).

John, Gottfried (August 29, 1942–September 1, 2014): Prolific German actor who portrayed ruthless general Arkady Grigorovich Ourumov, head of satellite operations for northern Russia in *GoldenEye*. Ourumov is actually a top operative of the Janus crime syndicate and an ally of Alec Trevelyan (Sean Bean). A native of Berlin, John made his motion picture debut in director Claude Autant-Lara's World War II drama

German actor Gottfried John as renegade general Ourumov in *GoldenEye*. *Courtesy of the Nicolás Suszczyk Collection*

Between Love and Duty (1960). His first role in an English-language feature was as Perebrodov in Rainer Werner Fassbinder's period drama *Despair* (1978). The following year, he portrayed Willi Klenze in Fassbender's *The Marriage of Maria Braun*.

Johnson, Lynn-Holly (December 13, 1958–   ): Blonde American actress and former champion figure skater who portrayed sex-crazed skater Bibi Dahl in *For Your Eyes Only*. Although Johnson brought to the film her winsome good looks and some very American mannerisms, her comic interaction with 007 (Roger Moore) does appear to be a bit out of place in a movie that features one of the most sinister groups of enemy villains since *From Russia with Love*. A Chicago native, Johnson made her feature film debut as an ice skater in director Donald Wrye's romantic sports drama *Ice Castles* (1978).

Perky Lynn-Holly Johnson portrayed competitive ice skater Bibi Dahl in *For Your Eyes Only*. *Courtesy of the David Reinhardt Collection*

"Jonah Set": Nickname for the huge interior of the *Liparus* supertanker designed by Ken Adam and built on the 007 Stage at Pinewood Studios for *The Spy Who Loved Me*. Since the plot involved a supertanker that swallows nuclear submarines, it was appropriate to name the set

Production designer Ken Adam's magnificent interior of the *Liparus* supertanker for *The Spy Who Loved Me*. It was nicknamed the "Jonah Set." *Courtesy of the David Reinhardt Collection*

after the biblical figure who was swallowed by a whale.

To build such a massive set, complete with a huge water tank to accommodate the nuclear submarines, Adam had initially thought he would need to look outside Pinewood. He considered using a World War II dirigible hangar, and even found a suitable one elsewhere in England. But the expense of converting it into a soundstage was equal to that of constructing an entirely new stage at Pinewood. And the cost of transporting crews back and forth between the studio and the hangar would be prohibitive. Adam reasoned that the only way to do things right was to follows the example of the *You Only Live Twice* volcano set and build the supertanker right on the lot.

Eon Productions thus entered the real estate business, investing in the 007 Stage, the biggest soundstage in the world at that time. Said Adam, "The stage was built to accommodate nuclear

submarines that were five-eighths the size of real submarines. A real nuclear submarine is about 425 feet long. To accommodate that size of vessel would have required a set in excess of 600 feet. I couldn't go that long because the relationship of the men to the ships would have been awkward." *

Adam constructed a model of the proposed set that was viewed with awe by the director and screenwriters. The script called for a huge battle to take place within the tanker when Bond (Roger Moore) releases the three captive submarine crews, who then attempt to take over the ship before enemy submarines can fire nuclear missiles on Moscow and New York City. The battle would rage over the entire dock area, along the catwalks, up staircases, and along the corridors, where the prisoners break out of the brig and

* Ken Adam, interview by the author, London, June 17, 1977.

Construction continues inside the 007 Stage on the "Jonah Set" in *The Spy Who Loved Me*. *Courtesy of the Michael VanBlaricum Collection*

gather weapons in the tanker's arsenal. When the special effects team was finished, the interior of the *Liparus* would be set ablaze with dozens of fires and explosions.

In one of the early scripts, the supertanker is controlled from a bridge area located on the surface of the tanker. Bond and his men battle to the surface and then attack the bridge along the deck of the ship. When Adam formulated the design for his interior set, however, it was decided to move the control room inside the tanker, where it would be attacked from the dock area.

"Much of the credit for the accuracy of the set and the swiftness in which it was constructed goes to the Pinewood construction crews, who were now used to the type of way-out set designs featured in a James Bond film," said Adam around the time of the film's release. "Over the years, they have organized themselves to cope with those sort of situations. I don't quite know what would happen if we tried to build such a set in another country. For one thing, the cost factor would be higher in Hollywood. The 007 Stage eventually cost about a half million dollars. For the biggest stage in the world, that isn't much. And it was built in four months." *

Upon completion, the 007 Stage measured 374 feet long, 160 feet wide, and 53 feet high. It included an interior tank into which Adam placed his nuclear submarine mock-ups. Like his *You Only Live Twice* volcano set, the supertanker interior was hyperrealistic and featured a working monorail, miles of steel girder work, and a final

* Ibid.

control room that strongly resembled Blofeld's communications center in the earlier film. Submarines had replaced the *Intruder* space rocket, but here again was movie design at its most impressive.

Jones, Grace (May 19, 1948–   ; birth name: Beverly Grace Jones): Jamaican American actress, singer, composer, and model who portrayed May Day, bodyguard/assassin/lover to Max Zorin (Christopher Walken) in *A View to a Kill*. Jones won the part after her strong appearance as Zula the fierce Amazonian warrior woman in *Conan the Destroyer* (1984).

As is the case in many 007 adventures, henchwoman May Day steals the scene from the main villain, her superior, Zorin. Quick as a cat and super strong, she ranks high among the rogues' gallery of Bond film henchwomen. Jones conceived of the character's unique look herself, explaining that she was initially worried that director John Glen would think her makeup and costumes too outrageous. To her delight, Glen embraced her stylistic vision for May Day, encouraging her to add even more color, especially reds to her face. Jones also performed some of her own stunts, which included keeping a right hand on the reins of a spooked thoroughbred and climbing up the broken structural supports of a ruined mine shaft—with a long drop to the stage floor where it was filmed.

Grace Jones took on the role of assassin May Day in *A View to a Kill*. *Courtesy of the David Reinhardt Collection*

Born in Spanish Town, Jamaica, and raised in Syracuse, New York, Jones made her feature film debut as Mary in actor/director Ossie Davis's crime adventure *Gordon's War* (1973).

Jones, Tom (June 7, 1940–   ; birth name: Thomas John Woodward): Sexy Welsh pop

superstar, nick-
named the Voice,
who warbled the
dynamic title tune to
Thunderball. Jones
was fairly new to
audiences when
the fourth James
Bond was released
on Christmas 1965.
He had recently
scored with his first
chart-busting single,
"It's Not Unusual"
(Decca Records).

Singer Tom Jones warbled
the full-throttle title tune to
*Thunderball. Courtesy of the
David Reinhardt Collection*

Jordan, Johnny (April 12, 1925–May 16, 1969):
British cameraman and aerial specialist who
filmed action sequences on *You Only Live Twice*
and *On Her Majesty's Secret Service*. During
location shooting in Japan on *You Only Live
Twice*, he was involved in a terrifying helicopter
collision.

Working with second unit director Peter Hunt,
Jordan was responsible for shooting the aerial
battle sequence that pits Bond (Sean Connery) in
his tiny autogyro Little Nellie against four armed
SPECTRE helicopters. Jordan would be filming
from inside one of the speedy French Alouette
copters, where a special Panavision camera
was rigged to the helicopter's metal skid. Four
Japanese stunt pilots would be flying the four
SPECTRE choppers, while Wing Commander Ken
Wallis, Little Nellie's inventor and the only person
who could fly the autogyro with any degree of
expertise, would be doubling Sean Connery.

On the afternoon of September 22, 1966, Jordan was filming above the little village of Ebino
when the four enemy helicopters began their
dive on Bond. Peter Hunt was on the ground,
observing the action from a jeep. "Our problem,"
Hunt remembered, "was that the helicopters were
always getting too spread out. Our Japanese
pilots were very nervous and wary of flying in too
close a formation. We had radio communication
with all the copters, and we were always yelling
at them to close up so we could get them all in
the same frame."*

At two o'clock that afternoon, Jordan's
Alouette was keeping pace with two black Hillers

when one of the action helicopters struck an
updraft, hurtling it toward the helpless camera
ship. Before the pilot could react, Jordan's ship
was struck by the Hiller's rotor blade, which
sliced through the Alouette's skids and Johnny
Jordan's extended leg.

Hunt watched the whole disaster speech-
lessly. "We were filming this close-order formation when suddenly there was a terrible crash and
the Alouette skidded on its side into a tree only
a few yards from us," said Hunt. "The pilot was
okay, but Johnny's foot was hanging by a thread.
Typical of a cameraman's mentality, he had photographed his own foot when it got hit, hoping
that it might be useful for the surgeons."

Coincidentally, Ebino was a health resort
for tubercular and bone disease patients. There
were a number of hospitals in the area, and
one of them sent out an ambulance to transport the injured aerial cameraman. Said Hunt,
"It just so happened that this hospital was one
of Japan's finest bone centers, and they were
doing operations that very day. The Japanese
surgeons rushed him into an operating room and
attempted to save his leg. At the time, there was
only one artery going strong. It was hopeless."
But they were able to stop the loss of blood
and preserve the leg until Jordan was returned
to England, where three months later it was
amputated.

The loss of Jordan completely demoralized
the second unit crew on *You Only Live Twice*, and
Peter Hunt soon requested that they temporarily abandon the helicopter stunts and return to
London at once. "It was a disaster," Hunt recalled.
"We were pretty early in the helicopter shooting
when Jordan was hit, and we had finished only
a couple of the establishing shots of the copters
moving across the volcanoes. We ended up doing
the rest of the fight over Spain, above Torremolinos on the Costa del Sol, before Christmas—
under those bright Spanish skies. We were lucky,
because behind Torremolinos there are many
volcanic mountains that perfectly matched our
locations on Kyushu." Jordan's work was completed by cameraman Tony Brown.

But Eon Productions had not heard the last of
Johnny Jordan. Equipped with an artificial limb,
Jordan returned to 007 service for *On Her Majesty's Secret Service*, working this time from a camera rig he designed himself, which hung down
from the belly of a helicopter like a parachute

---

* Peter Hunt, interview by the author, London, June 21, 1977.

Aerial cameraman Johnny Jordan films snow action from his personally designed helicopter rig in *On Her Majesty's Secret Service*. *Steve Rubin Collection*

Strangers Came (1949). Sadly, on May 16, 1969, Jordan was killed in a fall from the fuselage of a B-25 bomber during the filming of *Catch-22* (1970).

Jourdan, Louis (June 19, 1921–February 14, 2015; birth name: Louis Robert Gendre): Smooth French leading man who portrayed exiled Afghan prince Kamal Khan in *Octopussy*. Jourdan appears to have enjoyed himself in one of the most unsympathetic roles in his career. He had played cads before—especially in *The Best of Everything* (1959)—but that was nothing compared to the seething evil he projects in *Octopussy*. A native of Marseille, Jourdan made his feature film debut in director Marc Allégret's *Le corsaire* (1939). Eight years later, he made his English-language debut in Alfred Hitchcock's *The Paradine Case*. However, it was his role as playboy Gaston Lachaille opposite Leslie Caron in *Gigi* (1958) that won him international stardom.

French actor Louis Jourdan plays smarmy exiled Afghan prince Kamal Khan, a purveyor of all things illegal, in *Octopussy*. *Courtesy of the David Reinhardt Collection*

harness. By using such a platform, Jordan drifted above the treetops with complete freedom of movement and 360 degrees of traverse. He was responsible for some of the film's most beautiful aerial sequences, including the shots of the phony Red Cross helicopters of Marc-Ange Draco (Gabriele Ferzetti) headed across Switzerland for their attack on Ernst Stavro Blofeld's Piz Gloria stronghold, and the aerial view of the hair-raising bobsled chase in which Bond has one last chance to eliminate Blofeld.

A native of Oxfordshire, England, Jordan made his motion picture debut as a camera operator on director Alfred Travers's comedy *The*

Juarez (1939): Film on the life of Mexican revolutionary Benito Juarez (Paul Muni). Director William Dieterle's unusual introduction of the main character was so memorable to *Dr. No* director Terence Young that he borrowed it for his introduction of 007 (Sean Connery) in the first Bond feature. In the earlier film, Muni plays the whole first scene with his back to the camera, and then turns around when someone asks him his name. "Juarez," he sneers. For *Dr. No*, Young blocked James Bond's introduction in the Les Ambassadeurs gambling club in London the same way. His camera faces Sean Connery's back until the precisely worked-out moment when Sylvia Trench (Eunice Gayson) addresses him, and Bond is seen for the first time in a cloud of cigarette smoke, announcing himself as "Bond . . . James Bond."

Julienne, Rémy (April 17, 1930–   ): Top French auto-stunt coordinator whose frenetic car chases became an industry standard, thanks in large part to his work on the James Bond series. Julienne began his Bond association on *For Your Eyes Only*, for which he devised and coordinated the Citroën Deux Cheveux chase and the motorbike fight in Cortina d'Ampezzo. On *Octopussy*, his drivers took Bond (Roger Moore) on the wild chase through the German countryside to an American air force base. On *A View to a Kill*, Julienne took a car down concrete steps to the Seine River in Paris, then obliterated its windshield and eventually cut the car completely in half as Bond attempts to keep up with a parachuting May Day (Grace Jones). Later in the same film, his auto daredevils were put to work in downtown San Francisco during Bond's hook-and-ladder chase. In Mexicali, Mexico, on *Licence to Kill*, Julienne was intimately involved in the Kenworth tractor-trailer truck stunts.

Julienne's final Bond assignment was *GoldenEye*. As he recounted at the time, "I started with the James Bond series in 1980 [on] *For Your Eyes Only*. In *GoldenEye*, it's a very subtle race between two protagonists—a Ferrari 355, which is a real animal, and an Aston Martin DB5, which is a relatively ancient vehicle, a venerable machine. We were afraid to hurt it. . . . In order to match the performance of the two cars that have nothing in common is very complicated. We've had to use tricks—spikes on the tires to make it slide—it's the opposite of what we're used to doing. And this is precisely why the job is fascinating. In this chase scene—it is not a stunt, it is a chase scene—it must be very subtle to adapt to the actors's performances. And that's what makes it very difficult. But on the other hand it's also something wonderful to achieve."

He added, "Everything is always very dangerous. It requires a lot of skill in order to be very precise in relationship to the camera. The day before yesterday, we crashed both the Aston and the Ferrari. A small thing, but huge consequences. We were able to fix it during the night. . . . What is now wonderful is that we can now use all the technical craft we have acquired

on the race tracks, the Grand Prix, and use this knowledge for filmmaking, and I believe this is an outstanding accomplishment."[*]

A native of Cepoy, Loiret (in the Loire Valley, ninety-four kilometers from Paris), Julienne made his motion picture stunt debut on director André Hunebelle's crime comedy adventure *Fantomas* (1964). Three years later, he first served as a stunt coordinator on George Lautner's *Sorrel Flower*. However, it was his masterful work on Peter Collinson's *The Italian Job* (1969) that brought him international acclaim for his innovative car stunts.

Junkanoo: A festival similar to Mardi Gras celebrated in Nassau, Bahamas, complete with elaborate floats, marching bands, and a party in the streets—all of which become an elaborate backdrop to the action in *Thunderball*. In the story, Bond (Sean Connery) is captured by SPECTRE assassin Fiona Volpe (Luciana Paluzzi) and her thugs, who plan to transport him by car to the Palmyra estate of Emilio Largo (Adolfo Celi). On the way, they're held up by the parade, and a drunk happens to put his bottle of liquor in the window near Fiona, who is lighting her cigarette. Bond kicks outward and the liquor splashes into the car, allowing 007 to create a momentary distraction by igniting the liquor and dive out of the vehicle. Wounded in the ankle by a stray bullet, he limps his way through the parade and ends up in the bathroom at the Kiss Kiss Club, where a hasty tourniquet stops the bleeding.

Though the real Junkanoo was normally held on Boxing Day, December 26, the Nassau Junkanoo in *Thunderball* was staged during Easter 1965, when Eon Productions offered to back the whole affair with cash prizes for the most elaborate costumes. For the sequence, 548 locals were hired, along with 55 European extras. "The Junkanoo was a real parade," remembered Richard Jenkins, a third assistant director, who had also worked with Terence Young on *The Amorous Adventures of Moll Flanders* (1965). "Terence planned to film around the parade as it moved through downtown Nassau. He told us that whatever happened, we weren't to try to stop it or move it backward. We just had to shoot around it, doing the best we could. We all told Terence that his advice was very sensible. The parade was something like two miles long, traveling around

---

[*] Special features, *GoldenEye*, James Bond Ultimate Edition (1995; MGM, 2006), DVD.

in a big circle, and there were forty companies cosponsoring the event. To bring the whole thing to a halt might have caused a riot.

"As the parade moved through Nassau, there was this constant rhythm of *whistle, whistle, boom, boom.* And for two nights, that was all we heard. The performers were wild, and when their paper costumes began to loosen up, they would take them off and heat them over flames to make them stiff again. Several times, our camera picked up a crowd of people coming around a corner with nothing on. Well, this *whistle, whistle, boom, boom* had been going on for six hours the second night when Terence finally called out, 'I've got a headache, we must stop the parade for a little while.' And Terry Churcher, Robert Watts, and I just stood there, transfixed. There must have been forty-five thousand people watching the parade by then, and we were afraid to walk out there and stop the momentum. But we did it, and Terence was able to realign some cameras and continue shooting. I remember that later the same evening, Terence was sipping some champagne from a paper cup when he said, 'God, this is a rough location—my champagne is warm.'"*

Jurgens, Curt (December 13, 1915–June 18, 1982; birth name: Curd Gustav Andreas Gottlieb Franz Jürgens): Tall, accomplished German character

---
* Richard Jenkins, interview by the author, London, June 18, 1977.

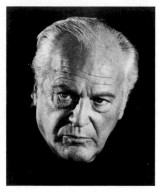

Character actor Curt Jurgens shines in *The Spy Who Loved Me* as billionaire shipping magnate Karl Stromberg, another megalomaniac with plans to end the world as we know it. *Courtesy of the David Reinhardt Collection.*

actor who portrayed billionaire shipping magnate and megalomaniac Karl Stromberg, the man with the webbed hands in *The Spy Who Loved Me*. A native of Munich, Jurgens made his big-screen debut in director Herbert Maisch's pre–World War II musical *Königswalzer* (1935). His first English-language role was as Emperor Joseph II in the biographical drama *The Mozart Story* (1948). His other feature credits include . . . *And God Created Woman* (1956), opposite Brigitte Bardot; *The Enemy Below* (1957), as the wily U-boat commander, with future Bond player David Hedison; *Me and the Colonel* (1958); *I Aim at the Stars* (1960), as rocket scientist Wernher von Braun; *The Longest Day* (1962), as General Gunther Blumentritt, adjutant to Field Marshal Von Rundstedt; and *Battle of Britain* (1969), for Bond producer Harry Saltzman.

Kabira, Yusef: Algerian boyfriend of Vesper Lynd (Eva Green)—the one she was trying to save by betraying Bond and MI6 in *Casino Royale*—portrayed by Simon Kassianides in *Quantum of Solace*. He was believed dead, washed up on a beach In Ibiza, but M (Dame Judi Dench) ordered a DNA check based on a lock of hair found in Vesper's apartment. It was not Kabira. He's later revealed as an agent of Quantum, turning up in Kazan, Russia, ready to seduce another woman—in this case, Canadian intelligence operative Corrine (Stana Katic). Bond captures him and turns him over to MI6.

Kalba, Max: Egyptian black-market trader and the owner of Cairo's Mojaba nightclub in *The Spy Who Loved Me*, portrayed by veteran character actor Vernon Dobtcheff. Following a clue he finds on the dead body of Aziz Fekkesh (Nadim Sawalha), Bond (Roger Moore) goes to the Mojaba Club to find Kalba and bid on a microfilm copy of a missing nuclear-submarine tracking system that he possesses.

Competing for the microfilm with KGB major Anya Amasova (Barbara Bach), Bond is prepared to offer a higher bid when Kalba is called to the phone. Instead of receiving a call, Kalba finds Jaws (Richard Kiel) waiting for him in the booth. He's "cut off," Jaws steals the film, Bond finds the body, Anya joins him, and both stow away in Jaws's phone utility truck as he drives off into the desert.

In an early treatment for *The Spy Who Loved Me*, the meeting with Kalba at the swank nightclub featured a tense, high-stakes game of backgammon in which Bond comes from behind to win 50,000 pounds from Kalba, who dies before he can pay up. Bond and Anya still go after Jaws, but this time they follow him in a sports car. The desert sequence was much more elaborate, with Bond and Amasova fighting off marauding bands of Tuareg bandits, with Anya's pearl necklace providing them with mini hand grenades. The unused backgammon sequence was later resurrected in *Octopussy*, when Bond battles the evil Kamal Khan (Louis Jourdan).

Kamen, Michael (April 15, 1948–November 18, 2003): American film composer and two-time Academy Award nominee who scored *Licence to Kill*. A native of New York City, Kamen received both his Oscar nominations for Best Original Song: "(Everything I Do) I Do It for You" from *Robin Hood: Prince of Thieves* (1991) and "Have You Ever Really Loved a Woman?" from *Don Juan DeMarco* (1994), sharing each nomination with Bryan Adams and Robert John Lange. Kamen made his motion picture composing debut on the action thriller *The Next Man* (1976), which starred Bond veterans Sean Connery and Adolfo Celi, and featured 007 stunt veteran Bob Simmons.

Kananga, Dr. (a.k.a. Mr. Big): Sinister foreign minister of the mythical island of San Monique in *Live and Let Die*, portrayed by American actor Yaphet Kotto. While he appears to be a mild-mannered third-world diplomat, Kananga is actually a resourceful, megalomaniacal drug lord who is about to corner the North American heroin market. He uses prosthetics to pose as Harlem drug kingpin Mr. Big. Kananga's plan is to cultivate two tons of San Monique heroin and distribute it free of charge through his chain of Fillet of Soul restaurants. Such a ploy would force his competitors out of business and double the number of addicts in the United States.

His entourage includes Baron Samedi (Geoffrey Holder), who may

Yaphet Kotto portrayed sinister island diplomat Dr. Kananga in *Live and Let Die*. Wearing prosthetics, he was also Mr. Big in Harlem. *Courtesy of the David Reinhardt Collection*

or may not be a supernatural being; Whisper (Earl Jolly Brown) and Tee Hee (Julius Harris), his principal assassins; and Solitaire (Jane Seymour), a fortune-teller whose tarot cards can predict the future of Kananga's evil deeds. Mr. Big / Kananga is eventually killed on San Monique when, in an underwater scuffle with Bond (Roger Moore), he is forced to swallow a bitter pill—a compressed air bullet that literally blows him to smithereens.

Kananga, Ross (June 7, 1945–January 30, 1978; birth name: Ross William Heilman): Amiable Jamaican of part-Seminole descent whose crocodile farm, the Jamaica Swamp Safari, became a principal location in *Live and Let Die*. Discovered on a location survey by director Guy Hamilton, art director Syd Cain, and writer Tom Mankiewicz, Kananga's ranch contained nearly fourteen hundred crocodiles and alligators. Since Mankiewicz was on the survey, it is logical to think that he borrowed the name of Kananga the crocodile farmer when writing the character of Kananga the drug lord. The real Kananga also performed the stunt in which James Bond (Roger Moore) jumps to safety across the backs of a group of hungry crocodiles.

Karl-Marx-Stadt, East Germany: City where Kamal Khan (Louis Jourdan) and General Orlov (Steven Berkoff) plant a nuclear device in a circus cannon in *Octopussy*. Using the traveling circus run by Octopussy (Maud Adams) as a cover, Orlov and Kamal plan to detonate the bomb on the US Air Force's Feldstadt Air Base across the border in West Germany and make Western Europe think the Americans triggered one of their nukes by mistake. Orlov is certain that this will force the US into unilateral nuclear disarmament along the border, opening the way for a massive Soviet invasion.

Unable to tap into a final briefing between Orlov and Kamal at the Monsoon Palace in Udaipur, India—because of the interference when Magda (Kristina Wayborn) uses her blow-dryer—Bond (Roger Moore) does hear the name Karl-Marx-Stadt and the reference to something happening in one week. Escaping from Kamal's palace, 007 makes it back to East Germany in time to defeat the insidious plan. After the reunification of Germany, Karl-Marx-Stadt reverted to its original name, Chemnitz, on June 1, 1990.

Kassianides, Simon (August 7, 1979–   ): British actor who portrayed Yusef Kabira, the Algerian agent of Quantum who seduced Vesper Lynd (Eva Green) and later shows up at the end of *Quantum of Solace*, ready to compromise another female agent. Born in London, Kassianides made his big-screen debut in director John Maybury's biographical drama *The Edge of Love* (2008). Subsequently, he played the recurring role of Sunil Bakshi in the television series *Agents of S.H.I.E.L.D.* (12 episodes, 2014–2017).

Kazakhstan: Former Soviet republic in Central Asia that is the site of King Industries' oil pipeline in *The World Is Not Enough*. Beset by local rebels who demand that the pipeline avoid cultural landmarks such as an ancient church, the pipeline is also a convenient terrorist target. That threat is a ruse, though: the terrorist, Renard (Robert Carlyle), and the oil company's owner, Elektra King (Sophie Marceau), are actually plotting to destroy three competing Russian pipelines instead.

keelhauling: How fiendish Aris Kristatos (Julian Glover) plans to torture and kill James Bond (Roger Moore) and Melina Havelock (Carole Bouquet) in *For Your Eyes Only*. The procedure, taken from Ian Fleming's novel *Live and Let Die*, involves tying Bond and Melina together, tossing them over the side of a motor launch, and dragging their bodies over a razor-sharp reef. The plot works until Bond and Melina dive under the water and use the reef to cut the towing rope. When they fail to surface, Kristatos mistakenly thinks they've become shark food and heads back to shore. Fortunately, Melina left an air tank near one of her father's archaeological excavations on the sea floor, which becomes a source of oxygen until Kristatos moves off.

Kent, England: City where Goldfinger (Gert Fröbe) runs a metallurgical facility, which is referenced but never visited in *Goldfinger*. According to Colonel Smithers (Richard Vernon) of the Bank of England, Goldfinger is a legitimate international jeweler who has authorization for a modest facility of this type. Unfortunately, he also uses it to illegally melt down gold and recast it as part of his Rolls-Royce's bodywork so he can smuggle it out of England.

Kenworth W900B: Huge eighteen-wheel American tanker truck, four of which are featured in the exciting conclusion to *Licence to Kill*. Filled with a 31,600-pound mixture of cocaine and gasoline, each truck is transporting a cargo of drugs worth more than $40 million. Headed down the highway from the drug laboratories of Franz Sanchez (Robert Davi) beneath the Olimpatec Meditation Institute, the cocaine convoy is virtually destroyed by James Bond (Timothy Dalton)—with a super assist from CIA fly girl Pam Bouvier (Carey Lowell).

The incredible chase was orchestrated by second unit director Arthur Wooster, 007 car chase veteran Remy Julienne, and special effects supervisor John Richardson, who spent seven weeks in the blazing desert mountains outside Mexicali, Mexico, near the California-Mexico border. The primary road was a deserted section of the Rumorosa mountain pass—an isolated, accident-prone mountain highway. Onto this treacherous terrain came a convoy of vehicles, including three Kenworth trucks that were specially modified for stunt use; five older Kenworths that were purchased and refurbished in Mexico; and a dozen tanker trailers, five of which were made out of wood for the explosion sequences.

Kerim Bey, Ali: Head of Station T–Turkey and right arm to Bond (Sean Connery) in Istanbul, portrayed by actor Pedro Armendariz in *From Russia with Love*. Kerim Bey is one of those wonderfully mysterious supporting characters, in the tradition of those played by Peter Lorre and Sydney Greenstreet, that populate the best spy stories. His moments on screen are unforgettable: the spying on the Russian consulate through a British periscope hidden in a Byzantine reservoir; an assignation with a ravishing brunette that is cut short by a limpet mine explosion; his assassination of Krilencu; the evening at the gypsy camp; and his expert movements on the Orient Express, where he helps Bond prepare for his escape across the border.

As to his background, the only thing we ever learn is that Kerim Bey started out in the circus as a strongman who broke chains and bent bars for a living. His cover in Istanbul is that of a Persian rug merchant.

Interestingly, a key scene involving Kerim Bey was cut out of *From Russia with Love*, according to director Terence Young. It would have

Delightful Mexican character actor Pedro Armendariz portrayed Ali Kerim Bey, an agent of British intelligence based in Istanbul, showing off his periscope under the Russian consulate to James Bond (Sean Connery) in *From Russia with Love*. *Courtesy of the David Reinhardt Collection*

occurred just before Bond meets Tanya on the Bosphorus ferryboat. Young could not save the sequence in postproduction, for a very good reason. Said Young, "We had a scene where everywhere Bond went, he was followed by this Bulgar, the man with the big mustache, the black beret, and the Citroën. In the scene, Bond has to go onto the ferry to meet the girl, and he has to shake off the opposition.

"He's in a taxi being followed by the Bulgar, when Bond suddenly leans across in front of the taxi driver and pumps the brakes. The taxi comes screeching to a halt, the Bulgar piles in behind, and he, in turn, is struck by a third car. Out of car number one steps James Bond; out of car number two steps the Bulgar, who's protesting that this is not protocol and this is not the way we behave, that such an act is unfair and dishonest. And out of the third car steps Kerim Bey.

"We ended up shooting ten takes. Pedro wanted an ash on the end of his cigar, and every time the Bulgarian expressed his shock, an ash would fall away from his cigar. On take ten, Pedro came out with his cigar with a long ash, and this Bulgarian turned on him, saying, 'You're the one responsible for this. This is an outrage. What am I going to do? Tell me, what am I going to do?' And Pedro took his cigar and tapped it, saying, 'My friend, this is life.' At that very moment, the big British embassy Rolls-Royce drove up, and Bond got in and drove away to his rendezvous with

Tanya. With his car locked between bumpers, the Bugarian could not follow 007 to the ferryboat. It was a perfect deception and certainly Armendariz's best scene."*

At some point, the entire ferryboat sequence was apparently moved later in the film than originally scripted, which brought about the Kerim Bey scene's fatal flaw. "We were running the picture later," said Young. "We had our final cut and our married print. United Artists had seen it and loved it. Everybody was happy. And my son, who was then age twelve, came and saw the picture at a private showing a week before the film came out. When it came time for the sequence with Pedro, my son turned to me and said, 'Daddy, that man with the beret was already killed. Robert Shaw killed him in St. Sophia Mosque behind the pillar.' And, of course, we all said, 'Yes, he did, didn't he?' So that was the end of that sequence."

Young recalled that when he later found out that actor Pedro Armendariz was dying of cancer, he went to his hotel and tried to say something dignified and meaningful, but could only stare at the walls. Once more, Armendariz had a cigar in his mouth. He leaned across, looked Young right in the eye, tapped an ash on the carpet, and said, "That, my friend, is life."

Kershner, Irvin (April 29, 1923–November 27, 2010): Acclaimed American film director who helmed *Never Say Never Again*. He's best known for directing the second *Star Wars* film, *The Empire Strikes Back* (1980). A native of Philadelphia, Kershner made his big-screen directorial debut on *Stakeout on Dope Street* (1958). His additional feature film credits include *The Luck of Ginger Coffey* (1964); *A Fine Madness* (1966), with Sean Connery; *Eyes of Laura Mars* (1978); and *RoboCop 2* (1990).

Keys, Alicia (January 25, 1981–   ; birth name: Alicia Augello Cook): American musician, singer, and songwriter who, alongside Jack White, warbled "Another Way to Die," the opening-titles song to *Quantum of Solace*. A New York City native, Keys first performed on a motion picture soundtrack with the song "Rear View Mirror," featured in *Dr. Dolittle 2* (2001). Her first major hit was the single "Fallin'" from her album *Songs in A Minor*, whch sold over twelve million copies

worldwide in 2001, and won her five Grammy Awards.

Khan, Prince Kamal: Exiled Afghan prince portrayed with a strong touch of evil by Louis Jourdan in *Octopussy*. In league with fanatical Russian general Orlov (Steven Berkoff), Kamal Khan is getting a treasure trove of Kremlin jewelry in return for his services in supplying the traveling circus of Octopussy (Maud Adams) as cover for Orlov's plan to detonate a nuclear device on a US Air Force base in West Germany. Octopussy herself is actually being kept in the dark about the bomb—she thinks she's involved in a simple jewelry smuggling operation.

Bond meets the suspicious Kamal Khan at Sotheby's, where he enters the auction for a jeweled Fabergé egg stolen by the conspirators and bids up the price considerably—Bond's colleague 009 nabbed the forged replacement egg from Octopussy's circus, so Orlov needs the real one back before the Kremlin realizes it's missing. Following Khan to Udaipur, India, 007 enters a backgammon game against the cheating prince and wins 200,000 rupees. In order to retrieve the real Fabergé egg that Bond stole from the auction—by carefully switching the forged version for the real thing—Khan employs the seductive Magda (Kristina Wayborn), who beds Bond and steals back the egg, which now contains a listening bug planted there by 007. Waving good-bye to the beautiful Swedish vamp, Bond is knocked unconscious by Khan's bodyguard Gobinda (Kabir Bedi). He wakes up in Kamal Khan's Monsoon Palace, where he is an imprisoned guest. When Orlov arrives for a final briefing, Bond attempts to listen in to their conversation, but Magda's blow-dryer jams the frequency. All he can hear is a place name: "Karl-Marx-Stadt."

Escaping from the palace, Bond becomes the prey in a festive tiger hunt, with Kamal Khan and Gobinda pursuing him atop elephants. Bond survives and eventually makes his way to Karl-Marx-Stadt, East Germany, where he sees Kamal Khan and General Orlov planting a nuclear device in the base of a cannon used in Octopussy's circus. He then follows the circus to Feldstadt Air Base and disarms the bomb with only seconds to spare.

After Octopussy's army of acrobatic women storm the Monsoon Palace and defeat Kamal Khan's garrison, he kidnaps Octopussy and

---

* Terence Young, interview by the author, London, June 25, 1977.

attempts his own form of escape aboard a twin-engine light plane. Bond follows on horseback (à la Indiana Jones) and eventually gets inside the cabin after an amazing fight with Gobinda atop the roof of the aircraft in flight. As Kamal Khan tries to land the disabled plane, Bond and Octopussy dive out of the cabin. The plane crashes into a hillside, killing Kamal Khan.

Khao Phing Kan: An unusually picturesque island off the coast of Thailand where filmmakers shot the home and solar energy complex of Scaramanga (Christopher Lee) in *The Man with the Golden Gun*. In the story, the island is located off the coast of China and is protected from interlopers by Red Chinese troops who man a neighboring island surveillance outpost. Scaramanga's refuge was built by Hai Fat (Richard Loo) and his Bangkok-based construction company. In addition to its solar station with its liquid helium-filled basins, the home also features an incredible "fun house" training maze, through which Scaramanga hunts his fully armed opponents.

Kidd, Mr.: Bookish, nearly bald, gay assassin, teamed with Mr. Wint (Bruce Glover) in *Diamonds Are Forever* and portrayed by musician Putter Smith. Working for Ernst Stavro Blofeld (Charles Gray), Kidd and Wint are eliminating the members of an international diamond smuggling operation one by one—a well-engineered plot that eventually brings them up against James Bond (Sean Connery), who is posing as a smuggler.

In the film's concluding scene aboard a luxury liner, Kidd, impersonating a waiter and about to attack Bond with flaming shish kebabs, is doused with wine and set afire. He then jumps overboard and drowns. In this last sequence, stuntman George Leech doubled Putter Smith. The sequence was done with the help of a very skillful special effects makeup department, which designed a mask made of fireproof rubber that was perfectly molded to the stuntman's features and that, on the outside, was the image of the bespectacled Smith. The mask also featured two copper gauze eyepieces through which Leech could see, and a copper gauze plate over the mouth so that he could breathe. Protecting the rest of his body was an asbestos automobile racing suit.

"When I first tried out the mask," said Leech, "I put on an asbestos apron and put the fiery gel in front of the mask. I brought the flame closer and closer until it caught on and enveloped my entire face. The mask was loose so that the moment I noticed something wrong I could throw it away. But it worked fine in the test. If something had gone wrong in the actual take, I couldn't have gotten out of the suit. I'd have to wait for someone to put the flame out with a handy fire extinguisher.

"When it came time to do the actual stunt, the effects man put so much of this liquid gel on me that I was really ablaze. He also threw in some aircraft dope, which is like gasoline. And I could smell that stuff, so I asked him what it was, and he said, 'It's only a little aircraft dope to give the flame some color.' And I told him, 'Get out of here with that stuff.'

"So here I was on fire, and I had to stagger around a little bit in front of the camera and then go over the edge of the boat set and supposedly jump onto a pad where a fireman stood by with an extinguisher. Before the scene, I told the fireman that as soon as I hit the pad, he was to put me out. So I hit the pad and I'm still lying there burning and nothing is happening. And I found this idiot waiting for the director to say 'cut.' Instead of having the extinguisher in his hand, he's got it a distance away. So he comes over and looks up at the director and looks down at me and then walks nonchalantly over and picks up the extinguisher and puts me out. The goon!

"By then, my hands were burning, because some of the gel had leaked down through my gloves. It took ages for them to heal. Although the gloves were made out of the same fireproof materials as the mask, they had cracked under the extreme heat, and the liquid had simply trickled down onto my hands. The gloves turned out to be the Achilles' heel of the entire outfit.

"Before the scene had started, the assistant director had told me, 'First we'll set fire to you, and then we'll run the camera.' And I had replied, 'No, first you'll run the camera, and when you've got the speed up, then you'll set fire to me.' Otherwise, they would have set the fire and I would have been waiting around while they got the right speed up. A guy would have appeared from nowhere and said, 'Does anyone want a chicken sandwich?' and all the while I'd be burning away. It's not a joke. I've seen it happen many times.

"Years ago, when I first came into the business, I relied on the assistants and the director. But they sometimes don't have all the answers, especially when it comes to stunt work. You end up having to watch out for yourself, because when your life's at stake, you can't rely on someone else to check the proper safety measures."*

Kiel, Richard (September 13, 1939–September 10, 2014): Tall American character actor, usually in villainous roles, whose career was given a huge boost in 1976 when producer Albert R. Broccoli signed him to play Jaws in *The Spy Who Loved Me*. He reprised the wild character in *Moonraker*. Outfitted with cobalt steel incisors, Jaws was the perfect fantasy villain for a new generation of James Bond fans, even though some purists felt the character was straight out of a comic book. Appearing in two of the most successful films in the series guaranteed that Jaws became one of the most memorable pop culture villains of the late 1970s.

A native of Detroit, Kiel made his feature debut as a US marine in director Jack Webb's *The D.I.* (1957). He also made quite an impression as a visiting Kanamit alien in the memorable *Twilight Zone* episode "To Serve Man" (1962). His feature work included a number of science fiction and fantasy credits, including *Eegah* (1962), in the caveman title role; *The Nutty Professor* (1963); *Two on a Guillotine* (1965); *The Human Duplicators* (1965); *The Giant of Thunder Mountain* (1991); *Inspector Gadget* (1999); and *Tangled* (2010). He was also well cast in the non-genre features *The Longest Yard* (1974); *Silver Streak* (1976); *Force 10 from Navarone* (1978), alongside Bond veterans Robert Shaw and Barbara Bach, for veteran Bond director Guy Hamilton; *Cannonball Run II* (1984); *Pale Rider* (1985); and *Happy Gilmore* (1996). In addition to his feature work, Kiel enjoyed recurring appearances on *The Wild Wild West* (3 episodes, 1965-1966), as Voltaire (he appeared one

It's amazing what a little dental work will do for a career. Actor Richard Kiel shows off Jaws' steel teeth, featured strongly in *The Spy Who Loved Me*. *Courtesy of the David Reinhardt Collection*

last time in 1968, in a different role); and *Barbary Coast* (14 episodes, 1975–1976), as Moose Moran.

Kincade: Elderly game warden and caretaker of the title property in *Skyfall*, portrayed by Albert Finney. Skyfall is the Bond family estate, located deep in the Scottish Highlands. It is here where Bond (Daniel Craig) takes M (Dame Judi Dench) to lure cyberterrorist Raoul Silva (Javier Bardem) into a final confrontation. However, due to poor planning, Bond's only ally proves to be Kincade, armed with a mere shotgun and woefully inadequate defenses. However, Bond and Kincade go way back, and with M's help, they devise an elaborate number of booby traps to waylay Silva's small army of thugs. According to *Skyfall* director Sam Mendes, there was initially some discussion about casting Sean Connery in the role of the Scottish game warden, but the idea was nixed because "I thought it would distract" to have the legendary Bond actor show up in a different role.*

King, Elektra: Stunningly beautiful but treacherous daughter of oil tycoon Sir Robert King (David Calder), portrayed by French actress Sophie Marceau in *The World Is Not Enough*. King was abducted by former KGB agent Renard (Robert Carlyle) before our story takes place, but on the advice of M (Dame Judi Dench), her father didn't pay the $5 million ransom and Elektra was forced to shoot her way out of captivity. At least that's what she's told the world's press. In reality, she's a victim of Stockholm syndrome, by which a kidnapping victim falls in love with her captor. Now partnered with Renard and intent on revenge like her mythological Greek namesake, Elektra helps the terrorist murder her father with a "compacted fertilizer bomb" deployed by Julietta the Cigar Girl (Maria Grazia Cucinotta) and then targets M for abduction and eventual assassination. Now in charge of her father's company, she also enlists Renard to take out three competing Russian oil pipelines—a plot that involves detonating a nuclear device in the Bosphorus.

Unaware that she's turned, M (who has been friends with the King family for many years)

---

* George Leech, interview by the author, London, June 23, 1977.

* Mike Ryan, "Sam Mendes, 'Skyfall' Director, on Bringing Humor Back to James Bond & Flirting with the Idea of Casting Sean Connery," *Huffington Post*, November 5, 2012, https://www.huffpost.com/entry/sam-mendes-skyfall_n_2074239.

Elektra King (Sophie Marceau) has James Bond (Pierce Brosnan) just where she wants him in a suspenseful moment from *The World Is Not Enough*. *Courtesy of the Luc Leclech Collection*

sends 007 (Pierce Brosnan) to Azerbaijan to protect Elektra from further trouble. When 007 saves her from marauding Parahawk hang gliders, Elektra thanks him with a hop in the sack. However, all of this is a plot to lure M to her doom. When Bond is also captured, Elektra places him in a medieval torture device that can snap his neck with the turn of a wheel. In one of the best torture sequences in the series since the encounter between Bond (Sean Connery) and the laser beam in *Goldfinger*, it looks like 007 has finally met his match. But he's rescued by casino owner Zukovsky (Robbie Coltrane), who, before Elektra kills him, shatters Bond's leg shackle with a single shot from the gun hidden in his cane.

Bond escapes, chasing Elektra through her Maiden's Tower hideaway in the Bosphorus and corners her in an upstairs bedroom. Ignoring her pompous comment that he could never kill a woman he made love to, Bond nails her with

a single shot from his Walther. Still, the look on 007's face says that he didn't enjoy it. Score a major victory for actor Pierce Brosnan, who really grew into the Bond role in this film.

Kinsale Street: Street in Kingston, Jamaica, that was the site of the cottage where Commander John Strangways (Tim Moxon) lived in *Dr. No*.

Kisch: One of Auric Goldfinger's henchmen, portrayed by Michael Mellinger in *Goldfinger*. It's Kisch who handcuffs James Bond (Sean Connery) to the ticking atomic device placed inside Fort Knox. When Goldfinger's troops are attacked by the surprisingly healthy US Army garrison, Kisch is locked inside the vault with Bond and Oddjob (Harold Sakata). When he threatens to disarm the bomb, Kisch is killed by the unreasonably loyal Oddjob, who tosses him off the top floor of the vault.

Director Guy Hamilton explains to Harold Sakata how the body of Kisch (Michael Mellinger) will be tossed over the railing during Fort Knox action in *Goldfinger Courtesy of the Anders Frejdh Collection*

Observing Blofeld's hidden base, Kissy (Mie Hama) and James Bond (Sean Connery) prepare for action in *You Only Live Twice. Courtesy of the David Reinhardt Collection*

Kiss Kiss Club: An outdoor nightclub in Nassau, Bahamas, that becomes a temporary shelter for a wounded James Bond (Sean Connery) in *Thunderball*. Chased by Fiona Volpe (Luciana Paluzzi) and her SPECTRE thugs, 007 takes a moment's rest in the club's bathroom, applies a tourniquet to his wounded ankle, and then mingles among the dancers. However, he's cornered again and soon finds himself in Fiona's arms on the dance floor, as a SPECTRE assassin prepares his silencer. As the bongo beat of the onstage combo (featuring real-life bongo player King Errisson) reaches its zenith, Bond spots the assassin and whirls Fiona around just in time for her to take the bullet. Dragging her body over to a table, he tells the seated patrons that his partner needs a break because "she's just dead."

Kissy: Lovely Japanese intelligence agent turned pearl diver portrayed by Mie Hama in *You Only Live Twice*. To make sure that James Bond (Sean Connery) has credible cover as an Ama Island boatman, she receives orders from Japanese

Secret Service chief Tiger Tanaka (Tetsuro Tamba) to become 007's bride in a mock ceremony. Backed by one of John Barry's most romantic musical compositions, the newlyweds then row out to the pearl beds and blend in with the other Ama Island couples. Later, they follow the trail of two dead islanders to the Rosaki Cave on the mainland, where they find lethal phosgene gas and a route to an extinct volcano—where Blofeld (Donald Pleasence) has built a secret rocket base.

NOTE: Although the character was created by Ian Fleming, who dubbed her "Kissy Suzuki" in his original novel, and her name is listed in the *You Only Live Twice* credits simply as "Kissy," she is actually never identified in the film itself.

Kitzmiller, John (December 4, 1913–February 23, 1965): American character actor who portrayed Quarrel, the Cayman Islander who helps James Bond (Sean Connery) in the first James Bond movie, *Dr. No*. Director Terence Young first saw Kitzmiller in director Luigi Zampa's *To Live in Peace* (1947), the actor's film debut. Born in Battle Creek, Michigan, Kitzmiller had settled in Italy after completing his US military service during World War II, and he spent his early career performing exclusively in Italian films. His first English-language film was Vincent Sherman's drama *The Naked Earth* (1958), which also featured future Bond player Laurence Naismith (*Diamonds Are Forever*).

Klebb, Colonel Rosa (a.k.a. Number 3): SPECTRE spymaster recruited from Soviet intelligence in *From Russia with Love*, portrayed by Lotte Lenya. Third in the SPECTRE hierarchy, she's ordered by Blofeld to execute the plan by Kronsteen (Vladek Sheybal) to humiliate James Bond (Sean Connery) and retrieve the Russian Lektor decoding machine used as bait for 007. Klebb recruits assassin Donald Grant (Robert Shaw), whose fitness she tests with a knuckle duster to the abdomen. She also recruits beautiful Russian cipher clerk Tatiana Romanova (Daniela Bianchi), who will seduce Bond in Istanbul.

After the plan fails, Klebb is nearly executed by Blofeld's assistant Morzeny (Walter Gotell), who kills Kronsteen instead. Given one more chance to eliminate Bond, Klebb impersonates a Venetian hotel maid and is about to shoot Bond when Tanya distracts her. Bond fights off Klebb, who attacks with the same poison-tipped shoe daggers that killed Kronsteen. Bond is eventually saved by Tanya, who shoots Klebb. "Horrible woman," she sighs. Bond replies, "Yes, she's had her kicks."

Lotte Lenya (right) costarred in *From Russia with Love* as SPECTRE agent Rosa Klebb, seen here with cipher clerk Tatiana Romanova (Daniela Bianchi), who has been recruited for a "real labor of love." *Courtesy of the David Reinhardt Collection*

Klein, Jordan (December 1, 1925–): Academy Award–winning underwater cameraman, inventor, and engineer who worked on *Thunderball*, *You Only Live Twice*, *Live and Let Die*, and *Never Say Never Again*. Klein's film career began in 1952, when he was hired by Barry & Enright Productions (this author's alma mater) to produce a pilot for an underwater series titled *20 Seconds to Zero*. The pilot subsequently bombed, but Klein learned some valuable lessons about the filmmaking process. Beginning in 1954, when he shot underwater stills on *The Creature from the Black Lagoon*, Klein became involved in virtually every major film and television show that featured underwater sequences.

His early association with Ivan Tors Studios on *Sea Hunt* and *Flipper* made him a natural choice to build all the underwater props for *Thunderball* in 1965. His original assignment called for the manufacture of the underwater A-bomb sled and six swift one-man scooters. The bomb carrier was designed by Ken Adam, who sent Klein a balsa wood model. From that basic model, Klein designed the fully operational carrier, which was equipped with a 12 horsepower motor. It was completed in five weeks.

In addition to contributing his engineering skill, Klein was recruited to share filming chores with cameraman Lamar Boren. He filmed mostly insert shots of crabs on the ocean floor, dead divers, spear hits, etc. He even ended up appearing on camera running the bomb carrier. That's him in the cockpit, wearing a gold Rolex. Klein explained that the sequence in which the Vulcan bomber crash-lands in the Bahamas was shot in miniature off Rose Island. The miniature bomber was launched down a wire from a 150-foot tower. The full-size bomber shell was lowered into the water off Clifton Pier.

Klein's surprise on the film was the underwater backpack he designed for Bond (Sean Connery). It was something he cobbled together over a weekend for the underwater battle sequence. The producers told him that if it wasn't ready for shooting at 8:30 AM Monday, it couldn't be used. Klein guaranteed its delivery, and it became a highlight of the shoot. The pack was equipped with two spearguns, which were actually stainless steel tubes with 12-gauge shotgun heads. The smokescreen was a yellow dye. The headlight never really worked, but since the battle was fought in daylight, it wasn't necessary. As for the pack's rocket motor, it was an effect. Connery's double, Frank Cousins, was actually pulled along by a piano wire attached to a high-speed motorboat.

On *You Only Live Twice*, Klein was once more teamed with Lamar Boren for the brief sequence in which British naval divers return the "corpse" of James Bond to a nuclear submarine. Klein built a small section of the submarine, which was placed on the ocean floor off Nassau, Bahamas.

Although some of his shark footage appears in *Live and Let Die*, his next major 007 assignment was for *Never Say Never Again*, for which he once again built a bomb carrier—this one designed to carry the SPECTRE-hijacked cruise missiles. In addition to the carrier, Klein built a huge section of the *Flying Saucer* yacht's hull, which was lowered into the waters of Silver Springs, Florida. Unlike the *Disco Volante* in *Thunderball*, this time the underwater hatch was located on the side of the ship rather than underneath it. It is through this side exit that the cruise missile carrier travels.

On both *Thunderball* and *Never Say Never Again*, Klein also worked with huge, sixteen-foot tiger sharks. On the latter film, he was assigned the task of installing electronic sensors on the sharks' dorsal fins. The sensors are attached to a homing device placed on Bond's scuba gear by the evil Fatima Blush (Barbara Carrera).

Kleinman, Daniel: Creative designer of movie title sequences who succeeded the late Maurice Binder to design the titles of *GoldenEye* and has continued in that capacity on *Tomorrow Never Dies*, *The World Is Not Enough*, *Die Another Day*, *Casino Royale*, *Skyfall*, *Spectre*, and *No Time to Die*. Kleinman is also well known as a top commercial and music video director.

Knight, Gladys (May 28, 1944–   ): Superstar singer, a multiple Grammy winner, who sang the title song in *Licence to Kill*. A native of Atlanta, Knight made her motion picture soundtrack debut performing "Double or Nothing" for *Rocky IV* (1985). Two of her singles made it to the top spot on the Billboard Hot 100, "Midnight Train to Georgia" by Gladys Knight and the Pips, and "That's What Friends Are For" with Dionne Warwick, Elton John, and Stevie Wonder.

Superstar pop singer Gladys Knight sang the title tune to *Licence to Kill*. *Courtesy of the David Reinhardt Collection*

Kohen, Muhammat: Turkish tour guide who portrayed himself during location sequences shot inside Istanbul's St. Sophia Mosque for *From Russia with Love*. It was his only film appearance.

Koskov, General Georgi: Renegade Russian general, portrayed by handsome Dutch leading man Jeroen Krabbé, who joins forces with arms dealer Brad Whitaker (Joe Don Baker) to perpetrate a huge drug deal in *The Living Daylights*. Actually, Koskov's story begins a million miles away from anything resembling a drug deal: he's introduced in Bratislava, Czechoslovakia, as a defecting Russian general. Bond (Timothy Dalton) is assigned to help him cross the border into Austria, and during the operation, he foils an assassination attempt on a beautiful blonde cellist named Kara Milovy (Maryam d'Abo). Bond is unaware that Koskov is Milovy's patron/lover and that he planned the assassination attempt to make his defection appear genuine. Koskov is actually partnered with Whitaker in the aforementioned drug deal.

Using a $50 million advance provided by the Russians for Whitaker's latest high-tech weapons, Koskov and Whitaker plan to convert the money into diamonds and trade them to the drug-dealing Snow Leopard Brotherhood of Afghanistan for a cache of raw opium. They will then sell the drugs on the open market, making enough of a profit to have enough money left over to supply the Russians with their arms. All they need is time, but KGB chief General Leonid Pushkin (John Rhys-Davies), already on the trail of Koskov, won't give it to them.

Arriving in England, Koskov is quartered at the heavily guarded Bladen safe house. There he quickly tells M (Robert Brown), Defence Minister Freddie Gray (Geoffrey Keen), and Bond that Pushkin is behind a fiendish plot called "Smiert Spionam," which is designed to kill off British and American spies. Soon after spilling this information, which compels M to order 007 to liquidate Pushkin, Koskov is abducted from the safe house by what appears to be a KGB agent. In actuality the agent, Necros (Andreas Wisniewski), is working for Koskov, and the abduction is another ruse designed to confuse both the British and the KGB.

Brought safely to Whitaker's house in Tangier, Koskov prepares to leave for Afghanistan and his drug deal. First, he informs Whitaker that Pushkin will be killed before Whitaker has to return the $50 million arms advance, but Whitaker's not convinced that the British will assassinate Pushkin. Koskov determines that another British agent must die before the British act. Necros then goes to Vienna, where he kills Saunders (Thomas Wheatley), the local British Secret Service section chief. Determined to stop "Smiert Spionam," Bond arrives in Tangier to kill Pushkin—but instead joins forces with the KGB general to expose the Koskov/Whitaker plot. Pushkin "dies" in a sham assassination at the hands of Bond.

But 007 forgets about Kara, who is tricked by Koskov into thinking that Bond is a KGB agent. Drugged by Kara, Bond is shipped to Afghanistan on Koskov's transport plane. Kara soon learns that she followed the wrong man's advice. Still,

she and Bond manage to escape from a Russian air base, and with the help of local mujahideen rebels, they're able to disrupt Koskov's drug deal, destroying a cargo plane full of raw opium. Koskov unbelievably survives a truly incredible head-on crash with a twin-engine plane, but is later captured in Tangier by Pushkin. His probable destination: Siberia.

Kotto, Yaphet (November 15, 1939–   ): American character actor who portrayed the villainous alter egos Dr. Kananga and Mr. Big in *Live and Let Die*. A native of New York City, Kotto made his credited big-screen debut as Jocko in director Michael Roemer's romantic drama *Nothing but a Man* (1964), which also featured his *Live and Let Die* costar Julius Harris. Kotto's additional feature film credits include *The Thomas Crown Affair* (1968); *The Liberation of L.B. Jones* (1970); *Bone* (1972); *Friday Foster* (1975); *Alien* (1979); *Brubaker* (1980), as convict Richard "Dickie" Coombes; *The Running Man* (1987); *Midnight Run* (1988), as no-nonsense FBI agent Alonzo Mosely; and *Witless Protection* (2008). He also starred as Lieutenant Al "Gee" Giardello in the critically acclaimed cop drama *Homicide: Life on the Street* (118 episodes, 1993–1999).

Actor Yaphet Kotto put quite a bit of gusto into the role of sinister island diplomat Kananga in *Live and Let Die. Courtesy of the Anders Frejdh Collection*

Krabbé, Jeroen (December 5, 1944–   ): Handsome Dutch leading man (his name is pronounced "yeh-ROON krah-BAY") who portrayed renegade Russian general Georgi Koskov in *The Living Daylights*. Krabbé, a marvelous actor, is actually too sympathetic as Koskov. He seems to spend most of the movie hugging his various associates, including Bond (Timothy Dalton), several times.

Born in Amsterdam, Krabbé made his motion picture debut in his native country in director Jef van der Heyden's comedy *Bicycling to the Moon* (1963). However, it was his charismatic performance as Dutch resistance fighter Guus LeJeune in Paul Verhoeven's World War II saga *Soldier of Orange* (1977) that brought him international attention. Krabbé's additional feature credits include *Spetters* (1980); *Crossing Delancey* (1988); *The Punisher* (1989); *Robin Hood* (1991); *The Prince of Tides* (1991); *The Fugitive* (1993), as duplicitous Dr. Charles Nichols opposite Harrison Ford; *Ocean's Twelve* (2004); and *Transporter 3* (2008).

Krest, Milton: Boozy drug runner, portrayed by Anthony Zerbe, who's masquerading as the head of a marine genetic engineering firm in *Licence to Kill*. The weak link in the enormous South American cocaine empire of Franz Sanchez (Robert Davi), Krest becomes the first target when James Bond (Timothy Dalton) launches his deadly scheme to avenge his mutilated CIA friend Felix Leiter (David Hedison), who was thrown into Krest's shark pen by Sanchez. Bond makes repeated assaults on Krest's Key West–based smuggling operation, eventually steals aboard his huge *Wavekrest* research vessel, and sabotages a drug run, destroying the cocaine and stealing $5 million of Sanchez's money. That princely sum becomes the key to Bond's plot to discredit and destroy Krest in Sanchez's eyes.

Kriegler, Erich: Powerfully built East German biathlon champion and henchman of Soviet agent Aris Kristatos (Julian Glover), portrayed by John Wyman in *For Your Eyes Only*. Bond (Roger Moore) first sees him when ice skater Bibi Dahl (Lynn-Holly Johnson) points him out during a biathlon competition in the snows of Cortina d'Ampezzo in the Italian Alps. Kriegler tries to kill Bond during a ski chase, but 007 escapes. Later, during the battle at St. Cyril's atop the Meteora cliffs in Greece, Bond pushes Kriegler through a window to his death.

Krilencu: Bulgarian assassin portrayed by Fred Haggerty in *From Russia with Love*. Working for the Soviets, Krilencu has a personal vendetta against Turkish spymaster Kerim Bey (Pedro Armendariz). He's given Station T–Turkey trouble before, but he's stayed out of Istanbul for over a year. It is Krilencu who places a limpet mine on the outside wall of Kerim Bey's office. He also leads the Bulgarian assault on the gypsy camp in an effort to assassinate his enemy. In return, Krilencu is himself gunned down by a wounded Kerim Bey, who uses 007's AR-7 sniper rifle to kill the Bulgar when he attempts to sneak out of his Istanbul apartment through a trapdoor—one that exits through the mouth of Anita Ekberg on a billboard for the Bob Hope comedy *Call Me Bwana* (produced by Albert R. Broccoli and Harry Saltzman).

Kristatos, Aris: Sinister millionaire tycoon who is working for the Russians in *For Your Eyes Only*. At first he introduces himself to Bond (Roger Moore) in Cortina, Italy, as an enthusiastic Anglophile who was a resistance fighter during World War II and won the King's Medal for his gallantry. He is also acting as patron to a young Olympic ice-skating hopeful (Lynn-Holly Johnson). He even tells Bond to watch out for Milos Columbo (Topol), a man he claims is a drug smuggler, sex trafficker, and contract murderer.

In reality, it's Kristatos who's a heroin smuggler and a top Russian agent charged with salvaging the ATAC device from the hulk of the sunken *St. Georges* surveillance vessel. On several occasions, his henchmen Locque (Michael Gothard) and Kriegler (John Wyman) try to kill Bond. Kristatos is also involved in a blood feud with Columbo, whom he betrayed during World War II while working as a double agent for the Nazis.

Kristatos eventually retrieves the ATAC from Bond, tries to kill him and Melina Havelock (Carole Bouquet) by keelhauling the pair, and later retreats to his aerie atop the Meteora cliff in Greece. In the film's finale, Bond assaults Meteora and Columbo kills Kristatos.

Kronsteen (a.k.a. Number 5): SPECTRE's director of planning, portrayed by Vladek Sheybal in *From Russia with Love*. Working under Blofeld (an uncredited Anthony Dawson), this sleepy-eyed nemesis plans SPECTRE's revenge against James Bond (Sean Connery) for killing their operative Dr. No. Kronsteen is introduced as a Czechoslovakian chess master who wins the Venice International Grandmasters Championship over MacAdams of Canada. Kronsteen plays the white pieces.

Kronsteen considers his plan to steal the Russian Lektor decoding machine and humiliate Bond in the process a foolproof one. Why? Because he's anticipated every possible countermove. The fact that he treats life like a chess game probably is the cause of his demise. Chess pieces do not carry concealed knives in their shoes, but Morzeny (Walter Gotell) does. Kronsteen is stabbed and poisoned to death after his plan fails miserably on the Orient Express.

Kurylenko, Olga (November 14, 1979–   ): Ukranian-born actress who portrayed Bolivian mystery woman Camille Montes in *Quantum of Solace*. Born in Berdyansk, Kurylenko made her motion picture debut as Iris in the French film *The Ring Finger* (2005), directed by Diane Bertrand. Her first English-language film was Xavier Gens's video game adaptation *Hitman* (2007). She later costarred opposite former 007 Pierce Brosnan in Roger Donaldson's crime thriller *The November Man* (2014), and alongside Rowan Atkinson in the spy comedy *Johnny English Strikes Again* (2018).

Olga Kurylenko portrayed revenge-minded Camille Montes in *Quantum of Solace*. *Courtesy of the Anders Frejdh Collection*

Kwang: Dedicated Hong Kong narcotics officer portrayed by Cary-Hiroyuki Tagawa in *Licence to Kill*. Working undercover as one of the Far

Eastern drug distributors of South American drug lord Franz Sanchez (Robert Davi), Kwang, in ninja garb, interrupts Bond (Timothy Dalton) as he attempts to assassinate Sanchez. Brought to a rural safe house outside Isthmus City, Bond is interrogated by Kwang and his attractive associate Loti (Diana Lee-Hsu). He learns that they've been planning an undercover operation for years, and they're not about to let a rogue agent blow it.

Tied to a table, Bond is incapable of lending a hand when the safe house is attacked and Loti is killed by Sanchez's men. To avoid capture, a badly wounded Kwang takes cyanide. The fact that Bond is tied to the table is a boon when Sanchez arrives with his security chief, Heller (Don Stroud). It helps bolster Bond's cover as a sympathetic unemployed British agent seeking security work.

Kwouk, Burt (July 18, 1930–May 24, 2016): British actor of Chinese heritage (his last name rhymes with "cluck") who portrayed Mr. Ling, the Red Chinese specialist in nuclear fission in *Goldfinger*. Kwouk also played one of the space scientists employed by Ernst Stavro Blofeld (Donald Pleasence) in *You Only Live Twice*, and one of the Chinese army officers who bids for compromising photographs during a madcap auction in the 1967 *Casino Royale* spoof. Kwouk is probably best known as Cato, fanatical martial arts instructor and sparring partner to Inspector Clouseau (Peter Sellers) in the *Pink Panther* film series. A native of Warrington, Cheshire, England, Kwouk made his credited big-screen debut as Li in director Mark Robson's *The Inn of the Sixth Happiness* (1958), working with future Bond players Curt Jurgens and Tsai Chin.

Actor Burt Kwouk. *Steve Rubin Collection*

La Rochefoucauld: French writer/philosopher quoted by Ernst Stavro Blofeld (Charles Gray) in *Diamonds Are Forever*. The quote, uttered to Bond (Sean Connery) on the oil rig is "As La Rochefoucauld once observed, 'Humility is the worst form of conceit.'" It was one of witty cowriter Tom Mankiewicz's favorite lines of dialogue in the film.

Lady in Bahamas: How actress Valerie Leon is identified in the credits of *Never Say Never Again*. Although nameless, she's a sexy sport-fishing enthusiast who "hooks" Bond (Sean Connery) in the Caribbean after 007 escapes from a group of radio-controlled man-eating sharks. Later in her hotel bed, she and Bond discover that SPECTRE agent Fatima Blush (Barbara Carrera) has blown up Bond's hotel suite—proving, of course, that for secret agents "Your place or mine?" is a pretty critical question.

Lady Rose, the: The name given to the Stradivarius cello played by scholarship cellist Kara Milovy (Maryam d'Abo) in *The Living Daylights*. Built by hand in 1724, it was sold at a New York auction for $150,000 to arms dealer Brad Whitaker (Joe Don Baker), who gave it to renegade Soviet general Georgi Koskov (Jeroen Krabbé) as a present for his protégée/lover Kara. The cello becomes a clue to Koskov's whereabouts. When Kara tells Bond (Timothy Dalton) that the cello is called the Lady Rose, Bond's local contact Saunders (Thomas Wheatley) identifies Whitaker as its most recent owner of record. Since Whitaker is based in Tangier, Bond knows where to find Koskov. During their madcap escape from Czech border troops, Bond and Kara actually use the expensive cello as an ersatz ski pole, guiding their descent down a treacherous mountainside.

Lake Mead: Nevada resort that would have been the site of a wild boat chase in an early draft of Richard Maibaum's screenplay for *Diamonds Are Forever*. Maibaum had discovered that each major hotel in Las Vegas maintained its own yacht on the lake for recreation and publicity purposes—Caesars Palace owned a Roman galley, the Riviera Hotel had a pirate frigate, etc. In the script's conclusion, Bond tracks an escaping Blofeld to the lake and watches as the SPECTRE chief takes off in a high-powered boat. Bond jumps on a powerboat himself, but before he gives chase, he speaks through a loudspeaker, summoning the captains of all the colorful yachts to do their duty for Las Vegas and blockade Blofeld's escape route. With that, the flotilla gives chase, eventually cornering Blofeld above the awesome Hoover Dam. Later drafts, however, abandoned the Lake Mead boat chase in favor of the climactic battle aboard the oil-drilling platform in Baja California.

Lake Toplitz: A lake located in the Salzkammergut region of Austria, mentioned in *Goldfinger*. According to the Bank of England, it's the rumored location of a hoard of Nazi gold secreted away at the end of World War II, one bar of which becomes the prize in a golf challenge between 007 (Sean Connery) and Auric Goldfinger (Gert Fröbe).

Lakefront Airport: Located in New Orleans, it's where filmmakers shot the wild chase between Bond (Roger Moore)—in his training Cessna—and killers working for Kananga (Yaphet Kotto) for *Live and Let Die*. Stunt coordinator Joie Chitwood organized the chase, which involved crashing cars into, over, and around airplanes. Chitwood's team even crashed the training Cessna through some partially closed hangar doors, which sheared off its wings.

L'Américain: Fictional hotel in Tangier where SPECTRE operative Mr. White (Jesper Christensen) keeps a secret room in *Spectre*. White informs Bond (Daniel Craig) that "L'Américain" is the key to tracking down his mysterious superior, Franz Oberhauser

(Christoph Waltz). White's daughter, Dr. Madeleine Swann (Léa Seydoux), leads 007 to the hotel, where, thanks to a field mouse's clue, he breaks through a wall and discovers the secret chamber. Clues there lead them to Oberhauser's base of operations in the Moroccan desert. Also among the mementos is Vesper Lynd's interrogation tape.

Lamont, Peter (November 12, 1929–   ): Oscar-winning British production designer whose association with 007 dates back to an assignment as a draftsman on *Goldfinger*. Hired on by art director Peter Murton, who would become production designer on *The Man with the Golden Gun*, Lamont moved steadily up the art department pyramid, through *Thunderball* (chief draftsman), *You Only Live Twice* (set decorator), *On Her Majesty's Secret Service* (set decorator), *Diamonds Are Forever* (set decorator), *Live and Let Die* (co–art director), *The Man with the Golden Gun* (art director), *The Spy Who Loved Me* (art director and Oscar nominee), and *Moonraker* (visual effects art director).

In 1980, Lamont was fortunate to be in the perfect position when fellow designer Ken Adam went to the United States to work on *Pennies from Heaven*. In need of a new production designer for the next Bond film, *For Your Eyes Only*, producer Albert R. Broccoli did what he liked to do best: he promoted from within, giving Lamont his first shot at the top spot. Lamont followed that success with production designer duties on *Octopussy*, *A View to a Kill*, *The Living Daylights*, *Licence to Kill*, *GoldenEye*, *The World Is Not Enough*, *Die Another Day*, and *Casino Royale*. He won his Oscar as production designer on James Cameron's blockbuster *Titanic* (1997).

Production designer Peter Lamont (center) at Pinewood Studios. *Steve Rubin Collection*

Lamora, Lupe: Hot-blooded South American drug lord's moll portrayed by Talisa Soto in *Licence to Kill*. Her tryst with Alvarez (Gerardo Albarrán), a local lothario, brings Franz Sanchez

There are certain disadvantages to being the girlfriend of a drug lord like Franz Sanchez (Robert Davi), especially when you're sleeping around on him, in *Licence to Kill*. *Courtesy of the David Reinhardt Collection*

(Robert Davi) to the Bahamas in the film's teaser sequence. After Dario (Benicio Del Toro) literally cuts out the man's heart, Sanchez whips Lupe, throws her into a jeep, and attempts to make his escape. When DEA agents intercept him and his men, a shoot-out occurs, and Lupe is separated from her boyfriend. Bond (Timothy Dalton) greets her momentarily while chasing after Sanchez.

Since there's no reason to hold Lupe—the authorities are unaware that she's Sanchez's squeeze—she's released, which allows her to join Sanchez's drug distributor, boozy Milton Krest (Anthony Zerbe), who will transport her back to Isthmus City aboard his research vessel, the *Wavekrest*. Bond sees Lupe again when he sneaks aboard the *Wavekrest*, and she begins to see him as another potential savior. Back in Isthmus City, as Bond worms his way into the confidence of Sanchez posing as a high-rolling gun for hire, he also finds himself prey to Lupe's seductive moves. Lupe eventually loses Bond to CIA agent Pam Bouvier (Carey Lowell), but she has her own happy ending as the new paramour of Isthmus City's President Lopez (Pedro Armendariz Jr.).

"Lara's Theme": Signature tune from the 1965 film *Dr. Zhivago*, which plays on the bedroom music box/communicator of KGB major Anya Amasova (Barbara Bach) in *The Spy Who Loved Me*.

Largo, Emilio (a.k.a. Number 2): SPECTRE's ruthless one-eyed spymaster, portrayed by Adolfo Celi in *Thunderball*. Posing as a wealthy businessman in Nassau, Bahamas, who collects predator fish for marine institutions, Largo is actually in charge of SPECTRE's ambitious "NATO project." The ultimate international blackmail sceme, the plan calls for the hijacking of two NATO atomic bombs from an English jet bomber, and a ransom demand for $280 million dollars (100 million pounds). If their demands are not met, SPECTRE will destroy a major city in either England or the United States.

With a large amphibious force under his command, Largo maintains his field headquarters aboard the *Disco Volante*, a huge pleasure yacht that can also convert to a speedy hydrofoil in emergency situations. His Palmyra estate is a few minutes from downtown Nassau.

But Largo is no match for Bond (Sean Connery). In quick order, he loses several games of baccarat; his mistress, Domino (Claudine Auger); his right arm, Vargas (Philip Locke), his fellow SPECTRE assassin Fiona Volpe (Luciana Paluzzi), and most of his command; his atomic bombs; and finally, his prize yacht, which crashes into a reef. Largo himself is speared by Domino in the film's thrilling finale.

SPECTRE's Number 2, Emilio Largo (Adolfo Celi) arrives at the organization's headquarters in Paris to brief his boss and fellow agents about their NATO project in *Thunderball*. *Courtesy of the David Reinhardt Collection*

Largo, Maximilian (a.k.a. Number 1): Billionaire entrepreneur who is also a psychotic SPECTRE master spy, portrayed brilliantly by Klaus Maria Brandauer in *Never Say Never Again*. Like Emilio Largo in *Thunderball* (of which this film is a remake), Maximilian Largo is involved in a nuclear blackmail scheme involving two hijacked NATO nuclear weapons. He also has a beautiful mistress named Domino Petachi (Kim Basinger). Largo reports to Blofeld (Max von Sydow), resides in the Bahamas, and travels aboard his huge oceangoing yacht, *The Flying Saucer*—the English translation of the Italian "Disco Volante." Born in Bucharest, Romania, in 1945, Largo has no criminal record or associations. His assets, worth $2.492 billion, include shipping, timber, and hotels.

When Captain Jack Petachi (Gavan O'Herlihy) helps arm two NATO cruise missiles with nuclear warheads, the weapons are directed to land in the Bahamas, where they're recovered by Largo's underwater troops. SPECTRE's scheme is to demand a ransom, equivalent to 25 percent of the annual oil purchases of each country in NATO (plus Japan), or one of the stolen warheads will be detonated. The bombs themselves have been planted under the White House and in the Tears of Allah archaeological excavation, which marks the beginning of a huge oil field in the Middle East.

Bond (Sean Connery) meets Largo and Domino in the south of France, where 007 survives a hair-raising video game called Domination, plus an assassination attempt by Largo's SPECTRE associate Fatima Blush (Barbara Carrera). Tracking Largo's yacht to his North African estate, Palmyra, Bond is captured and thrown into a medieval dungeon populated by bleached bones and hungry vultures. He escapes, rescues Domino from a group of sleazy Arab traders, boards a US Navy submarine, and heads for one final confrontation with Largo in his Tears of Allah dig. Attempting to escape with the one remaining cruise missile, Largo meets the identical fate of his *Thunderball* alter ego—he's speared by an avenging Domino.

Larson, Lola: American actress who portrayed Bambi, one of the athletic captors of billionaire Willard Whyte (Jimmy Dean) in *Diamonds Are Forever*. Teamed with Thumper (Trina Parks), she gets into an energetic fight with James Bond (Sean Connery). Her stunt double was Donna Garrett.

Las Vegas, Nevada: Predominant location in the seventh James Bond film, *Diamonds Are Forever*. The film actually combines location shooting at some of Las Vegas's classic 1970s-era landmarks, such as Fremont Street and the colorful Circus Circus Hotel and Casino, with the incredible interior creations of production designer Ken Adam.

Recalled director Guy Hamilton, "I'd been on honeymoon in Vegas having a look around, and I thought it was a very good place to shoot a picture. . . . [But for many years] the powers that be did not allow movies into Vegas. The reason being that the husband that was meant to be in Chicago on a business so-and-so would be seen in the casino by his wife and she would sue. . . . [But eventually] the doors opened and it was absolutely wonderful to shoot in Vegas. . . . Ken Adam burst into tears because we're looking around for the most awful suite of all the suites. And we went into every presidential suite and on top of . . . Caesar's Palace, there was a duplex, there were mirrors everywhere, anything that wasn't moving was painted gold. I mean, it

Sean Connery appears comfortable in the desert climate of Las Vegas in *Diamonds Are Forever*. *Courtesy of the Anders Frejdh Collection*

was glorious. And I said, 'Ken, can you imagine how much it would cost to build this set"? He said, 'Yes, lots of money.' I said, 'It's absolutely perfect. . . .' He said, 'But, Guy, you cannot shoot here.' I said, 'Why not? Ken, it's wonderful.' He said, 'But this is terrible taste.' I said, 'But that's the whole point.' He said, 'But they will think that I built it!'"* Hamilton later gave in and let Adam build the suite at Pinewood Studios.

laser: A popular weapon in the James Bond series, first introduced as a torture device in *Goldfinger*. In that film, Bond (Sean Connery) is captured and strapped onto a solid gold table, where the laser beam begins to eat away at the metal and is headed for 007's privates. "Do you expect me to talk?" Bond asks. "No, Mr. Bond," replies Goldfinger (Gert Fröbe), "I expect you to die." Fortunately, Bond saves his loins by uttering the magic words "Operation Grand Slam," the name of Goldfinger's supposedly top-secret plan to detonate a Red Chinese A-bomb inside Fort Knox. Fearing what 007 might know and have already shared with his colleagues in British intelligence, Goldfinger has him shot with a tranquilizer dart and shipped to Kentucky.

Laser beams reappear in *Diamonds Are Forever* when it is revealed that Blofeld (Charles Gray), posing as abducted billionaire aircraft manufacturer Willard Whyte (Jimmy Dean), is building a formidable space weapon that projects a deadly beam through a shield of diamonds. (According to the real Willard Whyte, the first laser was projected through a diamond.)

In *The Man with the Golden Gun*, Scaramanga (Christopher Lee) shows Bond (Roger Moore) how his solar energy collector can create a type of laser cannon, which he uses to obliterate 007's seaplane. In *Moonraker*, Q Branch builds a laser rifle that American space troops employ against Hugo Drax's space station. A similar laser is built into the nose of an American shuttle that Bond (Roger Moore) uses to destroy the deadly nerve gas spheres that are headed for the Earth's atmosphere.

In *Never Say Never Again*, Q-like engineer Algernon (Alec McCowen) supplies Bond (Sean Connery) with a tiny laser embedded in his wrist-

---

* Guy Hamilton, interview by Michael Apted, Directors Guild of America Visual History, accessed June 4, 2020, https://www.dga.org/Craft/VisualHistory/Interviews/Guy-Hamilton.aspx.

James Bond (Sean Connery) gets a quick science lesson in laser dynamics from a relaxed Auric Goldfinger (Gert Fröbe) in *Goldfinger*. *Courtesy of the David Reinhardt Collection*

watch, which can cut through manacles. In *Die Another Day*, billionaire environmentalist Gustav Graves (Toby Stephens) and his henchman Zao (Rick Yune) plan to torture captured NSA operative Jinx (Halle Berry) with multiple laser beams inside Graves's Ice Palace. Similar lasers are utilized by Ernst Stavro Blofeld (Christoph Waltz) on his foster brother James Bond (Daniel Craig) in his North African complex in *Spectre*.

Last Year at Marienbad (1962): Director Alain Resnais's art-house hit, which inspired director Terence Young's pre-credits teaser for *From Russia with Love*. The Resnais film featured some incredibly beautiful night shots in a garden surrounded by Greek statues. Young duplicated this setting on the Pinewood Studios backlot—next to the studio administration building—as SPECTRE assassin Donald Grant (Robert Shaw) tracks down and murders the phony Bond.

Laughing Water: The nickname of the hideaway estate of one Mrs. Minnie Simpson of Jamaica, a fan of Ian Fleming's 007 novels. In 1962, its fabulously exotic beach and nearby waterfalls portrayed the hostile shore of Crab Key, home of the title character's impenetrable fortress in *Dr. No*.

Lauterbrunnen: Swiss village that was the site of the humorous stock-car rally in *On Her Majesty's Secret Service*. Screenwriter Richard Maibaum carried forward the festive mood of the earlier

scenes set in nearby Grindelwald, where an escaping Bond (George Lazenby) is rescued by a resourceful Tracy (Diana Rigg), and created an auto rally on ice that is rudely interrupted when Tracy's Mercury Cougar and the big, lumbering SPECTRE Mercedes come smashing onto the racecourse. The cars continue their game of cat and mouse to the astonishment of the crowd and the consternation of the rally drivers, whose little compacts are being smashed around like toys.

The rally was shot on an icy track in Lauterbrunnen, only two miles from the village of Mürren. There, director Peter Hunt assigned racing specialist Anthony Squire to choreograph the race, which featured a number of spectacular crashes—one involving the SPECTRE Mercedes, which overturns and explodes. Shooting began on Sunday, February 2, 1969, and continued until ten o'clock that night, when heavy snows began to fall. On Friday, February 7, George Lazenby, Diana Rigg, and Peter Hunt braved a blizzard at London Airport and left for Lauterbrunnen to do their close-ups in the race, with cameras mounted on the hood of Tracy's Cougar.

Lawrence, Marc (February 17, 1910–November 27, 2005): Tough-guy American character actor and former opera singer who portrayed Rodney, the syndicate hit man who becomes the first victim that Scaramanga (Christopher Lee) hunts in his "fun house" in *The Man with the Golden Gun*. Lawrence had previously portrayed one of the Las Vegas diamond smuggling syndicate hoods in *Diamonds Are Forever*. After voluptuous Plenty O'Toole (Lana Wood) is unceremoniously tossed out of a Las Vegas hotel room window, Lawrence utters the immortal line "I didn't know there was a pool down there."

A native of New York City, Lawrence had a long and distinguished career in the movies, making his feature film debut as a henchman in the comedy drama *If I Had a Million* (1932). He was blacklisted in the 1950s and spent a decade working in Europe. His additional feature film credits include *San Quentin* (1937); *While New York Sleeps* (1938); *Johnny Apollo* (1940); *Hold That Ghost* (1941); *The Ox-Bow Incident* (1943); *Captain from Castile* (1947); *The Asphalt Jungle* (1950), as Cobby the bookie; *Abbott and Costello in the Foreign Legion* (1950); *Helen of Troy* (1956); *Krakatoa: East of Java* (1968); *The Kremlin Letter* (1970); and *Marathon Man* (1976).

***Lawrence of Arabia* theme**: Classic movie music that plays as Bond (Roger Moore) and Anya (Barbara Bach) trek into the desert in *The Spy Who Loved Me*. Aside from the whistling janitor's use of the *Goldfinger* theme in *On Her Majesty's Secret Service*, this was the first time in the series that familiar music from another film began to seep into the action of a Bond movie. It would happen again in the next film, *Moonraker*, when themes from *The Magnificent Seven* and *Close Encounters of the Third Kind* were used.

Composer Maurice Jarre's signature *Lawrence of Arabia* theme was appropriate accompaniment as Bond (Roger Moore) and Anya (Barbara Bach) trek across Egypt in *The Spy Who Loved Me*. *Steve Rubin Collection*

Lazenby, George (September 5, 1939–　　): Handsome Australian leading man who replaced Sean Connery as James Bond and made a strong impression in his one 007 adventure, *On Her Majesty's Secret Service*. Lazenby came to England in 1964 after a couple of successful years selling automobiles in his native country. Taking advice from photographer Chard Jenkins, Lazenby became a top male model in London. He gained some popularity with TV commercials for Big Fry Chocolate, in which he was seen carrying crates of chocolate on his back to give to children.

The commercials were seen by producers Albert R. Broccoli and Harry Saltzman as they began their search for a new Bond in 1968. And Lazenby already knew Broccoli indirectly; they were both customers of Kurt's Barber Shop in Mayfair. Unbeknownst to Lazenby, Broccoli had once mentioned to Kurt that he thought the young model would someday make an excellent James Bond. The producer often pointed to the way Lazenby walked—though he was a big man, he moved with the same catlike grace that had once sold Broccoli on Sean Connery.

Lazenby's agent, Maggie Abbott, sent him to the 007 auditions. It was a new experience for him; as he explained much later, "I had no acting experience—I didn't even know any actors. They were in a different class altogether, especially the young ones. A lot of these guys couldn't afford drinks, while I was making 500 and 600 pounds a week. But I was bored with modeling by then. There was no challenge in it."* Figuring that the best thing to do was to keep his Australian accent under wraps, Lazenby walked into the Audley Square offices of Eon Productions and pretended he was English.

Recalled Lazenby, "I walked right in and asked Harry Saltzman's assistant for an interview. He was on the phone with Harry that very moment. He put the phone down and asked me some quick questions." Lazenby lied and told the assistant that he was a playboy who raced sports cars for a living. He also mentioned his acting experience in Germany and Australia. The assistant repeated the information to Saltzman, who granted Lazenby an interview.

He was then escorted down a wood-paneled hallway to Saltzman's office. He found Saltzman behind his desk, talking on the phone, his shoeless feet draped over the top of his desk. Saltzman motioned Lazenby to a chair, but the nervous model instead walked over to a window and gazed out. Saltzman hung up the phone and looked over the newcomer. He was impressed.

"So you want to be James Bond?" Saltzman asked. "Yes," Lazenby replied. "Well," Saltzman continued, "You'll have to first meet our director, Peter Hunt. He'll be here tomorrow at four o'clock. Can you make it?" Lazenby hedged, saying, 'No, I'm sorry, I have to go back to Paris for a job."

"I don't know why I said that," remembered Lazenby. "I was just getting nervous sitting in Harry's big, plush office. You could tell there was a Rolls-Royce sitting outside, with a chauffeur standing next to it. I'd never been in touch with this kind of person before. Also, I guess I was stalling because I knew that when I met the director, he was going to know right away that I couldn't act."

---

* George Lazenby, interview by the author, Los Angeles, July 1, 1981.

Lazenby agreed to stay in town for a fee of 500 pounds. He eventually met Hunt and tested with another nonprofessional, Australian singer Trisha Noble, and did quite well. He was asked to stay in London for further testing on a retainer of 150 pounds a week.

By April 1968, Broccoli and Saltzman had narrowed the field down to five actors. Besides Lazenby, they were considering John Richardson, who had recently starred alongside Raquel Welch in *One Million Years B.C.*, and who was romantically linked with former Bond girl Martine Beswick; and three young English actors: Anthony Rogers, Robert Campbell, and Hans de Vries. All five were being tested individually on the stages at Pinewood Studios, along with the many young women who were also testing for parts in *On Her Majesty's Secret Service*.

It was a test fight sequence that proved decisive for Lazenby. Stunt coordinator George Leech picked the moment from the script in which Bond is surprised by a would-be assassin in the bedroom of a hotel on the Portuguese coast. Leech asked former wrestler Yuri Borienko to double the villain, a Union Corse gunman. Recalled Leech, "Yuri Borienko didn't have a lot of experience in film fighting, and Lazenby had virtually none at all. I had to instruct both of them in the basic mechanics. Yuri certainly didn't have to learn to fight, but he did have to learn how to react for the cameras. Lazenby was good physically, so he could learn how to punch easily enough. His main problem was learning not to flinch when a punch came his way."*

Progress was slow at first. The overly energetic Lazenby got carried away several times and actually bloodied Borienko's nose. The latter, a good-natured man, took the action in stride. For his patience, Borienko was rewarded with a significant part in the new film—that of Grunther, assistant to Blofeld (Telly Savalas). After three weeks of tough rehearsal, Hunt set up his cameras on Pinewood's Stage B and began shooting film on the test fight. In its finished form, the fight lasted two minutes and was so realistic that Hunt later regretted that he couldn't use it in the finished movie. (In the film, Lazenby would fight the same battle with actor Irvin Allen.)

Lazenby's ability with his fists eventually won him the part, with Broccoli and Saltzman agree-

* George Leech, interview by the author, London, June 23, 1977.

No actor looked better in his Bond debut than George Lazenby looked in 1968, when he took on the role in *On Her Majesty's Secret Service*. *Courtesy of the David Reinhardt Collection*

ing that of the five candidates, Lazenby was the perfect replacement. And after viewing the test-fight footage, United Artists in New York was inclined to agree. Negotiations were immediately halted with a number of other stars, and plans were finalized to go with George Lazenby when shooting began that fall.

Lazenby's film debut as Connery's replacement was, on the whole, a good one. Although he lacked the polish of a more experienced actor, he was very convincing as James Bond. And while his acting came up short in some key emotional sequences, especially his low-key response in the finale when his bride, Tracy (Diana Rigg), is murdered by Blofeld and Irma Bunt (Ilse Steppat), his agile movements worked amazingly well in the film's terrific action sequences. Lazenby could be a very physical actor, and director Peter Hunt played to this strength.

Unfortunately, besieged by worldwide press interest, and under the pressure of replacing one of the world's most popular sex symbols, Lazenby began to crack. His relationship with director Peter Hunt deteriorated over the course of filming, with Hunt preferring to leave Lazenby on his own most of the time, especially in the film's romantic sequences, when Bond falls in love with Tracy. Hunt later explained such a "hands-off" policy as part of his strategy for getting a good performance from a nonprofessional. "I wanted that feeling of isolation," said Hunt. "That is Bond. He's a loner. George wasn't experienced enough

to interpret this feeling of utter emptiness, especially the loss he feels when Tracy is killed. In that
sequence, I didn't want him bright and alert. I
wanted him beaten down and angry. I thus left
him entirely alone that day, hoping that he would
get angry at me and then show some of that
feeling in the scene."*

The strained relationship between actor and
director soon spread to other parts of the production, creating a long-running controversy that
was picked up and fueled by the voracious British
press. The reporters were particularly eager to
exploit an apparent rift between Lazenby and his
leading lady, Diana Rigg, especially when the latter announced she was going to eat garlic prior
to a key love scene.

Lazenby later acknowledged that he was the
cause of the eventual collapse of his relationship
with Hunt and the producers. "It was definitely an
ego thing on my part," said Lazenby. "The result
was that I did virtually the whole film without a
director, and if you look at the call sheet, you'll
find that I did almost every scene in one take. I
was practically a one-take man. If I made a goof,
the crew would shoot the scene from another
angle, and if that was good, that was what they
would print. So I never really got warmed up in
any of my scenes."

Lazenby's comments agree with those of
the London critics, who claimed that his version
of Bond was a mere shell of Connery's. Hunt,
though, had kinder words for Lazenby: "Apart
from one or two moments of frustration brought
about by his own feelings about his performance
in the film, which we worked out, I had no problem with George. In fact, I had fewer problems
with him during the shooting than I've had with
more established stars. And he did everything
in the film very well. It was only during the latter
part of the production, when he became involved
in quarrels and questions about his contract, that
he became difficult. Eventually, he began to hate
the film and, in consequence, me as well."

Hunt continually advised Lazenby to keep
a low profile and to wait until the film was
released—then his strengths could be acknowledged. But others advised Lazenby to take
advantage of his new image. Said Hunt, "Things
would have turned out differently if he had been
more sensible and not gone rushing around

Growing a beard during the prerelease period for
On Her Majesty's Secret Service was one clue that
George Lazenby was done with Bond. *Steve Rubin
Collection*

behaving in such a ridiculous way, saying all sorts
of unpleasant things about people. Whether they
were true didn't matter; he was still making a
spectacle of himself.

"The public will latch onto these things when
they hear them, and you've got to be a pretty
experienced person to be able to deal with the
press. You have to be able to turn those quotes
around so they don't become a knife in the back.
George wasn't capable of doing that, and the
result was that he got an incredible amount of
bad publicity—a fact that probably damaged his
career after *OHMSS*.

"As a young man who had never done a film
before, he was still good, and he came through in
the role. And you had to be a pretty mean critic
to find no talent in him. And I knew that if he

* Peter Hunt, interview by the author, London, June 21, 1977.

went on to make other Bond films, he would have grown into the role, as Roger Moore did. Unfortunately, George didn't have the experience at the time to realize this, and he was badly advised by others. I had too much on my plate to stand by him, to take him on as a friend and confidant. It was also a long shooting schedule, and on such a shoot, you expect everyone at certain moments to have outbursts and periods of anxiety. He was under a tremendous amount of pressure.

"For six years, the world had identified the character of James Bond with Sean Connery. The phenomenon of Bond had reached its peak under Connery's lead. To many, there could be no other James Bond."

Lazenby's feud with Hunt and the producers soured his chances of returning in the next movie, *Diamonds Are Forever*. During a publicity tour for *OHMSS*, he even refused to shave off a beard he had grown during his vacation. A decade later, Lazenby said, "Right now I could do it—I could sign a contract to do the Bond pictures for seven years. In those days, I couldn't, because I was too immature for it. I felt as if I was doing them a favor. After all, I used to think, 'I had a better life before I met you guys.' So I had this chip on my shoulder, and my attitude was entirely wrong. I wasn't looking toward the future.

"Also, in the beginning, I thought I was the only one with an ego. Now I know that everyone on a movie set has one. You have to tread very lightly through the vines. This was something I didn't understand originally, because I was moving around so much. I never stayed in one place long enough to wear out my welcome.

"In those days it also took something like twenty-four hours for me to learn a page of dialogue. Today it would take me maybe twenty minutes. And that takes a lot of pressure off. At least you have your lines and you feel a lot more secure with them."

After *On Her Majesty's Secret Service*, the word went out that Lazenby was unmanageable, and for a few years he found it impossible to get film work. He later went to Hong Kong, where he was in talks to work with Bruce Lee until that actor's untimely death. Lazenby's appearance in a number of low-budget kung fu films tided him over through the early 1970s, after which he went to the United States to play more serious roles. His post-007 feature credits include *Universal Soldier* (1971); *The Kentucky Fried Movie* (1977);

Saint Jack (1979); *Never Too Young to Die* (1986), with fellow Bond player Branscombe Richmond (*Licence to Kill*); and *Gettysburg* (1993), as Confederate brigadier general J. Johnston Pettigrew.

It should be noted that one of the pieces of advice that Lazenby was given in 1969 was that the time of Bond was over—that the series was nearing its end. As time has shown, it was probably the stupidest, most inaccurate piece of advice that anyone in show business was ever given.

Lee, Bernard (January 10, 1908–January 16, 1981; birth name: John Bernard Lee): British character actor who portrayed M, the retired admiral turned Bond's Secret Service superior in the first eleven James Bond movies. As with Desmond Llewelyn's character Q, M's serious demeanor was in direct contrast to 007's cavalier attitude toward bureaucratic authority and the British stiff upper lip. Born in Brentford, Middlesex, England, Lee made his feature film debut in director Leslie Howard Gordon's comedy *The Double Event* (1934). Lee's other feature credits include *The Third Man* (1949); *Sailor of the King* (1953); *Beat the Devil* (1953); *The Purple Plain* (1954); *Pursuit of the Graf Spee* (1956); *Fire Down Below* (1957); *The Key* (1958); *Sink the Bismarck!* (1960), as the uncredited firing officer; *The L-Shaped Room* (1962); *Dr. Terror's House of Horrors* (1965); *The Spy Who Came in from the Cold* (1965); and *Operation Kid Brother* (1967), starring Sean Connery's brother Neil, along with fellow Bond vets Daniela Bianchi, Adolfo Celi, Anthony Dawson, and Lois Maxwell).

Lee, Christopher (May 27, 1922–June 7, 2015) Tall, sinister British character actor, a veteran of countless horror films, who joined the James Bond series as Francisco Scaramanga, the title character in *The Man with the Golden Gun*. The part was a change of pace for Lee, who was used to playing the dark and horrifying side of every possible villain, but who, in *Golden Gun*, was given the opportunity to portray Scaramanga as a sexy, extremely suave, and sophisticated man about town who sleeps with Andrea Anders (Maud Adams), sunbathes on a private beach, and liquidates his clients' enemies for $1 million a shot. In fact, Lee is so likable in the role that some critics of the film pointed out that it was hard to accept him as Bond's deadly nemesis. After all, a man who wears jogging suits and tells stories about his pet elephant dying at the hands of an evil handler can't be all bad.

In a 1974 interview with *Cinefantastique*'s Chris Knight, Lee commented, "All villains should be slightly sympathetic. You should never play them 100 percent heavy. You should always play them with sympathy, sadness, loneliness, amusement, wit, charm, elegance, style or glamour. These traits make the character much more interesting. And in the role of Scaramanga, all of these qualities were able to come into play. He wasn't just a thug. Instead of playing him with no redeeming qualities at all, with no charm, I was able to play him as an educated, articulate man who killed because he liked money and women, and because he simply enjoyed killing.

"[Director] Guy Hamilton got something out of me in this picture which I've never been able to show on the screen. In his own words, he got the spook out of me. He got the Dracula out of me. Because, obviously, I can become very menacing, rather heavy, if I'm not careful, even with ordinary lines because I've done it so often. But on this picture, Guy got me to do Scaramanga in such a light way that you can hardly believe this man is as lethal as he is. He got me to smile and even made me laugh, something which, I admit, I haven't found very easy to do as an actor."*

Christopher Lee was destined to appear in the Bond series. He was the cousin of author Ian Fleming (Lee's stepfather, Harcourt Rose, was Fleming's uncle), and he was probably the inspiration for Fleming's character Dr. No. Born in Belgravia, London, Lee had a long and prolific film and television career, making his feature film debut for Bond director Terence Young in the mystery drama *Corridor of Mirrors* (1948), working with Lois Maxwell. He worked with Young again in the World War II drama *They Were Not Divided* (1950), alongside future Bond players Edward Underdown (*Thunderball*), Michael Brennan, Desmond Llewelyn, Anthony Dawson, and Peter Burton. It was his appearance as the creature in director Terence Fisher's acclaimed film *The Curse of Frankenstein* (1957) for Hammer Film Productions that firmly moved Lee into the world of horror cinema.

After decades of excellent work, Lee became even more popular in his later years when he

Perpetually tied to the horror genre, actor Christopher Lee was delighted to play Scaramanga, a suave million-dollar-a-hit assassin in *The Man with the Golden Gun. Courtesy of the David Reinhardt Collection*

played important characters in two hit film series: Saruman the wizard in *The Lord of the Rings* (2001–2003), and Count Dooku / Darth Tyranus *Star Wars: Episode II—Attack of the Clones* (2002) and *Episode III—Revenge of the Sith* (2005).

Lee, Will Yun (March 22, 1971–): Korean American actor who portrayed villainous Colonel Moon, a hot-tempered renegade North Korean officer and illegal arms merchant in *Die Another Day*. Born in Arlington, Virginia, and raised in such diverse environments as the Bronx and Hawaii, Lee is the son of a tae kwon do martial arts grandmaster. Beginning his career in American television, he made his feature film debut as Jimmy Nguyen in director Gurinder Chadha's romantic comedy *What's Cooking?* (2000). Following his Bond debut in 2002, Lee appeared in *Torque* (2004); *Elektra* (2005), with fellow Bond veteran Cary-Hiroyuki Tagawa (*Licence to Kill*); *Hers* (2007); *The King*

---

* Christopher Lee, interview by Chris Knight, *Cinefantastique*, 1974.

of *Fighters* (2010); *Total Recall* (2012); *Red Dawn* (2012); *The Wolverine* (2013); and *San Andreas* (2015). He also costarred with fellow Bond veteran Michelle Yeoh in the fifth season of the British action series *Strike Back* (5 episodes, 2015).

Leech, George (December 6, 1921–June 17, 2012): Top British stuntman and stunt coordinator who worked closely with stunt arranger Bob Simmons on many of the early Bond films, including *Dr. No* (as Joseph Wiseman's stunt double), *Goldfinger* (as Sean Connery's stunt double), *Thunderball*, *Casino Royale*, *You Only Live Twice*, *On Her Majesty's Secret Service* (as stunt arranger), *Diamonds Are Forever* (as Putter Smith's fiery stunt double), *The Spy Who Loved Me* (as the Lotus Esprit stunt driver), *For Your Eyes Only*, *Octopussy*, *Never Say Never Again*, and *A View to a Kill* (as Willoughby Gray's stunt double). A native of London, Leech got his start in big-screen stunt work riding war horses in the splashy MGM swashbucklers *Ivanhoe* (1952) and *Quentin Durward* (1955).

Leech, Wendy (November 30, 1949–   ): British stuntwoman, the daughter of Bond stunt veteran George Leech, who portrayed the heiress kidnapped by fanatical revolutionaries in the teaser for *Never Say Never Again*. Brainwashed by her captors, the heiress stabs James Bond (Sean Connery) with a knife after he rescues her—but the knife turns out to be phony, and the entire rescue just a training mission. Leech made her celebrated stunt debut doubling actress Holly Palance, whose character hangs herself from the mansion balcony in *The Omen* (1976).

Legrand, Michel (February 24, 1932–January 26, 2019): Three-time Academy Award–winning French film composer who contributed the score for *Never Say Never Again*, beating out up-and-coming American composer James Horner for the job. A Parisian native, Legrand received his Oscars for *The Thomas Crown Affair* (1968), Best Original Song for "The Windmills of Your Mind," shared with lyricists Alan and Marilyn Bergman; *Summer of '42* (1972), Best Original Dramatic Score; and *Yentl* (1983), Best Original Song Score or Adaptation Score, shared again with Alan and Marilyn Bergman. The prolific Legrand received ten other Academy Award

nominations, for *The Umbrellas of Cherbourg* (1964), three nominations; *The Young Girls of Rochefort* (1967); *The Thomas Crown Affair* (1968), Best Original Score; *The Happy Ending* (1969); *Pieces of Dreams* (1970); *Best Friends* (1982); and *Yentl* (1983), Best Original Song for "The Way He Makes Me Feel" and "Papa, Can You Hear Me?," with Alan and Marilyn Bergman. Legrand made his feature composing debut on director Henri Verneuil's romantic drama *The Lovers of Lisbon* (1954).

Leiter, Clarence: British agent portrayed by veteran character actor Michael Pate who joins James Bond (Barry Nelson) on a mission against Soviet master spy Le Chiffre (Peter Lorre) in the CBS TV adaptation of *Casino Royale* (1954). In essence, Leiter is a British version of Fleming's original American CIA agent, Felix Leiter—a logical move, since the adaptation made James Bond into an American intelligence operative. Leiter is an agent of Station S of the British Secret Service—specialists on the Soviet Union—working with the French Deuxième Bureau and the American Combined Intelligence Agency. His mission is to supply Bond with 26 million francs so he can bankrupt Le Chiffre at the baccarat table in Monte Carlo.

Leiter, Felix: James Bond's longtime friend and CIA compatriot. He's been portrayed by many different actors who took a number of approaches to the character. The first on-screen

Actor Jack Lord was the first to portray CIA agent Felix Leiter, here holding a gun on James Bond (Sean Connery) before 007 is informed that they're both fighting on the same side. *Courtesy of the David Reinhardt Collection*

take, in the 1954 TV adaptation of *Casino Royale*, was actually Australian actor Michael Pate, portraying a British intelligence operative named *Clarence* Leiter alongside an American James Bond. Producers Albert R. Broccoli and Harry Saltzman hired Jack Lord to play the first Felix Leiter in *Dr. No*. The film's tropical climate must have agreed with him, because he went on to spend most of his acting career in Hawaii as American detective Steve McGarrett in the television series *Hawaii Five-O*.

Canadian Cec Linder became the second actor to play CIA agent Felix Leiter in the Bond series. *Courtesy of the Anders Frejdh Collection*

Lord was succeeded in the part by Canadian Cec Linder (*Goldfinger*), who was the quintessential 1960s suit-and tie agent; Rik Van Nutter, a lanky, prematurely gray tropical Leiter (*Thunderball*); Norman Burton, another by-the-book suit-and-tie operative (*Diamonds Are Forever*); David Hedison, the debonair New England Leiter (*Live and Let Die*, *Licence to Kill*); Bernie Casey, in an underwritten role as the first African American Leiter (*Never Say Never Again*); and John Terry,

Rik Van Nutter was the third actor, and the most athletic, to play CIA agent Felix Leiter, here with James Bond (Sean Connery) searching the Caribbean for a hijacked NATO bomber in *Thunderball*. *Courtesy of the David Reinhardt Collection*

the youngest-looking Leiter ever, who seems like a kid off a Southern California beach (*The Living Daylights*). Most recently, Jeffrey Wright is intelligent and classy as the second African American to take on the role of Leiter; introduced as the American card player at the Texas hold'em tournament in *Casino Royale*, he's since returned in *Quantum of Solace* and *No Time to Die*.

Leiter's most central role in the series is Hedison's turn in *Licence to Kill*, when on the day of his wedding to Della Churchill (Priscilla Barnes), he's thrown into a shark pool by ruthless drug lord Franz Sanchez (Robert Davi). Leiter's mutilation—he loses his left leg below the knee—and Della's murder prompt James Bond (Timothy Dalton) to break away from the British Secret Service and stage his own revenge scheme.

Lektor decoding machine: Russian cipher device pursued by Bond (Sean Connery) in *From Russia with Love*. Referred to as a Spektor in Ian Fleming's original novel—the screenwriters changed it to Lektor when they made the criminal organization SPECTRE the villains of the film—it was based on the Enigma, an actual cipher machine used by the Germans to encrypt and decrypt secret messages during World War II. It proved key to Allied victory when Britain's Ultra program cracked the Enigma code.

The truth about the Enigma machine, Ultra, and Ian Fleming's part in the program wasn't revealed until 1975, when British wartime secrets were first declassified. Sir William Stephenson, the head of Ultra and a close friend of Fleming, revealed the secrets of Fleming's own contribution in his book *A Man Called Intrepid*. This concise history of British intelligence activities explained a great deal of the source material upon which Fleming based his James Bond novels, including the Spektor/Lektor decoder of *From Russia with Love*.

In the film, the Lektor weighs ten kilograms and is carried in a brown case like a typewriter. It has self-calibrating and manual capabilities, with a built-in compensator. There are twenty-four symbols and sixteen code keys on its keyboard. Inside, the mechanism includes a light and perforated copper disks. M states that the British Secret Service has been attempting to obtain a Russian Lektor for years. Now, according to their station contact in Istanbul—Ali Kerim Bey (Pedro Armendariz)—a Russian embassy cipher clerk named Tatiana Romanova (Daniela Bianchi) will steal the Lektor if James Bond (Sean Connery) comes to Istanbul and helps her defect. All of this, of course, is an intricate SPECTRE trap.

The Lektor is first seen in the communications room of the Russian embassy in Istanbul, where it is captured by Bond after the building is dynamited by Kerim Bey. Bond carries it aboard the Orient Express and eventually brings it to Venice, where it is nearly stolen back by Rosa Klebb (Lotte Lenya) before she is killed by Romanova.

Lenya, Lotte (October 18, 1898–November 27, 1981; birth name: Karoline Wilhelmine Charlotte Blamauer): Academy Award–nominated Austrian character actress and international singing star who portrayed one of the best villains in the James Bond series: SPECTRE agent number 3, Rosa Klebb, former head of operations for SMERSH (Soviet counterintelligence) in *From Russia with Love*. At the time, she was probably

Singer/actress Lotte Lenya took on a decidedly darker look as fiendish SPECTRE spymaster Rosa Klebb in *From Russia with Love*. *Courtesy of the David Reinhardt Collection*

best known as the performer of her late husband Kurt Weill's famous song repertoire. It's hard to picture the woman who portrayed Klebb as a world-famous entertainer, but it's true. The part of Klebb was apparently a romp for her, and her comfort in the role is evident.

Lenya truly inhabits the role of Rosa Klebb. Her military outfits and bearing, her whiplike screaming voice, her knuckle duster to the abdomen of Donald Grant (Robert Shaw), and her terror in the presence of Blofeld are riveting. At one point, Tatiana Romanova (Daniela Bianchi) balks at an espionage assignment, asking Klebb what the punishment will be if she refuses. Klebb turns to her and replies straightforwardly, "Then you will not leave this room alive." When Tanya agrees to the assignment, the film gets one of its biggest laughs.

Lenya, born in Vienna-Penzing, Austria-Hungary, made only a few motion picture and television appearances. Her motion picture debut was director Georg Wilhelm Pabst's *The 3 Penny Opera* (1931), filmed in German. She was nominated for the Academy Award for Best Supporting Actress for her English-language film debut, *The Roman Spring of Mrs. Stone* (1961), which also featured future Bond players Edward de Souza (*The Spy Who Loved Me*), Jill St. John, and Paul Stassino.

Leon, Valerie (November 12, 1943–   ): Curvaceous British actress who portrayed the Sardinian hotel receptionist in *The Spy Who Loved Me* and the sexy deep-sea fishing enthusiast who hooks Bond (Sean Connery) in *Never Say Never Again* (credited simply as "Lady in Bahamas"). Born in Islington, London, Leon is best known for performing in seven films in the popular *Carry On . . .* film series. She made her motion picture debut as Tove's secretary in director Desmond Davis's musical comedy *Smashing Time* (1967). That same year, she first appeared on television in the "To Kill a Saint" episode of the Roger Moore series *The Saint*.

Lewars, Margaret (1938–   ; a.k.a. Marguerite Lewars): Jamaican actress and former Miss Jamaica who portrayed the shapely and sinister freelance photographer who is determined to photograph Bond (Sean Connery) upon his arrival in Kingston in *Dr. No*. To date, it is her only professional acting credit.

Leyland RT: The make of the double-decker bus that was transported to Jamaica in 1972 to perform stunt chores in *Live and Let Die*. Fresh off of London's route 19 from Battersea, it was driven by London bus-driving instructor Maurice Patchett. The Leyland was equipped with a standard 98 horsepower engine, a thirty-five-gallon gasoline tank, and a coat of grayish-green paint simulating the colors of fictional San Monique Transport. It was impossible to discern that a team of metalworkers had actually sawed off the top half of the bus body, placed it on metal rollers, and reattached it to the lower body so that when Patchett (doubling Roger Moore) hit the low-clearance trestle bridge, the upper half would easily come smashing off.

Licence Revoked: Original title of *Licence to Kill*. The title was probably changed for fear that moviegoers either wouldn't understand what it meant for Bond's license to be "revoked" or wouldn't know what licence it was. Silly, isn't it—but a title can play a substantial part in the effectiveness of a film's marketing campaign.

 LICENCE TO KILL

(United Artists, 1989) ★★⌡ : The sixteenth James Bond film produced by Albert R. Broccoli, and the first to feature a title that is not taken from a work by Ian Fleming. US release date: July 14, 1989. Budget: $42 million. Worldwide box office gross: $156.2 million (US domestic gross: $34.7 million; international gross: $121.5 million).* Running time: 135 minutes.

THE SETUP

South American drug lord Franz Sanchez (Robert Davi) takes a risky journey to Key West, Florida, to catch his girlfriend, Lupe (Talisa Soto), in bed with her lover, Alvarez (Gerardo Albarrán). A few miles away, James Bond (Timothy Dalton) is attending the wedding of his good friend Felix Leiter (David Hedison) to Della Churchill (Priscilla Barnes) when Leiter is called into action to take down Sanchez. The drug lord is captured, but he escapes with the help of drug runner Milton Krest (Anthony Zerbe) and duplicitous DEA agent Ed Killifer (Everett McGill).

---

* "Licence to Kill (1989)," The Numbers, accessed June 8, 2020, https://www.the-numbers.com/movie/Licence-to-Kill.

Shockingly, Sanchez's thugs then murder Della and throw Leiter to the sharks. Ordered to Istanbul for a new mission, Bond defies his superior M (Robert Brown) and becomes a rogue agent—determined to take down Sanchez and his illegal drug operation. Helping along the way: resourceful CIA pilot and undercover operative Pam Bouvier (Carey Lowell) and a very present and active Q (Desmond Llewelyn).

BEHIND THE SCENES

Timothy Dalton returns as James Bond in *Licence to Kill*, the first Bond film to barely escape a restricted R rating from the MPAA for excessive violence. Unfortunately, the added violence featured in the film was unnecessary. It would have been one thing if Bond and Sanchez were involved in an incredibly violent fight à la *From Russia with Love*, but the violence is visited on supporting characters instead. Felix Leiter (David Hedison) is thrown to the sharks and loses a leg. The head of Milton Krest (Anthony Zerbe) inflates and explodes in a decompression chamber. Pam Bouvier (Carey Lowell) takes a bullet in the back and survives, courtesy of a Kevlar vest, and Bond narrowly avoids failling into a bag shredder that claims the life of knife-wielding Dario (Benicio Del Toro).

What the film needed wasn't over-the-top violence but a fresh story line. In the most serious Bond movie since *From Russia with Love*, writer Michael G. Wilson, working from an outline by Richard Maibaum (due to a Writers Guild of America strike, Maibaum was unable to write the script), eliminated some of the very elements that have contributed to the longevity of the series—namely, the dark humor, fascinating locations, and a grandiose scheme perpetrated by a larger-than-life villain. Robert Davi's Franz Sanchez is a suitably ruthless crime boss, but his international drug dealing is a bore, ripped from the headlines of the 1980s drug wars. The film is also claustrophobic; audiences used to the series' globe-trotting locations were disappointed by the bland trips to Key West and fictional Isthmus City.

The movie starts out with a good twist when Bond's longtime friend Felix Leiter is thrown to the sharks by Sanchez. Forsaking M and the Secret Service, Bond becomes a rogue agent seeking revenge at all costs—a great plot device, and one that harks back to *On Her Majesty's Secret Service*, which also involved a bride being murdered on her wedding day. Unfortunately, once 007 arrives in Isthmus City, the movie loses all of its tension and impact. Bond's attempt on Sanchez's life is stopped by a pair of Hong Kong narcotics agents. He's too easily accepted into Sanchez's inner circle as a friend and security adviser, and his efforts to slowly turn the drug kingpin against his confederates lack the ring of plausibility. There's also too much talk and not enough action. Even the tanker-trailer chase at the climax—despite some amazing stunt work—is lackluster. And the expected one-on-one show-down between Bond and Sanchez is over much too quickly.

Highlights: Dalton, who is once again serious and on target, although he could have been light-ened up a bit. Audiences who spend two-plus hours with Bond need to laugh once in a while. Thankfully, Q (Desmond Llewelyn), in his largest role in the series, is on hand to provide some cru-cial comic relief. Carey Lowell is delightful as Pam Bouvier, the resourceful, beautiful CIA operative who helps Bond at every turn—the best Bond girl in years. Her introduction in the Barrelhead Bar in Bimini is a classic. Benicio Del Toro's Dario is also an excellent villain.

THE CAST

James Bond	Timothy Dalton
Pam Bouvier	Carey Lowell
Franz Sanchez	Robert Davi
Lupe Lamora	Talisa Soto
Milton Krest	Anthony Zerbe
Sharkey	Frank McRae
Killifer	Everett McGill
Professor Joe Butcher	Wayne Newton
Dario	Benicio Del Toro
Truman-Lodge	Anthony Starke
President Hector Lopez	Pedro Armendariz Jr.
Q	Desmond Llewelyn
Felix Leiter	David Hedison
Della Churchill	Priscilla Barnes
M	Robert Brown
Miss Moneypenny	Caroline Bliss
Heller	Don Stroud
Hawkins	Grand L. Bush
Kwang	Cary-Hiroyuki Tagawa
Perez	Alejandro Bracho
Braun	Guy de Saint Cyr
Mullens	Rafer Johnson
Loti	Diana Lee-Hsu
Fallon	Christopher Neame

THE CREW

Director	John Glen
Screenplay	Michael G. Wilson
	Richard Maibaum
Producers	Albert R. Broccoli
	Michael G. Wilson
Associate Producers	Tom Pevsner
	Barbara Broccoli
Director of Photography	Alec Mills
Music composed and conducted by	Michael Kamen
Title song performed by	Gladys Knight
End titles song performed by	Patti LaBelle
Production Designer	Peter Lamont
Costume Designer	Jodie Tillen
Second Unit Direction and Photography	Arthur Wooster
Underwater scenes directed and photographed by	Ramon Bravo
Stunt Coordinator	Paul Weston
Driving stunts arranged by	Remy Julienne
Aerial Stunt Supervisor	Corkey Fornof
Title Designer	Maurice Binder
Special Visual Effects	John Richardson

Lienz Cossacks: Russian soldiers who fought on the side of the Nazis during World War II, as discussed in *GoldenEye*. They were captured, betrayed by the British, and mass murdered by Stalin's secret police. The parents of turncoat British agent Alec Trevelyan (Sean Bean) were Lienz Cossacks who committed suicide after they were betrayed—hence Trevelyan's ven-detta against England and James Bond (Pierce Brosnan).

limpet mine: An explosive device attached to the wall of the Istanbul office of Kerim Bey (Pedro Armendariz) by Bulgarian agent Krilencu (Fred Haggerty) in *From Russia with Love*. Thanks to the lovemaking pleas of his ravishing girlfriend (Nadja Regin), Kerim Bey retires to a settee and is saved from the blast.

Lin, Colonel Wai: Chinese secret agent and martial arts expert portrayed by Michelle Yeoh in *Tomorrow Never Dies*. Using her cover as a reporter for the New China News Agency, Wai Lin infiltrates the cable network of billionaire media mogul Elliot Carver (Jonathan Pryce) in Hamburg, where she meets another undercover operative, James Bond (Pierce Brosnan). They join forces to stop Carver from initiating World War III to increase his ratings.

Chinese actress Michelle Yeoh portrayed Chinese agent Wai Lin, who joins forces with James Bond (Pierce Brosnan) to prevent World War III in *Tomorrow Never Dies. Courtesy of the Anders Frejdh Collection*

Linder, Cec (March 10, 1921–April 10, 1992; birth name: Cecil Yekuthial Linder) Canadian character actor of Polish heritage—his first name is pronounced "CEESE," short for Cecil—who portrayed CIA field agent Felix Leiter in *Goldfinger*. Always dapper in a business suit and fedora, Linder's Leiter is a very businesslike, by-the-rules kind of guy who respects 007 (Sean Connery) and his risky, no-holds-barred form of espionage. In many ways, he's probably the quintessential working CIA man of the Kennedy era, more apt to make a phone call than use his fists. Leiter keeps track of Bond when he's captured by Goldfinger (Gert Fröbe), and it is Leiter who calls the shots during the US Army's

counterattack on Goldfinger's Operation Grand Slam at Fort Knox.

Linder was actually originally cast as Mr. Simmons, the mark whom Goldfinger cheats at cards, but at the last minute he was switched with the actor cast as Leiter, Austin Willis. Willis wasn't pleased to be moved into the much smaller role of Simmons. "He had a right to be upset," remembered Linder. "He got a few days on the picture, but I ended up with twelve weeks."*

Linder and Willis were the only two actors sent to Florida for the US shoot. Guy Hamilton's crew shot at the Fontainebleau Hotel pool, where producer Harry Saltzman loaned Linder his fedora for his introductory walk-by. They filmed the chase between Leiter and Oddjob, which concluded at a wrecking yard, with a double standing in for Harold Sakata. They also shot a brief sequence in front of a diner, where Leiter gets the word from his partner that Bond's signal is moving. Everything else with the actors was shot in England, including the thrilling assault on Fort Knox, which was built full size on the backlot at Pinewood Studios.

Unfortunately, Linder was not asked to play Leiter on the next film, *Thunderball*; he was replaced by the hunky Rik Van Nutter. Recalled Linder, "I guess they wanted a younger guy, someone who could fight sharks and that kind of thing."

A native of Timmons, Ontario, Linder appeared in a number of television shows before making his motion picture debut as Captain Dan Carver in director Sam Newfield's western *Flaming Frontier* (1958), which also featured future Bond player Shane Rimmer as Running Bear. Linder's additional feature film credits include *Crack in the Mirror* (1960), with his future *Goldfinger* mate Austin Willis; *Lolita* (1962), with fellow Bond players Irvin Allen (*On Her Majesty's Secret Service*), Lois Maxwell, and Ed Bishop; *The Verdict* (1964), with fellow Bond players Zena Marshall and Paul Stassino; *Zabriskie Point* (1970); *A Touch of Class* (1973); *Age of Innocence* (1977), with fellow *Goldfinger* veterans Honor Blackman and Lois Maxwell; and *Atlantic City* (1980).

Ling: Chinese girlfriend of James Bond (Sean Connery) portrayed by Tsai Chin in *You Only Live Twice*. After she gives 007 "very best duck,"

---

* Cec Linder, telephone interview by the author, July 17, 1989.

she pushes a button that swings her hide-a-bed, along with Bond, into the wall, and then allows two machine-gunning thugs into her apartment. After they're finished spraying the bed with lethal lead, it looks like 007 is dead. We know better. The sequence was filmed on a Pinewood Studios soundstage on the first day of shooting for *You Only Live Twice*, July 4, 1966. Joining the action that day, in addition to Sean Connery and Tsai Chin, were six Chinese extras, actors Patrick Jordan and Anthony Ainley—who were portraying two British military police officers—and stuntman Bob Simmons, who, doubling Connery, gets closed up in Ling's Murphy bed.

Ling, Mr.: Red Chinese specialist in nuclear fission, portrayed by Burt Kwouk in *Goldfinger*. Ling's government is providing Goldfinger (Gert Fröbe) with an atomic device he intends to explode inside Fort Knox, Kentucky, irradiating America's entire gold supply and essentially rendering it unusable for fifty-eight years. The hoped-for result: economic chaos in the West

for the Chinese, plus a tenfold increase in the value of Goldfinger's own smuggled gold cache. When the US infantry forces at Fort Knox launch their counterattack, Goldfinger, wearing an American officer's uniform, shoots Ling in front of them. Convinced that Goldfinger is one of them, the Americans move on and are promptly mowed down by the golden gunman.

Liparus: A supertanker belonging to billionaire shipping magnate Karl Stromberg (Curt Jurgens), the pride of his fleet and the linchpin in his scheme to destroy the world in *The Spy Who Loved Me*. The second largest tanker in the world at over a million tons—behind the Soviet ship *Karl Marx*—it is equipped with enormous bow doors that can swing open and swallow nuclear submarines whole. Hence, it isn't surprising that the interior set for the *Liparus*, built on the 007 Stage at Pinewood Studios, was dubbed the "Jonah Set"—after the biblical figure who was swallowed by a whale. Inside the *Liparus* is a fascinating mini-harbor with docking space for

Derek Meddings's special effects crew works with the large *Liparus* supertanker miniature during production on *The Spy Who Loved Me*. *Courtesy of the Brian Smithies Archive*

three submarines, a monorail, an armored control room, and a virtual army of sailors, some of whom will eventually gain control of two of the captured subs.

After noticing a model of the *Liparus* at Stromberg's Atlantis laboratory, Bond (Roger Moore) and KGB agent Anya Amasova (Barbara Bach) check up on the supertanker's history and discover that since it was fitted out nine months before, it has never once been in port—obviously, Stromberg's hiding something. After the billionaire takes captured Anya back to his Atlantis base and two subs exit the tanker, Bond makes his move. Stealing a ride in a monorail car, he clubs a guard (in a scene that is practically identical to one in *You Only Live Twice* inside Blofeld's volcano rocket base) and frees the three captured submarine crews.

Breaking into the armory, Bond and the escaping submariners outfit themselves with machine guns and hand grenades, and launch an all-out assault on the *Liparus* crew. The following battle sequence is one of the most impressive ever seen in the Bond series, a credit to director John Glen and his stunt and effects teams. Despite heavy casualties and the loss of the British submarine's commander (Bryan Marshall), 007's men succeed in breaking into the control room. Using a ship's computer, Bond sends new attack coordinates to the two enemy submarines so that when they launch their nuclear missiles, they will destroy each other instead. On fire from numerous internal explosions caused by the pitched battle, the *Liparus* eventually sinks, but not before the last sub, the USS *Wayne*, escapes—with Bond aboard.

The concept of a supertanker swallowing a nuclear submarine was not far-fetched, especially when the last scene in the film featured a real British naval vessel with the capability of flooding its cargo area to receive the Atlantis escape pod.

Lippe: Huge SPECTRE assassin portrayed by Pat Roach in *Never Say Never Again*. Unlike the well-groomed character of Count Lippe, portrayed by Guy Doleman in *Thunderball*, *Never Say Never Again*'s Lippe is a simple killing machine who practically destroys the lower level of the Shrublands health clinic in his attempts to kill Bond (Sean Connery). Aside from his pure strength, his most terrifying weapon is a razor-sharp metallic belt that can cut through metal

like a knife through butter. Eventually, cornered in a specimen storage room, Bond manages to stun Lippe by flinging a beaker full of yellow liquid in his face. Losing his balance, the giant falls against a rack of glass laboratory instruments and is impaled. As Lippe falls to the floor dead, a glass tube sticking out of his back, Bond looks at the beaker and realizes that it was his own urine specimen that did the job.

Lippe, Count: Sinister SPECTRE agent, portrayed by Guy Doleman, who engages in an unsuccessful game of cat and mouse with Bond (Sean Connery) at the Shrublands health clinic in *Thunderball*. Working with SPECTRE assassin Fiona Volpe (Luciana Paluzzi), Lippe is assigned the task of getting a plastic-surgery-aided duplicate of NATO aerial observer François Derval (Paul Stassino) onto a nuclear bomber. Unfortunately for SPECTRE, when Derval is murdered, Bond finds the bandage-wrapped body at Shrublands and begins to investigate.

Bond starts to suspect Lippe's involvement after he notices a telltale tong sign tattooed to his wrist. And the entire SPECTRE scheme to hijack the bomber is later jeopardized when Lippe tries unsuccessfully to kill Bond by sabotaging his motorized tracking table. For his bumbling, Blofeld orders Lippe assassinated—a job that is accomplished handily on the highway by a motorcycle-riding, rocket-firing Fiona Volpe.

Little Nellie (official name: Beagle-Wallis WA-116): The amazing portable autogyro (mini-helicopter) designed by Wing Commander Kenneth H. Wallis and flown by James Bond (Sean Connery) in *You Only Live Twice*. In the film, it's transported to Tokyo by Q (Desmond Llewelyn) in four suitcases and features an arsenal of weapons, including two fixed machine guns; two rocket launchers, forward firing on either side, with incendiary and high explosive capability; heat-seeking air-to-air missiles; two flame guns firing astern, range of eighty yards; two smoke ejectors; and aerial mines. Bond takes his new toy on a reconnaissance of Japan's volcano country, and runs into four SPECTRE helicopters that are no match for Nellie's deadly charms.

As to who discovered Wallis and his incredible mini-helicopter in reality, credit must be split between production designer Ken Adam, who

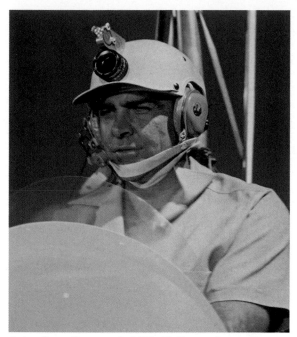

Actor Sean Connery in Little Nellie mode, on the blue screen stage at Pinewood. *Courtesy of the David Reinhardt Collection*

LIVE AND LET DIE

(United Artists, 1973) ★★⯨ : The eighth James Bond film produced by Albert R. Broccoli and Harry Saltzman. US release date: June 27, 1973. Budget: $7 million. Worldwide box office gross: $161.8 million (US gross: $35.4 million; international gross: $126.4 million).* Running time: 121 minutes.

—————— **THE SETUP** ——————

British agents are being systematically murdered in New York City, New Orleans, and fictional San Monique in the Caribbean. James Bond (Roger Moore) is sent to New York to investigate, where he contacts CIA spymaster Felix Leiter (David Hedison) and begins to follow the activities of San Monique's primary diplomat, Dr. Kananga (Yaphet Kotto). He also tracks Mr. Big, a Harlem drug kingpin who may also be connected to the murders. We soon discover that Kananga and Mr. Big are one and the same—a prodigious heroin trafficker with huge poppy fields on his native island, a throng of colorful bodyguards and thugs, and an expert tarot card reader named Solitaire (Jane Seymour).

—————— **BEHIND THE SCENES** ——————

Continuing their series in 1972 with another James Bond—their third in three films—producers Broccoli and Saltzman turned to Roger Moore, a successful television actor who was respected for his work in such series as *Maverick*, *The Persuaders!*, and especially *The Saint*. He could play a hero with a very light touch. Broccoli and Saltzman had considered him in 1962, but Moore was termed too much of a "pretty boy" in those days.[†] A decade later, he had matured, and considering that the series was going in the *Goldfinger* direction of outlandish plots, plenty of sexy women, and impossible stunts, Moore was considered the perfect 007 for the time.

Witty screenwriter Tom Mankiewicz, who had collaborated with Richard Maibaum on *Diamonds Are Forever*, returned as the sole writer on *Live*

heard a radio interview with Wallis, and producer Harry Saltzman, who saw the autogyro in an aviation magazine. During filming in Japan from August through October 1966, Wing Commander Wallis himself doubled Sean Connery, as he was the only one with the skill to fly Little Nellie. Close-ups of Connery were later shot against a blue screen on the special effects stage at Pinewood Studios. The tiny helicopter flew eighty-five sorties over Japan, for a total of forty-six hours in the air. Because it is against the law to fire guns—even phony ones—in midair over Japan, the Bond crew eventually completed the battle sequences in Spain near Torremolinos.

Little Nellie was an incredibly versatile flying machine, capable of a speed range of 14–130 mph. According to journalist Robin Harbour, who interviewed Wallis for a 1988 article in *007 Magazine*, Nellie weighed 250 pounds and could lift twice its own weight. Its range was 170 miles, and it could remain in the air for two and a half hours with a fuel consumption of seventeen liters per hour. Originally designed for the British Army as a reconnaissance aircraft, the autogyro carried the military serial number XR 943 and civil registration G-ARZB.

* "Live and Let Die (1973)," The Numbers, accessed June 8, 2020, https://www.the-numbers.com/movie/Live-and-Let-Die.
† Albert R. Broccoli, interview by the author, Los Angeles, April 10, 1977.

The new James Bond (Roger Moore) with the new Bond beauties, Rosie Carver (Gloria Hendry, left) and Solitaire (Jane Seymour, right) in *Live and Let Die*. *Courtesy of the David Reinhardt Collection*

and Let Die, his sensibilities perfectly matching Moore's own approach to the character. *Live and Let Die* plays like a Marvel comic book version of a James Bond film. Its plot is superfluous (something about drug smuggling that is never properly explained or dealt with), its characters are fantasy types (Whisper, Baron Samedi, Tee Hee), and its direction is uninspired. It does, however, have some good motorboat action sequences, a mysterious heroine in Jane Seymour's Solitaire, and a slam-bang title tune from Paul and Linda McCartney. A new era was about to begin.

James Bond (Roger Moore) races across Louisiana bayou country to escape drug gang killers in *Live and Let Die*. *Courtesy of the Anders Frejdh Collection*

THE CAST

James Bond	Roger Moore
Dr. Kananga / Mr. Big	Yaphet Kotto
Solitaire	Jane Seymour
Sheriff J. W. Pepper	Clifton James
Tee Hee	Julius Harris
Baron Samedi	Geoffrey Holder
Felix Leiter	David Hedison
Rosie Carver	Gloria Hendry
M	Bernard Lee
Miss Moneypenny	Lois Maxwell
Adam	Tommy Lane
Whisper	Earl Jolly Brown
Quarrel Jr.	Roy Stewart
Strutter	Lon Satton
Mrs. Bell	Ruth Kempf
Miss Caruso	Madeline Smith

THE CREW

Director	Guy Hamilton
Screenplay by	Tom Mankiewicz
Producers	Albert R. Broccoli
	Harry Saltzman
Director of Photography	Ted Moore
Music by	George Martin
Title song composed by	Paul McCartney &
	Linda McCartney
Supervising Art Director	Syd Cain
Costume Designer	Julie Harris
Production Supervisor	Claude Hudson
Assistant Director	Derek Cracknell
Stunt Coordinators	Bob Simmons
	Jerry Comeaux
	Ross Kananga
	Bill Bennet
	Eddie Smith
	Joie Chitwood
Choreographer	Geoffrey Holder
Title Designer	Maurice Binder
Special Effects	Derek Meddings
Editors	Bert Bates
	Raymond Poulton
	John Shirley

Cover of the 1960s era American paperback edition of Ian Fleming's *Live and Let Die*. *Steve Rubin Collection*

LIVING DAYLIGHTS, THE

(United Artists, 1987) ★★★: The fifteenth James Bond film produced by Albert R. Broccoli. US release date: July 31, 1987. Budget: $40 million. Worldwide box office gross: $191.2 million (US gross: $51.2 million; international gross: $140.0 million).* Running time: 131 minutes.

─────────── **THE SETUP** ───────────

Russian KGB general Georgi Koskov (Jeroen Krabbé) wants to defect to the West, and James Bond (Timothy Dalton) is sent to Bratislava, Czechoslovakia, to grease the wheels. Thanks to 007, Koskov's escape from a concert hall succeeds. Bond also shoots the sniper's rifle out of the hands of Kara Milovy (Maryam d'Abo), a beautiful cellist, who not only is protecting Koskov but is also his lover. In London, Koskov tells British intelligence that the KGB's General Pushkin (John Rhys-Davies) has invoked "Smiert Spionam," a plan to assassinate foreign spies, and advises that Pushkin be assassinated instead. In reality, this is all phony as a three-dollar bill. Koskov is working with arms trader Brad Whitaker (Joe Don Baker) to take $50 million in Russian funds earmarked for an arms purchase and use them for a giant drug deal.

─────── **BEHIND THE SCENES** ───────

Cheers for Timothy Dalton, who makes a stunning debut as James Bond in *The Living Daylights*! For those of us who grew up on Sean Connery's interpretation of 007, the Roger Moore era was a disappointment, largely because the films were just too jokey, the action sequences were not believable, and somehow Roger was just too nice to play a secret agent with a license to kill. Timothy Dalton brought back the

danger in Bond. You're never quite sure what he's going to do, and that makes his character intriguing. Dalton was a last-minute replacement after first choice Pierce Brosnan couldn't get out of his contract with the NBC series *Remington Steele*. *The Living Daylights* is also a very romantic film, thanks to the casting of Maryam d'Abo, who makes a very fetching Kara Milovy.

Unfortunately, the problem with the film is its lack of strong villains. As General Koskov, Jeroen Krabbé is too lovable to be dangerous—he hugs practically everyone he meets. Although Russians are stereotyped as being very demonstrative, the hugging begins to obscure the fact that Koskov is supposed to be a villainous drug trader.

The Living Daylights by Jeff Marshall. *Courtesy of Jeff Marshall*

─────────────────────────────────

* "The Living Daylights (1987)," The Numbers, accessed June 8, 2020, https://www.the -numbers.com/movie/Living-Daylights-The.

Brad Whitaker, meanwhile, is denied enough screen time to develop any true malice; he's an arms dealer who likes to play with toy soldiers. The only truly villainous character in the film is Koskov's henchman Necros, played effectively by Andreas Wisniewski, but he's also not on screen long enough to have any real impact. The result is that there's no real villain, at least not the kind you love to hate like Goldfinger or Blofeld.

The plot, meanwhile is another throwaway that would take an MIT graduate to figure out. Just as you're starting to figure out why Koskov and Whitaker are partners, the plot switches to a big drug deal in Afghanistan—talk about sharp left turns. But there are other highlights: the great teaser on Gibraltar, John Barry's warmly romantic music score, Art Malik's Kamran Shah, and Caroline Bliss's new Moneypenny.

THE CAST

James Bond	Timothy Dalton
Kara Milovy	Maryam d'Abo
General Georgi Koskov	Jeroen Krabbé
Brad Whitaker	Joe Don Baker
General Leonid Pushkin	John Rhys-Davies
Kamran Shah	Art Malik
Necros	Andreas Wisniewski
Saunders	Thomas Wheatley
Q	Desmond Llewelyn
M	Robert Brown
Minister of Defence	Geoffrey Keen
General Gogol	Walter Gotell
Miss Moneypenny	Caroline Bliss
Felix Leiter	John Terry
Rubavitch	Virginia Hey
Colonel Feyador	John Bowe
Rosika Miklos	Julie T. Wallace
Linda	Kell Tyler
Chief of Security, Tangier	Nadim Sawalha
Chief of the Snow Leopard Brotherhood	Tony Cyrus

THE CREW

Director	John Glen
Screenplay by	Richard Maibaum
	Michael G. Wilson
Producers	Albert R. Broccoli
	Michael G. Wilson
Associate Producers	Tom Pevsner
	Barbara Broccoli
Director of Photography	Alec Mills
Music by	John Barry
Title song performed by	a-ha
Production Designer	Peter Lamont
Second Unit Direction and Photography	Arthur Wooster
Action Sequence Supervisor	Paul Weston
Vehicle Stunt Coordinator	Remy Julienne
Title Designer	Maurice Binder
Special Effects Supervisor	John Richardson
Editors	John Grover
	Peter Davies

Llewelyn, Desmond (September 12, 1914–December 19, 1999): Tall, silver-haired Welsh character actor who effectively portrayed Q (a.k.a. Major Boothroyd), the long-suffering British Secret Service equipment officer. Llewelyn appeared in every James Bond film produced by United Artists from 1963 to 1995, except for *Live and Let Die*. Sadly, this fine actor died in a head-on traffic collision in East Sussex on December 19, 1999, as he was driving home from a book signing to promote his autobiography.

After actor Peter Burton briefly introduced the Major Boothroyd character in *Dr. No*, Llewelyn took over the role in *From Russia with Love*, where he introduced the iconic trick briefcase. A perfect foil to 007's frivolous attitude towards "gadgets," Q became one of the series' most enduring characters.

Born in Newport, Wales, Llewelyn made his credited motion picture debut in director and future Bond veteran Terence Young's World War II film *They Were Not Divided* (1950), working with future Bond players Edward Underdown (*Thunderball*), Michael Brennan, Anthony Dawson, Christopher Lee, and Peter Burton.

Actor Desmond Llewelyn and some of Q's gadgets, including the *From Russia with Love* briefcase. *Courtesy of the David Reinhardt Collection*

Lo Fat: Business partner of Hai Fat (Richard Loo) in one of screenwriter Tom Mankiewicz's early drafts of *The Man with the Golden Gun*. Thankfully, the character was later axed from the script.

Lochgilphead, Scotland: Hilly, rock-strewn location where the helicopter chase in *From Russia with Love* was shot. Piloting the SPECTRE chopper that day was former Royal Air Force captain John Crewdson.

Bond (Sean Connery) is chased by helicopter-borne SPECTRE gunmen in an iconic set piece in *From Russia with Love*. Director Terence Young was channeling director Alfred Hitchcock's crop duster plane chase in *North by Northwest*. *Courtesy of the David Reinhardt Collection*

Locke, Philip (March 29, 1928–April 19, 2004): Lean British character actor who portrayed Vargas, the sullen SPECTRE gunman and right arm of Emilio Largo (Adolfo Celi) in *Thunderball*. Born in St. Marylebone, London, Locke made his credited big-screen debut as the vicar in writer/director Jerome Epstein's comedy *Follow That Man* (1961).

Lockheed JetStar: Type of private jet owned by Goldfinger (Gert Fröbe) in the movie of the same name. Piloted by Miss Pussy Galore (Honor Blackman), it transports a tranquilized James Bond (Sean Connery) from Switzerland to Friendship Airport, Baltimore, and then continues on to Blue Grass Field, Kentucky. The stewardess on the flight is Mei-Lei (Mai Ling), and the copilot is Sydney (Tricia Muller).

Bond (Sean Connery) discovers he's being observed in the restroom aboard Goldfinger's Lockheed JetStar in *Goldfinger*. *Courtesy of the Anders Frejdh Collection*

Log Cabin Girl: Gorgeous Austrian blonde, portrayed by British actress Sue Vanner, who betrays Bond (Roger Moore) to the KGB in *The Spy Who Loved Me* pre-credits teaser.

London: Target of Mischa, a Russian satellite commandeered by the Janus crime syndicate and primed to destroy the city's electronic grid in *GoldenEye*. Janus crime syndicate head Alec Trevelyan (Sean Bean) and his cohorts plan to break into the Bank of England seconds before the satellite's GoldenEye weapons system destroys all records of transactions—not just bank records, but tax records and all land records—an event that will cause worldwide economic meltdown. It will also make them a *&^%load of cash.

Lonsdale, Michael (May 24, 1931–   ): French actor who portrayed billionaire industrialist Hugo Drax with a strong dose of dry wit and sarcasm in *Moonraker*. A Parisian by birth, Lonsdale made his motion picture debut as Sinclair in director Michel Boisrond's comedy *It Happened in Aden* (1956). His first English-language film was Orson Welles's thriller *The Trial* (1962). Lonsdale's additional feature appearances include *Is Paris Burning?* (1966); *The Day of the Jackal* (1973); *Chariots of Fire* (1981); *Enigma* (1982); *The Holcroft Covenant* (1985); *The Name of the Rose* (1986), working with Sean Connery; *The Remains of the Day* (1993); *Jefferson in Paris* (1995), as Louis XVI; *Ronin* (1998), alongside fellow Bond villains Sean Bean and Jonathan Pryce; and Steven Spielberg's *Munich* (2005), with Daniel Craig and Mathieu Amalric.

Loo, Richard (October 1, 1903–November 20, 1983): Chinese American character actor who portrayed sinister industrialist Hai Fat in *The Man with the Golden Gun*. Though Chinese by ancestry and Hawaiian by birth, Loo was the go-to Japanese villain in scores of wartime movies throughout the 1930s and 1940s. He made his credited feature debut as Charlie San in director Richard Thorpe's murder mystery *The Secrets of Wu Sin* (1932). Although Loo could sneer with the best Japanese Army screen villains, he could also play sympathetic characters, as he did in Sam Fuller's *The Steel Helmet* (1951), as American Sergeant Tanaka, and *Love Is a Many Splendored Thing* (1955).

L'Or Noir: Name of the casino in Azerbaijan run by Valentin Zukovsky (Robbie Coltrane) in *The World Is Not Enough*. In this casino everyone wears a gun, even the female playgirls (something we see thanks to Bond's X-ray glasses).

Lord, Jack (December 30, 1920–January 21, 1998; birth name: John Joseph Patrick Ryan): American tough-guy actor who was the first to portray CIA agent Felix Leiter when the character made its debut in *Dr. No* in 1962. Unlike some of the later Leiters, who were given comic support roles almost to the point of high camp, Lord's CIA man is strictly no-nonsense. The only time we get the hint of a smile is when Lord's Leiter finds Bond in a clinch with Honey Ryder (Ursula Andress) in the motorboat at the film's conclusion. From *Dr. No*, Lord went on to portray another serious detective in the tropics:

Steve McGarrett in the original hit series *Hawaii Five-O* (281 episodes, 1968–1980). A New York City native, Lord made his motion picture debut in writer/director Edward J. Montagne's action-drama *Project X* (1949).

Lorre, Peter (June 26, 1904–March 23, 1964; birth name: László Löwenstein): Distinctive-voiced Hungarian character actor who portrayed the first James Bond villain, Le Chiffre, in the CBS live television adaptation of *Casino Royale* in 1954. Lorre's nemesis is an Americanized James Bond portrayed by Barry Nelson. Born in Rózsahegy, Austria-Hungary (now Ružomberok, Slovakia), Lorre made his credited motion picture debut as Hans Beckert in director Fritz Lang's cele-brated crime drama *M* (1931). Three years later, he made his English-language debut as Abbott in Alfred Hitchcock's *The Man Who Knew Too Much* (1934). Lorre's desperate, unctuous presence was often played against the sinister, imposing Sydney Greenstreet in films such as *The Maltese Falcon* (1941) and *Casablanca* (1942).

Peter Lorre was the first Le Chiffre in the CBS TV version of *Casino Royale*. *Steve Rubin Collection*

Lotus Esprit submarine car: Fabulous trick sports car employed by James Bond (Roger Moore) in both *The Spy Who Loved Me* and *For Your Eyes Only*. Nicknamed "Wet Nellie," an homage to the weapon-laden autogyro Little Nellie in *You Only Live Twice*, the Lotus was another example of how the Bond team could rise to the occasion and top the effects of their previous films.

Motorized by Perry Oceanographics of Miami, the submarine car, which was referred to as "Esther Williams" in an early draft of the screenplay, was actually the product of two film geniuses: production designer Ken Adam and special effects supervisor Derek Meddings. Remembered Meddings, "When we decided to turn a sports car into a submarine, Ken Adam came to me with the suggestion that we use the

James Bond (Roger Moore) and his Lotus Esprit, which turned into a submarine in *The Spy Who Loved Me. Courtesy of the David Reinhardt Collection*

shell of the new Lotus Esprit. Neither of us knew anything about the aquadynamics of underwater driving, but we went ahead with the Lotus because it was the most beautiful car we could find in England—it had to be an English car, of course.

"The car was then given to us in shell form from the Lotus factory. We had five or six of the shells, and into each we built a special operating effect. First, to give the car the underwater streamlined effect, we had to create wheels that could disappear inside the body, and wheel arches that came down and filled in the space. We then built louvers that would go into place over the windshield, to create the impression of strengthening the glass against underwater pressure. The special modifications, such as the surface-to-air missile launcher, the underwater rockets, and the mine-laying panel, were all constructed and perfected in the Pinewood special effects shop."*

When the Pinewood unit had finished its modifications, Meddings transported the shell of the Lotus over to Miami and to Perry Oceanographics, a unique underwater engineering firm that built submarines and underwater scooters for the US Navy. They were the final authority on

Wet Nellie's seaworthiness. "Only one car was equipped to work underwater," Meddings remembered. "It had an engine, and you could drive it underwater like an airplane. When it turned, it would bank, and it would dive and climb. Two men were assigned to drive it."

These drivers would sit in an interior compartment that was completely flooded with water. Recalled Ken Adam, who was returning to the Bond series after a five-year layoff, "We didn't want a dry submersible. When you build something that has an air compartment, you have problems with ballast. You're faced with the problem of continually pumping ballast in and out of the car, and that was something we wanted to avoid." Instead, he said, "we went over to Miami, showed them the designs on our car, and asked them if they could motorize it and create a 'wet submersible.' . . . The plan was to go with two skin divers driving the vehicle. They would be wearing breathing apparatuses, but because of the louvers over the front windscreen, you wouldn't be able to see these devices clearly.

"The Perry people looked at our designs and said they could motorize the car. They also gave us the idea of having our divers use a rebreather unit that didn't leave a telltale trail of bubbles. However, we ended up going back to regular aqualungs, not only because they were much safer, but we realized that without any bubbles coming from the car, we were sacrificing a degree of realism. With the bubbles trailing the car from the aqualungs, we had a much more realistic picture of a car moving underwater. The last thing

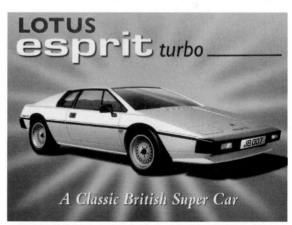

Catalog shot of James Bond's "Wet Nellie" Lotus Esprit from *The Spy Who Loved Me. Courtesy of the David Reinhardt Collection*

---

* Derek Meddings, interview by the author, London, June 27, 1977.

we wanted was the audience to get the impression we were using a model car in a studio tank."*

The underwater sequences with the motorized Lotus Esprit were filmed in the crystal-clear waters of the Bahamas by veteran underwater cinematographer Lamar Boren, who was also returning to the Bond series after a long absence.

Lovers, the: A tarot card featured in the deck of the mysterious Solitaire (Jane Seymour) in *Live and Let Die*. To Solitaire, it symbolizes the potential of romance and love between two strangers. In order to trick her into switching allegiances, James Bond (Roger Moore) brings a rigged deck of tarot cards to her sanctuary on the island of San Monique. When asked to pick a card, Solitaire picks the Lovers, unaware that the deck consists entirely of Lovers cards. Convinced that she is destined to lose her virginity and her power to Bond, Solitaire gives in. You'd think that a seer of her power would know better. In any case, this plot device would never work today, for obvious reasons.

low-grade iron pyrites: What Professor R. J. Dent (Anthony Dawson) disingenuously calls the radioactive ore samples discovered by John Strangways (Tim Moxon) in *Dr. No*.

Lowell, Carey (February 11, 1961–   ): Tall, beautiful American actress and former model who portrayed CIA undercover operative Pam Bouvier in *Licence to Kill*. Lowell is the highlight of the film, a fresh-faced, intelligent, gutsy fellow agent who lends Bond (Timothy Dalton) a resourceful hand against South American drug lord Franz Sanchez (Robert Davi). In many ways, she perfectly represented the new action woman of the 1980s—à la Sigourney Weaver in *Aliens* (1986)—who can handle herself just as well as a man and whose presence helps alleviate a dangerous situation rather than compounding it. A native of Huntington, New York, Lowell made her feature film debut as Julie in director Albert Pyun's crime thriller *Dangerously Close* (1986). Once married to actor Richard Gere, she is probably best known to TV viewers as ADA Jamie Ross on *Law & Order* (49 episodes, 1996–2001).

lox: Abbreviation for "liquid oxygen," a rocket propellant featured in *You Only Live Twice*. At first, Japanese Secret Service chief Tiger Tanaka (Tetsuro Tamba) thinks that the lox shipment identified on an invoiced order for naval stores is smoked salmon. Bond (Sean Connery) correctly identifies it as rocket fuel.

Lulu (November 3, 1948–   ; birth name: Marie McDonald McLaughlin Lawrie): Multitalented Scottish pop singer, actress, and media star who sang the bouncy title song to *The Man with the Golden Gun*. Prior to her Bond experience, the Glagow native had scored with the international hit song "To Sir with Love," which she sang in the popular 1967 film of the same name.

Lulu sang the zesty title song to *The Man with the Golden Gun*. *Steve Rubin Collection*

Lundigan, William (June 12, 1914–December 20, 1975): Distinctive-voiced American actor and former radio announcer who was hosting CBS's Climax Mystery Theater on the night of October 21, 1954, when Ian Fleming's *Casino Royale* made its debut as a live, one-hour television show. Lundigan was thus the first person to introduce the screen adventures of Ian Fleming's James Bond to the public.

Lundigan appeared on screen while holding a baccarat "shoe," the significance of which he explains in his opening remarks: "Good evening. This doesn't look dangerous, does it? But it's killed plenty of men and women. It's made beggars of many and millionaires of a few, mighty few. In French gambling casinos, this is called a shoe. It holds the cards for baccarat—king of gambling games—and its purpose is to make sure that no one can pull any funny business, like dealing from the bottom. The game to be played tonight is for the highest stakes of all. A man is going to wager his life. Climax presents *Casino Royale* from the bestseller by Ian Fleming. It stars Barry Nelson, Peter Lorre and Linda Christian. And now, *Casino Royale*."

---

* Ken Adam, interview by the author, London, June 17, 1977.

Lynch, Lashana

(November 27, 1987–   ):
British actress of film and
television who portrayed
Nomi, MI6's new agent
007 following the retire-
ment of James Bond
(Daniel Craig) in *No
Time to Die*. A woman of
Jamaican descent, Lynch
made her motion picture
debut as Belle Newman
in director Regan Hall's
sports drama *Fast Girls*
(2012). Prior to Bond,
she was best known for
playing the title charac-
ter's best friend, Maria
Rambeau, in the Marvel
blockbuster *Captain
Marvel* (2019).

Lashana Lynch
becomes the first
woman to take on the
double-0 prefix in *No
Time to Die*. *Courtesy
of the Anders Frejdh
Collection*

But Vesper later becomes a useful ally to
Bond, especially when she discovers him nearly
dead in his car from being poisoned by Le Chiffre's girlfriend, Valenka (Ivana Milicevic). Connect-
ing a wire from a portable defibrillator, Vesper
pushes the right button and brings 007 back, a
life-saving procedure that not only jump-starts
their romance but also revives his poker fortunes.
However, Vesper is much more than she appears.
In reality, she is a blackmail victim who will do
anything to save the life of her Algerian lover—
even sacrifice the life of James Bond and betray
the British Secret Service.

In the 1967 *Casino Royale* spoof, actress
Ursula Andress portrayed Vesper as a seductress
and double agent who lures British card expert
Evelyn Tremble (Peter Sellers) into her boudoir,
where they frolic to the moody strains of Dusty
Springfield's "The Look of Love."

Nomi (Lashana Lynch) outfitted for action in *No
Time to Die*. *Courtesy of United Artists Releasing*

Lynd, Vesper

Lynd, Vesper: Gorgeous international liaison
officer from Her Majesty's Treasury's Financial
Action Task Force, portrayed by Eva Green
in *Casino Royale*. She's assigned by M (Dame
Judi Dench) to make sure that James Bond
(Daniel Craig) adequately manages a hefty
gambling stake of 20 million pounds. Bond is
being bankrolled to take down Le Chiffre (Mads
Mikkelsen), an enemy agent with ties to major
terrorist organizations around the world, in a
high-stakes poker tournament. At first, Vesper is
cool to Bond, and the coolness increases when
Bond proceeds to lose his stake to Le Chiffre in a
disastrous hand of Texas hold'em.

Actress Eva Green brought a smoldering sexuality
to the role of British treasury agent Vesper Lynd in
Casino Royale. *Courtesy of the Anders Frejdh Collection*

M: James Bond's crusty superior and the head of the British Secret Service. Venerable British character actor Bernard Lee became the first M in *Dr. No* in 1962, and played him in every Eon Productions Bond movie until his death in 1981. As portrayed by Lee, M was a conservative, almost fatherly figure who put up with 007's increasingly outrageous behavior because he knew that Bond was his best agent, the only man he could trust on the most dangerous assignments.

M's office, disguised as Universal Exports in London, was always the starting point for Bond (Sean Connery)—a temporary haven where 007 traded double entendres with Miss Moneypenny (Lois Maxwell) and received his careful briefing from M. Today, there is something very nostalgic about that office—the leather double doors with the red and green warning lights; the warm, leathery naval decor of the room, with its ship models, paintings, and assorted bric-a-brac; and the quiet, low-key M himself—smoking his pipe, ready to send 007 out on one more impossible mission.

When Roger Moore took over the role of Bond in 1973, his relationship with M lost quite a bit of its subtlety. The sour interplay between M and Q (Desmond Llewelyn) in *The Man with the Golden Gun* was a definite low point. For Bernard Lee, however, the parts became a bit more mobile, with M and his secretary visiting Bond on location in Egypt and the Far East. And in *The Spy Who Loved Me*, he got a first name, Miles—a reference to his identity in the original Fleming novels, Admiral Sir Miles Messervy, KCMG.

When Lee died before filming began on *For Your Eyes Only*, producer Albert R. Broccoli's interim choice as Bond's superior was actor James Villiers, who portrayed Secret Service chief of staff Tanner. Robert Brown, who had earlier been introduced as Admiral Hargreaves in *The*

Beginning with *GoldenEye*, Dame Judi Dench brought her formidable acting experience to the role of M. *Courtesy of the Anders Frejdh Collection*

Bernard Lee introduced the role of M, the no-nonsense head of British MI6, in *Dr. No* and played him beautifully until his death in 1981. *Courtesy of the David Reinhardt Collection*

Ralph Fiennes brings his considerable acting skills to the role of M in *No Time to Die*. *Courtesy of the Anders Frejdh Collection*

Spy Who Loved Me, took over as the official new M in *Octopussy*—playing him in much the same manner as Lee.

The character was less helpful in the non-Eon Bond films. In producer Jack Schwartzman's *Never Say Never Again*, Edward Fox played M as a contemptuous bureaucrat. And in the 1967 *Casino Royale* spoof, played by John Huston in an incredibly bright red wig, M orders a mortar strike on the country manor of an uncooperative Sir James Bond (David Niven), and apparently dies when a barrage falls short.

The official series took a six-year hiatus from 1989 to 1995, after which Bond returned in the guise of Pierce Brosnan and Dame Judi Dench was introduced as the new M in *GoldenEye*. Dench, a brilliant actress, brought new dimension to the British Secret Service chief. She's the one who looks straight at James Bond and characterizes him as "a sexist, misogynist dinosaur, a relic of the Cold War." However, like her predecessors, she supports him in every way possible. In the script for *GoldenEye*, her character's real name is given as Barbara Mawdsley.

Her role in the James Bond films continued through the remaining Brosnan films and into the Daniel Craig era, reaching its peak in *Skyfall*, in which she teams with 007 to battle revenge-seeking Silva (Javier Bardem)—a confrontation that sadly leads to her demise in Bond's arms. On the box of the gift she leaves

for Bond in her will, it's possible to discern her real name—Olivia Mansfield, which suggests that Dench may have been playing a different M opposite Craig than in the Brosnan films.

Upon her death, Mansfield's duties were taken over by Gareth Mallory (Ralph Fiennes) who is the current M of record.

Macnee, Patrick (February 6, 1922–June 25, 2015): Dapper British actor, best known for the television series *The Avengers*, who joined James Bond (Roger Moore) as fellow agent and horse expert Sir Godfrey Tibbett in *A View to a Kill*. Working undercover as Bond's chauffeur, Tibbett provides much of the film's early comic relief as he stumbles around with 007's luggage and chafes at Bond's condescending remarks as they try to trick the security team of billionaire industrialist Max Zorin (Christopher Walken).

Born in Paddington, London, Macnee made his credited big-screen debut as Tony in director Mario Zampi's thriller *The Fatal Night* (1948). After years of film and television roles, Macnee struck gold when he assumed the role of British

Actor Patrick Macnee, a veteran of TV's *The Avengers* (with fellow Bond veteran Diana Rigg), joined the cast of *A View to a Kill*. *Steve Rubin Collection*

agent John Steed in *The Avengers* (159 episodes, 1961–1969). His first female partner was none other than Honor Blackman, who would soon take the iconic role of Pussy Galore in *Goldfinger*. When Blackman left the series to pursue her film career, she was replaced by a fetching Diana Rigg, who made a strong impression as the athletic Emma Peel. She would later leave the series herself to join James Bond (George Lazenby) in *On Her Majesty's Secret Service*.

Madagascar: Island off East Africa where Bond (Daniel Craig) tracks Mollaka (Sébastien Foucan), a terrorist bomb maker, in *Casino Royale*. He's introduced at an outdoor fighting competition between a cobra and a mongoose, surrounded by bettors. This is followed by an extraordinary foot chase through a construction site, employing the latest parkour moves. All of this was actually shot in the Bahamas on an abandoned hotel site at Coral Harbour. The same site was used to film hotel rooms for *Thunderball* and as a camera platform for Derek Meddings's special effects crew on *The Spy Who Loved Me*.

Madagascar black scorpion: The species of scorpion employed by Mr. Wint (Bruce Glover) to kill Dr. Tynan, the unfortunate South African dentist/smuggler in *Diamonds Are Forever*. For this sequence, which was shot in the desert outside Las Vegas, Glover was shown a selection of twenty-five scorpions, including the large Madagascar variety and its smaller yet more deadly California cousins. Fortunately, the little buggers were without their stingers, which had been conveniently clipped.

Madonna (August 16, 1958–   ; birth name: Madonna Louise Ciccone): American pop singing sensation—legendary for favorites like "Material Girl" and "Like a Virgin"—who performed the title tune in *Die Another Day* and made a decidedly low-key cameo appearance in the film as a fencing instructor at the Blades fencing club in London. A native of Bay City, Michigan, Madonna made her big-screen acting debut as a club singer in director Harold Becker's coming-of-age drama *Vision Quest* (1985). That same year, she made a more indelible impression opposite Rosanna Arquette, portraying the title character in director Susan Seidelman's

dramedy *Desperately Seeking Susan* (1985). Her performance as wisecracking women's league baseball player Mae Mordabito in director Penny Marshall's period dramedy *A League of Their Own* (1992) was also a standout.

Madsen, Michael (September 25, 1957–   ): Tough-guy American actor who portrayed no-nonsense NSA field commander Damian Falco in *Die Another Day*. Madsen told Empire Online that originally he was asked to play a character who "gets killed by a death ray from space"—presumably referring to the Icarus satellite laser deployed by smarmy billionaire Gustav Graves (Toby Stephens). But he held out for a role that might recur in subsequent Bond films. "They told me I could be introduced as a recurring character, so I'd come back in Bond 21 and 22, and then they said if I got tired of it, they'd assassinate me and Bond could use my death as a vengeful reason to do something," he laughed, saying his young sons would never let him live it down if he got killed off in a James Bond film.* Though Falco did indeed survive *Die Another Day*, with the end of the Pierce Brosnan era, the character never returned to the series. A native of Chicago, the prolific Madsen made his feature film debut as Cecil Moe in director Edward T. McDougal's biographical drama *Against All Hope* (1982). A favorite of writer/director Quentin Tarantino, Madsen has appeared in *Reservoir Dogs* (1992), *Kill Bill: Volume 1* (2003)

Actor Michael Madsen was NSA agent Damian Falco in *Die Another Day*. *Steve Rubin Collection*

---

* Willow Green, "Exclusive: Bond Talk—Empire Online Sits Down with Michael Madsen," Empire Online, June 23, 2002, http://www.empireonline.co.uk/news/news.asp?story=3988 (URL discontinued).

and *Kill Bill: Volume 2* (2004), *The Hateful Eight* (2015), and *Once Upon a Time in Hollywood* (2019).

Magda: Circus performer, seasoned pickpocket, card-carrying member of the Octopus Cult, and all-around girl Friday—second in command to Octopussy (Maud Adams) and assistant/mistress to Kamal Khan (Louis Jourdan)—portrayed by Swedish actress Kristina Wayborn in *Octopussy*. Magda first meets Bond (Roger Moore) briefly in London at a Sotheby's auction for a rare Fabergé egg. They're reunited in a casino in Udaipur, India, and they eventually spend a passionate night in 007's hotel suite—until Magda steals the genuine Fabergé egg Bond switched for a fake at the auction.

Magda's name is actually mentioned only once in the film—when Kamal formally introduces her to Bond at the Monsoon Palace dinner. On the East German border, she helps Octopussy prepare documents for the border guards, then performs magic tricks in the circus procession through Feldstadt Air Base. She even lifts the

Swedish beauty Kristina Wayborn portrayed Magda, Kamal Khan's girl Friday in *Octopussy*. *Steve Rubin Collection*

wallet of the US Air Force base commander (Bruce Boa)—unaware that Kamal Khan and his co-conspirator General Orlov (Steven Berkoff) are using the circus as cover to detonate a nuclear bomb. After 007 exposes the plot and disarms the bomb, the swift-kicking Magda returns to Udaipur, leading her fellow acrobats in the successful assault on Kamal's Monsoon Palace.

Maginot Line: A string of fortifications (named after French minister of war André Maginot) erected along the French-German frontier prior to World War II that were completely outflanked by Hitler's armored blitzkrieg through France and the Low Countries in the summer of 1940. During the winter of 1967–1968, Bond producer Harry Saltzman and production designer Syd Cain toured the line, searching for a possible redoubt for Ernst Stavro Blofeld in *On Her Majesty's Secret Service*.

Accompanied by a group of French officials, they were given a complete tour of a key position southeast of Metz. Saltzman and Cain trudged along miles of concrete tunnels, viewing the facilities that were designed to support a huge French army in static defense. After five and a half hours of walking among huge gun emplacements, underground airfields, and railroads, Saltzman turned to Cain and asked, "What do you think?" Replied Cain, "I think we can build all of this in the studio."[*]

In the end, Eon Productions was spared that chore when the unit discovered Piz Gloria, the marvelous mountaintop restaurant above Mürren, Switzerland, that eventually became the stronghold (and allergy research center) of Blofeld (Telly Savalas) in the film.

Maibaum, Richard (May 26, 1909–January 4, 1991): American scribe of stage and screen who wrote or cowrote thirteen James Bond movies, beginning with *Dr. No*. Maibaum was an honored New York playwright by the time he began his screenwriting career in the 1930s. Prior to the Bond films, he had worked for producer Albert R. Broccoli and his first producing partner, Irving Allen, on a number of adventure films, including *Paratrooper* (1953), *Hell Below Zero* (1954), and *Zarak* (1956). But it was the assignment of a lifetime—introducing James Bond to cinema

---

[*] Syd Cain, interview by the author, London, June 18, 1977.

Screenwriter Richard Maibaum (far left) joins the cast and creators of *The Man with the Golden Gun* (producer Albert R. "Cubby" Broccoli is at far right; director Guy Hamilton is to the right of Christopher Lee, center back). *Courtesy of the Paul Maibaum Collection*

audiences—that proved to be Maibaum's ticket to international acclaim.

It's not surprising that Broccoli chose an American to be the first to dramatize Bond for the big screen. Broccoli's contention all along, even as he and Saltzman were selling the series to United Artists, was that Bond had to possess the qualities that would appeal to an American audience. He had to be a ballsy Englishman, a sexy two-fisted agent in the style of Philip Marlowe and Sam Spade. Maibaum knew that character type well.

He also brought to the project an element that was not a part of Ian Fleming's novels: humor. Maibaum brightened the dark action of the books with clever lines—often placing them at the end of a particularly hair-raising stunt or set piece. Thus, having been taken to the edge of their seats, audiences were allowed to release their tension through laughter (or at least a

chuckle). It was called "throwaway humor"—a stylish, effective touch, especially when the lines were delivered by the sly and sexy Sean Connery.

Maibaum also shaped the films' approach to sex through his enthusiastic depiction of Bond's sexual appetites. Although it certainly helped that the films featured some of the most beautiful women ever seen on the silver screen, Maibaum was the one who established the playful antics of 007, with teasing love scenes that conveyed everything and showed nothing. Thanks to Maibaum's screenwriting skills, the early Bond movies moved flawlessly from danger to humor to sex and back again.

But the trendsetting style of the early Bonds couldn't survive the changing of the guard. After working on the first four Bond films, Maibaum became an off-and-on contributor to the series, and by the time Roger Moore took over the role of 007, the films, though still exciting and wonderfully inventive, had lost some of their early charm. After sitting out *Moonraker* in favor of Christopher Wood, who created the silliest yet one of the most successful films in the series, Maibaum returned on *For Your Eyes Only* to, in his own words, "pull the balloon down."* Working from two Ian Fleming short stories, "For Your Eyes Only" and "Risico," he anchored the story in a fascinating blood feud among former Greek partisans, reminiscent of *From Russia with Love*. The only scene in the entire film that rings false is the ridiculous encounter in the pre-credits teaser between Bond (Roger Moore) and a character obviously intended to be Blofeld (but, for legal reasons, not identified as such)—who, in return for sparing his life, offers Bond a "delicatessen in stainless steel." Maibaum later claimed that someone else wrote that embarrassing line.

Starting with *For Your Eyes Only*, Maibaum shared screenwriting duties with producer Michael G. Wilson (Albert R. Broccoli's stepson).

Screenwriter Richard Maibaum shares a point with author Ian Fleming and the Dutchess of Bedford during the premiere of *From Russia with Love*. *Courtesy of the Paul Maibaum Collection*

A lawyer and engineer, Wilson had worked on the Bond films in various capacities for the better part of two decades. Maibaum, who had been something of a lone-wolf writer in his career, told Cubby Broccoli that he was perfectly willing to work with Wilson. The result on *For Your Eyes Only* was, to quote Humphrey Bogart in *Casablanca*, the "beginning of a beautiful friendship."

"I think *For Your Eyes Only* turned out pretty well," remembered Maibaum, "except for the teaser, which was one of the worst in terms of audience reaction. I particularly liked Carole Bouquet, who played Melina. She was cool and beautiful, and she could hold her own alongside Bond. And the villains were very believable."[†]

For the next film, *Octopussy*, Maibaum once again worked with Wilson. And George MacDonald Fraser, who wrote the *Flashman* novels, also contributed a script draft. "We started with two elements," Maibaum remembered,

Screenwriter Richard Maibaum at home in his bar with its 007 wallpaper in Pacific Palisades, California. *Courtesy of the Paul Maibaum Collection*

---

* Richard Maibaum, interview by the author, Los Angeles, April 30, 1977.

† Ibid.

"Fleming's *Octopussy* novella, and a short story called 'The Property of a Lady.' That proved to be the springboard for the story.

"George came on and worked on a draft and came up with a lot of the elements dealing with the Fabergé eggs. He worked with Michael, then I was brought back to do the shooting script. We had a devil of a time coming up with a story about Octopussy, but it helped when we discovered that there actually is an organization in Japan composed entirely of women—a kind of female Mafia. And since we had once considered India as a location, it became the basis of this den of female thieves, led by a woman named Octopussy."

After *A View to a Kill*, the guard changed again with the arrival of Timothy Dalton as Bond. Says Maibaum, "We knew we had to get a younger man. Roger was maturing, and the film audiences were getting younger. It was time for a change." In actuality, *The Living Daylights* was written with Pierce Brosnan in mind rather than Dalton, but when Brosnan couldn't get out of his contract to the TV series *Remington Steele*, Dalton was a last-minute replacement.

That film was followed by *Licence to Kill*, Maibaum's final Bond credit. On that project, Maibaum was unable to do any rewriting on the script due to the Writers Guild strike of 1988. Faced with fan reaction that the film was too serious, that there wasn't enough humor, and that the story seemed bland, Maibaum pointed to the villain's scheme—a plot to render drug smuggling operations undetectable to international law enforcement—as a key problem. "There was very little fantasy about *Licence to Kill*," he said. "The villain's caper was bland when you compare it to destroying Fort Knox or the food supply of the world. And Bond shouldn't be so damn funereal. There should have been more humor."

Richard Maibaum was a New York City native. He made his motion picture writing debut on director Joseph Santley's comedy *We Went to College* (1936). That same year, he cowrote the musical comedy *Gold Diggers of 1937*.

Main Strike Mine: Abandoned Northern California silver mine purchased by Max Zorin (Christopher Walken) in *A View to a Kill*. Situated above the San Andreas Fault, it becomes the nucleus of Project Main Strike, Zorin's deadly plot to destroy Silicon Valley by creating a

Max Zorin (Christopher Walken) prepares to turn the Main Strike Mine into a catalyst for apocalypse in *A View to a Kill*. *Courtesy of the Luc Leclech Collection*

massive earthquake. Zorin intends to detonate a mountain of high explosives planted beneath the mine's principal shaft, thereby creating enough force to not only trigger a quake along the San Andreas Fault but also activate the nearby Hayward Fault as well. The twin killer quakes, timed to strike at the height of spring tide, will drown Silicon Valley under a massive lake.

Maitland, Marne (December 18, 1914–1992): Indian British character actor who portrayed Lazar, the Portuguese gunsmith who manufactures golden bullets for Francisco Scaramanga (Christopher Lee) in *The Man with the*

Actor Marne Maitland of *The Man with the Golden Gun*. *Steve Rubin Collection*

Golden Gun. Born in Calcutta, Maitland made his big-screen debut in director David MacDonald's crime drama *Cairo Road* (1950), which also featured future Bond players Eric Pohlmann (the voice of Blofeld in *From Russia with Love* and *Thunderball*) and Walter Gotell.

Malek, Rami (May 12, 1981–   ): Academy Award–winning American actor who portrayed principal villain Safin in *No Time to Die*. A Los Angeles native, Malek received his Oscar for his astonishing portrait of Freddie Mercury in *Bohemian Rhapsody* (2018).

Rami Malek brings the scarred Safin to life in *No Time to Die. Courtesy of United Artists Releasing*

Film audiences first noticed him as the pharaoh Ahkmenrah in *Night at the Museum* (2006), his feature film debut, and its two sequels. Malek also has a huge television following for his portrayal of hacker Elliot Alderson in the series *Mr. Robot* (45 episodes, 2015–2019).

Malik, Art (November 13, 1952–   ): Pakistani film and television actor, raised in England, who portrayed Kamran Shah, an Afghani mujahideen rebel leader who helps James Bond (Timothy Dalton) in *The Living Daylights*. A native of Bahawalpur, Pakistan, Malik made his motion picture debut in director Anthony Harvey's *Richard's Things* (1980), which also featured Bond veteran Peter Burton.

Actor Art Malik of *The Living Daylights. Steve Rubin Collection*

Mallet, Tania (May 19, 1941–March 30, 2019): Striking, highly paid British fashion model who reluctantly took the part of Tilly Masterson in *Goldfinger* as an experiment—securing her place in the pantheon of great Bond women—then returned to modeling. A native of Blackpool,

Sean Connery and Tania Mallet take a moment to relax between scenes in Switzerland in *Goldfinger Courtesy of the Anders Frejdh Collection*

Lancashire, England, Mallet played only one other screen role: the part of Sara on the television series *The New Avengers* (1 episode, 1976), starring Bond players Patrick Macnee (*A View to a Kill*) and Joanna Lumley (*On Her Majesty's Secret Service*).

Mallory, Gareth: The second M of the Daniel Craig era, portrayed by Ralph Fiennes and introduced in *Skyfall*. When SPECTRE agent Patrice (Ola Rapace) escapes from Bond with a stolen hard drive containing the names of NATO agents embedded in international terrorist organizations, the previous M (Dame Judi Dench) is dressed down by Mallory, who is introduced as the new chairman of Britain's Intelligence and Security Committee. She's told that she will be quietly relieved of her position—after a two-month transition, she'll receive the GCMG (Dame Grand Cross) and retire with full honors.

Ralph Fiennes joins MI6 in *Skyfall*, portraying British intelligence chief Gareth Mallory. *Courtesy of the Anders Frejdh Collection*

It's Golden Gun versus Walther, the ultimate show-down in *The Man with the Golden Gun*. *Courtesy of the David Reinhardt Collection*

But she vows to fight on—and ultimately dies at the hands of vengeful former agent Silva (Javier Bardem). Upon her death, Mallory is officially installed as the new M.

MAN WITH THE GOLDEN GUN, THE

(United Artists, 1974) ★★: The ninth James Bond film produced by Albert R. Broccoli and Harry Saltzman. US release date: December 20, 1974. Budget: $7 million. Worldwide box office gross: $97.6 million (US domestic gross: $21.0 million; international gross: $76.6 million).* Running time: 125 minutes.

THE SETUP

James Bond (Roger Moore) is summoned by M (Bernard Lee) and informed that he has received an unusual piece of mail: a solid gold bullet engraved with his number—007. Bond knows what this means: it's the ominous calling card of deadly assassin Francisco Scaramanga (Christopher Lee), a hired killer who charges his clients $1 million per shot. After Scaramanga murders a solar energy expert, Bond learns that the assassin may be responsible for stealing the "solex agitator," a device that can turn solar energy into a deadly beam weapon. From Beirut to Macao to Bangkok, to the exotic islands off the coast of Thailand, Bond trails Scaramanga—a chase that leads to the ultimate showdown.

* "The Man with the Golden Gun (1974)," The Numbers, accessed June 10, 2020, https://www.the-numbers.com /movie/Man-with-the-Golden-Gun-The.

BEHIND THE SCENES

The Man with the Golden Gun was a 007 misfire. Is director Guy Hamilton the same filmmaker who directed *Goldfinger*? Apparently not, because *The Man with the Golden Gun* is about as subtle as an elephant stampede—which would have been included in the film had producer Harry Saltzman gotten his way. (See "Saltzman and the elephant shoes.")

The biggest problem with the film is that the title villain, Scaramanga, portrayed by Christopher Lee, is much too sympathetic. In fact, the part was a respite for Lee, who for years had been typecast as fiendish horror villains like Dracula and Frankenstein's monster. As Scaramanga, by contrast, he's a dashing high-priced assassin with a great-looking girlfriend, a sleek wardrobe, and an incredible island home. At one point in the story, Scaramanga even tells Bond a tragic tale of how his pet elephant was brutally killed in the circus, and how he turned to a life of crime by bumping off the elephant's murderer. This type of story reveals the similarities between Bond and Scaramanga and how they should have been fighting on the same side—but does nothing to increase Scaramanga's potency as a classic Bond villain.

What's more, M and Q are reduced to a couple of insufferable magpies, Bond's Far Eastern secretary, Mary Goodnight, who was such a fine character in the books, is portrayed by Britt Ekland as a blundering buffoon, and the action sequences all lack credibility. One of the movie's most innovative stunts—the 360-degree bridge

James Bond (Roger Moore) joins forces with a couple of kung fu experts in *The Man with the Golden Gun*.
Courtesy of the David Reinhardt Collection

jump during a car chase in Thailand—is ruined by slow-motion photography, a slide whistle sound effect, and a gratuitous appearance by bumbling Louisiana sheriff J. W. Pepper (Clifton James) from *Live and Let Die*.

High points: Hervé Villechaize as Nick Nack, the perfect Bond henchman (a kind of miniature Oddjob); those incredible prehistoric islands off the coast of Thailand; and the crackling title track by pop star Lulu. A file-and-forget-it Bond adventure.

—— **THE CAST** ——

James Bond	Roger Moore
Francisco Scaramanga	Christopher Lee
Mary Goodnight	Britt Ekland
Andrea Anders	Maud Adams
Nick Nack	Hervé Villechaize
Sheriff J. W. Pepper	Clifton James
Hip	Soon-Taik Oh
Hai Fat	Richard Loo
Rodney	Marc Lawrence
M	Bernard Lee
Q	Desmond Llewelyn
Miss Moneypenny	Lois Maxwell
Lazar	Marne Maitland
Colthorpe	James Cossins
Chula	Chan Yiu Lam
Saida	Carmen Sautoy
Frazier	Gerald James
Naval Lieutenant	Michael Osborne
Communications Officer	Michael Fleming

—— **THE CREW** ——

Director	Guy Hamilton
Screenplay by	Richard Maibaum
	Tom Mankiewicz
Producers	Albert R. Broccoli
	Harry Saltzman
Associate Producer	Charles Orme

Roger Moore returns in *The Man with the Golden Gun*, once again in good female company. *Courtesy of the David Reinhardt Collection*

Mankiewicz, Tom (June 1, 1942–July 31, 2010): Sophisticated American screenwriter who cowrote *Diamonds Are Forever* and *The Man with the Golden Gun* with Bond veteran Richard Maibaum, and received solo credit on *Live and Let Die*. Known for his wit and his tongue-in-cheek approach to story-telling—later well suited to the first two Christopher Reeve *Superman* movies—Mankiewicz was just what the James Bond series needed in the early-to-mid 1970s, when Bond was slowly and inexorably moving away from the serious approach of the first few Sean Connery films.

After the relative box office failure of the very serious *On Her Majesty's Secret Service*, starring George Lazenby as Bond, the next films in the 007 series were destined to become globe-trotting extravaganzas with fantastic villains, incredible production design, and a light touch. The new direction was a good fit for the strengths of actor Roger Moore, who took over the Bond role in 1973, but even Sean Connery's return in *Diamonds Are Forever* two years earlier was a fantastic romp, with elements of pure whimsy—much of it supplied by Mankiewicz.

Mankiewicz wrote his first feature film in 1967, a surfing movie titled *The Sweet Ride* that starred a young Jacqueline Bisset. He followed it up with some work on Broadway, but Bond beckoned the young writer. "It turned out that Dick Maibaum had done a draft on *Diamonds* and was through with it," recalled Mankiewicz. "Cubby and Harry were thus looking for a young American writer—because this Bond took place largely in the United States—who had been around and also could write English dialogue. [United Artists executive] David Picker, who had seen my Broadway musical *Georgy Girl*, recommended me for the job."*

On a crisp fall morning in 1970, Mankiewicz arrived at Cubby Broccoli's mansion on Hillcrest Drive in Beverly Hills, and was greeted by both Broccoli and director Guy Hamilton, who had just

---

* Tom Mankiewicz, interview by the author, Los Angeles, November 7, 1977.

Directors of Photography	Ted Moore
	Oswald Morris
Music by	John Barry
Title song performed by	Lulu
Lyrics by	Don Black
Production Designer	Peter Murton
Art Directors	John Graysmark
	Peter Lamont
Production Supervisor	Claude Hudson
Assistant Director	Derek Cracknell
Location Manager (Thailand)	Frank Ernst
Location Manager (Hong Kong)	Eric Rattray
Special Effects	John Stears
Editors	John Shirley
	Raymond Poulton

Screenwriter Tom Mankiewicz (center), on the set of *The Man with the Golden Gun* with Roger Moore and director Guy Hamilton. *Courtesy of the Anders Frejdh Collection*

flown over from England. Within moments, the young screenwriter was signed to a two-week contract guaranteeing him $1,250 a week. After two weeks, Mankiewicz turned in the first forty pages of his script and was put on an indefinite retainer. For the next six months, he was completely engrossed in the world of James Bond. His relationship with 007 would continue for three more years.

A native of Los Angeles, Mankiewicz came from Hollywood royalty. His father was multi-Oscar-winning writer/director Joseph L. Mankiewicz (*A Letter to Three Wives*, *All About Eve*), and his uncle was Herman Mankiewicz, the cowriter of *Citizen Kane*. In addition to his stylish work on the Bond movies, Tom Mankiewicz also wrote *The Eagle Has Landed* (1976); *Superman*

(1978), uncredited; *Superman II* (1980), uncredited; *Ladyhawke* (1985); and *Dragnet* (1987).

Manson, Shirley (August 26, 1966–   ): Scottish singer, songwriter, musician, and actress who warbled the title tune to *The World Is Not Enough*. A native of Edinburgh, she leads the alternative rock band Garbage. She made her acting debut as Catherine Weaver, one of the titular killer robots on Fox's sci-fi series *Terminator: The Sarah Connor Chronicles* (17 episodes, 2008–2009).

Manticore: Yacht leased by the Janus crime syndicate, anchored in the Monte Carlo harbor in *GoldenEye*. It's where comely enemy agent Xenia Onatopp (Famke Janssen) takes Admiral

Chuck Farrell (Billy J. Mitchell) for a tryst. She then crushes him to death with her steel-like thighs. He does die with a smile on his face.

Manuela: Gorgeous British Secret Service agent based in Rio de Janeiro (Station VH), portrayed by Emily Bolton in *Moonraker*. Standing outside the Carlos & Wilmsberg import/expert warehouse while Bond (Roger Moore) searches inside, she's nearly killed by Jaws (Richard Kiel), but is saved by 007 at the very last moment.

Marceau, Sophie (November 17, 1966–   ): Accomplished French actress who portrayed duplicitous Elektra King in *The World Is Not Enough*. Marceau is dazzling as an orphaned billionaire's daughter and former kidnap victim who is apparently intent on completing the dangerous oil pipeline started by her father. In reality, she's suffering from Stockholm syndrome and in love with her former abductor, and deep into enacting revenge against her father and the person who advised him not to pay her

$5 million ransom: M (Dame Judi Dench). As a woman who knows her gifts and how to use them, Elektra proves to be a challenging adversary for Bond (Pierce Brosnan). And, despite the pain she puts Bond through, the audience understands the anguish on 007's face when he puts a bullet through her brain at the film's conclusion. It's a credit to Marceau's performance that she could create such an indelible impression.

A Parisian native, Marceau made her motion picture debut as Vic Beretton in director Claude Pinotau's romantic comedy *The Party* (1980), a film that also featured Bond player Jean Pierre Castaldi (*Moonraker*). She made her English-language debut as Bernardette in Bernard Schmitt's comedy *Pacific Palisades* (1990), and she first caught the eye of American audiences as the French noblewoman opposite Mel Gibson in *Braveheart* (1995).

Marie: Bikini-clad French jet-setter, portrayed by Denise Perrier, who is featured in the *Diamonds Are Forever* pre-credits teaser. Tipped off by a fez-wearing blackjack player (Frank Olegario)

Stunning Sophie Marceau played former kidnap victim Elektra King, a woman with unusual motives, in *The World Is Not Enough. Courtesy of the Luc Leclech Collection*

French actress Denise Perrier portrayed the curvaceous jet-setter whom James Bond (Sean Connery) "questions" in the *Diamonds Are Forever* pre-credits teaser. *Courtesy of the David Reinhardt Collection*

that she may have information on the where-abouts of Ernst Stavro Blofeld (Charles Gray), Bond (Sean Connery) confronts her on a beach in the Antibes, rips off her bikini top, and nearly strangles her with it until he gets the information he needs.

Marlohe, Bérénice Lim (May 19, 1979–   ): Tall, slender French actress who portrayed Severine, the former sex worker who becomes the kept woman of cyberterrorist Raoul Silva (Javier Bardem) in *Skyfall*. A native of Paris, Marlohe made her motion picture debut in director Guy Mazarguil's romantic comedy *L'art de séduire* (2011). *Skyfall* was her English-language debut.

Lovely Zena Marshall (right) has some out-of-frame fun with Sean Connery during a publicity shoot for *Dr. No. Courtesy of the Malcolm McNeil Collection*

Actress Bérénice Marlohe portrayed doomed Sever-ine in *Skyfall*. *Steve Rubin Collection*

Marshall, Zena (January 1, 1925–July 10, 2009): Sultry British leading lady with French ances-try who portrayed the seductive half-Chinese enemy agent Miss Taro in *Dr. No*. Her appear-ance fresh from the bath, wrapped in a towel

in the hallway of her Blue Mountains cottage, was certainly one of the film's highlights. Born in Nairobi, Kenya, Marshall grew up in Leicestershire, England, and made her motion picture debut as an Egyptian handmaiden in director Gabriel Pascal's 1945 production of *Caesar and Cleopatra*, which starred Claude Rains, Vivien Leigh, and Stewart Granger, and featured a young Roger Moore as a Roman soldier. Director Terence Young remembered her from a bit part as an Italian woman in David MacDonald's period drama *The Bad Lord Byron*, on which Young did uncredited writing work.

Martin, George (January 3, 1926–March 8, 2016): Academy Award–nominated British music pro-ducer, arranger, and composer who produced the Beatles' music until their breakup in 1969, and later scored *Live and Let Die*. A London native, Martin made his motion picture com-posing debut on director Ken Annakin's crime comedy *Crooks Anonymous* (1962). He had pre-viously gotten his start in motion picture music production on director Anthony Kimmins's comedy *Smiley* (1956), which featured future Bond player Guy Doleman. Martin received his Oscar nomination for Best Scoring of Music, Adaptation or Treatment for the Beatles' *A Hard Day's Night* (1964).

Masterson, Jill: Seductive girl Friday to Auric Goldfinger (Gert Fröbe) in Miami Beach, por-trayed by curvaceous actress Shirley Eaton in

Goldfinger. Bond (Sean Connery) finds her in Goldfinger's suite at the Fontainebleau Hotel, helping her boss cheat Mr. Simmons (Austin Willis) at gin. Equipped with a radio transmitter and a pair of high-powered binoculars, she is spying on Simmons's hand and feeding the results to Goldfinger via a receiver camouflaged as his hearing aid.

Dressed—or, shall we say, undressed—in a black bra and panties and lying sexily prone on a chaise lounge, she is surprised by Bond, who then forces Goldfinger to start losing to Simmons; otherwise, he'll report the scam to the Miami Beach police. Masterson, of course, falls in with Bond, and they go directly to his bedroom in the same hotel.

After switching allegiances, Masterson pays the ultimate penalty: death by skin suffocation when her entire body is painted gold by Oddjob (Harold Sakata), Goldfinger's mute Korean man-servant. Bond is later informed that such a death is not uncommon among cabaret dancers. To prevent such a demise, the movie claims, a small patch of skin must be left bare at the base of the spine so that the skin can breathe—a safety measure that was not performed in Miss Masterson's case.

Tania Mallet portrayed the quite fetching Tilly Masterson, here in her signature Mustang convertible in *Goldfinger*. *Courtesy of the Anders Frejdh Collection*

"I'm sorry, I can't. Something big's come up." James Bond (Sean Connery) spends some free time with Auric Goldfinger's girlfriend, Jill Masterson (Shirley Easton). *Courtesy of the David Reinhardt Collection*

Masterson, Tilly: Golden girl Jill Masterson's revenge-seeking sister (masquerading as Tilly Soames), portrayed by lovely Tania Mallet in *Goldfinger*. Determined to kill Goldfinger (Gert Fröbe), who had Oddjob (Harold Sakata)

murder Jill in Miami Beach, Tilly follows him to Switzerland, where on two occasions she tries to shoot him with a high-powered hunting rifle she keeps in a case inscribed with her initials: "T.M." Bond (Sean Connery) intercepts her and shreds the tires on her 1964 Mustang convertible. She introduces herself to him as Tilly Soames and says that the case contains her ice skates. After the truth comes out, they join forces against Goldfinger in a spectacular car chase. Unfortunately, Tilly runs afoul of Oddjob's razor-sharp bowler hat and is killed.

Mathis, Rene: Suave liaison to James Bond (Daniel Craig) in Montenegro, portrayed by Giancarlo Giannini in *Casino Royale*. Bond confides in the Frenchman, but later suspects him of having sold him out to Le Chiffre (Mads Mikkelsen). He's arrested but eventually cleared. Mathis returns in *Quantum of Solace*, in which he helps Bond penetrate the ranks of Quantum/SPECTRE spymaster Dominic Greene (Mathieu Amalric).

Mathis, Valerie: French double agent, portrayed by Linda Christian, who helps James

Bond (Barry Nelson) in the CBS live TV adaptation of *Casino Royale*. An ex-lover of Bond's, Mathis at first appears to be working for Soviet master spy Le Chiffre (Peter Lorre). In reality, she is a Deuxiéme Bureau agent assigned to support Bond's efforts to bankrupt Le Chiffre at the baccarat table in Monte Carlo. At a key moment in the game when Bond is wiped out, he suddenly receives an envelope containing 35 million francs. The money is from Mathis, and it's enough to keep Bond in the game. After bankrupting Le Chiffre, Bond discovers that Mathis has been captured by the Soviet master spy. Unless Bond gives Le Chiffre the check for his winnings—87 million francs—Mathis will be killed.

The character gets her name from the character of Rene Mathis in Ian Fleming's original novel, who was also an agent with the Deuxiéme Bureau.

Max: The Havelock family's pistachio-loving parrot in *For Your Eyes Only*. Quite the talker, Max leads James Bond (Roger Moore) and Melina Havelock (Carole Bouquet) to the aerie of Kristatos (Julian Glover) at St. Cyril's. Max also has a comical and potentially scandalous conversation with Prime Minister Margaret Thatcher (Janet Brown) at the film's conclusion.

Maxwell, Lois (February 14, 1927–September 29, 2007): Canadian leading lady who had a brief Hollywood career (1946–1948) before settling in England, where she portrayed M's iconic secretary Miss Moneypenny in fourteen James Bond films. During one of his frequent visits to the set of *Dr. No* in 1962, author Ian Fleming said to Maxwell, "You know, Miss Maxwell, when I visualized Miss Moneypenny in the James Bond stories, I saw her as a tall, distinguished-looking woman with the most kissable lips in the world. You, my dear, are exactly the woman I visualized."[*]

On Sean Connery, Maxwell told the *Sydney Morning Herald*, "I had first met Sean in Cubby's office back at the beginning. He had that wonderful atmosphere of menace and moved, as Cubby said, like a panther. But he was still a poor young actor in rumpled corduroys who looked like he lived in a bedsit. By 1964, however, when we had the party at the Dorchester

for the third film, 'Goldfinger,' he was very much his own man.

"He had been taught everything from how to dress and where to buy his shirts to table manners. His Scottish accent was ironed out. In 'Dr. No,' they had to film his dialogue one line at a time, but not now. At the party I went over to get some caviar. Sean was eating the caviar with a big serving spoon. I said: 'Sean, you mustn't eat from that.' He just turned round and said quite pleasantly: 'I can have caviar whenever I want now.'

"I think he was serious. I don't think he was drunk. I've never seen Sean drunk."[†]

A native of Kitchener, Ontario, Maxwell made her credited feature debut as Julia Kane opposite Ronald Reagan and a teenage Shirley Temple in director Peter Godfrey's drama *That Hagen Girl* (1947), a role that netted her a Golden Globe award for Most Promising Newcomer—Female. The following year, future Bond director Terence Young cast her in his mystery drama *Corridor of Mirrors* (1948), where she worked with future Bond player Christopher Lee. Among her many feature and television credits, Maxwell portrayed the wife of paranormal investigator Dr. John Markway (Richard Johnson) in director Robert Wise's classic horror thriller *The Haunting* (1963).

May Day: Steroid-enhanced guard/assassin/lover to Max Zorin (Christopher Walken), portrayed by singer Grace Jones in *A View to a Kill*. Wildly costumed and sporting the most unusual hairdos, May Day is one of 007's most formidable opponents. Bond (Roger Moore) first sees her at Ascot, the elegant British horse racetrack, where she's costumed like a character out of *Alice in Wonderland*—a soldier of the Red Queen, no doubt!

At the Eiffel Tower restaurant, she's in costume again, this time impersonating a nightclub puppeteer to assassinate Bond's French contact Aubergine (Jean Rougerie). Chased up the tower, with Bond blazing away at her with his Walther, May Day stops at the edge of one of the girders, hesitates for a split second, then jumps off the landmark, apparently to her doom. But a

---

[*] Lois Maxwell, interview by Mark Greenberg, *Bondage* 12 (1983).

[†] Lois Maxwell, interview with the *Sydney Morning Herald*, August 31, 1986, reprinted in "Moneypenny Dishes the Dirt," MI6: The Home of James Bond 007, August 31, 2016, https://www.mi6-hq.com/sections/articles/history-lois-maxwell-retires1.

May Day (Grace Jones) shows off her strength in *A View to a Kill. Courtesy of the Luc Leclech Collection*

parachute opens (just like Bond on the Asgard in *The Spy Who Loved Me*), and she makes a soft landing aboard a wedding-party barge on the river Seine.

Later betrayed and double-crossed, May Day joins forces with Bond, helping him remove a huge bomb from a bed of high explosives that could cause a major earthquake in Northern California. Hustling it onto a railroad handcar, May Day remains with the bomb so that she can keep a faulty hand brake in place. It turns out to be a noble yet suicidal act, as the car explodes safely outside the mine. Her last words to Bond: "Get Zorin for me!"

Mbale, Uganda: Site of a clandestine meeting between terrorist financier Le Chiffre (Mads Mikkelsen) and rebel leader Steven Obanno (Isaach De Bankolé) of the Lord's Resistance Army, orchestrated by the mysterious Mr. White (Jesper Christensen) in *Casino Royale*. Obanno is entrusting Le Chiffre with millions for investment purposes, which he stresses must be a no-risk proposition. However, Le Chiffre uses the entrusted funds to short the aerospace company Skyfleet, betting their stock will crash after he engineers the destruction of their new airliner prototype. When Bond thwarts his plan, Le Chiffre has no choice but to gamble the rest of Obanno's money in a high-stakes Texas hold'em poker tournament.

McCartney, Paul (June 18, 1942–   ): International superstar singer/composer and ex-Beatle who, with his wife Linda and their group Wings, composed and performed the vibrant title track for *Live and Let Die* in 1973. Ironically, producers Albert R. Broccoli and Harry Saltzman had the opportunity to produce the Beatles' first movie, *A Hard Day's Night* (1964), but they passed.

Live and Let Die's Paul McCartney *Steve Rubin Collection*

McClory, Kevin (June 8, 1926–November 20, 2006): Dapper, resourceful, and fabulously wealthy Irish film producer/director who was the first to collaborate with author Ian Fleming on a film script featuring his James Bond character. The collaboration would later turn sour and initiate one of the great legal battles in film history, as well as an important chapter in the history of the James Bond films.

McClory was introduced to Fleming by their mutual friend Ivar Bryce in 1959, shortly after McClory directed the drama *The Boy and the Bridge*. The hope was that a Bond adaptation would allow Bryce's film company, Xanadu Productions, to benefit from the UK's so-called Eady subsidies, which would underwrite the cost of a film shot on British soil with a largely British crew. Since McClory was also eager to film a story with underwater elements, the company could shoot in the lush Bahamas, which were part of the British Commonwealth and thus within Eady subsidy boundaries.

Much was made of McClory's experience in 1955 and 1956, when he worked with producer Mike Todd on *Around the World in 80 Days*, the colorful adventure that had reaped huge profits with its travelogue backgrounds and action-packed vignettes. McClory reasoned that Bond would also benefit from a story that took a broad, cosmopolitan view of the world.

The producer/director suggested that instead of using one of Fleming's previous Bond novels as the basis for a script, an entirely new adventure should be written that would feature plot and production values geared toward a film audience. Eventually, McClory, Fleming, and British screenwriter Jack Whittingham collaborated on a film script titled *Longitude 78 West*, which introduced the international criminal organization SPECTRE and its plan to hijack two atomic bombs from the NATO powers. When, in 1960, Ivar Bryce withdrew as a possible financial backer and McClory was unable to secure additional funds, Fleming left for his annual vacation in Jamaica, where he innocently wrote a novel based on the collaborators' film story. He called it *Thunderball*—from the NATO code name for the mission to recover the stolen A-bombs.

No sooner did McClory read an advance copy of the book than he and Whittingham petitioned the high court of London for an injunction to hold up publication. In their legal plea, they claimed that Fleming had infringed on their joint copyright by publishing a book based on the script without their approval.

The *Thunderball* infringement case dragged on for three years but was eventually a major victory for McClory, who won the film and television rights to *Thunderball* and all of its variations. Fleming, Whittingham, and McClory had written ten different versions of the story during their collaboration, and the rights to each of these drafts were now under McClory's control. Additionally, future published copies of Fleming's *Thunderball* novel would have to include the credit "This story is based on a screen treatment by K. McClory, J. Whittingham, and the author."

While McClory was battling Fleming for the *Thunderball* rights, producers Albert R. Broccoli and Harry Saltzman had, in 1961, acquired film rights to all the other available James Bond novels. (The *Casino Royale* rights were already owned by actor Gregory Ratoff, who would shortly sell them to agent turned producer Charles K. Feldman.) When McClory won the *Thunderball* case in 1963, Broccoli and Saltzman had already produced the first two films in the series, *Dr. No* and *From Russia with Love*, and actor Sean Connery was on the threshold of becoming an international sensation as 007. Their success proved to be an immediate roadblock for McClory, who could not interest any financial backer in making a *Thunderball* film that competed with the Broccoli/Saltzman Bond pictures.

Eventually, McClory went to Broccoli and Saltzman and proposed a collaboration. He would sell them the screen rights to *Thunderball* in exchange for a producer credit and a percentage of the profits. Why did Broccoli and Saltzman make the deal? "We didn't want anyone else to make *Thunderball*," said Broccoli. "We had the feeling that if anyone else came and made their own Bond film, it would have been bad for our series. After *Goldfinger*, we naturally felt that we knew more about Bond than anyone else.

"And this fact was certainly proven two years later when my dear friend Charles K. Feldman finally made *Casino Royale*. The making of that film, which everybody thought we made, ended up costing us a lot of customers. The public thought we had slipped. Early on, I could sense that happening with *Thunderball*. So I went ahead and made the deal with McClory to insure that the best of Fleming's stories could be our film."*

McClory was delighted. Not only was his film about to be produced with Sean Connery in the lead role, but it was getting out at the most auspicious time—the virtual pinnacle of worldwide Bond fever. With 20 percent of the film's profits coming to him per his contract with Broccoli and Saltzman, what more could he ask for?

There was one more thing. McClory insisted that the contract only prohibit him from producing a competing film version of *Thunderball* for ten years. The thought of another *Thunderball* a decade down the line didn't bother Broccoli and Saltzman enough to challenge the clause. The film was produced, it became the biggest hit in the series to date, and McClory deposited loads of profits in his bank account. And promptly in 1975, he announced a new *Thunderball* adaptation titled *James Bond of the Secret Service*.

Once again, Cubby Broccoli—now producing alone, having bought out Saltzman's shares in Eon Productions—refused to let a rival 007 production get off the ground. Legal armies began to assemble. Broccoli challenged McClory's right to make his own James Bond films independent of Eon. McClory, meanwhile, declared that because *Thunderball* had introduced SPECTRE, he alone owned the rights to the fictional organization, and that Broccoli could not use it in his latest 007 film, *The Spy Who Loved Me*. Broccoli succeeded in outgunning McClory legally and stalling his competitor's film plans, but he also instructed screenwriter Richard Maibaum to

* Albert R. Broccoli, interview by the author, Los Angeles, April 10, 1977.

remove any reference to SPECTRE or its leader Blofeld from *The Spy Who Loved Me*.

Between 1975 and 1981, McClory would occasionally announce *James Bond of the Secret Service*—sometimes under the alternate title *Warhead*—as an upcoming project, but he was unable to attract studio interest until he was introduced to entertainment lawyer turned film producer Jack Schwartzman. Schwartzman, a former production executive at Lorimar, was the perfect collaborator for McClory. A legal whiz, Schwartzman knew full well that McClory had the right to readapt *Thunderball*; he just needed to present his case properly, with enough financial muscle behind him to face off against Broccoli's equally determined legal army.

With the backing of Warner Bros., Schwartzman (who was married to actress Talia Shire of *Rocky* and *The Godfather* fame) allied himself with McClory, and paved the road to a remake of *Thunderball*. McClory would later take an executive producer credit on the film, which was titled *Never Say Never Again*, and which returned Sean Connery to the role he had made famous. Released in 1983, the film was just what Broccoli feared: a 007 film that competed with Eon's "official" series. Nevertheless, both *Never Say Never Again* and Broccoli's own 1983 Bond entry, *Octopussy*, were major international successes.

A native of Dublin, McClory made his motion picture debut as a location manager on director José Ferrer's World War II drama *The Cockleshell Heroes* (1955), working with future Bond player Christopher Lee and a script cowritten by Richard Maibaum. The following year he was an assistant director on *Moby Dick* and *Around the World in 80 Days*. Three years later, he wrote and directed *The Boy and the Bridge* (1959), which featured future Bond players Geoffrey Keen (Defence Minister Freddie Gray in the Moore and Dalton films), and Stuart Saunders (*Octopussy*).

Over the years, McClory spent a great deal of time in Nassau, Bahamas, where he owned a beautiful waterfront property. Visiting in 1978, I saw the rusting carcass of the original *Thunderball* A-bomb hijacking sled sitting in the tall grass. It was a small reminder of Kevin McClory's well-deserved place in the history of the Bond films.

NOTE: As Bond enters the casino in *Thunderball*, pay attention to the gentleman smoking a cigar in the foyer—that's Kevin McClory.

McGill, Everett (October 21, 1945–   ): Rugged American character actor who portrayed Ed Killifer, a duplicitous DEA agent who accepts a $2 million bribe to free convicted drug lord Franz Sanchez (Robert Davi) in *Licence to Kill*. A native of Miami Beach, Florida, McGill made his motion picture debut as a bigoted white soldier in director John Schlesinger's World War II drama *Yanks* (1979). McGill later made a strong impression as Naoh, a prehistoric man, in Jean-Jacques Annaud's acclaimed prehistorical drama *Quest for Fire* (1981). He's also well known as Big Ed Hurley in the television series *Twin Peaks* (24 episodes, 1990–1991, 2017).

Actor Everett McGill was smarmy DEA traitor Ed Killifer in *Licence to Kill*. *Steve Rubin Collection*

McRae, Frank (June 3, 1942–   ): American character actor and former professional football player who portrayed Sharkey, fisherman friend to Felix Leiter (David Hedison) in *Licence to Kill*. Born in Memphis, McRae had a brief career in the National Football League, playing six games for the Chicago Bears at defensive tackle. He made his credited motion picture debut as Osiat in director John Guillermin's *Shaft in Africa* (1973). McRae's other feature film credits include *Dillinger* (1973); *Hard Times* (1975); *Walking Tall Part II* (1975), with fellow Bond veteran Bruce Glover; *Big Wednesday* (1978); *Paradise Alley* (1978); *Norma Rae* (1979); *Rocky II* (1979); *1941* (1979), as Private Ogden Johnson Jones, one of Dan Aykroyd's fellow tank crewman; *48 Hours* (1982); *National Lampoon's Vacation* (1983); *Red Dawn* (1984), as Mr. Teasdale, the schoolteacher; and *Last Action Hero* (1993).

mechanical alligator: Reminiscent of the phony seagull on James Bond's head in *Goldfinger*, the alligator is another form of camouflage that allows Bond (Roger Moore) to approach the island home of Octopussy (Maud Adam) at night without being seen in *Octopussy*.

Meddings, Derek (January 15, 1931–September 10, 1995) Academy Award–nominated British special effects supervisor who joined the Bond team on *Live and Let Die* and later contributed extraordinary effects work to *The Man with the Golden Gun*, *The Spy Who Loved Me*, *Moonraker*, *For Your Eyes Only*, *The Living Daylights*, and *GoldenEye*. Meddings got his first Bond assignment while working on *Fear Is the Key* (1972), an adventure film based on the novel by Alistair MacLean. He recalled, "On *Fear Is the Key*, I was supervising all of the effects on the picture: the floor effects—explosions, etc.—as well as the model effects. It involved work with a crashing airplane, a bathyscaphe, and underwater sequences. And it was a very successful picture. Syd Cain was the production designer, and when he was assigned by Cubby Broccoli to *Live and Let Die*, Syd asked me to come along and work on the film's special effects."*

Meddings's principal contribution to *Live and Let Die* was the explosion of Kananga's poppy fields on mythical San Monique—a terrific fiery effect that was done completely in miniature on a Pinewood Studios effects stage. The producers were so pleased with the sequence that they offered Meddings an assignment on *The Man with the Golden Gun*, where he used his explosives expertise to expunge Scaramanga's solar reactor.

The model work that Meddings conceived on *The Spy Who Loved Me* qualifies as some of the best in the series, especially some terrific aerial shots of the *Liparus* supertanker swallowing the American nuclear submarine. In that particular sequence, both ships are beautifully realistic, appearing to cruise on a sparkling sea as if they were being photographed from ten thousand feet up.

Special effects chief Derek Meddings standing before his amazing tracking dish miniature for *GoldenEye*. *Courtesy of the Brian Smithies Archive*

"When we went on location in Nassau to look for a place to film the model sequences," Meddings recalled, "we found a place called Coral Harbour, which was ideal because it was right on the ocean and had these canals that led out to the sea where we could prepare our models. We wanted to be near the ocean because of its unlimited scope. With the sea, you don't have to go around wondering whether the camera is going to catch a bit of the studio tank or whether

---

* Derek Meddings, interview by the author, London, June 27, 1977

Derek Meddings's FX crew blows up a miniature bridge, simulating an Afghani span where Soviet troops are attempting to cross in *The Living Daylights*. *Courtesy of the Brian Smithies Archive*

the lighting is realistic or whether the water looks like real water. And since we were dealing with a sixty-three-foot-long tanker model, we needed a vast work area. The ocean next to Coral Harbour was perfect.

"One day, when we were planning the capture of the submarine and were looking for the right angles, I spotted a huge cement tower that was part of a nearby deserted hotel complex overlooking the ocean like a lighthouse. It had a staircase leading up to its concrete observation tower and had long since been abandoned. I went up there on an impulse to see what our tanker model would look like from that height and discovered a great shot. I knew that if we picked the right day, we would have a lovely, sparkling ocean, and it would look as if we were shooting the ship from an airplane. And that's exactly what happened."

In addition to the submarine miniatures that were filmed entering and leaving the tanker, Meddings was also working with a miniature Atlantis, the base of villain Karl Stromberg (Curt Jurgens) that, in the script, is destroyed by torpedoes; and

the little four-foot miniature version of Bond's Lotus submarine car, which appears in the brief sequence in which Bond (Roger Moore) drives up to the window of Atlantis to peer through a glass viewing port.

On *The Living Daylights*, Meddings and his team worked on the exciting sequence in which a Russian tank unit is obliterated on a bridge in Afghanistan. Later, one of his most exquisite miniature creations was the giant Cuban satellite dish that proved to be the final location in *GoldenEye*. *GoldenEye* director Martin Campbell explained, "We had a tight budget, I think the final budget came out to $57 to $58 million, which was quite a lot at the time. . . . A lot of the success of the movie—in terms of the scope of the movie—was as a result of Derek Meddings, because he's brilliant at doing models. The whole Arecibo dish at the end, even though we went to Arecibo [Observatory], Puerto Rico, to shoot this, an awful lot of the shots were created by Derek Meddings—it was something like a fifty-foot model, which was an exact replica of the dish and three-fourths of that sequence, if not more, was his model—rising up out of the water. Right at the beginning of the movie, there's the blowing up of the factory—that was all Derek. There were model helicopter shots coming down when we go to Russia. There's this big kind of secret station where the helicopter lands—all of that was models. He was one of these who with his models would give tremendous scope to the movie by economic means.

"Sadly, he died about four weeks after the end of the movie, and I remember him very, very fondly. He just had a genius for creating what looked like enormous sets but were actually very small models, perfectly in scale. He was a genius in a way and I've never worked with anyone like him."* Special effects supervisor John Richardson subsequently used some of those same miniature techniques on *Tomorrow Never Dies* and *Die Another Day*, working with members of Meddings's previous miniatures crew.

Born in Pancras, London, Meddings made his motion picture debut as a special effects supervisor on director Michael Campus's science fiction thriller *Z.P.G.* (1972). Meddings received his Oscar nomination for Best Visual Effects for his work on *Moonraker*—he lost to the special effects team behind *Alien*. The previous year, Meddings and his team shared a Special Achievement Award from the Academy of Motion Picture Arts and Sciences for their work on *Superman* (1978).

After his death in September 1995, a dedication was added in the closing credits of *GoldenEye*: "To the memory of Derek Meddings."

Medrano, General: Brutal renegade Bolivian general portrayed by Joaquín Cosio in *Quantum of Solace*. In his quest to become a major power in Bolivia, Medrano shot the father of Camille Montes (Olga Kurylenko), strangled her mother, and set her family house on fire. Like Melina Havelock in *For Your Eyes Only*, Camille is now dead set on revenge. The general is working with sinister international environmentalist Dominic Greene (Mathieu Amalric), who is engineering a coup that will make Medrano president of Bolivia in return for some desert land that Medrano believes is worthless. In reality, this land grab will help Greene develop a monopoly on Bolivia's freshwater supply—a plot by SPECTRE offshoot Quantum. Suspicious of Camille's intentions,

* Special features, *GoldenEye*, James Bond Ultimate Edition (1995; MGM, 2006), DVD.

Traitorous Bolivian general Medrano (Joaquín Cosio, left) is an influence peddler for Dominic Greene (Mathieu Amalric) in Bolivia in *Quantum of Solace*. *Courtesy of the Anders Frejdh Collection*

Greene turns her over to Medrano in Haiti, but Bond (Daniel Craig) rescues her. Agent 007 and Camille later track Greene and Medrano to an eco hotel in the desert of Bolivia, where Camille exacts her revenge.

Mei-Lei. The golden-clad stewardess portrayed by actress Mai Ling in *Goldfinger*. She works on the title character's private jet, informing 007 (Sean Connery) that his black attaché case did not survive the trip—it was "damaged when examined, so sorry."

Mellinger, Michael (May 30, 1929–March 17, 2004): German character actor of stage and screen, a longtime resident of Britain, who portrayed Kisch, an associate of Auric Goldfinger (Gert Fröbe) who poisons the "hoods convention" and locks Bond (Sean Connery) to the A-bomb in Fort Knox by his wrist. Born in Kochel, Bavaria, Mellinger

Actor Michael Mellinger was Kisch, Goldfinger's field commander in Kentucky in *Goldfinger*. *Steve Rubin Collection*

made his credited motion picture debut in director Jack Lee's crime adventure *The Golden Mask* (1953), working with future Bond players Marne Maitland and George Pastell.

Mendel: Official of Switzerland's Basel Bank, portrayed by Ludger Pistor in *Casino Royale*. Mendel is holding the $10 million deposits of all the poker players in a high-stakes, winner-take-all, no-limit tournament. Each player is asked to input a six-letter code, which will be utilized to retrieve winnings once the tournament concludes.

Mendes, Sam (August 1, 1965–   ): Academy Award–winning British film director and producer who helmed *Skyfall* and *Spectre*, two of the highest-grossing films in the James Bond series. A native of Reading, Berkshire, England, Mendes kicked off his feature film directing career with a bang: *American Beauty* (1999) won the Best Picture Oscar and netted Mendes a Best Director Oscar to boot. Mendes's additional feature directing credits include *Road to Perdition* (2002), *Jarhead* (2005), *Revolutionary Road* (2008), and *1917* (2019). For that last film he was again nominated for an Academy Award for Best Director (losing to *Parasite*'s Bong Joon Ho). He previously directed Dame Judi Dench in the play *The Cherry Orchard*, for which he won a Critics' Circle Award for Best Newcomer, and he went on to join the Royal Shakespeare Company, where he directed, among many others, Ralph Fiennes (in "Troilus and Cressida").

Mergui Archipelago: An island group off the coast of present-day Myanmar, where NATO will drop SPECTRE's $280 million diamond ransom in *Thunderball*. Per Blofeld's precise instructions, the cache must be delivered on May 27 at 2000 hours Greenwich mean time, at latitude 20 degrees north, longitude 60 degrees east. After verifying that the contents are flawless blue-white diamonds weighing between three and eight carats, SPECTRE will alert NATO on radio frequency 16.23 megacycles as to the location of the missing atomic bombs. NOTE: In actuality, following Blofeld's coordinates would depost the ransom in the Arabian Sea off the coast of Oman.

Meteora, the: Picturesque rock formations in central Greece where a famous fourteenth-century Eastern Orthodox monastery was built, which became an amazing location for the final action in *For Your Eyes Only*.

Director Sam Mendes brought a grounded feel to his Bond films, *Skyfall* and *Spectre*. *Courtesy of the Anders Frejdh Collection*

Sam Mendes guides Daniel Craig during production in Istanbul on *Skyfall*. *Steve Rubin Collection*

Greece's amazing Meteora rock structures, featured at the conclusion of *For Your Eyes Only*. *Steve Rubin Collection*

Meyer, David and Tony (July 24, 1947–   ): Twin British actors who portrayed Mischka and Grischka, knife-throwing circus performers and assassins who murder 009 (Andy Bradford) and participate in a renegade Soviet plot to start World War III in *Octopussy*. Natives of Watford, Hertfordshire, England, the brothers made their big-screen debut in director Celestino Coronado's avant-garde film version of *Hamlet* (1976), each portraying both Hamlet and Laertes alongside fellow Bond player Vladek Sheybal.

MI6 headquarters, London: Real-life headquarters of the British Secret Service at 85 Vauxhall Cross, along the Albert Embankment in Vauxhall, which has made an appearance in several Bond films. It's partially blown up in the pre-credits teaser of *The World Is Not Enough*—a scene that was apparently almost blocked by the real MI6. According to the *London Daily Telegraph*, when administrators learned that a scene from the film would be shot around their headquarters building, they tried to prohibit filming, citing a security risk. However, foreign secretary Robin Cook, at the urging of arts minister Janet Anderson, moved to overrule them and allow the shoot; the *Telegraph* quoted a source close to Cook as saying, "After all Bond has done for Britain, it was the least we could do for Bond."*

That same building is attacked again in *Skyfall*, when cyberterrorist Raoul Silva (Javier Bardem) hacks into MI6's computer systems and triggers a gas explosion to send a message to M (Dame Judi Dench). By the next film, *Spectre*, the damaged structure has been abandoned in favor of a new high-tech high-rise headquarters nearby. At the conclusion of the story, Blofeld (Christoph Waltz) triggers explosives that demolish the building and nearly kill Bond (Daniel Craig) and Madeleine Swann (Léa Seydoux).

microchip: Essential computer part manufactured by Max Zorin (Christopher Walken) in *A View to a Kill*, and the key to the film's plot. British intelligence fears that the magnetic pulse damage caused by a nuclear bomb exploded in space by the Russians could render all microchips useless. That's why they're so interested in a chip retrieved by Bond (Roger Moore) from the body of 003, who stole it from the Russians

in Siberia—it's impervious to micropulse damage.

Reasoning that Max Zorin might be supplying this new generation of chips to the Russians, M (Robert Brown) orders Bond to look into Zorin's activities. Later, in France, Bond and fellow agent Sir Godfrey Tibbett (Patrick Macnee) discover that Zorin has been using a surgically implanted microchip to covertly inject his horses with steroids. However, like Goldfinger's gold smuggling activities in the third James Bond film, Zorin's microchip antics with the Russians and his horses are just the tip of the iceberg. His real scheme is bigger: Project Main Strike.

In order to monopolize the world's supply of microchips, Zorin plans to utterly destroy Silicon Valley, where 80 percent of the planet's microchips are manufactured. His nefarious plan calls for using his oil wells on the California coast to pump seawater into the Hayward Fault, a major earthquake zone. Simultaneously, he's going to explode a bomb near the San Andreas Fault. The resulting double earthquake will turn Silicon Valley into a huge lake.

Like the "hoods convention" in *Goldfinger*, Zorin calls together a group of the world's microchip manufacturers and offers them an opportunity to join his new microchip cartel. The price: $100 million a franchise. One Taiwanese tycoon (Anthony Chin) becomes another Mr. Solo from *Goldfinger* when he declines. Instead of being crushed inside a Lincoln Continental, the tycoon is tossed out the exit door by May Day (Grace Jones). This exit, though, is in Zorin's blimp—five thousand feet up.

Mikkelsen, Mads (November 22, 1965–   ): Accomplished Danish actor who portrayed investment specialist, gambler, and SPECTRE agent Le Chiffre in *Casino Royale*. He is one of the best villains in the Bond series, bringing a sense of quiet menace to the role. A native of Copenhagen, Mikkelsen made his feature film debut as Tonny in director Nicolas Winding Refn's Danish crime thriller *Pusher* (1996). More recently, Mikkelsen

Actor Mads Mikkelsen.
Courtesy of photographer Kenneth Willardt

---

* Robert Shrimsley, "James Bond Turns the Big Guns on MI6," *London Daily Telegraph*, April 23, 1999.

Mads Mikkelsen brought his considerable charm to the role of Le Chiffre—he of the eye that drips blood—in *Casino Royale*. *Courtesy of the Anders Frejdh Collection*

played the key role of Galen Erso in *Rogue One: A Star Wars Story* (2016). He also portrayed the iconic Dr. Hannibal Lecter in the TV series *Hannibal* (39 episodes, 2013–2015).

Milicevic, Ivana (April 26, 1974–   ): Tall, statuesque American actress, born in what is now Bosnia and Herzegovina, who portrayed Valenka, the girlfriend of Le Chiffre (Mads Mikkelsen) in *Casino Royale*. Hailing from Sarajevo and raised in Michigan, Milicevic made her credited motion picture debut under the name Ivana Marina as a former girlfriend of the title character in *Jerry Maguire* (1996). Film audiences began to take note when she played Stacey, the "American Dreamgirl" in *Love Actually* (2003). She's also quite fetching as Katrina, Mark Ruffalo's sexy neighbor in *Just Like Heaven* (2005). In recent years, she has been shuttling between television series (*Banshee*, *The 100*) and film roles.

Milovy, Kara: Beautiful, wide-eyed Czechoslovakian cellist, portrayed by Maryam d'Abo, who falls in love with James Bond (Timothy Dalton) in *The Living Daylights*. Drawing from Ian Fleming's original short story, Kara is introduced as a Soviet sniper, supposedly assigned to liquidate defecting Russian general Georgi Koskov (Jeroen Krabbé). In reality, she's an innocent dupe whom her lover/patron Koskov talks into posing as a sniper to convince British intelligence that his defection is genuine.

Staring at her stunning features through the crosshairs of his own sniper rifle, Bond—on a mis-

sion to kill any potential assassin—hesitates and shoots the rifle out of Kara's hands instead. After Koskov is whisked away to England and safety, only to be quickly recaptured in what the British are supposed to think is a KGB operation, Bond returns to Bratislava to find Kara and question her. Again mesmerized by her beauty during an afternoon concert, 007 follows her and discovers that she's being shadowed by the KGB (they're suspicious of her supposed involvement with a defector).

Posing as a friend of the missing Koskov, Bond helps Kara escape into Austria—after a wild ride in his Aston Martin. Vienna is a treat for Kara, who has never been outside her native country but dreams of one day performing at Carnegie Hall. Bond buys her a beautiful evening gown ("Who will pay?" she asks; "Georgi, of course," he replies) and enjoys touring Vienna with her, including a romantic interlude on a Ferris wheel, where they kiss for the first time. They finally track Koskov to Tangier, where Bond joins forces with the KGB's General Pushkin (John

Kara Milovy (Maryam d'Abo) is an accomplished cellist in Czechoslovakia, but she's also the girlfriend of a renegade Soviet general in *The Living Daylights*. *Courtesy of the David Reinhardt Collection*

Rhys-Davies), who is also suspicious of Koskov's involvement with sinister arms dealer Brad Whitaker (Joe Don Baker).

mint julep: The favorite drink of Auric Goldfinger (Gert Fröbe) on his Auric Stud property in Kentucky. When offered the same drink, Bond (Sean Connery) instructs the waiter, "Sour mash, but not too sweet."

Mischka and Grischka: Formidable twin assassins and circus knife-throwing experts employed by Kamal Khan (Louis Jourdan), portrayed by twins David and Tony Meyer in *Octopussy*. The twins are a throwback to the serious killers of the early Bond films (*Dr. No, From Russia with Love*), bringing with them a realistic element of danger. They're introduced in the film's most atmospheric scene—their night chase through an East German forest in pursuit of clown-suited 009 (Andy Bradford). Everything recalls the moody Renaissance Garden exteriors in *From Russia with Love*'s pre-credits teaser: the proximity of the border, the stillness of the forest, 009's nervousness, the catlike grace of the twins. Even the bursting of one of 009's balloons recalls the snapping of a twig by Grant (Robert Shaw).

Caught by one of the twin killers, 009 is wounded, but he manages to karate-chop

The Meyer twins portrayed Mischka and Grischka, knife-throwing killers allied to Kamal Khan and General Orlov in *Octopussy*. *Steve Rubin Collection*

the twin to his knees. Running toward a border bridge, 009 quickly climbs up the girder but takes a well-aimed knife in his upper back. Stunned, he falls into a flood control basin. The agent survives long enough to drop a Fabergé egg at the feet of the British ambassador. The twins return to the circus. Later, Bond (Roger Moore) exacts his revenge by killing Mischka in the circus car in Germany, where he drops the cannon on his head, and later, Grischka in the forest, where Bond skewers the twin with one of his own throwing knives.

"Missing Duel, The": A sequence in *The Man with the Golden Gun* that ended up on the cutting room floor. It involved the tail end of the beach duel that pits Bond (Roger Moore) and his Walther against the golden automatic of Scaramanga (Christopher Lee). Lee explained the missing sequence: "In the duel, they cut out a great deal of footage that they felt would hold up the pace of the picture. As you recall, Bond turns around and Scaramanga is gone. The next time you see me, I'm coming around the corner of the 'fun house.' That was the way the final film came out.

"The way we shot it originally, you could see by the expression on my face that I wasn't going to play by the rules of the duel. So, as Bond is walking away from me, I dive out of the frame and just disappear. I had cheated, which presents an interesting psychological point, because if Scaramanga really thought he was the best assassin in the world, what was he doing cheating?

"Bond realizes I'm hiding in the rocks, and we have a long conversation, shouting at each other. Bond is thirty or forty yards away, also hiding behind some rocks. It's all very cat-and-mouse. Bond tries to flush me out by flinging a thermos of petrol in the air and exploding it above my head. We actually shot that, and it does appear in the trailer. I dodge the thermos, and we end up in the 'fun house.' But in the cutting room, they decided that two men standing behind rocks shouting at each other didn't work. And they were probably right. It was too conventional."*

Mitsouko (1943–March 1995; birth name: Maryse Guy): Actress of European and Japanese

* Christopher Lee, interview by the author, Los Angeles, February 15, 1989.

Mitsouko portrayed 007's French contact in *Thunderball*, here joining Bond (Sean Connery) at the "funeral" of SPECTRE agent Jacques Bouvar. "The coffin, it has your initials, J.B.," she says. *Courtesy of the David Reinhardt Collection*

descent, briefly active in films and television, who portrayed Mademoiselle LaPorte, French contact to James Bond (Sean Connery) in the *Thunderball* pre-credits teaser. She's waiting with the Aston Martin when Bond escapes from a chateau in a Bell jet pack. She made her film debut in director Max Pécas's French erotic drama *Sweet Violence* (1962). Sadly, she died by suicide in 1995.

Mollaka: Formidable African terrorist bomb-maker portrayed by Sébastien Foucan in *Casino Royale*. It is Mollaka whom Bond (Daniel Craig) identifies in a crowded bazaar on Madagascar, and pursues in one of the great chase scenes ever filmed. A master of the acrobatic art of parkour, Mollaka jumps, leaps, flies, and tumbles, and although he isn't nearly as skilled, Bond (Daniel Craig) matches him almost every step of the way—eventually tracking the elusive terrorist to an embassy compound, where he assassinates the man, a memorable villain in one of the most memorable sequences in the entire series.

By the way, that's really Foucan parkouring his way through the sequence—he's a master at the art.

Moneypenny, Miss: M's efficient, love-starved secretary, one of 007's most ardent admirers, portrayed solidly by Canadian actress Lois Maxwell in the first fourteen James Bond films from Eon Productions. Caroline Bliss took over the role in *The Living Daylights* and *Licence to Kill*. She was then followed by Samantha Bond in the four Pierce Brosnan Bonds—*GoldenEye*, *Tomorrow Never Dies*, *The World Is Not Enough*, and *Die Another Day*. Most recently, Naomie Harris has played her in the Daniel Craig Bond movies *Skyfall*, *Spectre*, and *No Time to Die*. Barbara Bouchet portrayed Moneypenny's daughter in the 1967 *Casino Royale* spoof, and Pamela Salem played Moneypenny in *Never Say Never Again*.

Starting with her introduction in *Dr. No* in 1962, Moneypenny's blatantly sexual repartee with Bond before and after a briefing with M became a staple of the series. Like M and Q, her character was less comedic in the early films, as was her relationship with Bond, and the most recent Moneypenny has returned to that more serious tone. This version, portrayed by Harris and given a full name for the first time—Eve Moneypenny—starts as a field agent who nearly

James Bond (Sean Connery) is about to tell Miss Moneypenny (Lois Maxwell) the secret of the world in *From Russia with Love*. *Courtesy of the Michael Van-Blaricum Collection*

In the Daniel Craig reboot of 007, Eve Moneypenny (Naomie Harris) starts out as a field agent, operating with Bond in Istanbul in *Skyfall*. *Steve Rubin Collection*

woman rescued by James Bond (Daniel Craig), portrayed by Olga Kurylenko in *Quantum of Solace*. Camille is determined to kill ambitious Bolivian general Medrano (Joaquín Cosio), who murdered her family. In order to get to Medrano, she's been sleeping with international environmentalist Dominic Greene (Mathieu Amalric), who is helping Medrano overthrow the Bolivian government, paving the way for a presidential bid. When Greene learns of Camille's true agenda, he targets her for assassination. However, her assassin, Edmund Slate (Neil Jackson), is killed by James Bond (Daniel Craig) in Haiti. Bond later rescues Camille a second time, and the two eventually make it to Bolivia to take down Medrano and thwart Greene's nefarious plan to corner the country's freshwater supply.

kills Bond in an abortive mission in *Skyfall*. She soon becomes one of his most trusted allies.

Montenegro: Southeastern European country on the Adriatic Sea that plays host to a high-stakes no-limit poker tournament in *Casino Royale*. Ten players, including James Bond (Daniel Craig), Le Chiffre (Mads Mikkelsen), and Felix Leiter (Jeffrey Wright) pay the $10 million buy-in, with the understanding that once that stake is exhausted, it will cost another $5 million to buy back in. It's a winner-take-all tournament, with a prize of more than $100 million. Since Le Chiffre has squandered the funds entrusted to him by rebel leader Steven Obanno (Isaach De Bankolé) in a disastrous stock play, he must win. Bond is determined to stop him.

Montes, Camille: Revenge-obsessed Bolivian mystery

James Bond (Daniel Craig) and Bolivian mystery woman Camille Montes (Olga Kurylenko) trek across the desert in *Quantum of Solace*. *Courtesy of the Anders Frejdh Collection*

Moon, Colonel Tan-Sun: Sinister North Korean military man and illegal arms trader, portrayed by Will Yun Lee, who is the superior of Zao (Rick Yune) in *Die Another Day*. Seemingly killed when Bond (Pierce Brosnan) escapes from Moon's North Korean border compound, the colonel goes through a radical surgical transformation and becomes Gustav Graves (Toby Stephens), an international billionaire with megalomaniac tendencies.

Moon Buggy No. 1: Comical getaway vehicle Bond (Sean Connery) uses to escape from Blofeld/Willard Whyte's Las Vegas–based Tectronics lab in *Diamonds Are Forever*. Designed for travel on the lunar surface, the moon buggy is hijacked by Bond, who finds it perfect for smashing through walls and gates and navigating across the Nevada desert.

Sean Connery prepares to pilot a moon buggy—one of his more unusual escape vehicles—in *Diamonds Are Forever*. *Courtesy of the Anders Frejdh Collection*

Moonraker: Line of US space shuttles, one of which is on loan to the British and hijacked off a Royal Air Force 747 airliner in the pre-credits teaser of *Moonraker*. Billionaire aerospace entrepreneur Hugo Drax (Michael Lonsdale) later admits to Bond (Roger Moore) that the vessel was hijacked to replace another Moonraker in his shuttle fleet that developed a fault during assembly. Its sister ship Moonraker 6 carries James Bond (Roger Moore) and Holly Goodhead (Lois Chiles) to Drax's space station when they stow away on the shuttle. They later steal Moonraker 5 and use its nose-mounted laser cannon to destroy the toxic-gas cylinders that could destroy all human life on Earth.

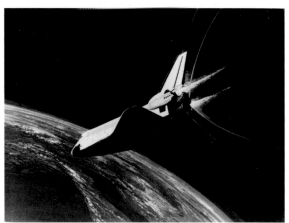

The Moonraker space shuttle becomes the pawn in Hugo Drax's plan to destroy the world. *Steve Rubin Collection*

MOONRAKER

(United Artists, 1979) ★★: The eleventh James Bond film produced by Albert R. Broccoli. US release date: June 29, 1979. Budget: $30 million. Worldwide box office gross: $210.3 million (US domestic gross: $70.3 million; international gross: $140.0 million).* Running time: 126 minutes

——————— **THE SETUP** ———————

Billionaire aerospace industrialist Hugo Drax (Michael Lonsdale) builds space shuttles, one of which, enroute to the UK aboard a 747 jetliner, disappears over the Yukon. British intelligence

* "Moonraker (1979)," The Numbers, accessed June 11, 2020, https://www.the-numbers.com/movie/Moonraker.

wants to know what happened to the missing shuttle, so they send James Bond (Roger Moore) to Drax's facility in California to investigate. Bond meets Drax, who says he also wants to know what happened to his shuttle, blaming the British for its disappearance, and icy US space scientist Holly Goodhead (Lois Chiles). Bond's investigations will lead him to Drax's deadly plot to destroy mankind with a toxin that will spare plants and animals but eliminate all human life on Earth. The only survivors: Drax's super-race, waiting out the destruction on a radar-proof space station that orbits the Earth.

— BEHIND THE SCENES —

Although producer Albert R. Broccoli was wise to follow the *Goldfinger* formula of less serious, more fantastical Bond adventures after the success of the lighthearted *Diamonds Are Forever* in 1971, *Moonraker* actually proved to be *too* fantastical. Not only did it send Bond into outer space, where no double-0 agent should ever go, but it also returned to *The Man with the Golden Gun*'s style of action sequences that lack all credibility. Except for the wild parachute jump in the pre-credits teaser, the action in the movie is just plain stupid, including the unbelievably dumb moment when Bond glides through Venice's St. Mark's Square on a gondola hovercraft. Even a pigeon did a double take. Interestingly, what could have been a great action sequence in the film—Bond flying a mini jet behind Angel Falls in Venezuela—was eliminated from the shooting script when the river dried up.

Steel-toothed assassin Jaws (Richard Kiel) returns and adds some tension, but his Wile E.

Roger Moore by Jeff Marshall. *Courtesy of Jeff Marshall*

Coyote antics are not as flavorful as they were in *The Spy Who Loved Me*. Lois Chiles is a cocky Bond heroine, but she's an ice machine in the charisma department. And Michael Lonsdale's Hugo Drax spends much of the film mumbling about Bond's ability to survive numerous assassination attempts—though one of those is actually the film's most effective sequence: the centrifuge trainer mishap.

High points include John Barry's score and Corinne Cléry's death scene in the forest, where she becomes lunch for Drax's Dobermans—a scene that found its way into the film's teaser trailer. The film's failings didn't hurt it at the box office; building upon the momentum of *The Spy Who Loved Me* and backed by an inspired marketing campaign, *Moonraker* became, to that point, the biggest moneymaker in Bond history.

─────────── **THE CAST** ───────────

James Bond	Roger Moore
Holly Goodhead	Lois Chiles
Hugo Drax	Michael Lonsdale
Jaws	Richard Kiel
Corinne Dufour	Corinne Cléry
M	Bernard Lee
Q	Desmond Llewelyn
Miss Moneypenny	Lois Maxwell
Frederick Gray	Geoffrey Keen
Manuela	Emily Bolton
Chang	Toshiro Suga
Dolly	Blanche Ravalec
Private Jet Pilot	Jean Pierre Castaldi
Private Jet Hostess	Leila Shenna
General Gogol	Walter Gotell
Cavendish	Arthur Howard
Blonde Beauty / Drax Girl	Irka Bochenko
Colonel Scott	Michael Marshall
Mission Control Director	Douglas Lambert
Consumptive Italian	Alfie Bass
Museum Guide / Drax Girl	Anne Lonnberg
US Shuttle Captain	Brian Keith
Captain Boeing 747	George Birt
RAF Officer	Kim Fortune

─────────── **THE CREW** ───────────

Director	Lewis Gilbert
Screenplay by	Christopher Wood
Executive Producer	Michael G. Wilson
Producer	Albert R. Broccoli
Associate Producer	William P. Cartlidge
Director of Photography	Jean Tournier
Music by	John Barry
Title song performed by	Shirley Bassey
Lyrics by	Hal David
Production Designer	Ken Adam
Costume Designer	Jacques Fonteray
Stunt Arranger	Bob Simmons
Title Designer	Maurice Binder
Special Effects	John Evans
	John Richardson
Visual Effects Supervisor	Derek Meddings
Visual Effects Art Director	Peter Lamont
Editor	John Glen

Moore, Roger (October 14, 1927–May 23, 2017): Dashing British actor who won the part of James Bond in *Live and Let Die* in 1973, and started his own dynasty that would last twelve years and seven films. Producers Albert R. Broccoli and Harry Saltzman had first considered Moore during their initial 007 casting search back in 1962, but he was considered too much of a "pretty boy" to play Bond.* He was also portraying *The Saint* on television and was thus unavailable to Eon Productions.

When Sean Connery left the Bond series after *Diamonds Are Forever*, the producers returned to Moore, and this time he was available and perfect for the role and the direction the series was now taking. The Moore years took a fantastical approach to the original Fleming stories, embracing globe-trotting adventure, tongue-in-cheek action, and witty repartee. Gone was the cruel sensuality of Connery epitomized by *Dr. No* and *From Russia with Love*. Moore was hardly the aristocratic snob that some critics claimed, but he did bring a more outwardly self-assured, confident, and polished take on 007.

As screenwriter Tom Mankiewicz, who would be involved in writing two of the Moore films, put it, "When Sean Connery walked into a bar, your immediate feeling was 'Uh oh, there's going to be trouble.' Sean can look like a bastard, especially when he's angry. Roger, on the other hand, looks like your typical nice-guy secret agent. There is no way that he can look evil. He is much more the Etonian dropout that Fleming once conjured, and in the Moore Bond films, we had to play to those strengths. While Sean could just look at somebody and they would back away, Roger has to come on with a line like 'Excuse me, haven't we met?'

"Sean, of course, could just be nasty and the audience loved him for it. He could sit at a table with a girl, and he could lean over the table and kiss her and then stick a knife into her under the table, saying to a nearby waiter, 'Excuse me, but I have nothing with which to cut my meat,' and the audience would go along with it. They would take that from Sean because he had that glint in his eye—that touch of the lorry driver in him—even though he was always the quintessential good guy inside. Audiences wouldn't take that kind of stunt from Roger.

─────────────

* Albert R. Broccoli, interview by the author, Los Angeles, April 10, 1977.

Roger Moore as 007 in the bright and energetic *Live and Let Die*. *Courtesy of the David Reinhardt Collection*

Roger Moore cut a dashing figure as agent 007—he would star in seven epic Bond adventures. *Courtesy of the David Reinhardt Collection*

"Roger, however, can have much more fun in a sophisticated setting. For instance, in the original script for *The Man with the Golden Gun*, Roger was pretending to be an ornithologist—which is really a conceit, because James Bond is named after an ornithologist. So Bond is at this party in Bangkok, and an ambassador comments to him, 'I understand you're doing a book on ornithology,' to which Roger replies, "Yes, sir," and the man asks, 'What is it called?" and Roger looks at the ambassador's beautiful wife, a Thai girl, and replies, '*Birds of the Far East*.'

"Now, Roger can say '*Birds of the Far East*' in a much more refined way than Sean ever could. Roger is a good comedian, and he can play direct comedy much better than Sean. Sean's strong point was not playing comedy at all. If he had played the comedy in the Bond films, it would have looked phony."*

* Tom Mankiewicz, interview by the author, Los Angeles, November 7, 1977.

One of Moore's first scenes is a perfect example of the new order described by Mankiewicz. In *Live and Let Die*, Bond tracks Kananga (Yaphet Kotto) to a nightclub in Harlem, where 007 is easily disarmed and captured by his enemies. He politely introduces himself to Solitaire (Jane Seymour), and they engage in a stoic repartee until local drug kingpin Mr. Big, who, unbeknownst to Bond, is Kananga in disguise, marks him for execution. Outside the club, Bond manages to distract and disable his two executioners, and he makes it out of Harlem with the help of Strutter (Lon Satton), a resourceful CIA man.

Given the same set of circumstances, Sean Connery's Bond would have probably approached the nightclub after dark, when he could camouflage his intentions more easily. Inside the club, he would have punched out a few people before surrendering to Mr. Big's minions. The introduction to Solitaire would have been less polite, and Bond wouldn't have responded so casually to the prospect of execution.

Critics and fans generally agree that Roger Moore grew into the James Bond role by his third go-around, in *The Spy Who Loved Me*. There is no question that the film was a cut above his previous two efforts; it even contained some subtle dramatic moments that surprised both the fans and the critics. The most impressive of these is the scene between Bond and Anya Amasova (Barbara Bach) in a Sardinian hotel suite, in which Anya learns that 007 has recently been to Berngarten in Austria, where her lover, a Russian agent,

Roger Moore was deemed "too pretty" to play James Bond in *Dr. No*. The producers embraced him ten years later in *Live and Let Die. Courtesy of the David Reinhardt Collection*

was killed. She shows him a picture of her lover, whom Bond doesn't recognize, but when Anya says that he was killed while on a mission, Bond confesses that he probably killed him. Anya turns cold and informs Bond that when their mission is over, she will kill him. It is one of Roger Moore's best scenes in the series, warmly reminiscent of the early Connery Bonds, when drama was ever present, even amid the fun. Director Lewis Gilbert later agreed that Moore had taken his character to a new level of honesty.

But what moviegoers responded to above all else was Moore's pure likability. The post-Vietnam, post-Watergate audience was looking for escapist fun, and nothing provided more of it than his Bond adventures. They won the series millions of new fans and turned Moore into an internationally famous movie star. Prior to the arrival of a new generation of science fiction and fantasy heroes in the late 1970s—in films like *Superman*, *Star Wars*, *Star Trek: The Motion Picture*, and *Alien*—Roger Moore's 007 was probably the most popular pop hero on the planet. And throughout the early 1980s, he maintained that status in the face of increasing competition. His retirement in 1985, after the release of his seventh film, *A View to a Kill*, was due primarily to age; producers thought it was time to enliven the series with a fresh face.

A London native, Roger Moore made his credited big-screen debut as a bon vivant tennis player opposite Elizabeth Taylor and Van Johnson in the romantic drama *The Last Time I Saw Paris* (1954). However, it was on the small screen that Moore found increasing traction, first as the title character in the British series *Ivanhoe* (39 episodes, 1958–1959), then as Silky Harris in *The Alaskans* (37 episodes, 1959–1960) and Beau Maverick in *Maverick* (16 episodes, 1959–1961). And then came *The Saint* (118 episodes, 1962–1969), which brought him his first international acclaim as wealthy adventurer Simon Templar—what turned out to be the perfect training ground for future Bond duty. His final series before Bond came calling was *The Persuaders!* (24 episodes, 1971–1972), in which Moore's English nobleman, Lord Brett Sinclair, teamed up with Tony Curtis's Bronx-born self-made man Danny Wilde.

One thing was certain: Roger Moore always looked like he was having fun on the Bond movies. He was. *Steve Rubin Collection*

Moore, Ted (August 7, 1914–1987): Academy Award–winning South African cinematographer who photographed *Dr. No*, *From Russia with Love*, *Goldfinger*, *Thunderball*, *Diamonds Are Forever*, *Live and Let Die*, and *The Man with the Golden Gun*. A native of Western Cape, South Africa, Moore broke into show business as a member of the camera crew on director Maurice Elvey's war drama *Sons of the Sea* (1939), which featured character actor Ian Fleming (no relation to the Bond author) as a naval intelligence officer. Three years later, he received his first opportunity as camera operator on Charles Frend's war drama *The Big Blockade* (1942). He continued in that discipline on a number of films, including three coproduced by Albert R. Broccoli: *Paratrooper* (1953), a.k.a. *The Red Beret*; *Hell Below Zero* (1954); and *The Black Knight* (1954).

After getting a break as second unit director of photography on Terence Young's *Safari* (1956), also produced by Cubby Broccoli, Moore won his solo DP spurs on another Broccoli production, *A Prize of Gold* (1955). He later received his Academy Award for Best Cinematography (Color) on *A Man for All Seasons* (1966). Moore was also director of photography on *Nine Hours to Rama* (1963); *Day of the Triffids* (1963); *Shalako* (1968), with Sean Connery; *The Golden Voyage of Sinbad* (1973), *Sinbad and the Eye of the Tiger* (1977), and *Clash of the Titans* (1981).

Cinematographer Ted Moore's crew captures Bond (Sean Connery) and Honey Ryder (Ursula Andress) navigating a river on Crab Key in *Dr. No. Courtesy of the David Reinhardt Collection*

Morgenthau, Henry, III (January 11, 1917–July 10, 2018): American multimillionaire producer and author who in 1956 collaborated with Ian Fleming on the idea for a television series entitled *Commander Jamaica*. When the concept failed to interest the networks, Fleming took the story idea and wrote his sixth James Bond novel, *Dr. No*.

Morzeny: SPECTRE operations chief portrayed by Walter Gotell in *From Russia with Love*. He's first seen in the pre-credits teaser, when he congratulates Donald Grant (Robert Shaw) on the murder of the phony James Bond. Later, he escorts Rosa Klebb (Lotte Lenya) around SPECTRE Island's training area, and he eventually leads the motorboat attack on Bond (Sean Connery) and Tanya Romanova (Daniela Bianchi). He also kills SPECTRE master planner Kronsteen (Vladek Sheybal) with a kick from his poisoned shoe blade.

Before he was promoted to General Gogol in later Bond adventures, actor Walter Gotell was Morzeny, a SPECTRE agent introduced in *From Russia with Love*, seen here with Lotte Lenya (right) and Peter Brayham (center). *Courtesy of the David Reinhardt Collection*

Mossberg "Rogue" shotgun: Formidable pump-action weapon employed by CIA undercover agent Pam Bouvier (Carey Lowell) during a wild brawl at the Barrelhead Bar in Bimini, Bahamas, in *Licence to Kill*. Eventually, she uses the gun to blow out a section of barroom wall, through which she escapes with Bond (Timothy Dalton).

motorized traction table: Also known as "the rack," this device is utilized by physical therapist Patricia Fearing (Molly Peters) to help James Bond (Sean Connery) stretch his spine in *Thunderball*. After strapping in 007 and turning on the mechanism, she excuses herself for fifteen minutes—during which SPECTRE agent Count Lippe (Guy Doleman) enters the room and resets the lever to its highest danger level. Bond is saved from assassination when Fearing returns in time to turn off the machine, after which Bond quips, "I must be six inches taller." Staggering into the steam room, Bond takes Fearing with him for additional recuperative value.

Mouton Rothschild 1955: The wine selected by SPECTRE assassins Mr. Wint (Bruce Glover) and Mr. Kidd (Putter Smith) when they bring dinner to James Bond (Sean Connery) and Tiffany Case (Jill St. John) in *Diamonds Are Forever*. Sniffing Wint's potent aftershave and remembering the scent from a previous encounter, Bond decides to test the man's knowledge of wines. He tastes the Mouton and deems it excellent. But he tells Wint that for such an elaborate meal, a claret wine would have been more suitable. Wint falls for the ploy and says that the ship's cellar is poorly stocked with clarets. Bond blows Wint's cover by explaining that the Mouton *is* a claret.

Moxon, Tim (June 2, 1924–December 5, 2006): Handsome British actor, briefly in films, who played Professor John Strangways, a doomed British undercover agent in *Dr. No*. A native of Kent, England, Moxon appeared in only one other film: director Marshall Stone's *Come Spy With Me* (1967).

Munro, Caroline (January 16, 1949–   ): Curvaceous British actress, a favorite of fantasy film fans, who portrayed Naomi, assistant and helicopter pilot to Karl Stromberg (Curt Jurgens) in *The Spy Who Loved Me*. The cat-and-mouse game between Bond (Roger Moore) in his trick Lotus submarine car and Naomi in her Jet Ranger helicopter is one of the film's highlights, capped delightfully by her knowing wink in the heat of battle. Born in Windsor, Berkshire, England, Munro made her credited motion picture debut as Madame Vendonne in director James Clavell's period crime film *Where's Jack?* (1969). Genre fans embraced

Caroline Munro portrayed Stromberg's comely helicopter pilot and executive assistant, Naomi in *The Spy Who Loved Me*. *Courtesy of the Luc Leclech Collection*

her for her performance as Margiana in Gordon Hessler's *The Golden Voyage of Sinbad* (1973), where she competed for screen time with Ray Harryhausen's marvelous special effects.

Murino, Caterina (September 15, 1977–   ): Stunningly beautiful Italian actress who portrayed the sultry Solange, wife of arms dealer and terrorist Alex Dimitrios (Simon Abkarian) in *Casino Royale*. A native of Cagliari, Sardinia, Murino made her big-screen debut in director Luis Sepúlveda's dramedy *Nowhere* (2002).

Casino Royale's Caterina Murino was a perfect choice for the cover of this 2006 issue of *High Roller* magazine. *Courtesy of the David Reinhardt Collection*

Mürren: A small, picturesque village in Switzerland, located beneath the Schilthorn peak, which became a principal location in *On Her Majesty's Secret Service* in 1968. It was atop the Schilthorn that a revolving restaurant, dubbed Piz Gloria, was constructed. It, too, became a location in the film, along with the fully functional cable car/funicular that connected the restaurant to Mürren below. Mürren proved to be an excellent location for other reasons. Not only were there excellent ski runs nearby, but it was a good place for the filmmakers to construct a working bobsled run, which was completed on the site of an older run that had been closed since 1937.

Murton, Peter (September 24, 1924–December 15, 2009): British production designer who served in that capacity on *The Man with the Golden Gun*. A native of London, Murton made his motion picture debut as an uncredited draftsman on director Leslie Arliss's romantic drama *A Lady Surrenders* (1944). After many years on the drawing board, Murton first rose to the position of art director on actor/director Peter Sellers's *I Like Money* (1961), a.k.a. *Mr. Topaze*. Three years later, Ken Adam asked him to join the *Goldfinger* team—again as art director, a capacity he continued in on *Thunderball*. Murton climbed the ladder again to production designer on director Peter Medak's pitch-black comedy *The Ruling Class* (1972). As a top production designer, he's also worked on films such as *The Eagle Has Landed* (1976), *Death on the Nile* (1978), *Superman II* (1980), *Superman III* (1983), and *Spies Like Us* (1985).

Nabila: Enormous, three-hundred-foot ocean-going yacht originally owned by billionaire arms trader Adnan Khashoggi in 1982, which became Maximilian Largo's yacht the *Flying Saucer* in *Never Say Never Again*. It was reportedly built by the Benetti yacht company for $100 million, and named after Khashoggi's daughter. Faced with financial struggles, Khashoggi eventually lost his ship to the sultan of Brunei as collateral for unpaid loans. Donald Trump purchased it from the sultan in 1987 for $29 million. He renamed it the *Trump Princess*. A few years later, Trump sold the yacht to Saudi prince al-Waleed bin Talal for $20 million.

Nambutu embassy, Madagascar: A fictional African nation's diplomatic headquarters, to which Bond (Daniel Craig) tracks the fleet-footed bomb maker Mollaka (Sébastien Foucan) in *Casino Royale*. Determined to stop another terrorist attack, 007 blasts his way in and out of the embassy, cornering Mollaka and taking him out—unfortunately, in full view of security cameras. He does recover Mollaka's pipe bombs and a cell phone with the mysterious "Ellipsis" message among its incoming texts.

Naomi: Luscious assistant and helicopter pilot to billionaire shipping magnate Karl Stromberg (Curt Jurgens), portrayed by Caroline Munro in *The Spy Who Loved Me*. When Bond (Roger Moore) and Major Anya Amasova (Barbara Bach) arrive in Sardinia for a visit with Stromberg, stunning, bikini-clad Naomi meets them at their hotel dock for a short motorboat trip to Atlantis—Stromberg's amphibious laboratory. Her obvious interest in 007 doesn't sit well with Anya at all, but a potential catfight is averted when Bond returns from his abbreviated visit with Stromberg.

Later, when 007 and Anya escape from killer motorcycles and cars, their final hurdle is Naomi herself, flying a machine-gun-equipped Jet Ranger helicopter that sticks to Bond's trick Lotus like glue—until he drives the car into the ocean and converts it into a submarine. One of the film's clever touches is Naomi winking at Bond while she's trying to kill him. Hovering over the ocean, however, Naomi is unfortunately a ripe target for a subsurface-to-air missile that obliterates her and her chopper. One of the most sympathetic of all of James Bond's adversaries, Naomi, nevertheless, took her paycheck from Stromberg—a fact that qualifies her for liquidation.

Nash, Captain: The unfortunate Yugoslavia-based British agent, portrayed by production manager Bill Hill, who is murdered by Donald Grant (Robert Shaw) in the restroom of the Zagreb train station in *From Russia with Love*. Grant then assumes his identity, stealing his wallet, hat, briefcase, and business cards. The masquerade works, and Bond is tricked into thinking that SPECTRE's deadliest assassin is a helpful Brit.

NATO project: SPECTRE's scheme in *Thunderball* to steal two atomic bombs from a NATO bomber and then blackmail the North Atlantic Treaty powers to the tune of $280 million. The plan involves substituting an exact duplicate for NATO aerial observer François Derval (Paul Stassino), who will then hijack a bomber to the Bahamas with two atomic weapons on board. There, off Nassau, using a small army of underwater troops, SPECTRE agent number 2 Emilio Largo (Adolfo Celi) will hide the bombs until NATO pays the ransom. If something goes wrong, Largo has orders to destroy Miami with one of the bombs.

Nelson, Barry (April 16, 1917–April 7, 2007; birth name: Haakon Robert Nielsen): Likable American stage and screen actor who was the first actor to play James Bond, making his debut in *Casino Royale*, a one-hour live television dramatization that was broadcast on CBS's Climax Mystery Theater on October 21, 1954. Little more than a year after Ian Fleming published his first Bond novel, and long before any semblance of a 007 following had been established in the United States, Barry Nelson's Bond was introduced as an American agent fighting against Soviet operatives in Monte Carlo. Not only did Bond debut in the States as a Yank counterspy, he was also given an outrageous nickname—"Card Sense Jimmy Bond"—by a British agent named Clarence Leiter (Michael Pate).

A native of San Francisco, Nelson made his credited motion picture debut opposite William Powell and Myrna Loy in director W. S. Van Dyke's *Shadow of the Thin Man* (1941). Two years later, he was a member of Robert Taylor's embattled US Army squad battling the Japanese in *Bataan*. Later generations will remember him as Dean Martin's fellow pilot Anson Harris in *Airport* (1970), and Ullman, the hotel manager who hires Jack Nicholson in Stanley Kubrick's horror thriller *The Shining* (1980).

American leading man Barry Nelson won the part of James Bond in the 1954 live television adaptation of *Casino Royale*. *Courtesy of the Michael VanBlaricum Collection*

Nene Valley Railway, Northhamptonshire, England: British railroad yard and station where filmmakers shot the chaotic sequence in which Bond (Roger Moore) escapes from Karl-Marx-Stadt, East Germany, in *Octopussy*. With the help of Peter Lamont's art department, the British station was equipped with German fences and East/West German crossing points. The same location was also the site of the sequences involving the armored train headquarters of Trevelyan (Sean Bean) in *GoldenEye*.

NEVER SAY NEVER AGAIN

(Warner Bros., 1983) ★★⟩ : A new adaptation of the novel *Thunderball*, this Bond film was produced by Jack Schwartzman. US release date: October 7, 1983. Budget: $36 million. Worldwide box office gross: $160.0 million (US domestic gross: $55.5 million; international gross: $104.5 million).* Running time: 137 minutes.

---

* "Never Say Never Again (1983)," The Numbers, accessed

THE SETUP

SPECTRE is at it again. Wicked assassin Fatima Blush (Barbara Carrera) has seduced US Air Force officer Jack Petachi (Gavan O'Herlihy) into helping the nefarious organization hijack two cruise missiles from England. Bond (Sean Connery) enters the picture when he spots Blush and Petachi at the Shrublands health clinic, where he's undergoing detoxification from alcohol and hard living. He later battles Lippe (Pat Roach), a giant of a SPECTRE assassin. After the cruise missiles are successfully hijacked, Bond heads for Nassau, where he meets the lovely Domino (Kim Basinger), the mistress of fabulously wealthy Maximilian Largo (Klaus Maria Brandauer)—who may or may not have a spectre at his shoulder.

BEHIND THE SCENES

Producer Kevin McClory won the film rights to *Thunderball* in 1963 after a three-year court battle with author Ian Fleming, who had based the original novel on a screen treatment he wrote with McClory and screenwriter Jack Whittingham. In 1965 McClory contracted with Albert R.Broccoli and Harry Saltzman to produce the movie version of *Thunderball*, under an agreement that required him to wait ten years before adapting the novel again in any future film. Promptly in 1975, he announced a new variation on *Thunderball* titled *James Bond of the Secret Service*. But Cubby Broccoli had been burned by the dreadful 1967 spoof *Casino Royale*, which many viewers thought his company had produced, and he wasn't about to let another competing Bond film happen again without a fight. With threats of legal action hanging over the project, McClory couldn't interest a studio in backing it—until he connected with Jack Schwartzman, a former production executive at Lorimar and an entertainment legal whiz who had known of McClory's project when it was first presented to and rejected by Lorimar. Schwartzman secured the backing of Warner Bros. and production began on a new *Thunderball* adaptation, now called *Never Say Never Again*—which would return Sean Connery to the role of 007.

But the production was handicapped by an uneven script that was still being rewritten

---

June 15, 2020, https://www.the-numbers.com/movie/Never-Say-Never-Again.

during filming, and inconsistent direction by Irvin Kershner—the first American filmmaker to direct a serious Bond feature. Legally speaking, the movie was required to follow the countours of the *Thunderball* story, but it falls woefully short of its predecessor. The hijacking of two cruise missiles, even with David Dryer's marvelous effects, was less than riveting, and compares unfavorably to the Vulcan bomber hijacking in the 1965 film. In fact, the entire plots lacks the sense of worldwide alarm that was so prevalent throughout *Thunderball*.

What the new film does have is one of the best casts ever assembled for a James Bond movie, with some wonderful performances that carry the film for a time. Certainly, the very presence of Connery made the whole project worthwhile. His assuredness in the role is remarkable, considering it had been twelve years since his last Bond outing. The throwaway humor, the playfulness, the confident sexuality, the two-fisted machismo—all the elements that had made him a success in the first place—are still present in good quantity. In fact, Connery looks better in this film than he did in *Diamonds Are Forever*. He's lean, tanned, and quick on his feet. And he can still deliver those quintessential Bond lines with aplomb. When Fatima Blush water-skis up to him in Nassau and apologizes, "I made you all wet," Bond replies, "Yes, but my martini is still dry." Only Connery could get away with a quip like that.

Klaus Maria Brandauer's Maximilian Largo is the most interesting villain since Auric Goldfinger. Handsome, debonair, and fabulously wealthy, he's extremely sympathetic until he starts to lose his mistress Domino (Kim Basinger) to Bond. And even in Largo's most psychotic moments, Brandauer maintains a level of control that makes his performance extremely resonant and believable. For that, both Brandauer and director Kershner must be given strong credit.

But it is Barbara Carrera's wild Fatima Blush who is truly the film's life force. Without a ticking bomb (and there really is no time frame for *Never Say Never Again*'s cruise missile warhead to explode), a key element in any Bond film is the final confrontation between Bond and the villain. Once Fatima Blush is killed, there really is no such confrontation, and the film's final act begins to die on the vine. A pitifully weak battle between Bond and Largo fails to generate much

tension and is cut short when Largo is impaled on Domino's spear. Though, in all fairness to Kershner, *Thunderball* director Terence Young faced a similar problem once Fiona Volpe (Lucianna Paluzzi) is killed.

Aside from the war game pre-credits teaser, the overblown battle with Lippe at Shrublands (will filmmakers ever do justice to Shrublands?), and a brief motorcycle chase, this is a talky outing—with characters grinning and growling at one another without much physical interplay. With Connery in the lead role, though, it's also a very sexy one—helped immensely by Kim Basinger and Valerie Leon, who's into sports fishing. High points: Carrera's Fatima Blush, the Domination video game, Basinger's dancing, the health club sequence in which 007 gives Domino a sexy rubdown, the tango, and Klaus Maria Brandauer. Low points: Edward Fox's shrill M and Michel Legrand's bland score.

THE CAST

James Bond	Sean Connery
Maximilian Largo	Klaus Maria Brandauer
Ernst Stavro Blofeld	Max von Sydow
Fatima Blush	Barbara Carrera
Domino Petachi	Kim Basinger
Felix Leiter	Bernie Casey
Algernon	Alec McCowen
M	Edward Fox
Miss Moneypenny	Pamela Salem
Lippe	Pat Roach
Patricia	Prunella Gee
Nigel Small-Fawcett	Rowan Atkinson
Captain Jack Petachi	Gavan O'Herlihy
Lady in Bahamas	Valerie Leon
Nicole—Agent 326	Saskia Cohen Tanugi
Captain Pederson	Billy J. Mitchell
Girl Hostage	Wendy Leech
Dr. Kovac	Milow Kirek

THE CREW

Director	Irvin Kershner
Screenplay by	Lorenzo Semple Jr.
Based on an original story by	Kevin McClory
	Jack Whittingham
	Ian Fleming
Executive Producer	Kevin McClory
Producer	Jack Schwartzman
Associate Producer	Michael Dryhurst
Director of Photography	Douglas Slocombe
Music by	Michel Legrand
Title song performed by	Lani Hall

Lyrics by	Alan Bergman
	Marilyn Bergman
Production Designers	Philip Harrison
	Stephen Grimes
Costume Designer	Charles Knode
Second Unit Director	Michael Moore
Underwater sequence directed by	Ricou Browning
Stunt Coordinators	Glenn Randall
	Vic Armstrong
Special Visual Effects Supervisor	David Dryer
Supervising Film Editor	Robert Lawrence

Newton, Wayne (April 3, 1942–   ): Superstar Las Vegas singer, entertainer, and recording artist who portrayed lecherous televangelist Joe Butcher in *Licence to Kill*. Newton is well cast in what could have been a distracting role as the seemingly devoted religious peddler who is actually a front for the cocaine empire of Franz Sanchez (Robert Davi). Born in Norfolk, Virginia, Newton made his motion picture debut in director Gerd Oswald's drama *80 Steps to Jonah* (1969). His trademark tunes, such as "Danke Schoen," have been featured on numerous film and TV soundtracks.

Nick Nack: Francisco Scaramanga's diminutive servant, portrayed by French actor and *Fantasy Island* veteran Hervé Villechaize in *The Man with the Golden Gun*. Nick Nack perfectly proves that you don't have to be seven feet tall to give James Bond (Roger Moore) big trouble.

Villechaize was a throwback to such distinctive, mysterious character actors of the 1930s as Sydney Greenstreet, Peter Lorre, and John Carradine. In *Golden Gun*, Nick Nack is fascinating to watch in his tiny waiter's outfit, delivering Tabasco sauce to the sunbathing Scaramanga (Christopher Lee) and Andrea (Maud Adams), or munching peanuts behind Bond at the kickboxing match. He's also quick on his feet as he plays with the controls that operate the "fun house" on Scaramanga's island or is chased around Bond's stateroom on the Chinese junk. Eventually, the pesky villain is netted and strung up in the junk's rigging, proving another adage: that what goes up—even if it doesn't go up very far—must eventually come down.

Ningpo: A Japanese cargo ship owned by Osato Chemical and bound from Shanghai to Kobe, Japan, a microphoto of which is stolen by James

He may be small in stature, but Nick Nack (Hervé Villechaize) gives 007 outsized trouble in *The Man with the Golden Gun*. *Courtesy of the David Reinhardt Collection*

Bond (Sean Connery) out of the Tokyo office safe of Mr. Osato himself (Teru Shimada) in *You Only Live Twice*. By enlarging the photo, Bond and Tanaka (Tetsuro Tamba) discover *ama* pearl divers in the background, which establishes the position of the ship near their island. Later at the Kobe docks, Bond finds the *Ningpo* loading containers of liquid oxygen (lox)—a rocket propellant that could be fueling SPECTRE's secret *Intruder* spaceship.

ninjas: Stealthy black-suited Japanese warriors featured in *You Only Live Twice*. Skilled in the arts of concealment and surprise, the commando-like ninjas are trained by Tiger Tanaka of the Japanese Secret Service at the famous Himeji Castle, and they participate in the climactic attack on SPECTRE's secret rocket base. A hundred of their number swarm into the crater of the extinct volcano like ants, avoid the machine gun fire of the automated guns, tie their ropes to the roof superstructure, and glide to the concrete floor like mountaineers. Led by Bond (Sean Connery) and Tiger, they eventually overwhelm the SPECTRE garrison and destroy the base.

To film this sequence inside the enormous rocket base set that production designer Ken Adam built at Pinewood Studios, practically every stuntman in England was summoned and trained, under the guidance of Bob Simmons and George Leech. Rappeling from the roof of the volcano base was a particularly dangerous stunt. Several of the men were required to ride down with one hand and fire a submachine gun with the other. Their progress on the rope was controlled by a mountaineering device: a piece of rubber hose that was squeezed to slow down their progress. Once a stuntman hit the ground, he had to move quickly, because a comrade was coming down right behind him.

"*You Only Live Twice*," recalled Leech, "was one of the most difficult experiences of my life. There were too many headaches, especially in getting more than a hundred stuntmen ready for the battle sequences. The worst thing was having to tell certain men that they weren't needed for the rope sequences. When the master shots were completed, we needed only forty men, and neither Bob nor I wanted to tell anyone to go home. Needless to say, the rejected ones weren't too happy, especially when the pay on the close-up stunts was very good.

"For the battle sequences, we used a number of new techniques to give the action a spectacular feel. About twelve of our best men were used on the trampoline. It was an interesting form of trampolining. It wasn't your expertise in tumbles and perfect somersaults that mattered. You just had to look as if you were being blown up—no pointed toes or classic positions. You went off screaming, with your arms and legs flailing every which way. You landed into a made-up bed about twenty feet away. The special effects team timed their real explosions to your jump."*

No, Dr.: Archenemy to James Bond (Sean Connery) portrayed by Joseph Wiseman in the first James Bond film, *Dr. No*. The son of a German missionary and a Chinese girl from a good family, No joined a tong—the Chinese

* George Leech, interview by the author, London, June 23, 1977.

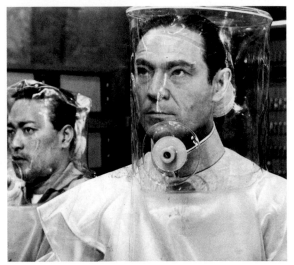

Actor Joseph Wiseman portrayed a nefarious SPECTRE operative intent on toppling US space rockets, the title character in the first James Bond movie. *Courtesy of the David Reinhardt Collection*

version of the Mafia—and escaped to American with $10 million of their loot. Turned away by both the US and Red Chinese scientific communities, No became a leading agent for SPECTRE.

Author Ian Fleming based Dr. No on the title character in author Sax Rohmer's Fu Manchu stories, and probably also on the screen roles portrayed by British character actor Christopher Lee, who was actually Ian Fleming's cousin. When both Lee and Fleming's friend Noël Coward turned down the role, it went to Wiseman. In the book, Fleming described Dr. No as an immense worm, clutching objects with his hooks and glaring at people with jet-black eyes. The character was so grotesque that screenwriters Richard Maibaum and Wolf Mankowitz, in their first draft script, actually gave the name Dr. No to a monkey who sat on the villain's shoulder. This bit of nonsense enraged producer Albert R. Broccoli, who was determined to make a serious spy story. Mankowitz would later leave the project, and Maibaum would finish the script, toning down Fleming's conception of Dr. No.

Helped by the makeup department and some exquisite Nehru jackets, Wiseman was also equipped with a pair of plastic hands, the result of what he calls an unfortunate accident. This impairment proves to be No's undoing in the final battle with Bond above the reactor pool.

NO TIME TO DIE

(United Artists Releasing/Universal, 2020): The twenty-fifth James Bond film produced by Eon Productions. US release date: November 20, 2020. Budget: $250+ million. Worldwide box office gross: N/A. Running time: 163 minutes.

THE SETUP

Five years have passed since the *Spectre* caper, but James Bond (Daniel Craig) and his main squeeze Dr. Madeleine Swann (Léa Seydoux) haven't managed to secure a happy ending. Bond is living in Jamaica, having retired from the British Secret Service. "On the surface, he's pretty happy," explained producer Barbara Broccoli. "He's living in a great place. But [he's] not entirely sure he's as happy as he could be. Felix Leiter, his buddy from the CIA shows up and asks him to do a favour."* That favor

---

* Shannon Connellan, "Everything We Know About 'No Time to Die' from Dropping by the Set," Mashable, February 7, 2020, https://mashable.com/article/james-bond-no-time-to-die-set-visit/.

involves tracking down a missing scientist, Valdo Obruchev (David Dencik). Bond agrees and winds up confronting his old nemesis: SPECTRE. Also returning is Bond's foster brother, imprisoned SPECTRE chief Ernst Stavro Blofeld (Christoph Waltz). The newcomers on the scene: CIA agent Paloma (Ana de Armas); mysterious genetic scientist Safin (Rami Malek), with whom Madeleine has a prior connection; and Nomi (Lashana Lynch), MI6's replacement for Bond as the new 007.

BEHIND THE SCENES

Needless to say, the twenty-fifth James Bond movie was a subject of intense speculation since moments after the release of the previous film, *Spectre*, in 2015. As fans gossiped and theorized—Daniel Craig was going to return for one more film, two more films, or none; he would be replaced by Tom Hiddleston (*Thor*) or Richard Madden (*Game of Thrones*), or by Idris Elba as the first black Bond—the filmmakers' journey to craft the film that became *No Time to Die* was just as convoluted. While Daniel Craig returned once more to the part he was born to play,

Producers Michael G. Wilson (far left) and Barbara Broccoli (far right) introduce the cast of *No Time to Die* in Jamaica, prior to the start of principal photography. Director Cary Fukunaga is third from the left. *Courtesy of the Anders Frejdh Collection*

Daniel Craig takes some last-minute instructions on location for *No Time to Die*. *Courtesy of the Anders Frejdh Collection*

A rare shot of James Bond (Daniel Craig) at leisure in *No Time to Die*. It won't last. *Courtesy of the Anders Frejdh Collection*

several crucial behind-the-scenes roles proved more difficult to fill. Initially, producers Barbara Broccoli and Michael G. Wilson enlisted director Danny Boyle (*Slumdog Millionaire*) and his writer John Hodge (*Trainspotting*), but after months of writing, they left the project over creative differences. Fortunately, Cary Fukunaga (*Beasts of No Nation*) was suddenly available, and the young, up-and-coming director came aboard as Boyle's replacement—becoming the first American to helm an Eon Productions 007 film.

On the writing front, Bond veterans Neal Purvis and Robert Wade had already delivered a draft of the screenplay, which was put on hold while Boyle and Hodge workshopped their own take on 007. Fukunaga would eventually return to the Purvis/Wade blueprint—with the inspired addition of ace British actor/writer/producer Phoebe Waller-Bridge, fresh off her acclaimed television series *Killing Eve* and *Fleabag*. The filmmakers also hired script doctor Scott Z. Burns to further hone the finished draft. For the film's title, meanwhile, the producers borrowed "No Time to Die" from a 1958 World War II drama coproduced by Albert R. Broccoli. Retitled *Tank Force* for its US release, the original *No Time to Die* was stacked with future Bond contributors, including director Terence Young, writer Richard Maibaum, and actress Luciana Paluzzi.

Script problems pushed the production's start date a number of times, but the film finally went before the cameras in Jamaica in April 2019. *No Time to Die* would also film on locations in England, Norway, and Italy. It was a challenging production; early on, Daniel Craig broke his ankle

during a chase scene, causing further delays. And when the film was finally finished, it became one of the first victims of the devastating coronavirus pandemic. As movie theaters closed all over the world to prevent the spread of the infection, the producers and studio executives at Universal Pictures, United Artists Releasing, and Annapurna Pictures decided to push the release date from April to November 2020. It was the first in a long line of major studio releases that scrapped their long-in-the-works marketing and distribution plans for 2020.

THE CAST

James Bond	Daniel Craig
Safin	Rami Malek
Madeleine Swann	Léa Seydoux
Paloma	Ana de Armas
Nomi	Lashana Lynch
M	Ralph Fiennes
Q	Ben Whishaw
Moneypenny	Naomie Harris
Ernst Stavro Blofeld	Christoph Waltz
Logan Ash	Billy Magnussen
Felix Leiter	Jeffrey Wright
Tanner	Rory Kinnear
Valdo Obruchev	David Dencik

THE CREW

Director	Cary Joji Fukunaga
Screenplay by	Neal Purvis & Robert Wade
	Cary Joji Fukunaga
	Phoebe Waller-Bridge
Producers	Barbara Broccoli
	Michael G. Wilson

Director of Photography	Linus Sandgren
Music by	Hans Zimmer
Title song performed by	Billie Eilish
Production Designer	Mark Tildesley
Art Directors	Andrew Bennett
	Neal Callow
	Dean Clegg
	Mark Harris
	Sandra Phillips
	Tamara Marini
Second Unit Director	Alexander Witt
Stunt Coordinator	Lee Morrison
Special Effects Supervisor	Chris Corbould
Editors	Tom Cross
	Elliot Graham

Sparkling comedy actress Margaret Nolan of *Goldfinger*. *Steve Rubin Collection*

Nolan, Margaret (October 29, 1943–   ): Voluptuous British actress who portrayed Dink the masseuse in *Goldfinger*. She was also featured as the golden girl in the film's opening titles and in numerous advertisements, trailers, and commercials for the film. Although her appearance was brief, with her dialogue consisting of only a half-dozen words, she managed to parlay it into a dramatically topless

Curvaceous British comedy actress Margaret Nolan made quite an impression as Dink, the Miami masseuse who attends to James Bond (Sean Connery) in *Goldfinger*. *Courtesy of the David Reinhardt Collection*

appearance in a 1965 *Playboy* magazine pictorial. Born in Hampstead, London, Nolan made her feature film debut as Julie in director Robert Hartford-Davis's musical comedy *Saturday Night Out* (1964), which also featured Bond players Bernard Lee and Martine Beswick. The following year she portrayed Miss Jones in Gerald Thomas's *Carry On Cowboy* (1965), her first of six *Carry On . . .* films.

Norman, Monty (London, April 4, 1928–   ): Top British composer who, for *Dr. No*, arranged all of the wonderful Jamaican calypso music ("Three Blind Mice," "Jump Up," and "Under the Mango Tree") that served the film so well. And, of course, he is credited with composing the James Bond theme—although history shows that another composer, John Barry (then of the pop group the John Barry Seven), augmented Norman's original theme with the plucked guitar signature that has since become world famous.

Norman began his career as a singer with the leading British dance bands of the late 1950s and early '60s and graduated to solo performer on stage, records, and television. He wrote pop songs for himself and other artists, and when his stage musical *Expresso Bongo* (1958) became a West End hit, he abandoned his singing career to become a composer. A string of stage musicals followed, including the long-running *Make Me an Offer*; *The Art of Living*; *Belle*; *Quick Quick Slow*; *Songbook*, which won the Evening Standard, SWET (Laurence Olivier), and Ivor Novello Awards for Best Musical, and a Tony nomination for Best Book; *Poppy*, which brought him yet another SWET Award for Best Musical; and

Pinocchio, his first children's musical. His film works include the songs for *The Two Faces of Dr. Jekyll* (1960); the beatnik music in *The Day the Earth Caught Fire* (1961); the score for *Call Me Bwana* (1963), produced by Cubby Broccoli and Harry Saltzman; and the lyrics in *Irma La Douce* (1963). Norman's songs have been recorded by scores of top British, American, and European artists, including Cliff Richard, Tommy Steele, Shirley MacLaine, Bob Hope, Mantovani, and Count Basie. His many television credits include *Against the Crowd* (1975) and *Dickens of London* (1976). In 1988, the British Academy of Song-writers, Composers, and Authors (now the Ivors Academy) honored him with the highly coveted Gold Badge of Merit, for services to British music.

Northolt: British airfield outside London that simulated Blue Grass Field, Kentucky, in *Goldfinger*. Formerly London's main airport, the field was also used in *Octopussy* to simulate a South American air force base.

NUMBERS AND FIGURES IN THE JAMES BOND SERIES

- **1 minute and 52 seconds**: The amount of time it takes SPECTRE assassin Donald Grant (Robert Shaw) to track and strangle the phony James Bond in the *From Russia with Love* pre-credits teaser.
- **2 moles on the left thigh**: The method by which 007 (Sean Connery) recognizes Domino (Claudine Auger) in *Thunderball*. He spots the identifying marks when she climbs into her motorboat.
- **2 white dots**: The familiar animated logo designed by title specialist Maurice Binder for the first James Bond film, *Dr. No*, in 1962. The logo is featured in each film in the series. Accompanied by John Barry's staccato signature 007 theme (which was continuously reorchestrated by succeeding composers), two dots—simulating the view down the scope of a sniper's rifle—roll across the screen, merging into one dot through which James Bond takes his patented walk. The dot itself then takes on the characteristics of the inside of a gun barrel. At a given point, 007 turns and fires at the screen, triggering a red shroud that slowly

covers the dot. As it wavers and begins to sink, indicating the death of the sniper, the single dot reappears, through which we see the first scene of the movie's pre-credits teaser. In the first three James Bond movies, which were projected on the screen in the 1.85:1 ratio—referred to in film jargon as "flat"—stuntman Bob Simmons portrayed James Bond. When *Thunderball* was planned as the first 2.35:1 widescreen Bond film—referred to in film jargon as "scope," for "Cinemascope"—title designer Maurice Binder was forced to create a new version of the 007 logo. He asked Sean Connery to take the patented "walk and fire." Since then, George Lazenby, Roger Moore, Timothy Dalton, Pierce Brosnan, and Daniel Craig have all taken the walk in the dot.

- **4 jacks**: Winning hand of Le Chiffre (Mads Mikkelsen) against Bond's full house (kings over aces), which cleans out Bond early in the no-limit Texas hold'em poker tournament in *Casino Royale*. Bond thought Le Chiffre was bluffing because he twitched— what Bond determined was the man's "tell." Unfortunately, 007 has been betrayed by one of his allies, who alerted Le Chiffre prior to the hand.

  Steve Rubin Collection

- **4 minutes**: The amount of time on the counter when Mr. Ling (Burt Kwouk) activates the atomic device that's set to explode inside Fort Knox in *Goldfinger*. When the bomb is deactivated, the timer stops, fittingly enough, at 007—even though Bond (Sean Connery) quips, "Three more ticks and Mr. Goldfinger would've hit the jackpot." Four minutes is also the amount of time that Bond (Roger Moore) has left to stop World War III when he enters the shattered command center of the *Liparus* supertanker in *The Spy Who Loved Me*. During Bond's rush to change the trajectory of the soon-to-be-launched nuclear missiles, a technical blooper occurs in the dialogue regarding the time remaining. Only ten seconds after the *Liparus*'s skipper (Sydney Tafler) says four minutes remain until the launch, Commander Carter (Shane Rimmer) says only three minutes are left.
- **4.2mm**: The unusual caliber of the automatic pistol used by Francisco Scaramanga (Christo-

pher Lee) in *The Man with the Golden Gun*. Its bullets are custom manufactured by a Macao gunsmith named Lazar (Marne Maitland).

- **6 hours**: The amount of time that the *Disco Volante*, the yacht belonging to Emilio Largo (Adolfo Celi), was out of Nassau Harbor on the night of the A-bomb hijacking in *Thunderball*.
- **13 Gs**: The amount of force that Bond (Roger Moore) endures in the sabotaged centrifuge trainer in *Moonraker*. According to Dr. Holly Goodhead (Lois Chiles), a normal human being will black out at 7 Gs.
- **58 days**: The number of days it took to shoot *Dr. No* in 1962. It is also the exact number of days, owing to bad weather in Switzerland and a complicated script, that *On Her Majesty's Secret Service* went over schedule in 1969.
- **58 years**: The amount of time the entire American gold reserve will remain radioactive if Goldfinger (Gert Fröbe) successfully explodes an atomic device inside Fort Knox, Kentucky, in *Goldfinger*.

© Kevynbj | Dreamstime.com

- **98.4 degrees**: The correct temperature for serving saki, according to James Bond (Sean Connery) in *You Only Live Twice*.
- **106 minutes**: The running time of *Quantum of Solace*, the shortest Bond film to date. *No Time to Die* is the longest at 163 minutes. NOTE: Running times tend to be much longer now, due mostly to the lengthy closing credit roll, which includes virtually everyone who worked on the film.

© Geotrac | Dreamstime.com

- **$1,000**: The amount of money paid to author Ian Fleming by CBS in 1954 for television rights to *Casino Royale*. The resulting one-hour dramatization, starring Barry Nelson as James Bond, was telecast live at 8:30 PM EST on October 21, 1954, as the third entry of the network's Climax Mystery Theater, an anthology series hosted by actor William Lundigan.
- **5,000 pounds**: The value of the gold bar loaned to 007 (Sean Connery) by the Bank of England, which becomes the prize in his high-stakes golf challenge match with Goldfinger (Gert Fröbe). The bar was smelted in 1940 at

the Weigenhaler Foundry in Essen, Germany. It was part of a smelt of six hundred ingots that were lost in 1944, near the end of World War II, but are now rumored to be lying at the bottom of Lake Toplitz in Austria's Salzkammergut region.

- **$6,000**: Actress Ursula Andress's salary for playing Honey Ryder in *Dr. No*—$1,000 a week for six weeks' work.
- **$15,000**: According to the terms dictated by James Bond (Sean Connery), it's the amount of money that Goldfinger (Gert Fröbe) must lose to Mr. Simmons (Austin Willis) in the rigged Miami Beach gin game in *Goldfinger*. Otherwise, 007 is calling the Miami Beach police.
- **22,000 pounds**: Both Sean Connery's salary for *Dr. No* and George Lazenby's salary for *On Her Majesty's Secret Service*.
- **41,000**: The number of US Army troops guarding the gold depository at Fort Knox, Kentucky, in *Goldfinger*. One of the gangsters who attends the "hoods convention" assembled by Goldfinger (Gert Fröbe) mistakenly guesses 35,000.

© Johncox1958 | Dreamstime.com

- **45,000 feet**: Cruising altitude of the doomed NATO jet bomber in *Thunderball*. Hijacked by SPECTRE mercenary Angelo Palazzi (Paul Stassino), it will drop below radar and land in the fictional Golden Grotto near Nassau, Bahamas.
- **50,000 carats**: The weight of the huge diamond cache that James Bond (Sean Connery) will smuggle from Amsterdam to Los Angeles in *Diamonds Are Forever*. Surprised when Tiffany Case (Jill St. John) mentions the size of the cache, Bond, posing as diamond smuggler Peter Franks (Joe Robinson), whom he's just killed, calculates that at 142 carats to the ounce, that's "a lot of ice." That "ice" will eventually fall into the hands of Ernst Stavro Blofeld (Charles Gray), who will use it to power his laser satellite. Bond/Franks receives $50,000 for smuggling the diamonds into the US.
- **$115,200**: Insured value of the jewelry worn by Talisa Soto to play Lupe Lamora in *Licence to Kill*. The antique chokers, bracelets, and rings were supplied to the production by a Los Angeles collector/dealer. Her name: Sheila Goldfinger.

- **$500,000**: What United Artists offered American producer Charles K. Feldman for the screen rights to *Casino Royale* in 1965. He refused and produced his spoof version two years later. It's also the value of the red poker plaque with which James Bond (Daniel Craig) tips the dealer after he wins everything in the Texas hold'em game in *Casino Royale*.

- **$1.25 million**: Sean Connery's salary on *Diamonds Are Forever*. To entice him back into the 007 role, United Artists production executive David Picker also agreed to finance two films of Connery's choice. Other elements of the unprecedented offer included a percentage of the film's profits and a provision that if the film went over its eighteen-week shooting schedule, Connery would get an extra $10,000 a week. The enormous length of the Bond production schedules had always irritated Connery, who did not like to spend so much of his time devoted to one project. *Diamonds Are Forever* was finished on schedule, sparing UA the extra cash outlay for its star.

Steve Rubin Collection

- **$115 million**: The amount in the final poker tournament pot in *Casino Royale*. Bond (Daniel Craig) beats Le Chiffre (Mads Mikkelsen) with a very impressive straight flush (4-5-6-7-8 of spades).

- **$280 million**: The amount of ransom that SPECTRE demands from NATO after hijacking two atomic bombs in *Thunderball*. In English currency in 1965, this amount translated to 100 million pounds sterling. The ransom, to be paid in flawless blue-white diamonds weighing between three and eight carats, was then to be dropped in the Mergui Archipelago off the coast of present-day Myanmar.

© *Marinini | Dreamstime.com*

- **$15 billion**: The amount of gold deposited in the Fort Knox gold repository when it becomes the target of Auric Goldfinger (Gert Fröbe) and his Operation Grand Slam in *Goldfinger*.

obeah: Term for the supernatural power of second sight that Solitaire (Jane Seymour) possesses in *Live and Let Die*. With her tarot cards, it allows her to predict the future for her boss, Dr. Kananga (Yaphet Kotto), a sinister island diplomat turned drug smuggler.

Oberhauser, Franz: Birth name of SPECTRE head Ernst Stavro Blofeld (Christoph Waltz) in *Spectre*, who in the course of the story is also revealed to be the foster brother of James Bond (Daniel Craig).

Octopus Cult: An old secret order of female bandits and smugglers that is revived by the title character (Maud Adams) in *Octopussy*. The sign of the cult is a blue-ringed octopus tattoo; Magda (Kristina Wayborn) has one of them on her buttocks, and Octopussy's barge flies the symbol on its pennant. The blue-ringed octopus, of the genus *Hapalochlaena*, produces a venom that is usually fatal in seconds.

Octopussy: The title character in the thirteenth James Bond film produced by Albert R. Broccoli. As portrayed by Maud Adams, Octopussy is the fabulously wealthy and resourceful leader of the Octopus Cult, a sect of acrobatic lady smugglers who live on a secluded island in the middle of Lake Pichola in Udaipur, India.

Octopussy is the daughter of Major Dexter Smythe, a former British Army officer and Secret Service agent who stole a cache of Chinese gold from North Korea and, in so doing, murdered his guide. Twenty years later, James Bond (Roger Moore) traced Smythe to Sri Lanka and gave him twenty-four hours to clear up his affairs before Bond brought him back to London for trial. Rather than face the disgrace of a court-martial, Smythe

committed suicide. Before he died, Smythe had become a leading authority on octopi. His pet name for his only daughter was "Octopussy."

When Smythe's gold ran out, the people of Hong Kong who helped dispose of it offered Octopussy a commission to smuggle some diamonds. Developing a talent for such illegal activities, she revived the old Octopus Cult and populated its ranks with a group of attractive young women who were searching for spiritual discipline. As her wealth increased, Octopussy diversified into shipping, hotels, carnivals, and circuses.

 OCTOPUSSY

(United Artists, 1983) ★★★⧸ : The thirteenth James Bond film produced by Albert R. Broccoli. US release date: June 10, 1983. Budget: $27.5 million. Worldwide box office gross: $187.5 million (Domestic gross: $67.9 million; international gross: $119.6 million).* Running time: 131 minutes.

--------- **THE SETUP** ---------

There are many ways to initiate World War III. Renegade Soviet general Orlov (Steven Berkoff) wants to make sure the Americans are blamed. His nefarious plan is to detonate a nuclear bomb on a US Air Force base in West Germany. He then predicts that this "accident" will force the West to dismantle its nuclear deterrent, allowing Soviet forces to overrun Europe. To fulfill this dream of Russian conquest, he offers up a fortune in Russian state jewels to renegade Afghan prince Kamal Khan (Louis Jourdan), who convinces a group of female circus performers and acrobats led by Octopussy (Maud Adams) to participate in the scheme. However, when one of the jewels—a Fabergé egg—is stolen by a mortally wounded 009 (Andy Bradford) and delivered to the British ambassador in East Berlin, British intelligence launches into the fray—sending James Bond (Roger Moore) to India on Operation Trove.

--------- **BEHIND THE SCENES** ---------

Continuing the 007 revival that began with *The Spy Who Loved Me* three films earlier, *Octopussy*

---
* "Octopussy (1983)," The Numbers, accessed June 18, 2020, https://www.the-numbers.com/movie/Octopussy.

Sultry Maud Adams returns to the James Bond series as the title character, a smuggler and circus entrepreneur, in *Octopussy. Courtesy of the David Reinhardt Collection*

ranked just behind its predecessor *Moonraker* at the US box office. Thanks to a risqué title, another inspired marketing campaign, and an interesting blend of *Goldfinger* glitz and *From Russia with Love* intrigue, it's an excellent entry that keeps up the momentum despite its excessive length.

Comfortably directed by John Glen, the film is filled with memorable set pieces that keep the plot moving, such as the mini jet pre-credits teaser, 009's final, fatal mission in East Germany, and Bond's attempts to disarm the A-bomb while dressed as a circus clown. Like the previous film, *For Your Eyes Only*, it's filled with henchmen and other characters with mystique, including Kamal Khan's deadly twin assassins, portrayed effectively by twins David and Tony Meyer, and Kabir Bedi's awesome Gobinda.

Low points: Maud Adams's Octopussy serves little purpose in the plot and takes a backseat to Kamal Khan's treachery. Kristina Wayborn's Magda actually steals the film out from under her. Although the sequences in India are suitably exotic, the chase through the streets of Udaipur is too silly, featuring another double-taking animal—this time, a camel. But once the film gets to Germany, it takes off, building incredible drama inside the circus tent as Bond disarms the nuclear bomb. Other high points include Steven Berkoff's strutting General Orlov, the John Barry score, and Rita Coolidge's opening-titles song, "All Time High."

THE CAST

James Bond	Roger Moore
Octopussy	Maud Adams
Kamal Khan	Louis Jourdan
Magda	Kristina Wayborn
Gobinda	Kabir Bedi
General Orlov	Steven Berkoff

The South American aircraft hangar built in miniature by Derek Meddings's effects crew for *Octopussy*. *Courtesy of the Brian Smithies Archive*

The same hangar after special effects explosives blow it apart. *Courtesy of the Brian Smithies Archive*

Mischka (Twin No. 1)	David Meyer	Kamp	Dermot Crowley
Grischka (Twin No. 2)	Anthony Meyer	Lenkin	Peter Porteous
Q	Desmond Llewelyn	Rublevitch	Eva Rueber-Staier
M	Robert Brown	Smithers	Jeremy Bullock
Miss Moneypenny	Lois Maxwell	Bianca	Tina Hudson
Penelope Smallbone	Michaela Clavell	Thug with Yo-Yo	William Derrick
General Gogol	Walter Gotell	Major Clive	Stuart Saunders
Vijay	Vijay Amritraj	British Ambassador	Patrick Barr
Sadruddin	Albert Moses	Borchoi	Gabor Vernon
Minister of Defence	Geoffrey Keen	Karl	Hugo Bower
Jim Fanning	Douglas Wilmer	Colonel Toro	Ken Norris
009	Andy Bradford	Francisco the Fearless	Richard Graydon
Auctioneer	Philip Voss	Circus Performers	The Hassani Troupe, the Flying
General	Bruce Boa		Cherokees, Carol and Josef Richter,
US Aide	Richard Parmentier		Vera and Shirley Fossett, Barrie Winship
Soviet Chairman	Paul Hardwick	Octopussy Girls	Mary Stavin, Carolyn Seaward,
Gwendoline	Suzanne Jerome		Carole Ashby, Cheryl Anne, Jani-Z,
Midge	Cherry Gillespie		Julie Martin, Joni Flynn, Julie Barth, Kathy Davies,

Helene Hunt, Gillian De Terville, Safira Afzal,
Louise King, Tina Robinson, Alison Worth, Janine
Andrews, Lynda Knight

Gymnasts   Suzanne Dando (supervisor), Teresa
Craddock, Kirsten Harrison,
Christine Cullers, Lisa Jackman, Jane Aldridge,
Christine Gibson, Tracy Llewellyn, Ruth Flynn

Thugs   Ravinder Singh Reyett, Gurdial Sira, Michael
Moor, Sven Surtees, Peter Edmund,
Ray Charles, Talib Johnny

THE CREW

Director	John Glen
Screenplay by	George MacDonald Fraser
Richard Maibaum & Michael G. Wilson	
Executive Producer	Michael G. Wilson
Producer	Albert R. Broccoli
Associate Producer	Tom Pevsner
Director of Photography	Alan Hume
Music by	John Barry
"All Time High" performed by	Rita Coolidge
Lyrics by	Tim Rice
Production Designer	Peter Lamont
Second Unit Direction and Photography	Arthur Wooster
Camera Operator	Alec Mills
Vehicle Stunt Coordinator	Remy Julienne
Title Designer	Maurice Binder
Special Effects Supervisor	John Richardson
Editor	John Grover

Oddjob: The prototypical villain's henchman, as portrayed by Japanese actor Harold Sakata

Oddjob (Harold Sakata) demonstrates his steel-rimmed bowler hat throwing ability for the benefit of James Bond (Sean Connery) and Auric Goldfinger (Gert Fröbe) in *Goldfinger*. *Courtesy of the David Reinhardt Collection*

in *Goldfinger*. A Korean by birth, and mute, the powerfully built Oddjob works for Auric Goldfinger (Gert Fröbe) as his bodyguard/chauffeur/assassin and sometime caddy. His trademark weapon is a bowler hat equipped with a razor-sharp steel brim, which in his hands becomes a sort of lethal Frisbee. Dressed impeccably in formal suits, with a perpetually wicked smile across his face, he's a formidable presence who nearly destroys Bond (Sean Connery) in the climactic fight inside glittering Fort Knox. Predating the karate/kung fu genre by a full decade, Oddjob was one of a series of Asian supervillains who are quite popular in the world-spanning 007 series.

O'Herlihy, Gavan (April 29, 1954–   ): Irish American character actor who portrayed US Air Force officer Captain Jack Petachi in *Never Say Never Again*. Perfectly cast as the nervous traitor who falls under the spell of vicious SPECTRE assassin Fatima Blush (Barbara Carrera), O'Herlihy's Petachi is a whimpering bundle of nerves forced into increasingly dangerous actions to save the life of his sister Domino (Kim Basinger). Born in Dublin, O'Herlihy is the son of actor Dan O'Herlihy (*Fail Safe*). He made his first major splash on American television when he was cast as Ron Howard's older brother Chuck Cunningham on *Happy Days* (7 episodes, 1974). He made his big-screen debut as Wilson Briggs in director Robert Altman's dramedy *A Wedding* (1978). Genre audiences may remember him as hunky Airk Thaughbaer, a rebel warrior in *Willow* (1988).

oil-rig battle: The pièce de résistance in *Diamonds Are Forever*, in which CIA helicopters raid the oil-rig command post of Blofeld (Charles Gray) in Baja California. Aboard the rig, Blofeld commands an orbiting laser satellite, powered by a huge diamond solar shield, that can wipe out any target on Earth.

As Blofeld waits for the Western powers to provide a huge ransom—otherwise Washington, DC, will be destroyed—Bond (Sean Connery) arrives inside a giant inflatable ball that has been dropped into the ocean near the oil rig. His mission is to somehow enter Blofeld's control room and substitute a phony command cassette for the one being used to guide the satellite. Why would Blofeld allow him anywhere near the navigation apparatus for the satellite? Because Bond villains notoriously reveal their plans to 007 before they kill him. It's an unspoken rule.

Bond achieves his mission—but, unfortunately, Tiffany Case (Jill St. John) misinterprets his subterfuge and actually switches back in the real cassette. By then, the CIA helicopters have launched their attack on the oil rig, which Blofeld defends using antiaircraft cannons, machine guns, and armor plating. The sudden attack—initiated by Bond, who thought the cassette swap was successful—actually confuses Blofeld and his missile expert Professor Dr. Metz (Joseph Furst). Thanks to some direct hits, the command center is blown apart, and the satellite's laser cannon is neutralized.

Bond, meanwhile, has found Blofeld trying to escape in his bathosub. Knocking out a crane operator, Bond assumes control of the winching mechanism and begins to have some torturous fun with the SPECTRE chief. Lifting the sub out of the water, he eventually slams it into the control room, supposedly killing Blofeld—although he returns briefly in a wheelchair in the pre-credits teaser of *For Your Eyes Only*, and is later resurrected for the Daniel Craig films.

The oil-rig battle was filmed aboard a studio-customized oil rig that was rented and placed off the coast of southern California, near Oceanside. The rig itself was a portable, floatable device built around a barge-like structure with enormous retractable sea legs. During filming, the crew was based in Oceanside at the Bridge Motel. Each morning, helicopters would transport the cast, director, and immediate production staff to the rig, while boats carried the extras and technical crew.

At a nearby dirt airfield, other choppers were being prepared to serve as the CIA attack force for their assault on the rig. Each one was outfitted with special effects weaponry, including metal tubes filled with electrically activated powder charges that simulated the *whoosh* of air-to-ground rockets, and small strobe lights that simulated the fire of machine guns. During one sequence that doesn't appear in the finished film, the helicopters dropped demolition-carrying frogmen into the water around the rig to prepare for the rig's final destruction. According to writer/director Robert Short, who observed some of the oil-rig sequence in 1971, the deleted sequence explains the presence of frogmen on the film's final release poster.

Old Albert: Huge crocodile featured in *Live and Let Die*. It's responsible for mauling Tee Hee (Julius Harris), costing him his right arm.

old man: The irritating term that Donald Grant (Robert Shaw) uses to refer to Bond (Sean Connery) on the Orient Express in *From Russia with Love*.

Olimpatec Meditation Institute (OMI): Oddly shaped, surreal religious retreat that is the home of televangelist Joe Butcher (Wayne Newton) in *Licence to Kill*. Located outside fictional Isthmus City, it also houses the cocaine laboratories of drug runner Franz Sanchez (Robert Davi)—it's where his drugs are being dissolved in gasoline. From this unusual location, Sanchez's tanker-truck convoy begins its ride to the ocean. In reality, the OMI complex, much of which is cone-shaped—hence the film's references to "cone power"—is the Centro Ceremonial Otomí, or Otomí Ceremonial Center, in Temoaya, Mexico, which the native Otomí people erected in 1980 to serve as a meeting place and to honor their religion and culture.

ON HER MAJESTY'S SECRET SERVICE

(United Artists, 1969) ★★★★: The sixth James Bond film produced by Albert R. Broccoli and Harry Saltzman. US release date: December 18, 1969. Budget: $8 million. Worldwide box office gross: $82.0 million (US domestic gross: $22.8 million; international gross: $59.2 million).* Running time: 140 minutes.

--- **THE SETUP** ---

James Bond (George Lazenby) is on holiday in coastal Portugal when he spies a lady in distress—the stunning Contessa Teresa "Tracy" di Vicenzo (Diana Rigg). Rescuing her from a possible suicide, and later from beach thugs, Bond ends up holding her shoes as she drives off, uttering, "This never happened to the other fellow." Later at the local casino, 007 covers Tracy's losses when she feigns poverty. This time, Bond's reward is a single night with Tracy.

* "On Her Majesty's Secret Service (1969)," The Numbers, accessed June 22, 2020, https://www.the-numbers.com /movie/On-Her-Majestys-Secret-Service.

Bond is later held at gunpoint and taken to Tracy's father, Marc-Ange Draco, the head of a powerful Italian crime organization, the Union Corse. He offers Bond a huge dowry if he'll marry Tracy, a ridiculous offer that 007 dismisses. Then, suddenly, 007 has an epiphany: If Draco can track down the whereabouts of one Ernst Stavro Blofeld of SPECTRE, he might agree to an arrangement.

The circa-1960s cover of the American paperback edition of *On Her Majesty's Secret Service*. *Steve Rubin Collection*

── BEHIND THE SCENES ──

If Sean Connery had stuck around for one more Bond film, *OHMSS* would have been his best. It offers 007 one of his most epic and yet most human stories, giving him the opportunity to finally meet his female match. Fans will always wonder what would have happened if Connery had been the one to fall in love and get married to Diana Rigg.

Instead, Bond was played by ex-model George Lazenby. He was no Sean Connery, but thanks to the careful direction of Peter Hunt and the fabulous script by Richard Maibaum, he comes across extremely well. Lazenby brought his own form of charisma to the role—he was handsome, capable, and light on his feet. He could play the droll humor and the two-fisted machismo. Had he not quit the series after one film, there is every reason to believe that he would have flourished in the role of Bond. *OHMSS* was his training ground for a continuing part that, unfortunately, never materialized.

The film marked the end of the training period for Peter Hunt, who had edited the first four films and shot second unit on *You Only Live Twice*, and finally earned his directing spurs. Tasked with adapting one of Fleming's best books, Hunt worked carefully with Maibaum to create one of the most carefully tuned Bond films. Once again, the set pieces are legendary, but they do not interfere with the story as they did in *You Only Live Twice*.

Lazenby's introduction is another classic moment, which takes place on the beach in Portugal with Bond rescuing Tracy from the surf. The fistfight in the water with a Draco henchman is a perfect example of Hunt's rapid-fire directing style. The Bond series has benefited greatly when its editors have been given the opportunity to direct. Peter Hunt, like John Glen, knew where to place his cameras for maximum effect.

Like *From Russia with Love* and *For Your Eyes Only*, *OHMSS* is filled with mysterious characters and realistic action. Blofeld's plot involves germ warfare—a very earthbound caper—and his stronghold this time is not a volcano rocket base but a converted Swiss allergy clinic. The action never lets up: ski chases, bobsled chases,

Diana Rigg and George Lazenby have some fun during a publicity shoot for *On Her Majesty's Secret Service*. *Courtesy of the Malcolm McNeil Collection*

car chases, helicopter attacks, fights in the surf, fights in the hotel, fights in the office. As with *Dr. No*, the producers wanted to keep the focus on movement to keep the audience from noticing any lapses in logic—in this case, the fact that Bond was now a completely different person. They succeeded.

Diana Rigg was an inspired bit of casting. She was a star in both Britain and America, thanks to her role as Emma Peel in the international-hit spy series *The Avengers*, and audiences were ready to accept her as Bond's potential mate. Telly Savalas's Blofeld was fair, though a European actor along the lines of Adolfo Celi would have been better. Gabriele Ferzetti was excellent as Marc-Ange Draco, the mafioso who joins forces with Bond to rescue his daughter, Tracy. And John Barry outdid himself with one of the series' best musical scores, including his rousing title instrumental.

The film boasted the series' longest running time to date—a record that would not be beaten until *Casino Royale* in 2006. Editor John Glen cut nearly 40 minutes of footage before he settled on the 140-minute cut, the length of which was kept a close secret from producers Broccoli and Saltzman. "Eventually," said director Peter Hunt, "I did have to tell them, and Harry was furious. I think they had told United Artists that the final print would be less than two hours long. Of course, with a longer running time, UA couldn't get in as many screenings. So there was this big song and dance about how long the film was and that it had to be cut.

"I was eventually saved from a major edit on the film by George Pinches, the booking manager of the Rank Organisation, who came to see the film in the little theater at Audley Square. Harry and Cubby told him to come and see them after the film. When it was over, George was very complimentary about the film's potential. Before anyone could say a word, I said to him, 'George, do you think I should cut the film anywhere? Is it too long?' And he said, 'Long? Long? How long have I been here, an hour and a half?' And I told him that he had been in the theater for almost two and a half hours. He told us not to touch a foot. This, of course, was said right in front of the producers, which ended any controversy over whether the film was going to be reedited."[*]

The assault on Piz Gloria in *On Her Majesty's Secret Service* by artist Paul Mann. *Courtesy of the Paul Mann Collection / Thomas Nixdorf*

The running time, however, did create a problem when the film was prepared for its US television debut on ABC. The network considered it too long for a standard two-hour time slot, even with the sorts of cuts that had been standard operating procedure for earlier Bond telecasts. Instead, without consulting Eon Productions or Peter Hunt, ABC decided to break the film in half for a two-night run. To fit the expanded running time, the network actually *added* footage, running certain sequences twice, once in their proper position and once earlier in the film. In the earlier instances, voiceover narration by a non-Lazenby "James Bond" attempted to explain the out-of-context scenes the viewers were seeing. It was an ill-conceived idea that confused and angered fans throughout the United States.

---

* Peter Hunt, interview by the author, London, June 21, 1977.

THE CAST

James Bond	George Lazenby
Tracy	Diana Rigg
Ernst Stavro Blofeld	Telly Savalas
Irma Bunt	Ilse Steppat
Marc-Ange Draco	Gabriele Ferzetti
Grunther	Yuri Borienko
Campbell	Bernard Horsfall
Sir Hilary Bray, Baronet	George Baker
M	Bernard Lee
Q	Desmond Llewelyn
Miss Moneypenny	Lois Maxwell
Ruby Bartlett	Angela Scoular
Nancy	Catherine Schell
Olympe	Virginia North

Piz Gloria Girls

American Girl	Dani Sheridan
Scandinavian Girl	Julie Ege
English Girl	Joanna Lumley
Chinese Girl	Mona Chong
Australian Girl	Anoushka Hempel
German Girl	Ingrid Black
Italian Girl	Jenny Hanley
Indian Girl	Zara
Jamaican Girl	Sylvana Henriques
Israeli Girl	Helena Ronee

Draco's Men

Toussaint	Geoffrey Cheshire
Che Che	Irvin Allen
Raphael	Terry Mountain
Kleff	Bill Morgan
Driver	Richard Graydon
Helicopter Pilot	John Crewdson

Blofeld's Men

Felsen	Les Crawford
Braun	George Cooper
Driver	Reg Harding
Gumbold (Swiss Lawyer)	James Bree
Manuel (Portuguese Hotel Manager)	Brian Worth
Janitor (who whistles "Goldfinger")	Norman McGlen
Hall Porter	Dudley Jones
Piz Gloria Receptionist	Joseph Vasa

At the Casino

American Guests	Bessie Love
	Elliott Sullivan
Greek Tycoon	Steve Plytas
Chef de Jeu	Robert Rietty
Chef de Jeu Hussier	Martin Leyden

THE CREW

Director	Peter Hunt
Screenplay by	Richard Maibaum
Producers	Albert R. Broccoli
	Harry Saltzman
Associate Producer	Stanley Sopel
Director of Photography	Michael Reed
Music composed and conducted by	John Barry
"We Have All the Time in the World" performed by	Louis Armstrong
Lyrics by	Hal David
Production Designer	Syd Cain
Art Director	Bob Laing
Construction Manager	Ronnie Udell
Set Dresser	Peter Lamont
Costume Designer	Marjory Cornelius
Production Supervisor	David Middlemas
Production Secretary	Golda Offenheim
First Assistant Director	Frank Ernst
Second Unit Director	John Glen
Stock-Car Sequence Director	Anthony Squire
Continuity	Joan Davis
Camera Operator	Alec Mills
Aerial Cameraman	Johnny Jordan
Ski Cameramen	Willy Bogner Jr.
	Alex Barbey
Camera Focus	Ron Drinkwater
Stunt Arranger	George Leech
Title Designer	Maurice Binder
Head Special Effects	John Stears
Sound Mixers	John Mitchell
	Gordon McCallum
Editor	John Glen

Onatopp, Xenia Zaragevna: Steel-thighed killer and former Soviet fighter pilot who now works for the Janus crime syndicate in Russia; portrayed by Famke Janssen in *GoldenEye*. Onatopp, a Georgian by birth, challenges Bond

Famke Janssen brought her strong sensuality and charisma to the role of steel-thighed Xenia Onatopp in *GoldenEye*. *Courtesy of the Luc Leclech Collection*

(Pierce Brosnan) to a wild road race outside Monte Carlo—Bond's trusty Aston Martin DB5 versus her red Ferrari. She later seduces and kills a Canadian admiral by crushing him with her thighs during lovemaking, steals a top-secret military helicopter prototype, and returns to Janus in St. Petersburg. She accompanies General Ourumov (Gottfried John) to Russia's Space Weapons Control Center in Severnaya, where she machine-guns the entire technology support staff, and then attempts to kill Bond in a St. Petersburg steam room. When Bond tracks Janus to Cuba, he runs into Onatopp, but this time he gets the better of her. When Onatopp rappels out of an enemy helicopter, she lands on top of Bond, who is groggy from a plane crash. Bond manages to pull his gun and shoot the helicopter pilot. When the chopper goes out of control, it drags Onatopp with it, slamming her against a tree and most likely snapping her spine.

OPENING-TITLES SONGS AND THE BILLBOARD HOT 100

When Duran Duran's title song for *A View to a Kill* hit number 1 on the *Billboard* Hot 100 singles chart in July 1985, it was the first time a song from the James Bond opening titles reached the top spot. Here's the record thus far of the Bond songs that have made the Hot 100:

Artist	Song	Highest No. On Top 100
Duran Duran	"A View to a Kill" (1985)	No. 1
Paul McCartney and Wings	"Live and Let Die" (1973)	No. 2
Carly Simon	"Nobody Does It Better" from *The Spy Who Loved Me* (1977)	No. 2
Sheena Easton	"For Your Eyes Only" (1981)	No. 4
Shirley Bassey	"Goldfinger" (1964)	No. 8
Madonna	"Die Another Day" (2002)	No. 8
Adele	"Skyfall" (2012)	No. 8
Billie Eilish	"No Time to Die" (2020)	No. 16
Dusty Springfield	"The Look of Love" from *Casino Royale* (1967)	No. 22
Tom Jones	"Thunderball" (1965)	No. 25
Herb Alpert and the Tijuana Brass	"Casino Royale" (1967)	No. 27
Rita Coolidge	"All Time High" (1983) from *Octopussy*	No. 36
Nancy Sinatra	"You Only Live Twice" (1967)	No. 44
Shirley Bassey	"Diamonds Are Forever"	No. 57
Sam Smith	"Writing's On the Wall" from *Spectre* (2015)	No. 71
Chris Cornell	"You Know My Name" from *Casino Royale* (2006)	No. 79
Jack White and Alicia Keys	"Another Way to Die" from *Quantum of Solace* (2008)	No. 81

Operation Bedlam: The British Secret Service code name for the Blofeld search in *On Her Majesty's Secret Service*. The worldwide hunt for the missing head of SPECTRE, last seen disappearing into the interior of his volcano rocket base in *You Only Live Twice*, is led by his most ardent foe: James Bond (George Lazenby).

Operation Grand Slam: The code name for the plan by Auric Goldfinger (Gert Fröbe) to detonate a Red Chinese atomic bomb in Fort Knox, a scheme he has spent fifteen years of his life developing. With America's entire gold reserve radioactive for fifty-eight years, economic chaos in the West will result, and Goldfinger's own gold will increase in value tenfold. Grand Slam has two tactical elements: the Grand Slam Task Force, which will break into Fort Knox and detonate the bomb, and Champagne Section, a flight of private planes that will spray the deadly Delta-9 nerve gas over the Fort Knox military reservation, eliminating the forty-one thousand American troops stationed there. The air support mission is code-named Operation Rockabye Baby. Thanks to screenwriters Richard Maibaum and Paul Dehn, this plot was a major improvement over the story in Ian Fleming's original novel, in which Goldfinger and his team of organized-crime bosses simply attempt to *steal* the gold.

Operation Passover: The CIA's plan to give smuggler Tiffany Case (Jill St. John) a cache of diamonds at the Circus Circus Hotel and Casino in *Diamonds Are Forever*. Once she has the diamonds, Felix Leiter (Norman Burton) plans to tail her to the next stop on the smuggling pipeline. Despite a net of CIA men, Tiffany gives them the slip when she sneaks out the back exit of the Zambora transformation show. Fortunately, Bond (Sean Connery) finds Tiffany at her desert house, where Plenty O'Toole (Lana Wood) has been drowned. Tiffany then helps Bond track the diamonds to an airport locker, where Bert Saxby (Bruce Cabot) picks them up and later gives them to Professor Dr. Metz (Joseph Furst) at a gas station. While Tiffany distracts Metz, Bond sneaks into the back of his van and takes a trip out to the Tectronics lab, where Blofeld (Charles Gray), posing as the lab's billionaire owner, Willard Whyte (Jimmy Dean), has supervised the construction of a laser satellite capable of blackmailing the world.

Operation Rockabye Baby: The code name for the plan by Auric Goldfinger (Gert Fröbe) to spray Delta-9 nerve gas into the atmosphere above the US Army installation at Fort Knox. Pussy Galore (Honor Blackman) will send five voluptuous female members of her Flying Circus to accomplish the mission in their Piper Cherokee monoplanes. Their flight moniker is Champagne Section. Neither Pussy Galore nor her pilots have any idea that Delta-9 nerve gas is fatal and that Operation Rockabye Baby will put forty-one thousand troops to sleep permanently. Fortunately, Pussy comes to her senses about Goldfinger's real motives and switches the gas canisters at the last minute.

Operation Trove: Mission assigned to James Bond (Roger Moore) in *Octopussy*. He's ordered by M (Robert Brown) to discover who's selling a priceless Fabergé egg, a fake of which was stolen by 009 (Andy Bradford) in East Berlin before he was murdered.

Operation Undertow: Mission assigned to James Bond (Roger Moore) in *For Your Eyes Only*. He's sent to recover the ATAC (Automatic Targeting Attack Communicator) from the sunken hulk of the surveillance ship *St. Georges*.

"Orbis Non Sufficit": Latin for "The World Is Not Enough," the motto of the Bond family, as revealed in both the novel and the film *On Her Majesty's Secret Service*. It also provides the title of the nineteenth James Bond film.

Orchidae nigra: The scientific name for the black orchid, the fictional, highly toxic jungle plant from which billionaire industrialist and madman Hugo Drax (Michael Lonsdale) has developed a nerve gas that could destroy all human, but not animal, life on Earth in *Moonraker*. According to Q (Desmond Llewelyn), who briefs Bond at a Brazilian jungle village, the orchid was thought to have been extinct but was brought back from Brazil's Tapirapé River by a missionary. Archaeological reports indicate that long-term exposure to the orchid's pollen caused sterility in the race of people who built the ancient city in the Amazon that is now Drax's space shuttle launch site.

Orient Express: The famous passenger train that is the setting for a good portion of *From Russia* *with Love.* Although its schedule has changed many times since its first trip on October 4, 1883, the Simplon Orient Express of the mid-1900s left Istanbul and traveled through Thessaloníki, Belgrade, Venice, Milan, and Lausanne, until it eventually arrived in Paris four days and five nights later. Bond (Sean Connery); Kerim Bey (Pedro Armendáriz), the head of the British Secret Service in Turkey; and defecting Soviet cipher clerk Tatiana "Tanya" Romanova (Daniela Bianchi) board the train in Istanbul after blowing up the Russian embassy and stealing the Lektor decoding machine. Unfortunately, two enemy agents follow them onto the train: Commissar Benz (Peter Bayliss), a Russian security agent, and Donald Grant (Robert Shaw), a ruthless SPECTRE assassin who, following the scheme of master planner Kronsteen (Vladek Sheybal), is intent on murdering Bond, Romanova, Kerim Bey, and Benz, as well as stealing back the Lektor decoder.

Trains have always provided a perfect setting for mysteries, and the Orient Express doesn't disappoint. Terence Young's direction is masterful, considering that the entire sequence was shot on a stationary soundstage at Pinewood Studios. You really believe you are on the actual Orient Express headed for exotic points west.

On the train, with Kerim Bey's help, Bond and Tanya prepare their escape near the Bulgarian frontier, where they will leave the train and catch a chartered plane to Athens and then a jet to London. Kerim Bey even corners Benz and decides to keep him company until his friends get across the border with the stolen decoder. But Grant steps in and destroys the plan's chances for success by killing Kerim Bey and Benz.

Thanks to the film's editor, Peter Hunt, much of the following sequences are intercut with scenes of the Orient Express making its way across the Balkans at night—with a map showing the train's position superimposed over the action. John Barry's moody score takes on the character of the Orient Express itself—penetrating, relentless, full throttle.

The train stops in Belgrade, and Bond informs one of Kerim Bey's sons about the fate of his father. Agent 007 asks for help from M (Bernard Lee), who must send an agent to the next stop—Zagreb. There help comes from local British agent Nash (Bill Hill), who unfortunately becomes Grant's next victim. Killing Nash in the station

Dining on the Orient Express in *From Russia with Love* are, left to right, James Bond (Sean Connery), Tatiana Romanova (Daniela Bianchi), and Donald Grant (Robert Shaw) posing as Captain Nash. *Courtesy of the David Reinhardt Collection*

restroom, Grant assumes his identity—the perfect cover as he continues to pursue his remaining quarry.

All of these sequences have a great reality and vitality about them, thanks to the no-nonsense acting of Sean Connery and Robert Shaw. First of all, both actors look good—tall, muscled, well dressed, and ready for action. The train has an ominous, unfriendly air about it; the stations, equally so.

Worming his way into 007's confidence, Grant drugs Tanya and knocks Bond unconscious, trapping 007 in what becomes one of the Bond series' most threatening situations. Disarmed and

Tanya (Daniela Bianchi) learns that negligees are not appropriate for Piccadilly Circus while traveling with James Bond (Sean Connery) on the Orient Express in *From Russia with Love. Courtesy of the David Reinhardt Collection*

on his knees, Bond finds himself looking down the long barrel of Grant's
silenced automatic.

Listen to the dialogue in this
sequence, and you will hear the gems
of screenwriter Richard Maibaum.
Bond is going to die; there's no way
he's going to survive the ruthless
Grant, who has murdered everyone
in sight thus far in the movie. Fortunately, Grant's greed and Q's trick
briefcase save the day. Staggered
by the briefcase's tear-gas cartridge,
Grant loses the initiative and is jumped
by Bond. One of the best fights in
cinema history begins, filmed expertly
by Terence Young and later edited to
a knife's edge by Peter Hunt. Hunt is
also the one who convinced Young
to add a free camera to catch much
of the action that spilled across two
compartments.

The men trade incredible punch
after punch after punch, until Grant
pulls out his "strangler's watch"
and nearly kills Bond, who has also
reached for a gadget: the throwing
knife hidden in the briefcase. He finally
stabs Grant in the arm. Staggered
by the blow, Grant drops his guard,
allowing Bond to strangle him with his
own watch.

With the barely conscious Tanya
and the Lektor decoder in tow,
Bond exits the train as it makes its
own unscheduled stop for what
was supposed to be Grant's escape
route. SPECTRE agent Rhoda (Peter
Brayham) has stalled his Chevrolet truck on the
tracks, a ploy that will stop the train long enough
for Grant to make good his own escape. Unfortunately for the agent, it is Bond who comman-
deers his vehicle and escapes.

Behind the scenes as General Orlov (Steven Berkoff) attempts to
make his escape to the West in *Octopussy*. *Steve Rubin Collection*

Orlov, General: Fanatical Russian general
portrayed by Steven Berkoff in *Octopussy*.
Determined to convince the detente-conscious
Soviet leadership that a successful military invasion of Western Europe is still possible, Orlov
plans to detonate a nuclear weapon on the US
Air Force's Feldstadt Air Base in West Germany
and blame the Americans. Such an "accident,"

Orlov believes, will force the West to disarm
unilaterally, destroying the nuclear deterrent
along the border and allowing Soviet tanks and
infantry to cross at will.

To accomplish this plot, Orlov makes a pact
with an exiled Afghan prince named Kamal Khan
(Louis Jourdan), whose associate Octopussy
(Maud Adams) owns an international circus that
can gain access to the American base. In return,
Orlov is offering a treasure trove of jewels stolen
from the Kremlin Art Repository and replaced
with duplicates created by his forgery expert,
Lenkin (Peter Porteous). One of these forgeries,
a jeweled Fabergé Easter egg, is stolen from East
Berlin by 009 (Andy Bradford). When it ends

up in the hands of the British Secret Service, Bond (Roger Moore) is sent on Operation Trove to find the egg's real owner.

Orlov is first seen by Bond when the general arrives by Soviet helicopter at Kamal Khan's Monsoon Palace in the mountains above Udaipur, India. Having escaped from his room, where he is being held prisoner, 007 tries to listen in on the Orlov/Kamal Khan conversation, but when the lovely Magda (Kristina Wayborn) uses her blow-dryer, it interferes with the bug that Bond has planted. All he hears is a time and a place: "one week" and "Karl-Marx-Stadt."

Bond hightails it to Karl-Marx-Stadt, East Germany, where Octopussy's circus is performing, and confronts Orlov, but the general escapes when his Soviet guards attack. Now pursued by fellow Russian general Gogol (Walter Gotell), who has discovered Orlov's forged jewelry operation, Orlov makes it to the West German border. But when he crosses illegally, he's gunned down by East German border guards. Gogol stands over him, branding him a thief and a disgrace to his uniform. With his dying gasp, Orlov says, "Yes, but tomorrow I shall be a hero of the Soviet Union."

James Bond (Sean Connery) and Plenty O'Toole (Lana Wood) by Jeff Marshall. *Courtesy of Jeff Marshall*

O'Toole, Plenty: Voluptuous Las Vegas floozy portrayed by Lana Wood in *Diamonds Are Forever*. When James Bond (Sean Connery) arrives in the Whyte House casino, she dumps her boyfriend, Maxie (Ed Call), who's broke, and hooks up with the well-heeled Bond. After introducing herself, Bond replies, "Named after your father, perhaps."

Following a successful night at the tables, after which Bond gives his new girlfriend a sizable bonus, the two arrive at 007's hotel suite, only to be greeted by three hoods from the diamond smuggling syndicate Bond has been investigating. Two of the goons literally throw poor Plenty out the window. When she lands in a swimming pool, Bond quips, "Exceptionally fine shot," to which one of the hoods (Marc Lawrence)

replies, "I didn't know there was a pool down there." Bond is then free to find Tiffany Case (Jill St. John) waiting for him in bed.

In a subsequent scene in the original script, Plenty actually returns to the hotel suite and finds Tiffany Case's purse, along with the address of her house in Las Vegas. This sequence was cut from the finished film, so audiences never really knew how Plenty turned up dead in Tiffany's pool.

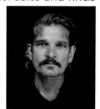

Götz Otto portrayed Stamper in *Tomorrow Never Dies*. *Steve Rubin Collection*

Otto, Götz (October 15, 1967–   ): Tall German actor, long in film and television in his native country, who portrayed the vicious Mr. Stamper, a chief henchmen to Elliot Carver (Jonathan Pryce) in *Tomorrow Never Dies*. Born in Dietzenbach, Hesse, Otto made his English-speaking motion picture debut as an SS guard in *Schindler's List* (1993).

Ourumov, General Arkady Grigorovich: Ruthless member of the Janus crime syndicate, portrayed by German actor Gottfried John in *GoldenEye*. As cover for his more sinister operations, Ourumov has a day job: he's head of the Russian Space Division, which controls orbiting satellite operations. With the aid of assassin Xenia Onatopp (Famke Janssen), Ourumov steals a secret helicopter prototype from a French missile frigate in Monte Carlo, then uses it to penetrate airspace above the Space Weapons Control Center at Severnaya, Russia. Inside, while Onatopp mows down the support staff, Ourumov inserts the "GoldenEye" computer device, which directs a space satellite to attack Severnaya with an electromagnetic pulse that obliterates the center. It's only a test—next time Janus is going to attack England.

General Ourumov (Gottfried John) holds Natalya Simonova (Izabella Scorupco) hostage on an armored train in *GoldenEye*. *Courtesy of the Nicolás Suszczyk Collection*

Palazzi, Angelo: SPECTRE-employed mercenary, portrayed by Paul Stassino, who for $100,000 agrees to undergo plastic surgery to become an exact duplicate of NATO aerial observer Major François Derval in *Thunderball*. After disposing of Derval with a blast of deadly gamma gas, Palazzi informs his SPECTRE co-conspirators Fiona Volpe (Luciana Paluzzi) and Count Lippe (Guy Doleman) that his payment must be increased to $250,000 or he will not go ahead with their plan to hijack an A-bomb-equipped NATO bomber to the Bahamas. They agree, and he succeeds in gaining entrance to a NATO air base by posing as Derval.

Aboard the Vulcan bomber, he murders his fellow crew members by inserting the gamma gas into their oxygen system, takes control of the plane, and lands it in the water near the *Disco Volante* yacht of SPECTRE spymaster Emilio Largo (Adolfo Celi). Its landing gear lowered, the plane gently floats to the sea floor of the Golden Grotto, a fictional area near Nassau, Bahamas, that is home to a deadly species of shark. When his seat belt becomes stuck, Angelo seeks the help of Largo, who has arrived in scuba gear. But instead of rescuing the mercenary, Largo takes his knife and cuts Palazzi's oxygen hose. Trapped by the malfunctioning seat belt, he drowns in the cockpit of the downed bomber.

When this sequence was shot in the water off Nassau's Clifton Pier, diver Courtney Brown, a member of the underwater film crew from Ivan Tors Studios, was doubling actor Paul Stassino. According to diving specialist and underwater cameraman/engineer Jordan Klein, Brown's actual air hose was cut; the diver was then supposed to rely on a "bailout bottle" of air once the shot was completed. However, during the sequence, Brown dropped his bailout bottle and nearly drowned before diving assistants brought him to the surface and took him to the hospital. After recovering from this accident, Brown went back to work for the climactic underwater battle, this time playing a SPECTRE diver—only to be injured by an explosive charge meant to simulate Bond (Sean Connery) firing his spear-gun at the character. The charge ignited under Brown's wet suit, causing a severe burn.

Pale King, the: Code name of SPECTRE operative Mr. White (Jesper Christensen), as revealed in *Spectre*. James Bond (Daniel Craig) infiltrates a SPECTRE conclave in Rome and learns of a plan by Franz Oberhauser (Christoph Waltz) to assassinate the Pale King.

Palisadoes Airport: Airport in Kingston, Jamaica, now known as Norman Manley International Airport, that served as the film series' first shooting location. There, on the morning of January 16, 1962, filmmakers shot James Bond (Sean Connery) arriving in Jamaica aboard Pan American Flight 323 for *Dr. No*.

Pallazzo Cardenza: Fictional site of the SPECTRE meeting in Rome in *Spectre*. Considering the limited amount of security and surveillance that greets Bond (Daniel Craig) when he arrives, you wonder if the evil organization is suffering a financial crunch. It's a long way from the secret chamber in *Thunderball* where SPECTRE shared their "area financial reports."

Palmyra: Huge seaside Nassau estate belonging to Emilio Largo (Adolfo Celi) in *Thunderball*. In one of its two swimming pools, Largo keeps his deadly Golden Grotto sharks (actually tiger sharks). Footage of the estate was shot at the Philadelphia summer home of Nicholas Sullivan and his family.

Palmyra is also the name of the North African estate/fortress of Maximilian Largo (Klaus Maria Brandauer) in *Never Say Never Again*. Traveling there from southern France as a guest on Largo's *Flying Saucer* yacht, Bond is later captured and shackled to the wall of a medieval dungeon filled with bleached bones and vultures. He breaks his bonds, thanks to his laser-equipped watch, steals a horse, and rescues Domino Petachi (Kim Basinger) from a group of sleazy Arab traders.

Chased across the ramparts of the fortress, Bond, Domino, and the horse dive into the Mediterranean as an American nuclear submarine blasts the traders with its deck cannon.

Paluzzi, Luciana (June 10, 1937–   ): Voluptuous, redheaded Italian leading lady who portrayed SPECTRE assassin Fiona Volpe in *Thunderball*. Luciana's introduction while wearing a sheer negligee in the bedroom of François Derval (Paul Stassino) was definitely an early highlight of the film. She's the perfect example of the type of woman the producers liked to cast as a ruthless villain in the early 007 thrillers: European, busty, and very sexy. A native of Rome, Paluzzi appeared in a number of international films before making her credited big-screen English-language debut as Carola in Bond director Terence Young's *Tank Force* (1958), a.k.a. *No Time to Die*, a World War II drama coproduced by Albert R. Broccoli and written by Young and Bond screenwriter Richard Maibaum—a part that surely put her on Mr. Young's radar for *Thunderball*.

Actress Luciana Paluzzi was a vision in black leather atop a rocket-firing SPECTRE motorcycle in *Thunderball*. *Courtesy of the David Reinhardt Collection*

Pan American Flight 323: The airliner James Bond (Sean Connery) takes from New York to Jamaica in *Dr. No*. In the late 1950s and early 1960s, it was common for transatlantic flights to stop in New York before the jaunt to the islands. Today, direct flights—London to Jamaica—are available.

Panama: The country where the yacht *Disco Volante* is registered in *Thunderball*. It's written on the ship's stern.

Parahawk: Enemy hang gliders that convert into deadly snowmobiles in *The World Is Not Enough*. A squadron of them, organized by Renard (Robert Carlyle), attack Bond and Elektra (Sophie Marceau) on the ski slopes not far from her Azerbaijan oil pipeline. But Bond takes them out in one of the film's more predictable set pieces. These air attack sequences haven't really worked since Sean Connery easily disposed of a fleet of killer helicopters during *You Only Live Twice* way back in 1967. Enough with the machine guns and the grenades. They never hit anyone anyway.

Paratrooper (1953): Alan Ladd wartime adventure film, a.k.a. *The Red Beret*, that influenced the motorboat chase scene in *From Russia with Love*. Coproduced by Albert R. Broccoli, directed by Terence Young, and written by Richard Maibaum—all future 007 mainstays—the film features a sequence in which Ladd's unit of soldiers is trapped in a minefield, and to escape one of the soldiers skims a bazooka rocket along the ground, touching off a row of lethal mines. *From Russia with Love*, also written by Maibaum, merely changed the location of the sequence to the sea. Bond (Sean Connery) dumps his speedboat's punctured gasoline drums overboard, watches them float among the SPECTRE boats, and then skillfully targets the gasoline with a flare. The skimming effect of the flare rocket ignites the gas, engulfing the enemy flotilla. *Paratrooper* was also the first film produced in Europe by Broccoli and his partner Irving Allen.

Paris: Location of the headquarters of SPECTRE in *Thunderball*. It's also where May Day (Grace Jones) skydives off the Eiffel Tower in *A View to a Kill*.

Roger Moore prepares for a little drive in Paris in pursuit of May Day in *A View to a Kill*. *Courtesy of the Luc Lecloch Collection*

parkour: Incredibly exciting movement discipline practiced by enemy bomb maker Mollaka (Sébastien Foucan) during the construction site chase at the beginning of *Casino Royale*. Running and jumping across treacherous gaps and at dizzying heights, it's a discipline that defies description. Needless to say, the sequence, which took six weeks to shoot, gets this James Bond movie off to an incredibly rousing start. Foucan is actually one of the originators of parkour.

Paso del Diablo: Spanish for "Devil's Pass," it's the location where drug runner Franz Sanchez (Robert Davi) and his cocaine tanker convoy rendezvous in *Licence to Kill*—a sequence that was shot at the isolated Rumorosa pass west of Mexicali, Mexico.

Pastell, George (March 13, 1923–April 4, 1976; birth name: Nino Pastellides): Cyprus-born Greek actor who portrayed the resourceful train conductor in *From Russia with Love*. It is his urgent voice, calling "Mr. Somerset, Mr. Somerset," that first alerts Bond (Sean Connery) to trouble on the Orient Express. Using his birth name, Pastell made his credited feature film debut in director Edward Dmytryk's drama *Give Us This Day* (1949).

Patchett, Maurice: London instructor for double-decker bus drivers who was hired by

Roger Moore stands atop the severed Leyland double-decker bus in Jamaica on *Live and Let Die*. *Courtesy of the Anders Frejdh Collection*

Eon Productions in 1972 to be a stunt driver in *Live and Let Die*. With five weeks leave from his job and double pay, Patchett and a Leyland RT double-decker bus, fresh off London's route 19 from Battersea, were transported to Jamaica, where they performed in the hair-raising chase between Bond (Roger Moore) and drug smuggler Kananga's henchmen riding in cars and motorcycles.

Patchett expertly skidded the bus on a small rural highway, forcing the motorcycles and cars off the road. He also drove the double-decker under a trestle bridge, shearing off its precut top deck. The fact that he bore a slight resemblance to Roger Moore helped Patchett win the job over twenty-four other instructors.

Pate, Michael (February 26, 1920–September 1, 2008; birth name: Edward John Pate): Prolific Australian-born character actor who portrayed Clarence Leiter, a British agent who assists an American James Bond (Barry Nelson) in the 1954 live television adaptation of *Casino Royale*. A native of Drummoyne, New South Wales, Pate made his credited motion picture debut as Shane O'Riordan in the Australian adventure drama *The Rugged O'Riordans* (1949). His many feature film credits include *Julius Caesar* (1953), as Flavius; *Hondo* (1953), as Vittorio; *The Court Jester* (1955), as Sir Locksley; *PT 109* (1963), as Lieutenant Reginald Evans, coastwatcher; and *Major Dundee* (1965), as Apache leader Sierra Charriba.

Patrice: SPECTRE agent, portrayed by Ola Rapace, who leads Bond (Daniel Craig) on a deadly chase across Istanbul and Turkey in *Skyfall*. With a stolen hard drive in his possession that can expose NATO agents embedded in terrorist groups around the world, Patrice makes it to a moving train, where he engages in a titanic battle with Bond until Eve Moneypenny (Naomie Harris) accidentally shoots 007 off the train. Referred to as a "ghost" in intelligence circles, Patrice has no known residence. The CIA has been chasing him for the murder of the Yemini ambassador. MI6 analyzed the shell fragments fired by Patrice, identifying them as depleted uranium shells—military grade, hard to get, and extremely expensive. Once recovered and returned to duty, Bond tracks Patrice to Shanghai, China, where 007 liquidates him after Patrice knocks off a prominent executive. He retrieves a gaming chip off the body, which leads Bond to Macao, where Bond redeems that one chip for 4 million Euros.

Pendik, Bay of: A body of water off the coast of Turkey near the Greek border that was the original shooting location for the motorboat chase in *From Russia with Love*. Bad weather, unserviceable boats, and an inexperienced group of local production assistants forced the move to Scotland, where filming was completed off the coastal town of Crinan.

Penfold Hearts: The brand of golf ball used by James Bond (Sean Connery) during his high-stakes challenge match against Goldfinger (Gert Fröbe).

Pepper, Sheriff J. W.: Bumbling Louisiana lawman portrayed by American character actor Clifton James in both *Live and Let Die* and *The Man with the Golden Gun*. A caricature of the tough-talking southern peace officer, Pepper was introduced in *Live and Let Die* as an outraged policeman who can't seem to halt a hair-raising motorboat chase between Bond (Roger Moore) and the water-borne henchmen of Kananga (Yaphet Kotto).

Having stopped Adam (Tommy Lane) for speeding, Pepper is about to make his first arrest when motorboats start flying over the highway. One of them crashes into his police car. Adam escapes, and Sheriff Pepper joins the chase, eventually catching up to 007, who introduces himself to local authorities as a "secret agent." Pepper is incredulous. "Secret agent?" he screams. "On whose side?"

Pepper was a popular element of the movie, so the producers brought him back in the next 007 film, *The Man with the Golden Gun*. This time, Pepper, vacationing in Thailand with his wife, thinks he sees Bond motoring down a causeway. *Nah*, he decides.

American character actor Clifton James played goofy Louisiana sheriff J. W. Pepper, who returns to action opposite 007 in *The Man with the Golden Gun*. *Courtesy of the David Reinhardt Collection*

In the film's most outrageous sequence, Pepper is admiring a new red AMC Hornet in a Bangkok showroom when Bond suddenly jumps into the car and drives it through a plate glass window. Bond does a double take when he sees Pepper, but he's in too much of a hurry chasing Scaramanga (Christopher Lee) to think about it. Aware of Bond's true identity, Pepper gets into the spirit of the chase to the point that he even flashes his Louisiana State Police ID to an approaching troop of angry Thai police officers, who promptly handcuff him.

And Pepper is in the passenger seat when Bond and his Hornet perform the famous 360-degree spiral jump over the collapsed Thai river bridge.

Petachi, Captain Jack: Traitorous US Air Force officer and brother of Maximilian Largo's mistress Domino (Kim Basinger), portrayed by Gavan O'Herlihy in *Never Say Never Again*. Attached to the ground staff of a cruise missile base in England, Petachi is bribed by SPECTRE and forced to undergo an unusual corneal implant operation that will give him the same right eye print as the president of the United States. With that capability, he can pass a top-level security check and arm two cruise missiles with nuclear warheads.

Petachi is assigned to "cruel mistress" Fatima Blush (Barbara Carrera). His addiction to heroin and her sexual demands gradually turn him into a nervous, pathetic mess. When Petachi sneaks a cigarette in his room at the Shrublands health clinic—an act that supposedly clouds his implant—Blush beats him up, then offers him a significant drug dose if he'll practice the security maneuver that will eventually arm the missiles. Bond (Sean Connery) observes this scuffle and begins to suspect Petachi.

Later, while searching Petachi's room, 007 finds a book of matches with the Largo emblem on the cover, a clue that leads him to Largo's home base in the Bahamas. Petachi completes his bomb-arming mission and drives off the base. Blush arrives to congratulate him but tosses a snake into his car instead. Losing control, Petachi slams head-on into a building and dies in the collision.

Petachi, Domino: Pampered mistress of Maximilian Largo (Klaus Maria Brandauer), portrayed by Kim Basinger in *Never Say Never Again*. She's also the sister of US Air Force captain Jack Petachi (Gavan O'Herlihy), who has defected to SPECTRE.

Secretly terrified of Largo's increasingly bizarre behavior, Domino is ripe for a new lover when she meets James Bond (Sean Connery) at a health spa in the south of France. The encounter—one of the film's best moments—occurs when 007 impersonates a masseur and gives Domino an especially arousing massage. They continue their flirtation at Largo's charity ball, where Bond beats Largo at his own game, a dangerous computerized showdown called Domination. Bond's "prize" is one dance with Domino.

During a rather conspicuous tango, Domino learns from 007 that Largo is responsible for her brother's death. Later, during a visit aboard Largo's yacht the *Flying Saucer*, Bond further humiliates Largo by kissing Domino tenderly in the ship's gym, which is visible via two-way in Largo's control room.

The psychotic SPECTRE master spy later retaliates by throwing Bond in a North African prison cell and selling Domino to Arab traders. Bond escapes—thanks to his laser watch—steals a horse, and rescues Domino from the traders. Joining 007 aboard a US nuclear sub, Domino eventually dives into the Tears of Allah archaeological dig and exacts her own revenge on Largo with a CO_2 speargun.

Peters, Molly (March 15, 1942–May 30, 2017): Sultry British actress, briefly in motion pictures

Actress Molly Peters gets some instruction from director Terence Young during bedroom scenes in *Thunderball*. *Courtesy of the David Reinhardt Collection*

and television, who portrayed Patricia Fearing, the comely physical therapist in *Thunderball*, her feature film debut. Born in Walsham-le-Willows, Suffolk, England, Peters made only two other films: the German crime thriller *Target for Killing* (1966), with fellow Bond players Karin Dor, Curt Jurgens, and Adolfo Celi; and *Don't Raise the Bridge, Lower the River* (1968), with fellow Bond girl Margaret Nolan.

Phidian: Artist employed by the London College of Arms in *On Her Majesty's Secret Service*, played by British actor Brian Grellis. When Bond (George Lazenby) arrives at the college, Sir Hilary Bray (George Baker) is complimenting Phidian on a coat of arms he has just completed on Bond's family tree. In the scenes that follow in the script, which never made the final cut of the film, Bond discovers a tiny radio-transmitting "homer" disguised inside a paperweight on Sir Hilary's desk. Realizing Phidian is a hireling of SPECTRE chief Blofeld and that he probably overheard Bond's plan to impersonate Bray, 007 gives pursuit. He chases Phidian out of the college, past St. Paul's Cathedral, and into London's main post office. Phidian is eventually struck and killed in an underground tunnel by one of the high-speed automated electric trolleys used to deliver mail. To make Phidian's death appear accidental to Blofeld, an elaborate ruse is devised: Phidian's body is recovered and, along with a dozen other corpses "borrowed" from morgues, planted on a St. Albans commuter train. A terrible train accident is staged, making it appear as if the train has jumped the tracks. It is reported that there are no survivors. Blofeld reads about Phidian's death and finds nothing suspicious. Obviously, these scenes would have added to the movie's already long running time, and therefore they were either never shot or deleted in the final edit.

phosgene gas: Lethal gas released into Japan's Rosaki Cave by Blofeld (Donald Pleasence) to discourage curiosity seekers in *You Only Live Twice*. According to the story that Kissy (Mie Hama) relates to Bond (Sean Connery), two Ama Islanders were exploring the cave when they were mysteriously killed. Later, when Bond and Kissy follow their route, they find the gas that killed the islanders—fortunately, they dive into the water before the gas can take effect.

Phuket: A city in Thailand that was the jumping-off point for the 007 filmmakers to discover the unusual islands featured in *The Man with the Golden Gun*. On a scouting trip near Phuket in 1974, the film's recon team discovered a chain of tiny islands so extraordinary in appearance that production designer Peter Murton thought they had crossed the time barrier and were back in the prehistoric age.

Covered with jungle foliage, shaped like overturned boulders, and appearing from the air like a series of giant stepping-stones, each island was a photographer's delight. One of these strange pieces of Thai geography was to become Scaramanga's island. It was called Khao Phing Kan, and it featured a lovely sandy beach fronting a grotto that would accommodate the seaplane flown by James Bond (Roger Moore), as well as be the site of the beach duel between Bond and Scaramanga (Christopher Lee).

In the background were smaller, unusually shaped islands that lent the entire scene a sense of exotic mystique far removed from anything the crew, let alone film audiences, had ever imagined. Coincidentally, the remote chain of islands was not far from the Mergui Archipelago (just up the coast a few hundred miles), which in *Thunderball* was designated as SPECTRE's drop zone for the diamond ransom.

Picker, David (May 4, 1931–April 20, 2019): American film producer and studio executive who helped engineer the deal that brought the James Bond series to United Artists in 1961. Working as a production executive at UA in the early 1960s, he'd actually tried to obtain the 007 film rights directly from Ian Fleming, only to be told that they were unavailable. Several months later, having been promoted to head of production, he took a meeting with producers Cubby Broccoli and Harry Saltzman, who wanted to talk to him about "something important," he recalled in a 2005 guest coumn in *Variety*. "After the usual pleasantries I was leaning back in my chair when they announced they owned the rights to Bond. . . . My chair hit the floor and I said in no uncertain terms that we would make a deal and that the key to the films would be spending enough money to maintain Fleming's tone in the sensuality, style, action and wit of the books."[*]

[*] David Picker, "How UA Bonded with Bond," *Variety*, May 4, 2005.

The gorgeous, prehistoric-looking islands off the coast of Phuket, Thailand. The center island houses Scaramanga's solar panels in *The Man with the Golden Gun*. *Steve Rubin Collection*

The producers were impressed with Picker's 007 knowledge, and after a courtesy call to Columbia Pictures, to whom Broccoli had previously pitched the project, the parties quickly reached a deal: $1.1 million upon script approval, a fifty-fifty split of the profits, and an agreement to hire an unknown to play Bond. In his *Variety* column, Picker marveled that Columbia had been unwilling to offer Broccoli and Saltzman more than $400,000 for the Bond film rights, then later went all in on the star-studded 1967 spoof version of *Casino Royale*, an infamous failure. "The Hollywood ending is that Columbia could have had Bond for $1 million in 1962."

Pickett's Charge: Confederate assault during the Battle of Gettysburg that arms dealer Brad Whitaker (Joe Don Baker) has incorrectly plotted on his diorama in *The Living Daylights*. Bond (Timothy Dalton), who has returned to Whitaker's home in Tangier to kill him, points out that Pickett's Charge took place up Cemetery Ridge, not Little Round Top as Whitaker has it. Whitaker retorts that he's fighting the battle the way he wants.

pig: A scouring plug designed to clean the interior of a natural-gas pipeline that is used by defecting Russian general Georgi Koskov (Jeroen Krabbé) as his escape route from Bratislava, Czechoslovakia, in *The Living Daylights*. This pig has been modified to carry a human being.

Pike, Rosamund (January 27, 1979–   ): Academy Award–nominated British film and television actress who portrayed icy double-0 agent and fencing champion Miranda Frost in *Die Another Day*, her big-screen debut. Born in Hammersmith, London, Pike received her Academy Award nomination for the role of Amy Dunne, Ben Affleck's missing wife in director David Fincher's *Gone Girl* (2014).

Pilatus Aircraft factory: Location outside Lucerne, Switzerland, that was used by the *Goldfinger* crew as the exterior of Auric Enterprises. Once Bond (Sean Connery) penetrates the compound, the sequences were shot on the Pinewood Studios lot, as was the incredible automobile chase involving 007's trick Aston Martin.

Pinewood Studios: Production studio outside London that has been the base of operations for nearly every James Bond film from *Dr. No* to the present day. SEE ALSO "007 Stage," "Renaissance Garden," "Stage D."

Piper Cherokees: The five single-engine monoplanes flown by the voluptuous blonde pilots of Pussy Galore's Flying Circus in *Goldfinger*. The aerial element of Auric Goldfinger's Operation Grand Slam, their mission is to immobilize Fort Knox by spraying Delta-9 nerve gas into the atmosphere above the base.

piranhas: The nasty aquatic pets of Blofeld (Donald Pleasence) in *You Only Live Twice*. They later consume SPECTRE agents Helga Brandt (Karin Dor) and Hans (Ronald Rich).

pistachio nuts: The favorite food of both Max the parrot and Columbo the smuggler (Topol) in *For Your Eyes Only*.

Pistor, Ludger (March 16, 1959–   ): German character actor who portrayed Mendel, the representative of Switzerland's Basel Bank, in *Casino Royale* (2006). Born in Recklinghausen, Pistor made his motion picture debut as one of the monks in director Jean-Jacques Annaud's medieval crime drama *The Name of the Rose* (1986), which starred fellow Bond players Sean Connery, Michael Lonsdale (*Moonraker*), and Vernon Dobtcheff (*The Spy Who Loved Me*).

piton gun: The helpful mountaineering device that Bond (Sean Connery) uses to gain entrance to the secretive suite of Willard Whyte (Jimmy Dean) at the Whyte House Hotel in *Diamonds Are Forever*. It fires a spike attached to a wire that allows 007 to swing over to a bathroom window. Inside the suite, he uses the same gun to fire a spike at the forehead of SPECTRE chief Blofeld (Charles Gray)—but it turns out to be a Blofeld clone.

Piz Gloria: The Alpine redoubt of Ernst Stavro Blofeld (Telly Savalas), and the revolving mountaintop restaurant in Switzerland that became the shooting location for the fortress, in *On Her Majesty's Secret Service*. The movie's Swiss production liaison, Hubert Fröhlich, suggested the site—perched atop the Schilthorn mountain,

The Piz Gloria restaurant atop the Schilthorn peak in Switzerland, site of amazing location filming for *On Her Majesty's Secret Service. Courtesy of the David Reinhardt Collection*

it was identical to the fictional fortress described in Ian Fleming's novel. The restaurant, which had just been completed and had yet to open, was ultimately named after the role it played in the film.

Construction of the revolving restaurant began in 1961 with the help of helicopters, which transported the building materials to the top of the Schilthorn. By Christmas 1967, the structure was finished, as was the cable-car run to the village of Mürren below. Everything was brand new, and plans were being made to furnish the restaurant's interior, when the James Bond crew arrived. A complicated series of negotiations began the following spring to secure the location for filming. Eon Productions agreed to furnish the interior, as well as to construct, next to the main building, a helicopter landing pad that could be used for rescue missions. In return, the filmmakers were given permission to film throughout the five-story mountaintop complex.

Production designer Syd Cain would be in charge of the operation that would eventually transform the bare restaurant into Blofeld's exotic allergy institute. It was not an expensive task, costing only 60,000 pounds, compared with the nearly 300,000 needed for Blofeld's rocket base in *You Only Live Twice*. The principal cost went to the construction of the heliport, which was accomplished by the Swiss government, working to Cain's designs.

Pleasence, Donald (October 5, 1919–February 2, 1995): Acclaimed British character actor who was the first to portray SPECTRE chief Ernst Stavro Blofeld on camera, in 1967's *You Only Live Twice*. Thanks to a makeup department scar, he was suitably evil-looking, but his slight form and decidedly low-key demeanor never matched the attributes of the enormously villainous character featured in the original Fleming novels. A native of Worksop, Nottinghamshire,

"This is my second life," says James Bond (Sean Connery) after Blofeld (Donald Pleasence, center) is surprised to see 007 alive. Blofeld replies, "You only live twice, Mr. Bond." *Courtesy of the David Reinhardt Collection*

England, the prolific Pleasence made his big-screen debut as Tromp in director Muriel Box's romantic comedy *The Beachcomber* (1954), which also featured future Bond player Michael Mellinger in a bit part. Pleasence's career included such iconic films as *The Great Escape* (1963), as Blythe the Forger; *Fantastic Voyage* (1966), as Dr. Michaels; *The Night of the Generals* (1967); *THX 1138* (1971); *The Eagle Has Landed* (1976), as Himmler; *Halloween* (1978), as Loomis; and *Escape from New York* (1981), as the president.

Top British character actor Donald Pleasence took on the role of Ernst Stavro Blofeld in *You Only Live Twice*, a part that comes with a white cat in tow. *Courtesy of the David Reinhardt Collection*

Pohlmann, Eric (July 18, 1913–July 25, 1979): Viennese character actor who dubbed the voice of Ernst Stavro Blofeld in *From Russia with Love* and *Thunderball*. Pohlmann made his motion picture debut as the search group leader in director Terence Fisher's thriller *Lost Daughter* (1949).

Port-au-Prince, Haiti: Island capital to which Bond (Daniel Craig) tracks tagged currency that links duplicitous MI6 agent Craig Mitchell (Glenn Foster) to assassin Edmund Slate (Neil Jackson) in *Quantum of Solace*. Bond learns that Slate's target is Camille Montes (Olga Kurylenko), whose lover is environmentalist/entrepreneur Dominic Greene (Mathieu Amalric).

Port Royal Road: A main highway out of Kingston, Jamaica, on which Bond (Sean Connery) drives in *Dr. No*. To visit Miss Taro (Zena Marshall) at her cottage in the Blue Mountains, 007 takes Port Royal Road to Windward Road, which he follows until he gets to a cement factory. He then turns left and follows the road up the hill and down the other side. Two miles farther on is Miss Taro's cottage on Magenta Drive, which is on the left. NOTE: When Miss Taro gives Bond directions to her house, she says she lives at "Magenta Drive 2391," but Bond later gives the address as "2171 Magenta Drive."

positive mental attitude, food, and shared bodily warmth: The three keys to survival that the KGB's Major Anya Amasova (Barbara Bach) learned in her Siberian survival course. She explains them to James Bond (Roger Moore) while aboard an Egyptian sailing vessel in *The Spy Who Loved Me*.

Potemkin: A Russian nuclear submarine swallowed by the *Liparus* supertanker in *The Spy Who Loved Me*. Its Soviet crew replaced by enemy submariners, the sub becomes a pawn in the plot by Karl Stromberg (Curt Jurgens) to destroy the world. Fortunately, Bond (Roger Moore) short-circuits the plot, and the *Potemkin* is blown apart before it can accomplish its mission.

Prague, Czech Republic: Where we first meet James Bond (Daniel Craig) in the pre-credits teaser of *Casino Royale*. He's there to assassinate Dryden (Malcolm Sinclair), a traitorous British agent selling secrets to the enemy.

"Property of a Lady, The": Reference in the Sotheby's auction catalog to the anonymous seller of a priceless Fabergé Easter egg in *Octopussy*. Arriving at the auction gallery, Bond (Roger Moore) at first thinks the lady might be Magda (Kristina Wayborn), the comely assistant of exiled Afghan prince Kamal Khan (Louis Jourdan). "The Property of a Lady" is also the title of one of Ian Fleming's Bond short stories, which was one of the inspirations for the film.

Pryce, Jonathan (June 1, 1947–   ): Academy Award–nominated Welsh character actor who portrayed megalomaniac billionaire Elliot Carver in *Tomorrow Never Dies*. Born in Holywell, Flintshire, Pryce made his big-screen debut as Joseph Manasse in director Stuart Rosenberg's pre–World War II drama *Voyage of the Damned* (1976), which also featured Bond players David de Keyser (*Diamonds Are Forever*), Milo Sperber (*The Spy Who Loved Me*), Max von Sydow (*Never Say Never Again*), and Emily Bolton (*Moonraker*). Pryce was so memorable as the bumbling bureaucrat in Terry Gilliam's *Brazil* (1985), and made an impression more recently as the pious High Sparrow in HBO's *Game of Thrones* (12 episodes, 2015–2016). He has given indelible performances in many films, including *Something Wicked This Way Comes* (1983); *The Adventures of Baron Munchausen* (1988); *Glengarry Glen Ross* (1992); *The Age of Innocence* (1993); *Evita* (1996), as Juan Perón; *Pirates of the Caribbean: At World's End* (2007); and *The Wife* (2017). Pryce received his Oscar nomination for playing one of the two leads in director Fernando Meirelles's *The Two Popes* (2019).

Pterois volitans: Species of exotic tropical fish with dangerous dorsal spines, identified by James Bond (Roger Moore) while posing as marine biologist Robert Sterling in *The Spy Who Loved Me*. The information does not impress 007's host, Karl Stromberg (Curt Jurgens), who already knows that Sterling is Bond.

Purvis, Neal (September 9, 1961–   ), and **Robert Wade** (1962–   ): British screenwriting duo who collaborated on the screenplays for *The World Is Not Enough*, *Die Another Day*, *Casino Royale*, *Quantum of Solace*, *Skyfall*, *Spectre*, and *No Time to Die*. As Purvis quipped after the release of *Skyfall* in 2013, "We have been doing it longer than Ian Fleming was writing Bond."[*]

Purvis and Wade, the latter of whom was born in Penarth, Wales, came to the attention of 007 producer Barbara Broccoli after they worked on director Jake Scott's period action comedy *Plunkett & Macleane* (1999), costarring future Bond player Robert Carlyle; Broccoli called their script "dark, witty, sexy and inventive."[†] The duo made their screenwriting debut on the crime drama *Let Him Have It* (1991), which featured Bond players James Villiers (*For Your Eyes Only*), Vernon Dobtcheff (*The Spy Who Loved Me*), and Serena Scott Thomas. They also collaborated on the screenplay for the spy spoof *Johnny English* (2003), starring Rowan Atkinson.

---

[*] Neal Purvis and Robert Wade, interview by ODE Entertainment, YouTube, February 18, 2013, https://www.youtube.com/watch?v=FcrCdVOoosg.

[†] Steven Priggé, *Movie Moguls Speak: Interviews with Top Film Producers* (Jefferson, NC: McFarland, 2004), 27.

Q: Bond's usually sarcastic equipment officer from Q Branch; Q stands for "quartermaster" in British military parlance. With only three exceptions—*Live and Let Die*, *Casino Royale*, and *Quantum of Solace*, in which no quartermaster was featured—Q has been a ubiquitous presence in the James Bond series. Actor Peter Burton introduced 007's first equipment officer, Major Boothroyd, in *Dr. No*, reciting the specs of his new Walther PPK pistol. Desmond Llewelyn took over for Burton in *From Russia with Love*. Though credited initially as "Boothroyd," he was

Bond historian Michael VanBlaricum, right, and actor Desmond "Q" Llewelyn, carrying the somewhat battered *From Russia with Love* briefcase. *Courtesy of the Michael VanBlaricum Collection*

generally referred to only as Q, and continued in the role through seventeen Bond films.

Llewelyn's most memorable appearance was in *Goldfinger*, in which he introduces Bond to the ultimate gadget: a modified Aston Martin DB5 sports car. When he finally mentions the passenger ejector seat, Bond replies, "Ejector seat, you're joking." To which Q responds in his typical deadpan, "I never joke about my work, 007." Llewelyn's appearance in *Licence to Kill* was his most lengthy, as he joins rogue agent James Bond (Timothy Dalton) in fictional Isthmus City. His bag of tricks proves to be the equalizer for outnumbered and outgunned 007.

Meanwhile, outside Eon Productions' James Bond series, Geoffrey Bayldon portrayed Q as a fop in the 1967 spoof version of *Casino Royale*. And Alec McCowen portrayed a Q-type, a witty engineer named Algernon, in the 1983 *Thunderball* remake *Never Say Never Again*.

In 1999, Desmond Llewelyn made his last appearance as Q in *The World Is Not Enough*, which also featured John Cleese as his assistant "R." When Llewelyn was killed in a traffic accident that same year, Cleese took over the role of Q in *Die Another Day*.

However, when Daniel Craig became the new Bond with 2006's *Casino Royale*, it was decided to forgo an equipment officer in his first two films. In *Skyfall*, the delightful Ben Whishaw was introduced as the youngest Q of the series. A brainy, energetic computer expert, engineer, scientist, and all-around genius, Whishaw's Q has added a degree of fun to the role of the equipment officer who becomes one of Bond's staunchest allies.

Q has always been and will always be a staple of the series—in essence, the voice of Ian Fleming, whose original novels were filled with the type of technical references that characterize the Q Branch equipment briefings.

Quantum: Mysterious criminal organization of which equally mysterious environmental entrepreneur Dominic Greene (Mathieu Amalric) is a member in *Quantum of Solace*. Eon Production initially created Quantum as a stand-in for the classic Bond adversary SPECTRE, the rights to which were controlled by *Thunderball* producer Kevin McClory. Once the filmmakers secured the rights from McClory in November 2013, they established that Quantum is a subsidiary of a newly rebooted SPECTRE, as revealed in the movie of the same name.

QUANTUM OF SOLACE

(Sony/MGM, 2008) ★★⌐ : The twenty-second film in the Eon Productions' James Bond series. US release date: November 14, 2008. Budget: $200 million. Worldwide box office gross: $591.7 million (US domestic gross: $169.4 million; international gross: $422.3 million).* Running time: 106 minutes.

THE SETUP

Having captured the mysterious criminal operative Mr. White (Jesper Christensen) at the end of *Casino Royale*, James Bond (Daniel Craig) and M (Dame Judi Dench) transport him to an MI6 field office in Siena, Italy. There they are betrayed by Craig Mitchell (Glenn Foster), an MI6 agent who's been turned by Quantum, the secret international crime organization Mr. White belongs to. Investigating the group, 007 undercovers a scheme by environmentally conscious entrepreneur Dominic Green (Mathieu Amalric), who is secretly plotting to destabilize Bolivia and eventually corner the world's freshwater supply.

BEHIND THE SCENES

When Daniel Craig was selected to play James Bond in *Casino Royale*, Bond producers Barbara Broccoli and Michael G. Wilson reestablished the international box office success of one of the most storied franchises in film history. It was indeed a new era, and Craig's first film launched the Bond series to new heights. Unfortunately, *Quantum of Solace* was a low-octane follow-up. Rather than craft an exciting new adventure, the filmmakers picked up exactly where *Casino Royale* left off, with Bond throwing the mysterious Mr. White into the trunk of his Aston Martin. Actually, the first twenty minutes of the film are pretty exciting as Bond chases Quantum bad guys, but once main villain Dominic Greene is introduced, the story just falls flat. The series has long centered around charismatic megalomaniacs like Dr. No, Goldfinger, Stromberg, and the like, but Dominic Greene is neither megalomaniacal nor charismatic. His scheme to corner the market on freshwater in Bolivia has to be the most tepid plot in the entire series. And the revenge plot pitting Bolivian mystery woman Camille Montes (Olga Kurylenko) against Greene's ally General Medrano (Joaquín Cosio) is tired and cliché.

Quantum cannot be entirely dismissed thanks to star Daniel Craig, who adds value to every scene as a tough and believable double-0, and whose relationship with M (Dame Judi Dench) is well developed. But there's not much here to recommend. The locations are bland and not very cinematic (particularly the eco hotel location at the end of the film), the characters are one dimensional, and there's no humor and very little sex. Sadly, it's a harbinger of things to come.

THE CAST

James Bond	Daniel Craig
Camille	Olga Kurylenko
Dominic Greene	Mathieu Amalric
M	Dame Judi Dench
Rene Mathis	Giancarlo Giannini
Strawberry Fields	Gemma Arterton
Felix Leiter	Jeffrey Wright
Gregg Beam	David Harbour
Mr. White	Jesper Christensen
Elvis	Anatole Taubman
Tanner	Rory Kinnear
Foreign Secretary	Tim Pigott-Smith
General Medrano	Joaquín Cosio
Mitchell	Glenn Foster
Guy Haines	Paul Ritter
Yusef	Simon Kassianides
Corrine	Stana Katic
Mr. Slate	Neil Jackson

THE CREW

Director	Marc Forster
Writers	Paul Haggis
	Neal Purvis & Robert Wade
Producers	Barbara Broccoli
	Michael G. Wilson
Director of Photography	Roberto Schaefer
Music by	David Arnold
Title song performed by	Alicia Keys
	Jack White
Production Designer	Dennis Gassner
Set Decorator	Anna Pinnock

---

* "Quantum of Solace (2008)," The Numbers, accessed June 29, 2020, https://www.the-numbers.com/movie/Quantum-of-Solace.

Director Marc Forster (far left) goes over a scene with actors Mathieu Amalric, Olga Kurylenko, and Daniel Craig for *Quantum of Solace*. *Courtesy of the Anders Frejdh Collection*

Costume Designer	Louise Frogley
Second Unit Director	Dan Bradley
Casting by	Debbie McWilliams
Stunt Coordinator	Gary Powell
Title Designer	Mk12
Editors	Matt Chesse
	Richard Pearson

Quarrel: Cayman Islander associate of James Bond (Sean Connery) portrayed by John Kitzmiller in *Dr. No*, one of the truly fun characters in the Bond series. Even in the early 1960s, Quarrel was a throwback to an earlier era when wide-eyed black sidekicks such as Eddie "Rochester" Anderson and Willie Best were common. But he's made of tougher stuff than those predecessors—Rochester would never have talked out of the side of his mouth with a cigarette hanging from it—and his scenes have a strong reality to them, no doubt due to the perfect casting of Kitzmiller.

A Cayman Island fisherman, Quarrel is working for CIA agent Felix Leiter (Jack Lord) when Bond meets him on the beach in Kingston.

Quarrel's seamanship, plus a bellyful of rum, gets 007 to Crab Key in a small sailboat. However, the trusty fisherman pays with his life when he's burned to death in the swamps by the flamethrower on Dr. No's "dragon."

Cayman Islander Quarrel (John Kitzmiller, center) joins a conversation in Puss-Feller's restaurant with James Bond (Sean Connery) and Felix Leiter (Jack Lord) in *Dr. No*. *Courtesy of the David Reinhardt Collection*

Queen Elizabeth I: British ocean liner that caught fire and partially sank under mysterious circumstances in Victoria Harbour, Hong Kong, on January 9, 1972. In *The Man with the Golden Gun*, the interior of the liner has been transformed into the Far East headquarters of the British Secret Service.

queen of cups: A tarot card in *Live and Let Die* that becomes an important clue to the true identity of CIA agent Rosie Carver (Gloria Hendry). According to Bond (Roger Moore), a queen of cups in the upside-down position means a deceitful, perverse woman, a liar or a cheat. Supplied to 007 by fortune-teller Solitaire (Jane Seymour), it helps him determine that Rosie is not a CIA operative at all but an agent of drug smuggler Kananga (Yaphet Kotto).

Queen's Club: The aristocratic-looking men's club in Kingston, Jamaica, where Commander John Strangways (Tim Moxon) plays bridge each day with his local cronies Principal Secretary Playdell-Smith (Louis Blaazer), Professor R. J. Dent (Anthony Dawson), and General Potter (Colonel Burton).

Quist: Henchman of Emilio Largo (Adolfo Celi) portrayed by Bill Cummings in *Thunderball*. He bungles an assassination attempt on Bond (Sean Connery) in 007's hotel room in Nassau, Bahamas. Disarmed, he's sent back to Largo with the message "The little fish I throw back into the sea." Largo subsequently throws poor Quist to his sharks.

radio-controlled sharks: Man-eating predators employed by SPECTRE assassin Fatima Blush (Barbara Carrera) to kill James Bond (Sean Connery) in *Never Say Never Again*. The sharks have been equipped with an electronic receiver that homes in on a transmitting device that Blush places on Bond's scuba equipment. Agent 007 discovers the ruse in time and tricks the sharks into following the homer into an undersea wreck.

Radio Operator: British Secret Service officer at MI6 communications headquarters, portrayed by John Hatton, who who loses contact with Commander John Strangways (Tim Moxon) in *Dr. No*. The London-based radio operator's call sign is G7W, while the call sign for Strangways's transmitter in Kingston, Jamaica, is W6N. When MI6 superiors ask the officer whether he's lost contact with Jamaica on both the main and the emergency frequencies, he tells them, "No joy on either"; "no joy" is a term dating from the Battle of Britain during World War II, which refers to a lack of success in receiving radio messages.

The role of the radio operator was John Hatton's feature film acting debut. After playing the robbery car driver in *On the Run* (1963), alongside future Bond players Patrick Barr (*Octopussy*), and Philip Locke (*Thunderball*), he was out of show business.

Rajadamnern Stadium: Bangkok, Thailand, location of the kickboxing match observed by James Bond (Roger Moore) in *The Man with the Golden Gun*. It's where 007 meets Scaramanga (Christopher Lee) for the first time.

Rapace, Ola (December 3, 1971–): Swedish actor who portrayed wily SPECTRE agent

Patrice in *Skyfall*. A native of Tyresö, Stockholm, Rapace made his motion picture debut as Lasse in director Lukas Moodysson's romantic dramedy *Together* (2000). More recently he was Major Gibson in Luc Besson's *Valerian and the City of a Thousand Planets* (2017).

Ratoff, Gregory (April 20, 1897–December 14, 1960): Russian actor/director, long in America, who purchased the feature film rights to *Casino Royale* from Ian Fleming for $6,000 in the mid-1950s. At one point, according to screenwriter Lorenzo Semple Jr., Ratoff was developing *Casino Royale* as a vehicle for a lady James Bond, to be played by actress Susan Hayward.[*] He would later sell the rights to American producer Charles K. Feldman, who produced *Casino Royale* as a spoof in 1967. Born in Samara, Russia, Ratoff made his motion picture acting debut in director Pyotr Chardynin's silent German film *Dubrowsky, der Räuber Ataman* (1921). Over a decade later, he made his English-speaking film debut as Meyer Klauber in director Gregory La Cava's drama *Symphony of Six Million* (1932). Ratoff made his directing debut on the drama *Sins of Man* (1936), sharing credit with Otto Brower.

Actor/director Gregory Ratoff was the first in Hollywood to recognize the talent of author Ian Fleming and the potential of the James Bond character. *Steve Rubin Collection*

rats: Ferocious denizens of the sixteen-hundred-year-old underground Byzantine cistern featured in *From Russia with Love*. A horde of these creatures chase Bond (Sean Connery), Tanya (Daniela Bianchi), and Kerim Bey (Pedro Armendariz).

Filming this sequence in England was a problem for producers Harry Saltzman and Albert R. Broccoli, because UK law forbade the use of

---

* Steven Gaydos, "Jane Bond? Scribe's-Eye View of 007 Pic Birth," *Variety*, May 11, 2012.

wild rats in film productions. Explained production designer Syd Cain, "We're not allowed to use wild rats in England, because if someone is bitten, we can have real trouble. We tried to use tame white rats that were dipped in cocoa to give them the proper color, but after we fixed our stage lights and dressed the set, they became terribly drowsy and wouldn't cooperate.

"Did you ever try to get a mouse to run? Here we were all standing around waiting for something to happen, and all they would do was lick chocolate coating off each other's bodies. So that was a bloody failure.

"We ended up going to Madrid, where you can film anything, and we hired a Spanish rat catcher who trapped two hundred of the little beggars. We then hired out a garage and built a tiny part of the Byzantine cistern there. Director Terence Young shot the rats coming down the tunnel, with a plate of glass in front of the camera protecting us from the rats. In the end, everybody was on chairs, even Cubby, who came down to watch. Why? Because all of the rats escaped and nobody wanted to be bitten."*

Even steel-toothed assassins need romance. Here Jaws (Richard Kiel) relaxes with Dolly (Blanche Ravalec). No photos please. *Courtesy of the David Reinhardt Collection*

Ravalec, Blanche (1954–   ): Buxom blonde French comedic actress who portrayed Dolly, girlfriend to Jaws (Richard Kiel) in *Moonraker*. Ravalec made her motion picture debut as Yveline in director Michel Lang's comedy *Holiday Hotel* (1978). More recently, she has done dubbing work for the French versions of American TV series, providing the French voice of actress Marcia Cross on television series such as *Melrose Place* and *Desperate Housewives*.

rebreather: A pocket-sized aqualung supplied to James Bond (Sean Connery) by Q (Desmond Llewelyn) in *Thunderball*. It holds four minutes of air, and Bond makes good use of it when he's trapped in the shark-infested pool at the estate of Emilio Largo (Adolfo Celi). After filming was completed, *Thunderball*'s art director, Peter Lamont, received a call from a commander in the British Royal Navy who was having difficulty with a design for a Navy rebreather and wanted the scoop on the film's unit. Lamont had to disappoint the naval officer by explaining that it was only a prop. It was not the first time that the military had become intrigued with a James

---

* Syd Cain, interview by the author, London, June 18, 1977.

Bond gadget only to find out it was a piece of movie magic.

red Chianti: The wine ordered by Donald Grant (Robert Shaw) on the Orient Express in *From Russia with Love*. Since Grant, posing as Captain Nash, has ordered the grilled sole as his dinner entree, this choice of wine immediately makes Bond (Sean Connery) suspicious. Any man of culture knows that when you order fish, you order a white wine to go with it.

Red Cross mercy flight: The cover for the Union Corse dawn helicopter assault on the Alpine fortress of Ernst Stavro Blofeld (Telly Savalas) in *On Her Majesty's Secret Service*. James Bond (George Lazenby), Marc-Ange Draco (Gabriele Ferzetti), and his men claim to be carrying blood plasma and emergency equipment to Rovigo to aid victims of the Italian flood disaster.

Red Dragon of Macao: One of the notorious Chinese tong societies, a criminal organization whose symbol is featured in a tattoo on the wrist of SPECTRE agent Count Lippe (Guy Doleman) in *Thunderball*. The telltale tong sign is enough to raise the suspicions of James Bond (Sean Connery), who encounters Lippe while spending some R&R time at rural England's Shrublands health clinic.

Regin, Nadja (December 2, 1931–April 6, 2019; birth name: Nadezda Poderegin): Yugoslavian actress who appeared in two James Bond films, first as the ravishing girlfriend of Kerim Bey (Pedro Armendariz) in *From Russia with Love*, then as Bonita, the fiery flamenco dancer in the pre-credits teaser of *Goldfinger*. A native of Nis, Serbia, Regin made her motion picture debut in *The Factory Story* (1949), a Yugoslavian film directed by Vladimir Pogacic. Nine years later,

Actress Nadja Regin, already a veteran of *From Russia with Love*, won the role of cabaret dancer Bonita in the *Goldfinger* teaser. *Courtesy of the Anders Frejdh Collection*

she made her English-language film debut as Odette Vernet in the sci-fi horror film *The Man Without a Body* (1957). She later retired from acting after appearing in two episodes of the BBC's *Comedy Playhouse* (1967–1968).

Reid, Milton (April 29, 1917–1987): Indian-born character actor, adept at playing exotic henchmen and villains, who portrayed one of the guards of Dr. No (Joseph Wiseman) in the first Bond film and came back in *The Spy Who Loved Me* to play Sandor the assassin. In the 1967 *Casino Royale* spoof, he played one of the Indian attendants of Mata Bond (Joanna Pettet). A native of Bombay who arrived in England in

1936, Reid started his career as a professional wrestler, then made his motion picture debut as Mac in director Francis Searle's crime drama *Undercover Girl* (1958). Three years later, he was Omar the bald-pated servant to Donald O'Connor's title character in *The Wonders of Aladdin*, and it was Reid who was neutralized by Charlton Heston's Major Matt Lewis during a Boxer sword-fighting exhibition in *55 Days at Peking* (1963). Reid returned to his native India late in life, and his death is shrouded in mystery. Some sources say that he died of a heart attack in 1982, but his family insists that he died somewhere on the subcontinent in 1987.

relevancy hearings: Public inquiry in Westminster, London, that will determine the future of MI6 and its clandestine operations after it allows information on vulnerable NATO agents around the world to fall into enemy hands in *Skyfall*. As M (Dame Judi Dench) defends her agency to members of Parliament, the meeting becomes a target for revenge-crazed Silva (Javier Bardem).

Renaissance Garden: An atmospheric standing location on the Pinewood Studios lot that was the background for the first pre-credits teaser sequence of the series in *From Russia with Love*. Tracked by SPECTRE assassin Donald Grant, the phony 007 in the Sean Connery mask tiptoes his way through an evocative setting of finely manicured bushes and trees, walkways, fountains,

Pinewood Studios' lush Renaissance Garden became the setting for an unusual manhunt in the *From Russia with Love* pre-titles teaser. *Courtesy of the David Reinhardt Collection*

and statuary. Director Terence Young, filming his second James Bond film, based the mood of this sequence on a similar setting used in the Alain Resnais film *Last Year at Marienbad* (1961). The Bond sequence began shooting on the night of April 12, 1963.

Renard (a.k.a. Victor Zokas, a.k.a. "the Anarchist"): Murderer, kidnapper, terrorist, and specialist in "chaos" portrayed by Robert Carlyle in *The World Is Not Enough*. Renard kidnapped Elektra King (Sophie Marceau), the daughter of billionaire oil magnate Sir Robert King, and, with the help of Stockholm syndrome, enticed her to join him in his mayhem. Having survived an assassination attempt by British intelligence, Renard has a bullet lodged in the medulla oblongata area of his brain. As a result, he has no feeling in his body and is impervious to pain. After joining forces with Elektra, this formidable killer embarks on his most ambitious plan: to steal plutonium from a dismantled Russian nuclear silo and deliver it to a commandeered Russian nuclear submarine anchored in the Bosphorus. When the plutonium is injected into the sub's reactor, it will melt down, destroying Istanbul and the tanker waterway to the Mediterranean and ensuring Elektra King's oil pipeline billions in new revenue. Fortunately, James Bond (Pierce Brosnan) thwarts Renard's plan by stealing aboard the sub and impaling him on his own plutonium rod.

Rhys-Davies, John (May 5, 1944–   ): Respected and prolific Welsh character actor who portrayed General Pushkin of the KGB in *The Living Daylights*. Having gained international popularity in *Raiders of the Lost Ark* (1981)—where he was delightful as Indiana Jones's Egyptian friend Sallah—Rhys-Davies was the perfect choice for Pushkin, the new head of the KGB. He later shone as Gimli the ferocious dwarf in director Peter Jackson's *Lord of the Rings* trilogy (2001–2003). A native of Ammanford, Wales, Rhys-Davies made his big-screen debut as a rugby player in director Jack Cardiff's thriller *Penny Gold* (1973). After appearing in dozens of British television shows, Rhys-Davies took on one of his first international roles as Stephanos Markoulis in Franklin Schaffner's mystery adventure *Sphinx* (1981), released the same year as his memorable appearance in *Raiders of the Lost Ark*.

Richards, Denise (February 17, 1971–   ): American film actress who portrayed sexy nuclear physicist Dr. Christmas Jones in *The World Is Not Enough*. Richards first came to the attention of American action audiences when she portrayed vivacious pilot cadet Carmen Ibanez in Paul Verhoeven's science fiction satire *Starship Troopers* (1997). As Christmas Jones, Richards was definitely a throwback to the curvy sexpots that were a mainstay of the 007 series in the 1960s, and she took quite a few brickbats for her casting as a brilliant nuclear weapons expert. But she's a lot of fun in a role that was never going to be played by a professorial type, and decently credible spouting a fountain of nuclear jargon while looking good in hiking shorts and work boots. She's also a credible action figure, jumping in to disarm bombs when the need arises. Born in Downer's Grove, Illinois, Richards made her motion picture debut as Elizabeth in

American actress Denise Richards costarred in *The World Is Not Enough* as Dr. Christmas Jones, a nuclear specialist who looks great in shorts. *Courtesy of the Anders Frejdh Collection*

director Guy Magar's crime drama *Lookin' Italian* (1994), which also featured Bond player Gloria Hendry. The former wife of actor Charlie Sheen, she made a big splash in John McNaughton's steamy thriller *Wild Things* (1998), and later had a brief cameo as "Carla, the real friendly one" in an ending scene in the celebrated Christmas classic *Love Actually* (2003).

Rietti, Robert (February 8, 1923–April 3, 2015): Nicknamed "the Man of a Thousand Voices," this British actor dubbed the voices of Emilio Largo in *Thunderball* and Tiger Tanaka in *You Only Live Twice*—and, finally, the pleading voice of the Blofeld-like figure in the pre-credits teaser of *For Your Eyes Only*. He also portrayed the Italian minister in *Never Say Never Again*. His first (uncredited) role was that of Fattorino the Page Boy in director Monty Banks's comedy *The Charming Deceiver* (1933).

Rigg, Diana (July 20, 1938–   ; birth name: Enid Diana Elizabeth Rigg): Sexy, athletic British actress who jumped from the hit British spy series *The Avengers* (51 episodes, 1965–1968) to the role of Tracy di Vicenzo in *On Her Majesty's Secret Service*. Unlike her Bond-girl predecessors, Tracy has a serious love affair with 007 (George Lazenby). And, to the astonishment of his fans, the secret agent eventually proposes marriage to her. In the film's conclusion, Bond and Tracy are married, but she is soon machine-gunned by Irma Bunt (Ilse Steppat), shooting from a car driven by Ernst Stavro Blofeld (Telly Savalas).

Was there a hotter female action star in the world in 1969 when Diana Rigg took on the role of Tracy in *On Her Majesty's Secret Service*? It is doubtful. After *The Avengers* TV series, her reputation was golden. *Courtesy of the David Reinhardt Collection*

For this crucial role, the producers decided for the first time that they should go with an established actress, someone who could work well with the fledgling Lazenby (an ex-model turned actor) and increase the power of the film's romantic scenes. Rigg fulfilled that requirement nicely. Not only did she look the part (three seasons on *The Avengers* had kept her in excellent shape), but she was a first-rate actress who rose to the occasion of playing the future Mrs. James Bond. Her much-publicized feud with Lazenby during the filming was more the product of tabloid imaginings than hard fact. SEE ALSO "garlic incident, the."

Rigg's best scenes include her arrival in Mürren to rescue 007, who is being hunted down by Blofeld's SPECTRE goons. Skating up to Bond at the rink, she falls into his arms, senses the danger that surrounds him, and then offers to help him escape in her red Mercury Cougar. Her driving ability and, later, her prowess on skis make her the consummate 007 mate. She even gets a chance to show off some of her hand-to-hand combat skills during a fight with Grunther (Yuri Borienko) at Blofeld's mountain fortress of Piz Gloria.

A native of Doncaster, Yorkshire, England, Rigg made her motion picture debut as Helena in

Diana Rigg by Jeff Marshall. *Courtesy of Jeff Marshall*

director Peter Hall's production of Shakespeare's *A Midsummer Night's Dream* (1968), which also featured future M Judy Dench. More recently, Rigg won a new legion of fans for her portrayal of proud Olenna Tyrell on HBO's mammothly successful series *Game of Thrones* (18 episodes, 2013–2017).

Rimmer, Shane (May 28, 1929–March 29, 2019): Canadian character actor who never seemed to play the same character twice in the James Bond series. In *You Only Live Twice*, he's the Hawaii radar operator. In *Diamonds Are Forever*, he's Tom, right-hand man to Willard Whyte (Jimmy Dean). In *Live and Let Die*, he's the uncredited voice of British agent Hamilton. And in *The Spy Who Loved Me*, he has his biggest role, as Commander Carter, the skipper of the American nuclear submarine captured by Stromberg (Curt Jurgens).

Born in Toronto, Ontario, Rimmer made his motion picture debut as Nancy's father in director Sidney J. Furie's teen drama *A Dangerous Age* (1957). His additional feature credits include *Dr. Strangelove or: How I Learned to Stop Worrying and Love the Bomb* (1964), as Captain "Ace" Owens; *The Bedford Incident* (1965); *Rollerball* (1975); *Twilight's Last Gleaming* (1977); *Star Wars: Episode IV—A New Hope* (1977); *The People That Time Forgot* (1977); *Warlords of the Deep* (1978); *Superman* (1978); *Reds* (1981); *Gandhi* (1982); *The Hunger* (1983); *A Kid in King Arthur's Court* (1995); and *Batman Begins* (2005).

Roach, Pat (May 19, 1937–July 17, 2004): Six-foot, six-inch British character actor who portrayed Lippe, the SPECTRE assassin who attacks Bond (Sean Connery) at Shrublands in *Never Say Never Again*. A native of Birmingham, England, Roach made his motion picture debut as a milk-bar bouncer in *A Clockwork Orange* (1971). He also portrayed Hephaestus in *Clash of the Titans* (1981), and he was the giant German mechanic who gets killed by the propeller blades in *Raiders of the Lost Ark* (1981).

Roberts, Tanya (October 15, 1955–   ; birth name: Victoria Leigh Blum): American actress and former costar of *Charlie's Angels* (16 episodes, 1980–1981) who portrayed geologist and oil heiress Stacey Sutton in *A View to a Kill*. Costumed mostly in long gowns, formal business attire, and mining coveralls, Roberts's shapely figure remained hidden throughout most of the film, making her the most conservatively portrayed Bond woman in the entire series. A Bronx native, Roberts made her motion picture debut as Nancy Ulman, the lead in director Jim Sotos's horror thriller *The Last Victim* (1976), a.k.a. *Forced Entry*.

Robinson, Joe (May 31, 1927–July 3, 2017; birth name: Joseph William Robinson Harle): Stuntman/actor and former wrestler who portrayed tough diamond smuggler Peter Franks in *Diamonds Are Forever*, his final big-screen role. In a vicious Amsterdam elevator fight, Franks battles James Bond (Sean Connery) and loses—a claustrophobic sequence that was one of the film's highlights. It was Joe and his brother Doug who taught actress and future Bond girl Honor Blackman her judo self-defense tactics for her part in the television series *The Avengers*. Born in Newcastle-upon-Tyne, England, Robinson made his motion picture debut as Sam Heppner in director Carol Reed's acclaimed family drama *A Kid for Two Farthings* (1955).

Rolls-Royce 1937 Phantom III: The model of Rolls-Royce owned by Auric Goldfinger (Gert Fröbe) and driven by his servant Oddjob (Harold Sakata) in *Goldfinger*. Its license plate number is AU 1.

Auric Goldfinger's Phantom III Rolls-Royce. *Steve Rubin Collection*

In order to smuggle his gold out of England, Goldfinger cleverly replaces the car's bodywork with an eighteen-karat-gold facsimile fabricated in his metallurgical plant in Kent; it will later be melted back into gold bars in Switzerland.

This is the car into which 007 (Sean Connery) places a homer—an electronic signaling device supplied by Q Branch that transmits the Rolls's position to a receiver in Bond's Aston Martin, thus allowing 007 to tail the sinister gold smuggler to his Swiss factory.

Rolls-Royce factory: Located at the Leavesden Aerodrome in Hertfordshire, England, forty minutes north of London, this enormous complex—in which British Mosquito fighter-bombers and Halifax bombers were built and test-flown during World War II—replaced Pinewood Studios as 007 headquarters for the filming of *GoldenEye*. At the time, Pinewood was overbooked with the production of the films *Mary Reilly* (with Julia Roberts) and *First Knight* (in which Sean Connery costars as King Arthur), so the producers relocated to the Rolls-Royce facility, which was considered the largest covered factory area in the world, featuring 1.2 million square feet of space. Converted into five soundstages and combined with exterior sets and a deserted Royal Air Force military airfield, that makes for 290 acres of studio space—about three times as big as Pinewood. Six hundred crew members were reported to be working on *GoldenEye* during its construction phase. The Leavesden studios were later the home of the *Harry Potter* film series, after which Warner Bros. purchased the property. Because of its early association with *GoldenEye*, the facility was briefly given the informal nickname of "Cubbywood," after Bond producer Albert R. "Cubby" Broccoli.

Romanova, Corporal Tatiana "Tanya": One of James Bond's sexiest women, she was portrayed by Italian beauty queen Daniela Bianchi in *From Russia with Love*. She becomes the innocent pawn in a deadly assassination and extortion plan concocted by SPECTRE.

Daniela Bianchi, a former Miss Rome, portrayed the stunningly beautiful Russian cipher clerk Tatiana Romanova in *From Russia with Love*. Her friends call her Tanya. *Courtesy of the David Reinhardt Collection*

Tatiana Romanova (Daniela Bianchi), voted Most Desirable Female to Share a Bedroom With on the Orient Express. *Courtesy of the David Reinhardt Collection*

Stationed in Istanbul and assigned to the Russian embassy's cryptographic section, where she works directly with the Lektor decoding machine, Romanova is a State Security corporal. Her friends call her "Tanya." She was originally stationed in Moscow, where she worked with the English decoding crew and where she first saw Colonel Rosa Klebb (Lotte Lenya), who is now a SPECTRE spymaster but whom Tanya thinks is still working for the Russians. Earlier in her life, Tanya was a ballet student who was disqualified for growing one inch over regulation height. Prior to meeting 007 in Istanbul, she had three lovers. Although Klebb orders her to seduce Bond in an Istanbul hotel suite—where, unbeknownst to her, the lovemaking will be filmed by a SPECTRE camera crew hiding in the *cabinet de voyeur*—she eventually falls in love with him.

Tanya joins Bond on the Orient Express with the Lektor decoding machine she has helped steal. Drugged by Donald Grant (Robert Shaw), she survives the flight on the train and the ensuing battles with SPECTRE assassins in helicopters and speedboats. She eventually saves Bond's life in Venice by shooting Rosa Klebb.

Screenwriter Richard Maibaum revived her character in an early draft of *The Spy Who Loved Me*, but she was replaced by Russian spy Major Anya "Triple X" Amasova (Barbara Bach) in the final script.

Actress Daniela Bianchi gets a touch-up before bedroom action in *From Russia with Love. Courtesy of the David Reinhardt Collection*

Rosaki Cave: A huge cave on the Japanese mainland located across the sea from Ama Island in *You Only Live Twice*. When two islanders are found dead in their boat, James Bond (Sean Connery) and his "wife," Kissy (Mie Hama), investigate and discover deadly phosgene gas in the cave. Diving into the water, they eventually find their way to an extinct volcano, which is the site of the secret rocket base of Blofeld (Donald Pleasence).

Rubavitch: Girlfriend of the KGB's General Leonid Pushkin (John Rhys-Davies), portrayed by Virginia Hey in *The Living Daylights*. Accompanying him to Tangier, Rubavitch is in the hotel room when Pushkin discovers that he's about to be killed by James Bond (Timothy Dalton). Pushkin eventually convinces 007 not to kill him, and they join forces to expose the plot of renegade Russian General Georgi Koskov (Jeroen Krabbé). As their first act, Pushkin is "assassinated" by Bond, a scam that stuns an already shaken Rubavitch. She is further stunned when Pushkin rises from his gurney and removes the fake-blood packs from under his uniform. NOTE: Rubavitch is not to be confused with General Alexis Gogol's lady friend, Rublevitch.

Rublevitch: Very sexy assistant to General Alexis Gogol (Walter Gotell), portrayed by Austrian

Eva Rueber-Staier portrayed General Gogol's girl Friday, Rublevitch, in *The Spy Who Loved Me*, *For Your Eyes Only*, and *Octopussy*. *Steve Rubin Collection*

actress Eva Rueber-Staier, who is introduced in *The Spy Who Loved Me* and who also appears in *For Your Eyes Only* and *Octopussy*.

Russhon, Charles Joseph Anthony "Rush" (March 23, 1911–June 26, 1982): Retired US Air Force lieutenant colonel who was a key production liaison on five James Bond films. Russhon's involvement with Eon Productions began in 1963 on *From Russia with Love* when he secured some US military aid during location shooting in Turkey. The following year, he was instrumental in securing permission from the US Army and four other government agencies for the *Goldfinger* production crew to film in and around Fort Knox, Kentucky—when Pussy Galore's Flying Circus puts the garrison to sleep. His relationship with President John F. Kennedy's press secretary, Pierre Salinger, helped cement the deal (it also helped that Kennedy was a huge Bond fan). In addition to opening the doors to the base, Russhon contacted the Piper Aircraft Company and secured free use of a group of Cherokee monoplanes for the film. As an inside joke and a nod to Russhon, the film crew put up a sign on one of the Fort Knox airplane hangars that can be seen during the air raid sequence: WELCOME, GENERAL RUSSHON.

On the next film, *Thunderball*, Russhon received $92,000 worth of free underwater gear from AMF. He also contacted the US Coast Guard, which participated in the final assault on Emilio Largo's SPECTRE flotilla, and the US Air Force aqua-para team, which jumped—free of charge—for the film. Russhon makes an appearance in *Thunderball* as a US Air Force officer who's present when the home secretary (Edward Underdown) briefs the double-0 section in London.

On *You Only Live Twice*, Russhon once again served as military liaison in Japan, his old stomping grounds. He joined the film crew for the initial reconnaissance, helped secure key transportation, and was a tremendous help on the logistically complicated shoot. He was even instrumental in working out a deal that brought Sony products into the film.

After a six-year absence, Russhon returned to the series on *Live and Let Die*. He helped secure key cooperation with the New York Police Department during location shooting in Manhattan.

Ryder, Honey: Voluptuous island girl portrayed by Ursula Andress in *Dr. No*. In Ian Fleming's original novel, she was referred to as Honeychile Ryder. The only child of a marine zoologist, Honey grew up all over the world, anywhere where her father could find sea life to study—the Philippines, Bali, Hawaii. Her school is the encyclopedia she has been reading since childhood; she's up to *T* when she meets Bond.

Honey and her father moved to Kingston, Jamaica, where her father reportedly drowned off Crab Key, though Honey believes that he was actually murdered by the henchmen of Dr. No (Joseph Wiseman). After she was orphaned, her seemingly kindly landlord allowed her to stay on for free—only to turn lecherous and assault her. For revenge, Honey placed a female black widow spider under his mosquito netting. Bitten, he took an entire week to die, a fact that 007 finds unsettling.

Honey knows Crab Key intimately, and she helps guide Bond (Sean Connery) and Quar-

Honey Ryder (Ursula Andress) and James Bond (Sean Connery) react to the engine of a high-powered boat off Crab Key in *Dr. No. Courtesy of the David Reinhardt Collection*

rel (John Kitzmiller) through the swamps until they're attacked by Dr. No's "dragon" tank.

Harold Sakata, a former professional wrestler, was well cast as Oddjob in *Goldfinger*. *Courtesy of the Anders Frejdh Collection*

Sadanoyama (February 18, 1938–April 27, 2017): Professional Japanese sumo wrestler who played himself as the Tokyo contact of James Bond (Sean Connery) in *You Only Live Twice*. Agent 007 meets Sadoyanama in the stadium locker room and the immense wrestler gives him a special reserved seat, which will put him adjacent to his next contact, Aki (Akiko Wakabayashi). His Bond appearance was one of only two films he made. In 1966, he was the fiftieth *yokozuna*—the highest rank in professional sumo wrestling in Japan.

Saigon, Vietnam: City where James Bond (Pierce Brosnan) and Colonel Wai Lin (Michelle Yeoh) of the Chinese Secret Service go to track down a killer stealth ship in *Tomorrow Never Dies*. This is a rare geographical identification error for the series. In reality, Saigon's name was changed to Ho Chi Minh City after the end of the Vietnam War in 1975 (even though locals apparently still call it Saigon).

Sakata, Harold (July 1, 1920–July 29, 1982; birth name: Toshiyuki Sakata; wrestling name: Tosh Togo): Powerfully built Hawaiian wrestler turned actor of Japanese descent who portrayed Oddjob, the iconic Korean henchman in *Goldfinger*, his film debut. Certainly one of the most memorable villains in screen history, Oddjob works for Auric Goldfinger (Gert Fröbe) as his manservant, chauffeur, and all around goon, battling James Bond (Sean Connery) from Miami to Switzerland to the bluegrass country of Kentucky. Their climactic battle in Fort Knox stands out as one of the Bond series' best set pieces. The following year, Sakata made his television debut opposite Robert Fuller, Robert Loggia, and Ann Blyth in the "Jungle of Fear"

episode of *Kraft Suspense Theater* (1965). Sakata's additional feature film credits include *The Poppy Is Also a Flower* (1966), for Bond director Terence Young; *Dimension 5* (1966); *The Phynx* (1970), billed as "Harold 'Oddjob' Sakata"; *Impulse* (1974), as Karate Pete; *The Wrestler* (1974), reprising the role of Oddjob for a bizarre bar fight scene; *Goin' Coconuts* (1978), opposite Donny and Marie Osmond; and *Invaders of the Lost Gold* (1982), his final performance.

Saltzman, Harry (October 27, 1915–September 27, 1994): Energetic Canadian producer, long in England, who coproduced the first nine James Bond films with Albert R. "Cubby" Broccoli. Born in Sherbrooke, Quebec, Saltzman was only two years old when his father, a Canadian flower grower, moved his family to New York City. During the Roaring Twenties, he supported his brood by selling miniature cactus plants to Manhattan dime stores. Harry attended elementary school in New York City but soon developed a passion for vaudeville. He would wander out to Long Island, where promoters were rehearsing their acts, and he'd simply hang around, hoping that someone would break him into the "business."

At ten, he was already dreaming of the future and a career as a big time vaudeville producer. His first break came when he was hired as a reporter for a local entertainment sheet called *Zit's Weekly*. *Zit's* was on the other side of the tracks from *Variety*. It constantly blackmailed the vaudeville houses, trading advertising for good reviews and blackballing shows that would not purchase ad space. Harry had been hired by a boozy newspaperman turned critic who needed a copy boy. As his columnist boss began to come to work drunk each day, young Saltzman would write the day's column for him. At a dollar a column, he began to make a good wage, and a few weeks after his thirteenth birthday he cleared $350 for a week's work. He was soon looking for vaudeville talent on his own.

With a bankroll, he purchased a franchise on one of the New York stages and began booking his own acts. By 1930, he was one of the most successful promoters on the East Coast vaudeville circuit, clearing $500 to $600 a week. Prepping his acts in Philadelphia and Washington, DC, he would bring the new talent into New York City and collect a sizable profit. Two years later, he moved to Paris and applied his savvy to the French music hall scene. He even managed a traveling circus. Whatever his position, Saltzman retained a clear eye for talent—a trait that would help him once he left vaudeville for the film world.

When World War II broke out in Europe, Saltzman joined the Royal Canadian Air Force as a flyer. He was given a medical discharge early in the war and returned to New York City to manage Henry Miller's Theatre. In 1942, he enlisted in the Office of Strategic Services (OSS), the precursor to the CIA. Assigned to the psychological warfare division, he spent the rest of the war in Europe.

He continued booking entertainment after World War II, expanding his reach into television. His most successful production, *Captain Gallant of the Foreign Legion* (1955–1957), starring Buster Crabbe, was filmed on location in North Africa and became a very popular program in America. His film career began in England in 1956 when he formed Woodfall Productions with playwright John Osborne and director Tony Richardson. Their partnership lasted three years and produced three of England's most critically acclaimed films of the era: *Look Back in Anger* (1959), which starred Richard Burton as an angry young man fighting the modern establishment; *The Entertainer* (1960), a brilliant study of an actor on the skids, with Laurence Olivier in the title role; and *Saturday Night and Sunday Morn-*

ing (1960), which brought instant stardom to young Albert Finney.

In a 1961 interview, Saltzman summarized his company's achievement as one flop (*Look Back in Anger*), one break-even enterprise (*The Entertainer*), and one blockbuster (*Saturday Night and Sunday Morning*). Although he admired the daring of his young creative team—both Osborne and Richardson were in their late twenties when Woodfall was formed—he criticized the stubbornness of the pair in refusing to make their films more commercial and thus more universally appreciated. Saltzman also explained that since England was really the last country to recover from the ravages of World War II, the English public were not ready for films that showcased their postwar squalor. Saltzman's discontent came to a head in the latter half of 1960, as Richardson developed his next project, *A Taste of Honey*. Unable to point his young partners in a more commercial direction, he resigned his position.

Saltzman began searching for his own film projects that were more in tune with audiences as he saw them. He wanted to produce adventure films along the lines of *Captain Gallant*—films that would transport an audience to another world where opulence not squalor was the norm, where bigger-than-life characters predominated, and where audiences could forget about their troubles. He was looking for escapism. He found what he was looking for in the James Bond novels of Ian Fleming.

Saltzman and Fleming shared the same lawyer, Brian Lewis, who had been assisting the author in setting up a pair of trust funds for his wife, Anne, and their son, Caspar. The lawyer had advised Fleming to make a deal for the film rights to his 007 novels; otherwise the trust value of his books would have to be based on the 1954 sale of *Casino Royale* to Gregory Ratoff for $6,000. Now it was Lewis who introduced Fleming to Saltzman.

The two men's fateful meeting took place at noon on a winter's day in 1960 at Les Ambassadeurs, a fashionable club in London's West End. As Saltzman began to discuss the films he had made at Woodfall with Tony Richardson and John Osborne, Fleming confessed that he didn't go to movies, and that the only film he had seen recently, *The Boy and the Bridge*, had resulted in a collaboration with the film's director,

Producer Harry Saltzman (center) on the set of *Live and Let Die* with partner Albert R. "Cubby" Broccoli (left) and Roger Moore (right). *Courtesy of the David Reinhardt Collection*

Kevin McClory, that ended in a chaotic impasse. Fleming came to the point and asked Saltzman what he could offer for the seven outstanding Bond books. Harry said that he could scrape together $50,000 for a six-month option, and if the project was picked up by a major studio, he would try to get Fleming $100,000 a picture, plus a percentage of the profits. The deal appealed to Fleming, who needed the option money to pay hospital bills. He may also have been compelled by his and Saltzman's shared history in covert operations during World War II. "I really strongly believe that he and my father shared some similar experiences," said Saltzman's daughter, Hilary. "Even though they couldn't publicize it, I really think Ian felt that this series was safe in my father's hands."* Fleming suggested that Saltz-

* David Kamp, "Harry the Spy: The Secret Pre-history of a James Bond Producer," *Vanity Fair*, September 18, 2012, https://www.vanityfair.com/culture/2012/10/fifty-years-of -james-bond.

man get in touch with his film agent, Bob Fenn at MCA, and work out the deal on paper.

Once the option was in place, Saltzman tried for five months to sell the studios on the idea of a series of James Bond movies. He encountered the same problems as Fleming: the studios would not touch the projects without the commitment of a major star, and no major star would commit himself to more than a couple of films. The frustration continued until one day in June 1961, with only twenty-eight days left on the option, Saltzman received a call from his writer friend Wolf Mankowitz, who wanted to introduce him to another film producer, Albert R. "Cubby" Broccoli. Saltzman had never met Broccoli, but he knew of his successful track record with coproducer Irving Allen in a series of action-packed films for Columbia Pictures. He thought it would be interesting to see Broccoli's offer.

Broccoli, meanwhile, was very interested in partnering up on a 007 series. Two years before, he had tried to interest his partner, Irving Allen, in purchasing the Bond film rights, but Allen had balked. (Ironically, Allen would go on to produce the Matt Helm spy series starring Dean Martin.) Although no two producers could be more different in background, style, and approach to the film business as Broccoli and Saltzman, they had one solid point in common: they knew in their hearts that the Bond books were perfect escapist movie fare. Agreeing to venture forth as a team (with a fifty-fifty split), and calling their company Eon Productions (EON standing for "Everything or Nothing"), Saltzman and Broccoli were able to make a deal with United Artists (after Columbia Pictures turned them down) for a series of Bond movies.

While the Bond films would become Broccoli's sole interest in the film business, Saltzman whistled a different tune. No sooner was Bond off and running than Saltzman was already searching for new projects. Early in production on the Bond series, he acquired the rights to thriller writer Len Deighton's Harry Palmer series, hired Michael Caine to play Palmer, and produced the three films away from the Eon banner. He also spent literally years on *The Battle of Britain*, which Guy Hamilton directed in 1969. Actually, the only time

Producer Harry Saltzman on the New Orleans location of *Live and Let Die* with Roger Moore. *Steve Rubin Collection*

Broccoli and Saltzman combined their efforts on a non-Bond project was on the Bob Hope comedy *Call Me Bwana*, which bombed in 1963—although its billboard pops up in a strategic spot in *From Russia with Love*.

Saltzman's outside interests not only began to interfere with his dedication to the Bond series, they also began to have an adverse effect on his financial condition. He fought for control of the film processing company Technicolor, but a sudden reversal in the corporation's fortunes in the mid-1970s eventually forced him to sell his share in Eon Productions to United Artists. *The Man with the Golden Gun* was his last Bond movie. Saltzman's additional film credits include *The Iron Petticoat* (1956), *The Ipcress File* (1965), *Funeral in Berlin* (1966), *Billion Dollar Brain* (1967), *Play Dirty* (1969), and *Nijinsky* (1980).

Saltzman and the elephant shoes: An amusing anecdote from the preproduction of *The Man with the Golden Gun*. Remembered screenwriter Tom Mankiewicz, "When *Golden Gun* was starting, producer Harry Saltzman went to Thailand. He wanted to have an elephant stampede in the picture. He told us that up in the Thai provinces, they use elephants for transport and work. He wondered whether Scaramanga could be working in the jungle, and when Bond arrives, they could chase each other on the back of elephants.

"Director Guy Hamilton didn't like the idea. He'd seen it before in ten thousand Tarzan films. But Harry disregarded us. He went down and found a guy who worked with elephants, and he learned that the elephants had to wear shoes when they worked—actually, they wore coverings for their feet that protected them in rough areas such as stone quarries. 'This is fabulous,' Harry told me. 'I've never seen an elephant shoe before.' So Cubby is down in Southeast Asia watching over the filming when some guy calls up and tells him that Eon's elephant shoes are ready. And Cubby says, 'What elephant shoes?'

Ever the showman, vaudeville veteran Harry Saltzman had a vision for an elephant stampede in *The Man with the Golden Gun. Courtesy of the Anders Frejdh Collection*

"As it turned out, Harry had ordered something like two thousand pairs of elephant shoes—even though there were no elephants in the script—which some guy had been working on for months. This guy still wanted his money."*

Salzkammergut, Austria: Lake region mentioned by Colonel Smithers (Richard Vernon) of the Bank of England in *Goldfinger*. It's the location of Lake Toplitz, the rumored site of a World War II Nazi gold hoard. One recovered bar of that hoard is used as bait by James Bond (Sean Connery) in the golf challenge match with Auric Goldfinger (Gert Fröbe).

Samedi, Baron: Giant henchman of drug smuggler Kananga (Yaphet Kotto) in *Live and Let Die*, portrayed by six-foot-six dancer/choreographer Geoffrey Holder. Holder plays the role in two distinctly different veins. At times, he is simply a conspicuous heavy of Kanaga's alter ego Mr. Big. But in several key sequences the henchman seems to become Baron Samedi ("Samedi" is French for "Saturday"), who in the mythology of voodoo is the god of cemeteries and the chief of the legion of the dead who cannot die.

Holder, with his powerful laugh and lithesome dancer movements, is nearly the symbol of the entire film, and viewers never quite know whether Samedi is a mortal or supernatural figure. At Bond's hotel on the fictional island of San Monique, he's merely a dancing, laughing character in an elaborate floor show. In a very atmospheric moment in the hinterlands of the island, he's a moody flute player, greeting Bond (Roger Moore) and Solitaire (Jane Seymour) and wishing them a good day. It is the mythical Samedi who officiates a sacrificial rite in which Solitaire is nearly murdered by snake-bearing

worshippers, but in the climactic fight to save her, Bond finds Samedi a very mortal opponent, defeating him by throwing him into a coffin full of snakes. But then, appropriately enough, the last character we see in the film is an uninjured, laughing Samedi riding on the front of Bond's homeward-bound train.

In fact, the appearance of Holder in the film's last scene was a late addition to the film. The filmmakers felt strongly that they risked alienating black Bond fans if they killed off practically all the black villains, so they added the final turn—little does 007 know who is sitting on the front of the train, warning us that the supernatural cannot be dismissed so lightly.

San Monique: Mythical and mystical Caribbean island represented at the United Nations by the

Striking actor/choreographer Geoffrey Holder portrayed the positively supernatural Baron Samedi, a confederate of Dr. Kananga in *Live and Let Die*. He also plays a mean flute. *Courtesy of the David Reinhardt Collection*

* Tom Mankiewicz, interview by the author, Los Angeles, November 7, 1977.

One thing you never want to do is get tied to a stake on an island full of voodoo worshippers, as seen here in *Live and Let Die*. *Courtesy of the Anders Frejdh Collection*

mysterious diplomat Dr. Kananga (Yaphet Kotto) in *Live and Let Die*. A nest of voodoo worshippers, San Monique is also the base of operations for a huge heroin smuggling operation run by Kananga, who masquerades as powerful Harlem crime kingpin Mr. Big.

Sanchez, Franz: Ruthless South American drug lord portrayed effectively by Robert Davi in *Licence to Kill*. Sanchez crosses paths with James Bond (Timothy Dalton) when he decides to sneak back into the US and confront his girlfriend, Lupe Lamora (Talisa Soto), who is having an illicit affair in Key West, Florida. Getting wind of Sanchez's arrival on US soil, CIA agent Felix Leiter (David Hedison) takes time out from preparing for his own wedding to Della Churchill (Priscilla Barnes) and enlists his best man, 007, to help him nail Sanchez. The combined CIA and DEA operation is successful, and Sanchez's plane is captured. Unfortunately, due to traitorous DEA agent Ed Killifer (Everett McGill), Sanchez escapes and exacts his revenge—murdering Della and maiming Leiter. Sanchez's act enrages Bond, who turns rogue and goes after

Robert Davi took on the role of suave drug lord Franz Sanchez in *Licence to Kill*. *Courtesy of the David Reinhardt Collection*

the drug lord, determined to take down him and his empire.

Sans Souci: The hotel in Ocho Rios, Jamaica, that housed the crew during the filming of *Dr. No*, and also served as the exterior location for the cottage in the Blue Mountains where Miss Taro (Zena Marshall) lures James Bond (Sean Connery). The same location was used as the hotel in fictional San Monique where Bond (Roger Moore) stays—and where Baron Samedi (Geoffrey Holder) puts on a nightclub floor show—in *Live and Let Die*.

SAS: Acronym for the Special Air Service, an elite British commando team (similar to the US Delta Force) that, in Ministry of Defence war games, is assigned the mission of defending a top-secret radar station on Gibraltar against three double-0 agents in the pre-credits teaser of *The Living Daylights*. Unfortunately, an enemy agent penetrates their security and kills 004 (Frederick Warder) and several SAS men before Bond (Timothy Dalton) gets just revenge.

Savalas, Telly (January 21, 1925–January 22, 1994; birth name: Aristotle Tsavalas): Acclaimed bald-pated American character actor of Greek extraction who portrayed a zealous Ernst Stavro Blofeld in *On Her Majesty's Secret Service*. Born in Garden City, New York, Savalas is internationally remembered for playing New York City detective Theo Kojak on the hit CBS television series *Kojak* (117 episodes, 1973–1978). A World War II US Army veteran, Savalas joined the US State Department's Information Service after the war, then went to work for ABC News, where he rose to senior director of news and special events, winning a Peabody Award for his series *Your Voice of America*.

Savalas was in his late thirties when he began a second career as an actor, first on TV and then also in feature films. Savalas's film credits include *Mad Dog Coll* (1961); *The Young Savages* (1961); *Cape Fear* (1962); *Birdman of Alcatraz* (1962), which earned him an Academy Award nomination for Best Supporting Actor; *The Interns* (1962); *The Man from the Diner's Club* (1963); *Love Is a Ball* (1963); *Johnny Cool* (1963); *The New Interns* (1964); *The Greatest Story Ever Told* (1965), as Pontius Pilate; *Genghis Khan* (1965); *Battle of the Bulge* (1965), as wisecracking tank sergeant

Guffy; *The Slender Thread* (1965); *Beau Geste* (1966); *The Dirty Dozen* (1967), as psychotic Archer Maggott; and *Kelly's Heroes* (1970), as Big Joe.

Savile Row: A famous street in London known for its expensive men's tailors, it's where 007 is fitted for his suits, as James Bond (Sean Connery) admits to Felix Leiter (Jack Lord) in *Dr. No*.

Clothes make the man, and in this case Sean Connery gets his dose of Savile Row finery before shooting begins on *Dr. No*. *Courtesy of the David Reinhardt Collection*

SB-5 nuclear torpedoes: Soviet atomic weapons aboard a Russian jet fighter on display at a terrorist's arms bazaar in *Tomorrow Never Dies*. Bond (Pierce Brosnan) steals the plane before a cruise missile, fired from a British missile frigate, can trigger a nuclear explosion.

Scaramanga, Francisco: Seemingly unstoppable hit man who charges $1 million per shot, suavely portrayed by Christopher Lee in *The Man with the Golden Gun*. Protected by Red Chinese interests, Scaramanga lives on a remote island off the coast of China, enjoys the pleasures of his girlfriend Andrea Anders (Maud Adams), hones his skills by challenging gunmen in his "fun house" maze, and continues his work as the world's most expensive killer. It's Scaramanga who murders a solar energy expert and steals his solex agitator, a device that can weaponize the sun's rays. And it is that murder that leads James Bond (Roger Moore) to the Far East, where he eventually tangles with Scaramanga and his diminutive servant Nick Nack (Hervé Villechaize).

You don't cross Francisco Scaramanga, "the Man with the Golden Gun," as his girlfriend, Andrea Anders (Maud Adams), soon discovers. *Courtesy of the David Reinhardt Collection*

Schwartzman, Jack (July 22, 1932–June 22, 1994): American producer and former entertainment lawyer who produced *Never Say Never Again* in 1983. Only a tenacious industry veteran like Schwartzman could have faced the seemingly impossible task of realizing fellow producer Kevin McClory's oft-postponed plans for a remake of *Thunderball*. Not only was the project an enormous creative challenge, but the project faced a potentially costly legal battle with Eon Productions and producer Albert R. "Cubby" Broccoli.

McClory, who collaborated with author Ian Fleming and screenwriter Jack Whittingham on the original story for *Thunderball*, controlled the novel's film rights, and his contract with Eon for the 1965 adaptation only prevented him from making a competing version for the next ten years. But from 1975 to 1981, Broccoli and a huge legal team had been fighting McClory's attempts at a remake, determined to prevent any rival Bond movies from hitting the marketplace. At one point, thriller writer Len Deighton and Sean Connery were working on a screenplay titled *Warhead*, which would feature the return of Connery in his iconic role. But no studio was willing to take a chance on the project—until Jack Schwartzman stepped in.

Schwartzman knew about McClory's pitch from when it was presented to and rejected by Lorimar, the company where he had worked as production executive. One year after Schwartzman left Lorimar to start his own company, Taliafilm (named after his wife, actress Talia Shire), he was contacted by an old friend, New York investment banker Philip Mengel, who was also McClory's financial advisor. Mengel wondered whether Schwartzman was interested in meeting with his client. Schwartzman was. He felt that Lorimar had made a mistake in rejecting the project. Despite the legal entanglements, the prospect of Sean Connery returning to the part he had created twenty years before was too good an opportunity to pass up.

Schwartzman met with McClory and read through his materials, but the *Warhead* screenplay didn't appeal to him. Instead, he persuaded McClory and Mengel to allow him to option the rights to the project and proceed with an entirely new screenplay. Thus was born *Never Say Never Again*, conceived as a remake of the *Thunderball* novel rather than the 1965 film. The story would also be updated to include the technology of the 1980s: B-1 bombers, cruise missiles, talking computers, and video games.

The first writer on the project was actually one of Schwartzman's associates at Lorimar, Julian Plowden. Plowden took a crack at the material, then recommended a friend, writer Lorenzo Semple Jr., for the job. Semple wrote the shooting script, although writers Dick Clement and Ian La Frenais were called up to add some comic elements to the final story and bridge some key scenes. They wrote the opening war game sequence and introduced the bumbling character of Nigel Small-Fawcett (Rowan Atkinson) from the British foreign office in Nassau, Bahamas. Schwartzman also received some help from his brother-in-law, director Francis Ford Coppola, who became a major collaborator on the project. Coppola, however, was never considered for the director's job. That went straight to Irvin Kershner, who had recently completed *The Empire Strikes Back*.

With a finished script in hand and Sean Connery set to return as Bond (for $3 million, not the $5 million that was reported in the press), Schwartzman started casting the other roles. Having attended a prerelease screening of *I, the Jury* (1982), a Mickey Spillane mystery starring Armand Assante, Schwartzman selected costar Barbara Carrera to portray wicked SPECTRE assassin Fatima Blush. Director Kershner, who was then serving on the Academy Award committee for foreign film selection, found Klaus Maria Brandauer in the critically acclaimed Hungarian film *Mephisto* (1981) and recommended

him for the part of main villain Maximilian Largo. For the part of Domino Petachi, Talia Shire suggested the actress wife of her own makeup man, Ron Britton: Kim Basinger, who had recently appeared as the prostitute (previously portrayed by Donna Reed) in the TV miniseries remake of *From Here to Eternity* (1979).

Despite a trememdous cast and an incredibly commercial property, the making of *Never Say Never Again* was something of a nightmare for Schwartzman. Weather problems delayed expensive underwater shooting in the Bahamas. Kershner's indecisiveness caused further delays and confusion, particularly in the art department. The budget mushroomed to $36 million. "It was the first film I produced on my own," Schwartzman remembered. "And I totally underestimated what I was getting into. There were substantial cost overruns, all of which came out of my own pocket—so, in effect, I paid the price of my own shortcomings."*

Had he been given the job to do all over again, Schwartzman admitted, he would have made the same picture but spent the money more efficiently and developed better relationships with his team. He would have also jettisoned Michel Legrand's musical score and hired a different composer. His original choice was up-and-comer James Horner, who would become one of America's brightest composers. Unfortunately, Sean Connery rejected Horner and chose Legrand, whose disastrous score nearly spoiled the picture.

Despite his later second-guessing, Schwartzman did contribute many creative elements to the film. His business relationship with the brother of Saudi billionaire Adnan Khashoggi helped secure the use of Khashoggi's huge yacht *Nabila* for ten days of shooting. It was also Schwartzman's idea to use a video game for the casino confrontation between Bond and Maximilian Largo. "Warner Brothers had given us a hundred Atari video arcade games for the casino sequence," Schwartzman remembered. "It was logical for these very wealthy French charity guests to be playing video games. And I thought it would be terrific for Bond to play Largo on video. By now, baccarat and chemin de fer were passé in Bond movies—we wanted to update

---

* Jack Schwartzman, interview by the author, Los Angeles, November 2, 1984.

what Fleming had originally conceived."* That sequence, built around a dangerous video game called Domination, is a highlight of the film.

While Schwartzman was busy shuttling between the film's many locations in France and the Bahamas, he was bracing for legal push-back from producer Cubby Broccoli. All was quiet until *Never Say Never Again* was about to open worldwide. Eon Productions then petitioned the High Court of London to stop the release of the film. This time, however, Broccoli's legal tactics failed. The judge simply asked, "Why did you wait until now?" The law was not about to stop Jack Schwartzman from releasing an already-completed film he'd spent $36 million to make. By waiting too long, Broccoli's legal team undercut any chance of stopping the rival Bond. Warner Bros., which had US distribution rights to the film, opened it during the Columbus Day holiday, October 7–10, 1983. Opening-weekend gross was a solid $11 million. The film would go on to gross $160 million worldwide, making it one of the most successful Bond movies of all time.

Schweizerhof: Elegant hotel in Bern, Switzerland, that served as the exterior of the office building of lawyer Gebrüder Gumbold (James Bree) in *On Her Majesty's Secret Service*.

Sciarra, Lucia: Voluptuous widow of terrorist Marco Sciarra (Alessandro Cremona), portrayed by Monica Bellucci in *Spectre*. After 007 (Daniel Craig) kills her husband in Mexico City, he arrives in Rome to attend the funeral, then, in true Bond fashion, saves her life and seduces her—gaining valuable information in the process.

Sciarra, Marco: Italian terrorist leader and SPECTRE operative, portrayed by Alessandro Cremona, who is tracked down by James Bond (Daniel Craig) in Mexico City and killed during an exciting helicopter chase above the city's Day of the Dead festivities.

Scorupco, Izabella (June 4, 1970–   ): Stunning Polish-born actress, singer, and ex-model who portrayed Natalya Fyodorovna Simonova, a computer expert who works for Russia's Space Weapons Control Center in *GoldenEye*. A native of Bialystok, Poland, who grew up in Sweden,

Polish leading lady Izabella Scorupco took on the role of Russian systems programmer Natalya Simonova in *GoldenEye. Courtesy of the David Reinhardt Collection*

Scorupco was originally discovered on the island of Gotland in the Baltic Sea and rose to popularity in Swedish films and advertisements. Her additional feature film credits include the Polish historical drama *With Fire and Sword* (1999); *Vertical Limit* (2000); *Reign of Fire* (2002), opposite Matthew McConaughey and Christian Bale; *Exorcist: The Beginning* (2004); *Among Us* (2010); and *Micke & Veronica* (2014), a.k.a. *Love Is a Drug*.

Scotch and water: The first cocktail ever ordered by James Bond, in the 1954 CBS TV version of *Casino Royale*. Bond (Barry Nelson) is seated in the bar of the Monte Carlo casino with British agent Clarence Leiter (Michael Pate), who orders a Scotch and soda for himself.

Scott, Andrew (October 21, 1976–   ): Irish actor who portrayed C, the director of Britain's new Joint Intelligence Service in *Spectre*. Born in Dublin, Scott made his motion picture debut as Eamon Doyle in director Cathal Black's *Korea* (1995). He may be best known as Professor Moriarty in the television series *Sherlock*

(8 episodes, 2010–2017), for which he won the BAFTA award for Best Supporting Actor.

Scoular, Angela (November 8, 1945–April 11, 2011): Lovely British actress who portrayed plucky Ruby Bartlett, one of the allergy patients Bond (George Lazenby) encounters in Blofeld's clinic in *On Her Majesty's Secret Service*. Ruby becomes 007's first conquest when she writes her room number in lipstick on his inner thigh. Scoular also portrayed Agent Buttercup, who takes a bath with Sir James

Angela Scoular was well cast as sexy Ruby Bartlett, an allergy patient in Blofeld's clinic in the Swiss Alps in *On Her Majesty's Secret Service*. *Courtesy of the David Reinhardt Collection*

Bond (David Niven) in the 1967 spoof version of *Casino Royale*. A native of London, Scoular made her feature film debut as a society girl in Charlie Chaplin's *A Countess from Hong Kong* (1967), then went on to appear in *The Adventurers* (1970), *Doctor in Trouble* (1970), *Adventures of a Taxi Driver* (1976), and *Adventures of a Private Eye* (1977), as well as a number of top British television series. Sadly, despondent over financial troubles and suffering from alcoholism, Scoular died by suicide in 2011. She was the wife of actor Leslie Phillips, who voiced the Sorting Hat in three *Harry Potter* films.

sea drill: Formidable weapon deployed by the stealth ship of billionaire Elliot Carver (Jonathan Pryce) in *Tomorrow Never Dies*. It penetrates the hull of the British warship HMS *Devonshire* and guts her like a fish. Thanks to electronic tampering initiated by Carver's techno-terrorist collaborator Henry Gupta (Ricky Jay), British intelligence is led to believe that the *Devonshire* was sunk by a Chinese aerial torpedo.

Semple, Lorenzo, Jr. (March 27, 1923–March 28, 2014): American playwright and screenwriter, a veteran of the 1960s *Batman* TV series, who penned *Never Say Never Again*. Born in Mount Kisco, New York, Semple made his feature film

writing debut on *The Honeymoon Machine* (1961), a Steve McQueen service comedy that costarred Brigid Bazlen (*How the West Was Won*) and was based on Semple's stage play. His other feature credits include *Fathom* (1967); *Pretty Poison* (1968); *The Sporting Club* (1971); *Papillon* (1973), again starring Steve McQueen; *The Super Cops* (1974); *The Parallax View* (1974); *Three Days of the Condor* (1975); *The Drowning Pool* (1976), cowritten with Tracy Keenan Wynn and Walter Hill; and *King Kong* (1976). In his later years, Semple cohosted a film review show on YouTube with former studio executive turned producer Marcia Nasatir titled *Reel Geezers*. He also revealed that, back in the 1950s, he worked with actor/producer Gregory Ratoff when the latter owned the feature film rights to Ian Fleming's first James Bond novel, *Casino Royale*. According to Semple, Ratoff was actually developing the project for actress Susan Hayward to play a female Bond.*

Sentinel: Remote-control submersible owned by Milton Krest (Anthony Zerbe) and used to transport illegal drugs underwater in *Licence to Kill*. Its cocaine cargo is sabotaged by Bond (Timothy Dalton). The *Sentinel* was portrayed by a real-life submersible, Perry Oceanographics' *Reef Hunter*. Its sister sub, the two-man *Shark Hunter II*, was also featured in the film.

Seven Mile Bridge: Causeway in the Florida Keys where traitorous DEA agent Killifer (Everett McGill) hijacks an armored truck carrying notorious drug runner Franz Sanchez (Robert Davi) in *Licence to Kill*. Driving off the bridge into the water, Killifer and Sanchez are rescued by scuba divers who work for local cocaine distributor Milton Krest (Anthony Zerbe).

Severine: Beautiful associate of SPECTRE agent Patrice (Ola Rapace) whom Bond (Daniel Craig) meets in a Macao casino, portrayed by Bérénice Marlohe in *Skyfall*. She's got a Beretta automatic strapped to her thigh and a tattoo on her wrist that indicates she was once ensnared in the local sex trade. Severine warns that Bond is about to be knocked off by her bodyguards and offers to help him if he will kill her employer—who turns out to be cyberterrorist Raoul Silva (Javier

---

* Steven Gaydos, "Jane Bond? Scribe's-Eye View of 007 Pic Birth," *Variety*, May 11, 2012.

In a rather chaste entry in the series, actress Léa Seydoux sashays down a train corridor in perhaps *Spectre*'s sexiest moment. *Courtesy of the Anders Frejdh Collection*

Bardem). Unfortunately, Silva is an unforgiving SOB, and Severine pays for her allegiance to Bond.

Actress Bérénice Marlohe portrayed the beautiful Severine, who leads James Bond (Daniel Craig) to Silva's lair in *Skyfall*. *Courtesy of the Anders Frejdh Collection*

Seydoux, Léa (July 1, 1985–   ): Sultry French actress who portrayed Dr. Madeleine Swann in *Spectre* and *No Time to Die*. A native of Paris, Seydoux made her motion picture debut as Aurore in director Sylvie Ayme's comedy *Girlfriends* (2006). International audiences first discovered her as Charlotte LaPadite in director Quentin Tarantino's World War II revenge fantasy *Inglourious Basterds* (2009). Director Woody Allen later cast her as Gabrielle,

Actress Léa Seydoux on location with Daniel Craig for *No Time to Die*. *Courtesy of the Anders Frejdh Collection*

a Parisian antiques dealer in *Midnight in Paris* (2011), in which she bonds with Owen Wilson. She's been on A-lists ever since, working in a variety of films, including *Mission: Impossible—Ghost Protocol* (2011); *Blue Is the Warmest Colour* (2013); *The Grand Budapest Hotel* (2014); *The Lobster* (2015); and *The Command* (2018), with fellow Bond player Max von Sydow (*Never Say Never Again*).

Seymour, Jane (February 15, 1951–   ; birth name: Joyce Penelope Frankenberg): Lovely British actress, the heroine of many films and miniseries, who portrayed the mystical Solitaire in *Live and Let Die*. Producers Albert R. Broccoli and Harry Saltzman originally spotted her in a popular British television series entitled *The Onedin Line*, a drama about the British shipping industry in the 1870s. On the set of the Bond film, Roger Moore referred to her as "Baby Bernhardt," a reference to the famous actress Sarah Bernhardt. She was an intelligent actress—perhaps too intelligent for the role.

Charismatic Jane Seymour took on the role of psychic Solitaire opposite Roger Moore's handsome James Bond in *Live and Let Die*. *Courtesy of the David Reinhardt Collection*

She quickly found that the producers wanted a psychic sex object who could escape the clutches of Dr. Kananga (Yaphet Kotto) by grabbing at Roger Moore's coattails. To fight such a one-dimensional characterization, she gave director Guy Hamilton a performance laced with forcefulness and sheer bravado, delivered in a straightforward tone of voice drawn from her years on the British stage and British radio. After a few weeks, the producers were threatening to redub all of her lines unless she adjusted her portrayal. She ultimately acceded, making the character more breathlessly sexy.

Once they succeeded in altering her performance, they also began to make her up like a living doll. "In one sequence," she recalled, "when I'm introduced at Mr. Big's headquarters in Harlem, they covered me with glitter, false eyelashes, and they gave me an exotic hairdo. That was their way of bringing in the occult. I was far more interested in the voodoo element in the story, because I had actually attended a ceremony in Jamaica with Geoffrey Holder [who played Baron Samedi], who knew a great deal about the supernatural. The Solitaire character could have been much more interesting if this voodoo element was brought out. After all, she was respected by everyone as having the power of second sight like her mother before her, and she lived all alone in that house on the cliff. It had fascinating possibilities."*

Despite her frustrations with the character, Seymour had the time of her life during filming, taking her acting career to places it had never been before. Terrified of gunshots, she was forced to undergo a strafing attack. Frightened of snakes, she was asked to stand perfectly still while someone shoved a fanged reptile right in her face. A nervous passenger, she actually sat calmly in the back of an imported double-decker bus while London busman Maurice Patchett rammed it under a low-clearance trestle bridge. Not one to perform readily at extreme heights, she still consented to be hoisted over the center of a Pinewood Studios soundstage, above a pool filled with sharks. To her credit, Baby Bernhardt survived all without a scratch.

Born in Hayes and Harlington, Middlesex, England, Seymour appeared on the big screen in films including *Oh! What a Lovely War* (1969),

---

* Jane Seymour, interview by the author, Los Angeles, April 16, 1979.

Jane Seymour was captivating as the mysterious Solitaire. *Steve Rubin Collection*

Young Winston (1972), *The Best Pair of Legs in the Business* (1973), *Sinbad and the Eye of the Tiger* (1977), *Somewhere in Time* (1980), *The New Swiss Family Robinson* (1998), *Wedding Crashers* (2005), *After Sex* (2007), *The Velveteen Rabbit* (2009), and *Fifty Shades of Black* (2016). She's appeared frequently on television, in TV movies such as *Frankenstein: The True Story* (1973) and *The Four Feathers* (1978); miniseries such as *Captains and the Kings* (1976), *East of Eden* (1981), and *War and Remembrance* (1988–1989); and series such as the original *Battlestar Galactica* (3 episodes, 1978), *Smallville* (6 episodes, 2004–2005), *Modern Men* (7 episodes, 2006), *Franklin & Bash* (4 episodes, 2012–2014), and *Jane the Virgin* (3 episodes, 2015–2016). She also starred in the hit western series *Dr. Quinn, Medicine Woman* (149 episodes, 1993–1998), for which she received two Emmy Award nominations for Outstanding Lead Actress, as well as two TV movie sequels in 1999 and 2001.

"shaken, not stirred": The martini order famously preferred by James Bond throughout the 007 series. It's the basis for one of the greatest bloopers in all the films: When Bond (Sean Connery) visits his colleague Dikko Henderson (Charles Gray) at his Japanese-furnished apartment in Tokyo in *You Only Live Twice*, the host offers him a martini, asking, "Stirred, not shaken?" Bond, without batting an eye, says it's fine, apparently forgetting his long-standing preference to the contrary.

Shaw, Maxwell (February 21, 1929–August 21, 1985): Bespectacled British actor who portrayed the foreman of signals in the communications room of the British Secret Service in London in *Dr. No*. He contacts MI6 radio security control when communication is broken with Commander John Strangways (Tim Moxon) in Jamaica. A London native, Shaw made his motion picture debut as Harry Jorgen in director Wilfred Eades's *Confess, Killer* (1957), which also featured Bill Nagy (Mr. Midnight in *Goldfinger*).

Shaw, Robert (August 9, 1927–August 28, 1978): Underrated British actor who portrayed ruthless SPECTRE assassin Donald Grant, one of 007's deadliest adversaries, in *From Russia with Love*. With his dyed-blond crew cut, Charles Atlas physique, and definite psychotic edge, Shaw is brilliant in the role. Grant's confrontation with Bond (Sean Connery) on the Orient Express is a masterful scene. After 007 insults him by asking from which lunatic asylum he's escaped, Grant sneers, "Don't make it tougher on yourself," stands up, and slaps Bond hard across the face. This is one of the few moments in the series when you seriously wonder whether Bond is finished. He's on his knees in a small train compartment, no friends in sight, looking down the barrel of a silenced automatic in the hands of a dangerous psychopath.

A native of Westhoughton, Lancashire, England, Shaw made his credited big-screen debut in director Michael Anderson's World War II drama *The Dam Busters* (1955), working with future Bond players Patrick Barr (*Octopussy*), Laurence Naismith (*Diamonds Are Forever*), and George Baker (*On Her Majesty's Secret Service*). Three years after playing Grant, Shaw was nominated for a Best Supporting Actor Oscar for his boisterous turn as Henry VIII in *A Man for All Seasons* (1966). However, he's best known as gritty shark hunter Quint in director Steven Spielberg's iconic horror classic *Jaws* (1975), which features Quint's memorable recollection of surviving the sinking of the USS *Indianapolis*. Shaw's additional credits include *Battle of the Bulge* (1965), as crack Nazi tank brigade leader Colonel Hessler; *Custer of the West* (1967), as General George Armstrong Custer; *Battle of Britain* (1969); *The Sting* (1973), as ruthless gangster Doyle Lonnegan; *The Taking of Pelham One Two Three* (1974), as hostage-taking mercenary Bernard Ryder, a.k.a. Mr. Blue; *Robin and Marian* (1976), as the Sheriff of Nottingham, once again facing off against Sean Connery; *Black Sunday* (1977); *The Deep* (1977); and *Force 10 from Navarone* (1978), with fellow Bond veterans Barbara Bach and Richard Kiel. Married three times with ten children, Robert Shaw died of a heart attack during the filming of *Avalanche Express* (1979). A successful novelist and playwright (*The Man in the Glass Booth*), he had suffered from alcoholism—a condition that perhaps contributed to his heart attack.

Shepridge, Johnny: London-based talent agent and former employee of Darryl Zanuck and Charles K. Feldman who is credited with sending Ursula Andress's famous "wet T-shirt" photograph to producer Albert R. Broccoli in January 1962. The eye-catching pic won Andress the part of Honey Ryder in *Dr. No*. Shepridge, whose nickname was "Ghoulash," later served as one of the executive producers on producer Feldman's comedy *What's New Pussycat* (1965).

Sheybal, Vladek (March 12, 1923–October 16, 1992): Sleepy-eyed character actor of Armenian, Scottish, and Austrian descent who portrayed SPECTRE master planner and chess wizard Kronsteen in *From Russia with Love*. When the film was released in 1963, a number of moviegoers who had never seen a James Bond movie before thought that Sheybal was Bond. After all, his character is introduced at the beginning of the film in an intense chess match, looking like a secret agent with his enigmatic expression and dapper attire, and he's summoned to a luxurious yacht anchored in the harbor in Venice. However, when he starts talking, you soon realize that this is one of a long series of Bond villains. Sheybal was perfectly cast in the role as the man who treats espionage as a chess game. He also appeared in the 1967 spoof version of *Casino Royale*, playing the associate of Le Chiffre (Orson Welles) who is sent to West Berlin

to auction off compromising photographs and state secrets, only to find his scheme short-circuited by Mata Bond (Joanna Pettet).

A native of Zgierz, Lódzkie, Poland, Sheybal made his motion picture debut in *Kanal* (1957), a Polish film that dramatized the events of the Warsaw Uprising during World War II. *From Russia with Love* was his English-language film debut. Sheybal's additional feature credits include *Billion Dollar Brain* (1967); *Journey to the Far Side of the Sun* (1969); *The Last Valley* (1971); *Puppet on a Chain* (1971); *Scorpio* (1973); *S*P*Y*S* (1974); *The Wind and the Lion* (1975), as the Bashaw of Tangier; *Avalanche Express* (1979); and *Red Dawn* (1984), as Bratchenko the Russian.

Shimada, Teru (November 17, 1905–June 19, 1988; birth name: Akira Shimada): Well-known Japanese character actor who portrayed the ruthless industrialist and SPECTRE agent Mr. Osato in *You Only Live Twice*. A native of Mito, Japan, Shimada made his uncredited motion picture debut as a Japanese dignitary in director Charles Brabin's romantic drama *The Washington Masquerade* (1932).

shoe knives: Retractable blade weapons dipped in a lethal nerve poison and embedded in the shoes of SPECTRE agents Rosa Klebb (Lotte Lenya) and Morzeny (Walter Gotell) in *From Russia with Love*. Morzeny kills Kronsteen (Vladek Sheybal) with his, and Klebb attempts to kill Bond (Sean Connery) with hers. Fortunately, Klebb is shot dead by Tanya (Daniela Bianchi) before Bond can be stabbed. Interestingly, in Ian Fleming's 1957 novel, Klebb comes after Bond with poisoned knitting needles. After she's disarmed, Bond's friend Rene Mathis escorts her out, but she manages to kick Bond with the poisoned shoe knife. Bond falls to the ground, and that's how the novel ends—giving rise to the theory that Fleming had originally intended to kill off 007 in *From Russia with Love* and end the series there. Since Fleming was very frustrated at that time over below-average book sales and the failure of any Bond movie deal to materialize, the theory does hold some water.

Shrublands: A pricey health clinic in rural England that is a principal location in the early scenes of *Thunderball* and *Never Say Never Again*. In *Thunderball*, Bond (Sean Connery)

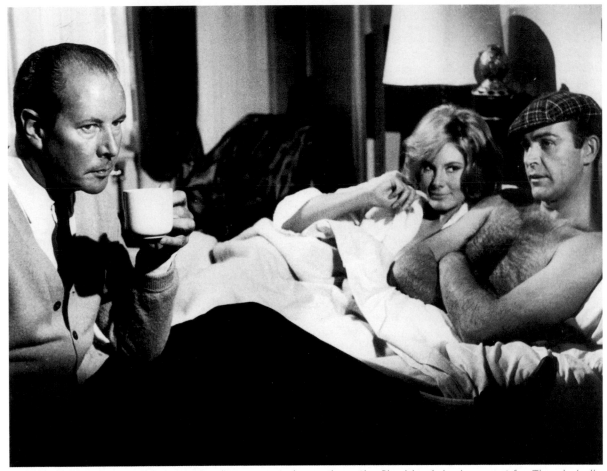

Director Terence Young (left) waits for the camera to be ready on the Shrublands bedroom set for *Thunderball*. Sean Connery and Molly Peters appear relaxed. *Courtesy of the David Reinhardt Collection*

goes to Shrublands to recover from wounds suffered in his fight with SPECTRE agent Jacques Bouvar (Bob Simmons). There he meets the very suspicious Count Lippe (Guy Doleman), who happens to have a telltale tong sign tattooed on his wrist. That, plus the appearance of the mysteriously bandaged "Mr. Angelo" (Paul Stassino), starts 007 on an investigation that leads to an incredible nuclear blackmail scheme. Along the way he battles Lippe and beds sexy Shrublands physical therapist Patricia Fearing (Molly Peters).

In Ian Fleming's original novel, Shrublands was patterned after the author's own experiences in the spring of 1956 when he was a recuperating patient at Enton Hall, a health resort located in a large, well-maintained Victorian mansion at the heart of the Surrey stockbroker belt. Production

designer Ken Adam and production manager David Middlemas had visited Enton Hall and had found it to be old, run down, and highly uncinematic—hardly a proper location for a James Bond film. They were looking for something a bit more streamlined and modern. Returning from Surrey, they discovered a converted hotel not far from their headquarters at Pinewood Studios. With its concrete driveways and well-trimmed hedgerows, it became the perfect Shrublands.

The clinic returns as a more dignified old-style English manor house in *Never Say Never Again*. This time Bond (Sean Connery again) has been sent to the health clinic to "purge" his body of free-radical toxins caused by too much white bread and red meat and too many dry martinis. While suffering through "lentil delight" and "goat's cheese," Bond smuggles in his own cuisine: beluga caviar, quail's eggs, fois gras from Strasbourg, and vodka—a meal that seduces the very willing nurse Patricia Fearing (Prunella Gee). During his stay, Bond also observes the suspicious activities of SPECTRE agent Fatima Blush (Barbara Carrera), who's masquerading as a private-duty nurse with a fearful corneal transplant patient named Jack Petachi (Gavan O'Herlihy). And Bond battles another SPECTRE agent, a giant named Lippe (Pat Roach), who comes after him with a razor-sharp belt. In an extremely violent encounter that practically destroys half the health clinic, Bond kills the SPECTRE assassin, first stunning him with a vial of 007's own urine to the face, and then impaling him on a group of glass laboratory instruments.

Siamese fighting fish: A species of deadly fish introduced at the beginning of *From Russia with Love* as Blofeld's pets. In the tank that sits behind Blofeld's desk, two Siamese fighting fish are locked in combat. In the next tank, a third fish watches, ready to pounce on the exhausted winner. Blofeld equates this tactic with the impending SPECTRE plan to outwit the Russians and the British by stealing a Soviet Lektor decoding machine and murdering James Bond.

Siberian separatists: The people General Ourumov (Gottfried John) names as suspects in the destruction of Russia's Space Weapons Control Center at Severnaya in *GoldenEye*. It's all a cover for Ourumov's own complicity in the attack.

Sidey, Hugh (September 3, 1927–November 21, 2005): American journalist and longtime political columnist for *Time* magazine who, while writing for *Life* magazine in 1961, noted that Ian Fleming's *From Russia with Love* novel was on President John F. Kennedy's reading list. The fact that the president of the United States had time to read about the adventures of 007 became a huge publicity windfall for Fleming's James Bond novels, and US sales began to rise spectacularly. Bond was no longer

Life magazine columnist Hugh Sidey. *Steve Rubin Collection*

being consumed solely by air travelers who browsed the shelves of airport book arcades. He was now entering the provinces of American youth, from grade school to college age—the core of the huge box office pool that would soon contribute to the success of the James Bond movies in America.

Siena, Italy: Where James Bond (Daniel Craig) takes a wounded Mr. White (Jesper Christensen) for MI6 interrogation in a dazzling opening chase in *Quantum of Solace*.

signature gun: Custom-built sniper rifle supplied to James Bond (Timothy Dalton) by Q (Desmond Llewelyn) in *Licence to Kill*. Made up of seemingly innocuous Hasselblad camera parts, the gun fires high-velocity .220 caliber shells and is equipped with an optical palm reader matched to the authorized user's right handprint. Once programmed, only James Bond can fire the weapon. It also has a Bushnell infrared gun sight. Unfortunately, Bond is captured by Hong Kong narcotics agents before he can put the signature gun to good use against drug runner Franz Sanchez (Robert Davi).

Silicon Valley: Area south of San Francisco that is the heartland of technology development in the United States, and the target of the scheme by psychotic industrialist Max Zorin (Christopher Walken) in *A View to a Kill*. Though it's better known today for its software companies, at the time of the film's release in 1985 it was the microchip capital of the world. Zorin estimates that the valley manufactures 80 percent of the world's supply—which is why he targets it with his Project Main Strike. Determined to monopolize the world's supply of microchips, Zorin plans to destroy Silicon Valley by triggering two powerful earthquakes in the region and burying more than 250 companies at the bottom of a giant lake.

Silva, Raoul: Charismatic, revenge-crazed cyberterrorist portrayed by Javier Bardem in *Skyfall*. Born Tiago Rodriguez, Silva was once an MI6 agent, assigned to Station H–Hong Kong between 1986 and 1997. He claims that he was a favorite of M (Dame Judi Dench) but M has a different recollection. According to her, he exceeded his orders, hacking into Chinese

Javier Bardem goes blond as former MI6 agent Silva in *Skyfall*. *Courtesy of the Anders Frejdh Collection*

intelligence as Great Britain was preparing to hand over control of Hong Kong to China. When the Chinese learned of his tricks, M was forced to give him up. In return, she got back six captured agents and ensured a peaceful transition. Silva chose to bite into the cyanide capsule hidden in his back left molar, but it didn't kill him, it only disfigured the inside of his mouth. Now Silva is determined to kill M and thoroughly disrupt British intelligence—in conjunction with, as we learn in the following film, his new allies in SPECTRE.

Simmons, Bob (March 31, 1922–October 21, 1987): Top British stunt coordinator and stuntman who not only doubled Sean Connery and Roger Moore but was also responsible for the action sequences in many James Bond films. In a sense, Simmons put the fists into producer Cubby Broccoli's two-fisted approach to Ian Fleming's secret agent. From the very beginning, the stunt sequences in the James Bond series were hard hitting, fast moving, and surprisingly realistic. With Simmons coordinating the action and Sean Connery throwing the punches, it was no surprise that the films appealed to action-hungry moviegoers, especially in America. And thanks to editor Peter Hunt cutting the action sequences to a razor's sharpness, there was no fat in Simmons's fights.

Simmons's first assignment for Cubby Broccoli was on *Paratrooper* (1953), a.k.a. *The Red Beret*. The stuntman told Richard Schenkman of *Bondage* magazine in 1980, "After doing one third of the picture, Cubby told me he'd employ me on all of his pictures. They used to bring over a stunt arranger from America, but after I'd worked on *The Red Beret*, they didn't bring him over any more. I got the job."*

According to director Terence Young, the handsome Simmons was actually considered as a candidate to play James Bond in *Dr. No*. When

---

* Bob Simmons, interview by Richard Schenkman, *Bondage* 9 (1980).

Connery won the role, Simmons, appropriately, became his stunt double and *Dr. No*'s stunt arranger. And in key fight sequences throughout the series, it's often Simmons versus Connery in the key fights—including the fight with Mr. Jones (Reggie Carter), the chauffeur in *Dr. No*, and the vicious clash with Jacques Bouvar in the *Thunderball* pre-credits teaser. In the climactic fight with Dr. No (Joseph Wiseman) in the reactor room, Simmons doubled Connery, while George Leech doubled Wiseman. In *From Russia with Love*, Simmons doubled Connery in the train compartment fight. In *Goldfinger*, Simmons doubled actor Michael Mellinger, who, as Kisch, is thrown off the top of Fort Knox by Oddjob (Harold Sakata). And for the assassination of Count Lippe (Guy Doleman) by Fiona Volpe (Luciana Paluzzi) in *Thunderball*, Simmons drove Lippe's car when it was struck by rockets from Volpe's motorcycle.

Remembered Simmons, "I was always looking for a better way. . . . I admired the American way of working. It's terribly professional, and that's what I've always tried to push into the people who work for me. I knew damn well if it hadn't been for the Americans we wouldn't be in the film industry today. I used to see people doing fight sequences in bars and they could never do it in one take because it wasn't rehearsed. I started choreographing fight sequences so you could repeat every movement. You could tell the director where to put the camera, because you knew where the action was going to be. I used to work with Sean very carefully. Sean used to say, 'What do I do and what do you do for me?' Generally, I used to do a master shot. I'd have the whole fight planned. We'd go right through it and film it with a double. We would then shoot Sean for the necessary inserts. But we'd do the whole thing as a master shot first, with doubles, because as [director] Raoul Walsh always said to me when I was a kid, 'If the action's good enough, it can be a monkey in top hat and spats.' As the film was progressing, I'd say to Sean, 'I want you to come and look at this sequence; I'll show you something.' He'd come out and say, 'Okay, let's work on it.' Sean would be in the studio sometimes until ten o'clock at night; we'd stay there on the set with just the house lights on, when everybody else had gone—just the night watchman was there. Sean was so keen, so good."*

---

* Ibid.

Born in Fulham, London, Simmons made his stunt debut on Alfred Hitchcock's *Jamaica Inn* (1939). He and fellow 007 stuntman George Leech both rode war horses in the jousting matches featured in *Ivanhoe* (1952). Simmons's additional stunt credits in the James Bond series include *You Only Live Twice*, *Diamonds Are Forever*, *Live and Let Die*, *The Spy Who Loved Me*, *For Your Eyes Only*, and *A View to a Kill*. He was also featured in the iconic gun-barrel title graphic for the first three Bond films. When *Thunderball* was shot in Cinemascope and the title graphic had to be redone, Sean Connery replaced him in the sequence.

Simmons, Mr.: The dupe with whom Goldfinger (Gert Fröbe) plays a rigged game of gin in Miami Beach, portrayed by a dapper Austin Willis in *Goldfinger*. Simmons is being systematically cheated by Goldfinger, who uses his girl Friday, Jill Masterson (Shirley Eaton), to spy on Simmons's hand with binoculars and then relay the information to him through a radio transmitter disguised as a hearing aid. Before Bond (Sean Connery) ferrets out the scam, Willis has lost $10,000. However, when 007 informs Goldfinger that the jig is up, the golden villain proceeds to lose back $15,000.

Miami resident Mr. Simmons (Austin Willis, right) continues to lose at gin to Goldfinger (Gert Fröbe). However, thanks to James Bond, that streak is about to end. *Courtesy of the Anders Frejdh Collection*

Simon, Carly (June 25, 1945–   ): Soulful pop singer-songwriter and Academy Award winner who sang one of the best James Bond theme songs, "Nobody Does It Better" from *The Spy Who Loved Me*. A native New Yorker who spawned decades of speculation with her number-one hit "You're So Vain," Simon made her feature film singing debut on director Milos Forman's musical comedy *Taking Off* (1971), which also featured future Bond player Vincent Schiavelli (*Tomorrow Never Dies*). Simon later won the Oscar for Best Original Song for the song "Let the River Run" from *Working Girl* (1988).

Songstress Carly Simon. *Steve Rubin Collection*

Simonova, Natalya Fyodorovna: Gorgeous Soviet systems programmer portrayed by Izabella Scorupco in *GoldenEye*. The only survivor of a Janus crime syndicate attack on the Space Weapons Control Center in Severnaya, Russia, Simonova forms an uneasy alliance with James Bond (Pierce Brosnan) when they are both captured by Janus in St. Petersburg. Simonova then accompanies Bond to Cuba, where they eventually foil the Janus plot to deploy the GoldenEye system and destroy England's economy.

Polish beauty Izabella Scorupco joined the cast of *GoldenEye*, portraying satellite technologist Natalya Simonova. *Courtesy of the Anders Frejdh Collection*

Sinatra, Nancy (June 8, 1940–   ): American pop singer, the daughter of Frank Sinatra, who sang the memorable title song to *You Only Live Twice* in 1967. Nancy recorded the song in London with composer John Barry conducting the London Philharmonic. The year before she worked on the Bond film, Sinatra made her motion picture singing debut on *The Ghost in the Invisible Bikini*, performing "Geronimo." Her number-one hit "These Boots Are Made for Walkin'" has been featured on the soundtracks of numerous films and television series, including the spy spoof *Austin Powers: International Man of Mystery* (1997).

Nancy Sinatra records the title tune for *You Only Live Twice*. *Courtesy of the David Reinhardt Collection*

Sirkeci Station: Istanbul's principal train station, featured in *From Russia with Love*. In addition to appearing as itself in night sequences for the film, it also stood in for stations in Belgrade and Zagreb.

Skyfall: The Bond family estate in the Scottish Highlands, which becomes a battleground at the conclusion of *Skyfall*. Determined to prevent the seemingly unstoppable Silva (Javier Bardem) from exacting his revenge on M (Dame Judi Dench), Bond (Daniel Craig) hatches a plan to lead the cyberterrorist and his murderous minions to Skyfall. Q (Ben Whishaw) and Tanner (Rory Kinnear) leave Silva an electronic trail to follow, while Bond transports M to Skyfall in his vintage Aston Martin DB5 with modifications. There they meet the property's long-serving gamekeeper, Kincade (Albert Finney), who helps 007 plant a series of booby traps. Considering the kind of firepower Silva has at his disposal, it's never clear why Bond doesn't hide a company of MI6 agents on the property. However, Bond and Kincade manage to kill off most of Silva's men amid a firestorm of destruction—some of which wounds M, leading to the film's downbeat conclusion in a deserted chapel on the property.

 **SKYFALL**

(Sony/MGM, 2012) ★★★⫧ : The twenty-third film in the Eon Productions James Bond series. US release date: November 9, 2012. Budget:

$200 million. Worldwide box office gross: $1.1 billion (US domestic gross: $304.4 million; international gross: $806.1 million).* Running time: 143 minutes.

―――――――――――― **THE SETUP** ――――――――――――

An enemy agent (Ola Rapace) has stolen a hard drive with a list of NATO agents embedded in international terrorist organizations. James Bond (Daniel Craig) tracks him down in Istanbul, but loses him when Eve Moneypenny (Naomie Harris), a field agent, accidentally shoots him instead of the target. M (Dame Judi Dench) is seriously criticized for allowing the list to fall into the wrong hands, and she's pressured by Gareth Mallory (Ralph Fiennes), the chairman of Britain's Intelligence and Security Committee, to retire. When MI6 headquarters in London is targeted by a terrorist bomb, Bond, battered physically and emotionally but not dead, returns

* "Skyfall (2012)," The Numbers, accessed July 9, 2020, https://www.the-numbers.com/movie/Skyfall.

Behind the scenes on a Turkish train roof as James Bond (Daniel Craig) battles enemy agent Patrice (Ola Rapace) in *Skyfall*. *Steve Rubin Collection*

to active duty (even though he fails every requalifying exam). He eventually follows clues that lead him to Asia and former MI6 agent Silva (Javier Bardem), now a rogue operative with a crime organization at his command, who is determined to enact revenge on the woman he blames for betraying him to the Red Chinese: M.

BEHIND THE SCENES

When new James Bond actors are introduced, they usually hit their stride in the third film. Sean Connery, exuding confidence and terrific timing, turned *Goldfinger* into an international smash in 1964. Roger Moore's third outing, *The Spy Who Loved Me* (1977), catapulted the Bond series to new heights of spectacular adventure, building a new generation of fans in the process. Daniel Craig's third film, *Skyfall*, became the most successful in the series financially—the first Bond to gross over $1 billion worldwide.

Producers Michael G. Wilson and Barbara Broccoli were determined to improve on *Quan-tum of Solace*, and their solution was to encourage writers Neal Purvis, Robert Wade, and John Logan to create a memorable villain—often the hallmark of a great Bond film. As Purvis recalled, "Either Sam Mendes or Daniel Craig suggested Javier Bardem as the perfect villain. So right from the very beginning we were writing for him."[*] Bardem is definitely a highlight, bringing to the role the same unstoppable malevolence that won him a Best Supporting Actor Oscar for the Coen brothers' *No Country for Old Men* (2007).

Purvis added, "It's great having someone like Sam Mendes directing, because he can get a hold of someone like Javier Bardem. It was also the first time that we already had a director in place when we started." Mendes was an unusual choice for the role, his previous experience more with straight drama than with blockbuster action. But he proved to be quite capable at bringing

[*] Neal Purvis and Robert Wade, interview by ODE Entertainment, YouTube, February 18, 2013, https://www.youtube.com/watch?v=FcrCdVOoosg.

All roads lead to Bond's ancestral home in Scotland in *Skyfall*. Where Bond goes, so does his vintage Aston Martin DB5 with modifications. *Courtesy of the Anders Frejdh Collection*

gripping suspense and believable emotion to this film, and his action sequences are first rate. With MI6 under siege from a mysterious organization that appears all-powerful, the movie's stakes are high, proving a great challenge to Bond and a thrilling ride for audiences.

THE CAST

James Bond	Daniel Craig
M	Dame Judi Dench
Silva	Javier Barden
Gareth Mallory	Ralph Fiennes
Eve Moneypenny	Naomie Harris
Severine	Bérénice Lim Marlohe
Kincade	Albert Finney
Q	Ben Whishaw
Tanner	Rory Kinnear
Patrice	Ola Rapace
Clair Dowar, MP	Helen McCrory
Dr. Hall	Nicholas Woodeson

THE CREW

Director	Sam Mendes
Writers	Neal Purvis & Robert Wade
	John Logan
Producers	Barbara Broccoli
	Michael G. Wilson
Director of Photography	Roger Deakins
Music by	Thomas Newman
Title song performed by	Adele
Production Designer	Dennis Gassner
Costume Designer	Jany Temime
Second Unit Director	Alexander Witt
Casting by	Debbie McWilliams
Stunt Coordinator	Gary Powell
Title Designer	Daniel Kleinman
Editor	Stuart Baird

Skyfleet S570 prototype: Fictional jumbo airliner—billed as the largest airplane in the world—that becomes a terrorist target in *Casino Royale*. Orchestrated by Le Chiffre (Mads Mikkelsen), the plot is to destroy the prototype while shorting Skyfleet stock. Le Chiffre plans to make a bundle on the move—he just doesn't figure on James Bond (Daniel Craig) gumming up the works. Le Chiffre's losses: $101,206,000. In the real world, the S570 was an augmented 747-200 that had originally been used by British Airways and flew for European Aviation Air Charter and Air Atlanta Europe before being retired from service.

Slazenger 1: The brand of golf ball used by Goldfinger (Gert Fröbe) during a high-stakes challenge match with James Bond (Sean Connery) in *Goldfinger*. Bond plays a Penfold Hearts.

Slazenger 7: The brand of golf ball found by James Bond (Sean Connery) during a golf match with Goldfinger (Gert Fröbe). Goldfinger

James Bond (Sean Connery) throws the wrong ball—a Slazenger 7—to Goldfinger (Gert Fröbe) during the famous golf match in *Goldfinger*. *Courtesy of the Anders Frejdh Collection*

also plays a Slazenger, but it's a Slazenger 1. When his adversary decides to make up for a bad lie by having his caddy, Oddjob (Harold Sakata), illegally drop a new ball on the main fairway, Bond decides to use the Slazenger 7 in a counter-cheating ploy. Pulling his Penfold Hearts and Goldfinger's Slazenger 1 from the cup, Bond substitutes the Slazenger 7 for the Slazenger 1, which Goldfinger promptly bangs onto the next fairway. Losing the final hole on purpose by blowing his last putt, Bond goes to the cup and announces that poor Goldfinger has been playing the wrong ball. Since strict rules of golf are in force, Bond's opponent must lose both the hole and the match.

Slumber Inc.: The Las Vegas mortuary run by Morton Slumber (David Bauer) in *Diamonds Are Forever*. It's actually a cover for an international diamond smuggling syndicate. When James Bond (Sean Connery) arrives in Los Angeles carrying a fifty-thousand-carat diamond cache—in the body of Peter Franks—he is greeted by a hearse and three goons from the syndicate. They transport him to the desert mortuary in Vegas—which, in real life, was actually one of the offices of the Las Vegas Visitors Bureau—where 007 meets Slumber. At Slumber Inc., James Bond has one of his most terrifying brushes with death. Knocked out by assassins Mr. Wint (Bruce Glover) and Mr. Kidd (Putter Smith), he's tossed into a coffin and placed in the mortuary's crematorium. In a frighteningly claustrophobic sequence, Bond fights to get out of the coffin, which is engulfed by flames. Fortunately, Slumber and Shady Tree (Leonard Barr) discover that the diamonds Bond has brought are phonies, and they retrieve him from the crematorium just in time.

Small-Fawcett, Nigel: Idiotic foreign service officer with an amazing upper-class accent who's attached to the British embassy in Nassau, Bahamas, and portrayed by comic actor Rowan Atkinson in *Never Say Never Again*. Small-Fawcett first meets Bond in Nassau Harbor, providing 007 with some useful information on the activities of billionaire philanthropist Maximilian Largo (Klaus Maria Brandauer). But by yelling Bond's name across the harbor, he of course eliminates any sense of secrecy about 007's visit. He also has the habit of communicating

with 007 at the wrong time. For instance, a phone call disturbs Bond while he's making love to his lady friend (Valerie Leon). And at the film's conclusion, Small-Fawcett stumbles into the jacuzzi where 007 and Domino Petachi (Kim Basinger) are relaxing.

The character of Small-Fawcett was created by uncredited writers Dick Clement and Ian La Frenais, who were hired by producer Jack Schwartzman to add humor to Lorenzo Semple Jr.'s original screenplay. Atkinson went on to play the very funny Johnny English in a series of spy spoofs.

smart blood: A nanotech tracking device that is injected into the bloodstream of James Bond (Daniel Craig) in *Spectre*. Having embarrassed MI6 and the British government with his unauthorized assassination operation in Mexico City, M (Ralph Fiennes) enacts this "post Mexico insurance policy," allowing the MI6 chief to keep track of 007 at all times.

"Smiert Spionam" Russian for "Death to Spies," it's the motto of a sinister KGB plot to kill American and British spies throughout the world—at least according to defecting Russian general Georgi Koskov (Jeroen Krabbé) in *The Living Daylights*. A tag with that phrase on it has already been found on the body of murdered British agent 004 (Frederick Warder) in Gibraltar. In reality, though, the plot has nothing to do with the KGB. It has actually been hatched by Koskov and his partner, arms dealer Brad Whitaker (Joe Don Baker), to get British intelligence to assassinate KGB chief Leonid Pushkin (John Rhys-Davies). Pushkin strongly suspects that Koskov is up to no good, and with him out of the way, Koskov can fly to Afghanistan and use local Soviet military personnel to consummate a huge diamonds-for-opium deal with the Afghan Snow Leopard Brotherhood.

To further convince the British and Bond (Timothy Dalton) that "Smiert Spionam" is indeed a Russian plot, Koskov's agent Necros (Andreas Wisniewski) kills the British Secret Service's Austrian section chief, Saunders (Thomas Wheatley), and once again leaves the "Smiert Spionam" motto near the body—printed on a balloon. When cornered by 007 in Tangier, Pushkin denies that "Smiert Spionam" exists. He refers to it as a Beria operation from Stalin's time (referring to

Lavrenty Pavlovich Beria, Stalin's feared head of internal security), but insists that it was deactivated twenty years earlier. Bond believes him, and eventually they join forces to go after Koskov and Whitaker.

In real life, "Smiert Spionam" was in fact the motto of Soviet counterintelligence during the Stalin era, and the motto was the source of the group's Russian acronym, SMERSH. Ian Fleming included a fictionalized version of SMERSH in his original 007 novels; it's the Russian counterintelligence agency scheming in the shadows of Bond's early adventures such as *Casino Royale* and *From Russia with Love*. Fleming's later novels replace it with the completely fictional criminal organization SPECTRE. In the film series, though SMERSH is mentioned in passing, SPECTRE is Bond's chief nemesis from the start.

Smith, Madeline (August 2, 1949–   ): Voluptuous British actress who portrayed Miss Caruso, the Italian Secret Service agent whom Bond (Roger Moore) beds at the beginning of *Live and Let Die*. She was the first in a long line of 007 conquests during the Moore years. Roger Moore described their intimate moments in his hysterically funny diary:

> A production point that seems to strike first-time visitors to a film studio is that sets built for interior shots rarely have roofs, so that light can blaze in from above. . . . Madeline and I were exposed to the draughts, which whistled around the stage, and the bed was icy. . . .
>
> I bounded and rebounded in and out of bed all morning, my feet freezing with every leap. It would have tarnished Bond's image to have worn wooly socks, and I envied Madeline, who, although bare from the waist up, could slide under the bed clothes; she squealed every time my cold feet made contact with the knees. . . .
>
> Miss Moneypenny has delivered Bond's intriguing magnetic timepiece. He embraces the *signorina*, then, holding the watch magnet near the long back zip on her dress, delicately draws his wrist down the line of her spine without touching her. The metal zip responds and the dress falls to the floor.
>
> "What a gentle touch you have, James," she whispers.

"Sheer magnetism," I reply.

> It may seem like money for jam pressed close to the beautiful Madeline Smith and taking her clothes off into the bargain, but on the twentieth take, your arm is aching, you've got cramp in your left foot, and your right knee is going to sleep. Part of the trouble was that Madeline's dress just would not fall far enough down. . . . Julie Harris, the costume designer, had to go down on her knees off camera and gently pull the dress down. As the watch is by no means magnetic, [another crew member] was also down there on his knees with his hands up Madeline's skirt, pulling a hidden wire attached to the end of the zip—so the floor around our feet was getting pretty crowded.*

* Roger Moore, *The 007 Diaries: Filming "Live and Let Die"* (Stroud, Gloucestershire, England: The History Press, 2018), loc. 2356 of 2729, Kindle.

Curvy British actress Madeline Smith portrayed Italian agent Miss Caruso, the first in a very long line of Roger Moore playmates, in *Live and Let Die*. *Courtesy of the David Reinhardt Collection*

A native of Hartfield, Sussex, England, Smith made her motion picture debut in director Robert G. Amram's romantic comedy *The Mini-Mob* (1967), which included fellow Bond players Stuart Saunders (*Octopussy*), Eric Pohlmann, Bruce Boa, and Milton Reid. Smith had previously worked with Roger Moore on the TV series *The Persuaders!* (1 episode, 1971).

Smith, Putter (January 19, 1941–   ): Nearly bald musician who portrayed the bookish gay assassin Mr. Kidd in *Diamonds Are Forever*, his film debut. A bassist for Thelonious Monk, Smith was discovered in a Los Angeles nightclub by director Guy Hamilton, who felt that his wild look was perfect for Kidd.

Musician Putter Smith took on the role of gay assassin Mr. Kidd in *Diamonds Are Forever*. *Courtesy of the Anders Frejdh Collection*

Smith, Sam (May 19, 1992–   ): British singer-songwriter who wrote and sang "Writing's on the Wall," the title tune to *Spectre*, and won the Oscar for Best Original Song. Born in Bishop's Stortford, England, Smith was first featured on a motion picture soundtrack in the German comedy film *Traumfrauen* (2015), performing the song "I'm Not the Only One." That same year, Smith wrote "Flashlight" for *Pitch Perfect 2*.

Smith & Wesson: The maker of the automatic pistol owned by Professor R. J. Dent (Anthony Dawson) in *Dr. No*. Equipped with a silencer, it holds six shots that Dent expels into what he thinks are the sleeping forms of Bond (Sean Connery) and Miss Taro (Zena Marshall), only to discover that it is a ruse and that Bond is seated right behind him. NOTE: In a prop error, Dawson

is actually wielding not a Smith & Wesson but a Colt M1911A1—which holds at least *seven* shots!

Another Smith & Wesson, a .45-caliber revolver, is carried by Pussy Galore (Honor Blackman) inside the private jet of her employer, Goldfinger (Gert Fröbe). When she points it at Bond, 007 explains to her that it's powerful enough to pass through him and puncture the plane's fuselage, creating rapid decompression. It's advice Goldfinger himself would have been wise to take later in the film, when he pulls his gold-plated gun on Bond inside the presidential jet.

Smithers, Colonel: Bank of England executive, portrayed by Richard Vernon, who briefs Bond (Sean Connery) and M (Bernard Lee) on the activities of the title character (Gert Fröbe) in *Goldfinger*. Smithers explains why Goldfinger has been smuggling his gold out of Britain: since the price of gold varies from country to country, smuggling allows Goldfinger to significantly increase the value of his loot. For instance, Smithers says, while the gold price in England is $30 per ounce, the price in Pakistan is $110. The colonel also loans Bond a bar of gold worth 5,000 pounds, which will be used as bait in the famous golf showdown between 007 and Goldfinger.

Character actor Richard Vernon portrayed the Bank of England's Colonel Smithers, here lecturing on Mr. Goldfinger's alleged smuggling activities, while Bond (Sean Connery) sniffs what Smithers calls a "rather disappointing brandy." *Courtesy of the David Reinhardt Collection*

Snooper: A doglike robot mounted on wheels that was developed by Q (Desmond Llewelyn) in *A View to a Kill*. Introduced in the office of M (Robert Brown) as the "prototype of a highly sophisticated surveillance machine," the Snooper returns at the story's conclusion to find James Bond (Roger Moore) showering with Stacey Sutton (Tanya Roberts).

Snow Leopard Brotherhood: Afghan drug wholesalers who are rumored to be the biggest opium dealers in the Golden Crescent in *The Living Daylights*. Dealing with renegade Russian general Georgi Koskov (Jeroen Krabbé) and his partner, arms dealer Brad Whitaker (Joe Don Baker), the brotherhood is about to be involved in a huge raw-opium-for-diamonds swap. Unfortunately for Koskov and Whitaker, James Bond (Timothy Dalton) hijacks the transport carrying the illegal drugs and jettisons the entire load.

Solange: Gorgeous neglected wife of terrorist arms dealer Alex Dimitrios (Simon Abkarian), portrayed by Caterina Murino in *Casino Royale*. Solange succumbs to the charms of James Bond (Daniel Craig) on Paradise Island in the Bahamas, after 007 wins her husband's Aston Martin DB5 in a poker game. It's a short tryst for Bond—and a ticket to the afterlife for Solange, who pays the ultimate penalty for her indiscretion. Like Kissy in *You Only Live Twice*, the character's name is never mentioned in the film itself but appears in the closing credits. The name Solange previously appeared in two Ian Fleming short stories: "007 in New York" and "From a View to a Kill," featured in the collections *Octopussy* and *For Your Eyes Only*, respectively.

solex agitator: A technological wonder introduced in *The Man with the Golden Gun*, it's a solar cell that can convert solar radiation into electricity with 95 percent efficiency. The British have it, a sinister industrialist named Hai Fat (Richard Loo) wants it, assassin Francisco Scaramanga (Christopher Lee) kills for it, and it's up to James Bond (Roger Moore) to recover it. As with plot elements in many James Bond films, the solex was inspired by current events. The year *The Man with the Golden Gun* was released, 1974, the United States was in the midst of an oil crisis, with many people forced to wait in long lines for gasoline. As Americans looked toward alternative forms of energy, the filmmakers decided to explore the promise of solar power.

The solex agitator plot point was added to the story by cowriter Richard Maibaum. It replaced a running duel between Bond and Scaramanga that was the center of earlier drafts by screenwriter Tom Mankiewicz. Said Maibaum, "As usual, we were looking for a world threat, and in the end it came down to either solar power or weather control. Harry Saltzman felt that weather control was not a good idea. He felt that it would just be a lot of special effects and stock footage showing hurricanes and tropical storms. He was right at the time." But just a few years after the film's release, when effects-driven sci-fi films surged to the top of the box office charts, Maibaum began to wonder how a weather-contol threat in a 007 movie would be received.*

---

* Richard Maibaum, interview by the author, Los Angeles, April 30, 1977.

Caterina Murino portrayed voluptuous Solange, who enjoys a brief tryst with James Bond (Daniel Craig) in the Bahamas in *Casino Royale*. *Courtesy of the Anders Frejdh Collection*

Scaramanga (Christopher Lee, left) shows off one of his solar energy weapons, powered by the solex agitator, to James Bond (Roger Moore) in *The Man with the Golden Gun*. *Courtesy of the David Reinhardt Collection*

Now, decades later, the Bond series still hasn't tapped the weather-control idea, but it has continued to draw inspiration from the headlines of the day—including the space shuttle missions in *Moonraker*, the international drug trade in *Licence to Kill*, and the international quest for safe drinking water in *Quantum of Solace*.

Solitaire: The mystical mistress of the tarot cards portrayed by Jane Seymour in *Live and Let Die*. Like her mother and grandmother before her, Solitaire has the supernatural power of the *obeah*—the "second sight." Because of this gift, she's a virtual slave to drug smuggler Kananga (Yaphet Kotto), who is relying on the amazingly accurate predictions of her cards to corner the North American heroin market. Her mother lost the power when she lost her virginity, and Solitaire faces that same fate when she meets James Bond (Roger Moore, in his first Bond appearance), who is not a strong believer in the occult. He tricks her into bed by using a fake deck of tarot cards—all of which depict the Lovers symbol. Deprived of her power, Solitaire falls in love with Bond and eventually helps him destroy Kananga's island empire.

In an early draft of the *Live and Let Die* script, writer Tom Mankiewicz departed from Ian Fleming's original description of Solitaire as a beautiful white fortune-teller. Said Mankiewicz, "This was at a time when *Shaft* had come out and there was a whole new wave of black exploitation films that were making a lot of money. So I thought that this time out, if we do *Live and Let Die*, Bond could get into bed with a black girl—in our case, Solitaire, who was of Haitian origin. Everybody said 'great,' and David Picker of United Artists went along with us. So, in my early script, Solitaire became this beautiful black girl." Meanwhile, CIA agent Rosie Carver, played in the finished film by African American actress Gloria Hendry, was originally white.

"At the last minute, however, United Artists changed their mind," Mankiewicz explained. "In their defense, I saw that they were very nervous about having a new James Bond and were unwilling to try something different when it came to a Bond girl. If Sean Connery had come back for this one, we wouldn't have had any problems. But in the back of UA's mind was the Lazenby affair, where the public didn't readily accept a new Bond right off, and they were very wary about

Solitaire (Jane Seymour) is threatened by a snake during a deadly ceremony on the island of San Monique in *Live and Let Die*. NOTE: Assistant director Derek Cracknell remembered that the snake wielder may have been more freaked out by the snake than Solitaire. *Courtesy of the David Reinhardt Collection*

Roger Moore's chances. He wasn't by any means a sure thing. Picker told me that although he liked the idea of a black Solitaire and felt it would work in progressive cities like New York and London, he felt that when the film was distributed in the places where the Bond movies had done very well—the so-called hinterlands—there would be a lot of people who didn't want Bond championing the cause of civil rights. Picker said that the decision was simply a matter of economic fact and that the studio wasn't making an *On the Waterfront* but a commercial James Bond film. 'And frankly,' Picker told me, 'with Roger, we're scared.' Of course, nobody bothered to tell me about the decision. I found out when suddenly I heard the studio execs mentioning Catherine Deneuve to play Solitaire, which I thought was pretty funny considering I had written her as being black."

The writer added, "I thought Jane Seymour was badly miscast as Solitaire. I think a much flashier girl should have been used, especially in Roger's first Bond film. Jane was so sweet and adorable looking that when Roger got into bed with her, it didn't work at all. It almost looked as if she was being taken advantage of. She's the type of girl you want to bring home to your mother, as opposed to a Bond girl who really knows her way around."[*]

---

[*] Tom Mankiewicz, interview by the author, Los Angeles, November 7, 1977.

Solo, Mr.: Mafia kingpin portrayed by actor Martin Benson in *Goldfinger*. In exchange for $1 million in gold, Solo arranges for a Red Chinese "atomic device" to be smuggled into the United States. Later, he is the only hood to turn down the chance to participate in the epic criminal scheme known as Operation Grand Slam. Electing to leave with his gold, he says good-bye to Goldfinger (Gert Fröbe) and Bond (Sean Connery) and is driven to the airport by Oddjob (Harold Sakata), who instead kills him with a silenced pistol. Solo's body and the entire Lincoln Continental in which he is riding are then crushed into a convenient lump of metal at a wrecking yard and returned to Auric Stud in the flatbed of a Ford Ranchero driven by Oddjob. In a nod to his host's previous remark, Bond quips, "As you said, he had a pressing engagement."

Goldfinger (Gert Fröbe, right) expresses his regret that Mr. Solo (Martin Benson) isn't willing to participate in the Fort Knox robbery in *Goldfinger*. *Courtesy of the Anders Frejdh Collection*

Soto, Talisa (March 27, 1967–   ; birth name: Miriam Soto): Sultry actress and cover-girl model of Puerto Rican descent who portrayed drug runner's moll Lupe Lamora in *Licence to Kill*. Soto looks great in the role and has a directness befitting a mobster's girlfriend, but her character never quite works due to the unbelievable manner in which she switches allegiances; although it's obvious that her relationship with Sanchez (Robert Davi) is a nightmare, the writers should have given her a little more time to get close to Bond (Timothy Dalton). A native of Brooklyn, Soto made her motion picture debut as a studio dancer in director Stuart Rosenberg's crime comedy *The Pope of Greenwich Village* (1984). Her additional feature credits include *The Mambo Kings* (1992), *Hostage* (1992), *Don Juan DeMarco* (1994), *Mortal Kombat* (1995), *Spy Hard* (1996), and *Piñero* (2001).

Sexy Talisa Soto scored many fans as drug lord moll Lupe Lamora in *Licence to Kill*. *Courtesy of the David Reinhardt Collection*

South China Sea: Potential battleground between the British fleet and the armed might of Red China in *Tomorrow Never Dies*—a fabricated conflict that could escalate to the real deal thanks to news-hungry media billionaire Elliot Carver (Jonathan Pryce). The evil Carver foments the confrontation between the two powers to build ratings for his new cable network.

souvenirs: The items that James Bond (George Lazenby) removes from his desk when he resigns from the British Secret Service in *On Her Majesty's Secret Service*. They include Honey Ryder's belt and knife from *Dr. No*, Donald Grant's strangler watch from *From Russia with Love*, and the miniature rebreather from *Thunderball*. Director Peter Hunt spotlights each keepsake while John Barry plays the appropriate theme music over each one. The scene was yet another of screenwriter Richard Maibaum's references to the rich 007 history that was taking a turn with the introduction of a new James Bond.

Space Weapons Control Center: Facility in Severnaya, Northern Russia, that employs computer analyst Natalya Fyodorovna Simonova (Izabella Scorupco) in *GoldenEye*. In a test of the capabilities of GoldenEye, a weapons system that can launch a deadly electromagnetic pulse from a roving space satellite, renegade Russian general Ourumov (Gottfried John) and his murderous associate Xenia Onatopp (Famke Janssen) destroy this space center after machine-gunning the crew. Only Natalya and her coworker Boris Grishenko (Alan Cumming) escape.

SPECTRE: The Special Executive for Counter-intelligence, Terrorism, Revenge, and Extortion, a huge international criminal organization headed by Ernst Stavro Blofeld, and James Bond's principal adversaries in a dozen Bond films and counting. SPECTRE has a long screen history dating back to 1958, when Ian Fleming worked with producer Kevin McClory to bring his James Bond character to film. Rather than adapt any of Fleming's existing Bond novels, McClory suggested creating a new story, an international caper that could use many different locations, not unlike his then recent experience on Mike Todd's epic film *Around the World in 80 Days*. In the early drafts of this story—conceived by McClory, Fleming, and screenwriter Jack Whittingham—the principal villains were the Mafia. Eventually the mob adversary was discarded and Fleming conceived of SPECTRE (which at first stood for Special Executive for Terrorism, Revolution, and Espionage), an immensely powerful, privately owned organization manned by former members of SMERSH (Soviet counterintelligence), the Gestapo, the Mafia, and the Black Tong of Peking. The idea struck a chord with the collaborators and became Bond's adversary in their story, the initial title of which was *Longitude 78 West*, after the coordinates where SPECTRE hides two A-bombs it has hijacked from NATO.

When McClory could not convince a major studio to finance the project, Fleming went ahead and used SPECTRE and other story elements in a novel titled *Thunderball*—the code name of Bond's mission to find the missing bombs. Claiming infringement of their collaboration, McClory and Whittingham sued Fleming in the British courts, and after a grueling three-year battle, they won. As a result, McClory and Whittingham were given the screen rights to *Thunderball* and co-credit on future editions of the popular book.

Meanwhile, producers Albert R. "Cubby" Broccoli and Harry Saltzman at Eon Productions had already featured SPECTRE as the organization behind the villains in their first two Bond films, *Dr. No* (1962) and *From Russia with Love* (1963), even though the organization was not featured in either of those original Fleming novels. (Origi-nally, Dr. No worked for the Russians, as did Rosa Klebb and Donald Grant in *From Russia with Love*.) Considering the state of the Cold War in the early 1960s, the producers wisely decided to avoid the cliché of casting the Soviets as their villains. The fictional, apolitical SPECTRE was the perfect umbrella organization for the types of fantastic schemes pulled off by the Eon series' villains.

As for McClory, with the film rights to *Thunderball* but no ability to mount a 007 film on his own, he eventually made a deal with Broccoli and Saltzman to produce *Thunderball* as part of their already thriving series. SPECTRE played a key role in *Thunderball* (1965) just as it had in the book, and Blofeld and SPECTRE returned in *You Only Live Twice* (1967), *On Her Majesty's Secret Service* (1969), and *Diamonds Are Forever* (1971).

But a new conflict soon arose regarding the SPECTRE concept. Under the agreement with Eon, McClory had agreed to wait ten years before producing another *Thunderball* adaptation. Promptly in 1975, he resurfaced with plans to bring a new project to the screen called *James Bond of the Secret Service*, a.k.a. *Warhead*. Burned once before by the release of a rival Bond movie—Charles K. Feldman's *Casino Royale* spoof in 1967—Cubby Broccoli was determined to stop McClory. A running battle began between the two producers, culminating in a number of lawsuits that stalled the McClory project on the one hand, and challenged Broccoli's use of the SPECTRE material on the other.

Early drafts of Eon's 1977 Bond entry *The Spy Who Loved Me* contained references to SPEC-TRE, which had now been updated to include members of the Baader-Meinhof Gang, the Japanese Red Army, and other modern terrorist organizations. Faced with a McClory suit about the unauthorized use of SPECTRE, Broccoli had his screenwriters remove these references, and villain Karl Stromberg (Curt Jurgens) became just another billionaire megalomaniac. Even soldiers in Stromberg's private army were given red uniforms to distinguish them from typical black-suited SPECTRE henchmen. Broccoli eventually introduced a Blofeld lookalike for Bond to kill off at the beginning of *For Your Eyes Only* (1981), but the film was careful not to actually identify the character as Blofeld.

But SPECTRE did make an appearance in Kevin McClory's renegade *Thunderball* adaptation, which producer Jack Schwartzman helped muscle into theaters over Broccoli's objections in 1983. In *Never Say Never Again* Max von Sydow portrays Ernst Stavro Blofeld. His SPECTRE, still based in Paris, is now heavily involved in the arms and terrorism business, with extensive operations in the Middle East and Central America. To provoke insurgency and revolution, armaments and missiles are indiscriminately supplied to rebels and government forces—a typical SPECTRE tactic. But with this movie a one-off proposition, and the Eon films steering clear of the *Thunderball* material for legal reasons, that was the last time SPECTRE was seen on screen until well after the turn of the millennium.

Then, on November 15, 2013, MGM and the McClory estate announced a deal: all rights to Blofeld and SPECTRE had been acquired by MGM and Danjaq LLC, Eon Productions' parent company. As a result, SPECTRE retroactively emerged as the principal nemesis of the Daniel Craig Bond movies. In 2015's *Spectre* we learn that the organization was the shadowy force behind the villains of the previous films: *Casino Royale*'s Le Chiffre (Mads Mikkelsen), *Quantum of Solace*'s Dominic Greene (Mathieu Amalric), and *Skyfall*'s Raoul Silva (Javier Bardem). *Spectre* also reintroduces Blofeld himself, now played by Christoph Waltz and suddenly revealed to be James Bond's foster brother. SPECTRE and Blofeld return in *No Time to Die*.

SPECTRE

(Sony/MGM, 2015) ★★⯨ : The twenty-fourth film in the Eon Productions James Bond series. US release date: November 6, 2015. Budget: $245 million. Worldwide box office gross: $879.5 million (US domestic gross: $200.1 million; international gross: $679.4 million).* Running time: 148 minutes.

THE SETUP

On a posthumous tip from the former M (Dame Judi Dench), James Bond (Daniel Craig) takes an unauthorized trip to Mexico City to foil another terrorist plot, this one engineered by one Marco Sciarra (Alessandro Cremona), whom Bond eliminates, recovering his unusual ring with a

distinctive octopus insignia. Investigating both Sciarra and the ring, 007 is eventually introduced to the international criminal organization that, it turns out, has been funding terrorism around the world, including the criminal activities of his defeated adversaries Le Chiffre (Mads Mikkelsen), Dominic Greene (Mathieu Amalric), and Raoul Silva (Javier Bardem). It's SPECTRE, and when it's involved, its ruthless leader, Ernst Stavro Blofeld (Christoph Waltz), can't be far behind—this time with an unusual personal history with Bond.

BEHIND THE SCENES

At the time the longest and most expensive James Bond movie ever made, *Spectre* was a huge grosser when it debuted—but not a hit with many die-hard fans. More a travelogue than a nail-biting adventure, it doesn't have a compelling threat with a ticking clock. What's more, its startling reveal—that Ernst Stavro Blofeld is actually James Bond's foster brother—hardly moves the emotional dial, since Blofeld remains just another sadistic bad guy who seems to enjoy torturing Bond.

For all its attempts to add more depth to Bond's story—including a more serious romantic interest in Dr. Madeleine Swann (Léa Seydoux)—*Spectre* scrimps on the qualities that have made Bond an international success story for nearly sixty years: action, sex, and violence. The heat between 007 and Swann is kept at a very low flame, and even a momentary tryst—emphasis on the "momentary"—with Italian bombshell Monica Bellucci barely registers. The much-touted car chase through Rome, with Bond battling Mr. Hinx (Dave Bautista), doesn't hold up next to modern high-octane competitors such as the *Fast and the Furious* films, while Bond's escape from Blofeld's Moroccan desert lair feels too easy to really get the adrenaline pumping.

THE CAST

James Bond	Daniel Craig
Ernst Stavro Blofeld	Christoph Waltz
Madeleine	Léa Seydoux
M	Ralph Fiennes
Lucia	Monica Bellucci
Q	Ben Whishaw
Moneypenny	Naomie Harris
Hinx	Dave Bautista
C	Andrew Scott
Tanner	Rory Kinnear

* "Spectre (2015)," The Numbers, accessed July 10, 2020, https://www.the-numbers.com/movie/Spectre.

After crashing his plane, James Bond (Daniel Craig) continues his attempts to rescue kidnapped Dr. Madeleine Swann (Léa Seydoux) in *Spectre*. *Courtesy of the Anders Frejdh Collection*

Mr. White	Jesper Christensen
Marco Sciarra	Alessandro Cremona
Estrella	Stephanie Sigman

THE CREW

Director	Sam Mendes
Writers	John Logan
	Neal Purvis & Robert Wade
	Jez Butterworth
Producers	Barbara Broccoli
	Michael G. Wilson
Director of Photography	Hoyte Van Hoytema
Music by	Thomas Newman
"Writing's on the Wall" performed by	Sam Smith
Production Designer	Dennis Gassner
Costume Designer	Jany Temime
Second Unit Director	Alexander Witt
Casting by	Debbie McWilliams
Stunt Coordinator	Gary Powell
Title Designer	Daniel Kleinman
Editor	Lee Smith

SPECTRE Island: The training ground for assassin Donald Grant (Robert Shaw) in *From Russia with Love*. Under the supervision of SPECTRE field agent Morzeny (Walter Gotell), the island is the setting for the pre-credits teaser sequence, in which Grant tracks a phony James Bond (Sean Connery) through the Renaissance Garden. Later in the story, we see Grant sunbathing on the island, while a bosomy masseuse (Jan Williams) works his deltoids. Rosa Klebb (Lotte Lenya) meets Grant there and tests his fitness with a knuckle-duster to the abdomen. She also views the SPECTRE training facilities, where agents perform feats of marksmanship, karate, and other acts of mayhem, using live targets. In reality, SPECTRE Island is located on the Pinewood Studios lot. The main building is actually the studio's administration building.

"Spiral Jump, the": An amazing 360-degree automobile jump that is a highlight of *The Man* *with the Golden Gun*. In the story, Bond (Roger Moore), is attempting to overtake Scaramanga (Christopher Lee) in a car chase through Bangkok, and he has to cross one of the narrow Thai canals, known as klongs, in a hurry. With no intact crossing in sight, resourceful 007 spies a fallen bridge, backs up his car and, rams it forward over the broken timbers. The car does a full 360-degree turn in the air and lands perfectly on the other side.

Designed by Jay Milligan, a member of stuntman Joie Chitwood's daredevil team, the jump was actually performed for real on location in Thailand. During preproduction, Milligan had worked out the stunt with the help of a computer at Cornell University: speed, car specifications, the length of the jump, and wind resistance were inputted, and out came the mathematical specifications for the jump. From this information, Milligan knew that he needed a set speed, a specially designed car, and takeoff and landing ramps designed to give the car the proper lift and turn so that it could land easily on all four tires.

Eon Productions purchased a two-year option on the stunt, which prohibited Milligan and any other stunt driver from performing it in public. It was something that had to be kept secret as much as possible—the producers were always nervous about quickie television productions stealing their stunts and other memorable moments. In Bangkok, production designer Peter Murton supervised the construction of specially designed takeoff and landing ramps over one of the local klongs. The ramps were skillfully disguised as a fallen bridge.

For a stunt that lasted all of fifteen seconds in the film, the producers spent a small fortune to build the fake bridge and the approach road, and to pay the salaries of Milligan's driving team. The cars for the stunt were provided by the American Motors Corporation, which was keenly aware that an appearance in a Bond film could easily boost the sales of its new line of AMC Hornets. Although the Hornet couldn't compete with Aston Martin in the styling department, it met Milligan's specifications perfectly. A team of engineers redesigned the car's chassis, placed the steering column in the center of the car, cut down the body in certain places and widened it in others, and monkeyed around with certain weight factors that could affect the eventual jump. By June 1974, the Hornet was ready to jump the klong.

Christopher Lee was one of hundreds of spectators who lined the canal on that summery day. "It was done right after lunch by Bumps Willard, one of Milligan's drivers," remembered Lee. "There were cranes and ambulances standing by should Willard end up in the water, and director Guy Hamilton had set up a number of cameras to catch the stunt from different angles. And then it just happened. The Hornet threw up a little dust, revved up its engine, and then hit the launch ramp. Before you knew it, it had flown across the canal, turned perfectly around and landed upright on four tires. He made it look easy. The stunt was so perfect that there was talk about doing it again. Some people worried that if it did look too easy, an audience might think it was faked. Any such talk was soon quashed, however, considering the added expense as well as the danger of putting Willard back in the car."[*] Interestingly, in the original script, screenwriter Richard Maibaum had wanted Bond to do the stunt twice: 007 jumps the klong and makes it to the other side, only to discover that Scaramanga is still on the opposite side of the klong. It was one Maibaum idea that was immediately dumped.

Unfortunately, the final film adds the sound of a slide whistle as as the car spirals through the air in slow motion—ruining the dramatic impact of one of the Bond series' greatest moments with a silly sound effect.

Spottiswoode, Roger (January 5, 1945–   ): Eclectic Canadian film director who helmed *Tomorrow Never Dies*. A native of Ottawa, Ontario, Spottiswoode started in Hollywood as an editor on films such as Sam Peckinpah's *Straw Dogs* (1971) and Karel Reisz's atmospheric *The Gambler* (1974) before making

Director Roger Spottiswoode directed Pierce Brosnan in his sophomore Bond appearance, *Tomorrow Never Dies. Courtesy of the David Reinhardt Collection*

---

[*] Christopher Lee, interview by the author, Los Angeles, February 15, 1989.

his directing debut on the low-budget horror film *Terror Train* (1980). In 1983, he directed the critically acclaimed *Under Fire*, a political drama that took Nick Nolte, Gene Hackman, and Joanna Cassidy into the hell of the Nicaraguan revolution. His acclaimed 1995 television mini-series *Hiroshima* is credited with dramatically increasing the profile of the American premium cable channel Showtime, which aired the production.

SPY WHO LOVED ME, THE

(United Artists, 1977) ★★★↗ : The tenth James Bond film produced by Eon Productions and the first produced solo by Albert R. Broccoli, Harry Saltzman having sold his share of Eon in 1975. US release date: August 3, 1977. Budget: $13.5 million. Worldwide box office gross: $185.4 million (US domestic gross: $46.8 million; international gross: $138.6 million).* Running time: 125 minutes.

THE SETUP

British and Russian nuclear submarines are disappearing into thin air—perhaps victims of a new submarine tracking system that is being auctioned off in the Middle East. Having successfully evaded Soviet assassins in Austria, James Bond (Roger Moore) is sent to Cairo to secure the tracking system and find the missing submarines. There he meets his opposite number, formidable Soviet agent Anya "Triple X" Amasova (Barbara Bach), and a terrifying nemesis, Jaws (Richard Kiel), a killer with cobalt steel teeth. Jaws is working for megalomaniac billionaire Karl Stromberg (Curt Jurgens), a marine enthusiast who has plans to destroy the entire world with nuclear weapons, allowing his planned undersea kingdom to flourish.

* "The Spy Who Loved Me (1977)," The Numbers, accessed July 13, 2020, https://www .the-numbers.com/movie/Spy-Who-Loved -Me-The.

BEHIND THE SCENES

The Spy Who Loved Me single-handedly revived the sagging Bond series in the mid-1970s. For a new generation of young viewers—fans who would soon be rooting for Indiana Jones, Superman, and E.T.—the film was an epic adventure with a way-out plot involving a worldwide threat, a submarine-swallowing supertanker, a steel-toothed assassin, and a resourceful and beautiful Russian agent who matches 007 play for play. Returning to the fantastical elements that had contributed to *Goldfinger*'s success, producer Albert R. Broccoli gave production designer Ken Adam a free hand to design the spectacular "Jonah Set," the massive interior of the *Liparus* supertanker. Meanwhile, Derek Meddings and Perry Oceanographics were designing the mid-1970s equivalent of Bond's classic Aston Martin: the Lotus Esprit submarine

Roger Moore and Barbara Bach made a striking pair in one of the best of the Moore Bond films, *The Spy Who Loved Me. Courtesy of the David Reinhardt Collection*

Divers on Derek Meddings's special effects team maneuver an American submarine as it departs the sinking *Liparus* in *The Spy Who Loved Me*. *Courtesy of the Brian Smithies Archive*

car. Producer Albert R. Broccoli had carefully updated the saga of 007, and the huge success of *The Spy Who Loved Me* guaranteed the series' longevity.

The cover of the 1960s-era American paperback edition of Ian Fleming's *The Spy Who Loved Me*—a story that was completely redone for the film version. *Steve Rubin Collection*

High points: the submarine car; Barbara Bach; Derek Meddings's special effects; and Carly Simon's theme song, "Nobody Does It Better." Low point: Jaws' invulnerability. Although the Jaws character contributed greatly to the film's success, compelling the producers to bring him back for *Moonraker*, it meant they had to make the character effectively unkillable. This took the film too far into comic book territory; Jaws became Wile E. Coyote to Bond's Road Runner.

THE CAST

James Bond	Roger Moore
Major Anya Amasova	Barbara Bach
Karl Stromberg	Curt Jurgens
Jaws	Richard Kiel
Naomi	Caroline Munro
General Gogol	Walter Gotell
Minister of Defence	Geoffrey Keen
M	Bernard Lee
Q	Desmond Llewelyn
Miss Moneypenny	Lois Maxwell
Captain Benson	George Baker
Sergei Barsov	Michael Billington
Felicca	Olga Bisera
Sheik Hosein	Edward de Souza
Max Kalba	Vernon Dobtcheff
Hotel Receptionist	Valerie Leon
Liparus Captain	Sydney Tafler
Fekkesh	Nadim Sawalha
Log Cabin Girl	Sue Vanner
Rublevitch	Eva Rueber-Staier
Admiral Hargreaves	Robert Brown
Stromberg's Assistant	Marilyn Galsworthy
Sandor	Milton Reid
Bechmann	Cyril Shaps
Markovitz	Milo Sperber
Barman	Albert Moses
Cairo Club Waiter	Rafiq Anwar
USS *Wayne* Captain	Shane Rimmer

THE CREW

Director	Lewis Gilbert
Screenplay by	Christopher Wood
	Richard Maibaum
Producer	Albert R. Broccoli
Associate Producer	William P. Cartlidge
Special Assistant to Producer	Michael Wilson
Director of Photography	Claude Renoir
Music by	Marvin Hamlisch
"Nobody Does It Better" performed by	Carly Simon
Lyrics by	Carole Bayer Sager
James Bond theme written by	Monty Norman
Production Designer	Ken Adam
Art Director	Peter Lamont
Production Manager	David Middlemas
Assistant Director	Ariel Levy
Second Unit Directors	Ernest Day
	John Glen
Underwater Cameraman	Lamar Boren
Ski sequence photographed and supervised by	Willy Bogner Jr.
Action Arranger	Bob Simmons
Ski jump performed by	Rick Sylvester
Title Designer	Maurice Binder
Special Visual Effects	Derek Meddings
Editor	John Glen

***Spy Who Loved Me* script wars**: The extended development process, featuring a parade of different writers, that led to a final shooting script for the tenth James Bond film, *The Spy Who Loved Me*. The difficulties began with Ian

Fleming's source material: in a departure from Fleming's other Bond stories, *The Spy Who Loved Me* is told through the eyes of a young Englishwoman who meets 007 only in the last few chapters. The format is so unusual, in fact, that it's the one novel the late author had never wanted to sell as a film project. But by the mid-1970s, producer Albert R. Broccoli was running out of 007 titles to adapt, so he went to the Fleming estate and requested permission to use only the novel's title. After a visit to Russia, Broccoli saw that an entirely new story could be built around a Russian agent who falls in love with James Bond.

The first person to take a crack at the screenplay was a New York City comic book writer named Cary Bates, who was recommended by celebrated author and *You Only Live Twice* screenwriter Roald Dahl. Bates's script was actually an adaptation of Fleming's novel *Moonraker*, which was also being considered for the next film. Bates took the Hugo Drax character from *Moonraker* and gave him a SPECTRE association with a huge underground base at Loch Ness in Scotland. The story focused on a SPECTRE plot to hijack a nuclear submarine and Bond's attempt to foil the plot with the help of Russian agent Tatiana Romanova, the cipher clerk in *From Russia with Love*. It was an interesting script, but Broccoli wasn't sold. Instead, he hired novelist Ronald Hardy to start fresh. Ironically, Hardy also developed a story about nuclear submarines, this time featuring a sophisticated electronic tracking device that allows the villain to pinpoint and capture enemy subs.

Though Broccoli again rejected the script, he did like the idea of the tracking device, which he decided to explore further with another screenwriter, Anthony Barwick. Barwick gave the tracking device to a villain named Zodiak. If the Western powers failed to surrender their art treasures, Zodiak intended to destroy fleets of nuclear submarines with his long-range torpedoes. But Barwick left the project as well. He was followed, in order, by Derek Marlowe; Stirling Silliphant; John Landis; and Anthony Burgess, the author of *A Clockwork Orange*. Burgess developed the most outrageous of all the scripts—an outright parody of the world of James Bond.

When Guy Hamilton was assigned to direct his fourth James Bond film in a row, another 007 vet was brought in to work on the script: Richard Maibaum. Maibaum decided to focus on SPECTRE as the main threat but get rid of the typical Blofeld-type old guard—literally. In the script's opening scenes, a group of villains burst into SPECTRE headquarters and assassinate the organization's leadership. This young cadre of international terrorists—members of the Red Brigade, the Baader-Meinhof Gang, the Black September Organization, and the Japanese Red Army—form a new SPECTRE that's no longer interested in blackmail or extortion. They're simply intent on destroying civilization by capturing a nuclear submarine and wiping out the world's oil fields.

Maibaum was finishing up his script with some location scouting in Budapest, Hungary, when Guy Hamilton suddenly left the project to direct *Superman*—the huge Warner Bros. film then in preproduction at Pinewood Studios (Hamilton was later replaced on *Superman* by Richard Donner). Lewis Gilbert was Broccoli's new choice for director, and he brought with him another writer, Christopher Wood, who began reworking Maibaum's draft.

Broccoli had liked Maibaum's script, but he felt that the young SPECTRE radicals were too political. Wood eliminated them and instead brought back a Blofeld-type character named Stavros, a SPECTRE-linked shipping magnate with a huge supertanker. The supertanker is equipped with special equipment in its bow that allows it to open up and swallow nuclear submarines. The tanker idea was Maibaum's, dating back to 1970 and the *Diamonds Are Forever* script, which originally had Blofeld commandeer a huge tanker as a firing platform for his laser cannon. In Wood's final draft for *The Spy Who Loved Me*, SPECTRE uses the special tracking system to capture a Russian and a British submarine. Bond and a Russian agent named Major Anya Amasova (whom Maibaum had also created) are sent to Cairo to find a SPECTRE traitor who is putting the tracking system on the open market. Each agent thinks the other is behind the hijacking. They play a game of spy versus spy in Cairo, until it is revealed that a third party has been playing them off against each other—a typical SPECTRE ploy reminiscent of their scheme in *From Russia with Love*. Bond and Anya join forces and eventually trace the tracking system to Stavros's base off the coast of Sardinia.

Leafing through the fifteen drafts of *The Spy Who Loved Me* offers a textbook look at script development. For Bond fans, the material is priceless, since it allows the reader to see how typical Bondian situations are workshopped. For instance, Stavros's chief henchman went through several changes until he became the Jaws character, a giant of a killer with cobalt steel teeth—played memorably by Richard Kiel in the final film. In the early scripts, there was an obsession with twins. Cary Bates's *Moonraker* treatment included a fearsome twosome named Pluto and Plato who work for Hugo Drax. Pluto is a chain smoker; Plato, an alcoholic. In the Anthony Barwick treatment, Zodiak is protected by three albino brothers named Tic, Tac, and Toe, all of whom are killed by 007. But however fascinating the idea of lookalike bodyguards may be, it would have created headaches for the casting director. The writers eventually settled on Jaws, who became a one-man, indestructible army and who would survive to return in *Moonraker*. And two films after that, the series would resurrect the original twin henchmen concept, introducing knife-throwing assassins Mischka and Grischka (David and Tony Meyer) in *Octopussy*.

Shortly before production began on *The Spy Who Loved Me* in 1976, one last script problem arose. Kevin McClory, the Irish film producer who owned the film rights to *Thunderball* and who was planning a new adaptation titled *James Bond of the Secret Service*, suddenly filed an injunction to hold up production of *The Spy Who Loved Me*. McClory claimed that the final Wood script improperly incorporated elements introduced into the Bond universe with *Thunderball*—namely, SPECTRE and its leader, Ernst Stavro Blofeld. To sidestep the legal challenge, Broccoli eventually told Wood to remove all traces of SPECTRE from the final shooting script. Stavros thus suddenly became billionaire shipping magnate Karl Stromberg, who plans to destroy the world without any help from SPECTRE. Even his supertanker security troops wear red rather than SPECTRE's black uniforms.

Such changes did not appease McClory. But there was little chance that he could stop Broccoli from filming, and a drawn-out attempt would be costly. He withdrew his injunction while he planned his own production, which eventually became 1983's *Never Say Never Again*, and the SPECTRE-free version of *The Spy Who Loved Me* made it to the screen in 1977.

St. Cyril's: Fictional monastery/fortress atop the steep Meteora cliffs in Greece, featured in *For Your Eyes Only*. In the film it's a personal retreat for Russian agent and heroin smuggler Aris Kristatos (Julian Glover). Bond (Roger Moore) learns from his friend and compatriot Milos Columbo (Topol) that the abandoned monastery used to be a favorite hiding place for the Greek resistance during World War II. Tipped off by Max the parrot, who keeps uttering the name "St. Cyril's," Bond, Melina Havelock (Carole Bouquet), Columbo, and his men, all disguised as monks, assault the fortress and overwhelm Kristatos's garrison, stealing back the Brits' top-secret ATAC computer, which 007 destroys before it falls into Russian hands. This sequence was filmed on location at Meteora's Holy Trinity Monastery—against the wishes of the local clergy, who even hung laundry over their buildings to disrupt the shoot. Stuntman Rick Sylvester, veteran of the ski jump in *The Spy Who Loved Me*, doubled James Bond during his precarious climb to the top of the Meteora cliff.

Max the parrot feeds James Bond (Roger Moore) some key information in *For Your Eyes Only*. *Courtesy of the David Reinhardt Collection*

St. Georges: A British electronic surveillance and communications ship disguised as a Greek fishing trawler in *For Your Eyes Only*. On board is ATAC, the Automatic Targeting Attack Communicator, a sophisticated electronic device that uses an ultra-low-frequency coded transmission to order nuclear submarines to launch their ballistic missiles. When the *St. Georges* is sunk by a mine that gets snared in her fishing nets—placed there by Soviet agent Aris Kristatos (Julian Glover)—technicians are unable to trigger the ATAC self-destruct mechanism. Thus, a race begins between the Russians and the British Secret Service to recover the ATAC from its watery grave off the coast of Albania.

St. John, Jill (August 19, 1940– ; birth name: Jill Oppenheim): Redheaded American actress who portrayed diamond smuggler Tiffany Case, the first American Bond girl, in *Diamonds Are Forever*. As a favor to attorney Sidney Korshak, who was setting up Las Vegas location deals for the film, producer Albert R. Broccoli had first considered her for the part of Plenty O'Toole. However, director Guy Hamilton deemed her too much of an actress for Plenty and suggested she play Tiffany Case instead. Broccoli agreed, and as it turned out she was excellent in the role. St. John had the versatility to be cool and detached when Bond (Sean Connery) first meets her in her Amsterdam apartment, then comically frightened when she accompanies Bond on the madcap car chase through downtown Las Vegas, and finally downright cocky when she creates the diversion in the Las Vegas gas station that allows Bond to sneak into the utility van of Dr. Metz (Joseph Furst), headed for the missile installation of Blofeld (Charles Gray). A rare performer who was actually born in Los Angeles, St. John made her film debut as a young English girl in the Alan Ladd / Deborah Kerr drama *Thunder in the East* (1952). Married to actor Robert Wagner, she's also appeared in *The Lost World* (1960), with future Bond player David Hedison; *The Roman Spring of Mrs. Stone* (1961),

Sexy American actress Jill St. John added additional dimensions to Ian Fleming's Tiffany Case character in *Diamonds Are Forever*. *Courtesy of the David Reinhardt Collection*

with Lotte Lenya; *Tender Is the Night* (1962); *Come Blow Your Horn* (1963); *Who's Minding the Store?* (1963); *Who's Been Sleeping in My Bed?* (1963); *Honeymoon Hotel* (1964); *The Liquidator* (1965); *The Oscar* (1966); *Tony Rome* (1967); *Banning* (1967); and *The Player* (1992).

St. Mary Star of the Sea Catholic Church: Known as the second-oldest Catholic church in Florida, this Key West landmark was the site of the wedding between Felix Leiter (David Hedison) and Della Churchill (Priscilla Barnes) in *Licence to Kill*.

St. Petersburg: Northwest Russian city, formerly known as Leningrad, that served as a primary filming location for *GoldenEye* in the spring of 1995. Located on the east end of the Gulf of Finland, the city hosted a full second unit crew, which captured backgrounds to blend with exterior sets built on the Rolls-Royce factory complex in Hertfordshire, England. These scenes included the destructive chase between a fleeing General Ourumov (Gottfried John) and Bond (Pierce Brosnan), piloting a captured Russian battle tank.

St. Sophia Mosque (a.k.a. Hagia Sophia Mosque): An Istanbul landmark, originally built as a church by the Roman emperor Justinian in the sixth century AD. In *From Russia with Love*, it becomes the drop-off point for a map of the Russian embassy, which Tatiana "Tanya" Romanova (Daniela Bianchi) hides in her compact and leaves for Bond (Sean Connery) at the foot of one of the mosque's columns. The plan is nearly foiled when a Bulgarian agent working for the Russians

On location with Sean Connery outside the St. Sophia Mosque in Istanbul for *From Russia with Love. Courtesy of the David Reinhardt Collection*

(Hasan Ceylan) intercepts the package, but he in turn is murdered by SPECTRE assassin Donald Grant (Robert Shaw), who is also lurking in the mosque. Bond is thus able to retrieve the stolen plans, crediting the Bulgar's death not to Grant but to Istanbul's reputation for being a tough town.

Stage D: Pinewood Studios soundstage where production designer Ken Adam created the Fontainebleau Hotel cabana area where Dink (Margaret Nolan) massages James Bond (Sean Connery) in *Goldfinger*. Designed to match exteriors shot on location in Miami Beach, the set was also used for close-ups of the gin game between Goldfinger (Gert Fröbe) and Mr. Simmons (Austin Willis), as well as the arrival of Felix Leiter (Cec Linder). Fifty-five extras were on hand for the shooting, which took place on Friday, April 24, and Saturday, April 25, 1964. Stage D also became the El Scorpio nightclub for the pre-credits teaser of *Goldfinger*.

Stanwell: Location, outside London, of a storage-tank complex that simulated the South American holdings of Mr. Ramirez in the pre-credits teaser of *Goldfinger*. When James Bond (Sean Connery) places his demolition charges inside one of the tanks, however, the interior is actually a Ken Adam–designed set at Pinewood Studios.

Stassino, Paul (1930–June 28, 2012): Greek Cypriot actor who portrayed dashing NATO aerial observer Major François Derval in *Thunderball*. He also portrayed Derval's plastic-surgery-aided duplicate, SPECTRE mercenary Angelo Palazzi, who, while posing as the NATO observer, hijacks a bomber to the Caribbean with nuclear bombs on board. A native of Limassol, Cyprus, Stassino made his big-screen debut in the action adventure *Night Ambush* (1957), which also featured future Bond players Christopher Lee (*The Man with the Golden Gun*) and George Pravda (*Thunderball*).

Stavin, Mary (August 20, 1957–   ): Striking Swedish actress, the former Miss World 1977, who portrayed gorgeous Kimberley Jones, a Secret Service colleague of James Bond (Roger Moore) who pilots the camouflaged iceberg launch in the pre-credits teaser for *A View to a Kill*. In addition, she was one of the Octopussy girls in the James Bond movie of the same name, her film debut. A native of Örebro, Sweden, Stavin also appeared in *House* (1985), *The Opponent* (1988), *Caddyshack II* (1988), *Howling V: The Rebirth* (1989), and *The Devil Takes a Holiday* (1996).

stealth ship: Radar-invisible warship operated by henchmen loyal to billionaire media mogul Elliot Carver (Jonathan Pryce) in *Tomorrow Never Dies*. Operating out of Southeast Asia, it attempts to provoke a nuclear confrontation between Britain and China when it sinks the HMS *Devonshire* in the South China Sea. It's later obliterated by Bond (Pierce Brosnan) and his partner, Colonel Wai Lin (Michelle Yeoh) of the Chinese Secret Service.

Stears, John (August 25, 1934–April 28, 1999): Two-time Oscar-winning British special effects expert who worked on the first six James Bond movies. Stears created and destroyed the miniature bauxite mine for *Dr. No*; blew up the SPECTRE helicopter and speedboats in *From Russia with Love*; flew the private and presidential jets in *Goldfinger*; and destroyed the *Disco Volante* hydrofoil and cocoon in *Thunderball*, for which he won his first Oscar. On *You Only Live Twice*, with its outer space sequences and helicopter chases, he would be kept particularly busy. And that space experience would be advantageous later in his career, when he was called on to create the effects for George Lucas's *Star Wars*, for which he won his second Oscar for special effects. Stears also worked on *On Her Majesty's Secret Service*. His crew throughout his Bond association included Frank George (engineer and effects), Jimmy Snow (floor effects and engineer), Bert Luxford (engineer), Joe Fitt (prop man and effects), and Charlie Dodds (effects rigger).

A native of Uxbridge, Hillingdon, Middlesex, England, Stears made his motion picture debut as a model aircraft builder for future 007 director Lewis Gilbert on the biographical war drama *Reach for the Sky* (1956), a film that featured future Bond players Sydney Tafler (*The Spy Who Loved Me*), Eric Pohlmann (*From Russia with Love*), and Peter Burton (*Dr. No*). He returned to work with Gilbert on the splendid *Sink the Bismarck!* (1960), then made his special effects

The large miniature of Elliot Carver's stealth ship, designed by Derek Meddings and his FX team, is prepared for water-tank filming for *Tomorrow Never Dies*. *Courtesy of the Brian Smithies Archive*

debut on producers Albert R. Broccoli and Harry Saltzman's Bob Hope comedy *Call Me Bwana* (1963).

Stephens, Toby (April 21, 1969–   ): British actor who portrayed duplicitous environmental entrepreneur Gustav Graves in *Die Another Day*. Stephens, who had previously played the young Clint Eastwood in *Space Cowboys* (2000), is the son of legendary actress Dame Maggie Smith and the late Sir Robert Stephens (so memorable as the title character in director Billy Wilder's *The Private Life of Sherlock Holmes*). A London native, Stephens made his motion picture debut as Othello in Sally Potter's 1992 adaptation of the Virginia Woolfe novel *Orlando*. More recently, Stephens portrayed space traveler John Robinson in the revival of the television series *Lost in Space* (19 episodes, 2018–2019).

Steppat, Ilse (November 30, 1917–December 21, 1969): German character actress who portrayed Frau Irma Bunt, personal secretary to Blofeld (Telly Savalas) in *On Her Majesty's Secret Service*. Steppat's only role in English, Bunt is a belligerent character who would have made

a great Gestapo chief—and she's the one who machine-guns 007's bride Tracy (Diana Rigg) to death in the film's tragic ending. Born in Barmen, Germany, the actress made her motion picture debut in director Kurt Maetzig's drama *Marriage in the Shadows* (1947). Sadly, Steppat died of a heart attack less than a week after the release of her Bond film debut.

Sterling, Mr. and Mrs. Robert: Cover identities used by James Bond (Roger Moore) and KGB major Anya Amasova (Barbara Bach) while visiting billionaire shipping magnate Karl Stromberg (Curt Jurgens) at his Atlantis facility off Sardinia in *The Spy Who Loved Me*. Robert is supposedly a marine biologist, with his wife as his assistant.

Stinger missiles: Deadly projectiles stolen from Nicaragua's Contra rebels by drug runner Franz Sanchez (Robert Davi) in *Licence to Kill*. Felix Leiter (David Hedison) has brokered a deal with Sanchez's chief of security, Heller (Don Stroud), to help return the missiles to the US government in exchange for immunity from prosecution. However, when Bond (Timothy Dalton) tries and fails to assassinate Sanchez, a spooked Heller changes his mind. The Stingers are used ineffectively against Bond in the wild tanker-truck chase.

Stock, James: Cover identity James Bond (Roger Moore) uses in San Francisco in *A View to a Kill*. Posing as a reporter with the *London Financial Times*, Bond is granted an interview with W. G. Howe (Daniel Benzali), a local official with the Divisions of Oil and Mines who is actually on the payroll of Zorin Industries.

Stockholm syndrome: The phenomenon by which kidnap victims develop feelings for their kidnappers, it helps explain why heiress Elektra King (Sophie Marceau) is conspiring with the terrorist Renard (Robert Carlyle), her former captor, in *The World Is Not Enough*.

Stoke Park: A country club in Buckinghamshire, England, where director Guy Hamilton filmed the golf match between James Bond (Sean Connery) and the titular villain (Gert Fröbe) in *Goldfinger*.

straight flush: Hand with which James Bond (Daniel Craig) defeats Le Chiffre (Mads Mikkelsen) in the poker tournament in *Casino Royale*. He wins with a 4-5-6-7-8 of spades to Le Chiffre's full house (three aces, two sixes).

strangler watch: The principal murder weapon of SPECTRE assassin Donald Grant (Robert Shaw) in *From Russia with Love*. The watch stem hides a retractable garrote wire that Grant uses to dispose of the phony James Bond in the pre-credits teaser and nearly kill the real 007 (Sean Connery) on the Orient Express, until Bond turns the watch on its keeper.

Strangways, Commander John: British Secret Service agent, portrayed by Tim Moxon, who is the head of station in Jamaica in *Dr. No*. With the help of a local Cayman Island fisherman named Quarrel (John Kitzmiller), Strangways has been gathering telltale ore samples on a nearby island called Crab Key. For his investigative work, Strangways and his new secretary are ruthlessly gunned down by Dr. No's assassins, the "Three Blind Mice." Strangways has the misfortune of

At the Stoke Park golf club in Buckinghamshire, England, James Bond (Sean Connery) has just told Goldfinger (Gert Fröbe) that because they are playing by the strict rules of golf, he's lost the hole and the match. *Courtesy of the Anders Frejdh Collection*

MI6 operative John Strangways (Tim Moxon) becomes a victim of Dr. No's hitmen—the "Three Blind Mice"—in the first James Bond film. *Courtesy of the David Reinhardt Collection*

being the first casualty in the United Artists 007 series.

strict rules of golf: The conditions under which Bond (Sean Connery) and Goldfinger (Gert Fröbe) undertake a high-stakes golf challenge match at an English country club. Although the terms are suggested by Goldfinger, it is the clever 007 who takes advantage of them. When Goldfinger tries to make up for his bad lie by having his caddy, Oddjob (Harold Sakata), plant a phony ball on the fairway and then calling it his own, 007 finds an alternative ball and tricks Goldfinger into playing it on his final tee shot. Bond loses the match on purpose, goes to the cup, and announces that Goldfinger has

Goldfinger discovers he played the wrong ball on the eighteenth fairway in *Goldfinger*. Since they're playing strict rules of golf, he loses the hole and the match! *Courtesy of the David Reinhardt Collection*

"accidentally" played the wrong ball somewhere on the course. Since strict rules of golf are in force, Bond is sorry to say that Goldfinger has lost the hole and the match.

Stromberg, Karl: Billionaire shipping magnate and megalomaniac ocean lover portrayed by Curt Jurgens in *The Spy Who Loved Me*. Stromberg is planning for a futuristic undersea kingdom by first destroying the rest of the planet with nuclear weapons.

German actor Curt Jurgens brought plenty of heft and gravitas to the role of Karl Stromberg in *The Spy Who Loved Me*. *The Steve Rubin Collecction*

Based off the coast of Sardinia on a huge amphibious structure called Atlantis, he commands a fleet of ships, including his prize, the *Liparus*—an enormous supertanker that is secretly capturing British, American, and Soviet nuclear submarines. To destroy the world, Stromberg plans to refit the submarines with his own crews and then launch their missiles on specified targets in the United States and Russia.

Bond (Roger Moore) tracks down Stromberg when 007 and his temporary partner, KGB major Anya Amasova (Barbara Bach), discover the Stromberg shipping-line logo while searching through a roll of microfilm containing a facsimile of a nuclear-sub tracking system that Stromberg's scientists have engineered. Surviving assassination attempts by Stromberg's two killers—Jaws (Richard Kiel) and Sandor (Milton Reid)—and his assistant Naomi (Caroline Munro), Bond eventually short-circuits the evil plan, obliterates the *Liparus* and Atlantis, and kills Stromberg with some well-aimed slugs from his Walther.

One of Stromberg's unusual traits is that he doesn't shake hands, probably because he doesn't want anybody to be shocked that his hands are webbed like a duck's feet.

stuffed sheep's head: The perfectly awful entree served by Kamal Khan (Louis Jourdan) to James

Bond (Roger Moore) at his Monsoon Palace in Udaipur, India, in *Octopussy*. At one point, Kamal actually plucks out one of the sheep's eyeballs and pops it into his mouth. A similarly repulsive dining experience is featured in Steven Spielberg's *Indiana Jones and the Temple of Doom* (1984), which was released the following year.

Sutton, Stacey: Beautiful blonde scientist, portrayed by Tanya Roberts, who battles Max Zorin (Christopher Walken) in *A View to a Kill*. Since she's in financial trouble, Stacey works as a geologist for the State of California, at the Divisions of Oil and Mines. However, there was a time when she was fabulously wealthy. Stacey's grandfather started Sutton Oil in the San Francisco Bay area, where oil is pumped out of the unstable Hayward Fault.

As the first step in Project Main Strike, a plot to destroy Silicon Valley by triggering a massive double earthquake, Zorin has taken control of Sutton Oil in a rigged proxy fight. To stop her

Played by former Charlie's Angel Tanya Roberts, Stacey Sutton is sheltered by James Bond (Roger Moore) atop San Francisco's Golden Gate Bridge in *A View to a Kill. Courtesy of the David Reinhardt Collection*

from challenging the takeover and convince her keep her mouth shut, Zorin offers Stacey the sum of $5 million. At his annual horse show in France, Zorin writes a check and gives it to Stacey—all of which is observed by James Bond (Roger Moore), who's peering through the tinted window with trick sunglasses.

Later, 007 slips into Zorin's office and photocopies the Sutton check, taking note of the huge sum. Posing as a journalist with the *London Financial Times*, Bond eventually sneaks into Stacey's mansion, in time to thwart a gang of Zorin's toughs who have been sent to pressure her into cashing the check and backing down. Ever the gentleman, Bond offers to cook her dinner and stand guard that night.

Suzuki, Kissy: See "Kissy."

Swadley: Fictional US Air Force base in England, headquarters of the Sixty-Third Tactical Air Command cruise missile unit in *Never Say Never Again*. Captain Jack Petachi (Gavan O'Herlihy) is a staff communications officer on the base—and a traitor who has gone over to SPECTRE. Having undergone an unusual corneal implant operation, Petachi now has the exact eye print of the president of the United States, which allows him to pass a top-level security procedure and arm two cruise missiles with nuclear warheads.

Swann, Dr. Madeleine: Clinical psychiatrist and the daughter of SPECTRE operative Mr. White (Jesper Christensen), portrayed by Léa Seydoux in *Spectre* and *No Time to Die*. Poisoned by his

French actress Léa Seydoux portrayed psychologist Dr. Madeleine Swann, daughter of the mysterious Mr. White, in *Spectre* and *No Time to Die. Courtesy of the Anders Frejdh Collection*

employer, the mysterious Franz Oberhauser (Christoph Waltz), a dying Mr. White exacts a promise from James Bond (Daniel Craig) to protect his daughter from suffering a similar fate. In return, he tells Bond that Madeleine can lead him to Oberhauser. Bond, indeed, rescues Madeleine from Mr. Hinx (Dave Bautista) and his murderous henchmen. Together they head for the L'Américain hotel in Tangier, where they discover White's secret room and further clues that lead them into the desert and a confrontation with Oberhauser—a.k.a. SPECTRE head Ernst Stavro Blofeld.

Sweetman, Captain Cyril: Pilot of the recon helicopter carrying director Terence Young and assistant art director Michael White that, on Saturday, July 6, 1963, was involved in an accident during a location survey off the coastal town of Crinan, Scotland, for *From Russia with Love*. Fortunately, there were only minor injuries.

Switchblades: Nickname given to twin stealth gliders utilized by James Bond (Pierce Brosnan) and Jinx (Halle Berry) in *Die Another Day*. In the story, they exit from the rear of a Chinook helicopter.

Sylvester, Rick: Top American stuntman who in July 1976 performed the incredible ski/parachute jump off Baffin Island's Asgard Peak for *The Spy Who Loved Me* teaser. The stunt was inspired by an advertisement for Canadian Club whisky in which Sylvester appeared to perform the same stunt—though he later admitted that the ad actually showed him jumping off El Capitan in Yosemite National Park. To perform the stunt for real in the film, Sylvester received $30,000. He later returned to perform a mountain-climbing stunt off Greece's Meteora cliffs in *For Your Eyes Only*.

Synthetic Turpentine: Phony label on Osato Chemical canisters in *You Only Live Twice*. They really contain liquid oxygen (lox), a rocket propellant destined for the secret volcano rocket base of Ernst Stavro Blofeld (Donald Pleasence).

T-55: Heavy Russian battle tank commandeered by James Bond (Pierce Brosnan) for a noisy, destructive chase through downtown St. Petersburg, Russia, in *GoldenEye*.

tactical fission device: The type of bomb Dr. Christmas Jones (Denise Richards) determines is on board an oil-pipeline shuttle car that is barreling at 70 mph toward an oil terminal in *The World Is Not Enough*.

Tafler, Sydney (July 31, 1916–November 8, 1979): British character actor and relative by marriage of director Lewis Gilbert, who cast him as the captain of the supertanker *Liparus* in *The Spy Who Loved Me*. Tafler, a London native, made his uncredited motion picture debut as an RAF officer in director Anthony Asquith's wartime comedy thriller *Bombsight Stolen*

Actor Sydney Tafler commanded the *Liparus* in *The Spy Who Loved Me*. *Steve Rubin Collection*

(1941). His first credited big-screen role was playing Morry Hyams in director Robert Hamer's crime drama, *It Always Rains on Sunday* (1947).

Talamone, Italy: Where James Bond (Daniel Craig) goes to find his former colleague Rene Mathis (Giancarlo Giannini) in *Quantum of Solace*. After supposedly betraying Bond in *Casino Royale*, Mathis was tortured and imprisoned. Later exonerated, he retired to Talamone, where MI6 bought him a villa as compensation.

He lives there with girlfriend, Gemma (Lucrezia Lante della Rovere). Mathis agrees to join Bond on a trip to La Paz, Bolivia, where Mathis has connections. He also supplies 007 with a new passport and credit cards—since they were revoked by MI6.

Tamahori, Lee (April 22, 1950–   ): New Zealand director who helmed the twentieth James Bond movie produced by the Broccoli family, *Die Another Day*. Tamahori actually began his career as a sound boom operator on the comedy *Skin Deep* (1978). Born in Wellington, Tamahori made his feature directorial debut on the crime drama *Once Were Warriors* (1994). Two years later, he scored with another crime drama, *Mulholland Falls* (1996), featuring Michael Madsen, whom he later cast in *Die Another Day*.

Tamba, Tetsuro (July 17, 1922–September 24, 2006; birth name: Shozaburo Tanba): Handsome Japanese actor who portrayed Tiger Tanaka, the head of the Japanese Secret Service, in *You Only Live Twice*. A Tokyo native, the prolific Tamba made his motion picture debut in director Hideo Suzuki's crime drama *Satsujin Yôgisha* (1952). He made his English-language film debut a decade later in director Etienne Périer's World War II drama *Bridge to the Sun* (1961). For *You Only Live Twice*, Tamba's voice was redubbed by British voice actor Robert Rietti.

Japanese Secret Service chief Tiger Tanaka (Tetsuro Tamba, left) goes into action with Kissy (Mie Hama) and James Bond (Sean Connery) during volcano base action in *You Only Live Twice*. *Courtesy of the David Reinhardt Collection*

Tanaka, Tiger: Japanese Secret Service chief, portrayed realistically by Tetsuro Tamba in *You Only Live Twice*. He's a resourceful spymaster who maintains his seclusion in an underground office complex in Tokyo, connected to a private train line. Assigned to help Bond (Sean Connery) track a missing American spacecraft, Tanaka introduces him to many aspects of the Japanese culture, including sophisticated electronics, bathing girls, ninja warriors, pearl divers, and, finally, a sham marriage to his agent Kissy (Mie Hama), one of the most beautiful women in the 007 series. With his ninjas, Tanaka leads the final attack on the secret rocket base of Blofeld (Donald Pleasence).

Tiger Tanaka (Tetsuro Tamba) demonstrates ninja weaponry for James Bond (Sean Connery) and Aki (Akiko Wakabayashi) in *You Only Live Twice*. *Courtesy of the David Reinhardt Collection*

Tangier, Morocco: North African city where arms dealer Brad Whitaker (Joe Don Baker) maintains his base of operations in *The Living Daylights*. It's here that Bond (Timothy Dalton) fakes the assassination of KGB chief General Leonid Pushkin (John Rhys-Davies)—a ploy to expose the real plot of Whitaker and renegade Russian general Koskov (Jeroen Krabbé). It works, although Bond is drugged, captured, and placed aboard a military air transport headed for Afghanistan.

Agent 007 returns to Tangier in *Spectre*, as Bond (Daniel Craig) and Dr. Madeleine Swann (Léa Seydoux) visit the city's L'Américain hotel, where Swann's father, Mr. White (Jesper Christensen), kept a secret room.

tarantula: Huge spider used unsuccessfully by Professor Dent (Anthony Dawson) to assassinate James Bond (Sean Connery) in *Dr. No*. Sweating out the insect's agonizingly slow crawl up his body, Bond waits for it to momentarily rest on a pillow, then dives off the bed, grabs his shoe, and pounds the spider to pulp. Traumatized by the event, 007 staggers into the bathroom and shuts the door—providing one of the film's best laughs.

The tarantula was portrayed by an arachnid actor nicknamed Rosie, who actually crawled on the body of stuntman Bob Simmons, pulled along by a string. If you watch the sequence closely, you can see that a sheet of glass separates Sean Connery from the tarantula in the final close-up, a similar effect to the one used in *Raiders of the Lost Ark* when Indiana Jones finds himself staring at a deadly asp. In Fleming's original novel, the tarantula was actually a deadly giant centipede.

Taro, Miss: Sexy secretary to British diplomat Playdell-Smith (Louis Blaazer), portrayed by actress Zena Marshall in *Dr. No*. Actually a

British actress Zena Marshall portrayed comely Miss Taro, a seductive agent of the title character in *Dr. No. Courtesy of the David Reinhardt Collection*

Something's going on behind the back of Miss Taro (Zena Marshall), thanks to James Bond (Sean Connery) *Courtesy of the David Reinhardt Collection*

spy for Dr. No (Joseph Wiseman), Miss Taro is ordered to lure Bond (Sean Connery) to her cottage on Magenta Drive in the Blue Mountains. Assassins in a black hearse will then run 007 off the road. However, the assassins are killed instead when, trying to avoid road-construction machinery, their hearse goes off a cliff. When her doorbell rings, Miss Taro is thus very surprised to greet Bond. Ordered via telephone to stall him, she consents to a tryst. Zena Marshall was the quintessential female adversary for the original 007—voluptuous (as producers Albert R. Broccoli and Harry Saltzman required), deadly, and expendable—although instead of facing death, she is arrested by the Jamaican police. She's the only one of Dr. No's agents to survive the film.

tarot cards: The mystical tools of Solitaire (Jane Seymour) in *Live and Let Die*. A virgin with the power of the *obeah* (the "second sight"), Solitaire uses the cards expertly to predict the future. Practically enslaved to Kananga (Yaphet Kotto) at first, Solitaire eventually sleeps with Bond (Roger Moore), switches allegiances, and loses her power. She also uses the cards to alert Bond to various dangers. For instance, when Bond meets an attractive CIA operative named Rosie Carver (Gloria Hendry), he also finds the queen of cups tarot card in the upside-down position. Since Bond knows that this means a deceitful, perverse woman, a liar, or a cheat, the card helps him realize that Carver is working for

Kananga. To help Bond rescue Solitaire from a voodoo sacrifice on the island of San Monique, three cards are left for him in the Fillet of Soul restaurant in New Orleans: the High Priestess (a reference to Solitaire herself), Death (meaning *great danger*), and the Moon (perhaps referring to the time of the planned sacrifice).

The tarot cards for *Live and Let Die* were beautifully painted for the movie by Scottish artist Fergus Hall, and they are featured prominently in the film's advertising campaign. Interestingly, the back side of each tarot card included the 007 logo. Even though the card backs never appeared in close-up in the film, you can plainly see the logo on the special cards that were sold to the public in a boxed set after the film's release in 1973. If you look closely enough, you can see the 007 logo on the film cards as well.

Taurus PT92: A 9mm, sixteen-round Brazilian handgun, a copy of the Italian Beretta, used by James Bond (Timothy Dalton) in the pre-credits teaser of *Licence to Kill*. What's 007 doing with what's practically a Beretta—a gun that was outlawed by M in *Dr. No*? It's on loan from a DEA agent. Remember, Bond was on his way to the wedding of Felix Leiter (David Hedison) and chose not to bring his Walther PPK with him.

Tears of Allah: Code name for the SPECTRE nuclear hijacking operation in *Never Say Never Again*. It's also the legendary place mentioned in the Arabic inscription on the priceless pendant that SPECTRE master spy Maximilian Largo (Klaus Maria Brandauer) gives to his mistress, Domino Petachi (Kim Basinger). As Largo explains, "The Prophet wept for the barrenness of the desert, and his tears made a well." The surface of the pendant is actually a map, with the diamond marking the site of the Tears of Allah, which is now a huge underground archaeological dig. The dig also marks the beginning of a huge Middle Eastern oil field—where SPECTRE places the second of its hijacked atomic bombs. Approaching the site via XT-7B flying platforms, James Bond (Sean Connery) and Felix Leiter (Bernie Casey) don wet suits and enter a well, traverse an underwater passageway, and arrive at the dig itself. Backed by divers from a US nuclear submarine, Bond and Leiter launch an attack against Maximilian Largo's SPECTRE forces.

TEASERS OF THE JAMES BOND FILMS

Teaser is a film term for a sequence that takes place before a movie's opening titles—a hallmark of the Eon Productions James Bond series. Pre-credits sequences can get a film off to a rousing start, and that's exactly how they're used in the 007 movies—though they weren't the first films to do so. One of the first action teasers was in the film *The Desert Fox: The Story of Rommel* (1951), depicting a commando raid on Rommel's headquarters in North Africa. The first Bond film, *Dr. No*, technically has no teaser sequence, but the assassination of John Strangways (Tim Moxon) after the opening credits works in much the same way. True Bond teasers began with the next film, and what follows is a brief summary of each one:

- *From Russia with Love*: James Bond (Sean Connery) is stalked by assassin Donald Grant (Robert Shaw), who ultimately kills his prey—only for it to turn out to be a phony Bond in a SPECTRE training session.
- *Goldfinger*: In the quintessential Bond teaser, 007 arrives on a beach in South America wearing a fake seagull atop his diving mask. After placing demolition charges in a heroin smuggler's lair, he visits the dressing room of the lovely Bonita (Nadja Regin), only to be attacked by the *capungo* (Alf Joint). The resulting fight is particularly vicious, culminating with the villain being thrown into the bathtub along with an electric heater that electrocutes him. Agent 007's classic comment, "Shocking, positively shocking," serves as the perfect segue into Shirley Bassey's title song.
- *Thunderball*: The film begins solemnly at a funeral, during which Bond discovers that the guest of honor, a supposedly deceased SPECTRE agent (Bob Simmons), is instead very much alive and disguised as his grieving widow. After a gruesome fight in which Bond eventually breaks the "widow's" neck, 007 steals away in a one-man Bell jet pack, ushering in the era of the super-gadgets. Bond then arrives back at his Aston Martin, which sprays three villains with water—the perfect prelude to Tom Jones's *Thunderball* theme song.

- *You Only Live Twice*: As the United States deals with the loss of one of its Jupiter space capsules, Bond seems to be enjoying some downtime in Hong Kong with his Chinese girlfriend Ling (Tsai Chin)—only to fall victim to an "assassination."
- *On Her Majesty's Secret Service*: The teaser serves to introduce a new Bond, model turned actor George Lazenby, who defeats a gang of hoods on the beach in southern France only to see his damsel in distress (Diana Rigg) drive away without saying a word—something that definitely didn't happen to the other guy.
- *Diamonds Are Forever*: After the murder of his wife in the previous film, a revenge-minded Bond (Sean Connery again) tracks Blofeld (Charles Gray) from Tokyo to Cairo and eventually attempts to bury him in boiling mud.
- *Live and Let Die*: Though the film introduces another new Bond (Roger Moore), he doesn't appear in the teaser, which instead focuses on the systematic assassination of three British agents in New York City, New Orleans, and the fictional Caribbean island of San Monique.
- *The Man with the Golden Gun*: In the very stylized teaser, assassin Scaramanga (Christopher Lee) kills a tough Mafia hit man (Marc Lawrence) in his fabulous "fun house" training ground.
- *The Spy Who Loved Me*: A ski-borne 007 shakes his enemy pursuers by jumping off an Austrian mountain peak and parachuting to safety. Ingeniously shot on the precarious slopes of Canada's Asgard Peak, it's the best of all Bond teasers and perhaps *the* daredevil sequence of all time.
- *Moonraker*: Another hijacked spaceship leads into another inventive skydiving stunt, as Bond must think fast when he's thrown from a plane without a parachute.
- *For Your Eyes Only*: In the first teaser sequence to actually get the film off on the wrong foot, Bond plays footsie with a Blofeld lookalike while trying to get out of a disabled helicopter. The bit in which he unceremoniously dumps Blofeld into a smokestack while Blofeld tries to bribe Bond with the offer of a "delicatessen in stainless steel" was a particular low point.
- *Octopussy*: The teaser introduces 007's Acrostar mini jet in a rousing battle between Bond and a Latin American dictator's private army.

- *A View to a Kill*: The teaser sequence returns to familiar ground with a ski chase—set to, of all things, the Beach Boys song "California Girls."
- *The Living Daylights*: The pre-credits sequence dazzles viewers with a war game battle on the Rock of Gibraltar while simultaneously introducing the next 007 (Timothy Dalton).
- *Licence to Kill*: Bond and Felix Leiter (David Hedison) are on their way to Leiter's wedding when they're suddenly ordered to capture a major drug kingpin (Robert Davi). Hopping aboard a US Coast Guard helicopter, Bond eventually chases and literally lassos the crook's private plane, towing it back to the base in very Bondian fashion.
- *GoldenEye*: The first 007 film of the 1990s introduces Pierce Brosnan as the latest Bond and flashes back to the Cold War, with 007 joining 006 (Sean Bean) for an attack on a Soviet chemical weapons depot. It's a thrilling sequence that involves both a bungee jump off the edge of a huge hydroelectric dam and a desperate free fall into a crashing plane that harks back to the Asgard Jump in *The Spy Who Loved Me*.
- *Tomorrow Never Dies*: In a flat teaser with no real heart-stopping moments, Bond prevents catastrophe by stealing a nuclear-armed Russian fighter jet from a terrorist arms bazaar.
- *The World Is Not Enough*: Bond takes on Julietta the Cigar Girl (Maria Grazia Cucinotta) in a splendid teaser involving a beautiful knife-throwing assassin, booby-trapped bank notes, and a jet boat chase on the Thames.
- *Die Another Day*: In another effective, audacious opening sequence, Bond surfs his way into North Korea, ends up in a high-speed hovercraft chase, and for once fails to pull off his escape, getting captured by the North Koreans and then tortured as the teaser segues into the title sequence and Madonna's opening song.
- *Casino Royale*: The series changed tone dramatically with the arrival of Daniel Craig as 007, and his debut teaser is a noirish black-and-white sequence in which Bond surprises Dryden (Malcolm Sinclair), a British double agent who has been selling his country's secrets. Since the series is essentially rebooting here, we learn from Dryden that to achieve double-0 status, an agent must make two kills.

Bond has already offed one of Dryden's associates, so Dryden's death will give him the final kill he needs.
- *Quantum of Solace*: The film begins five minutes after *Casino Royale* ended, with Bond pursued by agents of the criminal organization Quantum in a gripping car chase.
- *Skyfall*: This teaser involves another chase—this one mostly on foot in Istanbul, between Bond and the mercenary Patrice (Ola Rapace). It eventually leads to a battle atop a moving train, in which MI6 field agent Eve Moneypenny (Naomie Harris) takes a shot, misses Patrice, and hits Bond instead.
- *Spectre*: A message from the late M (Dame Judi Dench) leads Bond on an unauthorized mission to Mexico City to stop a terrorist bomb plot. The scale of the sequence is truly impressive, as 007's mission plays out in the streets of Mexico City during a massive Day of the Dead celebration.

The non-Eon Bond film *Never Say Never Again* doesn't have a pre-titles sequence. The film introduces Bond on a training exercise in the South American jungle (shot in the Bahamas), which serves as a teaser of sorts—but it takes place after the credits roll. Originally, however, the filmmakers planned to open the movie with one of the most interesting pre-credits teasers of all.

The film was meant to open at a spectacular medieval pageant and tournament. Horses ridden by fifteenth-century knights are charging at one another in a thrilling competition. The lances they use are wooden and nonlethal, but one of the knights suddenly picks up a lance that has a hidden metal-bladed tip. During the next competition, the metal lance kills one of the contestants.

Up until this point, the movie appears to be taking place six hundred years in the past. After the knight is killed, however, one of the other knights doffs his helmet, and we see that it's James Bond (Sean Connery). Bond jumps on his horse and chases after the murderous knight. As Bond's horse clears a fence, we're suddenly in the middle of a huge parking lot. He spies the killer—a woman—climbing into a sports car, and takes off after her. After a heart-pounding steeplechase across the parking lot, with Bond jumping car after car on his horse, the escaping assassin is caught and killed. This teaser could have been one of the best in the series; unfortunately, it was deemed too expensive and was dropped from the final shooting script.

The Bond teasers are the perfect embodiments of "Harry Houdini syndrome"—that is, the ongoing battle for the series to come up with ever more dangerous and death-defying stunts. The fact that, with few exceptions, the teasers have never ceased to be rip-roaring fun is a great credit to the skill and inventiveness of decades of Bond filmmakers.

Tee Hee: Chuckling associate of Harlem crime boss Mr. Big (Yaphet Kotto), portrayed by character actor Julius Harris in *Live and Let Die*. Literally the drug kingpin's right-hand man—he has a grasping hook for a right hand—Tee Hee lost his real hand in a fight with Old Albert, a Louisiana crocodile. In a climactic battle with Bond (Roger Moore) aboard a train destined for New York City, Tee Hee has the upper hand, until 007 manages to grab a pair of scissors and snip the wires controlling his hook. Unable to remove himself from a precarious position, Tee Hee is kicked out of the train window. A similar train compartment fight between James Bond and Jaws (Richard Kiel) was featured in *The Spy Who Loved Me*.

tell, the: Nervous twitch displayed by Le Chiffre (Mads Mikkelsen) in *Casino Royale*, which James Bond (Daniel Craig) concludes is a clue that his nemesis is bluffing. Unfortunately, one of Bond's allies betrays Bond's deduction to Le Chiffre, allowing the latter to win a huge pot that momentarily busts James Bond at the table.

Tennyson, Alfred Lord (August 6, 1809–October 6, 1892): English poet whose poem "Ulysses," is quoted as a source of strength by M (Dame Judi Dench) during the relevancy hearings in which she's forced to testify in *Skyfall*:

We are not now that strength which in old days
Moved earth and heaven; that which we are,
*   we are;*
One equal temper of heroic hearts,
Made weak by time and fate, but strong in will
To strive, to seek, to find, and not to yield.

Texas hold'em: Game played at the high-stakes poker tournament in Montenegro that becomes the major set piece of *Casino Royale*, replacing the game of baccarat (a.k.a. chemin de fer) in Ian Fleming's original novel. Although the tournament features a number of players, including undercover CIA agent Felix Leiter (Jeffrey Wright), the two main competitors are terrorist banker Le Chiffre (Mads Mikkelsen) and James Bond (Daniel Craig). Le Chiffre is desperate to win the tournament to pay an outstanding debt to African rebel leader Steven Obanno (Isaach De Bankolé). In his case, it could be win or die. Since Bond knows that Le Chiffre is involved with a mysterious international terrorist organization (which we later discover is SPECTRE), he gets the backing of Her Majesty's Treasury, which supplies him with his funds to challenge Le Chiffre. Representing the treasury is Vesper Lynd (Eva Green), international liaison officer for the Financial Action Task Force.

Thai klongs: A series of narrow canals that crisscross Bangkok, Thailand, which are featured in a boat chase in *The Man with the Golden Gun*. Instead of racing along in a swift motorboat, as he did in the previous film, *Live and Let Die*, Bond (Roger Moore) steals a relatively slow, knifelike Thai motor canoe for his getaway vehicle. Agent 007 actually gets better results with the canoe's propeller when it's out of the water—scaring the hell out of his pursuers—than when it's in the water. While racing by in the canoe, 007 is spotted by his old bayou buddy Sheriff J. W. Pepper (Clifton James), who's in Thailand on a vacation with his wife, Maybelle.

James Bond (Roger Moore) navigates a Thai klong in Bangkok in *The Man with the Golden Gun*. *Courtesy of the Anders Frejdh Collection*

Thames Lawn: A riverfront mansion not far from Pinewood Studios in Buckinghamshire that became the home of M (Bernard Lee) in *On Her Majesty's Secret Service*. The location reflects a new filmmaking style in producers Albert R. Broccoli and Harry Saltzman's sixth Bond film, thanks to their new director, former Bond editor Peter Hunt. Whereas on *You Only Live Twice* director Lewis Gilbert and screenwriter Roald Dahl had been more concerned with the fantasy elements of Bond's world—creating huge, workable sets and incredible stunts—Hunt pressed for a return to the basics of Ian Fleming's writing. This new emphasis is quite apparent in several sequences that were transferred to the screen almost word for word from Fleming's novel. One of these little bits of nostalgia was the visit to M's house.

Hunt had always wanted to show the admiral's home, complete with a sixteenth-century cannon guarding the driveway, a riverfront view, and a servant named Hammond. On *OHMSS*, he was given his chance, and Richard Maibaum wrote a sequence in which Bond (George Lazenby) comes to tell his chief that Blofeld (Telly Savalas) has been found in Switzerland. The exterior filming of the home, shot at Thames Lawn, was completed on Wednesday, April 9, 1969.

Thatcher, Margaret (October 13, 1925–April 8, 2013): British prime minister, the first woman to hold the post, portrayed by Thatcher lookalike Janet Brown in a humorous sequence at the end of *For Your Eyes Only*. Telephoning Bond (Roger Moore) in Corfu, Greece, to congratulate him on the success of his latest caper, Thatcher inadvertently starts speaking to Max, the parrot who does not count shyness among his qualities. "Give us a kiss, give us a kiss," he squawks. Slightly embarrassed by "007's" display of affection, Thatcher blushes, while her equally befuddled husband, Denis (John Wells), stands by.

"That's it . . .": The first line of dialogue ever uttered in an Eon Productions James Bond movie, from the first scene in *Dr. No*. It's uttered by MI6 operative John Strangways (Tim Moxon) as he finishes a hand of bridge.

third nipple (a.k.a. superfluous papilla): An anatomical abnormality displayed by super-assassin Francisco Scaramanga (Christopher Lee) in *The Man with the Golden Gun*. To gain an audience with ruthless industrialist Hai Fat (Richard Loo), Bond (Roger Moore) impersonates Scaramanga with the help of a prosthetic third nipple supplied by Q Branch. Hai Fat is impressed, saying that according to some, a third nipple is a sign of invulnerability and great sexual prowess.

"This never happened to the other fellow": Whimsical line of dialogue spoken by James Bond (George Lazenby) on a Portuguese beach at the beginning of *On Her Majesty's Secret Service*, after the girl he rescues (Diana Rigg) drives off and leaves him holding her shoes. It was screenwriter Richard Maibaum's ultimate wink to the audience, which was being introduced to a new James Bond. Said Maibaum, "It was the first time that we actually spoofed ourselves in the series. We decided this time that we would break the aesthetic distance for once. It was a different guy. We knew, and we knew the audience knew. So we decided, what the hell. Let's have a little fun. And the audience laughed and accepted it, and they were pleased that we didn't try some kind of phony B-picture thing to excuse the fact that we had a new James Bond."[*]

Thomas, Serena Scott (September 21, 1961–   ): British actress who portrayed MI6 physician Dr. Molly Warmflash in *The World Is Not Enough*. In decidedly non-PC fashion, Bond (Pierce Brosnan) takes her to bed to ensure that she declares him fit for duty after he separates his collarbone chasing Julietta the Cigar Girl (Maria Grazia Cucinotta). Born in Nether Compton, Dorset, England, Thomas made her motion picture debut in director Peter Medak's crime drama *Let Him Have It* (1991), which was written by veteran Bond writers Neal Purvis and Robert Wade.

Thomas, Varley (November 29, 1901–January 29, 1983; birth name: Margaret Ada Thomas): Silver-haired British actress who portrayed the friendly Swiss gatekeeper in *Goldfinger*, a tough little woman who later blasts away at Bond's Aston Martin with a submachine gun. A native of Wandsworth, Surrey, England, she made no other big-screen appearances.

Three Blind Mice, the: Trio of Jamaican assassins, portrayed by Eric Coverly, Charles Edghill, and Henry Lopez, who work for the title character in *Dr. No.* They're the first villains introduced in the Bond series, taking down British undercover operative John Strangways (Tim Moxon) in the film's opening scene. Their repeated attempts to kill James Bond (Sean Connery) go awry, however, and their last failed attempt, trying to run 007 off the road with their hearse, sends the vehicle over a cliff outside Kingston. As Bond quips, "They were on their way to a funeral."

Thumper: One of the acrobatic ladies whom Blofeld (Charles Gray) assigns the task of guarding Willard Whyte (Jimmy Dean) in *Diamonds Are Forever*. Portrayed by American actress Trina Parks, she and her partner Bambi (Lola Larson) give Bond (Sean Connery) plenty of trouble when he comes searching for the missing Whyte, until 007 gets the upper hand in the swimming pool.

Director Guy Hamilton goes over a Thumper move with actress Trina Parks in *Diamonds Are Forever*. *Courtesy of the Anders Frejdh Collection*

THUNDERBALL

(United Artists, 1965) ★★★☆ : The fourth James Bond film produced by Albert R. Broccoli and Harry Saltzman, this time in conjunction with producer Kevin McClory. US release date: December 29, 1965. Budget: $5.6 million. Worldwide box office gross: $141.2 million (US domestic gross: $63.6 million; foreign gross: $77.6 million).* Running time: 129 minutes.

THE SETUP

After liquidating SPECTRE assassin Jacques Bouvar (Bob Simmons) in a French chateau, James Bond (Sean Connery) is sent to the Shrublands health clinic for some much-needed R&R. There he meets sexy physical therapist Patricia Fearing (Molly Peters) and her patient Count Lippe (Guy Doleman), who sports a suspicious tattoo of a tong sign on his wrist. What Bond doesn't know is that Lippe is another enemy agent, working closely with assassin Fiona Volpe (Luciana Paluzzi), who has seduced NATO observer François Derval (Paul Stassino). Replacing him with an exact duplicate, SPECTRE plans to hijack a NATO jet bomber with two atomic weapons on board. The price to get those deadly nuclear weapons back: a $280 million ransom. Otherwise, a major city in the US or Great Britain will be destroyed. It's the most audacious and ambitious operation ever conducted by SPECTRE—an operation that leads Bond to Nassau in the Bahamas and to wealthy international businessman Emilio Largo (Adolfo Celi) and his voluptuous mistress, Dominique Derval (Claudine Auger), sister of François.

BEHIND THE SCENES

Thunderball is an epic film in every sense of the word—a big caper on a big canvas, capturing a worldwide sense of alarm that has never been duplicated in the series. The capers in other Bond films have been equally ambitious, but director Terence Young and screenwriter Richard Maibaum also managed to infuse this film with a very realistic menace. In *The Spy Who Loved Me*, Stromberg's nuclear threat is a fantasy. In *Thunderball*, you believe that SPECTRE can and will detonate an atomic device if their

* "Thunderball (1965)," The Numbers, accessed July 16, 2020, https://www.the-numbers.com/movie/Thunderball.

Thunderball by artist Jeff Marshall. *Courtesy of Jeff Marshall*

ransom is not paid. When Bond walks into the Secret Service briefing room and takes his seat with all the other double-0 agents in Europe, you sense that an incredible adventure is about to begin, with the fate of the planet potentially on the line.

As in the previous films in the series, there are simple touches in *Thunderball* that anchor the film in reality. The hijacking of the NATO bomber is treated realistically, as is the resulting concern that ripples through NATO command. And although Bond appears to be a bit cavalier at times—spending far too much time bedding one conquest after another—when duty calls, he responds quickly and decisively.

Much has been written over the years about how *Thunderball*'s underwater sequences slow down the pace of the film. Certain fight sequences are repetitive, but the underwater setting contributes enormously to the romance of this picture—particularly as a backdrop to the love affair between Bond and Domino. Nowhere is this more evident than in the sequence in which Bond first meets Domino in the waters

off Nassau. Directed by Ricou Browning, photographed by Lamar Boren, and scored beautifully by John Barry, this sequence has a poetic quality that perfectly establishes the interplay between the two future lovers.

Thunderball harnesses the romantic lure of Nassau throughout the film. One of the most evocative sequences is a brief moment when Bond arrives for a night of gambling at the Paradise Island casino. As he gets off the boat, he hears the laughter of a group of well-dressed vacationers who are leaving for the night. "See you tomorrow!" they shout, and the viewer suddenly gets a tremendous sense of the tropics—of carefree vacations, cool drinks, and moonlight romance.

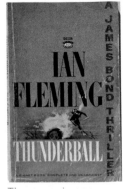

The cover image of the 1960s-era American paperback edition of Ian Fleming's original novel *Thunderball. Steve Rubin Collection*

There's also the super-confident quality that Sean Connery brings to the picture. After three films, the character of 007 has been firmly established. Now, it's time for Sean to have a little fun—for instance, the moment in the chateau when he kills Jacques Bouvar and takes time to throw flowers on the body, or the scene in Shrublands in which he discovers the dead Angelo and steals a bit of fruit as he leaves. Touches like these set *Thunderball* apart from other Bond movies.

The film also features one of the most beautiful women ever to grace a 007 adventure. Claudine Auger, a French beauty contest winner, has an electrifying presence on screen that matches Connery's own, ensuring that their romance never lacks for fire. Luciana Paluzzi is also fetching as Fiona Volpe, the voluptuous redheaded siren. The film's only real problem is the Shrublands sequence early in the film, which, aside from 007's interplay with the very desirable Patricia Fearing, is just too slow-moving to sustain audience interest.

THE CAST

James Bond	Sean Connery
Domino	Claudine Auger
Emilio Largo	Adolfo Celi
Fiona Volpe	Luciana Paluzzi
Felix Leiter	Rik Van Nutter
M	Bernard Lee
Paula Caplan	Martine Beswick
Count Lippe	Guy Doleman
Patricia Fearing	Molly Peters
Q	Desmond Llewelyn
Miss Moneypenny	Lois Maxwell
Foreign Secretary	Roland Culver
Pinder	Earl Cameron
Major Derval/Angelo	Paul Stassino
Madame Bouvar	Rose Alba
Jacques Bouvar	Bob Simmons
Vargas	Philip Locke
Kutze	George Pravda
Janni	Michael Brennan
Group Captain Pritchard	Leonard Sachs
Air Vice Marshall Sir John	Edward Underdown
Kenniston	Reginald Beckwith
Quist	Bill Cummings
Mademoiselle LaPorte	Mitsouko

THE CREW

Presented by	Albert R. Broccoli
	Harry Saltzman
Director	Terence Young
Screenplay by	Richard Maibaum
	John Hopkins
Based on an original screenplay by	Jack Whittingham
Based on the original story by	Kevin McClory, Jack Whittingham, and Ian Fleming
Produced by	Kevin McClory
Director of Photography	Ted Moore
Music by	John Barry
Title song performed by	Tom Jones
Lyrics by	Don Black
Production Designer	Ken Adam
Art Director	Peter Murton
Assistant Art Director	Michael White
Set Dresser	Freda Pearson
Costume Designer	Anthony Mendleson
Wardrobe Mistress	Eileen Sullivan
Wardrobe Master	John Brady
Makeup	Paul Rabiger
	Basil Newall
Hairstylist	Eileen Warwick
Production Manager	David Middlemas
Assistant Director	Gus Agosti
Underwater sequences by	Ivan Tors Studios
Underwater Director	Ricou Browning
Underwater Cameraman	Lamar Boren
Underwater Engineer	Jordan Klein
Continuity	Joan Davis
Camera Operator	John Winbolt
Location Manager	Frank Ernst
Stunt Director	Bob Simmons
Title Designer	Maurice Binder
Special Effects	John Stears
Sound Recordists	Bert Ross
	Maurice Askew
Supervising Film Editor	Peter Hunt

***Thunderball* continuity problems**: One of the major complaints about the 1965 James Bond movie is the presence of some glaring continuity errors. As editor Peter Hunt explained, "The whole film doesn't bear watching too closely. And as for continuity slips, there were many. One that I love is when Bond (Sean Connery) and Leiter (Rik Van Nutter) are looking for the Vulcan bomber from their helicopter. In one shot, Rik is sitting there with a hat on, and in another sequence, he has on a completely different set of clothes. And both sequences are cut together. It worked because nobody ever noticed it. My rationale is that if we had nothing else, we had to make it work.

"In another sequence, Bond, having lost his own blue diving mask, swims over to a dead SPECTRE frogman and grabs his black mask. However, in the next shot, Bond has his blue mask back on. Sometimes when it comes time to juxtapose certain bits of film, you can't. It's not possible, and that's how gaps occur. It's better to maintain the pace of the film than to worry about continuity."*

Thunderball title sequence: It was filmed by title specialist Maurice Binder in the Pinewood Studios water tank in July 1965. Micky De Rauch, Billie Bates, and Jean McGrath portrayed the nude swimmers—embodying the film's underwater theme.

Tibbett, Sir Godfrey: British Secret Service agent portrayed by Patrick Macnee in _A View to a Kill_. Working undercover as a chauffeur to James Bond (Roger Moore), Tibbett arrives at the sumptuous French estate of Max Zorin (Christopher Walken) to help 007 investigate Zorin's use of steroids to increase the racing abilities of his thoroughbreds.

Fooling the estate's security team with a tape-recorded conversation that plays in 007's bedroom, Bond and Tibbett sneak into Zorin's secret underground laboratory beneath his stables and discover a surgical suite where special microchips are being surgically inserted into the

---
* Peter Hunt, interview by the author, London, June 21, 1977.

Sir Godfrey Tibbett (Patrick Macnee, right) joins James Bond (Roger Moore) and Q (Desmond Llewelyn) at the Ascot racecourse in England for _A View to a Kill. Courtesy of the Luc Leclech Collection_

horses' legs to release a precise dose of steroids. They also discover a huge cache of microchips that Zorin is hoarding.

Returning to their quarters, Bond and Tibbett make plans to get the information to M (Robert Brown). Unfortunately, before Tibbett can make an important phone call, he's strangled by May Day (Grace Jones) in a nearby car wash. Bond is knocked unconscious and thrown into the backseat with his deceased fellow agent, while May Day pushes their Rolls-Royce into a nearby lake. Regaining his senses, Bond escapes from the sinking car and survives by sucking air from one of the Rolls's Michelin tires.

Tierra Project: Cover name for the ambitious plan by Dominic Greene (Mathieu Amalric) to corner the world's freshwater supply on behalf of the crime syndicate Quantum, later revealed to be a subsidiary of SPECTRE. The initial target is Bolivia, where Greene has made a deal with renegade general Medrano (Joaquín Cosio) to acquire what the latter believes is useless desert in return for installing him as the country's next president. To members of the international press, Greene claims that the Tierra Project is a small part of a global network of eco parks created to rejuvenate a world on the verge of collapse.

Tiger helicopter: Described as "Europe's answer to the electronic battlefield," this prototype aircraft is stolen off the deck of a French warship in the Monte Carlo harbor in _GoldenEye_. According to the briefing officer, the Tiger is impervious to all forms of electronic interference, radio jamming, and electromagnetic radiation.

Tokyo: Japanese capital city that figures in the plot of many James Bond movies. In _From Russia with Love_, it's where agents of SPECTRE capture and torture a British agent to get the Secret Service recognition code. In the same film, when Bond (Sean Connery) is asked to compare the sexual prowess of Tatiana Romanova (Daniela Bianchi) to that of the women he's known in the west, 007 remembers a time when he was in Tokyo with M (Bernard Lee); his story ends abruptly when M turns off Bond's tape-recorded conversation.

In _You Only Live Twice_, Tokyo is the film's principal location; it's where Bond meets Tiger

Tanaka (Tetsuro Tamba), the head of the Japanese Secret Service. During his stay, 007 visits a sumo wrestling match, where he meets Tanaka's agent Aki (Akiko Wakabayashi). And during a chase with agents of SPECTRE, one of Tanaka's helicopters uses its powerful electromagnet to lift the chasing vehicle into the air, after which it's dropped into Tokyo Bay.

TOMORROW NEVER DIES

(United Artists, 1997) ★★⁂ : Eighteenth James Bond movie produced by Eon Productions. US release date: December 16, 1997. Budget: $110 million. Worldwide box office gross: $339.5 million (US domestic gross: $125.3 million; international gross: $214.2 million).* Running time: 119 minutes.

THE SETUP

Spying on a terrorist arms bazaar on the Russian border, James Bond (Pierce Brosnan) discovers two nuclear torpedoes mounted on a Soviet L-39 Albatros aircraft. Unfortunately, British admiral Roebuck (Geoffrey Palmer), ignoring M's request that Bond be allowed to complete his reconnaissance, orders the bazaar destroyed. Bond escapes aboard the Albatros with the missiles, preventing a nuclear catastrophe—but, unbeknownst to Bond or British intelligence, a GPS encoder has been obtained at the bazaar by cyber-terrorist Henry Gupta (Ricky Jay) that could help provoke a war between China and the UK. The mastermind behind this brewing conflict is media baron Elliot Carver (Jonathan Pryce) who is operating a stealth warship in the South China Sea. That ship is responsible for sinking the British frigate HMS *Devonshire*, shooting down a Chinese J-7 fighter jet, and killing off the *Devonshire*'s survivors with Chinese weaponry. Carver's plan is to destroy the Chinese government with a stolen cruise missile, allowing a Chinese general to step in and stop war between Britain and China, but not before both sides destroy each other at sea. Once the war is over, Carver will be given

exclusive broadcasting rights in China for the next century. Bond eventually teams up with Red Chinese agent Wai Lin (Michelle Yeoh) to foil the psychotic scheme.

BEHIND THE SCENES

Pierce Brosnan suffered a sophomore slump in this flight of fancy, which features the series' most unbelievable storyline. We've seen Bond as Buck Rogers in outer space (*Moonraker*), we've seen Bond as a charter member of the Keystone Cops (*A View to a Kill*), and we've seen a joyless Bond impersonating a character on *Miami Vice* (*Licence to Kill*), but as lousy at times as those films were, at least they featured a credible villain. This film wants you to believe that a billionaire media mogul (Jonathan Pryce) would directly instigate World War III to increase

Tomorrow Never Dies by Jeff Marshall.
Courtesy of Jeff Marshall

* "Tomorrow Never Dies (1997)," The Numbers, accessed July 16, 2020, https://www.the-numbers.com/movie /Tomorrow-Never-Dies.

the ratings of his fledgling cable network. It's not Brosnan's fault—he's solid throughout and has a terrific action set piece, piloting a BMW 750iL from the backseat with his remote control—but he can't make up for a story that lacks all credibility.

We're also subjected to a number of elements that were handled better in other Bond films. Elliot Carver's stealth ship is just a pale imitation of Stromberg's supertanker in *The Spy Who Loved Me* (which was it itself a retread of SPECTRE's *Intruder* spaceship in *You Only Live Twice*). And the pre-credits teaser, in which Bond saves the day by stealing the Russian jet from the arms bazaar, is equally stale. Where's the ever more daring stunt we've come to expect from a 007 teaser? The end of the movie is just as dull as the beginning, failing to find much drama as Bond penetrates and destroys Carver's stealth ship.

It's the women who shine in this one. Fleet-footed Michelle Yeoh, who would later score in *Crouching Tiger, Hidden Dragon* (2000), is a perfect action companion to Bond: stylish, charismatic, capable. And Teri Hatcher has a few brassy moments as the villain's wife, and Bond's former flame, Paris Carver—but not enough of them. Other high points include the aforementioned BMW 750iL and two unusual casting coups—magician Ricky Jay's computer terrorist and eccentric Vincent Schiavelli as Paris Carver's assassin. (And keep an eye out for future *Downton Abbey* creator Julian Fellowes in a small part as the UK minister of defence, whom Elliot Carver provokes into sending the British fleet into the South China Sea.) Daniel Kleinman's opening titles were once again terrific, backed by Sheryl Crow's soulful title song. Unfortunately, the film went downhill fast from there.

THE CAST

James Bond	Pierce Brosnan
Elliot Carver	Jonathan Pryce
Colonel Wai Lin	Michelle Yeoh
Paris Carver	Teri Hatcher
Henry Gupta	Ricky Jay
Mr. Stamper	Götz Otto
Jack Wade	Joe Don Baker
Dr. Kaufman	Vincent Schiavelli
M	Dame Judi Dench
Q	Desmond Llewelyn
Miss Moneypenny	Samantha Bond
Charles Robinson	Colin Salmon
Admiral Roebuck	Geoffrey Palmer
Minister of Defence	Julian Fellowes
General Bukharin	Terence Rigby
Professor Inga Bergstrom	Cecilie Thomsen
Dr. Dave Greenwalt	Colin Stinton

THE CREW

Director	Roger Spottiswoode
Written by	Bruce Feirstein
Producers	Barbara Broccoli
	Michael G. Wilson
Director of Photography	Robert Elswit
Music by	David Arnold
Title song performed by	Sheryl Crow
Production Designer	Allan Cameron
Costume Designer	Lindy Hemming
Line Producer	Anthony Waye
Second Unit Director / Stunt Coordinator	Vic Armstrong
Casting by	Debbie McWilliams
Halo Jump Coordinator	B. J. Worth
Stunt Double for Ms. Yeoh	Wendy Leech

Pierce Brosnan and Michelle Yeoh make a formidable team in *Tomorrow Never Dies*. *Steve Rubin Collection*

Special effects technician Brian Smithies, part of John Richardson's miniatures team, works on detailing a Saigon, Vietnam, street for action in *Tomorrow Never Dies*. *Courtesy of the Brian Smithies Archive*

Stunt Double for Mr. Brosnan	Wayne Michaels
Title Designer	Daniel Kleinman
Special Effects Supervisor	Chris Corbould
Miniatures	John Richardson
Editors	Michel Arcand
	Dominique Fortin

Topol (September 9, 1935–   ; birth name: Chaim Topol): Charismatic Academy Award–nominated Israeli leading actor who portrayed Greek smuggler Milos Columbo in *For Your Eyes Only*. In a film that was a throwback to the earlier, more serious entries in the Bond series, Topol's Columbo was a fascinating character—very much in the vein of Kerim Bey (Pedro Armendariz) in *From Russia with Love*, and even earlier spy movie icons like Sydney Greenstreet and Peter Lorre. Playing a big man who's full of life and determined to destroy his enemy, Kristatos (Julian Glover), at all costs, Topol painted him with layers of likeability, down to his love for pistachio nuts. Born in Tel Aviv,

Topol made his motion picture debut as Mikha in director Peter Frye's Israeli dramedy *I Like Mike* (1961). A decade later, he won his most iconic role: Tevye the Milkman in director Norman Jewison's acclaimed *Fiddler on the Roof* (1971), for which he was nominated for the Best Actor Oscar (losing to Gene Hackman in *The French Connection*).

toppling: What Dr. No (Joseph Wiseman) is doing to American missiles launched from the Cape Canaveral base in Florida. As 007 (Sean Connery) defines it, "toppling" means throwing the gyroscopic controls of a guided missile off track with a radio signal. Dr. No's toppling operation is based on an island called Crab Key, where he has an atomic-powered radio beam secreted away in his fortress.

Toyota 2000GT: Futuristic white sports car driven by Aki (Akiko Wakabayashi) in *You Only Live Twice*. For the film, the Toyota Motor

Company offered to create a special version of their new 1966 2000GT sports car, complete with a convertible top—the first of its kind ever seen in Japan. Into this dream car, special effects chief John Stears added a functional closed-circuit television that allows Bond (Sean Connery) and Aki to communicate with Tiger Tanaka at the Tokyo headquarters of the Japanese Secret Service.

Tracy: Nickname of the spoiled daughter of Marc-Ange Draco (Gabriele Ferzetti), portrayed by Diana Rigg in Eon Productions' sixth James Bond film, *On Her Majesty's Secret Service*. Her formal name is Contessa Teresa di Vicenzo (her husband, an Italian count, died in a car crash with one of his mistresses). Introduced as a suicidal burnout case who's ready to end it all

in the ocean off Portugal, Tracy is rescued by Bond (George Lazenby). She gradually recovers during a whirlwind courtship with 007, until he leaves for the Swiss mountain hideaway of SPECTRE chief Ernst Stavro Blofeld (Telly Savalas).

Later, like a female version of the US Cavalry, she comes to Bond's aid, joining him in a mad escape from Switzerland, both in a car and later on skis. More than any other woman in the series, she displays the mental and physical skills needed to keep up with Bond.

Hiding out in a barn during a snowstorm, Bond expresses his love for Tracy. And, in one of the most dramatic pronouncements of the series, he proposes. However, their wedding plans are cut short when Tracy is captured by Blofeld's men. His love for Tracy, combined with his hate for Blofeld, leads Bond on a freelance mission—with the help of Draco—against Blofeld's Piz Gloria fortress (M and the Secret Service refuse to help). Masquerading as Red Cross workers headed for an Italian flood disaster, Draco's copter-borne attack force arrives at Piz Gloria, rescues Tracy, and obliterates the SPECTRE nest. In a thrilling bobsled chase, Bond disables Blofeld—at least temporarily.

Following their wedding, Bond and Tracy, now just another happy married couple, pull off a highway in Portugal to remove the conspicuous JUST MARRIED signs that have been plastered on 007's Aston Martin. As Bond throws them away,

The Contessa Teresa "Tracy" di Vicenzo by artist Jeff Marshall. *Courtesy of Jeff Marshall*

Wedding bells for Contessa Teresa "Tracy" di Vicenzo (Diana Rigg) and James Bond (George Lazenby) in *On Her Majesty's Secret Service. Courtesy of the David Reinhardt Collection*

a Mercedes driven by Blofeld drives by, and his henchwoman Irma Bunt (Ilse Steppat) opens fire with a machine gun. Bond returns to the car, but Tracy is already dead—shot right between the eyes. *OHMSS* ends on this sad note.

During the pre-credits teaser of *For Your Eyes Only*, the twelfth Eon Bond film, Bond (Roger Moore) pays an emotional visit to Tracy's grave, which bears the inscription

TERESA BOND

1943–1969

BELOVED WIFE OF JAMES BOND

WE HAVE ALL THE TIME IN THE WORLD

It's one of the few sentimental moments in the series' history. Unfortunately, it's followed by a ridiculous final confrontation with Blofeld—or at least, for legal reasons, an unidentified Blofeld lookalike.

Treadway Estate: A former Indian reservation in the Louisiana bayou country that was the site of the madcap motorboat chase through the wedding party in *Live and Let Die*. Three American stuntmen tried to ram their CV-19 powerboats through the wedding cake. After Murray Cleveland and Jerry Comeaux failed, it was Eddie Smith who tasted the icing—at a reduced speed of 60 mph.

Tree, Shady: Wisecracking Las Vegas lounge entertainer and smuggler portrayed by Leonard Barr in *Diamonds Are Forever*. He's the leader of a lounge act called Shady Tree and His Acorns, the latter being two showgirls. The withered old

Shady Tree (Leonard Barr, far right) of all people rescues James Bond (Sean Connery) from death by cremation in *Diamonds Are Forever*. *Courtesy of the Anders Frejdh Collection*

Tree saves Bond (Sean Connery) from a roasting in the crematorium at the Slumber Inc. mortuary when he demands to know what happened to the "real" diamonds. Later, while sequestered in his dressing room backstage at the Whyte House, Tree is assassinated by Blofeld's thugs Mr. Wint (Bruce Glover) and Mr. Kidd (Putter Smith).

Trench, Sylvia: Seductive English playgirl, amateur golfer, and card player portrayed by Eunice Gayson in *Dr. No* and *From Russia with Love*. Technically the first Bond girl in the Eon Productions 007 series, she meets James Bond (Sean Connery) at the baccarat table at

Society girl Sylvia Trench (Eunice Gayson) accepts a business card from James Bond (Sean Connery) after their spirited battle at a chemin de fer table in London in *Dr. No. Courtesy of the David Reinhardt Collection*

Actress Eunice Gayson returned to duty as Sylvia Trench, Bond's winsome girlfriend, in *From Russia with Love. Courtesy of the David Reinhardt Collection*

Eunice Gayson
borrowed James
Bond's dress shirt and
wrote herself into 007
history in *Dr. No.*
*Courtesy of the David
Reinhardt Collection*

Les Ambassadeurs in London, prompting his famous line "I admire your courage, Miss . . . ?" Unfortunately, 007 is usually in too much of a hurry to have more than a quick tryst with Sylvia, who looks quite fetching in a man's dress shirt and high heels.

TRESPASSERS WILL BE EATEN: Sign on the main gate of the alligator farm belonging to sinister drug smuggler Dr. Kananga (Yaphet Kotto) in *Live and Let Die*. A real sign, it belonged to farmer Ross Kananga, the actual owner of the land.

Trevelyan, Alec (a.k.a. 006, a.k.a. Janus): Former British double-0 agent and friend of James Bond (Pierce Brosnan) turned duplicitous traitor, portrayed by Sean Bean in *GoldenEye*. The son of Lienz Cossacks who were betrayed by the British after World War II, Trevelyan has sworn revenge on the country that was responsible for

The sign says it all, but Roger Moore just takes it in stride—because he is James Bond.
Courtesy of the Anders Frejdh Collection

his parents' suicide. Introduced as 006 and shown as Bond's comrade in a dangerous mission to destroy a Soviet chemical weapons depot, he's apparently killed by Colonel Ourumov (Gottfried John) before Bond obliterates the plant. The story picks up nine years later as Bond investigates a mysterious Russian crime figure, Janus, who is intent on destroying England with an electromagnetic pulse generated by a commandeered satellite. Janus, as Bond discovers in a graveyard of junked Communist-era statuary, is really Alec Trevelyan, who faked his death and became the head of a major Russian crime syndicate. Another reason for Trevelyan to seek revenge: Bond changed the timer on the demolition charges set at the chemical facility, so although Alec wasn't really killed by Ourumov, his face was badly scarred by the chemical explosion.

Before he turned traitor, Alec Trevelyan (Sean Bean) was a double-0 operative and a good friend of James Bond (Pierce Brosnan). *Courtesy of the Luc Leclech Collection*

Tropic Rover: Real-life name of the catamaran, anchored in Nassau Harbor, that provides James Bond (Sean Connery) with cover in *Thunderball*.

Tropicana Hotel: Las Vegas accommodations of James Bond (Sean Connery) in *Diamonds Are Forever*. It's where he meets Plenty O'Toole (Lana Wood), who is later thrown out of a hotel window by the diamond syndicate goons.

tulip: What James Bond (Sean Connery) promises to bring back to Miss Moneypenny (Lois Maxwell) from Amsterdam in *Diamonds Are Forever*. She had asked for a "diamond in a ring."

Turnbull & Asser: Famous menwear's shop located on Jermyn Street in London. It's where director Terence Young took Sean Connery for his initial 007 wardrobe in *Dr. No*. The tailor was Anthony Sinclair. The same company supplied Pierce Brosnan on *Tomorrow Never Dies*, *The World Is Not Enough*, and *Die Another Day* and Daniel Craig on *Casino Royale*.

Turner, Tina (November 26, 1939–   ): Sexy American-born song stylist who performed the title tune in *GoldenEye*. Born to poor black sharecroppers in Nutbush, Tennessee, Turner became one of the most successful rock artists of all time, with chart-topping hits such as "What's Love Got to Do with It." She was first featured in a motion picture when her song (with then husband Ike Turner) "Finger Poppin'" appeared on the soundtrack of the John Waters comedy *Mondo Trasho* (1969). She was also memorable as Aunty Entity in *Mad Max Beyond Thunderdome* (1985). She now lives in Switzerland.

Twiss, Peter (July 23, 1921–August 31, 2011; birth name: Lionel Peter Twiss): British test pilot and World War II Royal Air Force veteran who was the first man to fly a jet aircraft faster than 1,000 mph. Born in Lindfield, Sussex, England, and later an employee of Fairey Marine, he was put in charge of the motorboat flotilla at Crinan, Scotland in *From Russia with Love*, and drove one of the speedboats.

Type 23 Duke class frigate: Type of British anti-submarine warship featured in *Tomorrow Never Dies*. Interior shots of the vessels were all filmed at the HMS *Dryad* ship simulator at Portsmouth, Hampshire, England; most of the personnel in the background are real Royal Navy personnel.

Udaipur, India: Beautiful city on the subcontinent that became a principal filming location in *Octopussy*. Founded in 1559 by Maharana Udai Singh II, it is known as the City of Sunrise. Shooting began there on September 21, 1982, and continued for three weeks.

Udell, Ronald (August 20, 1911–????): Pinewood Studios construction manager, and production designer Ken Adam's right-hand man on many of the early James Bond films. Udell's motto, which Adam took literally, was "If you can draw it, we can build it." Udell and his team of craftsmen at Pinewood encouraged Adam during the early days of the Bond series to try out new materials and techniques that were within the series' initially low budgets. When the film series took off, Udell was intimately involved in the huge set constructions that became a trademark of the Bond films, including the interior and exterior of Fort Knox in *Goldfinger* and the huge volcano missile base in *You Only Live Twice*.

Udell's first film at Pinewood was the classic suspense thriller *Green for Danger* (1946). By the mid-1950s, he was one of six construction managers who supervised all construction at Pinewood. He worked closely with the other five: Harold Combden, Bill Surridge, Jock Lyall, Bert Mansell, and Ted Hughes. Each team moved from construction to construction, and there was a camaraderie among the various teams that is unknown today. It was common for Udell to be involved in as many as six to eight films at once. He was appointed chief construction manager for the studio in 1969.

Udell's relationship with Ken Adam had begun on *The Hidden Room* (1949), a suspense thriller directed by Edward Dmytryk. For *Dr. No* in 1962, Udell was delighted to work on the unusual sets designed by Adam for the film. "We had a budget of 17,000 pounds for all of the interiors," he recalled. "We had just enough money to finish everything except the most important set: Dr. No's reactor room. Since the producers were extremely happy with the rushes, they went back to United Artists and fought for another 7,000 pounds to finish the reactor room.

"We used a lot of fiberglass on *Dr. No*, which was a new material. We gave it a metallic finish with an Italian jewelry spray. For the reactor room, which was built on Stage E, Ken originally wanted one slick catwalk—where Bond has the fight with Chang, the fuel elements technician—with no visible means of suspension. For safety reasons, we convinced him to design two supports into the set."[*]

Though Bill Surridge supervised the constructions for *From Russia with Love*, Udell was heavily involved on *Goldfinger*. One of his initial assignments was to build a ramp for the out-of-control Mercedes-Benz that goes over a cliff and slams into a side of the Auric Enterprises building. "We went to the Harefield Quarry for the stunt," Udell remembered, "and we discovered that the only place we could build the ramp was over a pigsty. So that's exactly where we built it. While John Stears and his crew filled the car with petrol jelly, all of these pigs were constantly bleating."

Six months before *Goldfinger* began principal photography, Udell was planting an avenue of trees that would eventually lead up to his Fort Knox replica, which was built full scale in the Black Park woodland next to the studio. The trees were identical to ones photographed during a helicopter tour of the actual Fort Knox in Kentucky. Udell also remembered the difficulty of maneuvering the one-ton vault door from the interior stage to the outdoor set, where US troops battled Goldfinger's Grand Slam Task Force.

For *Thunderball*, Udell and his team journeyed to a Royal Air Force base in Alton, where a plaster mold was made of a full-scale Vulcan bomber. The mold was then taken to the Bahamas, where the bomber was constructed out of fiberglass and then lowered into the Caribbean off Nassau's Clifton Pier. A separate bomb bay was constructed and photographed from underneath for when Bond explores the wreck of the bomber.

---

[*] Ronald Udell, interview by the author, London, June 19, 1977.

Between February and May 1965, Udell was consumed by the *Thunderball* project—one of the most expensive films ever based at Pinewood to that point. But even *Thunderball* paled in comparison to *You Only Live Twice*, which involved the construction of a full-scale rocket base within the cone of an extinct volcano. Udell retired from Pinewood Studios in August 1976, a month before principal photography began on *The Spy Who Loved Me*. He has since passed away, but a date of death was not available at press time.

"Under the Mango Tree": Rhythmic island tune—reminiscent of "The Girl from Ipanema"—that is featured in *Dr. No*. In capturing the romantic mood of the tropics, "Under the Mango Tree" is one of the series' best songs, and in the absence of an opening-titles song, it really is the theme of *Dr. No*. It's sung at various times by Byron Lee and the Dragonaires at Puss-Feller's club and by Honey Ryder (Ursula Andress) and Bond (Sean Connery) on the beach at Crab Key—the only time that Connery ever sings in the series. A breezy instrumental version plays at the end of the movie. Credit composer Monty Norman for bringing this memorable tune to the series.

One of the most memorable screen meetings of all time takes place in *Dr. No*, when James Bond (Sean Connery) sees Honey Ryder (Ursula Andress) come out of the water on Crab Key, singing "Under the Mango Tree." *Courtesy of the David Reinhardt Collection*

underwater battle: The huge action-filled concluding sequence in *Thunderball*. It was filmed in segments over a period of six days in the waters off Nassau, with sixty divers from Miami-based Ivan Tors Studios. One important sequence was filmed around a sunken US Navy landing craft,

where Bond (Sean Connery) lures two SPECTRE frogmen to their deaths. The rest of the battle spread itself across the Nassau seascape.

Filming an underwater war was, at times, almost too realistic. In one scene, Bond flicks a switch on his trick backpack and fires an explosive spear at an enemy diver. In the actual sequence, Courtney Brown, portraying the SPECTRE diver, was given an explosive charge to place on the outside of his wet suit. When the spear was fired—on a line—it was designed to strike the charge and create an underwater explosion of black powder. Unfortunately, Brown placed the charge underneath his wet suit instead, so when the spear hit, it blew a hole right through the suit, severely burning his skin and landing him in Princess Margaret Hospital.

Bond's jet-propelled diving backpack—designed by Jordan Klein—which gives him super underwater speed, was actually a nonfunctional prop. A piano wire attached to a speedboat propelled Bond's double, Frank Cousins, through the water. If Cousins had turned his face at any moment, the force of being pulled at such speed would have torn the diver's mask from his face.

Most of the battle took place in twenty feet of water off Nassau's Clifton Pier. Into the battle, the producers threw every piece of equipment in the *Thunderball* arsenal, including the SPECTRE bomb sled, the scooters, and the scores of CO_2 guns that sprayed a lethal underwater rain of spears among the fighting ranks, the free-swimming, orange-suited US Navy aqua-paras versus the black-suited underwater SPECTRE flotilla. Seemingly invincible behind their spear-firing sleds, Emilio Largo's frogmen are systematically overwhelmed in hand-to-hand combat by Bond and his aqua-paras.

"The underwater sequences, especially the final battle, were too long," recalled director Terence Young, who became disenchanted with *Thunderball* during its final weeks of shooting. "The trouble was that people kept wondering what the hell was going on. Of all the Bond films, *Thunderball* was the only one where the audience had at least a half hour of meditation during those long underwater sequences. People began to ask questions that we didn't want them to ask until they were on their way home.

"I thought that the first underwater scenes were delightful, especially the opening sequence

Underwater engineer Jordan Klein's working A-bomb sled from *Thunderball* is put on display in London. *Courtesy of the Michael VanBlaricum Collection*

in which the *Disco Volante* sends out her divers to recover the hijacked atomic bombs. But in the later fight sequences, we kept repeating ourselves. There was nothing you could do except fire a spear at somebody, pull his mask off, or cut his lifeline. So when you've done that stuff forty-five times, the audience is naturally going to clamor for something new."*

Universal Studios backlot: Shooting site of the madcap parking-lot car chase in *Diamonds Are Forever*. It simulated the parking lot of downtown Las Vegas's Mint Hotel.

---

* Terence Young, interview by the author, London, June 25, 1977.

Upper Rissington: Site of a former RAF airfield in Gloucestershire, England, that was utilized to help complete a slippery car chase that began on the Vatnajökull ice cap in Iceland for *Die Another Day*. A two-hundred-person construction crew spent weeks prior to filming carefully setting up backdrops and building life-size 3-D icebergs, creating a set about the size of five soccer fields. Synthetic snow was added to complete the illusion.

US Navy aqua-paras: Adversaries of SPECTRE spymaster Emilio Largo (Adolfo Celi) in the final underwater battle of *Thunderball*. Outmanned and outgunned by the superior SPECTRE force of black-suited frogmen, the orange-suited aqua-paras hold their own until Bond (Sean Connery) arrives to even the odds.

USS *Wayne*: American submarine that is the third and last nuclear sub captured by megalomaniac Karl Stromberg (Curt Jurgens) with his *Liparus* supertanker in *The Spy Who Loved Me*. Captained by Commander Carter (Shane Rimmer), the sub is left behind when the other two hijacked craft, redesignated Stromberg 1 and Stromberg 2, leave on their apocalyptic mission. When Bond (Roger Moore) leads an eventually successful attack on the *Liparus*'s crew and command center, the surviving submariners board the *Wayne*, which escapes from the doomed supertanker.

Valenka: Slinky girlfriend of Le Chiffre (Mads Mikkelsen), portrayed by Ivana Milicevic in *Casino Royale*. It is Valenka who gets the scare of her life when rebel leader Steven Obanno (Isaach De Bankolé) threatens to cut her hand off in Le Chiffre's Montenegro hotel suite. She later succeeds in poisoning James Bond (Daniel Craig) via his martini—although he's saved from certain death by a handy defibrillator and Vesper Lynd (Eva Green).

Van Nutter, Rik (May 1, 1929–October 15, 2005; birth name: Frederick Allen Nutter): Handsome, silver-haired American actor, briefly in feature films, who portrayed Felix Leiter in *Thunderball*. Van Nutter (pronounced "Van NOOT-er") was married to actress Anita Ekberg in the early 1960s, and it was through the couple's friendship with Bond producer Albert R. "Cubby" Broccoli and his wife, Dana, that Van Nutter was first considered for the role of Leiter.

He may have had only a brief career, but in addition to being the former husband of bombshell Anita Ekberg (Bond related, because she's on the billboard through which Krilencu crawls to his doom in *From Russia with Love*) Rik Van Nutter made a strong impression as CIA agent Felix Leiter in *Thunderball*. *Courtesy of the David Reinhardt Collection*

"We were having one of those immense Italian dinners in London with Cubby and Dana," recalled Van Nutter, "when Cubby suddenly came out and said that I looked just like Felix Leiter. Now, I had read all of the Bond books, and I knew that Felix had straw-colored hair, blue eyes, and long legs. So I fit the bill physically. I later met [*Thunderball* director] Terence Young, who tested me with some of the Bond girls. The tests worked out fine, and I made plans to travel to Nassau that spring of 1965." A native of Los Angeles, Van Nutter made his uncredited motion picture debut as Victor in the Italian horror comedy *Uncle Was a Vampire* (1959), which also featured future Bond player Christopher Lee as Baron Roderico da Frankurten.

Vanner, Sue: Stunning British blonde, briefly in films and television, who played the Log Cabin Girl who betrays 007 (Roger Moore) to the KGB in the pre-credits teaser of *The Spy Who Loved Me*. Vanner made her feature film debut alongside fellow Bond girl Angela Scoular as a hostage in director Stanley Long's crime comedy *Adventures of a Taxi Driver* (1976).

Curvaceous Sue Vanner played the Log Cabin Girl in the pre-credits teaser for *The Spy Who Loved Me*. *Courtesy of the Luc Leclech Collection*

Vargas: Lean, sullen SPECTRE henchman portrayed by Philip Locke in *Thunderball*. According to his boss, Emilio Largo (Adolfo Celi), Vargas is a passionless man who doesn't drink, doesn't smoke, and doesn't make love. What does Vargas do? He's a killer, pure and simple. Agent

Actor Philip Locke portrayed SPECTRE henchman Vargas in *Thunderball*, a laconic man whose only interest . . . is killing. Here, he's about to "get the point." *Courtesy of the David Reinhardt Collection*

007 (Sean Connery) disposes of him on Love Beach with a well-aimed shot from his CO_2 speargun.

Vatnajökull ice cap, Iceland: Location of a thrilling car chase between Bond (Pierce Brosnan) and Zao (Rick Yune) in *Die Another Day*. The specific setting was Jökulsárlón, an ice lagoon one thousand feet deep with wind chill that comes off the glacier at temperatures around minus ten degrees Celsius (fourteen degrees Fahrenheit). The key question for the production team was whether the ice could accommodate heavy sports cars like the Aston Martin V12 Vanquish and the Jaguar XKR. Fortunately, the weather continued to provide favorable conditions for the production—specifically, a foot-thick ice cap on the lagoon that was growing every day—which allowed action unit director Vic Armstrong to get started on the sequence two days earlier than expected. However, some sections of ice were deemed too thin to accommodate the chase, so the production was forced to complete the sequence back in England,

moving into a business park in Bourton-on-the-Water, Gloucestershire, and a former RAF airfield in nearby Upper Rissington.

Vaux-la-Vicomte: Real castle located outside Paris, which served as Hugo Drax's French estate transplanted to California in *Moonraker*.

Vavra: Fiery gypsy leader portrayed by Francis De Wolff in *From Russia with Love*. Bond (Sean Connery) saves his life when Bulgarian assassins attack the gypsy camp. For that effort, Vavra honors 007 by letting him know he now considers Bond to be his "son."

Venice: Site of the Venice International Grandmasters chess tournament between Kronsteen (Vladek Sheybal) and McAdams (Peter Madden) in *From Russia with Love*. It's also the ultimate destination for Bond (Sean Connery) and Tanya (Daniela Bianchi) when they leave Yugoslavia in a stolen motorboat later in the same film. In *Moonraker*, Venice is a principal location and the site of a spirited gondola chase that eventually turns into a ridiculous hovercraft ride. In *Casino Royale*, it's where James Bond (Daniel Craig) recuperates with Vesper Lynd (Eva Green) before he retrieves his considerable poker winnings. Unfortunately, Vesper betrays him, steals the money, and prepares to give it to Mr. White (Jesper Christensen) and his SPECTRE henchmen. Bond chases her down, fights a swarm of bad guys, and destroys a

James Bond (Roger Moore) takes a comical glide through Venice's St. Mark's Square in *Moonraker*—and brings the dignity and practicality of being a secret agent to a new low. *Courtesy of the David Reinhardt Collection*

canal-adjacent building in the process—a building in which a guilt-ridden Vesper is trapped in a sunken freight elevator, and prefers to let herself drown rather than accept the help of the man she betrayed.

Vernon, Richard (March 7, 1925–December 4, 1997): Scene-stealing British character actor who portrayed the very intelligent and distinguished Colonel Smithers of the Bank of England in *Goldfinger*. Smithers briefs 007 (Sean Connery) and M (Bernard Lee) on the activities of Auric Goldfinger (Gert Fröbe)—both legal and very illegal. A native of Reading, Berkshire, England, Vernon, who looked much older than his years (was he really only thirty-nine when he portrayed Smithers?), made his credited motion picture debut in director Henry Watt's crime drama *Four Desperate Men* (1959). The following year, he was Sir Edgar Hargraves in Wolf Rilla's iconic science fiction drama *Village of the Damned*.

British character actor Richard Vernon portrayed the stylish head of the Bank of England who turns to MI6 to nail the ultimate smuggler in *Goldfinger*. *Courtesy of the David Reinhardt Collection*

Very pistol: A miniature signaling device supplied to Bond (Sean Connery) by Q (Desmond Llewelyn) in *Thunderball*. Trapped in an underwater grotto, 007 uses the pistol to signal Felix Leiter (Rik Van Nutter) and a US Coast Guard rescue helicopter. The Very pistol, invented by an American naval officer, Edward Wilson Very (1847–1910), launches flares, or "Very lights," that became a common signaling device among US warships. Bond also uses a handy Very pistol to torch the pool of gasoline that devastates the flotilla of speedboats commanded by SPECTRE agent Morzeny (Walter Gotell) in *From Russia with Love*.

Verzasca Dam: Hydroelectric dam in Locarno, Ticino, Switzerland, where the *GoldenEye*

filmmakers shot exteriors of the Arkangel Chemical Weapons Facility, target of James Bond (Pierce Brosnan) and his colleague 006 (Sean Bean) in the pre-credits teaser. It was here that 007 made his astonishing bungee jump down the 720-foot face of the dam.

"Vesper": The password that Bond (Daniel Craig) inputs into the encrypted server of Basel Bank representative Mr. Mendes (Ludger Pistor) before the Texas hold'em tournament in *Casino Royale*. It's how he retrieves his winnings at the end of the tournament, which at the table totaled $115 million but is somehow raised to $120 million when Mendel comes calling. "Vesper" is also the name that Bond gives to a cocktail he orders during the tournament. Taken from Ian Fleming's novel, it consists of three parts gin (Gordon's is 007's choice), one part vodka, and half part of Lillet. The ingredients are shaken over ice until cold, then served in a cocktail glass with a slice of lemon peel for garnish. Practically the entire table at the poker game orders the drink, with Felix Leiter (Jeffrey Wright) requesting his without "the fruit."

VIEW TO A KILL, A

(United Artists, 1985) ★: The fourteenth James Bond film produced by Albert R. Broccoli. US release date: May 24, 1985. Budget: $30 million. Worldwide box office gross: $152.6 million (US domestic gross: $50.3 million; international gross: $102.3 million).* Running time: 131 minutes.

THE SETUP

Recovering the body of agent 003 in Siberia, James Bond (Roger Moore) finds a unique microchip, impervious to damage from electromagnetic pulses, which Q traces to a company called Zorin Industries. Bond, now teamed with agent Sir Godfrey Tibbett (Patrick Macnee) first meets the company's owner, Max Zorin (Christopher Walken), and his bodyguard, May Day (Grace Jones), at the elegant Ascot Racecourse in England, where the agents uncover Zorin's plot to enhance the

---

* "A View to a Kill (1985)," The Numbers, accessed July 17, 2020, https://www.the-numbers.com/movie/View-to-a-Kill-A.

performance of his racehorses via steroid-releasing implants. Bond also meets California state geologist Stacey Sutton (Tanya Roberts), to whom Zorin gives a $5 million check. Zorin turns out to be a genetically enhanced former KGB agent gone rogue, who intends to corner the world's supply of microchips by destroying California's Silicon Valley with a massive double earthquake.

BEHIND THE SCENES

Despite the fact that the previous two Bond films, *For Your Eyes Only* and *Octopussy*, had found success by returning to the *From Russia with Love* formula of putting intrigue ahead of bombastic adventure, in *A View to a Kill* the filmmakers decided once again to return to the *Goldfinger* model of outrageous fantasy. In many ways, *A View to a Kill* is a veritable remake of *Goldfinger*—but it fails in every way that film succeeded.

Max Zorin, like Auric Goldfinger, is out to to corner the world market on a valuable commodity—microchips instead of gold bullion. Instead of nuking Fort Knox, he'll destroy Silicon Valley with earthquakes. It's a logical plan as the schemes of Bond villains go, considering the valley's proximity to the very dangerous San Andreas Fault—but the film makes no effort to establish the larger threat. In *Goldfinger*, a simple explanation uttered by Bond underscored the danger to the free world if the US gold supply were irradiated for fifty-eight years. But no one ever explains how Zorin's monopoly on microchips threatens life as we know it. As a result, there's no reason for the audience to care about microchips, Silicon Valley, or the story.

A more interesting plotline is teased early in the film: the notion that Zorin has developed a microchip that is impervious to magnetic pulse damage. A villain who could wipe out every computer in England, including early-warning systems, while his own systems are protected, is a credible and chilling threat. But the idea, once raised, is never elaborated upon. (Interestingly, the con-

Director John Glen (right) goes over a scene with Grace Jones and Christopher Walken during production on *A View to a Kill*. *Courtesy of the Luc Leclech Collection*

cept of an electromagnetic weapon targeting England would be resurrected a decade later as the ultimate goal of the Janus crime syndicate in *GoldenEye*.) Similarly, the entire sequence filmed in France at Zorin's estate has nothing to do with the film's main plot, though it's delightful to see Patrick Macnee in a largely comedic role.

Christopher Walken, meanwhile, was the ideal person to play the maniacal genius Zorin, but the character itself is bland and poorly realized. The sequence in which he and his henchman Scarpine (Patrick Bauchau) casually machine-gun his own workers in the Main Strike Mine is a case of literal overkill. And yet *A View to a Kill* is also a Bond movie with very little action. The snow-surfing sequence in the pre-credits teaser is well made, but once again it's ruined by a goofy musical score—the Beach Boys and James Bond just don't mix. The raging-fire sequence in San Francisco City Hall, though suspenseful, just rehashes what audiences had already seen in the disaster movies of the previous decade (e.g., *The Towering Inferno*). And the nutty fire-truck chase through San Francisco belongs in a *Ghostbusters* movie, not a Bond film. The action in the Main Strike Mine is fantastic, and includes some excellent production design work from Peter Lamont. But didn't Steven Spielberg cover the same ground in *Indiana Jones and the Temple of Doom* a year earlier?

A View to a Kill is also a surprisingly tame entry in the series romantically, perhaps presaging the safe-sex Bond films of the late 1980s. The only titillation comes from a brief liaison between Bond and KGB agent Pola Ivanova (Fiona Fullerton) in a hot tub. On the other hand, Tanya Roberts, a beautiful, sexy, and very photogenic actress, spends most of the film in conservatively cut formal dresses and coveralls—quite the miscalculation.

The few high points include the Main Strike Mine action—the best part of the film—and John Barry's score, which is reminiscent of *Goldfinger* and repeats instrumental elements of the catchy Duran Duran title song at key moments.

THE CAST

James Bond	Roger Moore
Max Zorin	Christopher Walken
Stacey Sutton	Tanya Roberts
May Day	Grace Jones
Sir Godfrey Tibbett	Patrick Macnee
Scarpine	Patrick Bauchau
Chuck Lee	David Yip
Pola Ivanova	Fiona Fullerton
Bob Conley	Manning Redwood
Jenny Flex	Alison Doody
Dr. Carl Mortner	Willoughby Gray
Q	Desmond Llewelyn
M	Robert Brown
Miss Moneypenny	Lois Maxwell
General Gogol	Walter Gotell
Minister of Defence	Geoffrey Keen
Achille Aubergine	Jean Rougerie
W. G. Howe	Daniel Benzali
Klotkoff	Bogdan Kominowski
Pan Ho	Papillon Soo Soo
Kimberley Jones	Mary Stavin
Butterfly Act Compere	Dominique Risbourg
Whistling Girl	Carole Ashby
Taiwanese Tycoon	Anthony Chin
Paris Taxi Driver	Lucien Jerome
US Police Captain	Joe Flood
The Auctioneer	Gérard Bühr
Venz	Dolph Lundgren
Mine Foreman	Tony Sibbald
O'Rourke	Bill Ackridge

THE CREW

Director	John Glen
Screenplay by	Richard Maibaum
	Michael G. Wilson
Producers	Albert R. Broccoli
	Michael G. Wilson
Associate Producer	Tom Pevsner
Director of Photography	Alan Hume
Music by	John Barry
Title song performed by	Duran Duran
Production Designer	Peter Lamont
Art Director	John Fenner
Construction Manager	Michael Redding
Set Decorator	Crispian Sallis
Costume Designer	Emma Porteous
Production Supervisor	Anthony Waye
Production Managers	Philip Kohler
	Serge Touboul
	Ned Kopp & Company
	Leonhard Gmür
	Jon Thor Hannesson
Assistant Director	Gerry Gavigan
Second Unit Direction and Photography	Arthur Wooster
Ski Sequence Director and Photographer	Willy Bogner Jr.
Camera Operator	Michael Frift
Casting by	Debbie McWilliams
Action sequences arranged by	Martin Grace
Driving stunts arranged by	Remy Julienne
Title Designer	Maurice Binder
Special Effects Supervisor	John Richardson
Sound Editor	Colin Miller
Editor	Peter Davies

Vijay: Amiable British Secret Service agent based in Udaipur, India, portrayed by professional tennis player Vijay Amritraj in *Octopussy*. Vijay is posing as a snake charmer when he meets Bond (Roger Moore) in an Udaipur street market. He gets Bond's attention with his rendition of the James Bond theme—perfect for the Roger Moore era of 007 films. Vijay actually hates snakes and prefers his other, more natural cover as a tennis pro at the resort club of exiled Afghan prince Kamal Khan (Louis Jourdan). His mean backhand comes in handy when Khan's henchman Gobinda (Kabir Bedi) and his men attack Bond's scooter in the streets of Udaipur. When 007 infiltrates the island home of Octopussy (Maud Adams) in the middle of Lake Pichola, Vijay stays behind on the mainland to keep watch. Unfortunately, he's jumped by local thugs and killed by the man with the horrifying buzz-saw yo-yo.

VILLAINS AND HENCHMEN

A deadly rogues' gallery has always been a 007 series hallmark.
Bond's enemies include the following:

Film	Name	Manner of Death
Casino Royale (TV)	Le Chiffre	Shot
Dr. No	Dr. No	Drowned
	Professor Dent	Shot
	Mr. Jones	Suicide
	Miss Taro	*Arrested*
	Three Blind Mice	Drive off a cliff
From Russia with Love	Rosa Klebb	Shot
	Grant	Strangled
	Kronsteen	Stabbed
	Morzeny	Blown up
	Krilencu	Shot
Goldfinger	Goldfinger	Blown out a window
	Oddjob	Electrocuted
	Mr. Solo	Shot and crushed
	Mr. Ling	Shot
	Kisch	Thrown to his death
Thunderball	Emilio Largo	Speared
	Fiona Volpe	Shot
	Vargas	Speared
	Angelo	Drowned
	Count Lippe	Blown up
	Quist	Eaten by sharks
You Only Live Twice	Blofeld	?
	Mr. Osato	Shot
	Helga Brandt	Eaten by piranhas
On Her Majesty's Secret Service	Blofeld	*Survives*
	Irma Bunt	*Survives*
	Grunther	Impaled
Diamonds Are Forever	Blofeld	?
	Mr. Wint	Blown up
	Mr. Kidd	Set on fire
	Bert Saxby	Shot
	Bambi and Thumper	?
Live and Let Die	Kananga	Blown up
	Rosie Carver	Shot
	Baron Samedi	*Survives*
	Tee Hee	Thrown out a train window
	Whisper	?
The Man with the Golden Gun	Scaramanga	Shot
	Nick Nack	*Captured*
	Hai Fat	Shot
The Spy Who Loved Me	Stromberg	Shot
	Jaws	*Survives*
	Sandor	Pushed off a building
	Naomi	Blown up
Moonraker	Drax	Tossed into outer space
	Jaws	*Survives*
	Chang	Tossed off a building
For Your Eyes Only	Kristatos	Knifed

Film	Name	Manner of Death
	Locque	Pushed off a cliff in his car
	Kriegler	Tossed out a window
	Gonzales	Speared
Octopussy	Kamal Khan	Plane crash
	Gobinda	Falls to his death
	Orlov	Shot
	Mischka	Crushed
	Grischka	Knifed
Never Say Never Again	Maximilian Largo	Speared
	Fatima Blush	Blown up
	Lippe	Impaled
A View to a Kill	Max Zorin	Falls to his death
	May Day	Blown up
	Scarpine	Blown up
	Carl Mortner	Blown up
The Living Daylights	Brad Whitaker	Crushed
	General Koskov	*Captured*
	Necros	Falls to his death
Licence to Kill	Sanchez	Immolated
	Milton Krest	Blown up
	Heller	Impaled
	Joe Butcher	*Survives*
	Dario	Shredded
GoldenEye	Alec Trevelyan	Blown up
	Xenia Onatopp	Crushed
	Ourumov	Shot
	Grishenko	Flash frozen
Tomorrow Never Dies	Elliot Carver	Drilled
	Stamper	Blown up
	Dr. Kaufman	Shot
	Henry Gupta	Shot
The World Is Not Enough	Renard	Impaled
	Elektra King	Shot
	Julietta	Blown up
Die Another Day	Gustav Graves	Shredded
	Zao	Impaled
	Miranda Frost	Stabbed
Casino Royale	Le Chiffre	Shot
	Vesper Lynd	Drowned
	Mr. White	*Survives*
	Mollaka	Shot
	Obanno	Strangled
	Carlos	Blown up
	Dimitrios	Stabbed
Quantum of Solace	Dominic Greene	Shot
	General Medrano	Shot
	Mr. White	*Survives*
	Yusef Kabira	*Arrested*
	Guy Haines	?
Skyfall	Raoul Silva	Stabbed
	Patrice	Falls to his death
Spectre	Blofeld	*Survives*
	Marco Sciarra	Falls to his death
	Mr. White	Suicide
	Hinx	Falls off train
	C	Falls to his death

Villechaize, Hervé (April 23, 1943–September 4, 1993): Three-foot-eleven French character actor who portrayed Nick Nack, clever and colorful servant to Scaramanga (Christopher Lee), in *The Man with the Golden Gun*. Villechaize is best known as Tattoo, Ricardo Montalban's partner on the popular US television series *Fantasy Island* (126 episodes, 1977–1983). A native of Paris, Villechaize was a fine artist in France when he decided to give show business a shot. He made his credited motion picture debut as Beppo in director James Goldstone's crime comedy *The Gang That Couldn't Shoot Straight* (1971). Sadly, he died by suicide in September 1993.

French actor Hervé Villechaize finds himself in good company on *The Man with the Golden Gun*. *Courtesy of the David Reinhardt Collection*

Villefranche-sur-Mer: City on the French Riviera whose narrow streets played host to the motor-cycle stunts in *Never Say Never Again*.

Virus Omega: A deadly germ-warfare agent that Ernst Stavro Blofeld (Telly Savalas) plans to spread in *On Her Majesty's Secret Service*. Omega creates total infertility in plants and animals and can destroy whole strains forever across entire continents in what Bond (George Lazenby) calls "epidemics of sterility." The virus will be spread by Blofeld's Angels of Death, a group of lovely allergy patients from all over the globe, who are unwittingly given atomizers filled with the virus as Christmas presents. Equipped with long-range radio transmitters and brain-washed to respond to a prearranged signal from Blofeld, the girls are programmed to destroy the agricultural and animal productivity of the entire world unless Blofeld gets his price: a full pardon for his past crimes and official acceptance of his claim to the title of Count de Bleuchamp.

vodka martini, dirty: Drink of choice for Dr. Madeleine Swann (Léa Seydoux) on the train to the base of operations of Ernst Stavro Blofeld (Christoph Waltz) in *Spectre*.

volcano rocket base: Fortress of Ernst Stavro Blofeld (Donald Pleasence) in *You Only Live Twice*. Hidden inside the cone of an extinct Japanese volcano, it harbors the formidable *Intruder* rocket that is systematically robbing the US and Soviet space programs of their manned space capsules. Its features include not only the rocket-firing platform but also a heliport; a steel curtain that covers the entire cone of the volcano and is camouflaged as a crater lake from the outside; a monorail that transports per-sonnel and equipment throughout the complex; numerous elevators and cranes; and a labyrinth of stairways and catwalks that ring the fortress.

The film's production designer, Ken Adam, designed and built the base as a full-size set on the Pinewood Studios lot at a cost of $1 million. Remembered Adam, "It was the first time that I had to build something that big. One of the problems on the Bond films is that if these big sets were written completely into the original screenplays, we could probably get away with building part of the sets full-size and faking the rest with models and matte paintings. But since we know only at the time of construction that the big finale or the big shoot-out takes place in the set, and nothing else, I've got to go for full size. We then work out the action as we go along. On *You Only Live Twice*, I designed the volcano rocket base and then [director] Lewis Gilbert and

Production designer Ken Adam's ultimate set: the marvelously functional volcano rocket base in *You Only Live Twice*. *Courtesy of the David Reinhardt Collection*

[screenwriter] Roald Dahl came along and helped plan the actual movements within the set.

"Since, by the time we made *You Only Live Twice*, we had a liberal budget for the set, our main problem was logistics. You can't afford to make any mistakes on a set of this size, especially when you're using an enormous amount of structural steel. You have to consult with structural engineers, who calculate your stress factors. And you can't keep changing your mind like you often do on an interior set. We had to create accurate models, and these had to be followed to a T. And when you work with steel, it has to be ordered three months ahead of time."*

In January 1967, the *Los Angeles Times* published a few of the project's more interesting statistics. In constructing the volcano rocket base at Pinewood, Adam's team used 200 miles of tubular steel, more than 700 tons of structural steel, 200 tons of plasterwork, 8,000 railway ties for the set's working monorail, and more than 250,000 square yards of canvas to protect the set from the elements. Two hundred and fifty men worked on the project, and on May 11, 1966, the first of the steel foundations was completed. The finished set was visible from the main London-Oxford highway some three miles away.*

"Such a set," said Adam, "represents both a dream and a nightmare in moviemaking. The nightmare comes from suddenly realizing that you have designed something that has never been done before in films, and that it is bigger than any set ever used before. Many times I woke up in the middle of the night wondering whether the whole thing would work. Sometimes the best possible construction engineers can't solve your problems. They may be qualified to build an Empire State Building or an Eiffel Tower—buildings that follow normal construction techniques—but we had to construct a set for which there were no precedents.

"But this type of set is also a designer's dream. To be given the mandate to plan such a complicated structure is a challenge no artist could resist. And seeing your drawings and ideas taking shape and becoming reality in steel, concrete, and plaster is like watching your own child grow into Superman."†

Adam, a veteran of many films in the Bond series, would go on to design the equally enormous supertanker interior—the so-called "Jonah Set"—for *The Spy Who Loved Me*.

Volpe, Fiona: Voluptuous, redheaded SPECTRE assassin portrayed by Luciana Paluzzi in *Thunderball*. She's a key figure in the organization's "NATO project." Using her feminine charms, Volpe seduces handsome NATO aerial observer François Derval (Paul Stassino), then arranges for him to be murdered by a mercenary

---

* Ken Adam, interview by the author, London, June 17, 1977.

* "007's Rocket Pad Out of This World," *Los Angeles Times*, January 15, 1967.
† Adam, interview by the author.

named Angelo Palazzi, who's been surgically altered to serve as Derval's exact duplicate.

After the replacement Derval hijacks a NATO bomber with nuclear bombs on board, Volpe's associate Count Lippe (Guy Doleman), who is keeping the real officer's body at the Shrublands health clinic, attempts to kill James Bond (Sean Connery), who also happens to be at Shrublands. For jeopardizing the mission with his personal vendetta, Fiona assassinates him with a rocket from her motorcycle. She then joins SPECTRE spymaster Emilio Largo (Adolfo Celi) in Nassau, Bahamas, where she meets Bond on the highway one night after his underwater investigation in the harbor. Giving him a ride to his hotel in her Mustang, Fiona tries to intimidate him by driving at high speed, but it doesn't work.

After kidnapping Bond's assistant Paula Caplan (Martine Beswick), who later poisons herself rather than submitting, Fiona steals into 007's hotel room during Nassau's Junkanoo celebration. Bond finds her relaxing in his bathtub. When she asks for "something to put on," he hands her some shoes. After their lovemaking, Fiona's SPECTRE goons arrive to take Bond away, but he later escapes into the crowd during the height of the Junkanoo parade.

When Bond is wounded by one of her assistants, Fiona follows 007's trail of blood to the Kiss Kiss Club, where she asks him for a dance. While in her arms, 007 sees an assassin lurking in the shadows and whirls Fiona around at the last moment. She gets a fatal bullet in the back.

Actress Luciana Paluzzi's portrayal of voluptuous SPECTRE assassin Fiona Volpe was a definite highpoint of *Thunderball*; she's seen here wrestling with Bond (Sean Connery) in his hotel bedroom in Nassau. *Courtesy of the David Reinhardt Collection*

In the *Thunderball* remake *Never Say Never Again*, Fiona's lethal charm is inherited by the luscious Fatima Blush (Barbara Carrera).

von Sydow, Max (April 10, 1929–March 8, 2020) Two-time Academy Award–nominated Swedish character actor, a former member of Ingmar Bergman's acting company, who portrayed Ernst Stavro Blofeld in *Never Say Never Again*. More a cameo part than an essential role in the film, von Sydow's Blofeld is an exquisitely mannered, bearded aristocrat type who presents SPECTRE's typical blackmail demands in return for the stolen NATO cruise missiles. A native of Lund, Skåne, Sweden, von Sydow made his motion picture debut in his native country as Nils in director Alf Sjöberg's drama *Only a Mother* (1949). His first film for director Ingmar Bergman was *The Seventh Seal* (1957), in which he played Antonius Block. Von Sydow's English-language debut was *The Greatest Story Ever Told* (1965), playing Jesus Christ. Von Sydow was also in two terrific spy films: *The Quiller Memorandum* (1966), as a neo-Nazi named Oktober (the film also featured a classic score from 007 composer John Barry), and *Three Days of the Condor* (1975), as freelance assassin Joubert opposite Robert Redford. Von Sydow received his Academy Award nominations for Best Actor in *Pelle the Conqueror* (1987) and Best Supporting Actor in *Extremely Loud & Incredibly Close* (2011).

Vulcan: Type of English jet bomber hijacked by SPECTRE mercenary Angelo Palazzi (Paul Stassino) during a NATO training flight in *Thunderball*. Cruising at 45,000 feet, with an identification code of RAFJET MBX-79, the plane has two MOS-type atomic bombs on board.

A Vulcan bomber with A-bombs onboard is hijacked by SPECTRE in *Thunderball*. *Steve Rubin Collection*

Wade, Jack: The '90s equivalent of Felix Leiter, he's a CIA agent portrayed comically by Joe Don Baker, introduced in *GoldenEye*. Interestingly, Baker debuted as a villain in the Bond series, playing arms trader Brad Whitaker in *The Living Daylights*. He returns briefly as Wade in *Tomorrow Never Dies*.

Wade, Kevin (March 9, 1954–   ): American playwright and screenwriter who contributed heavily to *GoldenEye*. Unfortunately, he received no credit on the final film. Wade first came to prominence in 1980 with his play *Key Exchange*, which was later adapted as a movie for 20th Century Fox. Wade is better known for his screenwriting work on the films *Working Girl* (1988), *True Colors* (1991), *Mr. Baseball* (1992), and *Junior* (1994). He first met Bond producer Barbara Broccoli in 1990 and attended her wedding to producer Fred Zollo. In August 1994, he was hired to do a rewrite on *GoldenEye*.

Wade was sent to London, and for five weeks—seven days a week—he worked on the script while holed up in the Eon Productions office in Piccadilly Circus (next to the Hard Rock Café). Wade was asked to work on the character of James Bond, who in the previous drafts of the script was more reactive than active. "I went to the bookshelf at Eon," says Wade, "and picked up three of the original Fleming novels. I would work from eight to six every day, and then I'd go home and read the books. It helped a lot. James Bond is a fatalistic action hero, and we wanted to give him the edge that Connery once presented when he did Bond. I had to make sure that Pierce Brosnan's Bond was a direct descendant of Connery's. When you read the Fleming novels, you see that Bond is always getting the crap beat out of him. He's a real character, not a comic book hero,

but unless you center the action around him, he becomes a mechanic."*

Wade also streamlined the plot of the film. A long interlude in a St. Petersburg weapons bazaar was reduced to a single scene. Wade, appropriately, also gave his surname to Bond's CIA contact in Russia, Jack Wade. Since he had pressing screenwriting duties with producer/director Ivan Reitman on the comedy *Junior*, Wade was unable to finish his work. Bruce Feirstein took over the rewrite.

Wade, Robert (1962–   ): See "Purvis, Neal."

Wakabayashi, Akiko (August 26, 1941–   ): Charming Japanese actress who portrayed Aki, a Japanese Secret Service agent in *You Only Live Twice* who is poisoned by SPECTRE. A Tokyo native, Wakabayashi made her motion picture debut in director Ishirô Honda's *Song for a Bride* (1958). *You Only Live Twice* was her English-language film debut.

Actress Akiko Wakabayashi poses in front of her character's Toyota 2000GT sports car during a break in the shooting on *You Only Live Twice*. *Courtesy of the David Reinhardt Collection*

Walken, Christopher (March 31, 1943–   ): Academy Award–winning American actor who portrayed psychotic industrialist Max Zorin in *A View to a Kill*. Walken, who has made a career out of playing quirky, often insane characters (he won a Best Supporting Actor Oscar for his Russian-roulette-playing Vietnam veteran in *The Deer Hunter*), was perfectly cast as Zorin, the

---

* Kevin Wade, telephone interview by the author, June 17, 1995.

Versatile American actor Christopher Walken took on the role of psychotic Max Zorin, a genetically engineered supergenius in *A View to a Kill. Courtesy of the David Reinhardt Collection*

product of an abortive Nazi steroid experiment to enhance intelligence in newborns. Walken had his hair bleached to portray the blond East German KGB operative turned French industrialist, who was created very much in the image of Auric Goldfinger—only with an interest in monopolizing the microchip market rather than gold.

Born in Astoria, Queens, Walken made his big-screen feature debut in director Michel Auder's comedy *Cleopatra* (1970). Film audiences discovered him as Diane Keaton's troubled brother Duane in Woody Allen's *Annie Hall* (1977). That led directly to Walken's stunning performance in *The Deer Hunter* (1978), which won the Best Picture Oscar that year and catapulted all its stars into the big leagues. His additional film credits include *Heaven's Gate* (1980); *Brainstorm* (1983); *The Dead Zone* (1983); *The Milagro Beanfield War* (1988); *Batman Returns* (1992); *True Romance* (1993), featuring his classic verbal mano a mano with Dennis Hopper; *Catch Me If You Can* (2002), which earned him another Oscar nomination for Best Supporting Actor; *Wedding Crashers* (2005); *Hairspray* (2007); and *Jersey Boys* (2014).

Wallis, Wing Commander Kenneth H. (April 26, 1916–September 1, 2013): Former Royal Air Force officer who designed, built, and flew Little Nellie, the autogyro that James Bond (Sean Connery) flies in *You Only Live Twice*. A native of Ely, Cambridgeshire, England, who served as a bomber pilot in World War II, Wallis reached the rank of wing commander and was later appointed a member of the Most Excellent Order of the British Empire.

Walther PPK: Semiautomatic pistol that is famously James Bond's weapon of choice in the 007 film series. In *Dr. No*, Bond (Sean Connery) originally prefers his Beretta 418, but MI6 armorer Major Boothroyd (Peter Burton) recommends the 7.65mm PPK for its superior stopping power. After M (Bernard Lee) orders Bond to make the switch, 007 quickly takes to the Walther, and continues to wield it through nearly all of his subsequent adventures.

In the Pierce Brosnan era, Bond trades his PPK for a Walther P99, a 9mm semiautomatic handgun that carries a fifteen-round magazine. He originally picks it up in the apartment of Colonel Wai Lin (Michelle Yeoh) in *Tomorrow Never Dies*, and hangs on to it through the rest of the film as well as the two that follow, *The World Is Not Enough*, and *Die Another Day*. The classic PPK returns to service in the Daniel Craig films.

Waltz, Christoph (October 4, 1956–   ): Two-time Academy Award–winning Austrian character actor who was given the plum role of Franz Oberhauser, a.k.a. Ernst Stavro Blofeld, vengeful supervillain and foster brother of James Bond (Daniel Craig) in *Spectre* and *No Time to Die*. A native of Vienna, Waltz made his uncredited motion picture debut as a paramedic in director Andrew V. McLaglen's World War II drama *Breakthrough* (1979), which also featured Bond veteran Curt Jurgens. After many years of toiling mostly on German and Austrian television, Waltz stepped into the big time when he met director Quentin Tarantino, who cast him as SS colonel Hans Landa in *Inglourious Basterds* (2009) and, two years later, as bounty hunter King Schultz

In a scene reminiscent of *Silence of the Lambs*, James Bond (Daniel Craig) comes to visit his foster brother Ernst Stavro Blofeld (Christoph Waltz) in a British prison in *No Time to Die*. *Courtesy of United Artists Releasing*

in *Django Unchained* (2012). Both roles netted Waltz Best Supporting Actor Oscars.

Warmflash, Dr. Molly: British Secret Service medical officer, portrayed by Serena Scott Thomas, who attends to James Bond (Pierce Brosnan) in *The World Is Not Enough*. Unlike the Brosnan era's Miss Moneypenny (Samantha Bond), who's more realistic about 007's romantic loyalties than her predecessors in the role, Warmflash has a real thing for 007. When he needs to be cleared for action after he separates his collarbone chasing Julietta the Cigar Girl (Maria Grazia Cucinotta), Dr. Warmflash is agreeable, provided they spend a little quality time together beforehand.

Waterloo: Historic land battle that ended the Napoleonic Wars, a miniature recreation of which is the final resting place for arms dealer and military history buff Brad Whitaker (Joe Don Baker) in *The Living Daylights*. He ends up pinned to the diorama after Bond (Timothy Dalton) sets off an explosion, toppling a heavy bust of Napoleon's enemy Lord Wellington into him.

Wavekrest: Marine research vessel, 155 feet long, owned by drug runner Milton Krest (Anthony Zerbe) in *Licence to Kill*. Like the *Disco Volante* in *Thunderball*, the *Wavekrest* is the

base of operations for a number of the villain's illegal underwater smuggling activities. Both a two-person minisub and the *Sentinel* remote-control underwater transport are housed inside the *Wavekrest*.

Wayborn, Kristina (September 24, 1950– ; birth name: Britt-Inger Johansson): Swedish beauty who portrayed Magda, the circus performer, pickpocket, and girl Friday to Kamal Khan (Louis Jourdan) in *Octopussy*. According to Graham Rye in his book *The James Bond Girls*, Wayborn was born on a small island in the Baltic Sea, where she was a Swedish track champion. Prior to her movie career, she led an adventurous life as a race car driver, jockey, horse and animal trainer,

Kristina Wayborn played the not entirely unsympathetic Magda, girl Friday to villain Kamal Khan in *Octopussy*. *Steve Rubin Collection*

and clothes designer.* Her acting break came when producer David Wolper chose her to play the young Greta Garbo in "The Silent Lovers," a segment of his 1980 miniseries *Moviola*.

"We Have All the Time in the World": Wonderful ballad sung by Louis Armstrong in *On Her Majesty's Secret Service*. Although it should have been the opening theme, producers Albert R. Broccoli and Harry Saltzman opted for a faster-paced instrumental piece from John Barry instead. Instrumental opening themes are uncommon in the series, having been featured in only three films: *Dr. No* (the end of which features the Byron Lee vocal tune "Three Blind Mice"), *From Russia with Love* (Matt Monro's title vocal was featured at the end of the film), and *On Her Majesty's Secret Service*.

weapons-grade plutonium: What Renard (Robert Carlyle) steals from a decommissioned Russian nuclear silo in *The World Is Not Enough*. He plans to fashion a plutonium rod that will be inserted into the reactor of a commandeered Russian submarine, causing a meltdown in the Bosphorus. The result: Istanbul will be destroyed and the Bosphorus will be closed to tanker traffic for decades, enabling him to make billions off his partner in crime—Elektra King—and her strategically placed oil pipeline.

WEBS: Fictional radio station serving Miami Beach, Florida, that is heard during the tryst between Bond (Sean Connery) and Jill Masterson (Shirley Eaton) in *Goldfinger*. According to its news report, "the president said he was entirely satisfied."

Wet Nellie: Nickname given to the Lotus Esprit submarine car in *The Spy Who Loved Me*. It was a reference to Little Nellie, the autogyro from *You Only Live Twice*.

---

* Graham Rye, *The James Bond Girls* (Secaucus, NJ: Citadel, 2000), 51.

Whishaw, Ben (October 14, 1980–): Respected British actor of stage, screen, and television who made his debut as a decidedly youthful Q in *Skyfall*, a role he reprised in both *Spectre* and *No Time to Die*. Born in Clifton, Bedfordshire, England, Whishaw studied at the Royal Academy of Dramatic Art and, six months after graduation in 2004 at the age of twenty-three, won the coveted role of Hamlet in Trevor Nunn's modern-dress production at the Old Vic in London. His acclaimed performance was just the beginning for the young thespian, who was being touted as one of the brightest of Britain's new generation of actors—an esteem that won him increasingly important roles in films and television shows. Whishaw had earlier made his feature film debut as Private James Deamis in writer/director William Boyd's taut World War I drama *The Trench* (1999), a film that starred Daniel Craig. He later won a role in *Layer Cake* (2004), another Daniel Craig starrer, and found himself in even more star-studded company as multiple characters in *Cloud Atlas* (2012), alongside such performers as Tom Hanks, Hugh Grant, and Bond veteran Halle Berry. He portrayed the young novelist Herman Melville in director Ron Howard's *In the Heart of the Sea* (2015) and Michael Banks in *Mary Poppins Returns* (2018).

One of the ways the James Bond films have stayed relevant over the years is through the

The Lotus submarine car, a.k.a. Wet Nellie, goes into action against enemy frogmen in *The Spy Who Loved Me*. *Courtesy of the Michael VanBlaricum Collection*

Ben Whishaw brings super intelligence to the role of Q in the Bond series. *Courtesy of the Anders Frejdh Collection*

ever-advancing technological wizardry of Q Branch. Whishaw is the youngest actor to play the role of Q, and he represents a next-generation equipment officer whose mind is alert, computer-centric, and ready to engage in the latest form of techno-espionage at a moment's notice. He admitted to the *London Daily Telegraph* that it was intimidating to step into the role after Desmond Llewelyn and John Cleese had given such iconic performances, but that he took lessons from his Shakespearean work on the need to detach from what's come before. "You can't just start from scratch," he explained. "You have to tick the boxes that people want ticked. Q has to be a bit snippy, tetchy and exasperated by Bond. But I felt very strongly from the script that this Q had to be something different from the past."

Whishaw understood that by casting someone of his his age in the role, the producers were aiming for a different dynamic with 007 (Daniel Craig). "In the past, Q would be rummaging around in some huge suitcase. He was brilliant, but ramshackle. This Q is definitely slicker. He's a

Zen character who likes everything to be simple and refined. He's pretty sharp, and Bond respects that."[*] And unlike the long-suffering, acerbic Q portrayed by Desmond Llewelyn, Whishaw's Q sees Bond as a mentor and friend.

Given all the techno-speak he is asked to recite for the role, it's surprising to learn that Whishaw confessed to not even owning a computer. "It was such fun for me to play an expert in an area where I'm completely not an expert," he explained. "I'm really hopeless with technology."[†] He also enjoyed, he said in another interview, "the excitement that it generates in people. Nothing else I've done has generated that much anticipation. And it's really been lovely because it's unusual to return to work with the same group of people on a different film."[‡]

---

[*] James Rampton, "Ben Whishaw on Playing Q in *Skyfall*," *London Daily Telegraph*, October 26, 2012.
[†] Ibid.
[‡] Gerard Gilbert, "Ben Whishaw Interview: *Spectre* Actor Talks Q, Avoiding Press Harassment and Freddie Mercury Biopic," *Independent*, October 23, 2015.

Whitaker, Brad: Smug international arms dealer and military history buff portrayed by Joe Don Baker in *The Living Daylights*. He joins forces with renegade Russian general Georgi Koskov (Jeroen Krabbé) to perpetrate a huge opium-for-diamonds deal. Based in Tangier, Whitaker lives in a mansion housing a virtual museum of wax military figures (Hitler, Napoleon, Attila, Caesar), toy-soldier dioramas, and ancient weaponry. It also hides a devil's cache of the newest weapons, all displayed in drawers operated electronically by a series of remote controls. Whitaker considers himself a brilliant military mind, but he's actually a pathetic little weasel who was thrown out of West Point for cheating.

Whitaker has made a huge arms deal with the Russians, who have given him a $50 million advance. However, instead of delivering the weapons in quantity to the Soviet Union, Whitaker and General Koskov have taken the advance and converted it into diamonds, which they use to purchase a huge heroin shipment from the Snow Leopard Brotherhood of Afghanistan. To conceal their treachery, the partners convince British intelligence that KGB chief General Leonid Pushkin (John Rhys-Davies) is behind a rash of killings that have targeted British agents. They plant the supposed evidence—the words "Smiert Spionam," Russian for "Death to Spies"—on or near the bodies of the dead agents.

White, Jack (July 9, 1975–   ): American singer-songwriter and actor who, with Alicia Keys, sang "Another Way to Die," the opening-titles song to *Quantum of Solace*. A native of Detroit, White has won twelve Grammys, including four for his alternative rock duo (with ex-wife Meg White) the White Stripes. White made his credited acting debut as Jack in the segment "Jack Shows Meg His Tesla Coil" from director Jim Jarmusch's anthology film *Coffee and*

Singer Jack White duetted with Alicia Keys on the opening-titles song to *Quantum of Solace*. *Courtesy of Endeavor*

Cigarettes (2003), which also featured future Bond player Isaach De Bankolé.

White, Mr.: Mysterious SPECTRE operative portrayed by Jesper Christensen in *Casino Royale*, *Quantum of Solace*, and *Spectre*. It is White who introduces Le Chiffre (Mads Mikkelsen) to African rebel leader Steven Obanno (Isaach De Bankolé), assuring the latter that Le Chiffre is an investment genius. When Le Chiffre blows Obanno's money in a stock scheme and a losing poker tournament against Bond (Daniel Craig), it is White who terminates his contract.

Jesper Christensen portrays mysterious SPECTRE agent Mr. White, who is captured temporarily by James Bond in *Quantum of Solace. Courtesy of the Anders Frejdh Collection*

White later recovers Bond's winnings in Venice, thanks to the coerced cooperation of Bond's colleague and lover Vesper Lynd (Eva Green). After Vesper commits suicide at the bottom of a Venetian canal, a vengeful Bond (Daniel Craig) tracks White to his Italian estate and shoots him.

The story picks up here in *Quantum of Solace*, as Bond throws White into the trunk of his Aston Martin and takes him to an MI6 safe house in Siena, Italy. But his interrogation by M (Dame Judi Dench) is interrupted by treacherous MI6 agent Craig Mitchell (Glenn Foster), allowing their prisoner to escape. In investigating the betrayal, Bond learns that Mr. White is a member of a mysterious international crime syndicate known as Quantum.

White's mystery deepens in *Spectre*, in which Bond discovers that Quantum is just one arm of an even more devious criminal organization called SPECTRE. Infiltrating a SPECTRE conclave in Rome, 007 learns that syndicate head Franz Oberhauser (Christoph Waltz) plans to assassinate White, whom he refers to as the Pale King. Getting a jump on the competition, 007 tracks White to a mountain lodge in Altaussee, Austria, where White is dying of thallium poisoning. Bond gives his enemy the opportunity to take his own life—shades of Bond's offer to Major Dexter Smythe, father of the title character (Maud

Adams) in *Octopussy*. Before he shoots himself with his own gun, White asks Bond to protect his daughter, psychiatrist Dr. Madeleine Swann (Léa Seydoux), who will have information on how to track down Oberhauser of SPECTRE—a.k.a. Ernst Stavro Blofeld.

white cat: Pet of SPECTRE chief Ernst Stavro Blofeld throughout the James Bond series. Introduced in *From Russia with Love*, the animal sits on the lap of Blofeld, whose face we never see. (Anthony Dawson was the actor; Eric Pohlmann provided the voice.) After explaining to Colonel Rosa Klebb (Lotte Lenya) the analogy of the Siamese fighting fish, Blofeld hands one of the dead fish to the cat, who chews it gratefully. The cat returns in *Thunderball*, once again sitting on the lap of the man whose face we never see. (Eric Pohlmann provided the voice again.)

When Donald Pleasence becomes the first on-screen Blofeld in *You Only Live Twice*, he had his cat, as did Telly Savalas in *On Her Majesty's Secret Service*. In *Diamonds Are Forever*, since plastic surgery has created multiple Blofelds (all played by Charles Gray), Bond (Sean Connery) attempts to use the cat to identify the real one. He frightens the creature into fleeing toward its master, then kills that Blofeld—only to discover that there are multiple white cats as well. "Right idea," the real Blofeld says, to which Bond responds, "But wrong pussy."

After a legal dispute with *Thunderball* producer Kevin McClory forced Albert R. Broccoli to remove Blofeld from the Eon Productions 007 series, the white cat disappeared as well—only to make one more appearance in *For Your Eyes Only* to help viewers identify a familiar-looking villain who carefully goes unnamed. After Bond (Roger Moore) dumps the Blofeld lookalike into a smokestack, it fell to McClory and his new producing partner Jack Schwartzman to bring back the white cat in their renegade Bond production *Never Say Never Again*. In that film, the cat sits on the lap of Max von Sydow, the last actor to portray the head of SPECTRE in the twentieth century. Three decades later, with the legal dispute finally resolved, Christoph Waltz took on the role of Blofeld in *Spectre*—and acquired the appropriate white cat.

Whittingham, Jack (August 2, 1910–July 3, 1972): British screenwriter who in 1959 collaborated with producer Kevin McClory and author Ian Fleming on an abortive James Bond film project. When the project fell apart and Fleming published the novel *Thunderball* based on their work without permission, Whittingham joined McClory in a major lawsuit against Fleming, which they won in 1963.

The project began with a story memorandum by Fleming's friend Ernest Cuneo, dated May 28, 1959, which outlined a Russian A-bomb hijacking caper. Fleming then wrote a treatment that changed the principal villain to the Mafia, which breaks into a US atomic base in England, steals a bomb, and transfers it from a helicopter to a tramp steamer to a flying boat and finally to a yacht in the Bahamas. Meanwhile, Fleming had Bond working with a fellow agent named Domino Smith, who infiltrates the Mafia in England.

In discussions, Whittingham had a number of problems with Fleming's treatment. He felt that the idea of three disguised Mafia henchmen sneaking onto an American base and making off with a bomb was straining reality, and that too much time was spent transferring the bomb from chopper to ship to plane to yacht. Whittingham suggested that, in place of all this, the Mafia operatives hijack a NATO bomber with *two* atomic bombs already on board. They could then crash-land the plane in the Bahamas, where the bombs could still be transferred aboard the Mafia yacht via frogmen. Furthermore, he didn't like Domino Smith's easy penetration of the Mafia gang or the counterespionage plot in which the British Secret Service sends only two men and a girl to the Bahamas.

Whittingham also pointed out that Fleming's story was told too much through dialogue, with not enough visuals to carry the filmic story along. In his revisions, he eliminated all Bond narration, took out an interlude at a public house in England, and removed 007's description of the Mafia. He planned to introduce the villains not through description but through action.

Whittingham decided to begin the script with a Mafia agent named Martelli who journeys to Nassau, Bahamas, to tell his employer, an imposing mafioso named Largo, that a NATO observer named Joe Petachi is now under their control. Largo is pleased, offers him a fee of $10,000, and then promptly has one of his bodyguards shoot Martelli in the back, after which his body is thrown to the sharks.

In the Whittingham script, Largo's home is called Xanadu, and Domino is replaced by a lazy American playgirl named Gaby. The head of the Sicilian-based Mafia, who had been named after Fleming's friend Cuneo, was renamed Bastico. Whittingham also introduced one of Largo's henchmen, Janni.

In this draft, Petachi hijacks the plane, but not before UK and American intelligence is able to get a faint trace of it in the mid-Atlantic. Bond is informed by M that this faint trace appears at longitude 78 west, so that is where Bond is sent. *Longitude 78 West* became the working title of the script.

Whittingham's script followed the basic Fleming outline once Bond and Felix Leiter arrive in Nassau—they lead the investigation on the island, where they come across Largo and other Mafia types at a convention. Whittingham added a scene, however, in which Bond fights it out with an underwater sentry while searching the hull of Largo's yacht (the name of which changed from the *Virginia* to the *Sorrento*). A British gunboat—replacing Fleming's submarine—shadows the *Sorrento* until the final underwater battle, which this time takes place off the missile base on the island of Grand Bahama. In the end, Largo flies off in a seaplane with the second hijacked atomic bomb, unaware that Gaby has reset the detonator. As Bond and a wounded Leiter observe, the plane is obliterated.

When the *Thunderball* lawsuit was concluded in 1963, McClory won the film rights to the novel, which he sold to producers Albert R. Broccoli and Harry Saltzman. As the producers prepared to make the long-gestating film project a reality, Whittingham's script was rewritten by American screenwriters Richard Maibaum and John Hopkins. However, the final film credit reads "Screenplay by Richard Maibaum and John Hopkins / Based on an original screenplay by Jack Whittingham / Based on the original story by Kevin McClory, Jack Whittingham and Ian Fleming."

A native of Scarborough, North Yorkshire, England, Whittingham made his motion picture writing debut by contributing the original story for the pre–World War II drama *Clouds over Europe* (1939), a.k.a. *Q Planes*. Because it is essentially a remake of *Thunderball*, Whittingham also received original story credit on *Never Say Never Again*.

Whyte, Willard: Billionaire recluse portrayed effectively by Jimmy Dean in *Diamonds Are Forever*. Based loosely on Howard Hughes, who was producer Albert R. Broccoli's boss in the 1940s, Whyte is the perfect kidnap victim for Ernst Stavro Blofeld (Charles Gray), who is once again at work on an international black-mail scheme. Since no one has seen Whyte for five years, Blofeld finds it easy to take over his global empire, especially when he's supplied with a computerized voice sampler that perfectly duplicates Whyte's vocal patterns. Whyte is involved in many fields, but it is his aerospace business and ties to the US Air Force that help Blofeld easily launch a laser satellite powered by the diamonds he has been stealing from a crime syndicate. That satellite becomes the instrument of Blofeld's latest blackmail scheme.

Whyte is finally rescued by James Bond (Sean Connnery), who has to get past his two acrobatic bodyguards, Bambi (Lola Larson) and Thumper (Trina Parks). Returning to his penthouse in Las Vegas, Whyte takes one look at a huge map of his holdings and discovers one element he doesn't recognize: an oil-drilling platform in Baja California, a clue that leads Bond to Blofeld's final command post.

Broccoli's familiarity with Howard Hughes was certainly a plus when it came time to create the character of Willard Whyte. In fact, a dream Broccoli had one night inspired the entire project. In the dream, Broccoli was paying a visit to Hughes in his permanent hotel suite at the Las Vegas Desert Inn. As Broccoli walked past a window, he saw the back of Hughes's head. However, when the man turned around, it wasn't Hughes. The vision jolted Broccoli and compelled him to contact Richard Maibaum, who was preparing the story for the new Bond film, and suggest the idea of someone replacing a reclusive billionaire. Maibaum had, at one point, considered introducing the evil twin brother of Auric Goldfinger as the villain in *Diamonds*, but Broccoli's dream was a more attractive idea, and thus Willard Whyte was born.

Whyte House: A Las Vegas hotel owned by billionaire recluse Willard Whyte (Jimmy Dean) in *Diamonds Are Forever*. Whyte is kidnapped and imprisoned by Ernst Stavro Blofeld (Charles Gray), who has literally taken over his global empire. When *Diamonds Are Forever* was filmed in Las Vegas in 1971, the Whyte House was actually the Las Vegas International Hotel. Today it's the Westgate Las Vegas Resort & Casino.

Williams, Esther (August 8, 1921–June 6, 2013): Actress and world-renowned swimming champion whose name, fittingly, served as the code designation for the Lotus Esprit submarine car in *The Spy Who Loved Me*. The code name was featured in an early draft of the screenplay but was dropped from the final film. The car was also called Wet Nellie—a reference to Little Nellie, the autogyro from *You Only Live Twice*.

Williams, Jan: English television actress and fashion model who portrayed Donald Grant's bosomy masseuse in *From Russia with Love*, her only credited feature film role.

Actress Jan Williams is attended to before giving Robert Shaw a massage on Spectre Island in *From Russia with Love. The Steve Oxenrider Collection*

Willis, Austin (September 30, 1917–April 4, 2004): Canadian film and television actor who portrayed Mr. Simmons, the cardplayer in *Goldfinger*. Well-tanned and dapper, Willis was perfect as the vacationing American who is being systematically cheated at gin by Goldfinger (Gert Fröbe). A native of Halifax, Nova Scotia, Willis made his motion picture debut as Red North in the adventure film *Bush Pilot* (1947). He later portrayed the US secretary of defense, in charge of negotiating with the tiny country of Grand Fenwick, in director Jack Arnold's hysterical comedy *The Mouse That Roared* (1959), a film that also featured three uncredited future Bond players: Fred Haggerty (*From Russia with Love*), Bill Nagy (*Goldfinger*), and Stuart Saunders (*Octopussy*).

Wilson, Michael G. (January 21, 1942–   ): American writer/producer, the stepson of Albert R. "Cubby" Broccoli, who has been involved almost exclusively in the production of the James Bond films since *The Spy Who Loved Me* in 1976. After the departure of Broccoli's

producing partner Harry Saltzman in 1975, it became clear that he was in need of an associate to begin sharing the producer chores on the enormously complicated 007 productions. Wilson fit the bill. He was an experienced lawyer and a former partner in a prestigious Washington, DC, and New York City law firm. He was also a college-trained electrical engineer with an interest in photography and scuba diving.

Producer Michael Wilson has guided the film future of 007 alongside his half sister, Barbara, for decades. *Courtesy of the Nicolás Suszczyk Collection*

The son of actor Lew Wilson, who was cinema's first Batman in 1943, Michael G. Wilson became part of the Broccoli clan when his mother, Dana, married Cubby in 1959. His first experience with the Bond series actually came in February 1964, when he became a production assistant on *Goldfinger* during location shooting in the United States. Wilson was vacationing in London and about to start law school when Broccoli invited him to join him in the United States for sequences shot at Fort Knox. Wilson bought cases of beer for the American GIs participating in the sequence in which the entire base is put to sleep by Pussy Galore's Flying Circus.

A decade later, Wilson left his law practice to become assistant to the producer on *The Spy Who Loved Me*. He rose to executive producer on *Moonraker*, and he continued in that position on *For Your Eyes Only* and *Octopussy*. He has been a producer on every James Bond film since, working closely with Broccoli's daughter, Barbara, with whom he shares producing chores and credit. Meanwhile, starting with *For Your Eyes Only*, Wilson began to work alongside veteran writer Richard Maibaum on the Bond scripts. He continued in that capacity on *Octopussy*, *A View to a Kill*, *The Living Daylights*, and *Licence to Kill*.

Wilson has also made it a tradition to cameo in the films he works on. In *GoldenEye*, he's a Russian official sitting at the table when General Ourumov (Gottfried John) presents his report on the destruction of the Russian space weapons center at Severnaya. In *Tomorrow Never Dies*, he's a media associate of Elliot Carver (Jonathan Pryce), helping to blackmail the US president into raising cable television rates; in *The World Is Not Enough*, he's a casino patron; and in *Die Another Day* he's General Chandler in the US command center in South Korea. He's the local chief of police in *Casino Royale* who's arrested for corruption, a man sitting in a chair in the Haitian hotel lobby in *Quantum of Solace*, a pallbearer in *Skyfall*, and he's a man in the corridor when M (Ralph Fiennes) and C (Andrew Scott) meet in *Spectre*.

Wint, Mr.: Soft-spoken gay assassin employed by Ernst Stavro Blofeld (Charles Gray) in *Diamonds Are Forever*, portrayed by veteran character actor Bruce Glover. Wint's partner is fellow assassin Mr. Kidd (Putter Smith). Together they give 007 (Sean Connery) plenty of trouble.

Wint and Kidd's first priority is to infiltrate a diamond smuggling operation that stretches from South Africa to the United States. The diamonds will be used by Blofeld to create a huge laser satellite capable of blackmailing the entire planet. Disposing of one agent after another, Wint and Kidd first meet Bond—posing as smuggler Peter Franks—at the Las Vegas mortuary of Morton Slumber (David Bauer), where they knock him out and place him in the crematorium. In one of the most terrifying and desperate situations of the series, 007 is about to be burned to death, when he's saved by diamond smugglers Slumber and Shady Tree (Leonard Barr), who are upset over Bond's phony diamond cache.

After killing a duplicate of Blofeld in the penthouse of Willard Whyte (Jimmy Dean), 007 is overcome by sleeping gas and thrown into the back of Wint's car. Wint also manages to drop his aftershave lotion in the process, which is smashed under 007's body. Thus, when the assassins stuff the unconscious Bond into a concrete pipe that is being placed in an underground flood control line, 007 smells like, in his own words, "a tart's handkerchief." The smell of Mr. Wint's aftershave is an important clue in the film's final scene, when Wint and Kidd try to assassinate Bond one last time. Posing as waiters on a luxury ocean liner, the pair have planted a bomb inside Bond's "surprise" dessert. A suspicious 007 first smells Wint's very familiar aftershave, then trips up the "waiter" with a comment about

Bruce Glover (right) joined forces with Putter Smith (left) to bring life to the unique gay assassins Mr. Wint and Mr. Kidd, who cause James Bond all sorts of trouble in *Diamonds Are Forever*. *Courtesy of the Michael VanBlaricum Collection*

the wine selection, which Wint fails to comprehend. A fight ensues, and both Kidd and Wint are disposed of—the latter with the bomb attached to his torso.

The idea of a pair of gay assassins was a tad spicy in 1971, when *Diamonds Are Forever* was released. In actuality, the personal aspect of Wint and Kidd's relationship was touched upon only slightly, and in a tongue-in-cheek fashion. The scene in which they walk off into the South African desert holding hands was one of the film's biggest laughs (a scene that ABC edited out when the film debuted on on American network television). The campy portrayal of Wint and Kidd's relationship is echoed in Charles Gray's effeminate take on Blofeld—and the scene in which the archvillain escapes from the Whyte House by dressing in drag.

Wiseman, Joseph (May 15, 1918–October 19, 2009): Canadian character actor who portrayed Dr. No in the Bond film of the same name. Made up to appear half Asian—reflecting the character's German/Chinese heritage—and outfitted with a stylish wardrobe and black metal hands, Wiseman set the tone for every future Bond villain. The measured way in which Wiseman delivered his dialogue—using an unemotional, monotone "voice of doom"—was a marvelous and memorable touch. As the story goes, author Ian Fleming wrote the character with his cousin, actor Christopher Lee, in mind. But producers

Albert R. Broccoli and Harry Saltzman wanted Wiseman. Although he had made his feature film debut in *With These Hands* (1950), which dramatized the infamous Triangle Shirtwaist Factory fire of 1911, it was his role as the crazed thief/drug addict Charley Gennini in director William Wyler's *Detective Story* (1951) that ensured his place among the great character actors of his era. His feature credits include *Les Misérables* (1952), *The Garment Jungle* (1957), *The Unforgiven* (1960), *Bye Bye Braverman* (1968), *The Valachi Papers* (1972), *The Apprenticeship of Duddy Kravitz* (1974), and *The Betsy* (1978). A native of Montreal, Wiseman made his television debut opposite Tom Ewell and Anne Bancroft in the *Lights Out* episode "The Deal" (1951). He later appeared in the miniseries *Masada* (1981) and played the recurring role of Manny Weisbord in *Crime Story* (18 episodes, 1986–1988).

Wisniewski, Andreas (July 3, 1959–   ): Tall, blond West German actor who portrayed Necros, the formidable assassin who battles Bond (Timothy Dalton) on the cargo nets in *The Living Daylights*. Born in West Berlin, Wisniewski made his motion picture debut as Fletcher in director Ken Russell's fanciful horror drama *Gothic* (1986). After his James Bond film experience, Wisniewski was cast as Tony, one of the thieves working for Hans Gruber (Alan Rickman) in the original *Die Hard* (1988)—the first to be taken down by John McClane (Bruce Willis).

Andreas Wisniewski played Necros in *The Living Daylights*. *Steve Rubin Collection*

WOMEN OF THE JAMES BOND FILMS

Film	Character	Actress
Casino Royale (TV)	Valerie Mathis	Linda Christian
Dr. No	Honey Ryder	Ursula Andress
	Sylvia Trench	Eunice Gayson
	Miss Taro	Zena Marshall
	Miss Moneypenny	Lois Maxwell
From Russia with Love	Tatiana Romanova	Daniela Bianchi
	Sylvia Trench	Eunice Gayson
	Kerim's Girl	Nadja Regin
	Zora	Martine Beswick
	Vida	Aliza Gur
	Miss Moneypenny	Lois Maxwell
Goldfinger	Pussy Galore	Honor Blackman
	Jill Masterson	Shirley Eaton
	Tilly Masterson	Tania Mallet
	Bonita	Nadja Regin
	Dink	Margaret Nolan
	Miss Moneypenny	Lois Maxwell
Thunderball	Domino	Claudine Auger

Film	Character	Actress
	Fiona Volpe	Luciana Paluzzi
	Paula Caplan	Martine Beswick
	Patricia Fearing	Molly Peters
	Miss Moneypenny	Lois Maxwell
You Only Live Twice	Kissy	Mie Hama
	Aki	Akiko Wakabayashi
	Helga Brandt	Karin Dor
	Ling	Tsai Chin
	Miss Moneypenny	Lois Maxwell
On Her Majesty's Secret Service	Tracy	Diana Rigg
	Ruby	Angela Scoular
	Nancy	Catherine Von Schell
	Miss Moneypenny	Lois Maxwell
Diamonds Are Forever	Tiffany Case	Jill St. John
	Plenty O'Toole	Lana Wood
	Marie	Denise Perrier
	Bambi	Lola Larson
	Thumper	Trina Parks
	Miss Moneypenny	Lois Maxwell
Live and Let Die	Solitaire	Jane Seymour
	Miss Caruso	Madeline Smith
	Rosie Carver	Gloria Hendry
	Miss Moneypenny	Lois Maxwell
The Man with the Golden Gun	Mary Goodnight	Britt Ekland
	Andrea	Maud Adams
	Saida	Carmen Sautoy
	Miss Moneypenny	Lois Maxwell
The Spy Who Loved Me	Major Anya Amasova	Barbara Bach
	Naomi	Caroline Munro
	Hotel Receptionist	Valerie Leon
	Log Cabin Girl	Sue Vanner
	Miss Moneypenny	Lois Maxwell
Moonraker	Holly Goodhead	Lois Chiles
	Corinne Dufour	Corinne Cléry
	Manuela	Emily Bolton
	Private Jet Hostess	Leila Shenna

Film	Character	Actress
	Miss Moneypenny	Lois Maxwell
For Your Eyes Only	Melina Havelock	Carole Bouquet
	Lisl	Cassandra Harris
	Bibi Dahl	Lynn-Holly Johnson
	Miss Moneypenny	Lois Maxwell
Octopussy	Octopussy	Maud Adams
	Magda	Kristina Wayborn
	Miss Moneypenny	Lois Maxwell
	Bianca	Tina Hudson
Never Say Never Again	Domino	Kim Basinger
	Fatima Blush	Barbara Carrera
	Lady in Bahamas	Valerie Leon
	Agent 326	Saskia Cohen Tanugi
	Miss Moneypenny	Pamela Salem
A View to a Kill	Stacey Sutton	Tanya Roberts
	May Day	Grace Jones
	Pola Ivanova	Fiona Fullerton
	Kimberley Jones	Mary Stavin
	Miss Moneypenny	Lois Maxwell
The Living Daylights	Kara Milovy	Maryam d'Abo
	Miss Moneypenny	Caroline Bliss
Licence to Kill	Pam Bouvier	Carey Lowell
	Lupe Lamora	Talisa Soto
	Della Churchill	Priscilla Barnes
	Miss Moneypenny	Caroline Bliss
GoldenEye	Natalya Simonova	Izabella Scorupco
	Xenia Onatopp	Famke Janssen
	M	Dame Judi Dench
	Miss Moneypenny	Samantha Bond
Tomorrow Never Dies	Wai Lin	Michelle Yeoh
	Paris Carver	Teri Hatcher
	M	Dame Judi Dench
	Miss Moneypenny	Samantha Bond
The World Is Not Enough	Elektra King	Sophie Marceau
	Dr. Christmas Jones	Denise Richards
	M	Dame Judi Dench
	Julietta the Cigar Girl	Maria Grazia Cucinotta

Film	Character	Actress
	Miss Moneypenny	Samantha Bond
Die Another Day	Jinx	Halle Berry
	Miranda Frost	Rosamund Pike
	M	Dame Judi Dench
	Miss Moneypenny	Samantha Bond
Casino Royale	Vesper Lynd	Eva Green
	Solange	Caterina Murino
	Valenka	Ivana Milicevic
	M	Dame Judi Dench
Quantum of Solace	Camille	Olga Kurylenko
	Strawberry Fields	Gemma Arterton
	M	Dame Judi Dench
Skyfall	M	Dame Judi Dench
	Eve Moneypenny	Naomie Harris
	Severine	Bérénice Marlohe
Spectre	Madeleine Swann	Léa Seydoux
	Lucia	Monica Bellucci
	Eve Moneypenny	Naomie Harris
No Time to Die	Madeleine Swann	Léa Seydoux
	Eve Moneypenny	Naomie Harris
	Nomi, Agent 007	Lashana Lynch
	Paloma	Ana de Armas

Roger Moore, surrounded by the usual bevy of beauties—in this case, the female astronauts from *Moonraker*. *Courtesy of the David Reinhardt Collection*

Lois Chiles was perfectly cast as icy Holly Goodhead, an astrophysicist, in *Moonraker*. *Courtesy of the David Reinhardt Collection*

The desirable duo of *Never Say Never Again*: Barbara Carrera (left) as Fatima Blush and Kim Basinger as Domino Petachi. *Courtesy of the David Reinhardt Collection*

Maryam d'Abo joined 007 newcomer Timothy Dalton in *The Living Daylights*. *Courtesy of the David Reinhardt Collection*

Kristina Wayborn and Roger Moore take time out from circus action in *Octopussy*. *Steve Rubin Collection*

Pierce Brosnan and his two leading ladies from *The World Is Not Enough*: Sophie Marceau (left) and Denise Richards (right). *Courtesy of the Luc Leclech Collection*

Famke Janssen (left) and Izabella Scorupco joined Pierce Brosnan in *GoldenEye*. *Courtesy of the Luc Leclech Collection*

The ladies of *No Time to Die*. Left to right: Léa Seydoux, Ana de Armas, Naomie Harris, and Lashana Lynch. *Courtesy of the Anders Frejdh Collection*

Wood, Christopher (November 5, 1935–May 9, 2015): British screenwriter/novelist, a favorite of director Lewis Gilbert, who wrote *The Spy Who Loved Me* (with Richard Maibaum) and *Moonraker*. A London native, Wood made his motion picture writing debut on director Val Guest's comedy *Confessions of a Window Cleaner* (1974), based on Wood's novel.

Wood, Lana (March 1, 1946–   ): American actress who portrayed Las Vegas party girl Plenty O'Toole in *Diamonds Are Forever*. Born in Santa Monica, California, Wood made her credited motion picture debut as the young Debbie Edwards in John Ford's classic western *The Searchers* (1956), in which her sister, Natalie Wood, played the older version of the character.

Voluptuous Lana Wood played Vegas floozy Plenty O'Toole in *Diamonds Are Forever. Courtesy of the David Reinhardt Collection*

"World Is Not Enough, The": The motto on the Bond family coat of arms—in Latin, *"Orbis Non Sufficit"*—as related by Sir Hilary Bray (George Baker) to 007 (George Lazenby) in *On Her Majesty's Secret Service*. According to the records of the London College of Arms, Bray says, Bond's lineage can be traced back to 1387. The coat of arms was that of Sir Thomas Bond, who died in 1734. It consisted of an "argent on a chevron sable, with three bezants," or gold balls.

WORLD IS NOT ENOUGH, THE

(United Artists, 1999) ★★★⯪ : The nineteenth James Bond film produced by Eon Productions. US release date: November 19, 1999. Budget: $135 million. Worldwide box office gross: $361.7 million (US domestic gross: $126.9 million; international gross: $234.8 million).* Running time: 128 minutes.

THE SETUP

To retrieve money for oil tycoon Sir Robert King (David Calder), a friend of M (Dame Judi Dench), James Bond (Pierce Brosnan) journeys to a Swiss bank in Bilbao, Spain. However, the banker is killed and, unbeknownst to Bond, the money is booby-trapped. When 007 returns with it to London, King is killed by the resulting explosion inside MI6 headquarters. Bond eventually traces the deadly bank notes to Victor "Renard" Zokas (Robert Carlyle), a KGB agent turned terrorist. Following an earlier attempt on his life by MI6, Renard was left with a bullet in his brain that is gradually destroying his senses, making him immune to pain. Bond is assigned to protect King's daughter, Elektra (Sophie Marceau) against Renard, who had previously kidnapped her. He teams up with nuclear physicist Dr. Christmas Jones (Denise Richards) to foil Renard's latest attempt at nuclear terrorism.

BEHIND THE SCENES

After the crummy *Tomorrow Never Dies*, the producers came back strong with this epic Bond adventure, which is sweeping in scope, intelligent in its plotting, and, thanks to director Michael Apted, full of interesting characters and situations. Pierce Brosnan plays a truly beaten-down Bond, who shows the strain of his double-0 job more acutely than any 007 had in decades. Timothy Dalton had moments like this, especially in *Licence to Kill*, but he just couldn't

* "The World is Not Enough (1999)," The Numbers, accessed July 20, 2020, https://www.the-numbers.com/movie/World-is-Not-Enough-The.

One of John Richardson's amazing miniature landscapes—a Russian oil field from *The World Is Not Enough. Courtesy of the Brian Smithies Archive*

An explosion rips up a section of the Thames during action filming on *The World Is Not Enough. Courtesy of David Williams, Bondpix*

inspire audiences with his physicality. Brosnan is a much more credible action hero, which plays perfectly off his moments of humanizing failure.

In fact, the film begins with a spectacular defeat for Bond. Not only does he carry a bomb into MI6 headquarters—killing a prominent British businessman and taking out a chunk of the building in the process—but also he fails to capture the killer who ignited it. And not for lack of trying; there's a fantastic boat chase on the Thames between 007 and the knockout Maria Grazia Cucinotta, who turned many heads in *Il Postino* (1994). Saddled with sour feelings, a dislocated collarbone, and a desire for his own special brand of revenge, Bond gets his chance when he's assigned to protect the stunning but conflicted Elektra King, portrayed by Sophie Marceau, the most interesting woman in the Bond series since Pussy Galore. Suffering from Stockholm syndrome, Elektra has actually fallen in love with the man who kidnapped her—the villainous Renard. Though a true madman, he too comes across as sympathetic, robbed of the ability to feel both pain and pleasure by the bullet that's slowly killing him.

Speaking at a press conference in Hong Kong prior to the film's premiere, Brosnan described *The World Is Not Enough* as a strong note on which to end the Bond saga of the 1990s. He credited the film's success to his "wonderful rapport" with director Michael Apted, who collaborated with his lead actor to create "a film that has character and style and wit and charm." He marveled at the development of the series since his first film, *GoldenEye*—of which many observers were initially skeptical. "That's a good progression, good growth in character, confidence, and assuredness," he said. Though he expressed an eagerness to continue on as Bond, he acknowledged the need for a break, saying, "I'd like to have time for recovery beginning of next year, make a couple of my own films." And whatever was to come for him (one more Bond film, *Die Another Day*, as it turned out), he seemed to see his first three movies as a satisfying whole: "*GoldenEye* was act 1. *Tomorrow Never Dies* was act 2, act 3 is this. I'm very happy."[*]

Some critics persisted in their negativity, especially when it came to Denise Richards as nuclear physicist Dr. Christmas Jones. But she's a fun character if taken in the proper spirit— she's gorgeous, looks great in hiking shorts, and doesn't embarrass herself delivering some complicated scientific jargon. High points of the movie include the fabulous boat-chase teaser; Elektra King's torture chair, which puts Bond in the type of dire straits we haven't seen since his privates were threatened by Goldfinger's laser beam; the title song by Garbage; and Robbie Coltrane's inspired black-marketeer Valentin Zukovsky, returning to the 007 fold with some choice repartee. The only major low point is the Parahawk hang-glider chase, which lacks credibility, leaning heavily on the pyrotechnic effect of blasting machine guns—which never manage to hit Bond. Do they ever?

---

[*] Special features, *The World Is Not Enough*, James Bond Ultimate Edition (1999; MGM, 2006), DVD.

THE CAST

James Bond	Pierce Brosnan
Elektra King	Sophie Marceau
Victor "Renard" Zokas	Robert Carlyle
Dr. Christmas Jones	Denise Richards
Valentin Zukovsky	Robbie Coltrane
M	Dame Judi Dench
Q	Desmond Llewelyn
R	John Cleese
Julietta the Cigar Girl	Maria Grazia Cucinotta
Miss Moneypenny	Samantha Bond
Bill Tanner	Michael Kitchen
Charles Robinson	Colin Salmon
Mr. Bullion	Goldie
Sir Robert King	David Calder
Dr. Molly Warmflash	Serena Scott Thomas
Security Chief Sasha Davidov	Ulrich Thomsen
Gabor	John Seru
Dr. Mikhail Arkov	Jeff Nuttall
Coptic Priest	Diran Meghreblian
Nina	Daisy Beaumont
Verushka	Nina Muschallik

THE CREW

Director	Michael Apted
Screenplay	Neal Purvis & Robert Wade
	Bruce Feirstein
Story by	Neal Purvis & Robert Wade
Producers	Barbara Broccoli
	Michael G. Wilson
Associate Producer	Nigel Goldsack
Director of Photography	Adrian Biddle
Music by	David Arnold
Title song performed by	Garbage
Production Designer	Peter Lamont
Costume Designer	Lindy Hemming
Line Producer	Anthony Waye
Production Coordinator	Elena Zokas
Second Unit Director	Vic Armstrong
Casting by	Debbie McWilliams
Stunt Coordinator	Simon Crane
Aerial Coordinator	Marc Wolff
Title Designer	Daniel Kleinman
Special Effects Supervisor	Chris Corbould
Miniatures	John Richardson
Editor	Jim Clark

World's Greatest Marches: Misleading label on the master satellite control tape in *Diamonds Are Forever*. It contains the code that Blofeld (Charles Gray) needs to guide his laser satellite. Bond (Sean Connery) first spots it at the laboratory of Professor Dr. Metz (Joseph Furst) at Tectronics. Later, on Blofeld's oil-drilling platform, 007 tries unsuccessfully to substitute a phony tape for the real one.

Worth, B. J. (1952–   ): American stuntman and skydiving expert who jumped off the Eiffel Tower and parachuted to safety in *A View to a Kill*. Worth was doubling Grace Jones's character, May Day. For the subsequent sequence in which May Day parachutes onto a wedding barge on the Seine, he actually jumped twice from a stationary helicopter. Worth had previously worked as a skydiving stunt double for the pilot in the *Moonraker* pre-credits teaser, and stunt double for Gobinda (Kabir Bedi) in *Octopussy*'s midair final battle. He was later the aerial stunt arranger on *The Living Daylights* (for the parachute assault on Gibraltar in the teaser), the parachute stunt coordinator on *Licence to Kill* (for Bond and Felix's arrival at the latter's wedding), the free fall skydiving double for Pierce Brosnan in *GoldenEye*, and the halo jump coordinator on *Tomorrow Never Dies*.

Wright, Jeffrey (December 7, 1965–   ): Emmy Award–winning American actor who portrayed CIA agent Felix Leiter in *Casino Royale*, *Quantum of Solace*, and *No Time to Die*. A native of Washington, DC, Wright made his motion picture debut as a prosecuting attorney in director Alan J. Pakula's *Presumed Innocent* (1990). He earned critical acclaim for playing the title character in Julian Schnabel's biographical drama *Basquiat* (1996), and won both a Tony and an Emmy for starring in

Jeffrey Wright brought a touch of intelligence and class to the role of Felix Leiter in the Daniel Craig films. *Courtesy of the Anders Frejdh Collection*

Tony Kushner's *Angels in America*, first onstage and then in HBO's 2003 miniseries adaptation. More recently, he returned to HBO in the role of scientist Bernard Lowe on the popular science fiction series *Westworld* (27 episodes, 2016–2020), for which he has been nominated for two more Emmy Awards, one for Outstanding Supporting Actor and one for Outstanding Leading Actor.

X-ray glasses: What Bond (Pierce Brosnan) uses to help spot enemy weapons inside the casino run by Valentin Zukovsky (Robbie Coltrane) in *The World Is Not Enough*. He also sees a lot of frilly female underwear.

XT-7B: Designation of the jet-propelled flying platforms utilized by James Bond (Sean Connery) and Felix Leiter (Bernie Casey) in *Never Say Never Again*. Launched via a US nuclear submarine's Polaris missile tubes, the hovering platforms transport Bond and Leiter to the mainland, where they can then dive into a well that connects to the underground Tears of Allah archaeological dig of nuclear-equipped madman Maximilian Largo (Klaus Maria Brandauer).

Yeoh, Michelle (August 6, 1962–   ; birth name: Yeoh Chu-Kheng): Athletic and charismatic Malaysian actress who portrayed feisty Chinese secret agent Colonel Wai Lin in *Tomorrow Never Dies*. Yeoh was even more memorable a few years later in the martial arts classic *Crouching Tiger, Hidden Dragon* (2000). A native of Ipoh, Perak, Malaysia, who was named Miss Malaysia in 1983, Yeoh made her motion picture debut as Miss Yeung in director Sammo Hung's action comedy *The Owl vs. Bumbo* (1984). More recently, Yeoh took on the key role of Captain Philippa Georgiou in the television series *Star Trek: Discovery* (16 episodes, 2017–2019), she was Aleta Ogord in *Guardians of the Galaxy Vol. 2* (2017), and she played wealthy, hard-nosed matriarch Eleanor Young in the enormously popular feature *Crazy Rich Asians* (2018). Her terrific performance opposite fellow Bond player Will Yun Lee in the British action series *Strike Back* (9 episodes, 2015) is also a career highlight.

Actress Michelle Yeoh portrayed athletic Chinese agent Wai Lin in *Tomorrow Never Dies. Courtesy of the David Reinhardt Collection*

YOU ONLY LIVE TWICE

(United Artists, 1967) ★★★: The fifth James Bond film produced by Albert R. Broccoli and Harry Saltzman. US release date: June 13, 1967. Budget: $9.5 milion. Worldwide box office gross: $111.6 million (US domestic gross: $43.1 million;

international gross: $68.5 million).*
Running time: 117 minutes.

────────── THE SETUP ──────────

SPECTRE is up to its old blackmail
tricks. This time, resourceful Ernst
Stavro Blofeld (Donald Pleasence) is
operating out of a rocket base hidden
inside the cone of an extinct Japanese
volcano—launching rockets that are
capturing US and Soviet space capsules. World War III is imminent unless
British intelligence can find the source
of the SPECTRE plot. To free up his
movements in Japan, James Bond
(Sean Connery) is "assassinated" by
machine gun–wielding killers in Hong
Kong, buried at sea, and rescued by
British naval divers. He then arrives
incognito in Tokyo, where he teams up
with the head of the Japanese Secret
Service, Tiger Tanaka (Tetsuro Tamba)
to track down Blofeld.

────────── BEHIND THE SCENES ──────────

Every film series has its highs and lows.
It's extremely difficult to maintain
quality in an ongoing film series—especially given the creative aspirations of
filmmakers, who are always looking for
new paths and challenges. To make the
same type of film every two years is not
an attractive thought for any serious
artist. Sean Connery was already feeling the urge to move on when he began
work on *You Only Live Twice* in 1966.
And he wasn't the only one ready for a
change.

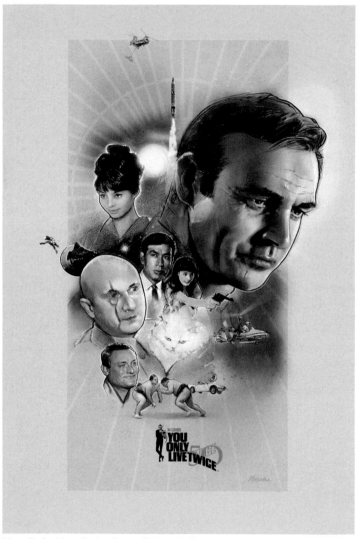

You Only Live Twice by Jeff Marshall. *Courtesy of Jeff Marshall*

For the fifth James Bond film, producers
Albert R. Broccoli and Harry Saltzman changed
their lineup considerably. Gone were director
Terence Young, writer Richard Maibaum, cinematographer Ted Moore, and editor Peter Hunt
(although Hunt was brought back to shoot second
unit footage and to supervise the editing process).
The new team included director Lewis Gilbert,
cinematographer Freddie Young, and screenwriter
Roald Dahl (yes, the legendary children's author).
It was a difficult shoot, and the result is a step

down for the series. While *Thunderball*'s SPECTRE
nuclear blackmail scheme is believable, Blofeld's
scheme to capture US and Soviet spaceships with
the *Intruder* rocket is pure science fiction. If the
007 films have demonstrated anything, it's that
James Bond's adventures should take place on
Earth, not in outer space.

The scale of the film is undeniably impressive. Following *Thunderball*'s enormous success—it grossed more than $60 million in the US
alone—the emphasis was once again on big, epic
adventure. The story centers on another worldwide threat of nuclear destruction. Production
designer Ken Adam was given carte blanche to

────────

* "You Only Live Twice (1967)," The Numbers, accessed July
20, 2020, https://www.the-numbers.com/movie/You-Only
-Live-Twice.

create his enormous volcano rocket-base set. And the filmmakers skipped across the Japanese mainland, filming at many picturesque locations (surrounded at all times by the Japanese press corps). The movie does capture the allure of Japanese culture—its beautiful women, ancient customs, and emerging technologies.

But the film's story is a less than compelling one. Elaborate set pieces take center stage at the expense of a solid dramatic structure. The best Bond films establish the villain and his plot early in the story, and everything moves toward a final confrontation between Bond and his enemy. But *You Only Live Twice* bounces from villain to villain, escapade to escapade, until the final assault on the volcano rocket base puts 007 up against Blofeld for the first time. The action sequences are also more like those found in comic books, and Connery—so glib and light-footed in *Thunderball*—is given very little to do. The helicopter battle above volcano country, pitting the Little Nellie autogyro against a flight of SPECTRE killer helicopters, is one of the least dramatic action sequences in the entire series. Reduced to pushing the buttons on his autogyro's defensive controls, Bond becomes a very passive hero.

The women in *You Only Live Twice* are actually much more interesting than Bond. Japanese secret agent Aki (Akiko Wakabayashi), SPECTRE assassin Helga Brandt (Karin Dor), and 007's undercover "bride" Kissy (Mie Hama) are the advance guard of the new Bond girl, less breathless and more capable of standing toe to toe with the men. Other high points include John Barry's lush score and Freddie Young's cinematography.

Thanks to a long and complicated production schedule, *You Only Live Twice* was scheduled for release in the summer of 1967 instead of Christmas 1966. That meant it was beaten to the theaters by Charles K. Feldman's huge, lumbering 007 spoof *Casino Royale*, which opened on April

To thwart more of Blofeld's treachery, James Bond (Sean Connery) goes undercover in Japan with Japanese Secret Service agent Kissy (Mie Hama) in *You Only Live Twice*. *Courtesy of the David Reinhardt Collection*

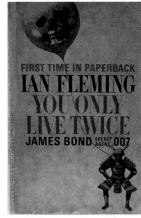

The cover of the 1960s-era American paperback edition of Ian Fleming's *You Only Live Twice*. *Steve Rubin Collection*

28, 1967. *Casino Royale*'s failure to duplicate the success of the serious Bond films had a definite negative effect on the release of *You Only Live Twice*. Although Broccoli and Saltzman's Bond was no failure, it did not repeat the success of *Thunderball*, and the Bond series began a downward spiral at the box office that would last a decade. With the exception of 1971's *Diamonds Are Forever*, Bond would not return to big-money box office success until 1977 with the lavish *The Spy Who Loved Me*.

THE CAST

James Bond	Sean Connery
Aki	Akiko Wakabayashi
Tiger Tanaka	Tetsuro Tamba
Kissy	Mie Hama
Osato	Teru Shimada
Ernst Stavro Blofeld	Donald Pleasence
Helga Brandt	Karin Dor
Miss Moneypenny	Lois Maxwell
M	Bernard Lee
Q	Desmond Llewelyn
Dikko Henderson	Charles Gray
Ling	Tsai Chin
American President	Alexander Knox
President's Aide	Robert Hutton
SPECTRE No. 3	Burt Kwouk
SPECTRE No. 4	Michael Chow
Hans	Ronald Rich

THE CREW

Director	Lewis Gilbert
Screenplay by	Roald Dahl
Producers	Harry Saltzman
	Albert R. Broccoli
Director of Photography	Freddie Young
Music by	John Barry
Title song performed by	Nancy Sinatra
Lyrics by	Leslie Bricusse
Production Designer	Ken Adam
Art Director	Harry Pottle
Production Supervisor	David Middlemas
Assistant Director	William P. Cartlidge
Second Unit Director	Peter Hunt
Technical Adviser	Kikumaru Okuda
Second Unit Cameraman	Bob Huke
Aerial Unit Cameraman	John Jordan
Underwater Cameraman	Lamar Boren
Action sequences by	Bob Simmons
Title Designer	Maurice Binder
Special Effects	John Stears
Editor	Thelma Connell

Dapper as always, director Terence Young takes a break with his *Dr. No* stars Ursula Andress and Sean Connery, on location in Jamaica. *Courtesy of the David Reinhardt Collection*

Young, Freddie (October 9, 1902–December 1, 1998): Three-time Academy Award–winning British cinematographer whose exquisite work can be viewed in *You Only Live Twice*. He was part of the new team brought in by producers Albert R. Broccoli and Harry Saltzman to freshen up the series in 1966. A London native, Young made his motion picture debut as a film development technician on the silent film fantasy *The First Men in the Moon* (1919). Three years later, he was a camera assistant on director W. P. Kellino's adventure *Rob Roy* (1922), another silent. He made his debut as a director of photography on M. A. Wetherell's silent war drama *Victory* (1928). His sound debut as a DP was on Victor Saville's wartime adventure film *The W Plan* (1930). Young received his Academy Awards for Best Cinematography for *Lawrence of Arabia* (1962), *Doctor Zhivago* (1965), and *Ryan's Daughter* (1970), all directed by David Lean. He also received Oscar nominations for *Ivanhoe* (1952) and *Nicholas and Alexandra* (1971).

Young, Terence (June 20, 1915–September 7, 1994): Urbane Irish film director and screenwriter who directed three of the best films in the 007 series: *Dr. No*, *From Russia with Love*, and *Thunderball*. Since he was the first director on the United Artists series, he was very much responsible for setting the style of the films and guiding Sean Connery in the role that made him an international star.

In many ways, Young *was* James Bond. While Ian Fleming was serving his country as an intelligence officer, Young was a dashing young tanker with the Irish Guards Armoured Division. Like Fleming, he was a connoisseur of the finer things in life—gourmet meals, expensive wines, beautifully appointed homes, travel, and adventure. He always surrounded himself with an eclectic group of artists, authors, filmmakers, and other VIPs who appreciated his keen wit, sense of humor, and boyish enthusiasm for filmmaking. When he was tapped to direct *Dr. No*, Young had been reading Fleming's novels for years and thus was very familiar with the world of 007. Combining Young's sophisticated talents with the contributions of American screenwriter Richard Maibaum and editor Peter Hunt, producers Albert R. Broccoli and Harry Saltzman created a true hybrid of early-1960s filmmaking: a stylish international film series with well-crafted production values and action sequences that American audiences could appreciate. In 1977, Young noted with pride that he "directed the first James Bond film (*Dr. No*), the best James Bond film (*From Russia with Love*), and the most successful James Bond film of all (*Thunderball*)."[*]

---

[*] Terence Young, interview by the author, London, June 25, 1977.

One of Young's earliest films was about the Irish Guards and was titled *They Were Not Divided* (1950). It featured several actors who would become players in the Bond series, including Peter Burton, Anthony Dawson, Desmond Llewelyn, and Michael Brennan. His involvement with Broccoli and Maibaum dated back to the Alan Ladd World War II adventure *Paratrooper* (1953), a.k.a. *The Red Beret*. Born in Shanghai, the Cambridge-educated Young started his career as a screenwriter, making his film debut on director Brian Desmond Hurst's *The Fugitive* (1939) a.k.a. *On the Night of the Fire*, which he adapted from F. L. Green's novel. His first original screenplay was Hurst's *Suicide Squadron* (1941). Young made his film directing debut on *Corridor of Mirrors* (1948), a mystery drama that featured future Bond players Christopher Lee and Lois Maxwell.

Youngstein, Max (March 21, 1913–July 8, 1997): American production executive who, as a vice president with United Artists, made an early, unsuccessful attempt to bring Ian Fleming's James Bond novels to the big screen. A native New Yorker, Youngstein was turned on to the idea by an English filmmaker named Victor Saville. Saville had been a successful producer/director with MGM when he left the studio to join United Artists in the early 1950s. Youngstein and UA brought him aboard because they were looking for low-budget productions that had a guaranteed audience, and Saville held the rights to a series of pseudoerotic, slam-bang Mickey Spillane thrillers. Saville eventually produced several Spillane films for UA, including *I, the Jury* (1953) and *Kiss Me Deadly* (1955). But the lack of a bankable lead kept the films from becoming the sort of hits Youngstein was hoping for. "We could never find the right Mike Hammer," he recalled. "We had Ralph Meeker and Biff Elliot. Some of the productions were better than others—Robert Aldrich directed one—but they were B movies without a name lead."* A personality conflict with UA president Arthur Krim eventually proved the end of Saville's relationship with UA.

Yet Saville did approach Youngstein with one more possible project for the studio. "He walked into my office," Youngstein remembered, "and said, 'Did you ever hear of James Bond?' He then pulled out a paperback of *From Russia with Love* and we started to talk about the cinematic potential of the books. I knew about James Bond, because I had close contacts with every book editor in New York. I had read the Fleming books and found them to be terrific, but I didn't have the money for an option. I told him to take the books in to Arthur and see what kind of result he would get." Unfortunately, Krim wasn't interested.

Youngstein left United Artists in the early 1960s, and another Bond fan, David Picker, was promoted to head of production. Then, in 1961, Albert R. Broccoli and Harry Saltzman set up a meeting with Picker and Arthur Krim to pitch a James Bond film series—and the rest is history.

Yune, Rick (August 22, 1971–): American actor of Korean descent who portrayed North Korean agent and henchman Zao in *Die Another Day*. Prior to the Bond experience, he made a strong impression as Johnny Tran in the summer 2001 car-racing film *The Fast and the Furious*, a surprise hit. He played another North Korean villain—terrorist Kang Yeonsak, who launches an attack on the White House—in Antoine Fuqua's action thriller *Olympus Has Fallen* (2013). A native of Washington, DC, Yune made his motion picture debut as Kazuo Miyamoto in director Scott Hicks's period drama *Snow Falling on Cedars* (1999).

* Youngstein, Max, telephone interview by the author, February 15, 1990.

Zambora: A real-life sideshow attraction at Las Vegas's Circus Circus Hotel and Casino that figures in the plot of *Diamonds Are Forever*. Zambora is a performer who seems to transform magically into a rampaging gorilla. Having given Tiffany Case (Jill St. John) a cache of diamonds, Felix Leiter (Norman Burton) and his fellow CIA agents hope to trace her to the next stop on a diamond smuggling pipeline. Unfortunately, while the agents are distracted by the Zambora transformation, Tiffany slips out the back exit, and they lose her.

Zao: Sinister North Korean agent, henchman, and sports car aficionado portrayed by Rick Yune in *Die Another Day*. He works for

Rick Yune as henchman Zao in *Die Another Day*.
Courtesy of the Anders Frejdh Collection

Colonel Moon (Will Yun Lee), a renegade North Korean army officer who is determined to invade the South. In the film's exciting pre-credits teaser, Bond (Pierce Brosnan) is captured by Zao when he attempts to penetrate the villain's lair inside the demilitarized zone between North and South Korea. Bond is tortured and imprisoned, but Zao is badly disfigured by 007, a setback that leads the Korean to Cuba, where he undergoes a novel type of treatment: DNA replacement therapy. How novel is this therapy? It could allow a person to dramatically change his or her appearance, the perfect option for a master of disguise. Later in the story, Zao chases Bond's Aston Martin V12 Vanquish across a frozen ice cap in Iceland while driving one of his most intimidating vehicles, a machine gun–equipped Jaguar XKR.

Zerbe, Anthony (May 20, 1936–   ): Emmy Award–winning American character actor who portrayed boozy drug runner Milton Krest in *Licence to Kill*. A native of Long Beach, California, Zerbe made his motion picture debut as Dog Boy in director Stuart Rosenberg's acclaimed Southern chain gang film *Cool Hand Luke* (1967). Zerbe's long and eclectic career includes roles in *Will Penny* (1967); *The Molly Maguires* (1970), opposite Sean Connery; *The Liberation of L.B. Jones* (1970); *They Call Me Mister Tibbs!* (1970); *The Omega Man* (1971), as Matthias the mutant leader; *Papillon* (1973), as Toussaint the leper; *Rooster Cogburn* (1975); *The Turning Point* (1977); *The Dead Zone* (1983); and *Star Trek: Insurrection* (1998). Zerbe received his Emmy for Best Supporting Actor for the television series *Harry O* (30 episodes, 1975–1976).

Zero Zero: Nickname bestowed upon James Bond (Sean Connery) by Japanese Secret Service chief Tiger Tanaka (Tetsuro Tamba) in *You Only Live Twice*.

Zokas, Victor: Real name of Renard, the villain portrayed by Robert Carlyle in *The World Is Not Enough*.

Zora: Gypsy woman, portrayed by Martine Beswick in *From Russia with Love*, who is involved in the famous girl fight with fellow gypsy Vida (Aliza Gur).

Zorin, Max: Billionaire industrialist and horse breeder, portrayed by Christopher Walken, who intends to monopolize the world's supply of microchips by destroying Silicon Valley in *A View to a Kill*. Born in Dresden, Zorin was the product of a cruel Nazi experiment conducted by Dr. Carl Mortner (Willoughby Gray) on pregnant concentration camp inmates. Attempting to prove his theory that steroid injections could enhance the intelligence of children, Mortner succeeded in killing most of the newborns. Those that survived were, indeed, born with phenomenal IQs, but they each suffered a glaring side effect: they were all psychotic.

Zorin fled East Germany in the 1960s on a French passport. By then he was a top KGB agent, working for General Gogol (Walter Gotell). Zorin Industries, his brainchild, was financed by the Russians, who hoped to benefit from its new technologies. Zorin's wealth increased as he made his first fortunes in oil and gas trading, continuing on to electronics and high technology. Perceived in France as a top industrialist and

A formidable duo: megalomaniac Max Zorin (Christopher Walken) and May Day (Grace Jones), up to no good in *A View to a Kill*. *Courtesy of the Luc Leclech Collection*

anti-Communist, Zorin continued his work for Mother Russia, but those ties began to weaken. Surrounded by wealth and power, Zorin mentally snapped when he conceived of Project Main Strike—a plan to destroy Silicon Valley and thereby gain a monopoly on the world's microchip manufacturing.

That plan is short-circuited by James Bond (Roger Moore), who tracks Zorin and his henchwoman May Day (Grace Jones) from France to San Francisco and on to the Main Strike silver mine. There, 007 manages to stop a bomb from detonating along the San Andreas Fault. That explosion, combined with the pumping of seawater from Zorin's oil wells into the nearby Hayward earthquake fault, could have turned Silicon Valley into a lake.

Bond battles his way aboard Zorin's blimp, and during a climactic fight above the Golden Gate Bridge, he forces the psychotic industrialist to lose his footing and fall to his death. NOTE: Singer/actor David Bowie was considered at one point for the role of Zorin, eventually losing out to Christopher Walken.

Zukovsky, Valentin Dmitrovich: Black-market criminal, opportunist, and defiant capitalist based in St. Petersburg, Russia, portrayed by rotund Robbie Coltrane in *GoldenEye* and *The World Is Not Enough*. A former KGB agent, Zukovsky met Bond (Pierce Brosnan) on one of 007's previous, unnamed missions. Bond wounded him, so he walks with a limp. Although there's obviously no love lost between the two men, there is a grudging respect between them. Valentin is reminiscent of Milos Colombo, the colorful smuggler portrayed by Topol in *For Your Eyes Only*. By the time Zukovsky returns in *The World Is Not Enough*, he's also running a casino in Baku, Azerbaijan. He saves James Bond's life when Elektra King (Sophie Marceau) nearly snaps Bond's neck in a medieval torture machine—at the cost of his own life.

Zurich, Switzerland: In *Goldfinger*, one of four cities (along with Amsterdam, Caracas, and Hong Kong) in which Auric Goldfinger (Gert Fröbe) has stashed the 20 million in pounds sterling worth of gold he has been smuggling out of Great Britain, according to Colonel Smithers (Richard Vernon) of the Bank of England.

BIBLIOGRAPHY

Books

Brosnan, John. *James Bond in the Cinema*. 2nd ed. San Diego: A. S. Barnes, 1981.

Burlingame, Jon. *The Music of James Bond*. Oxford: Oxford University Press, 2012.

Moore, Roger. *The 007 Diaries: Filming "Live and Let Die."* Stroud, Gloucestershire, England: The History Press, 2018. Kindle.

Priggé, Steven. *Movie Moguls Speak: Interviews with Top Film Producers*. Jefferson, NC: McFarland, 2004.

Rye, Graham. *The James Bond Girls*. Secaucus, NJ: Citadel, 2000.

Articles

Connellan, Shannon. "Everything We Know About 'No Time to Die' from Dropping by the Set." Mashable, February 7, 2020. https://mashable.com/article/james-bond-no-time-to-die-set-visit/.

Cerulli, Mark. "Welcome to Japan, Mr. Bond: You Only Live Twice at Fifty." *Cinema Retro* 13, no. 39 (2017).

Craig, Daniel (actor). Interview by Gabrielle Donnelly. *Hello!*, November 20, 2006.

Craig, Daniel (actor). Interview by David Sheff. *Playboy*, November 2008.

Duncan, Paul. "The Gold Standard." *Taschen*, Winter 2012.

Elle. "Emerging Icon: Naomie Harris." November 2013.

Fackler, Martin. "From Bond Girl to 'a Normal Life.'" *New York Times*, March 5, 2017.

Fullerton, Fiona. "The Day a Stalker Came to Kill Me." *Daily Mail*, August 3, 2008. https://www.dailymail.co.uk/femail/article-1041249/The-day-stalker-came-kill-Fiona-Fullerton-reveals-terrifying-ordeal.html.

Gaydos, Steven. "Jane Bond? Scribe's-Eye View of 007 Pic Birth." *Variety*, May 11, 2012.

Gilbert, Gerard. "Ben Whishaw Interview: *Spectre* Actor Talks Q, Avoiding Press Harassment and Freddie Mercury Biopic." *Independent*, October 23, 2015.

Green, Willow. "Exclusive: Bond Talk—Empire Online Sits Down with Michael Madsen." Empire Online, June 23, 2002. http://www.empireonline.co.uk/news/news.asp?story=3988 (URL discontinued).

Jamaica Gleaner. "Icon: Reggie Carter—the Famous Mr Blackburn." April 15, 2008. http://old.jamaica-gleaner.com/gleaner/20080415/ent/ent3.html.

Kamp, David. "Harry the Spy: The Secret Prehistory of a James Bond Producer." *Vanity Fair*, September 18, 2012. https://www.vanityfair.com/culture/2012/10/fifty-years-of-james-bond.

Katz, David. "Bond Is Dead, Long Live Bond!" *Esquire*, September 2006.

Lee, Christopher (actor). Interview by Chris Knight. *Cinefantastique*, 1974.

London Daily Telegraph. Item on how 007 got his number. September 18, 1991.

Los Angeles Times. "007's Rocket Pad Out of This World." January 15, 1967.

Mann, Roderick. "Actresses Unruffled in the Battle of the Bonds." *Los Angeles Times*, August 31, 1982.

Maxwell, Lois (actress). Interview by Mark Greenberg. *Bondage* 12 (1983).

Maxwell, Lois (actress). Interview by the *Sydney Morning Herald*, August 31, 1986. Reprinted in "Moneypenny Dishes the Dirt." MI6: The Home of James Bond 007, August 31, 2016. https://www.mi6-hq.com/sections/articles/history-lois-maxwell-retires1.

Numbers, The. Nash Information Services, 1997–2020. https://www.the-numbers.com.

Picker, David. "How UA Bonded with Bond," *Variety*, May 4, 2005.

Radio Times. "Spectre: Naomie Harris on Playing Miss Moneypenny, 'the Only Person Bond Can Trust.'" November 8, 2017. https://www .radiotimes.com/news/2015-10-28/naomie -harris-revamped-miss-moneypenny-for-a -21st-century-james-bond-and-transformed -her-career-too/.

Rampton, James. "Ben Whishaw on Playing Q in *Skyfall*." *London Daily Telegraph*, October 26, 2012.

Retroculturati (blog). "How 007 Got His His Name." May 4, 2019. https://retroculturati .com/2019/05/04/how-007-got-his-name/.

Ryan, Mike. "Sam Mendes, 'Skyfall' Director, on Bringing Humor Back to James Bond & Flirting with the Idea of Casting Sean Connery." *Huffington Post*, November 5, 2012. https:// www.huffpost.com/entry/sam-mendes -skyfall_n_2074239.

Shrimsley, Robert. "James Bond Turns the Big Guns on MI6." *London Daily Telegraph*, April 23, 1999.

Simmons, Bob (stunt coordinator). Interview by Richard Schenkman, *Bondage* 9 (1980).

Simpson, George. "James Bond Villain Robert Davi 'Timothy Dalton Is the Father of Daniel Craig's Darker 007.'" *Daily Express*, June 11, 2019.

Weber, Bruce. "Robert Rietti, a Familiar Voice, Dies at 92." *New York Times*, May 5, 2015.

Movies

Diamonds Are Forever. James Bond Ultimate Edition. 1971; MGM, 2006. DVD.

Dr. No. James Bond Ultimate Edition. 1962; MGM, 2006. DVD.

GoldenEye. James Bond Ultimate Edition. 1995; MGM, 2006. DVD.

Goldfinger. James Bond Ultimate Edition. 1964; MGM, 2006. DVD.

Living Daylights, The. James Bond Ultimate Edition. 1987; MGM, 2006. DVD.

World Is Not Enough, The. James Bond Ultimate Edition. 1999; MGM, 2006. DVD.

You Only Live Twice. James Bond Ultimate Edition. 1967; MGM, 2006. DVD.

Interviews by the Author

Adam, Ken (production designer). London, June 17, 1977.

Barry, John (composer). Los Angeles, December 12, 1977.

Beswick, Martine (actress). Los Angeles, November 12, 1977.

Binder, Maurice (title designer). London, June 16, 1977.

Boren, Lamar (underwater cinematographer). La Jolla, CA, August 17, 1976.

Broccoli, Albert R. (producer). Los Angeles, April 10, 1977.

Cain, Syd (production designer). London, June 18, 1977.

Cartlidge, William P. (associate producer). London, June 2, 1977.

Dahl, Roald (screenwriter). London, June 19, 1977.

Feirstein, Bruce (screenwriter). Telephone interview, June 1, 1995.

France, Michael (screenwriter). Telephone interview, June 15, 1995.

Gayson, Eunice (actress). London, June 1977.

Gilbert, Lewis (director). London, June 15, 1977.

Glover, Bruce (actor). Los Angeles, December 1, 1977.

Hill, Bill (production manager). London, June 20, 1977.

Hunt, Peter (director/editor). London, June 21, 1977.

Jenkins, Richard (assistant director). London, June 18, 1977.

Lazenby, George (actor). Los Angeles, July 1, 1981.

Lee, Christopher (actor). Los Angeles, February 15, 1989.

Leech, George (stuntman). London, June 23, 1977.

Linder, Cec (actor). Telephone interview, July 17, 1989.

Maibaum Richard (screenwriter). Los Angeles, April 30, 1977.

Mankiewicz, Tom (screenwriter). Los Angeles, November 7, 1977.

Meddings, Derek (special effects supervisor). London, June 27, 1977.

Schwartzman, Jack (producer). Los Angeles, November 2, 1984.

Seymour, Jane (actress). Los Angeles, April 16, 1979.

Sylvester, Rick (stuntman). Los Angeles, January 15, 1978.

Udell, Ronald (construction manager). London, June 19, 1977.

Wade, Kevin (screenwriter). Telephone interview, June 17, 1995.

Young, Terence (director). London, June 25, 1977.

Youngstein, Max (production executive). Telephone interview, February 15, 1990.

Additional Interviews

Berry, Halle (actress). Interview. *Entertainment Tonight*, Paramount Domestic Television, November 18, 2002.

Dalton, Timothy (actor). Interview by Craig Modderno. Los Angeles, June 30, 1989.

Glen, John (director). Interview by Craig Modderno. Los Angeles, June 30, 1989.

Hamilton, Guy (director). Interview by Michael Apted. Directors Guild Visual History, accessed June 4, 2020. https://www.dga.org/Craft/VisualHistory/Interviews/Guy-Hamilton.aspx.

Purvis, Neal, and Robert Wade (screenwriters). Interview by ODE Entertainment, YouTube, February 18, 2013. https://www.youtube.com/watch?v=FcrCdVOoosg.

Sean Connery's iconic 007 set the tone for more than half a century of Bond movies
Courtesy of the David Reinhardt Collection